BACKLASH

BACKLASH

*The Undeclared War
Against Women*

SUSAN FALUDI

Chatto & Windus
LONDON

First published in Great Britain by
Chatto & Windus Ltd
20 Vauxhall Bridge Road
London SW1V 2SA

The publisher gratefully acknowledges permission to reprint lines from
The Man in the Black Coat Turns, published by Dial/Doubleday Press, New
York, in 1981, copyright © 1981 by Robert Bly. Reprinted by permission
of the author.

Susan Faludi has asserted her right to be identified as the author of this work.

A CIP Catalogue record for this book is available from the British Library.

ISBN 0 7011 4643 5

Phototypeset by Intype, London

Printed and bound in Great Britain by
Mackays of Chatham PLC Chatham, Kent

To my mother,
Marilyn Lanning Faludi

Contents

Acknowledgements

As the years have mounted in much-belaboured preparation of this book, so have the debts. It's a wonder authors have any friends by the time they get around to the acknowledgements. I am enormously fortunate to have had such a kind, and forgiving, cheering squad.

This project began as a 1986 magazine story on the Harvard–Yale 'man shortage' study, written while I was on the staff at *West*, the Sunday magazine of the *San José Mercury News*, and *West* editor Jeffrey Klein proved an early and invaluable supporter. He greatly eased the research and writing process by arranging for a year-long leave and by agreeing to publish a string of magazine stories on women's status that became an important element in *Backlash*. My good luck continued under the auspices of Greg Hill, my bureau chief at the *Wall Street Journal*, who held open a job for months so I could finish the book and who granted weeks off for various rewrites. My colleagues at the *Journal*'s San Francisco office have also been an understanding and supportive crew.

Edie Gelles, American scholar with Stanford University's Institute for Research on Women and Gender, gave much-needed intellectual sustenance, bringing me into the visiting scholars programme at the institute, which provided a wonderful forum in which to test ideas, and lending a sensitive and intelligent ear as I fumbled around for the book's thesis. I am grateful to all the scholars at the institute for their thoughtful suggestions and criticism.

My agent Sandra Dijkstra was willing to take a chance on what was initially a pretty fuzzy proposal, and I am grateful to her for backing the idea so indefatigably. At Crown Publishers, Jane Von Mehren was an enthusiastic and gracious editor, putting up with several false starts and telephone-book-sized early drafts. I am also indebted to Betty Prashker, who gave her personal support to the project from the outset. I also would like to give special thanks to Irene Prokop, Andrea Connolly and Penny Simon, as well as the many others at Crown who guided the book through its final paces and suffered through my many last-minute inserts and changes. Christina Pattarelli and Rebecca Carroll also were lifesavers, hunting down a last round of books and periodicals and helping with fact checking at the eleventh hour.

I would not have made much headway without the quiet cooperation of the many people, from Census Bureau demographers to mental-health epidemiologists, whom I called upon in my research for this book. With few exceptions, they gave ungrudgingly of their time, submitting to lengthy interviews and providing a vast store of documentation. Nor would I have progressed very far without the work of many feminist writers and researchers, whose impressive body of scholarship provided both inspiration and critical foundation blocks.

Many friends have been salvations. Sarah Winterfield read through unwieldy first manuscripts and dispensed sometimes daily pep talks; Phil Winterfield tamed an often-petulant computer. Barbara McIntosh, Lisa Scalapino, Kathy Holub, Sara Frankel, Peggy Orenstein, and Cathy and David Massey came to my rescue countless times. So did Robert Faludi, who coaxed me out of writing doldrums with perpetual good humour. To Gary Kamiya goes heartfelt thanks for his endless enthusiasm for the project, his tender loving care, and his kitchen wizardry. I have a special and incalculable debt to Scott Rosenberg, whose clarity of thinking and meticulous editing are felt throughout *Backlash*.

I am enormously grateful to Jane Hill, whose diligent and thorough research efforts for the British edition have greatly enriched the book's scope and significance for non-American readers. Beth Humphries copy-edited the book with great care, under pressure. And Carmen Callil had the vision to create an Anglicized version of *Backlash* – and the determination to make it happen despite the time pressures and difficulties of distance.

In gathering material on the UK I have had generous help from many individuals and institutions, in particular: Lesley Abdela; Dr Jack Glatt of the Infertility Advisory Centre; the Labour Party; the Women's Aid Federation; the Family Policy Studies Centre; the Women's International Resource Centre; Women's Health; Claire Messud and the *Guardian*; Rosie Boycott; the Low Pay Unit; Maternity Alliance; *Spare Rib*; the National Magazine Company (for *Cosmopolitan*, *Company*, *She* and *Good Housekeeping*); IPC (for *Options* and *Woman's Journal*); the Family Planning Association Resource Centre; the Birth Control Trust; the British Heart Foundation; the Independent Television Commission, especially Lesley Aston, Patricia Albans, Jane Aldridge and the library staff; Dr Sonia Livingstone; Sheila Whittaker; Janet Fielding; Lynda Myles; Maggie Sanson; Jane Harris; Mark Shivas; *Broadcast* magazine; Cancerlink; the Health Education Authority; the Equal Opportunities Commission; and Mary Walker.

For information on Australia I am indebted to the Rt Hon. Franca Arena; Dr Marian Sawer; Quentin Bryce AO; Valerie Pratt; Margaret McDonald; Eva Cox; Adele Horin; Sue Neales; and Peter McDonald. For material on New Zealand I am especially grateful to Sue Elliott; Lesley Haynes; and Raewyn Good.

This book is dedicated to my mother, who as a young woman fought to preserve her independence in the face of her own era's 'feminine mystique' backlash. And it is written in the hopes that the next generation of women might not have to fight another round.

Preface

Some time ago I received a call from a journalist on a Sunday newspaper inviting me to write an article. It was twenty years since the publication of *The Female Eunuch*, she said, and the paper would like to run a major piece arguing that feminism had failed. No one, she continued, published or read feminist books any more, and even women like herself who were sympathetic to the aims of feminism had to concede that they had not been achieved. I pointed out the flaws in this generalization, listing the changes that had taken place over the last two decades and naming several successful feminist books, but it did not deter her from finding someone else to articulate her 'feminism is finished' thesis.

Eighteen months later the *Spectator* took a diametrically opposite view, devoting its front cover to an illustration of 'the battle of the sexes' and running an alarmist three-page article on the 'growing threat of militant feminism'. The author stigmatized feminists as a 'totalitarian' group whose sinister ideas had permeated the media, publishing, government, business and the legal profession to an astonishing degree; indeed the Law Lords had so far fallen under feminist influence that they had recently taken the extraordinary step of banning rape in marriage.

These two examples are a perfect illustration of the phenomenon Susan Faludi describes in *Backlash*. The successes of the women's movement are inscribed on the charge sheet alongside its failures, imagined or otherwise, and both are magnified to suit the purposes of its detractors. Women are told they are unhappy because feminism has 'gone too far', giving them more independence than they can handle and wrecking their relationships with men; at the same time they are asked to dismiss it as a well-meaning experiment doomed to founder on the rocks of biological difference. In the *Daily Telegraph* and on Channel 4 television, the right-wing journalist Minette Marrin ponders on the small number of women who get to the top in the City and in the professions and asks whether the old doctrine of women's inferiority isn't valid after all. (The same faulty logic could be used to explain the under-representation of black people in many walks of life but such an argument is probably too explosive even for the *Daily Telegraph*.)

The brilliance of *Backlash* is that Susan Faludi sees these strategies for what they are: an attempt to divide and isolate women at a crucial moment in the struggle for equality, independence and autonomy. She documents the failures, but also shows why they have happened. It is the vast corporations determined to use their power and wealth to fight equal pay claims which have kept down women's wages, not some minor difference in the size of the hypothalamus; it is the hostility and overt aggression of male colleagues in blue-collar jobs which have driven women away from manual work, not women's feminine distaste for getting their hands dirty. It is the necessity to fight, on both sides of the Atlantic, to defend those advances we have already made that has kept us from turning our energies to other matters; in the quarter-century since abortion was legalized in Britain, women have faced *sixteen* attempts to restrict or recriminalize it.

In a sense, as Susan Faludi points out, the strength and scope of the backlash against feminism are compliments to it. Her suggestion that it is the opponents of feminism who truly understand its radical potential is spot-on; if feminist ideas were not perceived as popular and threatening, why make such a fuss about them? One particular manifestation of the backlash, the attempt by the poet Robert Bly to re-establish separate spheres for men and women through his 'wild man' cult, has been slower to get off the ground in Britain than in the United States, but a handful of English journalists – among them the Old Etonian editor of *Punch* – have recently attracted media attention with claims that they have been victimized, stifled and oppressed by feminism. One is tempted to say 'you ain't seen nothing yet', but that is precisely the point; it is not so much what feminism has already accomplished in this country – 19 female circuit judges out of 426, for instance, hardly constitutes a revolution – but its potential which causes such fright.

The greatest achievement of feminism in the last two decades – as demonstrated by the individual testimony of many women in Susan Faludi's book – is the change it has brought about in female consciousness. Her interviews with shop assistants, factory workers, journalists and academics show that the founding aims of the women's movement – reproductive choice, equal pay, access to childcare and freedom from sexual abuse – are now supported by vast numbers of women who might not, especially in the present repressive climate, identify themselves as feminists. It is precisely because this precondition for more radical change exists that we are experiencing a backlash, and Susan Faludi is right to warn that the same old cycle of progress followed by setbacks and demoralization is on the verge of repeating itself.

It can happen, but it requires our cooperation. It requires that we believe everything we are told about the damage we are doing to men, about the misery which is the invariable lot of working mothers, single and childless women. It happened in ancient Rome, where a period of relative freedom for women was followed by centuries in which they were expunged from history. It is happening now in those states, like Algeria, where recent improvements in the status of women are under threat from fundamentalist Islam. *Backlash*, with its sharp historical sense, its clear-sighted perception of the opposition, and its faith in the willpower of women, is the balance-sheet which tells us, in a period of concerted anti-feminist propaganda, exactly where we stand.

Joan Smith
Oxford, 1992

Chapter One

Introduction: Blame It on Feminism

To be a woman at the close of the twentieth century – what good fortune. That's what we keep hearing, anyway. The barricades have fallen, politicians assure us. Women have 'made it', the style pages cheer. Women's fight for equality has 'largely been won', *Time* magazine announces. Enrol at any university, join any law firm, apply for credit at any bank. Women have so many opportunities now, corporate leaders say, that we don't really need equal opportunity policies. Women are so equal now, lawmakers say, that we no longer need equal rights legislation. 'The battle for women's rights has been largely won,' Mrs Thatcher has proclaimed. 'The days when they were demanded in strident tones should be gone forever.' Even American Express ads have saluted a woman's freedom to charge it. At last, women have received their full citizenship papers.

And yet . . .

Behind this celebration of women's victory, behind the news, cheerfully and endlessly repeated, that the struggle for women's rights is won, another message flashes. You may be free and equal now, it says to women, but you have never been more miserable.

This bulletin of despair is posted everywhere – at the newsagent's, on the TV set, at the cinema, in advertisements and doctors' offices and academic journals. Professional women are suffering 'burn-out' and succumbing to an 'infertility epidemic'. Single women are grieving from a 'man shortage'. The *New York Times* reports: childless women are 'depressed and confused' and their

1

ranks are swelling. *Newsweek* says: unwed women are 'hysterical' and crumbling under a 'profound crisis of confidence'. The health advice manuals inform: high-powered career women are stricken with unprecedented outbreaks of 'stress-induced disorders', hair loss, bad nerves, alcoholism, and even heart attacks. The psychology books advise: independent women's loneliness represents 'a major mental health problem today'. Even founding feminist Betty Friedan has been spreading the word: she warns that women now suffer from a new identity crisis and 'new "problems that have no name"'.

How can women be in so much trouble at the same time that they are supposed to be so blessed? If the status of women has never been higher, why is their emotional state so low? If women got what they asked for, what could possibly be the matter now?

The prevailing wisdom of the past decade has supported one, and only one, answer to this riddle: it must be all that equality that's causing all that pain. Women are unhappy precisely *because* they are free. Women are enslaved by their own liberation. They have grabbed at the gold ring of independence, only to miss the one ring that really matters. They have gained control of their fertility, only to destroy it. They have pursued their own professional dreams – and lost out on the greatest female adventure. The women's movement, as we are told time and again, has proved women's own worst enemy.

'In dispensing its spoils, women's liberation has given my generation high incomes, our own cigarette, the option of single parenthood, rape crisis centers, personal lines of credit, free love, and female gynecologists,' Mona Charen, a young American law student, writes in the *National Review*, in an article titled 'The Feminist Mistake'. 'In return it has effectively robbed us of one thing upon which the happiness of most women rests – men.' The *National Review* is a conservative publication, but such charges against the women's movement are not confined to its pages. 'Our generation was the human sacrifice' to the women's movement, *Los Angeles Times* feature writer Elizabeth Mehren contends in a *Time* cover story. Baby-boom women like her, she says, have been duped by feminism: 'We believed the rhetoric.' In the UK *Cosmopolitan* in 1985, writer Erica Jong claims: 'We have won the

2

right to be terminally exhausted', and finds herself agreeing with Nora Ephron that 'the main achievement of the woman's movement is the Dutch treat'. In *Newsweek*, writer Kay Ebeling dubs feminism 'the Great Experiment That Failed' and asserts 'woman in my generation, its perpetrators, are the casulties'. Even the beauty magazines are saying it: *Harper's Bazaar* accuses the women's movement of having 'lost us [women] ground instead of gaining it'.

In the last decade, publications from the *New York Times* to *Vanity Fair* have issued a steady stream of indictments against the women's movement, with such headlines as WHEN FEMINISM FAILED or THE AWFUL TRUTH ABOUT WOMEN'S LIB. They hold the campaign for women's equality responsible for nearly every woe besetting women, from mental depression to meagre savings accounts, from teenage suicides to eating disorders to bad complexions. The *Today* show says women's liberation is to blame for bag ladies. A guest columnist in the *Baltimore Sun* even proposes that feminists produced the rise in slasher movies. By making the 'violence' of abortion more acceptable, the author reasons, women's rights activists made it all right to show graphic murders on screen.

At the same time, other outlets of popular culture have been forging the same connection: in Hollywood films, of which *Fatal Attraction* is only the most famous, emancipated women with condominiums of their own slink wild-eyed between bare walls, paying for their liberty with an empty bed, a barren womb. 'My biological clock is ticking so loud it keeps me awake at night,' Sally Field cries in the film *Surrender*, as, in an all too common transformation in the cinema of the eighties, an actress who once played feisty working heroines is now showcased grovelling for a groom. In prime-time television shows, from *thirtysomething* to *Coronation Street*, single, professional or feminist women are humiliated, turned into harpies, or hit by nervous breakdowns; the wise ones recant their independent ways by the closing sequence. In popular novels, from Gail Parent's *A Sign of the Eighties* to Stephen King's *Misery*, unwed women shrink to snivelling spinsters or inflate to fire-breathing she-devils; renouncing all aspirations but marriage, they beg for wedding rings from strangers or swing sledgehammers at reluctant bachelors. We 'blew it by waiting', a typically remorseful careerist sobs in Freda Bright's *Singular Women*; she and her sister professionals are 'condemned to be childless forever'. Even Erica Jong's high-flying independent heroine literally crashes by the end of the decade, as the author supplants *Fear of Flying*'s saucy Isadora Wing, a symbol of female sexual emancipation in the seventies, with an embittered careerist-turned-recovering-'co-dependent' in *Any Woman's Blues* – a book that is intended, as the narrator bluntly states, 'to demonstrate what a deadend the so-called sexual revolution had become, and how desperate so-called free women were in the last few years of our decadent epoch'.

Popular psychology manuals peddle the same diagnosis for contemporary female distress. 'Feminism, having promised her a stronger sense of her own identity, has given her little more than an identity *crisis*,' the bestselling advice manual *Being a Woman* asserts. The authors of the era's self-help classic *Smart Women/Foolish Choices* proclaim that women's distress was 'an unfortunate consequence of feminism', because 'it created a myth among women that the apex of self-realization could be achieved only through autonomy, independence, and career'.

In the Reagan and Bush years, US government officials have needed no prompting to endorse this thesis. Reagan spokeswoman Faith Whittlesey declared feminism a 'straitjacket' for women, in the White House's only policy speech on the status of the American female population – entitled 'Radical Feminism in Retreat'. Law enforcement officers and judges, too, have pointed a damning finger at feminism, claiming that they can chart a path from rising female independence to rising female pathology. As a California sheriff explained it to the press, 'Women are enjoying a lot more freedom now, and as a result, they are committing more crimes.' The US Attorney-General's Commission on Pornography even proposed that women's professional advancement might be responsible for rising rape rates. With more women in college and at work now, the commission members reasoned in their report, women just have more opportunities to be raped.

Some academics have signed on to the consensus, too – and they are the 'experts' who have enjoyed the highest profiles on

4

the media circuit. On American news and talk shows, they have advised millions of women that feminism has condemned them to 'a lesser life'. Legal scholars have railed against 'the equality trap'. Sociologists have claimed that 'feminist-inspired' legislative reforms have stripped women of special 'protections'. Economists have argued that well-paid working women have created 'a less stable family'. And demographers, with greatest fanfare, have legitimized the prevailing wisdom with so-called neutral data on sex ratios and fertility trends; they say they actually have the numbers to prove that equality doesn't mix with marriage and motherhood.

Finally, some 'liberated' women themselves have joined the lamentations. In confessional accounts, works that invariably receive a hearty greeting from the publishing industry, 'recovering Superwomen' tell all. In *The Cost of Loving: Women and the New Fear of Intimacy*, Megan Marshall, a Harvard-pedigreed writer, asserts that the feminist 'Myth of Independence' has turned her generation into unloved and unhappy fast-trackers, 'dehumanized' by careers and 'uncertain of their gender identity'. Other diaries of mad Superwomen charge that 'the hard-core feminist viewpoint', as one of them puts it, has relegated educated executive achievers to solitary nights of frozen dinners and closet drinking. The triumph of equality, they report, has merely given women hives, stomach cramps, eye-twitching disorders, even comas.

But what 'equality' are all these authorities talking about?

If women are now so equal, why are they much more likely to be poor, especially in retirement? Why are over 6.5 million of the 10 million workers in the UK who earn below the Council of Europe's decency threshold women? Why does the average working woman, in both the UK and the US, still earn only just over two-thirds what men do for the same work? Why in 1990 was the average hourly rate for a part-time worker – and in the UK 86 per cent of part-time workers are women – little more than half that of male full-time earnings?

If women have 'made it', then why are 80 per cent of all workers in catering, cleaning, hairdressing and other personal services still women, and 78 per cent of all workers in clerical jobs? Conversely, why are there only 19 female circuit-court judges out of 426, two female high court judges out of 83, and no female Law Lords?

Why, of 1,200 surgeons in the UK, are there only ten women? Why for every woman given a public appointment by the government are there four men? Why, of the 48 per cent non-industrial civil servants who are women, have only 3 per cent reached the top two grades? Why are there still only 44 women Members of Parliament in the House of Commons, out of 650 MPs? Why in the US are there only three female state governors and two female senators, the same number as in the 1930s? Why in the UK are there only two female general secretaries out of a total of 71 affiliated unions in the TUC? And why in 1989 were only 11 per cent of British managers women?

If women 'have it all', then why don't they have the most basic requirements to achieve equality in the work force? The US government provides no family-leave or childcare programmes. The UK has the lowest provision of paid maternity leave in Europe, and is bottom of the European childcare league. In the House of Commons there is a shooting gallery, but no nursery. Prime Minister John Major opted out of signing the Social Chapter, and has maintained strong opposition to EC Directives emanating from the Social Action Programme – which effectively vetoes maternity leave on full pay for British women as well as rights for part-time workers and a maximum 48-hour week. Even in Australia, which overall has a more progressive approach to equal opportunities than the UK and more government monitoring bodies, an Institute of Family Studies maternity leave survey found that there was 'a deep-seated prejudice against working mothers'. Despite winning the right to equal pay for work of equal value in 1972, Australian women in 1990 still earned only 83 per cent of the average earnings of Australian men; and women from Aboriginal backgrounds earned substantially less. Likewise, the Equal Pay Act of 1972 in New Zealand has yet to remove the pay gap between men and women's earnings. Over 50 per cent of women are in the lowest 40 per cent of income earners.

The Conservative government in Britain had to be forced by the European Court to update the law to include the idea of equal pay for work of equal value – even so, the law is weak and cases can take up to four years, with no certainty of success. In the US, a campaign for equal pay for work of equal value was quickly derailed in the courts and denounced by Reagan officials as 'the looniest idea since "Looney Tunes" '. Though business leaders say they are aware of and deplore sex discrimination, corporate Britain, like corporate America, has yet to make an honest effort towards eradicating it. In September 1991 the Hanson Trust announced the appointment of three more non-executive directors to its all-male board. All three were men, even though Sir Gordon Booth, who was responsible for the appointments, admitted that 'Amidst the 100 serious candidates there were certainly a sufficient number of women to allow us to get one out of three or three out of three' – had they wished to.

If women are so 'free', why are their reproductive freedoms in greater jeopardy today than a decade earlier? Why do women who want to postpone childbearing now have fewer options than ten years ago? The availability of different forms of contraception has declined, research for new birth control has virtually halted, and in the US new laws restricting abortion – or even *information* about abortion – for young and poor women have been passed, and the Supreme Court has shown little ardour in defending the right it granted in 1973.

Nor is women's struggle for equal education over; as a 1989 study found, three-quarters of all American high schools still violate the federal law banning sex discrimination in education. In colleges, undergraduate women receive only 70 per cent of the aid undergraduate men get in grants and work-study jobs – and women's sports programmes receive a pittance compared with men's. In Britain, the number of women undergraduates at university fell in 1984 for the first time in years – despite the fact that in the sixth form 9 per cent more girls than boys wanted to go on to higher education.

Nor do women enjoy equality in their own homes, where they still shoulder 70 per cent of the household duties. The 1988 British Attitudes Survey found that in 81 per cent of households where a woman works full time, she is still responsible for the washing and ironing. The only major change in the last fifteen years is that now middle-class men *think* they do more around the house. (In fact, a US poll finds the ranks of women saying their husbands share equally in childcare shrunk to 31 per cent in 1987 from 40

7

per cent three years earlier.) Furthermore, in thirty states it is still generally legal for husbands to rape their wives. (It was not considered a crime in the UK until the House of Lords ruling in October 1991. A month later a man who raped his wife was sentenced at the Old Bailey to six years in prison.) In Canada in 1991 the Supreme Court overturned the so-called 'rape shield' law which protected rape victims from being questioned in court about their previous sexual activity. Only ten US states have laws mandating arrest for domestic violence – even though battering was the leading cause of injury of women in the late eighties. Women who have no other option but to flee find that isn't much of an alternative either. Federal funding for battered women's shelters has been withheld and one third of the million battered women who seek emergency shelter each year can find none. Blows from men contributed far more to the rising numbers of 'bag ladies' than the ill effects of feminism. In the 1980s, almost half of all homeless women (the fastest-growing segment of the homeless) were refugees of domestic violence.

The word may be that women have been 'liberated', but women themselves seem to feel otherwise. Repeatedly in surveys, majorities of women say they are still far from equality. Nearly 70 per cent of women polled by the *New York Times* in 1989 said the movement for women's rights had only just begun. A clear majority of women in a 1991 *Guardian* survey believed that neither men's attitudes to women nor levels of sexual discrimination in the workplace have changed in the past twenty-one years – and for under-thirty-fives the figure rose to almost two-thirds. In poll after poll, overwhelming majorities of women have said they need equal pay and equal job opportunities, they need the right to an abortion without government interference, they need guaranteed maternity leave, they need decent childcare services. They have none of these. So how exactly have we 'won' the war for women's rights?

Seen against this background, the much ballyhooed claim that feminism is responsible for making women miserable becomes absurd – and irrelevant. As we shall see in the chapters to follow, the afflictions ascribed to feminism are all myths. From 'the man shortage' to 'the infertility epidemic' to 'female burn-out' to 'toxic day care', these so-called female crises have had their origins not in the actual conditions of women's lives but in a closed system that starts and ends in the media, popular culture and advertising – an endless feedback loop that perpetuates and exaggerates its own false images of womanhood.

Women themselves don't single out the women's movement as the source of their misery. To the contrary, in national surveys 75 to 95 per cent of women credit the feminist campaign with *improving* their lives, and a similar proportion say that the women's movement should keep pushing for change. Less than 8 per cent think the women's movement might have actually made their lot worse.

What actually is troubling the female population, then? If the many ponderers of the Woman Question really wanted to know, they might have asked their subjects. In public opinion surveys, women consistently rank their own *inequality*, at work and at home, among their most urgent concerns. Over and over, women complain to pollsters about a lack of economic, not marital, opportunities; they protest that working men, not working women, fail to spend time in the nursery and the kitchen. The Roper Organization's survey analysts find that men's opposition to equality is 'a major cause of resentment and stress' and 'a major irritant for most women today'. It is justice for their gender, not wedding rings and cradles, that women believe to be in desperately short supply. When the *New York Times* polled women in 1989 about 'the most important problem facing women today', job discrimination was the overwhelming winner; none of the crises the media and popular culture had so assiduously promoted even made the charts. In the 1990 Virginia Slims opinion poll, women were most upset by their lack of money, followed by the refusal of their men to shoulder childcare and domestic duties. By contrast, when the women were asked where the quest for a husband or the desire to hold a 'less pressured' job or to stay at home ranked on their list of concerns, they placed them at the bottom.

As the last decade ran its course, women's unhappiness with inequality only mounted. In US polls, the ranks of women protesting against discriminatory treatment in business, political and personal life climbed sharply. The proportion of women complaining of unequal employment opportunities jumped more than ten points from the 1970s, and the number of women complaining of unequal barriers to job advancement climbed even higher. By the end of the decade, 80 per cent to 95 per cent of women said they suffered from job discrimination and unequal pay. Formal applications to the UK's Equal Opportunities Commission for funding to pursue sex discrimination charges rose nearly 60 per cent in the Thatcher years. In the home, a much increased proportion of women complained to pollsters of male mistreatment, unequal relationships, and male efforts to, in the words of the Virginia Slims poll, 'keep women down'. The share of women in the Roper surveys who agreed that men were 'basically kind, gentle, and thoughtful' fell from almost 70 per cent in 1970 to 50 per cent by 1990. And outside their homes, women felt more threatened, too: in the 1990 Virginia Slims poll, 72 per cent of women said they felt 'more afraid and uneasy on the streets today' than they did a few years ago. Lest this be attributed only to a general rise in criminal activity, by contrast only 49 per cent of men felt this way.

While the women's movement has certainly made women more aware of their own inequality, the rising chorus of female protest shouldn't be written off as feminist-induced 'oversensitivity'. The monitors that serve to track slippage in women's status have been working overtime since the early 1980s. Government and private surveys are showing that women's already vast representation in the lowliest occupations is rising, their tiny presence in higher-paying trade and craft jobs stalled or backsliding, their minuscule representation in upper management posts stagnant or falling, and their pay dropping in the very occupations where they have made the most 'progress'. The status of women lowest on the income ladder has plunged most perilously; government budget cuts in the first four years of the Reagan administration alone pushed nearly 2 million female-headed families and nearly 5 million women below the poverty line. And the prime target of government rollbacks has been one sex only: one-third of the Reagan budget cuts, for example, came out of programmes that predominantly serve women – even more extraordinary when one considers that all these programmes combined represent only 10 per cent of the federal budget. In Britain, over a million women – single, separated, divorced or widowed – are bringing up children on their own. (Nine out of ten lone parents are women.) Cutbacks in local government, health and welfare services have disproportionately affected women, who are more likely to need and use them.

The alarms aren't just going off in the work force. In US politics, the already small numbers of women in both elective posts and political appointments fell during the eighties. John Major succeeded Margaret Thatcher and chose to exclude women entirely from his first Cabinet. In private life, there has been a 50 per cent drop in the proportion of one-parent families on benefit who receive child maintenance: from 50 per cent to 23 per cent between 1981 and 1988. Domestic-violence shelters in the US recorded a more than 100 per cent increase in the numbers of women taking refuge in their quarters between 1983 and 1987. And government records chronicled a spectacular rise in sexual violence against women. Reported rapes more than doubled from the early seventies – at nearly twice the rate of all other violent crimes and four times the overall crime rate in the United States. While the homicide rate declined, sex-related murders rose 160 per cent between 1976 and 1984. And these murders weren't simply the random, impersonal by-product of a violent society; at least one-third of the women were killed by their husbands or boyfriends, and the majority of that group were murdered just after declaring their independence in the most intimate manner – by filing for divorce and leaving home.

By the end of the decade women were starting to tell pollsters that they feared their sex's social status was once again beginning to slip. They believed they were facing an 'erosion of respect', as the 1990 Virginia Slims poll summed up the sentiment. After years in which an increasing percentage of women had said their status had improved from a decade earlier, the proportion suddenly shrank by 5 per cent in the last half of the 1980s, the Roper Organization reported. And it fell most sharply among women in their thirties – the age group most targeted by the media and advertisers – dropping about ten percentage points between 1985 and 1990.

Some women began to piece the picture together. In the 1989 *New York Times* poll, more than half of black women and a quarter of white women put it into words. They told pollsters they believed men were now trying to retract the gains women had made in the last twenty years. 'I wanted more autonomy', was how one woman, a thirty-seven-year-old nurse, put it. And her estranged husband 'wanted to take it away'.

The truth is that the last decade has seen a powerful counter-assault on women's rights, a backlash, an attempt to retract the handful of small and hard-won victories that the feminist move-ment did manage to win for women. This counterassault is largely insidious: in a kind of pop-culture version of the Big Lie, it stands the truth boldly on its head and proclaims that the very steps that have elevated women's position have actually led to their downfall.

The backlash is at once sophisticated and banal, deceptively 'progressive' and proudly backward. It deploys both the 'new' findings of 'scientific research' and the sentimental moralizing of yesteryear; it turns into media sound bites both the glib pro-nouncements of pop-psych trend-watchers and the frenzied rhet-oric of New Right preachers. The backlash has succeeded in fram-ing virtually the whole issue of women's rights in its own language. Just as Reaganism and Thatcherism shifted political discourse far to the right and demonized liberalism, so the backlash convinced the public that women's 'liberation' was the true contemporary scourge – the source of an endless laundry list of personal, social and economic problems.

But what has made women unhappy in the last decade is not their 'equality' – which they don't yet have – but the rising pres-sure to halt, and even reverse, women's quest for that equality. The 'man shortage' and the 'infertility epidemic' are not the price of liberation; in fact, they do not even exist. But these chimeras are the chisels of a society-wide backlash. They are part of a relentless whittling-down process – much of it amounting to out-right propaganda – that has served to stir women's private anxieties and break their political wills. Identifying feminism as women's enemy only furthers the ends of a backlash against women's equality, simultaneously deflecting attention from the backlash's central role and recruiting women to attack their own cause.

Some social observers may well ask whether the current pressures on women actually constitute a backlash – or just a continuation of Western society's longstanding resistance to women's rights. Certainly hostility to female independence has always been with us. But if fear and loathing of feminism is a sort of perpetual viral condition in our culture, it is not always in an acute stage; its symptoms subside and resurface periodically. And it is these episodes of resurgence, such as the one we face now, that can accurately be termed 'backlashes' to women's advancement. If we trace these occurrences in history, we find such flare-ups are hardly random; they have always been triggered by the perception – accurate or not – that women are making great strides. These outbreaks are backlashes because they have always arisen in reaction to women's 'progress', caused not simply by a bedrock of misogyny but by the specific efforts of contemporary women to improve their status, efforts that have been interpreted time and again by men – especially men grappling with real threats to their economic and social well-being on other fronts – as spelling their own masculine doom.

The most recent round of backlash first surfaced in the late 1970s on the fringes, among the evangelical right. By the early 1980s the fundamentalist ideology had shouldered its way into government. By the mid-eighties, as resistance to women's rights acquired political and social acceptability, it passed into the popular culture. And in every case the timing coincided with signs that women were believed to be on the verge of breakthrough.

Just when women's quest for equal rights seemed closest to achieving its objectives, the backlash struck it down. Just when a 'gender gap' at the voting booth surfaced in the US in 1980, and women in politics began to talk of capitalizing on it, the Republican Party elevated Ronald Reagan, and both political parties began to shunt women's rights off their platforms. Just when support for feminism and the Equal Rights Amendment reached a record high in 1981, the amendment was defeated the following year. Just when women were starting to mobilize against battering and sexual assaults, the federal government stalled funding for battered-women's programmes, defeated bills to fund shelters, and shut down its Office of Domestic Violence – only two years after opening it in 1979. Just when record numbers of younger women were supporting feminist goals in the mid-1980s (more of them, in fact, than older women) and a majority of all women were calling themselves feminists, the media declared that feminism was the flavour of the seventies and that 'post-feminism' was the new story – complete with a younger generation who supposedly reviled the women's movement.

In other words, the anti-feminist backlash has been set off not by women's achievement of full equality but by the increased possibility that they might win it. It is a pre-emptive strike that stops women long before they reach the finishing line. 'A backlash may be an indication that women really have had an effect,' feminist psychologist Dr Jean Baker Miller has written, 'but backlashes occur when advances have been small, before changes are sufficient to help many people . . . It is almost as if the leaders of backlashes use the fear of change as a threat before major change has occurred.' In the last decade some women did make substantial advances before the backlash hit, but millions of others were left behind, stranded. Some women now enjoy the right to legal abortion – but most of the millions of women who depend on government health services for their medical care will not qualify for a 'free' one. Some women can now walk into high-paying professional careers – but not the millions still in the typing pools or behind the department-store sales counters. (Contrary to popular myth about the 'have-it-all' baby-boom women, the largest percentage of women in this generation remain typists and clerks.)

As the backlash has gathered force, it has cut off the few from the many – and the few women who have advanced seek to prove, as a social survival tactic, that they aren't so interested in advancement after all. Some of them parade their defection from the women's movement, while their working-class peers founder and cling to the splintered remains of the feminist cause. Longtime activist Jane Fonda announced she had decided to give up making movies for a while because of her new relationship. 'Ted Turner is not a man that you leave to go on location,' she says. 'He needs you there all the time.' While a very few affluent and celebrity women who are profiled in news articles boast, like Maeve Haran, that their lives are 'fuller, richer, happier' than they ever were when they were 'pretending to Have It All', the many working-class women appeal for their economic rights – flocking to unions in record numbers, striking on their own for pay equity and establishing their own fledgling groups for working women's rights. In 1986, while 41 per cent of upper-income women were claiming in the Gallup poll that they were not feminists, only 26 per cent of low-income women were making the same claim.

Women's advances and retreats are generally described in military terms: battles won, battles lost, points and territory gained and surrendered. The metaphor of combat is not without its merits in this context and, clearly, the same sort of martial accounting and vocabulary is already surfacing here. But by imagining the conflict as two battalions neatly arrayed on either side of the line, we miss the entangled nature, the locked embrace, of a 'war' between women and the male culture they inhabit. We miss the reactive nature of a backlash, which, by definition, can exist only in response to another force. As Brenda Polan put it in the *Guardian*, 'Post-feminism is the backlash. Any movement or philosophy which defines itself as post whatever came before is bound to be reactive. In most cases it is also reactionary.'

In times when feminism is at a low ebb, women assume the reactive role – privately and most often covertly struggling to assert themselves against the dominant cultural tide. But when feminism itself becomes the tide, the opposition doesn't simply go along with the reversal: it digs in its heels, brandishes its fists, builds walls and dams. And its resistance creates countercurrents and treacherous undertows.

The force and fury of the backlash churn beneath the surface, largely invisible to the public eye. On occasions in the last decade they have burst into view. We have seen New Right politicians condemn women's independence, anti-abortion protesters fire-bomb women's clinics, fundamentalist preachers damn feminists as 'whores' and 'witches'. Other signs of the backlash's wrath, by their sheer brutality, can push their way into public consciousness for a time – the sharp increase in rape, for example, or the rise in pornography that depicts extreme violence against women.

More subtle indicators in popular culture may receive momentary, and often bemused, media notice, then quickly slip from social awareness: a report, for instance, that the image of women on prime-time TV shows has suddenly degenerated. A survey of mystery fiction finding the numbers of female characters tortured and mutilated mysteriously multiplying. The puzzling news that, as one commentator put it, 'So many hit songs have the B-word [bitch] to refer to women that some rap music seems to be veering toward rape music.' Or word that, in 1987, the American Women in Radio & Television couldn't award its annual prize for ads that feature women positively: it could find no ad that qualified.

These phenomena are all related, but that doesn't mean they are somehow coordinated. The backlash is not a conspiracy, with a council dispatching agents from some central control room, nor are the people who serve its ends often aware of their role; some even consider themselves feminists. For the most part, its workings are encoded and internalized, diffuse and chameleonic. Not all of the manifestations of the backlash are of equal weight or significance either; some are mere ephemera, generated by a culture machine that is always scrounging for a 'fresh' angle. Taken as a whole, however, these codes and cajolings, these whispers and threats and myths, move overwhelmingly in one direction: they try to push women back into their 'acceptable' roles – whether as Daddy's girl or fluttery romantic, active nester or passive love object.

Although the backlash is not an organized movement, that doesn't make it any less destructive. In fact, the lack of orchestration, the absence of a single string-puller, only makes it harder to see – and perhaps more effective. A backlash against women's rights succeeds to the degree that it appears *not* to be political, that it appears not to be a struggle at all. It is most powerful when it goes private, when it lodges inside a woman's mind and turns her vision inward, until she imagines the pressure is all in her head, until she begins to enforce the backlash, too – on herself.

In the last decade the backlash has moved through the culture's secret chambers, travelling through passageways of flattery and fear. Along the way, it has adopted disguises: a mask of mild derision or the painted face of deep 'concern'. Its lips profess pity for any woman who won't fit the mould, while it tries to clamp the mould around her ears. It pursues a divide-and-conquer strategy: single versus married women, working women versus housewives, middle- versus working-class. It manipulates a system of rewards and punishments, elevating women who follow its rules, isolating those who don't. The backlash remarkets old myths about women as new facts and ignores all appeals to reason. Cornered, it denies its own existence, points an accusatory finger at feminism, and burrows deeper underground.

Backlash happens to be the title of a 1947 Hollywood movie in which a man frames his wife for a murder he's committed. The backlash against women's rights works in much the same way: its rhetoric charges feminists with all the crimes it perpetrates. The backlash line blames the women's movement for the 'feminization of poverty' – while the backlash's own instigators in Washington and London and elsewhere pushed through the budget cuts that helped impoverish millions of women, fought pay equity proposals and undermined equal opportunity laws. The backlash line claims the women's movement cares nothing for children's rights – while its own representatives have blocked one attempt after another to improve childcare. (In the UK publicly funded childcare provision is virtually non-existent. Local authority nurseries provide places for less than 2 per cent of children under two. The Conservative government froze Child Benefit from April 1988 to April 1991, and have still not reinstated its full value – leading many to suspect that their aim is to abolish it altogether.) The backlash line accuses the women's movement of creating a generation of unhappy single and childless women – but its purveyors in the media are the ones guilty of making single and childless women feel like circus freaks.

To blame feminism for women's 'lesser life' is entirely to miss the point of feminism, which is to win women a wider range of experience. Feminism remains a pretty simple concept, despite repeated – and enormously effective – efforts to dress it up in greasepaint and turn its proponents into gargoyles. As Rebecca West wrote sardonically in 1913, 'I myself have never been able to find out precisely what feminism is: I only know that people call me a feminist whenever I express sentiments that differentiate me from a doormat.'

The meaning of the word 'feminist' has not really changed since it first appeared in a book review in the *Athenaeum* of April 27, 1895, describing a woman who 'has in her the capacity of fighting her way back to independence'. It is the basic proposition that, as Nora put it in Ibsen's *A Doll's House* a century ago, 'Before everything else I'm a human being.' It is the simply worded sign hoisted by a little girl in the 1970 US Women's Strike for Equality: I AM NOT A BARBIE DOLL. Feminism asks the world to recognize at long last that women aren't decorative ornaments, worthy vessels, members of a 'special-interest group'. They are half (in fact, now more than half) of the population, and just as deserving of rights and opportunities, just as capable of participating in the world's events, as the other half. Feminism's agenda is basic: it asks that women not be forced to 'choose' between public justice and private happiness. It asks that women be free to define themselves – instead of having their identity defined for them, time and again, by their culture and their men.

The fact that these are still such incendiary notions should tell us that women have a way to go before they enter the promised land of equality.

Part One
Myths and Flashbacks

Chapter Two

Man Shortages and Barren Wombs: The Myths of the Backlash

By the end of the 1980s many women had absorbed the teachings of the media and were bitterly familiar with various 'statistical' developments, most notably a 'man shortage'; a 'devastating' plunge in economic status for women divorcing under new 'no-fault' laws; an 'infertility epidemic'; and a 'great emotional depression' and 'burn-out' attacking, respectively, single and career women.

The source for the 'man shortage' that is supposedly endangering women's opportunities for marriage was a famous 1986 marriage study by Harvard and Yale researchers. It claimed that a college-educated, unwed woman at the age of thirty has a 20 per cent likelihood of marriage, at thirty-five a 5 per cent chance, and at forty no more than a 1.3 per cent chance. The alleged dive in status for today's divorcing women came from a 1985 study by a sociologist then at Stanford University. It found that the average American woman suffers a 73 per cent drop in her living standard a year after divorce, while the average man enjoys a 42 per cent rise. And the so-called 'infertility epidemic' striking professional women who postpone childbearing was based on a 1982 study by two French researchers. It made the alarming claim that women between thirty-one and thirty-five stand a 39 per cent chance of not being able to conceive – a big 13 per cent jump from women in their late twenties. 'Burn-out' was a contention rather than a quasi-scientific theory; it held that women's mental health has never been worse – and is declining in direct proportion to women's tendency to stay single or devote themselves to careers.

These are the fundamental arguments that have supported the backlash against women's quest for equality. They have one thing in common: they aren't true.

That no doubt sounds incredible. We've all heard these facts and figures so many times, as they've bounced back and forth through the backlash's echo chamber, that it's difficult to discount them. How is it possible that so much distorted, faulty or plain inaccurate information can become so universally accepted? Before turning to these myths, a quick look at the way the media handled two particular statistical studies may help in part to answer that question.

Statistics and a Tale of Two Social Scientists

In 1987 the American media had the opportunity to spotlight the work of two social scientists. One of them had exposed hostility to women's independence; the other had endorsed it.

'The picture that has emerged of Shere Hite in recent weeks is that of a pop-culture demagogue', the November 23, 1987 issue of *Newsweek* informed its readers, under the headline MEN AREN'T HER ONLY PROBLEM. Shere Hite had just published the last instalment of her national survey on sexuality and relationships, *Women and Love: A Cultural Revolution in Progress*, a 922-page compendium of the views of 4,500 women. The report's main finding: most women are distressed and despairing over the continued resistance from the men in their lives to treat them as equals. Four-fifths of them said they still had to fight for rights and respect at home, and only 20 per cent felt they had achieved equal status in their men's eyes. Their quest for more independence, they reported, had triggered mounting rancour from their mates.

This was not, however, the aspect of the book that the press chose to highlight. The media were too busy attacking Hite personally. Most of the evidence they marshalled against her involved tales that, as *Newsweek* let slip, 'only tangentially involve her work'. Hite was rumoured to have punched a cab-driver for calling her 'dear' and phoned reporters claiming to be Diana Gregory, Hite's assistant. Curious behaviour, if true, but behaviour that suggests a personality more eccentric than demagogic. Nonetheless, the nation's major publications pursued tips on the feminist researcher's peculiarities with uncharacteristic ardour. The *Washington Post* even brought in a handwriting expert to compare the signatures of Hite and Gregory.

Certainly Hite's work deserved scrutiny; many valid questions could be raised about her statistical approach. But Hite's findings were largely held up for ridicule, not inspection. 'Characteristically grandiose in scope', 'highly improbable', 'dubious' and 'of limited value' was how *Time* dismissed Hite's report in its October 12, 1987, article 'Back Off, Buddy' – leading one to wonder why, if the editors felt this way, they devoted the magazine's cover and six inside pages to the subject. The book is full of 'extreme views' from 'strident' women who are probably just 'malcontents', the magazine asserted. Whether their views were actually extreme, however, was impossible to determine from *Time*'s account: the lengthy story squeezed in only two two-sentence quotes from the thousands of women that Hite had polled and quoted extensively. Yet the same article gave plenty of space to Hite's critics – far more than to Hite herself.

When the media did actually criticize Hite's statistical methods, their accusations were often wrong or hypocritical. Hite's findings were 'biased' because she distributed her questionnaires through women's rights groups, some articles complained. But Hite sent her surveys through a wide range of women's groups, including church societies, social clubs and senior citizens' centres. The press charged that she used a small and unrepresentative sample. Yet, as we shall see, the results of many psychological and social science studies that journalists report uncritically are based on much smaller and non-random samples. And Hite specifically states in the book that the numbers are *not* meant to be representative; her goal, she writes, is simply to give as many women as possible a public forum to voice their intimate, and generally silenced, thoughts. The book is actually more a collection of quotations than numbers.

While the media widely characterized these women's stories

about their husbands and lovers as 'man-bashing diatribes', the voices in Hite's book are far more forlorn than vengeful: 'I have given heart and soul of everything I am and have . . . leaving me with nothing and lonely and hurt, and he is still requesting more of me. I am tired, so tired.' 'He hides behind a silent wall.' 'Most of the time I just feel left out – not his best friend.' 'At this point, I doubt that he loves me or wants me . . . I try to wear more feminine nightgowns and do things to please him.' 'In daily life he criticizes me for trivial things, cupboards and doors left open . . . I don't like him angry. So I just close the cupboards, close the drawers, switch off the lights, pick up after him, etc., etc., and say nothing.'

From these personal reports Hite culls some data about women's attitudes toward relationships, marriage and monogamy. That the media find this data so threatening to men is a sign of how easily hysteria about female 'aggression' ignites under an anti-feminist backlash. For instance, should the press really have been infuriated – or even surprised – that the women's number-one grievance about their men is that they 'don't listen'?

If anything, the media seemed to be bearing out the women's complaint by turning a deaf ear to their words. Maybe it was easier to flip through Hite's numerical tables at the back of the book than to digest the hundreds of pages of rich and disturbing personal stories: stories which Tom Hibbert, looking back at *The Hite Report* in the British magazine *Options*, characterized as 'a collection of lurid vignettes concerning the female anatomy'. In reporting the attacks on Hite in the States Hibbert adopted a sneering tone – even to the point of describing her voice as being that of 'a "dippy chick". Bimboid almost.' Perhaps some journalists just couldn't stand hearing what these women had to say; the overheated denunciations of Hite's book suggest an emotion closer to fear than fury – as do the illustrations accompanying *Time*'s story, which included a woman standing on the chest of a collapsed man, a woman dropping a shark in a man's bathwater, and a woman wagging a viperish tongue in a frightened male face. Tom Hibbert went as far as to sympathize with Hite's husband, Friedrich Horicke: 'Poor Fred. Compliant and crushed.'

At the same time the press was pillorying Hite for suggesting that male resistance might be partly responsible for women's grief, it was applauding another social scientist whose theory – that women's equality was to blame for contemporary women's anguish – was more consonant with backlash thinking. Psychologist Dr Srully Blotnick, a *Forbes* magazine columnist and much quoted media 'expert' on women's career travails, had directed what he called 'the largest long-term study of working women ever done in the United States'. His conclusion: success at work 'poisons both the professional and personal lives of women'. In his 1985 book, *Otherwise Engaged: The Private Lives of Successful Women*, Blotnick asserted that his twenty-five-year study of 3,466 women proved that achieving career women are likely to end up without love, and their spinsterly misery would eventually undermine their careers as well. 'In fact,' he wrote, 'we found that the anxiety, which steadily grows, is the single greatest underlying cause of firing for women in the age range of thirty-five to fifty-five.' He took some swipes at the women's movement, too, which he called a 'smoke screen behind which most of those who were afraid of being labeled egomaniacally grasping and ambitious hid'.

The media received his findings warmly – he was a fixture everywhere from the *New York Times* to the *Donahue* show – and national magazines like *Forbes* and *Savvy* paid him hundreds of thousands of dollars to produce still more studies about these anxiety-ridden careerists. None doubted his methodology, even though there were some fairly obvious grounds for scepticism – such as Blotnick's claims that he had 'three tons of files' (a larger data base than any federal study) and had been conducting surveys since 1958, when he would have been only seventeen years old.

In the mid-1980s Dan Collins, a reporter at *US News & World Report*, was assigned a story on that currently all-popular media subject: the misery of the unwed. His editor suggested he call the ever-quotable Blotnick, who had just appeared in a similar story on the woes of singles in the *Washington Post*. After his interview, Collins recalls, he began to wonder why Blotnick had seemed so nervous when asked for his academic credentials. The reporter looked further into Blotnick's background and found what he thought was a better story: the career of this national authority was built on sand. Not only was Blotnick not a licensed psychologist, almost nothing on his résumé checked out; even the professor that he cited as his current mentor had been dead for fifteen years. But Collins's editors at *US News* had no interest in that story – a spokeswoman explained later that they didn't have a news 'peg' for it – and the article was never published.

The press's treatment of Hite's and Blotnick's findings suggests that the statistics the popular culture chooses to promote most heavily are the very statistics we should view with the most caution. They may well be in wide circulation not because they are true but because they support widely held media preconceptions.

Under the backlash, statistics became prescriptions for expected female behaviour, cultural marching orders to women describing only how they *should* act – and how they would be punished if they failed to heed the call. These 'data' were said to reflect simply 'the way things are' for women, a bedrock of demographic reality that was impossible to alter; the only choice for women was to accept the numbers and lower their sights to meet them.

As the backlash consensus solidified, statistics on women stopped functioning as social barometers. The data instead became society's checkpoints, positioned at key intervals in the life course of women, dispatching warnings on the perils of straying from the appointed path. This prescriptive agenda, certainly in the US, governed the life span of virtually every statistic on women in the 1980s, from initial gathering to final dissemination. In the Reagan administration, US Census Bureau demographers found themselves under increasing pressure to generate data for the government's war against women's independence, to produce statistics 'proving' the rising threat of infertility, the physical and psychic risks lurking in abortion, the dark side of single parenthood, the ill effects of day care. 'People I've dealt with in the [Reagan] government seem to want to recreate the fantasy of their own childhood,' Martin O'Connell, chief of the Census Bureau's fertility statistics branch, says. And results that didn't fit that fantasy were discarded, like a government study finding that federal affirmative action policies have a positive effect on corporate hiring rates of women and minorities. The Public Health Service censored information on the beneficial health effects of abortion and demoted and fired federal scientists whose findings conflicted with the administration's so-called pro-family policy.

'Most social research into the family has had an immediate moral purpose – to eliminate deviations like divorce, desertion, illegitimacy and adultery – rather than a desire to understand the fundamental nature of social institutions,' social scientist Kingsley Davis wrote in his 1948 classic, *Human Society*. More than forty years later it is one of the few statements by a demographer that has held up.

The Man Shortage: A Tale of Two Marriage Studies

Valentine's Day 1986 was coming up, and at the Stamford *Advocate* it was reporter Lisa Marie Petersen's turn to produce that year's story on Cupid's slings and arrows. Her 'angle', as she recalls later, would be 'Romance: Is It In or Out?' She went down to the Stamford Town Center mall and interviewed a few men shopping for flowers and chocolates. Then she put in a call to the Yale sociology department, 'just to get some kind of foundation,' she says. 'You know, something to put in the third paragraph.'

She got Neil Bennett on the phone – a thirty-one-year-old unmarried sociologist who had recently completed, with two colleagues, an unpublished study on women's marriage patterns. Bennett warned her the study wasn't really finished, but when she pressed him he told her what he had found: college-educated women who put schooling and careers before their wedding date were going to have a harder time getting married. 'The marriage market unfortunately may be falling out from under them,' he told her.

Bennett brought out the numbers: never-married college-educated women at thirty had a 20 per cent chance of being wed; by thirty-five their odds were down to 5 per cent; by forty, to 1.3 per cent. And black women had even lower odds. 'My jaw just dropped,' recalls Petersen, who was twenty-seven and single at the time. Petersen never thought to question the figures. 'We usually just take anything from good schools. If it's a study from Yale, we just put it in the paper.'

The *Advocate* ran the news on the front page. The Associated

Press immediately picked up the story and carried it across the nation and eventually around the world. In no time, Bennett was fielding calls from Australia.

In the United States, the marriage news was absorbed by every outlet of mass culture. The statistics received front-page treatment in virtually every major newspaper and top billing on network news programmes and talk shows. They wound up in sitcoms from *Designing Women* to *Kate and Allie*; in movies from *Crossing Delancey* to *When Harry Met Sally* to *Fatal Attraction*; in women's magazines from *Mademoiselle* to *Cosmopolitan*; in dozens of self-help manuals, dating-service mailings, night-class courses on relationships, and greeting cards. Even a transit advertising service, 'The Street Fare Journal', plastered the study's findings on display racks in city buses around the USA, so single straphangers on their way to work could gaze upon a poster of a bereft lass in a bridal veil, posed next to a scorecard listing her miserable nuptial odds.

Bennett and his colleagues, Harvard economist David Bloom and Yale graduate student Patricia Craig, predicted a 'marriage crunch' for baby-boom college-educated women for primarily one reason: women marry men an average of between two and three years older. So, they reasoned, women born in the first half of the baby boom between 1946 and 1957, when the birthrate was increasing each year, would have to scrounge for men in the less populated older age brackets. And those education-minded women who decided to get their degrees before their marriage licences would wind up worst off, the researchers postulated – on the theory that the early bird gets the worm.

At the very time the study was released, however, the assumption that women marry older men was rapidly becoming outmoded; federal statistics now showed first-time brides marrying grooms an average of only 1.8 years older. (In England and Wales the 'age gap' was similarly small, and actually narrower in 1986 than ten years before.) But it was impossible to revise the Harvard–Yale figures in light of these changes, or even to examine them – since the study wasn't published. This evidently did not bother the press, which chose to ignore a published study on the same subject – released only a few months earlier – that came to the opposite conclusion. That study, an October 1985 report by researchers at the University of Illinois, concluded that the marriage crunch in the United States was minimal. Their data, the researchers wrote, 'did not support theories which see the marriage squeeze as playing a major role in recent changes in marriage behavior'. (In fact, in their historical and geographic review of marital data, they could find 'marriage crunches' only in a few European nations back in the 1900s and in some Third World countries in more modern times.)

In March 1986 Bennett and his co-researchers released an informal 'discussion paper' that revealed they had used a 'parametric model' to compute women's marital odds – an unorthodox and untried method for predicting behaviour. Princeton professors Ansley Coale and Donald McNeil had originally constructed the parametric model to analyse marital patterns of elderly women who had already completed their marriage cycle. Bennett and Bloom, who had been graduate students under Coale, thought they could use the same method to predict marriage patterns. Coale, asked about it later, was doubtful. 'In principle, the model may be applicable to women who haven't completed their marital history,' he says, 'but it is risky to apply it.'

As news of the 'man shortage' study raced through the media, Jeanne Moorman, a demographer in the US Census Bureau's marriage and family statistics branch, kept getting calls from reporters seeking comment. She decided to take a closer look at the researchers' paper. A college-educated woman with a doctoral degree in marital demography, Moorman was herself an example of how individual lives defy demographic pigeonholes: she had married at thirty-two, to a man nearly four years younger.

Moorman sat down at her computer and conducted her own marriage study, using conventional standard-life tables instead of the parametric model, and drawing on the 1980 Population Census, which includes 13.4 million households, instead of the 1982 survey that Bennett used, which includes only 60,000 households. The results: at thirty, never-married college-educated women have a 58 to 66 per cent chance of marriage – three times the Harvard–Yale study's predictions. At thirty-five the odds were 32 to 41 per cent, seven times higher than the Harvard–Yale figure.

At forty the odds were 17 to 23 per cent, *twenty-three* times higher. And she found that a college-educated single woman at thirty would be *more* likely to marry than her counterpart with only a high-school diploma.

In June 1986 Moorman wrote to Bennett with her findings. She pointed out that more recent data also ran counter to his predictions about college-educated women. While the marriage rate has been declining in the general population, the rate has actually risen for women with four or more years of college who marry between the ages of twenty-five and forty-five. 'This seems to indicate delaying rather than forgoing marriage,' she noted.

Moorman's letter was polite, almost deferential. As a professional colleague, she wrote, she felt obliged to pass along these comments, 'which I hope will be well received.' They were received with silence. Two months passed. Then, in August, writer Ben Wattenberg mentioned Moorman's study in his syndicated newspaper column and noted that it would be presented at the Population Association of America Conference, an important professional gathering for demographers. Moorman's findings could prove embarrassing to Bennett and Bloom before their colleagues. Suddenly, a letter arrived in Moorman's mailbox. 'I understand from Ben Wattenberg that you will be presenting these results at PAA in the spring,' Bennett wrote; would she send him a copy 'as soon as it's available'? When she didn't send it off at once, he called and, Moorman recalls, 'He was very demanding. It was, "You have to do this, you have to do that."' This was to become a pattern in her dealings with Bennett, she says. 'I always got the feeling from him that he was saying, "Go away, little girl, I'm a college professor; I'm right and you have no right to question me."' (Bennett refuses to discuss his dealings with Moorman or any other aspect of the marriage study's history, asserting that he has been a victim of the over-eager media, which 'misinterpreted [the study] more than I had ever anticipated'. Neither Neil Bennett nor David Bloom have ever agreed that any error was made.)

Meanwhile at the Census Bureau, Moorman recalls, she was running into interference from Reagan administration officials. The head office handed down a directive, ordering her to quit speaking to the press about the marriage study because such critiques were 'too controversial'. She was told to concentrate instead on a study that the White House wanted – about how poor unwed mothers abuse the welfare system.

By the winter of 1986 Moorman had put the finishing touches to her marriage report with the more optimistic findings and released it to the press. The media relegated it to the inside pages, when they reported it at all. At the same time, in an op-ed piece printed in the *New York Times*, the *Boston Globe* and *Advertising Age*, Bennett and Bloom roundly attacked Moorman for issuing her study, which only 'further muddled the discussion', they complained. Moorman and two other Census Bureau statisticians wrote a response to Bennett and Bloom's op-ed article. But the Census Bureau held up its release for months. 'By the time they finished blue-lining it,' Moorman recalls, 'it said nothing. We sent it to the *New York Times*, but by then it was practically the next December and they wouldn't print it.'

Bennett and Bloom's essay had criticized Moorman for using the standard-life tables, which they labelled a 'questionable technique'. So Moorman decided to repeat her study using the Harvard–Yale men's own parametric model. She took the data down the hall to Robert Fay, a statistician whose speciality is mathematical models. Fay looked over Bennett and Bloom's computations and immediately spotted a major error. They had forgotten to take account of the different patterns in college- and high-school-educated women's marital histories. (High school-educated women tend to marry in a tight cluster right after graduation, making for a steep and narrow bell curve skewed to the left. College-educated women tend to spread out the age of marriage over a longer and later period of time, making for a longer and lower curve skewed to the right.) Fay made the adjustments and ran the data again, using Bennett and Bloom's mathematical model. The results this time were nearly identical to Moorman's.

So Robert Fay wrote a letter to Bennett. He pointed out the error and its significance. 'I believe this reanalysis points up not only the incorrectness of your results,' he wrote, 'but also a necessity to return to the rest of the data to examine your assumptions more closely.' Bennett wrote back the next day. 'Things have gotten grossly out of hand,' he said. 'I think it's high time that we get together and regain at least some control of the situation.' He blamed the press for their differences and pointedly noted that 'David [Bloom] and I decided to stop entirely our dealings with all media', a hint perhaps that the Census researchers should do the same. But Bennett needn't have worried about his major error making headlines: Moorman had, in fact, already mentioned it to several reporters, but no one was interested.

Three and a half years after the Harvard–Yale study made nationwide headlines, the actual study was finally published – without the marriage statistics. Bennett told the *New York Times*: 'We're not shying away because we have anything to hide.' The famous statistics were deleted, Bennett said, because 'Right now my colleagues and I don't know whether we can stand behind our results or whether they warrant alteration or what have you.'

In all the reportorial enterprise expended on the Harvard–Yale study, the press managed to overlook a basic point: there was no man shortage. As a simple check of the latest Census population charts would have revealed, there were about 1.9 million more bachelors than unwed women between the ages of twenty-five and thirty-four and about half a million more between the ages of thirty-five and fifty-four. (The 1986 Census for England and Wales bears these figures out – in the two age groups there were, respectively, 464,000 and 275,000 more single men than single women.) In fact, the proportion of never-married men was larger than at any time since the Census Bureau began keeping records in 1890. If anyone faced a shortage of potential spouses, it was *men* in the prime marrying years: between the ages of twenty-four and thirty-four there were 119 single men for every hundred single women. In 1991 *Woman's Journal* reported that 'By the age of 40, only one woman in 20 but one man in 11 remains single.'

A glance at past Census charts would also have dispelled the notion that the USA was awash in a record glut of single women. The proportion of never-married women, about one in five, was lower than it had been at any time in the twentieth century except the 1950s, and even lower than the mid- to late nineteenth century, when one in three women was unmarried. In Victorian England, one-third of the female population could anticipate a single life, whereas today the figure is fewer than one woman in twelve. If one looks at never-married women aged forty-five to fifty-four (a better indicator of lifelong single status than women in their twenties and thirties, who may simply be postponing marriage), the number of unwed British women in 1985 was, in fact, smaller than in 1891, and smaller even than in the marriage-crazed 1950s. In fact, the only place where a 'surplus' of unattached women could be said to exist in the eighties was in retirement communities. What was the median age of American women living alone in 1986? Sixty-six years old. (The median age of single men, by contrast, was forty-two.)

Conventional press wisdom held that single women of the 1980s were desperate for marriage – a desperation that mounted with every passing unwed year. Surveys of real-life women told a different story. A massive study of women's attitudes by Battelle Memorial Institute in 1986, which examined fifteen years of national surveys of 10,000 women, found that marriage was no longer the centrepiece of women's lives and that women in their thirties were not only delaying but actually dodging the wedding rings. The 1985 Virginia Slims poll reported that 70 per cent of women believed they could have a 'happy and complete' life without a wedding ring. In the 1989 'New Diversity' poll by Langer Associates and Significance Inc., that proportion had jumped to 90 per cent. *Cosmopolitan* in the UK reported in 1988 that 'a whacking majority' (81 per cent) of their readers surveyed enjoyed being single. A 1989 Loius Harris poll of older single women – between forty-five and sixty – found that the majority of them said that they didn't want to get married. A review of fourteen years of US National Survey data charted an 11 per cent jump in happiness among 1980s-era single women in their twenties and thirties – and a 6.3 per cent *decline* in happiness among married women of the same age. If marriage had ever served to boost personal female happiness, the researchers concluded, then 'those effects apparently have waned considerably in the last few years'.

In lieu of marriage, more women were choosing to live with their loved ones. The cohabitation rate in Britain tripled between 1979 and 1988. In Australia, by 1991, 7 per cent of all couples were cohabiting, and in New Zealand the number of people in 'de facto unions' rose by nearly a third between 1981 and 1986. In some European countries the levels of cohabitation are even higher. In Norway, France, Germany and Finland, for example, between 10 and 15 per cent of all couples in 1989 were thought to be cohabiting.

More people, too, and especially women, were opting to live on their own. Single-person households in Britain have grown from an eighth of the total in 1961 to more than a quarter in 1990, much of the growth due to an increasing number of career women, who get the satisfaction from work that previously came only from a family. *The Times* reported: 'But there is a cost. By their mid-30s, career women find that most eligible men are married. Many of the remaining men are poorly educated, suffering from a chronic illness or lacking in social graces.'

The more women are paid, the less eager they are to marry. A 1982 study of 3,000 singles found that women earning high incomes are almost twice as likely to *want* to remain unwed as women earning low incomes. 'What is going to happen to marriage and childbearing in a society where women really have equality?' Princeton demographer Charles Westoff wondered in the *Wall Street Journal* in 1986. 'The more economically independent women are, the less attractive marriage becomes.'

Men in the 1980s, on the other hand, were a little more anxious to marry than the press accounts let on. Single men far outnumbered women in dating services, matchmaking clubs and the personals columns, all of which enjoyed explosive growth in the decade. In the mid-eighties video dating services were complaining of a three-to-one male-to-female sex ratio in their membership rolls. In fact it had become common practice for dating services to admit single women at heavily reduced rates, even free memberships, in hopes of remedying the imbalance.

Personal ads were similarly lopsided. In an analysis of 1,200 ads in 1988, sociologist Theresa Montini found that most were placed by thirty-five-year-old heterosexual men and the vast majority 'wanted a long-term relationship'. Dating service directors reported that the majority of men they counselled were seeking spouses, not dates. These men had good cause to pursue nuptials; if there's one pattern that psychological studies have established, it's that the institution of marriage has an overwhelmingly salutary effect on men's mental health. 'Being married,' the prominent government demographer Paul Glick once estimated, 'is about twice as advantageous to men as to women in terms of continued survival.' Or, as family sociologist Jessie Bernard wrote in 1972:

> There are few findings more consistent, less equivocal, [and] more convincing, than the sometimes spectacular and always impressive superiority on almost every index – demographic, psychological, or social – of married over never-married men. Despite all the jokes about marriage in which men indulge, all the complaints they lodge against it, it is one of the greatest boons of their sex.

Bernard's observation still applies. As Ronald C. Kessler, who tracks changes in men's mental health at the University of Michigan's Institute for Social Research, says: 'All this business about how hard it is to be a single woman doesn't make much sense when you look at what's really going on. It's single men who have the worst of it. When men marry, their mental health massively increases.'

The mental health data, chronicled in dozens of studies that have looked at marital differences in the last forty years, are consistent and overwhelming: the suicide rate of single men is twice as high as that of married men. Single men suffer from nearly twice as many severe neurotic symptoms and are far more susceptible to nervous breakdowns, depression, even nightmares. And despite the all-American image of the carefree single cowboy, in reality bachelors are far more likely to be morose, passive and phobic than married men.

When contrasted with single women, unwed men fared no better in mental health studies. Single men suffer from twice as many mental health impairments as single women; they are more depressed, more passive, more likely to experience nervous breakdowns and all the designated symptoms of psychological distress – from fainting to insomnia. In one study, one third of the single men scored high for severe neurotic symptoms; only 4 per cent of the single women did.

In 1987 news surfaced in the USA that women's age at first

marriage had dropped slightly and, reversing a twenty-year trend, the number of family households had grown faster between 1986 and 1987 than the number of non-family households. (The increase in family households, however, was a tiny 1.5 per cent.) These small changes were immediately hailed as a sign of the comeback of traditional marriage. 'A new traditionalism, centered on family life, is in the offing,' Jib Fowles, University of Houston professor of human sciences, cheered in a 1988 opinion piece in the *New York Times*. Fowles predicted 'a resurgence of the conventional family by the year 2000 (father working, mother at home with the children)'. This would be good for American industry, he reminded business magnates who might be reading the article. 'Romance and courtship will be back in favor, so sales of cut flowers are sure to rise,' he pointed out. And 'a return to home-making will mean a rise in supermarket sales.'

This would also be good news for men, a point that Fowles skirted in print but made plain enough in a later interview: 'There's not even going to have to be a veneer of that ideology of subscribing to feminist thoughts,' he says. 'Men are just going to feel more comfortable with the changed conditions. Every sign that I can see is that men feel uncomfortable with the present setup.' He admits to being one of them: 'A lot of it has to do with my assumptions of what it is to be a male.'

But will his wife embrace the 'new traditionalism' with equal relish? After having recently given birth to their second child, she returned immediately to her post as secondary education coordinator for a large Texas school district. 'She's such a committed person to her job,' Fowles says, sighing. 'I don't think she'd give up her career.'

The No-Fault Disaster: A Tale of Two Divorce Reports

In the 1970s, many states in the US passed new 'no-fault' divorce laws that made the process easier: they eliminated the moralistic grounds required to obtain a divorce and divided up a marriage's assets based on needs and resources without reference to which party was held responsible for the marriage's failure. In the 1980s these 'feminist-inspired' laws came under attack: the New Right painted them as schemes to undermine the family, and the media and popular writers portrayed them as inadvertent betrayals of women and children, legal slingshots that 'threw thousands of middle-class women', as a typical chronicler put it, 'into impoverished states'.

Reform proposals for 'no-fault' divorce in England and Wales, recommended by the Law Commission in 1990, have also come under fire. The Lord Chancellor, Lord Mackay, reported that during consultations, reactions had mostly been favourable, but even so: 'there is quite a strong feeling in some people's minds that the Law Commission did not recognize sufficiently clearly the need to strengthen the institution of marriage.' He plans to publish his own reform proposals – but not until after the 1992 general election.

At present, 70 per cent of divorces are granted on the fault-based grounds of adultery, unreasonable behaviour or desertion. The government's backtracking on no-fault divorce was welcomed by the *Daily Mail*, whose front-page headline crowed, 'BRAKES GO ON DIVORCE, Innocent spouses will get new veto'. As seven out of ten divorces are granted to wives, most of these unwilling, 'innocent' spouses are their husbands. The prospect of the law being liberalized had, the *Mail* declared, 'brought a fierce backlash from MPs and pro-family organisations who believe that the divorce legislation of the 60s and 70s undermined marriage and ignored the misery inflicted on children'. The paper quoted a recent report that broken marriages cost Britain £10 billion a year and threaten its economic recovery.

Mrs Valerie Riches, director of the Family Education Trust, says: 'If you make divorce easy, people think it's OK to do it. If the government says marriage and the family are important, it makes people think a bit harder about breaking them up.' According to Lord Mackay, it is now likely that a contested divorce will only be granted after a longer separation period than the five years obligatory in 1991. Dr Jack Dominian, director of the marriage research body One Plus One, says the current level of divorce in Britain is 'mad for the couples, mad for the children, mad for society. Any change in the law that doesn't defend marriage as much as possible is moving in the wrong direction.'

Elsewhere in the world, some progressive governments have made divorce more accessible. Australia, for example, introduced no-fault divorce in 1976, under the terms of the Family Law Act (1975). The Act allows couples to dissolve their marriage on the grounds of irretrievable breakdown after twelve months of separation. Likewise, in New Zealand, the Family Proceedings Act (1980) made the sole ground for divorce irreconcilable breakdown, evidenced in this case by living apart for two years. In both countries, costs and stress have been reduced by transferring the proceedings to 'family courts'.

Perhaps no one person did more to fuel the attack on US divorce-law reform in the backlash decade than sociologist Lenore Weitzman, whose 1985 book, *The Divorce Revolution: The Unexpected Social and Economic Consequences for Women and Children in America*, supplied the numbers quoted by everyone assailing the new laws. From Phyllis Schlafly to Betty Friedan, from the *National Review* to the *CBS Evening News*, Weitzman's 'devastating' statistics were invoked as proof that women who sought freedom from unhappy marriages were making a big financial mistake: they would wind up poorer under the new laws – worse off than if they had divorced under the older, more 'protective' system, or if they had simply stayed married.

If the media latched on to Weitzman's findings with remarkable fervour, they weren't solely to blame for the hype. Weitzman wasn't above blowing her own trumpet. Until her study came along, she writes in *The Divorce Revolution*, 'No one knew just how devastating divorce had become for women and children.' Her data, she asserts, 'took years to collect and analyze' and constituted 'the first comprehensive portrait' of the effects of divorce under the new laws.

This is Weitzman's thesis: 'The major economic result of the divorce-law revolution is the systematic impoverishment of divorced women and their children.' Under the old 'fault' system, Weitzman writes, the 'innocent' party stood to receive more than half the property – an arrangement that, she says, generally worked to the wronged wife's benefit. The new system, on the other hand, hurts women because it is too equal – an evenhandedness that is hurting older housewives most of all, she says. '[T]he legislation of equality actually resulted in a worsened position for women and, by extension, a worsened position for children.'

Weitzman's work does not say feminists were responsible for the new no-fault laws, but those who promoted her work most often acted as if her book indicts the women's movement. *The Divorce Revolution*, *Time* informed its readers, shows how forty-three states passed no-fault laws 'largely in response to feminist demand'. A flurry of anti-no-fault books, most of them imitations of Weitzman's work, blamed the women's movement for divorced women's poverty. 'The impact of the divorce revolution is a clear example of how an equal-rights orientation has failed women,' Mary Ann Mason writes in *The Equality Trap*. '[J]udges are receiving the message that feminists are sending.'

Actually, feminists had almost nothing to do with divorce-law reform – as Weitzman herself points out. The 1970 California no-fault law, considered the most radical for its equal-division rule, was drafted by a largely male advisory board. The American Bar Association, not the National Organization for Women, instigated the national 'divorce revolution' – which wasn't even much of a revolution. At the time of Weitzman's work, half the states still had the traditional 'fault' system on their books, with no-fault only as an option. Only eight states had actually passed community property provisions like the California law, and only a few required equal property division.

Weitzman argued that because women and men are differently situated in marriage – that is, the husbands usually make more money and, upon divorce, the wives usually get the kids – treating the spouses equally upon divorce winds up overcompensating the husband and cheating the wife and children. On the surface this argument seems reasonable enough, and Weitzman even had the statistics to prove it: 'The research shows that on the average, divorced women and the minor children in their households experience a 73 percent decline in their standard of living in the first year after divorce. Their former husbands, in contrast, experience a 42 percent rise in their standard of living.'

These figures seemed alarming, and the press willingly passed them on – without asking two basic questions: were Weitzman's statistics correct? And, even more important, did she actually show that women fared *worse* under the new divorce laws than the old?

In the summer of 1986, soon after Lenore Weitzman had finished testifying before Congress on the failings of no-fault divorce, she received a letter from Saul Hoffman, an economist at the University of Delaware who specializes in divorce statistics. He wrote that he and his partner, University of Michigan social scientist Greg Duncan, were a little bewildered by her now famous 73 per cent statistic. They had been tracking the effect of divorce on income for two decades and they had found the changes following divorce to be nowhere near as dramatic as she described. They found a much smaller 30 per cent decline in women's living standards in the first year after divorce and a much smaller 10 to 15 per cent improvement for men. Moreover, Hoffman observed, they found the lower living standard for many divorced women to be temporary. Five years after divorce, the average woman's living standard was actually slightly *higher* than when she was married to her ex-husband.

After Weitzman failed to respond to various requests to share her data, Duncan and Hoffman tried repeating her calculations using her numbers in the book. But they still came up with a 33 per cent, not a 73 per cent, decline in women's standard of living. The two demographers published this finding in *Demography*. 'Weitzman's highly publicized findings are almost certainly in error,' they wrote. Not only was the 73 per cent figure 'suspiciously large', it was 'inconsistent with information on changes in income and per capita income that she reports'. The press response? The *Wall Street Journal* acknowledged Duncan and Hoffman's article in a brief item in the newspaper's demography column. No one else picked it up.

Weitzman never responded to Duncan and Hoffman's critique. 'They are just wrong,' she says in a phone interview. 'It does compute.' She refuses to answer any additional questions put to her. 'You have my position. I'm working on something very different and I just don't have the time.'

Confirmation of Duncan and Hoffman's findings came from the US Census Bureau, which issued its study on the economic effects of divorce in March 1991. The results were in line with Duncan and Hoffman's. '[Weitzman's] numbers are way too high,' says Suzanne Bianchi, the Census Study's author. 'And that seventy-three percent figure that keeps getting thrown around isn't even consistent with other numbers in [Weitzman's] work.'

How could Weitzman's conclusions have been so far off the mark? There are several possible explanations. First, her statistics, unlike Duncan and Hoffman's, were not based on a national sample, although the press widely represented them as such. She drew the people she interviewed from Los Angeles County divorce court. Second, her sample was remarkably small – 114 divorced women and 114 divorced men. Finally, Weitzman drew her financial information on these divorced couples from a notoriously unreliable source – their own memories. 'We were amazed at their ability to recall precisely the appraised value of their house, the amount of the mortgage, the value of the pension plan, etc.,' she writes in her book. Memory, particularly in the emotion-charged realm of divorce, is hardly a reliable source of statistics; one wishes that Weitzman had been a little less 'amazed' by the subjects' instant recall and a little more dogged about referring to the actual records.

To be fair, the 73 per cent statistic is only one number in Weitzman's work. And a 30 per cent decline in women's living standard is hardly ideal, either. Although the media fixed on its sensational implications, the figure has little bearing on her second and more central point – that women are *worse* off since 'the divorce revolution'. This is an important question because it gets to the heart of the backlash argument: women are better off 'protected' than equal.

Yet, while Weitzman's book states repeatedly that the new laws have made life 'worse' for women than the old ones, it concludes by recommending that legislators should keep the new divorce laws with a little fine-tuning. And she strongly warns against a return to the old system, which she calls a 'charade' of fairness. '[I]t is clear that it would be unwise and inappropriate to suggest that California return to a more traditional system,' she writes.

Needless to say, this conclusion never made it into the press coverage of Weitzman's study. A closer reading explains why

Weitzman had little choice but to abandon her theory on no-fault divorce: she had conducted interviews only with men and women who divorced after the 1970 no-fault law went into effect in California. She had no comparable data on couples who divorced under the old system – and so no way of testing her hypothesis. (A later 1990 study by two law professors reached the opposite conclusion: women and children, they found, were slightly better off economically under the no-fault provisions.)

Nonetheless, Weitzman suggests she had two other types of evidence to show that divorcing women suffered more under no-fault law. Divorcing women, she writes, are less likely to be awarded alimony under the new legislation – a loss most painful to older housewives who are ill equipped to enter the work force. Second, women are now often forced to sell the family house. Yet Weitzman fails to make the case on either count.

National data collected by the US Census Bureau show that the percentage of women awarded alimony or maintenance payments (all told, a mere 14 per cent) is not significantly different from what it was in the 1920s. Weitzman argues that, even so, one group of women – long-married traditional housewives – have been hurt by the new laws, caught in the middle when the rules changed. Yet her own data show that older housewives and long-married women are the *only* groups of divorced women who actually are being awarded alimony in greater numbers under the new laws than the old. The increase that she reports for housewives married more than ten years is a remarkable 21 per cent.

Her other point is that under no-fault 'equal division' rules, the couple is increasingly forced to sell the house, whereas under the old laws, she says, the judge traditionally gave it to the wife. But the new divorce laws don't require house sales and, in fact, the authors of the California law explicitly stated that judges shouldn't use the law to force single mothers and their children from the home. If more women are being forced to sell the family home, the new laws aren't to blame.

The real source of divorced women's woes can be found not in the fine print of divorce legislation but in the behaviour of ex-husbands and judges. Between 1978 and 1985 the average amount of child support that divorced men in the US paid fell nearly 25 per cent. Divorced men are now more likely to meet their car payments than their child support obligations – even though, as one study in the early 1980s found, for two-thirds of them, the amount owed their children is *less* than their monthly car loan bill.

A survey in the UK in 1989 found that only three lone parents in ten were receiving child maintenance payments regularly, and their average weekly payment even so was very low, at just under £27. Although the number of lone parents on benefit doubled during the eighties, the Department of Social Security collected 9 per cent less child maintenance in real terms in 1988–9 than in 1981–2. Both the National Audit Office and the Public Accounts Committee put the blame on the DSS, who cut the number of staff devoted to collection by one-third during that period. As sociologist Arlie Hochschild has observed, economic abandonment may be the new method some divorced men have devised for exerting control over their former families: 'The "new" oppression outside marriage thus creates a tacit threat to women inside marriage,' she writes. 'Patriarchy has not disappeared; it has changed form.'

At the same time, public and judicial officials weren't setting much of an example. A 1988 US audit found that thirty-five states weren't complying with federal child support laws. And judges weren't even upholding the egalitarian principles of no-fault. Instead, surveys in several states found that judges were wilfully misinterpreting the statutes to mean that women should get not one-half but *one-third* of all assets from the marriage. Weitzman herself reached the conclusion that judicial antagonism to feminism was aggravating the rough treatment of contemporary divorced women. 'The concept of "equality" and the sex-neutral language of the law,' she writes, have been 'used by some lawyers and judges as a mandate for "equal treatment" with a vengeance, a vengeance that can only be explained as a backlash reaction to women's demands for equality in the larger society.'

In the end, the most effective way to correct the post-divorce inequities between the sexes is simple: correct pay inequality in the work force. If the wage gap were wiped out between the sexes, a federal advisory council concluded in 1982, half of female-headed households would be instantly lifted out of poverty. 'The dramatic increase in women working is the best kind of insurance against this vulnerability,' Duncan says, observing that women's access to better-paying jobs saved a lot of divorced women from a far worse living standard. And that access, he points out, 'is largely a product of the women's movement'.

While the social scientists whose views were promoted in the 1980s harped on the 'devastating consequences' of divorce on women, we heard virtually nothing about its effect on men. This wasn't for lack of data. In 1984, demographers on divorce statistics at the University of Michigan's Institute for Social Research reviewed three decades of data on men's mental health, and flatly concluded – in a report that got little notice – the following: 'Men suffer more from marital disruption than women.' No matter where they looked on the mental spectrum, divorced men were worse off – from depressions to various psychological impairments to nervous breakdowns, from admissions to psychiatric facilities to suicide attempts.

From the start, men are less anxious to untie the knot than women: in surveys, less than a third of divorced men say they were the spouse who wanted the divorce, while women report they were the ones actively seeking divorce 55 to 66 per cent of the time. Men are also more devastated than women by the breakup – and time doesn't cure the pain or close the gap. A 1982 survey of divorced people a year after the breakup found that 60 per cent of the women were happier, compared with only half the men; a majority of the women said they had more self-respect, while only a minority of the men felt that way. America's largest study on the long-term effects of divorce found that five years after divorce, two-thirds of the women were happier with their lives; only 50 per cent of the men were. By the ten-year mark, the men who said their quality of life was no better or worse had risen from one-half to two-thirds. While 80 per cent of women ten years after divorce said it was the right decision, only 50 per cent of the ex-husbands agreed. 'Indeed, when such regrets [about divorcing] are heard, they come mostly from older men,' the study's director, Judith Wallerstein, observed.

Nonetheless, in her much-publicized 1989 book, *Second Chances: Men, Women and Children a Decade After Divorce* – hailed by such New Right groups as The Family in America and promptly given the cover of the *New York Times Magazine* – Wallerstein chooses to focus instead on her belief that children are worse off when their parents divorce. Her evidence for this is purely anecdotal since she did no original statistical research herself. Her 300-page book explains in a footnote: 'Because so little was known about divorce, it was premature to plan a control group,' Wallerstein writes, adding that she figured she would 'generate hypotheses' first, then maybe conduct the control-group study at a later date – a shoot-first, ask-questions-later logic that sums up the thinking of many backlash opinion makers.

'It's not at all clear what a control group would be,' Wallerstein explains later. One would have to control for other factors that might have led to the divorce, like 'frigidity and other sexual problems', she argues. 'I think people who are asking for a control group are refusing to understand the whole complexity of what a control group is,' she says. 'It would just be foolish.'

By the end of the decade, however, Wallerstein was feeling increasingly queasy about the ways her work was being used – and distorted – by politicians and the press. At a congressional hearing, she was startled when Senator Christopher Dodd proposed that, given her findings, the government should perhaps impose a mandatory delay on all couples seeking a divorce. And then national magazines quoted her work, wrongly, as saying that most children from divorced families become delinquents. 'It seems no matter what you say,' she sighs, 'it's misused. It's a very political field.'

If the campaign against no-fault divorce had no real numbers to make its case, then relentless promotion against divorce in the 1980s served as an effective substitute. Americans were finally convinced. Public support for liberalizing divorce laws, which had been rising since 1968, fell 8 per cent from the 1970s. And it was men who contributed most to this downturn; nearly twice as many men as women told pollsters they wanted to make it harder for couples to divorce.

The Infertility Epidemic: A Tale of Two Pregnancy Studies

On February 18, 1982, the *New England Journal of Medicine* reported that women's chances of conceiving dropped suddenly after the age of thirty. Women between the ages of thirty-one and thirty-five, the researchers claimed, stood a nearly 40 per cent chance of being infertile. This was unprecedented news indeed: virtually every study up until then had found that fertility didn't start truly declining until women reached at least their late thirties or even early forties.

The supposedly neutral *New England Journal of Medicine* didn't just publish the report. It served up a paternalistic three-page editorial, exhorting women to 'reevaluate their goals' and have their babies before they started careers. The *New York Times* put the news on its front page that day, in a story that extolled the study as 'unusually large and rigorous' and 'more reliable' than previous efforts. Dozens of other newspapers, magazines and TV news programmes quickly followed suit. NEW STUDY SHOWS RISK OF DELAY IN STARTING A FAMILY, warned *The Times* in London. By the following year, the statistic had found its way into alarmist books about the 'biological clock'. And like the children's game of Chinese whispers, as the 40 per cent figure got passed along, it kept getting larger. A self-help book was soon reporting that women in their thirties now faced a 'shocking 68 per cent' chance of infertility – and promptly faulted the feminists, who had failed to advise women of the biological drawbacks which went with a successful career.

For their study, French researchers Daniel Schwartz and M. J. Mayaux had studied 2,193 Frenchwomen who were infertility patients at eleven artificial-insemination centres, all of which were run by a federation that sponsored the research. The patients they used in the study were hardly representative of the average woman: they were all married to completely sterile men and were trying to get pregnant through artificial insemination. Frozen sperm, which was used in this case, is far less potent than the naturally delivered, 'fresh' variety. In fact, in an earlier study that Schwartz himself had conducted, he found women were more than four times more likely to get pregnant having sex regularly than by being artificially inseminated.

The French study also declared any woman infertile who had not become pregnant after one year of trying. (The twelve-month rule is a recent development, partly inspired by 'infertility specialists' marketing experimental and expensive new reproductive technologies; the definition of infertility used to be set at five years.) The one-year cutoff is widely challenged by demographers, who point out that it takes young newlyweds a mean time of eight months to conceive. In fact, only 16 to 21 per cent of couples who are defined as infertile under the one-year definition actually prove to be, a congressional study found. Time is the greatest, and certainly the cheapest, cure for infertility. In a British longitudinal survey of more than 17,000 women, one of the largest fertility studies ever conducted, 91 per cent of the women eventually became pregnant after thirty-nine months.

After the French study was published, many prominent American demographers disputed its results in a round of letters and articles in the professional literature. John Bongaarts, senior associate of the Population Council's Center for Policy Studies, called the study 'a poor basis for assessing the risk of female sterility' and largely invalid. Three statisticians from Princeton University's Office of Population Research also debunked the study and warned it could lead to 'needless anxiety' and 'costly medical treatment'. Even the French research scientists were backing away from their own study. At a professional conference later that year, they told their colleagues that they never meant their findings to apply to all women. But neither their retreat nor their peers' disparaging assessments attracted press attention.

Three years later, in February 1985, the US National Center for Health Statistics unveiled the latest results of its nationwide fertility survey of 8,000 women. It found that American women between thirty and thirty-four faced only a 13.6 per cent, not 40 per cent, chance of being infertile. Women in this age group had a mere 3 per cent higher risk of infertility than women in their *early* twenties. In fact, since 1965 infertility had *declined* slightly among women in their early- to mid-thirties – and even among women in their forties. Overall, the percentage of women unable to have babies had actually fallen – from 11.2 per cent in 1965 to 8.5 per cent in 1982.

As usual, this news made no media splashes. And in spite of the federal study's findings, Yale medical professor Dr Alan DeCherney, the lead author of the *New England Journal*'s sermonizing editorial, says he stands by his comments. Asked whether he has any second thoughts about the editorial's message, he chuckles: 'No, none at all. The editorial was meant to be provocative. I got a great response. I was on the *Today* show.'

In seeking the source of the 'infertility epidemic', the media and medical establishment considered only professional women, convinced that the answer was to be found in the rising wealth and independence of a middle-class female population. A *New York Times* columnist blamed feminism and the careerism it supposedly spawned for creating 'the sisterhood of the infertile' among middle-class women. Writer Molly McKaughan admonished fellow career women, herself included, in *Working Woman* (and, later, in her book *The Biological Clock*) for the 'menacing cloud' of infertility. Thanks largely to the women's movement, she charged, we made this mistake: 'We put our personal fulfilment first.'

At the same time, gynaecologists began calling endometriosis, a uterine ailment that can cause infertility, the 'career woman's disease'. It afflicts women who are 'intelligent, living with stress [and] determined to succeed at a role other than "mother" early in life,' Niels Lauersen, a New York Medical College obstetrics professor at the time, asserted in the press. (In fact, epidemiologists find endometriosis no more prevalent among professional women than any other group.) Others warned of high miscarriage rates among career women. (In fact, professional women typically experience the lowest miscarriage rate.) Still others reminded women that if they waited, they would be more likely to have stillbirths or premature, sick, retarded or abnormal babies. (In fact, a 1990 study of 4,000 women found women over thirty-five no more likely than younger women to have stillbirths or premature or sick newborns; a 1986 study of more than 6,000 women reached a similar conclusion. Women under thirty-five now give birth to children with Down's syndrome at a higher rate than women over thirty-five.)

Exercising the newly gained right to a legal abortion became another favourite 'cause' of infertility. Gynaecologists warned their middle-class female patients that if they had 'too many' abortions, they risked developing infertility problems later, or even becoming sterile. More than 150 epidemiological research efforts in the last twenty years have searched for links between abortion and infertility. But, as a research team who conducted a worldwide review and analysis of the research literature concluded in 1983, only ten of these studies used reliable methods, and of those ten, only one found any relation between abortion and later pregnancy problems – and that study looked at a sample of Greek women who had undergone dangerous, illegal abortions. Legal abortion methods, the researchers wrote, 'have no adverse effect on a woman's subsequent ability to conceive'. Dr Jack Glatt, Medical Director of London's Infertility Advisory Centre, agrees. 'There is no evidence,' he says, 'that abortion causes infertility.'

In reality, women's quest for economic and educational equality has only improved reproductive health and fertility. Better education and bigger salaries breed better nutrition, fitness and health care, all important contributors to higher fecundity. Statistics confirm that college-educated and higher-income women have a lower infertility rate than their high-school-educated and low-income counterparts.

The 'infertility epidemic' among middle-class career women over thirty was a political programme – and, for infertility specialists, a marketing tool – not a medical problem. The same White House that promoted the infertility threat allocated no funds toward preventing infertility – and, in fact, rebuffed all requests for aid. That the backlash's spokesmen showed so little interest in the decade's *real* infertility epidemics should have been a tipoff. In the US the infertility rates of young black women tripled between 1965 and 1982. The infertility rates of young women of all races in their early twenties more than doubled. In fact, by the 1980s, women between twenty and twenty-four were suffering from 2 per cent more infertility than women nearing thirty. Yet we heard little of this crisis and its causes – which had nothing to do with feminism or yuppie careerists.

This epidemic, in fact, could be traced in large part to the negligence of doctors and government officials, who were shockingly slow to combat the sexually transmitted disease of chlamydia; infection rates rose in the early eighties and were highest among young women between the ages of fifteen and twenty-four. This illness, in turn, triggered the breakneck spread of pelvic inflammatory disease, which was responsible for a vast proportion of the infertility in the decade and afflicted an additional 1 million women each year. Chlamydia became the number-one sexually transmitted disease in the US, afflicting more than 4 million women and men in 1985, causing at least half of the pelvic inflammatory infections, and helping to quadruple life-threatening ectopic pregnancies between 1970 and 1983. By the mid- to late 1980s as many as one in six young sexually active women were infected; infection rates ran as high as 35 per cent in some inner-city clinics. Yet chlamydia is one of the most poorly publicized, diagnosed and treated illnesses. F. M. Graham and J. Ellis of New Zealand's National Women's Hospital declare: 'Of all the causes of infertility, infection-related causes are certainly the most preventable ones and the increase in incidence over the past 20 years must give rise to major concern.'

A 1987 *British Medical Journal* editorial surveyed all the published infertility data available and concluded that in the age group thirty to thirty-four only 16 per cent of women studied remained childless. Dr Glatt's experience is that right up until the woman is thirty-six, 65 per cent of couples will conceive within six months of trying and 85 per cent within one year; there is no significant decline in fertility at the age of thirty. At the Infertility Advisory Centre, whose waiting room is papered with photos of 'miracle' babies, Dr Glatt sees patients of all ages and from all backgrounds. 'There has been no epidemic of any particular description,' he says. 'Looking at the causes of infertility in general, postponed motherhood pales into insignificance.' There are a whole range of causes of infertility, from ovulation disorders and blocked tubes in women, to weak or absent sperm in semen. Ageing problems, in his view, are only of the order that *any* physical condition can appear the longer you live. Indeed, one study shows that 70 per cent of women seeking infertility treatment had secondary infertility, i.e. they had already had at least one child.

The elderly 'prima gravida' is defined as having 'more than double' the chance of having a Down's syndrome baby – but it must be remembered, Dr Glatt insists, that this is the doubling of a very small number. 'There is still only a very small chance of there being a problem, even at age forty-two. Blood pressure during pregnancy is perhaps the greatest problem for the older age group, but even so, most of these women do all right.' He is keen to point out that for *any* fertile woman under the age of thirty-six who is having sex regularly, however young she is, the chance per month of a pregnancy going to term is only 20 per cent. Human beings, he says wryly, are 'very inefficient reproductive animals' compared with dogs or cats, for whom the equivalent chances are 90–95 per cent.

While policy-makers wring their hands over the so-called 'infertility epidemic', they have been notably less willing to fund available treatments for infertility. If women go to the National Health Service for fertility assistance, they are likely to be charged substantial sums: up to £800 per cycle, excluding the cost of drugs. And now there's a move to eliminate NHS funding for infertility services altogether.

The medical establishment and the press in the eighties also seemed uninterested in signs of another possible infertility epidemic. This one involved men. Men's sperm count appeared to have dropped by more than half in thirty years, according to the few studies available. (Poor semen quality is a principal cause of infertility.) The average man's sperm count, one researcher reported, had fallen from 200 million sperm per millilitre in the 1930s to between 40 and 70 million by the 1980s. The alarming depletion has many suspected sources: environmental toxins, occupational chemical hazards, excessive X-rays, drugs, tight underwear, even California-style hot tubs. But the causes are murky because research in the area of male infertility is so scant, even though it is much more significant as the cause of a couple's infertility than most of them realize. A 1988 congressional study on infertility concluded that, given the lack of information on male infertility, 'efforts on prevention and treatment are largely guesswork'.

The US government still does not include men in its national fertility survey. 'Why don't we do men?' William D. Mosher, lead demographer for the federal survey, repeats the question as if it's the first time he's heard it. 'I don't know. I mean, that would be another survey. You'd have to raise money for it. Resources aren't unlimited.'

If the 'infertility epidemic' was the first round of fire in the pronatal campaign of the 1980s, then the 'birth dearth' was the second. At least the leaders of this campaign were more honest: they denounced liberated women for choosing to have fewer or no children. They didn't pretend that they were just neutrally reporting statistics; they proudly admitted that they were seeking to manipulate female behaviour. 'Most of this small book is a speculation and provocation,' Ben Wattenberg freely concedes in his 1987 work, *The Birth Dearth*. 'Will public attitudes change soon, thereby changing fertility behavior?' he asks. 'I hope so. It is the root reason for writing this book.'

Instead of hounding women into the maternity ward with now-or-never threats, the birth dearth theorists tried appealing to society's baser instincts – xenophobia, militarism and bigotry, to name a few. If white educated middle-class women didn't start reproducing, the birth-dearth men warned, paupers, fools and foreigners would. Harvard psychologist Richard Herrnstein predicted that the genius pool would shrink by nearly 60 per cent and the American population with IQs under 70 would swell by a comparable amount, because the 'brighter' women were neglecting their reproductive duties to chase after college degrees and careers – and insisting on using birth control. 'Sex comes first, the pains and costs of pregnancy and motherhood later,' he harrumphed. If present trends continue, he grimly advised, 'it could swamp the effects of anything else we may do about our economic standing in the world.' The documentation he offered for this trend? Casual comments from some young students at Harvard who seemed 'anxious' about having children, grumblings from some friends who wanted more grandchildren, and dialogue from movies like *Baby Boom* and *Three Men and a Baby*.

The birth dearth's creator and chief cheerleader was Ben Wattenberg, a syndicated columnist and senior fellow at the American Enterprise Institute, who first introduced the birth dearth threat in 1986 in the conservative journal *Public Opinion* – and tirelessly promoted it in an endless round of speeches, radio talks, television appearances and his own newspaper column.

His inflammatory tactics constituted a notable departure from the levelheaded approach he had advocated a decade earlier in his book *The Real America*, in which he chided population-boom theorists for spreading 'souped-up scare rhetoric' and 'alarmist fiction'. The fertility rate, he said, was actually in slow decline, which he saw then as a 'quite salutary' trend, promising more jobs and a higher living standard. The birth dearth, he enthused then, 'may well prove to be the single most important agent of a massive expansion and a massive economic upgrading' for the middle class.

Just ten years later, the 53-year-old father of four was sounding all the alarms about this 'scary' trend. 'Will the world backslide?' he gasped in *The Birth Dearth*. 'Could the Third World culture become dominant?' According to Wattenberg's treatise – subtitled 'What Happens When People in Free Countries Don't Have Enough Babies' – the United States would lose its world power status, millions would be put out of work, multiplying minorities would create 'ugly turbulence', smaller tax bases would diminish the military's nuclear weapons stockpiles, and a shrinking army would not be able 'to deter potential Soviet expansionism'.

When Wattenberg got around to assigning blame, the women's movement served as the prime scapegoat. For generating what he now characterized as a steep drop in the birthrate to 'below replacement level', he faulted women's interest in postponing marriage and motherhood, women's desire to advance their education and careers, women's insistence on the legalization of abortion and 'women's liberation' in general. To solve the problem, he lectures, women should be urged to put their careers off until after they have babies. Nevertheless, he actually maintains, 'I believe that *The Birth Dearth* sets out a substantially pro-feminist view.'

Wattenberg's birth-dearth slogan was quickly adopted by New

Right leaders, conservative social theorists and presidential candidates, who began alluding in ominous – and racist – tones to 'cultural suicide' and 'genetic suicide'. These men were as anxious to stop single black women from procreating as they were for married white women to start. The rate of illegitimate births to black women, especially black teenage girls, was reaching 'epidemic' proportions, conservative social scientists intoned repeatedly in speeches and press interviews. The pronatalists' use of the disease metaphor is unintentionally revealing: they considered it an 'epidemic' when white women *didn't* reproduce or when black women *did*. In the case of black women, their claims were simply wrong. Illegitimate births to both black women and black teenagers were actually declining in the 1980s; the only increase in out-of-wedlock births was among white women.

The birth-dearth theorists were right that women have been choosing to limit family size in record numbers. They were wrong, however, when they said this reproductive restraint has sparked a perilous decline in the birthrate. The fertility rate in the USA fell from a high of 3.8 children per woman in 1957 to 1.8 children per woman in the 1980s. But that 1957 peak was the aberration. The national fertility rate has been declining gradually for the last several centuries; the 1980s rate simply marked a return to the status quo. Furthermore, the fertility rate didn't even fall in the 1980s; it held steady at 1.8 children per woman – where it had been since 1976. Similarly, the number of live births in England has increased each year since 1982 apart from 1989, and the fertility rate was higher in 1990 than in 1980. The peak birth rate was in 1964, followed by a decline which came to a halt in 1977.

Wattenberg arrived at his doomsday scenarios by projecting a declining birthrate two centuries into the future. In other words, he was speculating on the number of children of women who weren't even born – the equivalent of a demographer in pre-industrial America theorizing about the reproductive behaviour of an eighties career woman. Projecting the growth rate of a *current* generation is tricky enough, as post-Second World War social scientists discovered. They failed to predict the baby boom – and managed to underestimate that generation's population by 62 million people.

The Great Female Depression: Women on the Verge of a Nervous Breakdown

In the backlash yearbook, two types of women were named as most likely to break down: the unmarried and the gainfully employed. According to dozens of news features, advice books and women's health manuals, single women were suffering from 'record' levels of depression and professional women were succumbing to 'burn-out' – a syndrome that supposedly caused a wide range of mental and physical illnesses from dizzy spells to heart attacks.

In the mid-1980s, several epidemiological mental health studies noted a rise in mental depression among baby boomers, a phenomenon that soon inspired popular-psychology writers to dub the era 'The Age of Melancholy'. Casting about for an explanation for the generation's gloom, therapists and journalists quickly fastened upon the women's movement. If baby-boom women hadn't received their independence, their theory went, then the single ones would be married and the careerists would be home with their children – in both cases, feeling calmer, healthier and saner.

The rising mental distress of single women 'is a phenomenon of this era, it really is,' psychologist Annette Baran asserted in a 1986 *Los Angeles Times* article, one of many on the subject. 'I would suspect,' she said, that single women now represent 'the great majority of any psychotherapist's practice', precisely 'sixty-six percent' her hunch told her. The author of the article agreed, declaring the 'growing number' of single women in psychological torment 'an epidemic of sorts'. A 1988 article in *New York Woman* issued the same verdict: single women have 'stampeded' therapists' offices, a 'virtual epidemic'. The magazine quoted psychologist Janice Lieberman, who said, 'These women come into treatment convinced there's something terribly wrong with them.' And, she assured us, there is: 'Being single too long is traumatic.'

In fact, no one knew whether single women were more or less depressed in the 1980s; no epidemiological study had actually tracked changes in single women's mental health. As psychological researcher Lynn L. Gigy, one of the few in her profession to study single women, has noted, social science still treats unmarried women like 'statistical deviants'. They have been 'virtually ignored in social theory and research'. But the lack of data hasn't discouraged advice experts, who have been blaming single women for rising mental illness rates since at least the nineteenth century, when leading psychiatrists described the typical victim of neurasthenia as 'a woman, generally single, or in some way not in a condition for performing her reproductive function'.

As it turns out, social scientists have established only one fact about single women's mental health: employment improves it. The 1983 landmark 'Lifeprints' study in the US found poor employment, not poor marriage prospects, to be the leading cause of mental distress among single women. Researchers from the Institute for Social Research and the National Center for Health Statistics, reviewing two decades of data on American women's health, came up with similar results: 'Of the three factors we examined [employment, marriage, children], employment has by far the strongest and most consistent tie to women's good health.' Single women who worked, they found, were in far better mental and physical shape than married women, with or without children, who stayed at home. Finally, in a rare longitudinal study that treated single women as a category, researchers Pauline Sears and Ann Barbee found that of the women they tracked, single women reported the greatest satisfaction with their lives – and single women who had worked most of their lives were the most satisfied of all.

While demographers haven't charted historical changes in single women's psychological status, they have collected a vast amount of data comparing the mental health of single and married women. None of it supports the thesis that single women are causing the 'age of melancholy': study after study shows single women enjoying far better mental health than their married sisters (and, in a not unrelated phenomenon, making more money). The warning issued by family sociologist Jessie Bernard in 1972 still holds true: 'Marriage may be hazardous to women's health.'

The psychological indicators are numerous and they all point in the same direction. Married women in these studies report about 20 per cent more depression than single women and three

times the rate of severe neurosis. Married women have more nervous breakdowns, nervousness, heart palpitations and inertia. Still
other afflictions disproportionately plague married women:
insomnia, trembling hands, dizzy spells, nightmares, hypochon-
dria, passivity, agoraphobia and other phobias, unhappiness with
their physical appearance and overwhelming feelings of guilt and
shame. A twenty-five-year longitudinal study of college-educated
women found that wives had the lowest self-esteem, felt the least
attractive, reported the most loneliness and considered themselves
the least competent at almost every task – even childcare. A 1980
study found that single women were more assertive, independent
and proud of their accomplishments. The Mills Longitudinal
Study, which tracked women for more than three decades,
reported in 1990 that 'traditional' married women ran a higher
risk of developing mental and physical ailments in their lifetime
than single women – from depression to migraines, from high
blood pressure to colitis. A *Cosmopolitan* survey of 106,000
women found that not only do single women make more money
than their married counterparts, they have better health and are
more likely to have regular sex. Finally, when noted mental health
researchers Gerald Klerman and Myrna Weissman reviewed all
the depression literature on women and tested for factors ranging
from genetics to PMS to birth-control pills, they could find only
two prime causes for female depression: low social status and
marriage.

If mentally imbalanced single women weren't causing the 'age of
melancholy', then could it be worn-out career women? Given that
employment improves women's mental health, this would seem
unlikely. But the 'burn-out' experts of the eighties were ready to
make a case for it anyway. 'Women's burnout has come to be a
most prevalent condition in our modern culture,' psychologists
Herbert Freudenberger and Gail North warned in *Women's Burn-
out*, one of a raft of potboilers on this 'ailment' to hit the book-
shops in the decade. 'More and more, I hear about women pushing
themselves to the point of physical and/or psychological collapse,'
Marjorie Hansen Shaevitz wrote in *The Superwoman Syndrome*.
'A surprising number of female corporate executives walk around

with a bottle of tranquilizers,' Dr Daniel Crane alerted readers in *Savvy*. Burn-out's afflictions were legion. As *The Type E Woman* advised, 'Working women are swelling the epidemiological ranks of ulcer cases, drug and alcohol abuse, depression, sexual dysfunction and a score of stress-induced physical ailments, including backache, headache, allergies, and recurrent viral infections and flu.' But that's not all. Other experts added to this list baldness, menstrual difficulties, heart attacks, strokes, hypertension, nervous breakdowns, suicides and cancer. 'Women are freeing themselves up to die like men,' asserted Dr James Lynch, author of several burn-out tomes, pointing to what he claimed was a rise in rates of drinking, smoking, heart disease and suicide among career women.

The experts provided no evidence, just anecdotes – and periodic jabs at feminism, which they quickly identified as the burn-out virus. 'The women's liberation movement started it' with 'a full-scale female invasion' of the work force, *Women Under Stress* maintained, and now many misled women are belatedly discovering that 'the toll in stress may not be worth the rewards'. The authors warned, 'Sometimes women get so enthused with women's liberation that they accept jobs for which they are not qualified.'

Ex-hippie writer Richard Neville told *Evening Standard* readers that in the past decade women have been working so hard that 'they've grown moustaches and turned their children into strangers', all for 'an image of success as outmoded as the Roman Empire'.

The message behind all this 'advice'? Go home. 'Although being a full-time homemaker has its own stresses,' Georgia Witkin-Lanoil wrote in *The Female Stress Syndrome*, 'in some ways it is the easier side of the coin.' Psychotherapist Vera Diamond told *She* magazine that in her experience career women were often in conflict with their femininity. After relaxation therapy, many would burst into tears and discover that 'what they really want to do is chuck it all in and have a baby.'

Yet the actual evidence – dozens of comparative studies on working and non-working women – all point the other way. Whether they are professional or blue-collar workers, working women experience less depression than housewives; and the more challenging the career, the better their mental and physical health.

Women who have never worked have the highest levels of depression. Working women are less susceptible than housewives to mental disorders big and small – from suicides and nervous breakdowns to insomnia and nightmares. They are less nervous and passive, report less anxiety and take fewer psychotropic drugs than women who stay at home. 'Inactivity,' as a study based on the US Health Interview Survey data concludes, ' . . . may create the most stress.'

Career women in the 1980s were also not causing a female rise in heart attacks and high blood pressure. In fact, there was no such rise: heart disease deaths among women in the USA, Australia, England and Wales – and even in Scotland and Northern Ireland where the overall heart disease rate is still appreciably higher – were lower in 1987 (in America and Australia *much* lower) than in 1972, when women's labour-force participation rate took off. Only the lung cancer rate has increased, and that is the legacy not of feminism but of the massive midcentury ad campaign to hook women on smoking. The proportion of adult smokers in the UK has been falling over the last twenty years but the decline is slow and the decrease in female smoking from 1976 to 1986 has been smaller than that among males. This may have something to do with the appetite-suppressing effects of smoking – in countries where most post-pubescent women are 'on a diet', their addiction to nicotine is less surprising.

The importance of paid work to women's self-esteem is basic and longstanding. Even in the 'feminine mystique' 1950s, when married women were asked what gave them a sense of purpose and self-worth, two-thirds said their jobs; only one-third said homemaking. In the 1980s, 87 per cent of women said it was their work that gave them personal satisfaction and a sense of accomplishment. In short, as one large-scale study concludes, 'Women's health is hurt by their *lower* [my emphasis] labor-force participation rates.'

By helping to widen women's access to more and better employment, the women's rights campaign led to vast improvements in women's mental health over the last three decades, as several landmark US surveys have shown. The famous 1980 Midtown Manhattan Longitudinal Study found that adult women's rate of mental health impairment had fallen 50 to 60 per cent since the early 1950s. Midtown Manhattan project director Leo Srole concluded that the changes 'are not mere chance coincidences of the play of history, but reflect a cause-and-effect connection between the partial emancipation of women from their 19th-century status of sexist servitude, and their 20th-century advances in subjective well-being'.

If anything threatened women's emotional well-being in the 1980s, it was the backlash itself, which worked to undermine women's social and economic status – the two pillars on which good mental health are built. As even one of the 'burn-out' manuals concedes, 'There is a direct link between sexism and female stress.' How the current counterassault on women's rights will affect women's rate of mental illness, however, remains to be seen: because of the time lag in conducting epidemiological studies, we won't know the actual numbers for some time.

While the effects of the women's movement may not have depressed women, they did seem to trouble many men. In a review of three decades of research literature on sex differences in mental health, social scientists Ronald C. Kessler and James A. McRae, Jr, with the University of Michigan's Institute for Social Research, concluded, 'It is likely that men are experiencing more rapidly role-related stresses than are women.' The role changes that women have embraced 'are helping to close the male–female mental-health gap largely by increasing the distress of men'. While women's improving mental health stems from their rising employment rate, the researchers said, at the same time 'the increase in distress among men can be attributed, in part, to depression and loss of self-esteem related to the increasing tendency of women to take a job outside the home.' For many men in the 1980s this effect was exacerbated by that other well-established threat to mental health – loss of economic status – as millions of traditional 'male' jobs that once yielded a living wage evaporated. Observing the dramatic shifts in the mental-health sex ratios that were occurring in manufacturing communities, Jane Murphy, chief of psychiatric epidemiology at Massachusetts General Hospital, wrote in 1984: 'Have changes in the occupational structure of this society created a situation that is, in some ways, better for the goose than for the gander . . . ?' As Kessler says in an interview, researchers who focus on the female side of the mental health equation are probably missing the main event: 'In the last thirty years, the sex difference [in mental illness] is getting smaller largely because *men* are getting worse.'

Numerous mental health reports published in the last decade support this assertion. A 1980 study finds husbands of working women reporting higher levels of depression than husbands of housewives. A 1982 study of 2,440 adults at the University of Michigan's Survey Research Center finds depression and low self-esteem among married men closely associated with their wives' employment. A 1986 analysis of the federal Quality of Employment Survey concludes that 'dual earning may be experienced as a downward mobility for men and upward mobility for women'. Husbands of working women, the researchers found, had greater psychological distress, lower self-esteem and greater depression than men married to housewives. 'There lies behind the facade of egalitarian lifestyle pioneering an anxiety among men that cannot be cured by time alone,' they concluded. The fact is, they wrote, 'that conventional standards of manhood remain more important in terms of personal evaluation than contemporary rhetoric of gender equality'.

A 1987 study of role-related stresses, conducted by a team of researchers from the University of Michigan, the University of Illinois and Cornell University, makes the same connection and observes that men's psychological well-being appears to be significantly threatened when their wives work. 'Given that previous research on changing gender roles has concentrated on women to the neglect of men,' they wrote, 'this result suggests that such an emphasis has been misleading and that serious effort is needed to understand the ways changing female roles affect the lives and attitudes of men.' This warning, however, went virtually unheeded in the press. When *Newsweek* produced its cover story on depression, it put a grim-faced woman on the cover – and, inside, all but two of the nine victims it displayed were female, too.

The Day Care Demons: Make Your Own Statistics

The anti-childcare headlines practically shrieked in the 1980s: 'MOMMY, DON'T LEAVE ME HERE!' THE DAY CARE PARENTS DON'T SEE. DAY CARE CAN BE DANGEROUS TO YOUR CHILD'S HEALTH. WHEN CHILD CARE BECOMES CHILD MOLESTING: IT HAPPENS MORE OFTEN THAN PARENTS LIKE TO THINK. CREEPING CHILD CARE . . . CREEPY.

The spokesmen of the New Right, of course, were most denunciatory, labelling day care 'the Thalidomide of the '80s'. Reagan's men didn't mince words either, like the top military official who proclaimed, 'American mothers who work and send their children to faceless centers rather than stay home to take care of them are weakening the moral fiber of the Nation.' But the press, more subtly but just as persistently, painted devil's horns both on mothers who use childcare and childcare workers themselves.

In 1984 a *Newsweek* feature warned of an 'epidemic' of child abuse in childcare facilities, based on allegations against directors at a few day care centres – the most celebrated of which were later found innocent in the courts. Just in case the threat had slipped women's minds, two weeks later *Newsweek* was busy once more, demanding WHAT PRICE DAY CARE? in a cover story. The cover picture featured a frightened, saucer-eyed child sucking his thumb. By way of edifying contrast, the eight-page treatment inside showcased a Good Mother – under the title AT HOME BY CHOICE. The former bond seller had given up her career to be at home with her baby and offer wifely assistance to her husband's career. 'I had to admit I couldn't do [everything],' the mother said, a view that clearly earned an approving nod from *Newsweek*. Still later, in a special issue devoted to the family, *Newsweek* ran another article on 'the dark side of day care'. That story repeatedly alluded to 'more and more evidence that child care may be hazardous to a youngster's health', but never got around to providing it. This campaign was one the press managed to conduct all by itself. Researchers were having a tough time linking day care with deviance. So the press circulated some antiquated 'research' and ignored the rest.

At a press conference in the spring of 1988 the University of New Hampshire's Family Research Laboratory released the largest and most comprehensive study ever on sexual abuse in day care centres – a three-year study examining the reported cases of sexual abuse at day care facilities across the US. One would have assumed from the swarm of front-page stories on this apparent threat that the researchers' findings would rate as an important news event. But the *New York Times* response was typical: it noted the study's release in a modest article on the same page as the classifieds. (Ironically, it ran on the same page as an even smaller story about a Wisconsin father beating his four-year-old son so brutally that the child had to be institutionalized for the rest of his life for brain injuries.) Why such little interest? The study concluded that there was no epidemic of child abuse at childcare centres. In fact, if there was an abuse crisis anywhere, the study pointed out, it was at home – where the risk to children of molestation is almost twice as high as in childcare. Children are far more likely to be beaten, too, at the family hearth, the researchers found; and the physical abuse at home tends to be of a longer duration, more severe and more traumatic than any violence children faced in childcare centres. In 1986, 1,500 children died in the USA from abuse at home. 'Day care is not an inherently high-risk locale for children, despite frightening stories in the media,' the Family Research Laboratory study's authors concluded. 'The risk of abuse is not sufficient reason to avoid day care in general or to justify parents' withdrawing from the labor force.'

Research over the last two decades has consistently found that if childcare has any long-term effect on children, it seems to make them slightly more gregarious and independent. Day care children also appear to be more broad-minded about sex roles; girls interviewed in day care centres are more likely to believe that housework and child rearing should be shared by both parents. A National Academy of Sciences panel in 1982 concluded that children suffer no ill effects in academic, social or emotional development when mothers work.

Yet the childcare 'statistics' that received the most press in the 1980s were the ones based more on folklore than research. Illness, for example, was supposedly more pervasive in childcare centres than in the home, according to media accounts. The actual studies on childcare and illness indicate that while children in day care are initially prone to more illnesses, they soon build up immunities and actually become sick less often than kids at home. Childcare's threat to bonding between mother and child was another popular myth. But the research offers scant evidence of diminished bonds between mother and child – and suggests that children profit from exposure to a wider range of grown-ups, anyway. (No one ever worries, it seems, about childcare's threat to paternal bonding.)

With no compelling demographic evidence to support an attack on childcare for toddlers, critics of childcare turned their attention to infants. Three-year-old toddlers may survive childcare, they argued, but newborns would surely suffer permanent damage. Their evidence, however, came from studies conducted on European children in wartime orphanages and war refugee camps – environments that were hardly the equivalent of contemporary childcare facilities, even the worst variety. One of the most commonly quoted studies in the press wasn't even conducted on human beings. Psychologist Harry Harlow found that 'infants' in day care suffer severe emotional distress. His subjects, however, were baby monkeys. And his 'day care workers' weren't even surrogate adult monkeys: the researchers used wire-mesh dummies.

Finally, in 1986, it loked as if childcare critics had some hard data they could use. Pennsylvania State University psychologist and social researcher Jay Belsky, a prominent supporter of day care, expressed some reservations about day care for infants. Up until this point, Belsky had said that his reviews of the child development literature yielded few if any significant differences between children raised at home and in day care. Then, in the September 1986 issue of the childcare newsletter *Zero to Three*, Belsky suggested that placing children in day care for more than twenty hours a week in their first year of life might be a 'risk factor' that could lead to an 'insecure' attachment to their mothers. The press and conservative politicians hurried to the scene. Soon Belsky found himself making the network rounds – *Today*, *CBS Morning News* and *Donahue* – and fielding dozens of press calls a month. And, much to the liberal Belsky's discomfort, 'conservatives embraced me'. Right-wing scholars cited his findings. Conservative politicians sought out his Congressional testimony at childcare hearings – and got furious when he failed to spout 'what they wanted me to say'.

Belsky peppered his report on infant childcare with qualifications, strongly cautioned against over-reaction, and advised that he had only a 'trickle', 'not a flood' of evidence. He wrote that only a 'relatively persuasive *circumstantial* [all italics are his] case can be made that early infant care *may* be associated with increased avoidance of mother, *possibly* to the point of greater insecurity in the attachment relationship'. And, he added, 'I cannot state strongly enough that there is sufficient evidence to lead a judicious scientist to doubt this line of reasoning.' Finally, in every press interview, as he recalls later, he stressed the many caveats and emphasized that his findings underlined the need for better funding and standards for childcare centres, and were not grounds for eliminating day care. 'I was not saying we shouldn't have day care,' he says. 'I was saying that we need *good* day care. Quality matters.' But his words 'fell on deaf ears'. And once the misrepresentations of his work passed into the media it seemed impossible to root them out. 'What amazed me was the journalists just plagiarized each other's newspaper stories. Very few of them actually read my article.'

Social scientists *could* supply plenty of research to show that one member of the family, at least, is happier and more well adjusted when mum stays home and looks after the children. But that person is dad – a finding of limited use to backlash publicists. Anyway, by the end of the decade the press was no longer even demanding hard data to make its case. By then the public was so steeped in the lore of the backlash that its spokesmen rarely bothered to round up the usual statistics. Who needed proof? Everybody already believed that the myths about eighties women were true.

Chapter Three

Backlashes Then and Now

A backlash against women's rights is nothing new. Indeed, it's a recurring phenomenon: it returns every time women begin to make some headway towards equality, a seemingly inevitable early frost to the brief flowerings of feminism. 'The progress of women's rights in our culture, unlike other types of "progress," has always been strangely reversible,' American literature scholar Ann Douglas has observed. Women's studies historians over the years have puzzled over the 'halting gait', the 'fits and starts', the 'stop–go affair' of feminism. 'While men proceed on their developmental way, building on inherited traditions,' women's historian Dale Spender writes, 'women are confined to cycles of lost and found.'

Yet in the popular imagination the history of women's rights is more commonly charted as a flat dead line that, only twenty years ago, began a sharp and unprecedented incline. Ignoring the many peaks and valleys traversed in the endless march towards liberty, this mental map of women's progress presents instead a great plain of 'traditional' womanhood, upon which women have roamed helplessly and 'naturally', the eternally passive subjects until the 1970s women's movement came along. This map is in itself harmful to women's rights; it presents women's struggle for liberty as if it were a one-time event, a curious and even noxious by-product of a postmodern age. It is, as poet and essayist Adrienne Rich has described it, 'the erasure of women's political and historical past which makes each new generation of feminists appear as an abnormal excrescence on the face of time'.

An accurate charting of Western women's progress through

history might look more like a corkscrew tilted slightly to one side, its loops inching closer to the line of freedom with the passage of time – but, like a mathematical curve approaching infinity, never touching its goal. Woman is trapped on this asymptotic spiral, turning endlessly through the generations, drawing ever nearer to her destination without ever arriving. Each revolution promises to be '*the* revolution' that will free her from the orbit, that will grant her, finally, a full measure of human justice and dignity. But, each time, the spiral turns her back just short of the finish line. Each time, she hears that she must wait a little longer, be a little more patient – her hour on the stage is not yet at hand. And worse yet, she may learn to accept her coerced deferral as her choice, even to flaunt it.

Whenever this spiral has swung nearer to equality, women have believed their journey to be drawing to a close. 'At the opening of the twentieth century,' American suffragist Ida Husted Harper rejoiced, the female condition was 'completely transformed in most respects'. Soon the country would have to open a Woman's Museum, feminist Elsie Clews Parsons mused in 1913, just to prove 'to a doubting posterity that once women were a distinct social class'. Still later, at the close of the Second World War, a female steelworker declared in a government survey, 'The old theory that a woman's place is in the home no longer exists. Those days are gone forever.'

Yet in each of these periods the celebrations were premature. This pattern of women's hopes raised only to be dashed is peculiar neither to America nor to modern times. Different kinds of back-lash against women's mostly tiny gains – or against simply the perception that women were in the ascendancy – may be found in the rise of restrictive property laws and penalties for unwed and childless women of ancient Rome, the heresy judgments against female disciples of the early Christian Church, or the mass witch burnings of medieval Europe.

But if we look at the compressed history of the United States we see that backlashes have surfaced with striking frequency and intensity – and they have evolved their most subtle means of persuasion. In a nation where class distinctions are weak, or at least submerged, maybe it's little wonder that gender status is more highly prized and hotly defended. If the American man can claim no ancestral coat of arms by which to elevate himself from the masses, perhaps he can fashion his sex into a sort of pedigree. In America, too, successfully persuading women to collaborate in their own subjugation is a tradition of particularly long standing. White European women first entered the American colonies as 'purchase brides', shipped into Virginia and sold to bachelors for the price of transport. This transaction was billed not as servitude but choice because the brides were 'sold with their own consent'. As a perplexed Alexis de Tocqueville observed, the single woman in early nineteenth-century America seemed to have more freedom than her counterpart in Europe, yet also more determination to relinquish it in confining marriages: 'It may be said that she has learned by the use of her independence to surrender it without a struggle.' Such a trait would prove especially useful in the subsequent periodic campaigns to stymie women's progress, as American women were encouraged to use what liberty they did have to promote their own diminishment. As scholar Cynthia Kinnard observes in her bibliographical survey of American anti-feminist literature, about one-third of the articles and nearly half the books and pamphlets denouncing the campaign for women's rights have issued from a female pen.

While American backlashes can be traced back to colonial times, the style of backlash that surfaced in the last decade has its roots most firmly in the nineteenth century. The Victorian era gave rise to mass media and mass marketing – two institutions that have since proved more effective devices for constraining women's aspirations than coercive laws and punishments. They rule with the club of conformity, not censure, and claim to speak for female public opinion, not powerful male interests.

If we retrace the course of women's rights back to the Victorian era we wind up with a spiral that has made four revolutions. A struggle for women's rights gained force in the mid-nineteenth century, the early 1900s, the early 1940s and the early 1970s. In each case, the struggle yielded to backlash.

The All-American Repeating Backlash

The 'woman movement' of the mid-nineteenth century, launched at the 1848 Seneca Falls women's rights convention and articulated most famously by Elizabeth Cady Stanton and Susan B. Anthony, pressed for suffrage and an array of liberties – education, jobs, marital and property rights, 'voluntary motherhood', health and dress reform. But by the end of the century a cultural counterreaction crushed women's appeals for justice. Women fell back before a barrage of warnings virtually identical to today's, voiced by that era's line-up of Ivy League scholars, religious leaders, medical experts and press pundits. Educated women of this era, too, were said to be falling victim to a man shortage; 'the redundancy of spinster gentlewomen', in the parlance of the time, inspired debate in state legislatures and frenzied scholarly 'research'. A marriage study even made the rounds in 1895, asserting that only 28 per cent of college-educated women could get married. They, too, faced a so-called infertility epidemic – this one induced by 'brain–womb' conflict, as a Harvard professor's best-selling book defined it in 1873. And Victorian women who worked were likewise said to be suffering a sort of early career burn-out – 'exhaustion of the feminine nervous system' – and losing their femininity to 'hermaphroditism'.

Then as now, late-Victorian religious and political leaders accused women who postponed childbearing of triggering a 'race suicide' that endangered (white) America's future; they were, in the words of President Theodore Roosevelt, 'criminals against the race' and 'objects of contemptuous abhorrence by healthy people'. Married women who demanded rights were charged, then as now, with creating a 'crisis of the family'. The media and the churches railed against feminists for fuelling divorce rates, and state legislatures passed more than a hundred restrictive divorce laws between 1889 and 1906. South Carolina banned divorce outright. And a band of 'purity' crusaders, like the contemporary New Right brigade, condemned contraception and abortion as 'obscene' and sought to have it banned. By the late 1800s they had succeeded: Congress outlawed the distribution of contraceptives and a majority of states criminalized abortion – both for the first time in the nation's history.

In the early 1910s women's rights activists resurrected the struggle for suffrage and turned it into a nationwide political campaign. The word 'feminism' entered the popular vocabulary – even silent film vamp Theda Bara was calling herself one – and dozens of newly formed women's groups hastened to endorse its tenets. The National Woman's Party organized in 1916, a campaign for an Equal Rights Amendment began and working women formed their own trade unions and struck for decent pay and better working conditions. The International Ladies' Garment Workers Union, founded in 1900, grew so quickly that it was the American Federation of Labor's third largest affiliate by 1913. Margaret Sanger led a national birth-control movement. And Heterodoxy, a sort of feminist intelligentsia, began conducting early versions of consciousness-raising groups.

But just as women had won the right to vote and a handful of state legislatures had granted women jury duty and passed equal pay laws, another counterassault on feminism began. The US War Department, with the aid of the American Legion and the Daughters of the American Revolution, incited a red-baiting campaign againt women's rights leaders. Feminists like Charlotte Perkins Gilman suddenly found they couldn't get their writings published; Jane Addams was labelled a communist and a 'serious threat' to national security; and Emma Goldman was exiled. The media maligned suffragists; magazine writers advised that feminism was 'destructive of woman's happiness'; popular novels attacked 'career women'; clergymen railed against 'the evils of woman's revolt'; scholars charged feminism with fuelling divorce and infertility; and doctors claimed that birth control was causing 'an increase in insanity, tuberculosis, Bright's disease, diabetes, and cancer'. Young women, magazine readers were informed, no longer wanted to be bothered with 'all that feminist pother'. Post-feminist sentiments first surfaced, not in the 1980s media, but in the 1920s press. Under this barrage, membership of feminist organizations soon plummeted, and the remaining women's groups hastened to denounce the Equal Rights Amendment or simply converted themselves to social clubs. 'Ex-feminists' began issuing their confessions.

In place of equal respect, the nation offered women the Miss

America beauty pageant, established in 1920 – the same year in which women won the vote. In place of equal rights, lawmakers, labour and corporate leaders, and eventually some women's groups, endorsed 'protective' labour policies, measures that served largely to protect men's jobs and deny women equal pay. The 1920s eroded a decade of growth for female professionals; by 1930 there were fewer female doctors than in 1910. When the Depression hit, a new round of federal and state laws forced thousands of women out of the work force, and new federal wage codes institutionalized lower pay rates for women.

'All about us we see attempts being made, buttressed by governmental authority, to throw women back into the morass of unlovely dependence from which they were just beginning to emerge,' feminist Doris Stevens wrote in1933, in *Equal Rights*, the National Woman's Party publication. 'It looks sometimes as if pre-suffrage conditions even might be curiously reversed and the grievance held by women against men be changed into a grievance held by men against women,' Margaret Culkin Banning remarked in an essay in *Harper's* in 1935. But like today, most social commentators held that the feminists' tents were folding only because their battle was over – women's rights had been secured. As political science scholar Ethel Klein writes of the 1920s, 'The dissipation of interest in the women's movement was taken as a sign not of failure but of completion.'

The spiral swung around again in the 1940s as a wartime economy opened millions of high-paying industrial jobs to women, and the government even began to offer minimal day care and household assistance. Federal brochures saluted the hardy working woman as a true patriot. Strong women became cultural icons; Rosie the Riveter was revered and, in 1941, Wonder Woman was introduced. Women welcomed their new economic status; 5 to 6 million poured into the work force during the war years, 2 million into heavy-industry jobs; by the war's end they would represent a record 57 per cent of all employed people. Seventy-five per cent reported in government surveys that they were going to keep their jobs after the war – and, in the younger generation, 88 per cent of the 33,000 girls polled in a *Senior Scholastic* survey said they wanted a career, too. Women's political energies revived; working-

class women flooded unions, protested for equal pay, equal seniority rights, and day care; and feminists launched a new campaign
for the ERA. This time, the amendment won the endorsements of
both political parties, and, in the course of the war, for the first
time since the ERA had been proposed in 1923, the Senate
Judiciary Committee voted it to the Senate floor three times. In a
record outpouring of legislative goodwill, the 1940s-era Congress
passed thirty-three bills serving to advance women's rights.

But with the close of the Second World War, efforts by industry,
government and the media converged to force a female retreat.
Two months after a US victory had been declared abroad, women
were losing their economic beachhead as 800,000 were fired from
the aircraft industry; by the end of the year, 2 million female
workers had been purged from heavy industry. Employers revived
prohibitions on hiring married women or imposed limits on female
workers' salaries; and the federal government proposed giving
unemployment assistance only to men, shut down its day care
services, and defended the 'right' of veterans to displace working
women. An anti-ERA coalition rallied its forces, including the
federal Women's Bureau, forty-three national organizations, and
the National Committee to Defeat the UnEqual Rights Amendment. Soon they had killed the amendment – a death sentence
hailed on the *New York Times* editorial page. 'Motherhood cannot
be amended and we are glad the Senate didn't try,' the newspaper
proclaimed. When the United Nations issued a statement supporting equal rights for women in 1948, the United States government
was the only one of the twenty-two American nations that
wouldn't sign it.

Employers who had applauded women's work during the war
now accused working women of incompetence or 'bad attitudes'
– and laid them off at rates that were 75 per cent higher than
men's. Advice experts filled book shops with the usual warnings:
education and jobs were stripping women of their femininity and
denying them marriage and motherhood; women were suffering
'fatigue' and mental instability from employment; women who
used day care were selfish 'fur-coated mothers'. Yet another Ivy
League marriage study drew headlines: this Cornell University
study said college-educated single women had no more than a 65

per cent chance of getting married. Better watch out, the Sunday magazine *This Week* advised its female readers; a college education 'skyrockets your chances of becoming an old maid'. Feminism was 'a deep illness' that was turning modern women into a woebegone 'lost sex', the era's leading advice book warned. Independent-minded women had got 'out of hand' during the war, Barnard sociologist Willard Waller decreed. The rise in female autonomy and aggressiveness, scholar and government officials agreed, was causing a rise in juvenile delinquency and divorce rates – and would only lead to the collapse of the family. Childcare authorities, most notably Dr Benjamin Spock, demanded that wives stay at home, and colleges produced new curricula to train women to be good housewives.

Advertisers reversed their wartime message – that women could work and enjoy a family life – and claimed now that women must choose, and choose only home. As a survey of women's images in postwar magazine fiction would later find, careers for women were painted in a more unattractive light in this era than at any time since the turn of the century; these short stories represented 'the strongest assault on feminine careerism' since 1905. On the comics pages, even the postwar Wonder Woman was going weak at the knees.

Again, a few defenders of women's rights tried to point out signs of the gathering political storm. In 1948 Susan B. Anthony IV remarked that there appeared to be a move afoot to 'crack up' the women's movement. Margaret Hickey, head of the federal Women's Advisory Committee to the War Manpower Commission warned that a 'campaign of undercover methods and trumped up excuses' was driving women from top-paying government jobs. But most women's rights groups were disowning their own cause. Soon Hickey herself was declaring, 'The days of the old, selfish, strident feminism are over.' Meanwhile, a younger generation of women, adrift in a TV-shaped dreamscape of suburban patios and family dens, donned padded bras and denied personal ambition. Before long, the majority of young college women were claiming they were on campus only to find husbands. Their age at first marriage dropped to a record low for the century; the number of their babies climbed to a record high.

The 1950s era of the 'feminine mystique' is amply chronicled, most famously in Betty Friedan's 1963 account. But in fact the much publicized homebound image of the fifties woman bore little relation to her actual circumstances. This is an important distinction that bears special relevance to the current backlash, the effects of which have often been discounted, characterized as benign or even meaningless because women continue to enter the work force. In the 1950s, while women may have been hastening down the aisle, they were also increasing their numbers at the office – soon at a pace that outstripped even their wartime work participation. And it was precisely women's unrelenting influx into the job market, not a retreat to the home, that provoked and sustained the anti-feminist uproar. It was the reality of the nine-to-five working woman that heightened cultural fantasies of the compliant homebody and playmate. As literary scholars Sandra M. Gilbert and Susan Gubar observe of the postwar era, '[J]ust as more and more women were getting paid for using their brains, more and more men represented them in novels, plays, and poems as nothing but bodies.'

These cultural images notwithstanding, the proportion of women working doubled between 1940 and 1950, and for the first time the majority of them were married – forcing the average man to face the spectre of the working woman in his own home. Even at the very peak of the postwar industries' expulsion of female workers, women were quietly returning to the workplace through a back door. While 3.25 million women were pushed or persuaded out of industrial jobs in the first year after the end of the Second World War, 2.75 million women were entering the work force at the same time, in lower-paid clerical and administrative positions. Two years after the war, working women had recouped their numerical setbacks in the job market, and by 1952 more women were employed than at the height of the war economy's output. By 1955 the *average* wife worked until her first child was born and went back to work when her children started school.

The backlash of the feminine-mystique years did not return working women to the home (and, instructively, almost none of the wartime *clerical* work force was laid off after VJ Day). Instead the culture derided them; employers discriminated against them;

government promoted new employment policies that discriminated against women; and eventually women themselves internalized the message that, if they must work, they should stick to
typing. The ranks of working women didn't shrink in the 1950s,
but the proportion of them who were relegated to low-paying
jobs rose, their pay gap climbed, and occupational segregation
increased as their numbers in the higher-paying professions
declined from one-half in 1930 to about one-third by 1960. The
fifties backlash, in short, didn't transform women into full-
time 'happy housewives'; it just demoted them to poorly paid
secretaries.

Women's contradictory circumstances in the 1950s – rising
economic participation coupled with an embattled and diminished
cultural stature – is the central paradox of women under a backlash. At the turn of the century, concerted efforts by university
presidents, politicians and business leaders to purge women from
the campus and the office also failed; between 1870 and 1910 both
the proportion of college women and the proportion of working
women doubled. We should not, therefore, gauge a backlash by
losses in women's numbers in the job market, but by attacks on
women's rights and opportunities within that market, attacks that
serve to stall and set back true economic equality. As a 1985 AFL-
CIO [American Federation of Labour and Congress of Industrial
Organizations] report on workers' rights observed of women's
dubious progress in the 1980s job market: 'The number of working
women has grown to about 50 million today, but there has been
no similar growth in their economic status.'

To understand why a backlash works in this contrary manner
we need to go back to our tilted corkscrew model of female
progress. In any time of backlash, cultural anxiety inevitably centres on two pressure points in that spiral, demographic trends that
act like two arrows pushing against the spiral, causing it to lean
in the direction of women's advancement but also becoming the
foci of the backlash's greatest wrath.

A woman's claim to her own salary is one of these arrows. The
proportion of women in the paid labour force has been rising with
little interruption since the Victorian era. In a society where
income is the measure of social strength and authority, women's

growing presence in the labour force can't help but mitigate women's secondary standing. But it hasn't brought full equality. Instead, with each turn of the spiral the culture simply redoubles its resistance, if not by returning women to the kitchen, then by making the hours spent away from their stoves as inequitable and intolerable as possible: pushing women into the worst occupations, paying them the lowest wages, laying them off first and promoting them last, refusing to offer childcare or family leave, and subjecting them to harassment.

The other straight arrow pressing against but never piercing the backlash corkscrew is a woman's control over her own fertility – and it, too, sets up the same paradox between private behaviour and public attitudes. As Henry Adams said of the furore over women's increasing propensity to limit family growth in his day, '[T]he surface current of social opinion seemed set as strongly in one direction as the silent undercurrent of social action ran in the other.' With the exception of the postwar baby boom, the number of childbirths per household has gradually declined in the last century. The ability to limit family size has certainly improved women's situation, but it, too, has only inspired countervailing social campaigns to regulate pregnant women's behaviour and stigmatize the childless. In periods of backlash, birth control becomes less available, abortion is restricted, and women who make use of it are painted as 'selfish' or 'immoral'.

The 1970s women's movement made its most substantial progress on the twin fronts of employment and fertility   forging historic and record numbers of equal employment and anti-discrimination policies, forcing open the doors to lucrative and elite 'male' professions, and ultimately helping to legalize abortion. And now, once again, as the backlash crests and breaks, it crashes hardest on these two shores – dismantling the apparatus for enforcing equal opportunity, gutting crucial legal rulings for working women, undermining abortion rights, halting birth-control research, and promulgating 'foetal protection' and 'foetal rights' policies that have shut women out of lucrative jobs, caused them to undergo invasive obstetric surgeries against their will, and thrown 'bad' mothers in jail.

*

The attack on women's rights that has developed in the last decade is perhaps most remarkable for how little it has been remarked upon at all. The press has largely ignored the mounting evidence of a backlash – and promoted the 'evidence' that the backlash invented instead. The media have circulated make-believe data on marriage and infertility that linked women's progress to marital and fertility setbacks, or unquestioningly passed along misleading government and private reports that concealed increasing inequities and injustice – such as the US Labor Department's claim that women's wage gap has suddenly narrowed or the Equal Employment Opportunity Commission's claim that sexual harassment on the job is declining or a Justice Department report that rape rates are static.

In place of factual reporting on the political erosion in women's lives, the mass media have offered us fictional accounts of women 'cocooning', a so-called new social trend in which the *Good Housekeeping*-created 'New Traditionalist' gladly retreats to her domestic shell. Cocooning is little more than a resurgence of the 1950s 'back-to-the-home movement', itself a creation of advertisers and, in turn, a recycled version of the Victorian fantasy that a new 'cult of domesticity' was bringing droves of women home. Not surprisingly, the cocooning lady has been invented and exalted by the same institutions that have sustained the heaviest financial blow from women's increasingly non-cocooning habits. Traditional women's magazine publishers, television programmers and the marketers of fashion, beauty and household goods have all played central roles – all merchandisers who still believe they need 'feminine passivity' and full-time housework to sell their wares.

The very choice of the word 'cocooning' should suggest to us the trend's fantastical nature. A cocoon is a husk sloughed upon maturity; butterflies don't return to their chrysalis – nor to a larval state. The cultural myth of cocooning suggests an adult woman who has regressed in her life cycle, returned to a gestational stage. It maps the road back from the feminist journey, which was once aptly defined by a turn-of-the-century writer as 'the attempt of women to grow up'. Cocooning's infantile imagery, furthermore, bears a vindictive subtext, by promoting a retreat from female adulthood at the very time when the largest proportion of the female population is entering middle age. Feminine youth is elevated when women can least ascend its pedestal; cocooning urges women to become little girls, then mocks them mercilessly for the impossibility of that venture.

The false feminine vision that has been unfurled by contemporary popular culture in the last decade is a sort of vast velveteen curtain that hides women's reality while claiming to be its mirror. It has not made women cocoon or become New Traditionalists. But its thick drapery has both concealed the political assault on women's rights and become the impossible standard by which women are asked to judge themselves. Its false front has encouraged each woman to doubt herself for not matching the image in the mass-produced mirror, instead of doubting the validity of the mirror itself and pressing to discover what its non-reflective surface hides.

As the backlash has gained power, instead of fighting and exposing its force many women's groups and individual women have become caught up with fitting into its fabricated backdrop. Feminist-minded institutions founded a decade earlier, from The First Women's Bank to Options for Women, camouflaged their intent with new, neutral-sounding names; women in politics have claimed they are now only interested in 'family issues', not women's rights; and career women with Ivy League degrees have eschewed the feminist label for public consumption. Instead of assailing injustice, many women have learned to adjust to it. Instead of getting angry, they have become depressed. Instead of uniting their prodigious numbers, they have splintered and turned their pain and frustration inward, some in starkly physical ways.

In turn, this female adjustment process to backlash pressures has yielded record profits for the many 'professionals' who have rushed in to exploit and exacerbate it: advice writers and pop therapists, matchmaking consultants, plastic surgeons and infertility specialists have both fuelled and cashed in on women's anxiety and panic under the backlash. Millions of women have sought relief from their distress only to wind up in the all-popular counselling of the era where women learn not to raise their voices but to lower their expectations and 'surrender' to their 'higher power'.

Today's woman has not yet slipped into a cocoon, but she has tumbled down a rabbit hole into sudden isolation. In Wendy Wasserstein's 1988 Broadway hit *The Heidi Chronicles*, her heroine, Heidi Holland, delivers what would become one of the most quoted lines by women writing about the female experience in America in the 1980s: 'I feel stranded, and I thought the point was that we wouldn't feel stranded,' the once feminist art historian says. 'I thought we were all in this together.' As women's collective quest for equal rights smacks into the backlash's wall of resistance, it breaks into a million pieces, each shard a separate woman's life. The backlash has ushered in not the cosy feeling of 'family togetherness', as advertisers have described it, but the chilling realization that it is now every woman for herself. 'I'm alone,' a secretary confides in an article surveying contemporary women, an article that is filled with such laments. 'I know a lot of people [are] dealing with the same problems, but I guess we're just dealing with them by ourselves.' Both young and old women, non-ideological undergraduates and feminist activists alike, have felt the pain of this new isolation – and the sense of powerlessness it has bred. 'I feel abandoned,' an older feminist writes in the letters column of *Ms.*, 'as if we were all members of a club that they have suddenly quit.' 'We don't feel angry, we feel helpless,' a young woman bursts out at a college board on women's status.

The loss of a collective spirit has proven far more debilitating to women than what is commonly characterized as the overly taxing experience of a liberated life. Backlash-era conventional wisdom blames the women's movement for women's 'exhaustion'. The feminists have pushed forward too fast, backlash pundits say; they have brought too much change too soon and have worn women out. But the malaise and enervation that women are feeling today aren't induced by the speed of liberation but by its stagnation. The feminist revolution has petered out, leaving so many women discouraged and paralysed by the knowledge that, once again, the possibility for real progress has been foreclosed.

When one is feeling stranded, finding a safe harbour inevitably becomes a more compelling course than struggling against social currents. Keeping the peace with the particular man in one's life becomes more essential than battling the mass male culture. Saying one is 'not a feminist' (even while supporting quietly every item of the feminist platform) seems the most prudent, self-protective strategy. Ultimately in such conditions, the impulse to remedy social injustice can become not only secondary but silent. 'In a state of feeling alone,' as feminist writer Susan Griffin has said, 'the knowledge of oppression remains mute.'

To expect each woman, in such a time of isolation and crushing conformism, to take a solitary feminist stand is asking too much. 'If I were to overcome the conventions,' Virginia Woolf wrote, 'I should need the courage of a hero, and I am not a hero.' Under the backlash, even a heroine can lose her nerve, as the social climate raises the stakes to an unbearable degree and as the backlash rhetoric drives home, time and again, the terrible penalties that will befall a pioneering woman who flouts convention. In the last decade, all the warnings and threats about the 'consequences' and 'costs' of feminist aspiration have had their desired effect. By 1989 almost half the women in a *New York Times* poll on women's status said they now feared they had sacrificed too much for their gains. The maximum price that their culture had forced them to pay for minimal progress, they said, was just too high.

A Crisis in Confidence . . . But Whose Crisis?

> And when women do not need to live through their husbands and children, men will not fear the love and strength of women, nor need another's weakness to prove their own masculinity.
>
> BETTY FRIEDAN, *The Feminine Mystique*

This stirring proclamation, offered in the final page of Friedan's classic work, is one prediction that never came to pass. Feminists have always optimistically assumed that once they demonstrated the merits of their cause, male hostility to women's rights would evaporate. They have always been disappointed. 'I am sure the emancipated man is a myth sprung from our hope and eternal aspiration,' feminist Doris Stevens wrote wearily in the early 1900s. 'There has been much accomplishment,' Margaret Culkin

Banning wrote of women's rights in 1935, ' . . . and more than a few years have passed. But the resentment of men has not disappeared. Quietly it has grown and deepened.'

When author Anthony Astrachan completed his seven-year study of American male attitudes in the 1980s, he found that no more than 5 to 10 per cent of the men he surveyed 'genuinely support women's demands for independence and equality'. In 1988 the American Male Opinion Index, a poll of 3,000 men conducted for *Gentlemen's Quarterly*, found that less than a quarter of men supported the women's movement, while the majority favoured traditional roles for women. Sixty per cent said wives with small children should stay at home. Other studies examining male attitudes toward the women's movement – of which, regrettably, there are few – suggest that the most substantial share of the growth in men's support for feminism may have occurred in the first half of the 1970s, in that brief period when women's 'lib' was fashionable, and slowed since. As the American Male Opinion Index observed, while men in the 1980s continued to give lip service to such abstract matters of 'fair play' as the right to equal pay, 'when the issues change from social justice to personal applications, the consensus crumbles'. By the eighties, as the poll results made evident, men were interpreting small advances in women's rights as big, and complete, ones; they believed women had made major progress toward equality – while women believed the struggle was just beginning. This his-and-hers experience of the equal-rights campaign would soon generate a gulf between the sexes.

At the same time that men were losing interest in feminist concerns, women were gaining and deepening theirs. During much of the 1970s there had been little divergence between American men and women in polling questions about changing sex roles, and men had even given slightly more support than women to such issues as the Equal Rights Amendment. But as women began to challenge their own internalized views of a woman's proper place, their desire and demand for equal status and free choice began to grow exponentially. By the 1980s, as the polls showed, they outpaced men in their support for virtually every feminist position.

The pressures of the backlash only served to reinforce and broaden the divide. As basic rights and opportunities for women became increasingly threatened, especially for female heads of households, the ranks of American women favouring not just a feminist but a social-justice agenda swelled. Whether the question was affirmative action, the military buildup or federal aid for health care, women were becoming more radical, men more conservative. This was especially apparent among younger women and men; it was younger men who gave the most support to Reagan. (Contrary to conventional wisdom, the rise of 'the conservative youth' in the early eighties was largely a one-gender phenomenon.) Even in the most liberal baby-boom populations, male and female attitudes were polarizing dramatically. A national survey of 'progressive' baby boomers (defined as the 12 million who support social-change groups) found that 60 per cent of the women called themselves 'radical' to 'very liberal', while 60 per cent of the men described themselves as 'moderate' to 'conservative'. The pollsters identified one prime cause for this chasm: the majority of women surveyed said they felt the 1980s had been a 'bad decade' for them (while the majority of men disagreed) – and they feared the next decade would be even worse.

The divergence of men's and women's atttitudes passed several benchmarks in 1980. For the first time in American history, a gender voting gap emerged over women's rights issues. For the first time, polls found men less likely than women to support equal roles for the sexes in business and government, less likely to support the Equal Rights Amendment – and more likely to say they preferred the 'traditional' family where the wife stayed at home. Moreover, some signs began to surface that men's support for women's rights issues was not only lagging but might actually be eroding. A national poll found that men who 'strongly agreed' that the family should be 'traditional' – with the man as the breadwinner and the woman as the housewife – suddenly jumped four percentage points between 1986 and 1988, the first rise in nearly a decade. (The same year, it fell for women.)

By the end of the decade, the National Opinion Research poll was finding that nearly twice the proportion of women as men thought a working mother could be just as good a parent as a mother who stayed at home. In 1989, while a majority of women in the *New York Times* poll believed American society had not changed enough to grant women equality, only a minority of men agreed. A majority of the men *were* saying, however, that the women's movement had 'made things harder for men at home'. Just as in previous backlashes, American men's discomfort with the feminist cause in the last decade has endured – and even 'quietly grown and deepened'.

While pollsters can try to gauge the level of male resistance, they can't explain it. And unfortunately our social investigators have not tackled 'the man question' with a tenth of the enterprise that they have always applied to 'the woman problem'. The works on masculinity would barely fill a bookshelf. We might deduce from the lack of literature that manhood is less complex and burdensome, and that it requires less maintenance than femininity. But the studies that are available on the male condition offer no such assurance. Quite the contrary, they find masculinity a fragile flower – a hothouse orchid in constant need of trellising and nourishment. 'Violating sex roles has more severe consequences for males than females,' social researcher Joseph Pleck concluded. '[M]aleness in America,' as Margaret Mead wrote, 'is not absolutely defined; it has to be kept and reearned every day, and one essential element in the definition is beating women in every game that both sexes play.' Nothing seems to crush the masculine petals more than a bit of feminist rain – a few drops are perceived as a downpour. 'Men view even small losses of deference, advantages, or opportunities as large threats,' wrote William Goode, one of the many sociologists to puzzle over the peculiarly hyperbolic male reaction to minuscule improvements in women's rights.

'Women have become so powerful that our independence has been lost in our own homes and is now being trampled and stamped underfoot in public.' So Cato wailed in 195 BC, after a few Roman women sought to repeal a law that forbade their sex to ride in chariots or to wear multicoloured dresses. In the sixteenth century, just the possibility that two royal women might occupy thrones in Europe at the same time provoked John Knox to issue his famous diatribe, 'The First Blast of the Trumpet Against the Monstrous Regiment of Women'.

By the nineteenth century the spokesmen of male fears had mostly learned to hide their anxiety over female independence behind masks of paternalism and pity. As Edward Bok, the legend-ary Victorian editor of the *Ladies' Home Journal* and guardian of women's morals, explained to his many female readers, the weaker sex must not venture beyond the family sphere because their 'rebellious nerves instantly and rightly cry out, "Thus far shalt thou go, but no farther".' But it wasn't female nerves that were rebelling against feminist efforts, not then and not now.

A 'crisis of masculinity' has erupted in every period of backlash in the last century, a faithful quiet companion to the loudly voiced call for a 'return to femininity'. In the late 1800s a blizzard of literature decrying the 'soft male' rolled off the presses. 'The whole generation is womanized,' Henry James's protagonist Basil Ransom lamented in *The Bostonians*. 'The masculine tone is pass-ing out of the world; it's a feminine, a nervous, hysterical, chatter-ing, canting age . . . The masculine character . . . that is what I want to preserve, or rather, as I may say, to recover; and I must tell you that I don't in the least care what becomes of you ladies while I make the attempt!' Child-rearing manuals urged parents to toughen up their sons with hard mattresses and vigorous athletic regimens. Billy Sunday led the clerical attack on 'feminized' religion, promoting a 'muscular Christianity' and a Jesus who was 'no dough-faced, lickspittle-proposition' but 'the greatest scrapper that ever lived'. Theodore Roosevelt warned of the national peril of losing the 'fiber of vigorous hardiness and masculinity' and hardened his own fibre with the Rough Riders. Martial swaggering prevailed on the political platform; indeed, as sociologist Theodore Roszak writes of the 'compulsive masculinity' era that culminated in the First World War, 'The period leading up to 1914 reads in the history books like one long drunken stag party.'

The masculinity crisis would return with each backlash. The fledgling Boy Scouts of America claimed one-fifth of all American boys by 1920; its founder's explicit aim was to staunch the feminiz-ation of the American male by removing young men from the too-powerful female orbit. Chief Scout Ernest Thompson Seton feared that boys were degenerating into 'a lot of flat-chested ciga-rette-smokers, with shaky nerves and doubtful vitality'. Again, in the years following the Second World War, male commentators and literary figures were panicking over reduced masculine powers. At home, 'momism' was siphoning virile juices. Philip Wylie's best-selling *Generation of Vipers* advised, 'We must face the dynasty of the dames at once, deprive them of our pocket-books' before the American man degenerated into 'the Abdicating Male'. In what was supposed to be a special issue on 'The American Woman', *Life* magazine became fixated on the weak-kneed American man. Because women had failed to live up to their feminine duties, the 1956 article charged, 'the emerging American man tends to be passive and irresponsible'. In the business world, the *Wall Street Journal* warned in 1949 that 'women are taking over'. *Look* decried the rise of 'female dominance': first, women had grabbed control of the stock market, the magazine complained, and now they were advancing on 'authority-wielding executive jobs'.

In the 1980s male nerves rebelled once more, as 'a decline in American manhood' became the obsession of male clergy, writers, politicians and scholars all along the political spectrum, from the right-wing Reverend Jerry Falwell to the leftist poet and lecturer Robert Bly. Anti-abortion leaders such as Randall Terry rallied thousands of men with their visions of a Christ who was a muscle-bound 'soldier', not a girlish 'sheep'. A new 'men's movement' drew tens of thousands of followers to all-male retreats, where they rooted out 'feminized' tendencies and roused 'the wild man within'. In the UK, *Punch* editor David Thomas and journalist Neil Lyndon have spearheaded a counterattack on what they perceive as 'thirty years of feminist orthodoxy – an orthodoxy that nowadays makes communism look broad-minded and flexible'. In a prominent *Sunday Times Magazine* article in autumn 1990, Neil Lyndon dismissed feminist complaints – 'It is hard to think of one example of systemic and institutionalized discrimination against women today' – and asserted that men are the new 'second-class citizens'. Not only are men 'suffering from systemic disadvantages' themselves, but their manhood has been trivialized. 'The penis is *not* taken seriously. It *is* treated as a crude mechanism . . . It is, in fact, the subject of institutionalized neglect.'

In the American press, male columnists bemoaned the rise of the 'sensitive man'. *Harper's* editor Lewis Lapham advocated all-male clubs to tone sagging masculinity: 'Let the lines of balanced

tension go slack and the structure dissolves into the ooze of androgyny,' he predicted. In films and television, all-male macho action
shows so swamped the screen and set that the number of female
roles in this era markedly declined. In fiction, violent macho action
books were flying off the shelves, in a renaissance of this genre
that Bantam Books' male-action-adventure editor equated with
the 'blood-and-thunder pulp dime novels of the nineteenth
century'. In apparel, the masculinity crisis was the one bright spot
in this otherwise depressed industry: sales boomed in safari outfits,
combat gear and the other varieties of what *Newsweek* aptly
dubbed 'predatory fashion'. In US politics, the 1988 presidential
campaign turned into a testosterone contest. 'I'm not squishy soft,'
Michael Dukakis fretted, and leapt into a tank. 'I'm very tough.'
George Bush, whose 'wimpiness' preoccupied the press,
announced, 'I'm the pitbull of SDI.' He stocked his wardrobe
with enough rugged togs to adorn an infantry, and turned jogging
into a daily photo opportunity. Two years into his presidency,
George Bush's metaphorical martial bravado had taken a literal
and bloody turn as his administration took the nation to war; it
might be said that Bush began by boasting about 'kicking a little
ass' in his debate with Geraldine Ferraro and ended by, as he
himself put it, 'kicking ass' in the Persian Gulf.

Under this backlash, like its predecessors, an often ludicrous
over-reaction to women's modest progress has prevailed. 'The
women are taking over' is again a refrain many working women
hear from their male colleagues – after one or two women are
promoted at their company, but while top management is still
solidly male. In newsrooms, white male reporters routinely complain that only women and minorities can get jobs – often at
publications where women's and minorities' numbers are actually
shrinking. 'At Columbia,' literature professor Carolyn Heilbrun
has observed, 'I have heard men say, with perfect sincerity, that
a few women seeking equal pay are trying to overturn the university, to ruin it.' At Boston University, president John Silber fumed
that his English department had turned into a 'damn matriarchy'
– when only six of its twenty faculty members were women.
Feminists have 'complete control' of the Pentagon, a brigadier-
general complained – when women, much less feminists, rep-

resented barely 10 per cent of the armed services and were mostly relegated to the forces' lowest levels.

But what exactly is it about women's equality that even its slightest shadow threatens to erase male identity? What is it about the way we frame manhood that, even today, it still depends so much on 'feminine' dependence for its survival? A little-noted finding by the Yankelovich Monitor survey, a large American poll that has tracked social attitudes for the last two decades, takes us a good way toward a possible answer. For twenty years the Monitor's pollsters have asked its subjects to define masculinity. And for twenty years, the leading definition, ahead by a huge margin, has never changed. It isn't being a leader, athlete, Lothario, decision-maker, or even just being 'born male'. It is simply this: being a 'good provider for his family'.

If establishing masculinity depends most of all on succeeding as the prime breadwinner, then it is hard to imagine a force more directly threatening to fragile manhood than the feminist drive for economic equality. And if supporting a family epitomizes what it means to be a man, then it is little wonder that the backlash erupted when it did – against the backdrop of the 1980s economy. In this period, the 'traditional' man's real wages shrank dramatically and the traditional male breadwinner himself became an endangered species (representing less than 8 per cent of all American households). That the ruling definition of masculinity remains so economically based helps to explain, too, why the backlash has been voiced most bitterly by two groups of men: blue-collar workers, devastated by the shift to a service economy, and younger baby boomers, denied the comparative riches their fathers and elder brothers enjoyed. The 1980s was the decade in which factory closures put blue-collar men out of work by the million, and only 60 per cent found new jobs – about half at lower pay. It was a time when, of all men losing earning power, younger baby-boom men were losing the most. Inevitably, these losses in earning power would breed other losses. As pollster Louis Harris observed, economic polarization spawned the most dramatic change in attitudes recorded in the last decade and a half: a spectacular doubling in the proportion of Americans who describe themselves as feeling 'powerless'.

When analysts at Yankelovich reviewed the Monitor survey's annual attitudinal data in 1986 they had to create a new category to describe a large segment of the population that had suddenly emerged, espousing a distinct set of values. This segment, now representing a remarkable one-fifth of the study's national sample, was dominated by young men, median age thirty-three, disproportionately single, who were slipping down the income ladder – and furious about it. They were the younger, poorer brothers of the baby boom, the ones who weren't so celebrated in 1980s media and advertising tributes to that generation. The Yankelovich report assigned the angry young men the euphemistic label of 'the Contenders'.

The men who belonged to this group had one other distinguishing trait: they feared and reviled feminism. 'It's these downscale men, the ones who can't earn as much as their fathers, who we find are the most threatened by the women's movement,' Susan Hayward, senior vice-president at Yankelovich, observes. 'They represent 20 per cent of the population that cannot handle the changes in women's roles. They were not well employed, they were the first ones laid off, they had no savings and not very much in the way of prospects for the future.' Other surveys would reinforce this observation. By the late 1980s the American Male Opinion Index found that the *largest* of its seven demographic groups was now the 'Change Resisters', a 24 per cent segment of the population that was disproportionately underemployed, 'resentful', convinced that they were 'being left behind' by a changing society, and most hostile to feminism.

To single out these men alone for blame, however, would be unfair. The backlash's public agenda has been framed and promoted by men of far more affluence and influence than the Contenders, men at the helm in the media, business and politics. Poorer or less-educated men have not so much been the creators of the anti-feminist thesis as its receptors. Most vulnerable to its message, they have picked up and played back the backlash at distortingly high volume. In the US the Contenders have dominated the ranks of the militant wing of the eighties anti-abortion movement, the list of plaintiffs filing reverse-discrimination and 'men's rights' lawsuits, the steadily mounting police rolls of rapists and sexual assailants. They are men like the notorious Charles Stuart, the struggling fur salesman in Boston who murdered his pregnant wife, a lawyer, because he feared that she – better educated, more successful – was gaining the 'upper hand'. They are young men with little or no prospects like Yusef Salaam, one of six charged with raping and crushing the skull of a professional woman jogging in Central Park; as he later told the court, he felt 'like a midget, a mouse, something less than a man'. They are men like George Hennard, a thirty-five-year-old unemployed merchant marine, who stormed into a diner in Belton, Texas, in autumn 1991 and assassinated twenty-two people – all but a few of whom were women – because, he said, he wanted to 'prevail over the female vipers'. And they are men like Marc Lepine, the unemployed twenty-five-year-old engineer who gunned down fourteen women in a University of Montreal engineering classroom because they were 'all a bunch of fucking feminists'.

The economic victims of the era are men who know someone has made off with their future – and they suspect the thief is a woman. At no time did this seem more true than in the early 1980s, when, for the first time, women outranked men among new entrants to the work force and, for a brief time, men's unemployment outdistanced women's. The start of the eighties provided not only a political but an economic hair trigger to the backlash. It was a moment of symbolic crossover points for American men and women: the first time white men became less than 50 per cent of the work force, the first time no new manufacturing jobs were created, the first time more women than men enrolled in college, the first time more than 50 per cent of women worked, the first time more than 50 per cent of married women worked, the first time more women with children than without children worked. Significantly, 1980 was the year the US Census officially stopped defining the head of household as the husband.

To some of the men falling back, it certainly has looked as if women have done the pushing. If there has been a 'price to pay' for women's equality, then it seems to these men that they are paying it. The man in the White House during much of the 1980s did little to discourage this view, and neither, it must be said, did the right-wing woman in No. 10 Downing Street. 'Part of the unemployment is not as much recession,' Ronald Reagan said in a 1982 address on the economy, 'as it is the great increase of the people going into the job market, and – ladies, I'm not picking on anyone but . . . – because of the increase in women who are working today.'

In reality, the past decade's economic pains most often took a disproportionate toll on women, not men. And working women's so-called gains under Reagan and Thatcher had precious little to do with men's losses. About a third of the new jobs were at or below the poverty level, up from a quarter a decade earlier, and lowly 'female' service jobs in retail and service industries accounted for 77 per cent of the total net job growth in the 1980s. The so-called job growth occurred in such areas as sweatshop labour, home-based work with below-minimum wages, the sales-clerk and fast-food career track of no security and no benefits. These were not positions men were losing to women; these were the bottom-of-the-barrel tasks men turned down and women took out of desperation – to support families where the man was absent, out of work or underemployed.

The eighties economy thinned the ranks of middle-income earn-ers and polarized the classes to the greatest extreme since the US government began keeping such records in 1946. In this climate, the only way a middle-class family maintained its shaky grip on the income ladder was with two salaries. Household income would have shrunk three times as much in the decade if women hadn't worked in mass numbers. And this fact dealt the final blow to masculine pride and identity: not only could the middle-class man no longer provide for his family, the person who bailed him out was the wife he believed he was meant to support.

To the men who were suffering, the true origins of economic polarization seemed remote or intangible: a binge of mergers and takeovers that piled up debt and spat out jobs; a speculative boom that collapsed in the 1987 Black Monday stock market crash; a shift to offshore manufacturing and office automation; a loss of union power; the massive spending cuts for the poor and tax concessions for the rich; low wages that placed a family of four at the poverty level; the impossible cost of housing that consumed almost half an average worker's income. These are also conditions, it's worth noting, that to a large degree echo economic circumstances confronting workers in previous backlash eras: mass financial speculation led to the panic of 1893 and the 1929 crash; under the backlashes of the late nineteenth-century and Depression era, wage earners also reeled under waves of corporate mergers, unions lost their clout, and wealth was consolidated in the hands of the very few.

When the enemy has no face, society will invent one. All that free-floating anxiety over declining wages, insecure employment and overpriced housing needs a focus, and in the 1980s much of it fixed itself on women. 'There had to be a deeper cause [for the decade's materialism] than the Reagan era and Wall Street,' a former newspaper editor wrote in the *New York Times Magazine* – then concluded, 'The women's movement had to have played a key role.' Seeking effigies to hang for the eighties excesses of Wall Street, the American press and public hoisted highest a few female investment bankers in this largely white male profession. 'FATS' ('Female Arbitrageurs Traders and Short Sellers') was what a particularly vindictive 1987 column in *Barron's* labelled them. When the *New York Times Magazine* got around to decrying the avidity of contemporary brokers, the publication reserved its fiercest attack for a minor female player: Karen Valenstein, an E. F. Hutton vice-president who was one of Wall Street's 'pre-eminent' women. (In fact, she wasn't even high enough to run a division.) The magazine article, which was most critical of her supposed failings in the wife-and-motherhood department, unleashed a torrent of rage against her on Wall Street and in other newspapers (the *New York Daily News* even ran an unpopularity poll on her), and she was ultimately fired, blacklisted on Wall Street, and had to leave town. She eventually opened a more ladylike sweater shop in Wyoming. Still later, when it came time to vent public wrath on the haves of the decade, Leona Helmsley was the figure most viciously tarred and feathered. She was dubbed 'the Wicked Witch of the West' and a 'whore' by politicians and screaming mobs, scalded in a *Newsweek* cover story (entitled RHYMES WITH RICH), and declared 'a disgrace to humanity' (by, of all people, real-estate king Donald Trump). On the other hand, Michael Milken, whose multibillion-dollar manipulations dwarf Helmsley's comparatively petty tax evasions, enjoyed fawning full-page ads from many admirers, kid-gloves treatment in national magazines such as *Vanity Fair*, and even plaudits from civil rights leader Jesse Jackson.

For some high-profile men in trouble, women, especially feminist women, became the all-purpose scapegoats – charged with crimes that often descended into the absurd. Beset by corruption and awash in weaponry boondoggles, US military brass blamed the Defense Department's troubles on feminists who were trying 'to reduce combat effectiveness' and on 'the feminization of the American military'; commanding officers advised the Pentagon that pregnancy among female officers – a condition affecting less than 1 per cent of the total enlisted force at any one time – was the armed services' 'single biggest readiness problem'. Mayor Marion Barry blamed a 'bitch' for his cocaine-laced fall from grace – and one of his more vocal defenders, writer Ishmael Reed, went further, recasting the whole episode later in a play as a *feminist* conspiracy. Joel Steinberg's attorney claimed that the notorious batterer and child-beater had been destroyed by 'hysterical feminists'. And even errant Colonel Oliver North blamed his legal troubles in the Iran–Contra affair on 'an arrogant army of ultra-militant feminists'.

The Nature of Today's Backlash

Once a society projects its fears on to a female form, it can try to cordon off those fears by controlling women – pushing them to conform to comfortingly nostalgic norms and shrinking them in the cultural imagination to a manageable size. The demand that women 'return to femininity' is a demand that the cultural gears shift into reverse, that we return to a fabled time when everyone was richer, younger, more powerful. The 'feminine' woman is forever static and childlike. She is like the ballerina in an old-fashioned music box, her unchanging features tiny and girlish, her voice tinkly, her body stuck on a pin, rotating in a spiral that will never grow.

In times of backlash, images of the restrained woman line the walls of the popular culture's gallery. We see her silenced, infantilized, immobilized or, the ultimate restraining order, killed. She is a frozen homebound figure, a bedridden patient, an anonymous still body. She is 'the Quiet Woman', the name on an eighties-vintage wine label that depicted a decapitated woman. She is the comatose woman on display in ads for Opium perfume, or the plumaged exotic bird who is shackled at the ankle in ads for Chanel's Coco. She is Laura Palmer, the dead girl of *Twin Peaks*, whom *Esquire* picked for the cover of its 'Women We Love' issue. While there have been a few cases – like the pop icon Madonna – where a female figure who is loud and self-determined has challenged the popular consensus, these are the exceptions. More commonly, outspoken women on screen and stage have been hushed or, in a case like Roseanne Barr's, publicly shamed – and applause reserved for their more compliant and whispery sisters. In this past decade, the media, the movies, the fashion and beauty industries, have all honoured most the demure and retiring child-woman – a neo-Victorian 'lady' with a pallid visage, a birdlike creature who stays indoors, speaks in a chirpy small voice and clips her wings in restrictive clothing. Her circumstances are, at least in mainstream culture, almost always portrayed as her 'choice'; it is important not only that she wear rib-crushing garments but that she lace them up herself.

The restrained woman of the current backlash distinguishes herself from her predecessors in earlier backlashes by appearing to choose her condition twice – first as a woman and second as a feminist. Victorian culture peddled 'femininity' as what 'a true woman' wants; in the marketing strategy of contemporary culture it's what a 'liberated' woman craves, too. Just as Reagan and Thatcher appropriated populism to sell a political programme that favoured the rich, politicians, the mass media and advertising adopted feminist rhetoric to market policies that hurt women or to peddle the same old sexist products or to conceal anti-feminist views. Bush promised 'empowerment' for poor women – as a substitute for the many social-service programmes he was slashing; Major promised a classless society and backed 'Opportunity 2000' while presiding over rising unemployment and an all-male Cabinet. Even *Playboy* claimed to ally itself with female progress. Women have made such strides, the magazine's spokeswoman assured the press, 'there's no longer a stigma attached to posing'.

The eighties culture stifled women's political speech and then redirected self-expression to the shopping mall. The passive consumer was reissued as an ersatz feminist, exercising her 'right' to buy products, making her own 'choices' at the checkout. 'You *can* have it all', a Michelob ad promised a nubile woman in a bodysuit – but by 'all' the brewing company meant only a less-filling beer. Criticized for targeting young women in its ads, an indignant vice-president of Philip Morris cigarettes claimed that such criticism was 'sexist', because it suggested that 'adult women are not capable of making their own decisions about whether or not to smoke'. The feminist entreaty to follow one's own instincts became a merchandising appeal to obey the call of the market – an appeal that diluted and degraded women's quest for true self-determination. By returning women to a view of themselves as devoted shoppers, the consumption-obsessed decade succeeded in under-cutting one of the guiding principles of feminism: that women must think for themselves. As Christopher Lasch (who would himself soon be lobbing his own verbal grenades at feminists) observed in *The Culture of Narcissism*, consumerism undermines women's progress most perniciously when it 'seems to side with women against male oppression'.

> The advertising industry thus encourages the pseudo-emancipation of women, flattering them with its insinuating reminder, 'You've come a long way, baby' and disguising the freedom to consume as genuine autonomy . . . It emancipates women and children from patriarchal authority, however, only to subject them to the new paternalism of the advertising industry, the industrial corporation, and the state.

The contemporary counterassault on women's rights contributes still another unique tactic to the old backlash strategy books: the pose of a 'sophisticated' ironic distance from its own destructive ends. To the backlash's list of faked emotions – pity for single women, worry over the fatigue level of career women, concern for the family – the current onslaught adds a sneering 'hip' cynicism toward those who dare point out discrimination or anti-female messages. In the era's entertainment and advertising, aimed at and designed by baby boomers, the self-conscious cast of characters constantly let us know that *they* know their presentation of women is retrograde and demeaning, but what of it? To make a fuss about sexual injustice is more than unfeminine; it is now uncool. Feminist anger, or any form of social outrage, is dismissed breezily – not because it lacks substance but because it lacks 'style'.

It is hard enough to expose anti-feminist sentiments when they are dressed up in feminist clothes. But it is far tougher to confront a foe that professes not to care. Even the unmitigated fury of an anti-abortion 'soldier' may be preferable to the jaundiced eye of the sitcom spokesmen. Feminism is 'so seventies', the pop culture's ironists say, stifling a yawn. We're 'post-feminist' now, they assert, meaning not that women have arrived at equal justice and moved beyond it, but simply that they themselves are beyond even pretending to care. It is an indifference that may, finally, deal the most devastating blow to women's rights.

Part Two
The Backlash in Popular Culture

Chapter Four

The 'Trends' of Anti-feminism: The Media and the Backlash

The first action of the new women's liberation movement to receive front-page coverage was a demonstration against the Miss America pageant in 1968. Protests against beauty contests would follow in many other countries, from Miss New Zealand to Miss World, but none caused quite the furore that this one did. Many feminist marches for jobs, pay equity and coeducation had preceded it, but they didn't attract anything like the amount of media attention. The reason this event got so much ink: a few women tossed some padded brassières in a rubbish bin. No one actually burned a bra that day – as a journalist erroneously reported. In fact, there's scant evidence of underwear torchings at women's rights demonstrations in the decade. (The only two such displays that came close were both organized by *men*, a disc jockey and an architect, who tried to get women to fling their bras into a barrel and the Chicago River as 'media events'. Only three women cooperated in the river stunt – all models hired by the architect.) Yet, according to press accounts of the time, the bonfires of feminism nearly cremated the lingerie industry.

Mostly, editors at the reigning publications in the late sixties and early seventies preferred not to cover the women's movement at all. The 'grand press blitz', as some feminists jokingly called the media's coverage of the movement, lasted three months; by 1971 the press was already declaring this latest 'fad' a 'bore' or 'dead'. All that 'bra burning', the media perversely said of its own created myth, had alienated ordinary women. And publications where editors were forced to recognize the women's movement – they were under internal pressure from women on their own staff – often deployed reporters to discredit it. At *Newsday*, a male editor assigned reporter Marilyn Goldstein a story on the women's movement with these instructions: 'Get out there and find an authority who'll say this is all a crock of shit.' At *Newsweek*, Lynn Young's 1970 story on the women's movement, the magazine's first, was rewritten every week for two months, then killed. Finally *Newsweek* commissioned a freelancer for the job, the wife of a senior editor and a self-professed anti-feminist. (This tactic backfired when she changed her mind after 'my first interview' and embraced the movement.)

By the mid-1970s the media and advertisers had settled on a line that served to neutralize and commercialize feminism at the same time. Women, the mass media seemed to have decided, were now equal and no longer seeking new rights – just new lifestyles. Women wanted self-gratification, not self-determination – the sort of fulfilment best serviced at a shopping mall. Soon periodicals and, of course, their ad pages, were bristling with images of 'liberated single girls' stocking up on designer swimsuits for their Club Med vacations, perky 'Superwomen' flashing credit cards at the slightest provocation. 'She's Free. She's Career. She's Confident', a jewellery ad enthused. Prestige launched a brand of tights in New Zealand called 'Freedom Lovers' with an ad featuring a model in hot pants pretending to be restrained by two policemen, her placard proclaiming FREEDOM FOR WOMEN upside down at her feet. The copy line read: 'Now feel as free as a bird should be'. SUCCESS! was the stock headline on magazine articles about women's status – as if all barriers to women's opportunity had suddenly been swept aside. UP THE LADDER, FINALLY! *Business Week* proclaimed, in a 1975 special issue on 'the Corporate Woman' – illustrated with a lone General Electric female vice-president enthroned in her executive chair, her arms raised in triumph. 'More women than ever are within striking distance of the top', the magazine asserted – though, it admitted, it had 'no hard facts' to substantiate that claim.

The media's pseudo-feminist cheerleading stopped suddenly in the early 1980s – and the press soon struck up a dirge. Feminism is 'dead,' the banner headlines announced, all over again. 'The women's movement is over,' began a cover story in the *New York Times Magazine*. In case readers missed that issue, the magazine soon ran a second obituary, in which Ivy League students recanted their support for the women's movement and assured readers that they were 'not feminists' because those were just women who 'let themselves go physically' and had 'no sense of style'.

This time around, the media did more than order a quiet burial for the feminist corpse. They went on the rampage, smashing their own commercial icons of 'liberated' womanhood, tearing down the slick portraits that they themselves had mounted. Like graffiti artists, they defaced the two favourite poster girls of the seventies press – spray-painting a downturned mouth and shrivelled ovaries on the Single Girl, and adding a wrinkled brow and ulcerated stomach to the Superwoman. These new images were, of course, no more realistic than the last decade's output. But their effect on live women would be quite real and damaging.

The press first introduced the backlash to a national audience – and made it palatable. Journalism replaced the 'pro-family' diatribes of right-wing commentators, like Mary Whitehouse in the UK, with sympathetic and even progressive-sounding rhetoric. It cosmet-icized the scowling face of anti-feminism while blackening the feminist eye. In the process, it popularized the backlash beyond the New Right's wildest dreams.

The press didn't set out with this, or any other, intention; like any large institution, its movements aren't premeditated or programmatic, just grossly susceptible to the prevailing political currents. Even so, the press, carried by tides it rarely fathomed, acted as a force that swept the general public, powerfully shaping the way people would think and talk about the feminist legacy and the ailments it supposedly inflicted on women. It coined the terms that everyone used: 'the man shortage', 'the biological clock', 'the mommy track' and 'post-feminism'. Most importantly, the press was the first to set forth and solve for a mainstream audience the paradox in women's lives, the paradox that would become so central to the backlash: women have achieved so much yet feel so dissatisfied; it must be feminism's achievements, not society's resistance to these partial achievements, that is causing women all this pain. In the 1970s the press had held up its own glossy picture of a successful woman and said, 'See, she's happy. That must be because she's liberated.' Now, under the reverse logic of the backlash, the press airbrushed a frown into its picture of the successful woman and announced, 'See, she's miserable. That must be because women are too liberated.' The backlash showed itself in the UK even as the emerging women's movement was barely under way. The *Daily Mail*'s women's page shrieked, as early as 1975, 'Is this the price *we* have to pay for our liberation?'

'What has happened to American women?' ABC asked with much consternation in its 1986 special report. The show's host Peter Jennings promptly answered, 'The gains for women sometimes come at a formidable cost to them.' *Newsweek* raised the same question in its 1986 story on the 'new problem with no name'. And it offered the same diagnosis: 'The emotional fallout of feminism' was damaging women; an 'emphasis on equality' had robbed them of their romantic and maternal rights and forced them to make 'sacrifices'. The magazine advised: ' "When the gods wish to punish us, they answer our prayers," Oscar Wilde wrote. So it would seem to many of the women who looked forward to "having it all".' (This happens to be the same verdict *Newsweek* reached when it last investigated female discontent – at the height of the feminine-mystique backlash. 'American women's unhappiness is merely the most recently won of women's rights,' the magazine reported then.)

The press might have looked for the source of women's unhappiness in other places. It could have investigated and exposed the buried roots of the backlash in the New Right and misogynistic governments, in a chilly business community and intransigent social and religious institutions. But the press chose to peddle the backlash rather than probe it.

The media's role as backlash collaborator and publicist is a familiar one. The first article sneering at a 'Superwoman' appeared not in the 1980s press but in an American newspaper headline at the turn of the century. Feminists, according to the late Victorian press, were 'a herd of hysterical and irrational she-revolutionaries', 'fussy, interfering, faddists, fanatics', 'shrieking cockatoos' and 'unpardonably ridiculous'. Feminists had laid waste the American female population; any sign of female distress was surely another 'fatal symptom' of the feminist disease, the periodicals reported. WHY ARE WE WOMEN NOT HAPPY? the male-edited *Ladies' Home Journal* asked in 1901 – and answered that the women's rights movement was debilitating its beneficiaries.

As American studies scholar Cynthia Kinnard observed in her bibliography of American anti-feminist literature, journalistic broadsides against women's rights 'grew in intensity during the late 19th century and reached regular peaks with each new suffrage campaign'. The arguments were always the same: equal education would make women spinsters, equal employment would make women sterile, equal rights would make women bad mothers. With each new historical cycle, the threats were simply updated and sanitized, and new 'experts' enlisted. The Victorian periodical press turned to clergymen to support its brief against feminism; in the 1980s the press relied on therapists.

The 1986 *Newsweek* backlash article, FEMINISM'S IDENTITY CRISIS, quoted many experts on women's condition – sociologists, political scientists, psychologists – but none of the many women supposedly suffering from this crisis. The closest the magazine came was two drawings of a mythical feminist victim: a dour executive with cropped hair is pictured first at her desk, grimly pondering an empty family-picture frame, and then at home, clutching a clock and studying the hands – poised at five minutes to midnight.

The absence of real women in a news account that is allegedly about real women is a hallmark of 1980s backlash journalism. The press delivered the backlash to the public through a series of 'trend stories', articles that claimed to divine sweeping shifts in female social behaviour while providing little in the way of evidence to support their generalizations. The trend story, which may go down as late twentieth-century journalism's prime contribution to its craft, professes to offer 'news' of changing mores, yet prescribes more than it observes. Claiming to mirror public sentiment, its reflections of the human landscapes are strangely depopulated.

Pretending to take the public's pulse, it monitors only its own heartbeat – and its advertisers'.

Trend journalism attains authority not through actual reporting but through the power of repetition. Said enough times, anything can be made to seem true. A trend declared in one publication sets off a chain reaction, as the rest of the media scramble to get the story too. The lightning speed at which these messages spread has less to do with the accuracy of the trend than with journalists' propensity to repeat one another. And repetition became especially hard to avoid in the 1980s, as the 'independent' press fell into a very few corporate hands.

Fear was also driving the media's need to dictate trends and determine social attitudes in the eighties, as print and broadcast audiences, especially female audiences, turned to other news sources and advertising plunged. Anxiety-ridden media managements became preoccupied with conducting market research studies and 'managing' the fleeing reader, now renamed 'the customer' (just like former 'patients', 'passengers' and 'ratepayers'). And their preoccupations eventually turned up in the way the media covered the news. 'News organizations are moving on to the same ground as political institutions that mold public opinion and seek to direct it,' Bill Kovach, former editor of the *Atlanta Journal-Constitution* and the Nieman Foundation's curator, observed. 'Such a powerful tool for shaping public opinion in the hands of journalists accustomed to handling fact is like a scalpel in a child's hands: it is capable of great damage.'

Journalists first applied this scalpel to women. While trend stories of the 1980s occasionally considered the changing habits of men, these articles tended to cover men's latest hobbies and whimsies – fly fishing, cell phones and the return of the white shirt. The 1980s female trends, by contrast, were the failure to find husbands, get pregnant, or properly bond with their children. NBC, for instance, devoted an entire evening news special to the pseudo-trend of 'bad girls', yet ignored the real trend of bad boys: the crime rate among boys was climbing twice as fast as for girls. (In New York City, right in the network's backyard, rape arrests of young boys had jumped 200 per cent in two years.) Female trends with a more flattering veneer surfaced in women's magazines and newspaper 'style' pages in the decade, each bearing, beneath new-and-improved packaging, the return-to-gender trade-mark: 'the New Abstinence', 'the New Femininity', 'the New High Monogamy', 'the New Morality', 'the New Madonnas', 'the Return of the Good Girl'. While anxiety over AIDS has certainly helped fuel promotion of these 'new' trends, that's not the whole story. While in the 1980s AIDS remained largely a male affliction, these media directives were aimed almost exclusively at women. In each case, women were reminded to re-embrace 'traditional' sex roles – or suffer the consequences. For women, the trend story was no news report; it was a moral reproach.

The trends for women always came in instructional pairs – the trend that women were advised to flee and the trend that they were pushed to join. For this reason, the paired trends tended to contradict each other. As one woman writer observed wryly in an *Advertising Age* column, 'The media are having a swell time telling us, on the one hand, that marriage is "in" and, on the other hand, that women's chances of marrying are slim. So maybe marriage is "in" because it's so hard to do.' Three contradictory trend pairs, concerning work, marriage and motherhood, formed the backlash media's triptych: Superwoman 'burn-out' versus New Traditionalist 'cocooning'; 'the spinster boom' versus 'the return of marriage'; and 'the infertility epidemic' versus 'the baby boomlet'. In these female trend stories, fact and forecast traded places. These articles weren't chronicling a retreat among women that was already taking place; they were compelling one to happen.

The trend story is not always labelled as such, but certain characteristics give it away: an absence of factual evidence or hard numbers; a tendency to cite only three or four women, typically anonymously, to establish the trend; the use of vague qualifiers like 'there is a sense that' or 'more and more'; a reliance on the predictive future tense ('Increasingly, mothers will stay home to spend more time with their families'); and the invocation of 'authorities' such as consumer researchers and psychologists, who often support their assertions by citing other media trend stories. Just as the decade's trend stories on women pretended to be about facts while offering none, they served a political agenda while telling women that what was happening to them had nothing to do with political events or social pressures. In the 1980s trend analysis, women's conflict was no longer with her society and culture but only with herself. Single women were simply struggling with personal problems; they were 'selfish' or 'too choosy'.

The only external combat the press recognized was woman on woman. THE UNDECLARED WAR, a banner headline announced on the front page of the *San Francisco Examiner*'s Style section: 'To work or not divides mothers in the suburbs'. *Child* magazine offered THE MOMMY WARS and *Savvy*'s WOMEN AT ODDS informed readers that 'the world is soon to be divided into two enemy camps and one day they may not be civil toward each other'. Media accounts encouraged married and single women to view each other as opponents – and even confront each other in the ring on *The Oprah Winfrey Show*. IS HE SEPARABLE? was the title of a 1988 *Newsday* article that warned married women to beware the husband-poaching trend; the man shortage had driven single women into 'brazen' overtures and wives were advised to take steps to keep 'the hussy' at bay.

Trend journalists in the 1980s were not required to present facts for the same reason that ministers aren't expected to support sermons with data. The reporters were scripting morality plays, not news stories, in which the middle-class woman played the Christian innocent, led astray by a feminist serpent. In the final scene, the woman had to pay – repenting of her ambitions and 'selfish' pursuit of equality – before she could reclaim her honour and her happiness. The trend stories were strewn with judgemental language about the wages of feminist sin. The ABC report on the ill effects of women's liberation, for example, referred to the 'costs' and 'price' of equality thirteen times. Like any cautionary tale, the trend story offered a 'choice' that implied only one correct answer: take the rocky road to selfish and lonely independence or the well-paved path to home and flickering hearth. No middle route was visible on the trend story's map of the moral feminine universe.

Cocooners, New Traditionalists and Mummy Trackers

MANY YOUNG WOMEN NOW SAY THEY'D PICK FAMILY OVER CAREER, the front page of the *New York Times* announced in 1980. Actually, the 'many' women were a few dozen Ivy League undergraduates who, despite their protestations, were heading for medical school and fellowships at Oxford. The *Times* story managed to set off a brief round of similar back-to-the-home stories in the press. But with no authority to bless the trend, return-to-nesting's future looked doubtful. Then, midway through the decade, a media expert surfaced spectacularly in the American press. Her name, which soon became a household word, was Faith Popcorn.

A former advertising executive, Popcorn had reinvented herself as a 'leading consumer authority' and launched her own market research firm, BrainReserve, which had this speciality: 'trend identification'. In 1986, Faith Popcorn managed to please the media trend writers and her corporate clients at the same time with the coining of a single word, 'cocooning'. The word 'just popped into my head' in the middle of an interview with the *Wall Street Journal*, Popcorn recalls. 'It was a prediction . . . It hadn't happened.' But that wasn't quite how she marketed it to the media at the time.

Cocooning was *the* national trend for the eighties, she told the press. 'We're becoming a nation of nesters . . . We like to stay home and cocoon. Mom foods, like meat loaf and chicken potpie, are very big right now.' Her food industry clients were more than happy to back her up on that. As one enthusiastic spokesman for Pillsbury told *Newsweek*, 'I believe in cocooning.' 'Cocooning', or 'nesting', was no gender-neutral concept; thanks to the media, it became a female trend – defined not as *people* coming home but as *women* abandoning the office. As Popcorn advised the press, 'Fewer women will work. They will spend their time at home concentrating on their families.' The press feminized this trend even further, envisaging not only cocooning but the cocoon itself as female. 'Little in-home wombs', was how the *Los Angeles Times* described these shells to which women were supposed to be retreating.

Female cocooning might have shown up on Popcorn's trend

metre but it had yet to make a blip on US Bureau of Labor Statistics charts. Women steadily increased their representation in the work force in the 1980s – from 51 to 57 per cent for all women, and to more than 70 per cent for women between the ages of twenty-five and forty-four. And the increase in working mothers was the steepest. Opinion polls didn't support her theory either: they showed adult women increasingly more determined to have a career with a family (63 per cent versus 52 per cent a decade earlier) and less interested in having a family with no career (26 per cent versus 38 per cent a decade earlier). And 42 per cent of the women who weren't working said they would if there were more childcare centres in the vicinity.

Popcorn herself is no model of the trend she has so avidly promoted. Past forty, she is happily unmarried and childless – and puts her career first. 'I'm hooked on my work,' she confesses, laughing, in an interview. Though she has had many men in her life, she says, marriage has never appealed to her: 'I didn't want somebody to own me.' The women in her family, she proudly reports, have valued professionalism and financial independence for at least three generations. Her grandmother owned and managed New York City real estate – and pronounced marriage 'dumb' and 'boring'. Popcorn's mother, a negligence lawyer in the 1920s who started her own firm when no one would hire her, took a similarly low view of traditional femininity. 'She was really a cowgirl, rough and tough,' Popcorn recalls with admiration. 'She was teeny, five feet, but you'd never know it.'

Despite her assertions that, as a trend, feminism is out – 'it's seen as a step back' – Popcorn describes herself as 'still a seventies feminist'. She explains, 'I think we still have a long way to go. I think we have a lot of prejudice and a lot of discrimination. I think we need to organize.' She says she started BrainReserve because prejudice was stalling her progress at a male-run advertising agency. 'I didn't like how I was being treated . . . And I wanted to be noticed, I wanted the top title, I wanted the recognition, just like any guy.'

What made Popcorn think that 'cocooning' was a trend? In the press, she cited the following evidence: the improving sales of 'mom foods', the popularity of 'big comfortable chairs', the ratings of the *Cosby* show, and one statistic – 'a third of all the female MBA[Master of Business Administration]s of 197[6] have already returned home'. But the sales spurt in 'mom foods' was the consequence, not the cause, of her relentless 'cocooning' promotions; if it had been the other way around, Campbell's Soup wouldn't have needed her services. Only the last statistic had anything remotely to do with gauging women's actual behaviour – and that statistic, as it happened, was highly dubious.

Popcorn borrowed the MBA figure from what was, at the time, a celebrated trend article – a 1986 *Fortune* cover story entitled WHY WOMEN ARE BAILING OUT. The article, about businesswomen trained at elite schools fleeing the corporate suite, inspired similar 'bailing out' articles in *Forbes*, *USA Today* and *US News & World Report*, among others.

The *Fortune* story left an especially deep and troubling impression on young women aspiring to business and management careers; after all, it seemed to have hard data. A year later at Stanford University's Graduate School of Business, women were still talking about the article and the effect it had had on them. Phyllis Strong, a Stanford MBA candidate, said she now planned to look for a less demanding career, after reading how 'you give up too much' and 'you lose that sense of bonding and family ties' when you take on a challenging business job. Marcia Walley, another MBA candidate, said that she now understood 'how impossible it is to have a successful career and a good family life. You can't have it all and you have to choose.' A group of women at the business school even wrote a musical number on this theme for the senior play. Set to the tune of Paul Simon's 'You Can Call Me Al', the bitter little anthem provoked tears from young women in the audience:

> When I was at B-school, they said . . .
> Girl, you can have it all. But I
> Didn't think I'd lose so much.
> Didn't want such long hours.
> Who'd think my only boyfriend
> Would be a blow-up doll? . . .

Where are my old boyfriends now?
Nesting, nesting,
Getting on with their lives,
Living with women who get off at five.

The year after *Fortune* launched the 'bailing out' trend, the proportion of women applying to business schools suddenly began to shrink – for the first time in a decade.

Fortune's 1986 cover photo featured Janie Witham, former IBM systems engineer, seated in her kitchen with her two-year-old daughter on her lap. Witham is 'happier at home', *Fortune*'s cover announced. She has time now to 'bake bread'. She is one of 'many women, including some of the best educated and most highly motivated', wrote the article's author, *Fortune* senior writer Alex Taylor III, who are making 'a similar choice' to quit work. 'These women were supposed to lead the charge into the corridors of corporate power,' he wrote. 'If the MBAs cannot find gratification there [in the work force], can *any* [his italics] women?'

The *Fortune* story originated in some cocktail chatter at a *Fortune* editor's class reunion. While mingling with Harvard Business School classmates, Taylor's editor heard a couple of graduates say they were staying at home with their newborns. Suspecting a trend, he assigned the story to Taylor. 'He had this anecdotal evidence but no statistics,' Taylor recalls. So the reporter went hunting for numbers.

Taylor called Mary Anne Devanna, research coordinator at Columbia Business School's Center for Research in Career Development. She had been monitoring MBA women's progress for years – and she saw no such trend. 'I told him, "I don't believe your anecdotes are right,"' she recalls. '"We have no evidence that women are dropping out in larger numbers." And he said, "Well, what would convince you?"' She suggested he ask *Fortune* to commission a study of its own. 'Well, *Fortune* apparently said a study would cost $36,000 so they didn't want to do one,' she says, 'but they ended up running the story anyway.'

Instead of a study, Taylor took a look at graduation records for the Class of '76 from seventeen top business schools. But these numbers did not support the trend either: in 1976, the same proportion of women as men went to work for large corporations or professional firms, and ten years later virtually the same proportion of women and men were still working for these employers.

Nonetheless, the story that Taylor wrote stated, 'After ten years, significantly more women than men dropped off the management track.' As evidence, Taylor cited this figure: 'Fully 30 per cent of the 1,039 women from the class of '76 reported they are either self-employed or unemployed, or they listed no occupation.' That would seem newsworthy but for one inconvenient fact: 21 per cent of the *men* from the same class were also self-employed or unemployed. So the 'trend' boiled down to a nine-percentage-point difference. Given that working women still bear primary responsibility for childcare and still face job discrimination, the real news was that the gap was so *small*.

'The evidence is rather narrow,' Taylor concedes later. 'The drop-out rates of men and women are roughly the same.' Why then did he claim that women were fleeing the work force in 'disquieting' numbers? Taylor did not actually talk to any of the women in the story. 'A [female] researcher did all the interviews,' Taylor says. 'I just went out and talked to the deep thinkers, like the corporate heads and social scientists.' One woman whom Taylor presumably did talk to, but whose example he did not include, is his own wife. She is a director of corporate communications and, although the Taylors have two children, three years old and six months old at the time of the interview, she's still working. 'She didn't quit, it's true,' Taylor says. 'But I'm struck by the strength of her maternal ties.'

The *Fortune* article passed lightly over political forces discouraging businesswomen in the 1980s and concluded that women flee the work force because they simply would 'rather' stay at home. Taylor says he personally subscribes to this view: 'I think motherhood, not discrimination, is the overwhelming reason women are dropping out.' Yet even the ex-IBM manager featured on the cover didn't quit because she wanted to stay at home. She left because IBM refused to give her the flexible schedule she needed to care for her infant. 'I wish things had worked out,' Witham told the magazine's interviewer. 'I would like to go back.'

Three months later, *Fortune* was back with more of the same. 'A woman who wants marriage and children,' the magazine warned, 'realizes that her Salomon Brothers job probably represents a choice to forgo both.' But *Fortune* editors still couldn't find any numbers to support their retreat-of-the-businesswoman trend. In fact, in 1987, when they finally did conduct a survey of business managers who seek to hold back career for family life, they found an even smaller 6 per cent gender gap, and 4 per cent *more* men than women said they had refused a job or transfer because it would mean less family time. The national pollsters were no help either: they couldn't find a gap at all; while 30 per cent of working women said they might quit if they could afford it, 30 per cent of the men said that too. And contrary to press reports about 'the best and brightest' burning out, the women who were well educated and well paid were the least likely to say they yearned to go home. A 1989 survey of 1,200 Stanford business-school graduates found that among couples who both hold MBAs and work, the husbands 'display more anxiety'.

Finally *Fortune* just turned its back on these recalcitrant career women and devoted its cover instead to the triumph of the 'trophy wife', the young and doting second helpmate who 'make[s] the fifty- and sixty-year-old CEOs [chief executive officers] feel they can compete' – unlike that selfish first wife who failed to make her husband 'the focus of her life' and 'in the process loses touch with him and his concerns'. *Fortune* wasn't the only publication to resort to this strategy. *Esquire*, a periodical much given to tirades against the modern woman, devoted its entire June 1990 issue to a dewy tribute to 'the American Wife', the traditional kind only. In one memorable full-page photo, a model homemaker was featured on her knees, happily scrubbing a toilet bowl.

While women in business management faced the most pressure to abandon their careers – the corporate boardroom being the most closely guarded male preserve – the media flashed its return-to-the-nest sign at all working women. WHY 90S WOMEN NOW SAY NO TO CAREERS, the *Daily Mail* announced in 1990, offering us the image of the 'New Feminist' who has 'thrown away the shoulder pads and picked up the carry cot'. The feature cited as examples only three women, of whom two had in fact returned to work; the other had missed the stimulation of her job for a full year and admitted to feeling worthless at drinks parties. *Options* asked in 1985, 'Is motherhood a full-time job?' and concluded that yes, it could well be, even if the author of the piece had herself worked full- or part-time for most of her ten-year-old son's life. She also reported that two-thirds of graduate working mothers surveyed by researchers at Bristol University said they worked because they enjoyed it, not out of financial necessity. *Company* said 'Goodbye to all that' in 1986, referring to the 'unreal expectations' implanted in young women by feminism in the 1970s. 'Already, thankfully,' the author of the piece breathed in relief, 'there are clear signs of a backlash as reports of superwoman burnout crop up worldwide.' Of the women this journalist had spoken to, 'all had learned to make choices and focus their energies on what was important to them' – top priorities going to their partners and children. Even so, one of those interviewed, an actress, confessed: 'The problem is there are days when I'm desperate for acting and the outside world', and said that she missed tremendously having her own money.

High-profile women in the media were in the forefront of the droves supposedly abandoning their careers for full-time motherhood. Kathy Gyngell, Editor of TV-AM's *After Nine*, wrote in the *Daily Mail* of her decision to give up her job a year after the birth of her first son, and followed up two years later with another article, entitled 'Why Must We Treat Mothers as Second-class Citizens?' Rather than a campaign for improved childcare facilities to help the lot of working mothers, this was part of her movement to 'raise the status and appreciation of the full-time mother'. She accused the women's movement of 'browbeating' women into avoiding motherhood altogether and losing sight of 'the importance of feminine goals'. This clarion call to motherhood closed, without a hint of irony, with the words: 'One child I know said to her mother, "I don't like it when you work. You become a different person. Even when you're at home your mind is elsewhere." '

Maeve Haran, a television producer with LWT's *Six O'Clock Show*, was given two bouts of publicity – once when she was signed up, for a six-figure sum, to write a blockbuster novel called *Having It All*, and again when the book was published. Her intention was to give up her high-pressure television job to spend more time with her two children – and write a bestseller while she was about it, based on the 'dilemma' of career versus motherhood. After a hotly contested publishers' auction, the *Observer* gave Haran space to announce her own good fortune, and pictured her smilingly at home with the kids. (Naturally, the photograph did not show her bent over her word processor with the door shut while a nanny cared for her children elsewhere.)

When the novel was published it gave the media a figurehead, and a controversy, that they had been waiting for. Even though the heroine of *Having It All* sets up her own successful business, the press was more interested in Maeve Haran's role-model status as back-to-the-nest mother. 'Maeve Haran has broken rank, and a good thing, too,' said the *Independent*. Angela Neustatter in the *Guardian* went further, defending Haran and women like her who 'remain close enough to their emotions to act on it if they prefer being with their children to being dynamic in an executive suite'. She declared: 'Those sisters who bay for their blood and decry their right to say that having it all may be having too little are guilty of female fascism.' The *Daily Mail* predictably weighed in for 'poor old Maeve Haran' and suggested that 'the novel proves that having it all is a myth.' Libby Purves in *The Times* was one of the few to demur. 'Why do women cooperate with people who turn their lives into a series of lurid, improbable caricatures?' she asked, and warned working mothers to brace themselves for a wave of hype.

In the States, the media jumped when Felice Schwartz, the founder of Catalyst – a consulting firm to corporations on women's careers – claimed that 'most' women are 'willing to trade some career growth and compensation for freedom from the constant pressure to work long hours and weekends'. Not only was Schwartz a bona fide expert, she was taking her stand in the esteemed *Harvard Business Review*.

The 'mommy-tracking' trend, as the media immediately coined it, became front-page news; Schwartz personally fielded seventy-five interviews in the first month and her words inspired more than a thousand articles. It wasn't as dramatic as women 'bailing out' of the work force altogether, but it was better than nothing. 'Across the country, female managers and professionals with young families are leaving the fast track for the mommy track,' *Business Week* proclaimed in a cover story. Their numbers are 'multiplying'. It offered no actual numbers, only a few pictures of women holding children's books and stuffed animals, and quotes from four part-time workers. The media in other countries picked up the story; the *Guardian*, for example, reported it in April 1989 under the headline CAREERING OFF THE MUMMY TRACK.

If the media had scant evidence that the mummy trackers were multiplying, so did Felice Schwartz. She merely speculated that the majority of women, whom she called 'career-and-family women', were 'willing' and 'satisfied' to give up higher pay and promotions. Corporations should somehow identify these women and treat them differently from 'career-primary' women, allotting them fewer hours, bonuses and opportunities for advancement. That this would amount to discrimination didn't seem to occur to Schwartz. In fact, at a conference sponsored by traditional women's magazines, she proposed that young women ignore Title VII of the Civil Rights Act and review their child-rearing plans with prospective employers; women need to move beyond 'insistence on the rights women achieved in an era when we weren't valued', she told her audience.

Women with this mummy-track mind-set were, in reality, vastly in the minority in the workplace: in the 1984 *Newsweek* Research Report on Women Who Work, for example, more than 70 per cent of women interviewed said they would rather have high-pressure jobs in which advancement was possible than low-pressure jobs with no advancement. And a year after Schwartz's article was published, when the 1990 Virginia Slims poll specifically asked women about 'mommy tracking', 70 per cent of the women called it discriminatory and 'just an excuse for paying women less than men'.

Corporations, Schwartz asserted, had cause to be impatient with female employees; as she put it in the first sentence of her *Harvard Business Review* article, 'The cost of employing women in management is greater than the cost of employing men.' As evidence she vaguely alluded to two studies, neither published, conducted by two corporations which she refused to identify. One of them, a 'multinational corporation', claimed its rate of turnover in management positions was two and a half times higher among top-performing women than men. Its women managers, in her view, were fleeing not because they were mummy tracking but because 'until the last few years, it was a company that was not responsive to women'. Only in 1989 did the company even get around to modifying its leave-of-absence policy to allow its employees to work a reduced working week temporarily to care for sick children or elderly parents, its employee policy manager concedes. But, he maintains, the company is very accommodating towards its women: 'We're a very paternalistic company.'

'I was not writing a research piece,' Schwartz says in her defence. 'I was writing as an expert in the field.' But as an expert, Ms Schwartz, it would seem, would have access to the research in the field. Statistics that have compared the cost of employing men and women find no significant differences between the sexes; men and women take about the same amount of sick leave. Schwartz herself seems to have come around to that view. In an about-turn that was as ignored in the press as her mummy-track credo was celebrated, she issued a ten-page statement hotly denying that she ever supported mummy tracking. Her recantation didn't register, even with the *Harvard Business Review* editors still busy defending the article. 'She speaks with a tone of authority,' the *Review*'s executive editor Timothy Blodgett told *Ms*. 'That comes through.' Later that spring, the *Review*'s managing editor Alan M. Webber wrote an op-ed piece in the *New York Times* that may help explain why he was so willing to trumpet the mummy-track message in his magazine. In his essay, entitled 'Is the American Way of Life Over?' Webber wrung his hands over 'the demise' of motherhood and charged that critics of Schwartz's article were too fixated on women's rights and didn't care about the future of American maternity. Fears over declining female fertility, not cheers for rising mummy tracking, was apparently the trend weighing heaviest on his mind.

If scaring women with tales of sleepless nights and 'emotional strain' didn't prompt women to leave the full-time work force, maybe they could be flattered into an exodus. That seemed, anyway, to be the premise behind *Good Housekeeping*'s massive 'New Traditionalist' ad campaign, launched in America in 1988 with double-page ads in dozens of publications. The New Traditionalist woman wasn't even real, but she set off another round of trend stories in the media, similar ad campaigns by publications from the *New York Times* to *Country Living*, and similar sales pitches by merchandisers from Ralph Lauren to Wedgwood. The *New York Times* even held up Barbara Bush as an example of the New Traditionalist trend, a case of a real woman living up to the standards of a fake one.

The New Traditionalist ads presented grainy photos of former careerists cuddled up in their renovated Cape Codder homes, surrounded by adoring and well-dressed children. The accompanying text dished out predictable women's magazine treacle about the virtues and 'deep-rooted values' of any woman who 'found her identity' by serving home, husband and kids. But this homage to feminine passivity was cleverly packaged in activist language, a strategy that simultaneously acknowledged women's desire for autonomy and co-opted it. The New Traditionalist, the ads said, was an independent thinker who 'made her own choices' and 'started a revolution'. The magazine's ads assured readers, 'She's not following a trend. She *is* the trend . . . In fact, market researchers are calling it the biggest social movement since the sixties.'

Praising women for their 'choices' was hardly the purpose of this ad campaign. As *Good Housekeeping* publisher Alan Waxenberg himself asserted, women today 'don't need all that choice'. The 'social movement' that *Good Housekeeping* had in mind would lead not only to the home but, more important, to the magazine's subscription office. To salvage its profit margins, *Good Housekeeping* might have tried a more obvious strategy. It could simply have recognized women's changed status, and changed with it. In 1987 *Good Housekeeping*'s management was, in fact, considering a move in that direction. Maybe, some of its top editors proposed at the time, the magazine should appeal to working women. After all, even 65 per cent of *Good Housekeeping*'s current readership worked. But when the magazine's managers turned to an outside advertising agency for help, they were quickly talked out of such an unorthodox solution. 'The problem, as they perceived it, was that they were considered old-fashioned and they thought they needed to be more contemporary,' recalls Malcolm MacDougall, the advertising executive commissioned to overhaul the magazine's image. MacDougall, vice-chairman of Jordan, McGrath, Case & Taylor, told them to think again; 'neotradition-alism' was coming and they'd best be ready for it. He had a key source – the Yankelovich Monitor poll of 2,500 Americans. Some of the New Traditionalist ads even footnoted this survey, lending a pseudo-scholarly touch. 'When I looked at that study,' MacDougall says of the Yankelovich report, 'the numbers just jumped out at me. It's a pretty dramatic shift. It's a trend going back five years, it's very real and it can be backed up. So I went back to *Good Housekeeping* and I said, this is not a problem, it's an opportunity.'

But at Yankelovich, the researchers are still trying to figure out just what numbers jumped out at him. 'I cheerfully disavow any connection with those *Good Houskeeping* ads,' Susan Hayward, senior vice-president at Yankelovich, says. '*Good Housekeeping* is a client of ours. They looked at the Monitor study and we did a proprietary study for them, too. And they seemed to have misinterpreted both.' Neither study shows any signs of women leaving work or even fantasizing about leaving work. The percentage of women who want to work in the Yankelovich poll is as high as ever. And the proportion of women who describe motherhood as 'an experience every woman should have' stands at 53 per cent; in 1974, when non-traditionalism was more in vogue, it was 54 per cent.

But doubts about neotraditionalism's validity don't faze MacDougall. 'You can argue forever that people aren't this way but it doesn't work because they are,' he says. Pressed to offer something more substantial, he gets a little huffy: 'I'm selling a magazine based on home values. C'mon. We're in business here. I'm not going to give in to a few angry women.'

The British *Good Housekeeping* featured articles in 1989 on traditional crafts such as making tassels, rag rugs and quilted cushions. It spoke of 'the charm of the old' and declared that 'the crafts of our great-grandmothers are enjoying a comeback'. Whether or not anyone actually made a tassel in response to this 'trend', it is true that the homecrafts magazine *Prima*, launched in October 1986, immediately became one of the UK's top monthly sellers, with a peak Audit Bureau Circulation figure for July to December 1987 of over 1 million copies. Brenda Polan, in the *Guardian*, explained the success of the new 'häusfrau' magazines as giving women permission to indulge their domestic fantasies. She was clear that fantasy, and not a real return to domesticity, was the appeal: 'Research shows that very few readers *make* any of the incredibly useful thingummajigs for which copious step-by-step instructions plus easy-to-follow diagrams are included. But they love thinking they *might*.'

The Spinster Boom: The Sorrow and the Pity

'In all respects, young single American women hold themselves in higher regard now than a year ago,' the *New York Times* noted in 1974. Single women are more 'self-assured, confident, secure'. The article concluded, 'The [women's] movement, apparently, is catching on.'

Such media views of single women were certainly catching on in the seventies. *Newsweek* quickly elevated the news of the happy single woman to trend status. 'Within just eight years, singlehood has emerged as an intensely ritualized – and newly respectable – style of American life,' the magazine ruled in a 1973 cover story. 'It is finally becoming possible to be both single and whole.' In fact, according to *Newsweek*, the single lifestyle for women was more than 'respectable'; it was a thrill a minute. The cover photo featured a grinning blonde in a bikini, toasting her good fortune at the poolside. Inside, more singles beamed as they sashayed from sun decks to moonlit dances. 'I may get married or I just may not,' a flight attendant, who described her single status as 'pretty groovy', told the magazine. 'But if I do, it will be in my own time and on my own terms . . . I see nothing wrong with staying single for as long as you please.' And even *Newsweek*'s writers, though betraying some queasiness at such declarations, ultimately gave a round of applause to these spunky new singles who weren't 'settling for just any old match'.

The many features about giddy single women in the early seventies left the impression that these unwed revellers rarely left their beach towels. The stereotype got so bad that one bachelor grumbled in a 1974 *New York Times* article, 'From reading the press, you'd think that every girl is 36-24-36 . . . and every guy lounges by a poolside and waits for the beautiful blondes to admire his rippling muscles.'

Married life, on the other hand, acquired a sour and claustrophobic reputation in the early seventies press. DROPOUT WIVES – THEIR NUMBER IS GROWING, a 1973 *New York Times* trend story advised, asserting that droves of miserable housewives were fleeing empty marriages in search of more 'fulfilled' lives. The *Times*'s portrait of the wedded state was bleak: it featured husbands who cheat, criticize and offer 'no communication', and wives who obsessively drink and pop pills. According to *Newsweek*, married couples were worse than troubled – they were untrendy: 'One sociologist has gone so far as to predict that "eventually married people could find themselves living in a totally singles-oriented society." '

A dozen years later, these same publications were sending out the opposite signals. *Newsweek* was now busy scolding single women for refusing to 'settle' for lesser mates, and the *New York Times* was reporting that single women are 'too rigid to connect' and suffer from 'a sickness almost'. Single women were no longer the press's party girls; with a touch of the media's wand, they were turned back into the scowling scullery maids who couldn't go to the ball. TOO LATE FOR PRINCE CHARMING? the *Newsweek* headline inquired sneeringly, over a drawing of a single woman sprawled on a lonely mattress, a teddy bear her only companion. The magazine now offered only mocking pity for women shut out of the marital bedroom, which press accounts of the 1980s enveloped in a heavenly, and tastefully erotic, glow. On the front page of the *New York Times* the unwed woman stalked the empty streets like Typhoid Mary; though 'bright and accomplished', she 'dreads nightfall, when darkness hugs the city and lights go on in warm kitchens'. It's clear enough why she fears the dark: according to the 1980s press, nightmares are a single girl's only bedmate. *New York* magazine's 1984 cover story on single women began with this testimony from 'Mary Rodgers', which the magazine noted in small print was not her real name: 'Last night, I had a terrible dream. The weight of the world was on my shoulders, and it was pressing me into the ground. I screamed for help, but nobody came. When I woke up, I wanted somebody to hold me. But it was just like the dream. There was no husband. No children. Only me.'

'Mary' was an executive in a garment firm. Like most of the ailing single women that the media of this time chose to pillory, she was one of the success stories from the women's movement now awakening to the error of her independent ways. She was single because, as the story's own headline put it, she was one of those women who 'expect too much'.

The campaign for women's rights was, once more, identified as the culprit; liberation had depressed single women. LOVELESS, MANLESS: THE HIGH COST OF INDEPENDENCE, read one women's magazine headline. 'Feminism became a new form of defensiveness' that drove men away, explained a 1987 *Harper's Bazaar* article, entitled ARE YOU TURNING MEN OFF?: DESPERATE AND DEMANDING. An *Options* feature in 1989, headlined THE SINGLE WOMAN'S LAMENT, urged single women in their thirties and forties to set their sights a bit lower and not to hold out for their 'ideal' man. *New York*'s story on grim-faced single women summoned an expert, psychotherapist Ava Siegler, who said the women's movement should be blamed for 'failing to help women order their priorities'. Siegler charged, 'It [the women's movement] didn't outline the consequences. We were never told, "While you're climbing up the corporate ladder, don't forget to pick up a husband and child." '

ABC's 1986 special, *After the Sexual Revolution*, also told single women to hold feminism responsible for their marital status. Women's success has come 'at the cost of relationships', co-host Richard Threlkeld said. Even married women are in danger, he advised: 'The more women achieve in their careers, the higher their chances for divorce.' Co-host Betsy Aaron concurred: Feminists never 'calculated *that* as a price of the revolution, freedom and independence turning to loneliness and depression'. It wasn't a trade-off Aaron could have deduced from her own life: she had a successful career and a husband – co-host Threlkeld.

The media's preoccupation with single women's miseries reared up suddenly in the mid-1980s. Between 1980 and 1982, as one study has noted, American magazines ran only five feature articles about single women; beween 1983 and 1986, they ran fifty-three – and almost all were critical or pitying. (Only seven articles about single men ran in this same period.) The headlines spoke bleakly of THE SAD PLIGHT OF SINGLE WOMEN, THE TERMINALLY SINGLE WOMAN and SINGLE SHOCK. To be unwed and female was to succumb to an illness with only one known cure: marriage.

The press contributed to single women's woes as much as it reported on them, by redefining single women's low social status as a personal defect. The media spoke ominously of single women's 'growing isolation' – but it was an isolation that trend journalism helped create and enforce. In the 1970s, the media's accounts featured photos and stories of real single women, generally in groups. In the 1980s the press offered drawings of fictional single women and tales of 'composite' or 'anonymous' single women – almost always depicted alone, hugging a tear-stained pillow, or gazing forlornly from a garret window. *McCall's* described the prototype this way: 'She's the workaholic, who may enjoy an occasional dinner with friends but more likely spends most of her time alone in her apartment, where she nightly retreats as her own best friend.'

Just as the press had ignored the social inequalities that cause career women to 'burn out', it depoliticized the situation of single women. While seventies press reports had chipped away at the social stigma that hurt single women, the eighties media maintained, with the aid of pop psychologists, that single women's troubles were all self-generated. As a therapist maintained in the *New York Times* story on single women, 'Women are in this situation because of neurotic conflicts.' This therapist was even saying it about herself; she told the *Times* she had entered 'intensive analysis' to cure herself of this singular distaff disorder.

The media's presentation of single women as mental patients is a well-worn backlash tradition. In the late Victorian press, single women were declared victims of 'andromania' and 'marriage dread'. After briefly rehabilitating single women as sprightly 'bachelor girls' in the early 1900s, the press condemned them to the mental ward once more for the duration of the Depression. In the 1930s, *Good Housekeeping* conducted a poll of single career women that looked for signs of psychic distress. When the single women all said they were quite satisfied with their lives, the magazine inquired hopefully, 'May not some of them have hidden a longing that hurt like a wound . . . as they bent above some crib and listened to the heavy sleeping breath that rhythmed from rosy lips?' And yet again, in the 1950s, a parade of psychoanalysts led by Marynia Farnham and Ferdinand Lundberg, authors of the 1947 leading manual, *Modern Woman: The Lost Sex*, marched through the women's magazines, declaring single women 'defeminized' and 'deeply ill'.

When the backlash press wasn't labelling single women mental misfits, it was busy counting the bodies. Not only were single women sick, the media pundits warned, they were outnumbered – a message that only helped to elevate anxiety levels. The late Victorian press was obsessed with calculating the exact number of 'excess' or 'redundant' single women; national periodicals printed graphs and tables listing the overabundance of unaccounted-for women. 'Why Is Single Life Becoming More General?' the *Nation* pondered in 1868, noting that the issue 'is fast getting into the category of topics of universal discussion'. The ratio was so bad, *Harper's Bazaar* exclaimed in 1874, that men could get 'wives at discount', and 'eight melancholy maids' clung to the same bachelor's arm at parties. 'The universal cry is "No husbands! No husbands!" ' (Feminist ideas, the magazine was quick to add, were to blame for this 'dreadful' situation: 'Many "advanced women" forgot that there can be no true progress for them save in the company of, not in opposition to, men.')

By the mid-1980s the media was busy once more counting heads in the single-woman pool and issuing charts that supposedly proved a surplus of unattached women, which the press now called 'the spinster boom'. The most legendary tally sheet appeared in *Newsweek*. IF YOU'RE A SINGLE WOMAN, HERE ARE YOUR CHANCES OF GETTING MARRIED, the headline on *Newsweek*'s June 2, 1986 cover helpfully announced. The accompanying graph plunged like the north face of the Matterhorn, its colour scheme changing from hot red to frigid blue as it slid past thirty – and into Old Maid free-fall. 'The traumatic news came buried in an arid demographic study,' *Newsweek*'s story began, 'titled innocently enough, "Marriage Patterns in the United States." But the dire statistics confirmed what everybody suspected all along: that many women who seem to have it all – good looks and good jobs, advanced degrees and high salaries – will never have mates.'

Newsweek took the flawed and unpublished Harvard–Yale marriage study and promoted it to cover-story celebrity status. A few months later the magazine received the more comprehensive US Census Bureau marriage study and shrank it to a two-paragraph item buried in the 'Update' column. Why? Eloise Salholz, *Newsweek*'s lead writer on the marriage study story, later explains the promotion of the Harvard–Yale study in this way: 'We all knew this was happening before that study came out. The study summarized impressions we already had.'

The *New York Times* assigned a staff writer to the Harvard–Yale study and produced a lengthy story. But when it came time to cover the Census Bureau study, the *Times* didn't even waste a staff writer's time; it just used a brief wire story and buried it. And almost a year after demographers had discredited the Harvard–Yale study, the *New York Times* ran a front-page story on how women were suffering from this putative man shortage, citing the study as proof. Asked to explain this later, the story's author, Jane Gross, says, 'It was untimely, I agree.' But the story was assigned to her, so she made the best of it. The article dealt with the fact that the study had been invalidated by dismissing the entire critique as 'rabid reaction from feminists'.

Some of the press's computations on the marriage crunch were at remedial levels. The *Newsweek* story declared that single women 'are more likely to be killed by a terrorist' than marry. Maybe *Newsweek* was only trying to be metaphorical, but the terrorist line was repeated with sombre literalness in many women's magazines, talk shows and advice books. 'Do you know that . . . forty-year-olds are more likely to be killed by a terrorist than find a husband?' gasped the press release that came with

Tracy Cabot's *How to Make a Man Fall in Love with You*. A former *Newsweek* trainee journalist who was involved in the story's preparation later explains how the terrorist analogy wound up in the magazine: 'What happened is, one of the bureau reporters was going around saying it as a joke – like, "Yeah, a woman's more likely to get bumped off by a terrorist" – and next thing we knew, one of the writers in New York took it seriously and it ended up in print.'

Newsweek's 'marriage crunch' story, like its story on a 'mother's choice', was a parable masquerading as a numbers report. It presented the 'man shortage' as a moral comeuppance for independent-minded women who expected too much. *Newsweek*'s preachers found single women guilty of at least three deadly sins: greed – they put their high-paying careers before the quest for a husband; pride – they acted 'as though it were not worth giving up space in their closets for anything less than Mr. Perfect'; and sloth – they weren't really out there beating the bushes; 'even though they say they want to marry, they may not want it enough.'

Now came judgment day. 'For many economically independent women, the consequences of their actions have begun to set in,' *Newsweek* intoned. 'For years bright young women singlemindedly pursued their careers, assuming that when it was time for a husband they could pencil one in. They were wrong.' *Newsweek* urged young women to learn from the mistakes of their feminist elders: 'Chastened by the news that delaying equals forgoing, they just may want to give thought to the question [of marriage] sooner than later.'

For the further edification of the young, *Newsweek* lined up errant ageing spinsters like sinners before the confessional and piously recorded their regrets: 'Susan Cohen wishes she had been able to see her way clear to the altar. "Not being of sound mind," she refused several marriage proposals when she was younger.' Paediatrician Catherine Casey told the magazine's inquisitors, 'I never doubted I would marry, but I wasn't ready at twenty-two. I was more interested in going to school . . . Now my time clock is striking midnight.'

Parading the penitent unwed became a regular media tearjerker, and it was on the network news programmes that the melodrama enjoyed its longest run. *CBS Morning News* devoted a *five*-day special in 1987 to the regrets of single women. Just like the *Newsweek* story, the show was graciously aired in the wedding month of June. 'We thought we were going to be dating for twenty-five years,' one woman moaned. 'We'll be sitting here in our forties and our biological clocks will have stopped,' wailed another. The relentless CBS newscaster behaved as if she were directing an on-air group therapy session. 'Have you always been this way?' she pressed her patients. 'What are you scared of?' 'Do you all have strong relationships with your dads?' 'Did you learn to talk as kids?'

ABC took television psychiatry one step further in its three-hour special in 1986. Not only did the network hire a psychiatrist to serve as a behind-the-scenes consultant, the newscaster managed to badger one of the programme's subjects into an on-camera breakdown. Laura Slutsky, thirty-seven and single, the president of her own company, tried to explain that, while living alone could be a 'difficult challenge', she was determined to 'make my life work'. 'I'll do it,' she said, 'I'll be classy about it, at times.' But the interviewer would have none of it and kept at her. Finally:

Interviewer: Face that fear a minute for me.
Slutsky: Wait a second, this is not easy stuff. [starts to cry] The fear of being alone is not – I don't like it. I'll do it though. Why am I crying? I don't know why I'm crying . . . These are hard questions . . . But I'll do it. I'll do it. I don't want to do it. I don't want to do it.

Apparently still not sated, ABC aired another special the following year, this one the four-day *Single in America*. Co-anchor Kathleen Sullivan set the tone in the opening segment: 'Well, when I first heard that we were going to do this,' she announced on the air, 'I said, so what? I mean, who cares about singles? They don't have responsibilities of family. They're only career-motivated.' But, she added generously, she's learned to pity them: 'I at first wasn't compassionate, but now I am.'

Compassion seemed only appropriate given that, as Sullivan's report amply demonstrated, a single woman's life is a gallery of horrors:

Day One – 'Singles have to go to industries to provide them with some way to meet people.'

Day Two – 'Today, we'll look at singles and sex, how the fatal disease AIDS is redefining some of their choices.' (A gory clip from the singles bar-hopping movie *Looking for Mr Goodbar* follows, with Sullivan's advisory voiceover: 'Indiscriminate dating can be dangerous. In this case it killed.')

Day Three – 'Single parents can be sexual, but . . . better think twice [unless] you want your child to sleep around with anyone when they get older.'

Day Four – 'Today we'll have a more positive outlook for you . . . ' followed by: 'But there are some overwhelming concerns. One is economics. It's not that easy on a single income to buy a home. [And] there is an overwhelming and a very saddened concern about the AIDS virus, and that this deadly disease is changing the sexual habits of singles.'

When all was said and done, Sullivan could only find one 'positive' development in single women's lives: they could now sign themselves up to the 'self registry' in Bloomingdale's – just like a bride. But even here her co-host Charles Gibson chimed in with the downside: 'I'm not sure who goes out to buy you presents if you're not getting married.'

Despite the title *Single in America*, the network programme never addressed the status of single men. The omission was typical. The promotional literature for ABC's *After the Sexual Revolution* actually promised to discuss the impact on men. But it never did. Asked to explain the omission later, co-host Richard Threlkeld says, 'There wasn't any time. We only had three hours.'

When the press did manage to fit the single man into its busy schedule, it was not to extend condolences. On the cover of the *New York Times* Sunday magazine, a single man luxuriated in his well-appointed bachelor pad. Reclining on his parquet floor, his electric guitar by his side, he was casually reading a book and enjoying (much to the joy of the magazine's cigarette advertisers, no doubt) a smoke. WHY WED? was the headline. Inside, the story's author Trip Gabriel clucked patronizingly about the 'worries' of 'the army of single women in their thirties'. Of single men, however, he had this to say: 'I was impressed by the men I talked with' and 'I came away thinking bachelorhood a viable choice.' Even the men who seemed to be avoiding women altogether earned his praise. He saw nothing wrong, for example, with a thirty-year-old man who recoiled from Saturday-night dates because 'Sunday's my game day.' Nor did he wonder about a thirty-five-year-old single sports photographer who told him, 'To me, relationships always seemed very stifling.' Instead, Gabriel praised his bachelorhood as a 'mature decision'.

Having whipped single women into high marital panic – or 'nuptialitis', as one columnist called it – the press hastened to soothe fretted brows with conjugal tonic. In what amounted to an enormous dose of free publicity for the matchmaking and bridal industries, the media helped peddle professional introduction agencies and how-to-get-married manuals. 'Time is running out for single people,' a *San Francisco Chronicle* columnist (himself an ageing bachelor) advised, and then turned his column over to a dating service owner who was anxious to promote her new business: 'There's a terrific scramble going on now,' she alerted single women, 'and in two years there just isn't going to be anyone left out there. There aren't going to be all these great surplus older guys.' The media even offered their own coaching and counselling assistance. *New York* trotted out inspirational role models – single women who managed to marry after forty. 'When they really decided to set their sights on a marriageable man,' the article, entitled 'Brides at Last', declared, 'they found one.' *USA Today* even played doctor, offering a special hot line for troubled singles – with psychologists working the phones. The telephone monitors confessed to being 'startled' at the results: lovelorn male callers outnumbered women – by two to one.

Women's magazines rose most grandly to the occasion. Nuptialitis was, after all, their speciality. *Options* offered 'Love Forty', a profile of three high-powered women who succumbed with 'girlish glee' to become starry-eyed newly-weds. In 'How to Get Married in a Year' *She* gave advice on how to 'throw the noose around the man you're after' and reported: 'The Americans started it but now that dating agencies and marriage brokers are boom industries it seems the single Brit is ripe for a determined marriage-making.' *Cosmopolitan*'s February 1989 issue offered an eleven-page guide to oiling the husband trap, under the businesslike title 'How to Close the Deal'. The magazine lectured, 'You've read the statistics: More women than men practically everywhere but San Quentin . . . You have to tidy up your act. *Starting right now.*' Its get-married-quick pointers were all on loan from the last back-lash's advice books. Among them: pretend to be less sexually experienced than you are, play up your knitting and cooking skills, let him do most of the talking, and be 'extremely accepting'. At *Mademoiselle*, similar 1950s-style words of wisdom were on tap: the magazine promoted 'The Return of Hard-to-Get', advised women to guard their 'dating reputation', and reminded them, 'Smart Cookies Don't Phone First'. And a *New Woman* cover story by Dr Joyce Brothers offered some old advice for wedding-ring hunters: 'Why You Shouldn't Move In With Your Lover'.

While the press was busy pressing single women into marriage, it was simultaneously ordering already married women to stay put. One effective holding action: spreading fear about life after divorce. In 1986, NBC ran a special report that focused exclusively on 'the negative consequences of divorce'. *Cosmopolitan* offered a four-page feature wholly devoted to divorce's drawbacks. 'Singlehood seems so tempting when you're wrangling bitterly,' it instructed. 'But be forewarned: More and more marital veterans and experts in the field are cautioning potential divorcées to be wary – extremely wary – of eight common, dangerous delusions [about divorce].' *She* cautioned, 'Whatever you do don't get divorced': 'It's horrendously painful, agonisingly long and drawn out, disastrous for your financial security, devastating for your self-esteem and terribly traumatic for the children.' For women, the press reported over and over again, broken wedding vows lead to severe depression, a life of loneliness and an empty bank account.

To stave off divorce, the media once more came to the rescue with friendly advice and stern moral lectures. CBS revived *Can This Marriage Be Saved?* – the old *Ladies' Home Journal* feature – as a nationwide talk show in 1989, offering on-air reconciliation for couples with rocky relations. HOW TO STAY MARRIED was

Newsweek's offering – a 1987 cover story replete with uplifting case studies of born-again couples who had gone 'right to the edge' before finding 'salvation', usually through a therapist's divine intervention. Several marital counsellors made promotional appearances in these pages, one hawking a sixteen-week marital improvement programme – for newlyweds.

'How times have changed!' *Newsweek* wrote. 'Americans are taking marriage more seriously.' The magazine had no evidence that a marital boom was in progress. All it could produce was this flimsy statistic: an insignificant 0.2 per cent drop in the divorce rate.

Infertility Illness and Baby Fevers

'Is this surge in infertility the yuppie disease of the eighties?' NBC correspondent Maria Shriver asked in a 1987 special report. Could it be, she worried, turning to her line-up of experts, that barren wombs have become 'the curse of the career woman'? Her experts, infertility doctors hawking costly experimental cures, were only too happy to agree.

By now the trend journalists had it down; they barely needed an expert to point out the enemy. If it was a woman's problem, then they knew women's quest for independence and equality must be to blame. In the case of the 'curse of the career woman', the witch casting the spell must be carrying her own wallet. The headlines made it clear why women's wombs were drying up: HAVING IT ALL: POSTPONING PARENTHOOD EXACTS A PRICE and THE QUIET PAIN OF INFERTILITY: FOR THE SUCCESS-ORIENTED, IT'S A BITTER PILL. As a *New York Times* columnist asserted, the infertile woman today is 'a walking cliché' of the feminist generation, 'a woman on the cusp of forty who put work ahead of motherhood'. 'Have You Left It Too Late to Have a Baby?' asked *Options. She* investigated infertility in its August 1989 issue and concluded that as women 'become less content with housewifery and more determined to have a fulfilling career outside the home' they are postponing motherhood. 'Wait as long as you like to have your baby, but don't expect nature to play,' it admonished. 'When you do get round to it, you may have to wait longer than you anticipated.'

Newsweek devoted two cover stories to the 'trend of childless-ness'. Between shots of lone career women in corner offices and lone teddy bears in empty cribs, the magazine warned that as many as 20 per cent of women in their early to mid-thirties will end up with no babies of their own – and 'those numbers will be even higher for women with high-powered careers, the experts say'. The expert that *Newsweek* used to support this point was none other than Harvard economist David Bloom, co-author of the infamous Harvard–Yale marriage study. Now he was saying that 30 per cent of all female managers will wind up childless.

Not to be upstaged in the motherhood department, *Life* issued its own special report, 'Baby Craving', which said that 'millions' of career women will 'pay a price for waiting'. *Life* produced photographic evidence: Mary Chase, a forty-two-year-old writer and producer, who stared contritely at an empty cot. In sub-sequent snapshots Mary was examined by an infertility specialist, bared her back to an acupuncturist attempting to 'stimulate the energy', sought counsel from a male psychic claiming to have inspired one pregnancy, stood on her head in her underwear after having sex, and opened her mouth wide for husband Bill, who peered in and tried 'to uncover early traumas that might block Mary's ability to conceive'. The couple didn't know the cause of their fertility troubles, so it was just as likely that Bill's 'early traumas' were the problem. (Infertility odds are the same for both sexes.) But the *Life* story never dealt with that possibility.

As in all trend stories, the data supporting the infertility epi-demic were nonexistent, so the magazines had to fudge. 'It's hard to tell, but infertility may be on the rise,' *Newsweek* said. 'There are few good statistical measures of how infertility has overtaken our lives,' *Life* said. Of course, plenty of good statistical measures existed; they just didn't uphold the story of the 'curse of the career woman'. Some magazine articles got round the lack of proof by simply shifting to the future tense. *Mademoiselle*, for example, offered this prediction – in upper-case type: THE INFERTILITY EPIDEMIC IS COMING. And a 1982 feature in the *New York Times* just cast aspersions on all sceptics. Women in their thirties who don't believe their infertility odds are high must be suffering 'on an emotional level' from 'a need to deny the findings'.

The week that this *New York Times* feature ran, women who subscribed to both the *Times* and *Time* magazine must have been bewildered. While the *Times* was busy bemoaning the empty wombs of thirty-plus professional women – it ran, in fact, two such stories that week – *Time* was burbling about all the inhabited ones. The news weekly was pushing the other half of the trend pair: a baby boomlet. 'Career women are opting for pregnancy and they are doing it in style,' the magazine cheered in its cover story entitled 'The New Baby Bloom'. Once again, federal Census numbers didn't bear *Time* out; the birthrate had not changed for more than a decade. But that was beside the point. The baby-boomlet trend was only a carrot for the infertility epidemic's stick. *Time* made that clear when it complemented its boomlet story with this cautionary article: 'The Medical Risks of Waiting'.

To get round the lack of data, *Time* resorted to the familiar trend euphemisms: 'More and more career women,' it asserted, 'are choosing pregnancy before the clock strikes twelve.' Then it quickly directed readers' attention to a handful of pregnant movie stars and media celebrities. Former *Charlie's Angels* actress Jaclyn Smith and Princess Diana were expecting, so it must be a national phenomenon.

Time wasn't the only publication to substitute a few starlets for many numbers. *McCall's* gushed over 'Hollywood's Late-Blooming Moms'. *Vogue*'s story on 'baby fever' exulted over still another mom from the *Charlie's Angels* set: 'Motherhood is consuming Farrah Fawcett. All she wants to talk about is breast-feeding.' Actress Patricia Hodge announced there was 'no contest' between family life and her career. 'Pregnancy is like a drug,' she told the *Daily Mail* – which cheered, ACTRESS READY TO SACRIFICE HER CAREER. *Vanity Fair* gave its front cover to a naked, seven months' pregnant Demi Moore and caused a sensation. Interviewed in the *Sunday Express* magazine in December 1991, Moore said, 'I was trying to tell people I feel it's possible to have a career, be a mother and still be very sexy.' Nevertheless, it is likely to have been magazine sales rather than 'having it all' that *Vanity Fair* was interested in.

The mythical 'baby bloom' inspired even more florid tributes on the press's editorial pages. The *San Francisco Chronicle* waxed eloquent:

> In our personal life, we must observe, we have noted an absolute blossoming of both marriages and of births to many women who seemed, not all that long ago, singlemindedly devoted to the pursuit of personal careers. It's nice to hear again the sound of wedding bells and the gurgles of contented babies in the arms of their mothers.

In less purply prose, the *New York Times* conveyed the same sentiments:

> Some college alumnae answered 25th reunion questionnaires with the almost-guilty admission that they were 'only' wives and mothers. But before long, other women found that success at jobs traditionally held by men doesn't infallibly produce a fulfilling life. Motherhood started to come back in style.

If the articles didn't increase the birthrate, they did increase women's anxiety and guilt. 'You can't pick up a magazine without reading about another would-be-mom with a fertility problem that might have been less complicated if she had just started at an earlier age,' a young woman wrote in an op-ed essay in the *New York Times*, entitled 'Motherhood's Better Before Thirty'. She was upset, but not with the media for terrorizing women. She was mad at the older women who seemed to think it was safe to wait. 'I believe it is my birthright to follow a more biologically sound reproductive schedule,' she sniffed, sounding suspiciously businesslike under those maternity clothes.

Simply being able to recognize the media onslaught put that young writer ahead of a lot of other women readers who, wondering why they suddenly felt desperate, unworthy and shameful for failing to reproduce on the media's schedule, decided the signals were coming exclusively from their bodies, not their newspapers. 'I wasn't even thinking about having a child, and suddenly, when I was about thirty-four, it gripped me like a claw,' a woman confided in *Vogue*. 'It was as if I had nothing to do with it, and these raging hormones were saying, "Do what you are supposed to do, which is reproduce." It was a physical feeling more than a mental feeling.'

In the end, this would be the press's greatest contribution to the backlash: not only dictating to women how they should feel, but persuading them that the voice barking orders was only their uterus talking.

True *Ms.*-Confessions

While the media promoted the backlash, who covered it? The mainstream press wasn't doing a very good job. In the US, the formerly quasi-feminist forum, the 'Hers' column in the *New York Times*, was now printing stories on such politically charged topics as what it's like to have a makeover, why a woman really wants a big engagement ring, and the restorative powers of bathtub cleaning. And many smaller-circulation feminist newspapers were closing up shop; even in the San Francisco Bay area, once a mecca for women's rights periodicals, most of the publications had folded by 1989.

Surely, however, women could still turn to the flagship of feminist journalism, *Ms.*, for the real scoop on the backlash. But as the eighties advanced, *Ms.*'s readers would find the magazine retreating almost as quickly as the culture around it.

'We give you permission to have nicely plucked eyebrows,' *Ms.* chirped in the October 1989 issue, in a three-page feature on grooming. Also OK now, according to *Ms.*: uprooting unsightly hairs with painful electrolysis treatments, and applying Accutane, a suspected carcinogen, to vanquish 'adult acne'. All this from a magazine that used to be critical of the beauty industry.

Although the magazine still investigated sexual harassment, domestic violence, the prescription-drug industry and the treatment of Women in Third World countries, the new management of *Ms.* in the late 80's launched a regular fashion column, featured Hollywood stars on more than 25% of its covers, and delivered the really big news – pearls are back. The first magazine to run the pulpy face of a battered wife on the cover now pulled a photo of battered wife Hedda Nussbaum from its cover to pacify advertisers. (The cover that replaced it: a soft-focus shot of a naked woman).

What was most curious about *Ms.*'s escalation of celebrity reporting was that it ocurred after the magazine jettisoned its non-profit status – a course the editors took precisely so they could be 'more political'. As a for-profit venture, *Ms.* could endorse candidates, founding editor Gloria Steinem told the press at the time of the changeover. Indeed, they did. And Anne Summers did start a *Ms.* bureau in Washington to cover national politics and produced numerous dispatches on the 1988 presidential election.

When Summers took over from Steinem in 1987 she decided, much like *Good Housekeeping*'s editors, that *Ms.*'s image needed 'updating'. What it seemed to add up to, though, was taking up-market – a strategy the magazine's previous management had already begun to embrace by the mid-80's. Now that *Ms.* was a profit-making concern, the magazine was primarily interested in gaining women readers with high incomes. This point was stated clearly enough in the promotional literature it sent to potential advertisers, such as the one in 1986 which promised to deliver readers who 'shop in gourmet stores more than anybody' – and later illustrated its pitch with a photo of a woman falling, upside down, off a couch, credit card and other signs of affluence spilling from her pockets. (It was, weirdly, the exact same pose that *Connoisseur* magazine used on its cover about the same time – for a story on expensive lingerie).

To further the upmarket move of *Ms.*, Summers hired a market research firm to conduct consumer focus groups around the country. Only women in households making more than $30,000 a year were invited. The researchers asked these women to assess women's magazines currently on the market. Summers recalls, 'They complained that the women's magazines were partronizing and condescending. They were sick of reading about celebrities. They wanted a magazine that made them feel good, valued, honoured.' Judging by the subsequent covers, *Ms.* paid scant attention to the women's anti-celebrity sentiments. In her first five covers Ms Summers experimented with non-celebrities and with issues. The circulation dropped dramatically. By the sixth issue celebrities began to return. But the magazine's editor did take very seriously one comment the women made. 'One of the things that emerged from the groups was that – especially in the young age groups – there was this incredible resistance to the word "feminist",' Summers says. One might have thought *Ms.*'s whole mission was to tackle that resistance, to show women that 'feminist' was a word they might embrace instead of fear, to explain how American culture had demonized that word precisely because it offered such potential power for women. The magazine could, in fact, have helped fight the backlash by exposing it and driving home the point that feminism simply meant supporting women's rights and choices. This was, after all, an agenda that the women in the focus group uniformly supported; every woman interviewed said she believed she shouldn't have to choose between family and career.

But instead of revitalizing the word, the magazine began using it less and less frequently. 'I think we have to be very careful in the ways we use it,' Summers said in 1988. 'Often you can say "woman" and it means the same thing.' But, as subsequent issues of *Ms.* would make abundantly clear, 'woman' and 'feminist' are not inter-changeable. While the traditionally feminist issues were still being covered, the offending word hardly applied to many of the stories the magazine was now printing. Who needs to talk about feminism in features about 'Cookbooks To Dream About' or 'Laundry Daze', an article about 'Stain-removal rules'.

Indeed, by the end of the decade *Ms.* readers were encountering sentiments in its pages not very different from the moral judgements issued by the backlash press. In an under-reported but overheated cover-story assault on the misdeeds of Bess Myerson, the former Miss America and Mayor Koch aide, writer Shana Alexander informed her audience:

> As for the Women's Movement, I often think we may have opened Pandora's Box. We wanted to be equal. We insisted. We did it . . . We forgot that we are different from men; we are *other*; we have different sensibilities. Today young women are paying for our error.

Newsweek couldn't have said it better.

Women in the *Ms.* focus groups complained about another phenomenon: the backlash. 'The main thing we learned is that women are having a hard time out there,' Summers says, 'and we should be more sympathetic.' One wishes her magazine had been less sympathetic and more analytical. After the Supreme Court issued the *Webster* decision restricting women's reproductive rights, *Ms.* did truly rouse itself and declare IT'S WAR! on the cover of the August 1989 issue. The abortion cover was seen as *too* political by some advertisers, who were looking for an excuse in a softening consumer market to bail out anyway. Meanwhile, the magazine's publishers had been losing many of their biggest advertisers at their other venture, *Sassy*, which the year before had become the target of a fundamentalist letter-writing campaign after printing some frank stories on teenage sexuality. Finally, with *Sassy's* advertising exodus threatening to push both magazines into financial collapse, male publisher Dale Lang took control of the female-run magazine in October 1989. Summers remained to fight for her staff and the preservation of the magazine, but was let go as Editor-in-Chief in December by Lang. He then shut it down for eight months, diverted circulation to his other publications, and finally reissued *Ms.* as a bimonthly journal with no ads, a tiny distribution network – and an impossibly high annual subscription price (a move that cut circulation by half).

Happily, the fate of the feminist press elsewhere has been different. *Spare Rib* in the UK, founded in 1972 by, among others, Rosie Boycott and Marsha Rowe, has been owned by numerous collectives over the years, and since the abolition of the Greater London Council has been completely unfunded. Nevertheless, it has maintained a circulation of around 25,000 copies a month and has achieved its aim of putting women's liberation on the newsstands. Relaunched with a full-colour cover, self-mocking cartoons and more film, television and book reviews, *Spare Rib* made itself more attractive without losing its seriousness, kept up consistently high standards throughout the 1980s, and retained its internationalist, socialist, feminist perspective. Where other, short-lived, feminist magazines like *Red Rag*, *Scarlet Woman* and *Shrew* expired in the 1970s, *Spare Rib*, says Rosie Boycott, 'has got more radical as it's gone on. The first few issues were very mild.' Where in the beginning *Cosmopolitan* in the UK pursued good times and advocated getting the best out of men, *Spare Rib* occupied, as it still does, a clear cultural space opposing the mainstream. Other magazines, like *Honey* under editor Carol Sarler, tried to sell a mix that combined fashion with more serious issues including feminism, but after three years she was sacked. In *Spare Rib*'s view this was because of a combination of outspoken anti-Conservative politics and a penchant for showing models without make-up – which was bound to upset cosmetics advertisers. After her departure, *Honey* changed direction. *Spare Rib*, like current affairs magazine *Everywoman* and the more culture-based *Women's Review*, never depended on consumer advertising and was therefore free of the pressure to couple 'feminist' content with the imagery of consumption.

British *Cosmopolitan* 'came out' as feminist under editor Deirdre McSharry and still aligns itself with feminist concerns, and in January 1991 published an eighteenth-birthday tribute to *Spare Rib*, congratulating it on being 'one of the world's longest running and most widely read feminist magazines' and praising its 'hard-edge political thinking'. Collectives in other parts of the world continue to produce similar magazines, however great the financial difficulties. *Broadsheet*, in New Zealand, for example, has survived as a progressive women's periodical, and in Australia, the equally long-lived and lively *Refractory Girl* continues to publish.

But the circulation of these magazines is nowhere near that of the glossies. With *Ms.* no longer a major player in the mainstream circulation would any of the new magazines launched in the late 1980s dare to challenge the backlash? Not *Men* or *Men's Life* (for the 'real man') or *M. Inc.* (for the 'powerful' man) or any of the other new men's magazines, like *Arena* and *GQ* and the British version of *Esquire*, which hit the news-stands in a sudden burst at the end of the eighties: they featured stories on why men prefer blondes, and what was so repulsive about the 'the sensitive man'. Not *Elle*, the slick periodical of fashion and beauty trends for young women: it maintained that the new generation of women 'no longer needs to examine the whys and hows of sexism' and, anyway, 'all those ideals that were once held as absolute truths – sexual liberation, the women's movement, true equality – have been debunked or debased'. The only new periodical in America that showed even the vaguest interest in tackling the concerns of real women was *Lear's*, a magazine targeted to women over forty, and one of the few run by a female-owned firm. 'We want to use characters who are real, with lines on their faces,' publisher Frances Lear announced (though this didn't stop her from running ads of flawless women half her readers' age). But by the decade's end she, too, was beginning to make backlash noises. At a speech at the 1988 Women in Communications convention, Lear spoke out against materialistic values – then declared, 'I blame the women in the movement . . . the feminist preoccupation with filling one's own needs.' At last, the media's leaders had found a way to pin even the crass commercialism that they themselves had encouraged on female independence.

Chapter Five

Fatal and Foetal Visions:
The Backlash in the Movies

'Punch the bitch's face in,' a moviegoer shouts into the darkness of the Century 21 Theater, as if the screenbound hero might hear, and heed, his appeal. 'Kick her ass,' another male voice pleads from the shadows.

The cinema in suburban San Jose, California, is stuffy and cramped, every seat taken, for this Monday night showing of *Fatal Attraction* in October 1987. The story of a single career woman who seduces and nearly destroys a happily married man has played to a full house here every night since its arrival six weeks earlier. 'Punch the bitch's lights out! I'm not kidding,' a man up front implores actor Michael Douglas. Emboldened by the chorus, a man in the back row cuts to the point: 'Do it, Michael. Kill her already. Kill the bitch.'

Outside in the lobby, the teenage ushers sweep up sweet wrappers and exchange furtive quizzical glances as their elders' bellows penetrate the padded doors. 'I don't get it really,' says Sabrina Hughes, a high-school student who works the Coke machine and finds the adults' behaviour 'very weird', an anthropological event to be observed from a safe distance. 'Sometimes I like to sneak into the theater in the last twenty minutes of the movie. All these men are screaming, "Beat that bitch! Kill her off now!" The women, you never hear them say anything. They are all just sitting there, real quiet.'

Hollywood joined the backlash a few years later than the media;

140

movie production has a longer lead time. Consequently, the film industry had a chance to absorb the 'trends' the 1980s media flashed at independent women – and reflect them back at moviegoers at twice their size. 'I'm thirty-six years old!' Alex Forrest, the homicidal single career woman of *Fatal Attraction*, moans. 'It may be my last chance to have a child!' As Darlene Chan, a 20th Century-Fox vice-president, puts it: '*Fatal Attraction* is the psychotic manifestation of the *Newsweek* marriage study.'

The escalating economic stakes in Hollywood in the 1980s would make studio executives even more inclined to tailor their message to fit the trends. Rising financial insecurity, fuelled by a string of corporate takeovers and the double threat of the cable-television and home-VCR invasions, fostered Hollywood's conformism and timidity. Just like the media's managers, moviemakers were relying more heavily on market research consultants, focus groups and pop psychologists to determine content, guide production and dictate the final cut. In such an environment, portrayals of strong or complex women that went against the media-trend grain were few and far between.

The backlash shaped much of Hollywood's portrayal of women in the eighties. In typical themes, women were set against women; women's anger at their social circumstances was depoliticized and displayed as personal depression instead; and women's lives were framed as morality tales in which the 'good mother' wins and the independent woman gets punished. And Hollywood restated and reinforced the backlash thesis: women were unhappy because they were too free; their liberation had denied them marriage and motherhood.

The movie industry was also in a position to drive these lessons home more forcefully than the media. Filmmakers weren't limited by the requirements of journalism. They could mould their fictional women as they pleased; they could make them obey. While editorial writers could only exhort 'shrill' and 'strident' independent women to keep quiet, the movie industry could actually muzzle its celluloid bad girls. And it was a public silencing ritual in which the audience might take part; in the anonymity of the dark cinema, male moviegoers could slip into a dream state where it was permissible to express deep-seated resentments and fears about women.

'It's amazing what an audience-participation film it's turned out to be,' *Fatal Attraction*'s director Adrian Lyne would remark that autumn, as the film continued to attract record crowds, grossing more than $100 million in four months. 'Everybody's yelling and shouting and really getting into it,' Lyne said. 'This is a film everyone can identify with. Everyone knows a girl like Alex.' That women weren't 'participating', that their voices were eerily absent from the yelling throngs, only underlined Lyne's film message; the silent and impassive female viewers were serving as exemplary models of the 'feminine' women that the director most favoured on screen.

Efforts to hush the female voice in American films have been a perennial feature of cinema in backlash periods. The words of one outspoken independent woman, Mae West, provoked the reactionary Production Code of Ethics in 1934. It was her caustic tongue, not her sexual behaviour, that triggered these censorship regulations, which banned premarital sex and enforced marriage (but allowed rape scenes) on screen until the late 1950s. West infuriated the guardians of the nation's morals – publisher William Randolph Hearst called her 'a menace to the sacred institution of the American family' – because she talked back to men in her films and, worse yet, in her own words; she wrote her dialogue. 'Speak up for yourself, or you'll end up a rug,' West tells the lion she tames in *I'm No Angel*, summing up her own philosophy. In the 1930s she herself would wind up as carpeting, along with the other overly independent female stars of the era: Marlene Dietrich, Katharine Hepburn, Greta Garbo, Joan Crawford and West were all officially declared 'box office poison' in a list published by the president of Independent Theater Owners of America. West's words were deemed so offensive that she was even banned from radio.

Having stopped the mouth of the forty-year-old West and the other grown-up actresses, the thirties studios brought in the quiet good girls. The biggest Depression female star, Shirley Temple, was not yet school age – and got the highest ratings from adult men. When she played Marlene Sweetrick in *War Babies*, she was playing a version of the autonomous Dietrich, shrunk now to a compliant tot.

During the Second World War, in a brief burst of enthusiasm for strong and working women, a handful of Rosie-the-Riveter characters like Ann Sothern's aircraft worker in *Swing Shift Maisie* and Lucille Ball's *Meet the People* flexed muscles and talked back, and many female heroines were now professionals, politicians, even executives. Throughout the 1940s some assertive women were able to make themselves heard: Katharine Hepburn's attorney defended women's rights in the courtroom in *Adam's Rib*, and Rosalind Russell's single reporter in *His Girl Friday* huskily told a fiancé who wanted her to quit work and move to the country, 'You've got to take me as I am, instead of trying to change me. I'm not a suburban bridge player; I'm a newspaperman.'

But even in this decade the other Hollywood vision of woman-hood vied for screen time, and it began to gain ground as the backlash built. Another group of women on screen began to lose their voices and their health. A crop of films soon featured mute and deaf-mute heroines, and the movie women took to their beds, wasting away from brain tumours, spinal paralysis, mental illness and slow poisons. As film historian Marjorie Rosen observes, 'The list of forties female victims reads like a *Who's Who* hospital roster.' The single career women on screen, a brittle, dried-up lot, were heading to the doctor's office, too, for psychiatric treatment. In movies like *Dark Mirror*, *Lady in the Dark*, and later *The Star*, they all received the same medical prescription: quit work and get married.

By the 1950s the image of womanhood surrendered had won out, its emblem the knock-kneed and whispery-voiced Marilyn Monroe – a sort of post-lobotomized 'Lady in the Dark', no longer fighting doctor's orders. Strong women were displaced by good girls like Debbie Reynolds and Sandra Dee. Women were finally silenced in fifties cinema by their absence from most of the era's biggest movies, from *High Noon* to *Shane* to *The Killing* to *Twelve Angry Men*. In the 1950s, as film critic Molly Haskell wrote, 'There were not only fewer films about emancipated women than in the thirties or forties, but there were fewer films about women.' While women were relegated to mindless how-to-catch-a-husband movies, men escaped to womanless landscapes. Against the backdrop of war trenches and the American West, they triumphed at last – if not over their wives then at least over Indians and Nazis.

In late-1980s Hollywood, this pattern would be repeated, as filmmakers once again became preoccupied with toning down independent women and drowning out their voices – sometimes quite literally. In *Overboard*, an unexceptional product of the period, Goldie Hawn's character, a rich city loudmouth (like *Fatal Attraction*'s antiheroine, also named Alex), plunges off a yacht and suffers a spell of amnesia. A rural carpenter she once tongue-lashed rescues her – and reduces her to his squeaky-voiced Hausfrau: 'Keep your mouth closed,' orders the carpenter (played, curiously, by Hawn's real-life husband Kurt Russell), and she learns to like it. In *The Good Mother*, the wisecracking Babe, who resists marriage and bears an illegitimate child, winds up drowning in a lake. Her punishment parallels that of the film's heroine, Anna, a repressed single mother who dares to explore her sexuality – and, as a result, must sacrifice her six-year-old daughter. Fittingly, this was the decade in which Henry James's *The Bostonians* was brought to the screen; Basil Ransom's vow to 'strike dumb' the young women's rights orator had renewed market appeal.

Glenn Close's character in *Fatal Attraction* was not the only independent working woman whose mouth gets clamped shut in a Lyne production. In *9½ Weeks*, released a year before *Fatal Attraction*, a single career woman plays love slave to a stockbroker, who issues her this command: 'Don't talk.' And soon after *Fatal Attraction*'s triumph at the box office, Lyne announced plans for another film – about a literally mute black prostitute who falls for a white doctor. The working title, he said, was *Silence*.

The plots of some of these films achieve this reverse metamorphosis, from self-willed adult woman to silent (or dead) girl, through coercion, others through the female character's own 'choice'. In any case, only for domestic reasons – for the sake of family and motherhood – can a woman shout and still come out a heroine in the late-1980s cinema. The few strong-minded, admirable women are rural farm mothers defending their broods from natural adversity (*Places in the Heart*, *The River* and *Country*) and housewives guarding their families from predatory single women (*Tender Mercies*, *Moonstruck*, *Someone to Watch Over Me* and *Terms of Endearment*). The tough-talking space engineer who saves an orphan child in *Aliens* is sympathetically portrayed, but her wilfulness, too, is maternal; she is protecting the child – who calls her 'Mommy' – from female monsters.

In Hollywood, 1987 was a red-letter year for the backlash against women's independence. In all four of the top-earning films released that year, women are divided into two groups – for reward or punishment. The good women are all subservient and bland housewives (*Fatal Attraction* and *The Untouchables*), babies or voiceless babes (*Three Men and a Baby* and *Beverly Hills Cop II*). The female villains are all women who fail to give up their independence, like the mannish and child-hating shrew in *Three Men and a Baby*, the hip-booted gunwoman in *Beverly Hills Cop II*, and the homicidal career woman in *Fatal Attraction*. All of these films were also produced by Paramount – ironically, the studio that had been saved from bankruptcy half a century earlier by Mae West.

Of all Paramount's offerings that year, *Fatal Attraction* was the one that most mesmerized the national media. Completing the feedback loop, the press even declared the movie's theme a trend and scrambled to find real live women to illustrate it. Story after story appeared on the '*Fatal Attraction* phenomenon', including seven-page cover stories in both *Time* and *People*. A headline in one supermarket tabloid even dubbed the film's single-woman character the MOST HATED WOMEN IN AMERICA. Magazine articles applauded the movie for starting a monogamy trend; the film was supposedly reinvigorating marriages, slowing the adultery rate and encouraging more 'responsible' behaviour from singles. *People* promoted this trend with cautionary case studies of 'Real Life Fatal Attractions' and warned, 'It's not just a movie: All too often, "casual" affairs end in rage, revenge, and shattered lives.' Though in real life such assailants are overwhelmingly male – a fact surely available to the six reporters assigned this apparently important story – all but one of the five aggressors *People* chose as examples were women.

Fatal Attraction, Before and After

British director and screenwriter James Dearden first dreamed up the story that became *Fatal Attraction* one solitary weekend in London in the late 1970s. He was battling writer's block; his wife was out of town – and he wondered to himself, 'What if I picked up that little black address book and rang that girl who gave me her number at a party six months ago?' The original plot was simple. Dearden recalls it this way:

> A writer takes his wife to the station in the morning with their child and sees them off. Then he picks up the phone and rings a girl whose number he's got. He takes her out to dinner, takes her to bed. He thinks that's the end of it, but the phone rings the next day and it's her. So he goes over to see her and spends Sunday with her. And Sunday evening she freaks out completely and cuts her wrists . . . He stays the second night and gets home early in the morning. His wife gets back. The phone rings and it's the girl. He fobs her off and the phone rings again and the wife goes to pick up the phone and you know that's going to be it. She's going to find out about the affair. The wife picks up the phone and says hello, and the screen goes black.

Dearden says he intended the story to explore an individual's responsibility for a stranger's suffering: he wanted to examine how this man who inflicted pain, no matter how unintentionally, must eventually hold himself accountable. In 1979 Dearden turned his screenplay into a forty-five minute film called *Diversion*, highly acclaimed at the Chicago Film Festival the following year.

In the early 1980s American producer Stanley Jaffe was in London looking for new talent, and he paid Dearden a call. The former president of Paramount had recently teamed up with Sherry Lansing, former president of production at 20th Century-Fox, to launch an independent movie production company that would be affiliated with Paramount. Lansing had left Fox in 1982, where she was the first woman ever to be put in charge of production at a major film studio, because she wanted more authority than Fox was willing to grant her. Jaffe returned from London with a stack of scripts for Lansing. 'I kept coming back to *Diversion*,' she recalls. It was the film's potential to deliver a feminist message that appealed to her most, she says:

> I always wanted to do a movie that says you are responsible for your actions . . . And what I liked in the short film was that the man is made responsible. That there are consequences for him. When I watched that short film, I was on the single woman's side. And that's what I wanted to convey in our film. I wanted the audience to feel great empathy for the woman.

Lansing invited Dearden to Los Angeles to expand the story into a feature film, a story from the woman's point of view with a turning-of-the-tables message: the Other Woman shouldn't be getting all the blame; let the adulterous man take the fall for a change.

But Paramount didn't want to make that kind of movie. '[Paramount president] Michael Eisner turned it down because he thought the man was unsympathetic,' director Adrian Lyne recalls. When Eisner left Paramount in 1984, Lansing tried again, and this time the studio agreed to take the film. Almost immediately, however, the old objections were raised. 'My short film was a moral tale about a man who transgresses and pays the penalty,' Dearden says. 'But it was felt, and it was a feeling I didn't particularly agree with, that the audiences would not be sympathetic to such a man because he was an adulterer. So some of the onus for the weekend was taken off his shoulders and placed on the girl's.' With each rewrite, Dearden was pressured to alter the characters further; the husband became progressively more lovable, the single woman more venomous. Dearden finally did away with the man's little black address book and made the single career woman the initiator of the affair. 'As we went along, Alex became much more extreme,' Dearden says. 'She ended up having a kind of predatory quality. It weakened her case and strengthened his.'

'The intent was to soften the man,' a studio executive who was involved in the development discussions explains. 'Because if you saw him shtup a different woman every week, then people would see him as cold and deliberate, and obviously you had to feel for him.' Apparently no one had to feel for the single woman. The feelings of another man were involved, too: Michael Douglas, who was cast early on to play the husband, made it clear to *Fatal Attraction*'s producers that he was not going to play 'some weak unheroic character,' Dearden recalls.

With Douglas on board, the next task was finding a director. Adrian Lyne was the producers' first choice – a peculiar one for a film that was supposed to empathize with women. Of course, they chose him not for his perspective on the opposite sex but for his record at the box office. In 1983 Lyne directed *Flashdance*, a hit MTV-style musical in which the dancing women's rumps received far more screen time than their faces.

Following *Flashdance*'s commercial success, Lyne had also directed *9½ Weeks*, which attracted media attention for its glossy depiction of sadomasochism and for a particularly graphic episode, ultimately excised from all but the video version, in which the masochistic woman is forced to grovel for money at her stockbroker boyfriend's feet. During the filming, the humiliation continued between takes. Kim Basinger, the actress who played the woman, was cringing not only before her character's lover but also from the ministrations of Lyne, who waged an intimidation campaign against the actress – on the theory that an 'edge of terror' would 'help' prepare her for the role. At one point, heeding Lyne's instructions that 'Kim had to be broken down', co-star Mickey Rourke grabbed and slapped Basinger to get her in the mood.

Much as he would later invert *Fatal Attractions*'s theme, Lyne tried to reverse the original message of *9½ Weeks*. The story of that film was drawn from a real woman's 1978 memoirs, which recounted her devastating descent into sexual masochism. In the original script the woman finally rejects the humiliation and walks away from her tormentor. But Lyne tried to change the ending so that she winds up learning to love the abuse. Only a mass protest by the women on the set prevented Lyne from shooting this version.

'Where is the new Kim Basinger?' casting agent Billy Hopkins recalls Lyne demanding throughout the auditions for *Fatal Attrac-*

tion. 'Get me the new Kim Basinger.' The casting agents went after several name actresses, including Debra Winger and Jessica Lange, who turned them down. Meanwhile, they kept getting calls from Glenn Close's agent. Close was determined to have the role; she was even willing to come in for a screen test, an unheard-of gesture for a major star. Close was anxious to shed the good-girl image of her previous roles, from the nurse-mother in *The World According to Garp* to the lady in white in *The Natural*. And late-eighties Hollywood offered actresses only one option for breaking typecasts: trading one caricatured version of womanhood for another.

Once Close was hired, the casting agents turned their attention to the character of the wife. In the original script she was a side character, unimportant. But the producers and Lyne wanted her remade into an icon of good wifery. Producer Stanley Jaffe says, 'I wanted her to be – and I think this is the way she turned out – a woman who is sensitive, loyal, and acts in a way that I would be proud to say, "I would like to know that lady."' Casting agent Risa Bramon recalls that she was told to find an actress who 'projected incredible warmth and love and strength in keeping the family together'. Meanwhile, Dearden was sent back to his desk to turn the two women into polar opposites – as he puts it, 'the Dark Woman and the Light Woman'. Originally the wife, Beth, had a job as a teacher that she was anxious to resume. But by the final version all traces of a career were excised and Beth was transformed into the complete Victorian hearth angel (*à la* prototypical Victorian 'Beth' of *Little Women*), sipping tea, caressing piano keys, and applying cosmetics with an almost spiritual ardour.

Concurrently, Lyne was pushing Close in the other direction, transforming her character, as he describes it, into 'a raging beast underneath'. It was his idea to dress her up in black leather and turn her apartment into a barren loft in New York's meat market district, ringed by oil drums that burned like witches' cauldrons.

To inspire this modern version of the Dark Woman, Lyne says he 'researched' the single women of the publishing world. 'I was mostly interested in their apartments,' he says. He looked at Polaroids of dozens of single women's studios. 'They were a little sad, if you want me to be honest. They lacked soul.' His 'research' didn't involve actually talking to any of the inhabitants of these apartments; he had already made up his mind about unmarried career women. 'They are sort of overcompensating for not being men,' he says. 'It's sad, you know, because it kind of doesn't work.' Sadness, however, is not Lyne's dominant feeling for single professional women, particularly when it comes to the handful of career women he confronts in Hollywood.

> I see it with the executives within the studio area. The other day, I saw a woman producer who was really quite powerful; and she railroaded, walked all over this guy, who was far less successful and powerful than her. She just behaved as if this man wasn't there because her position was more powerful than his. And it was much more disconcerting because it was a woman doing it. It was unfeminine, you know?

In Lyne's analysis, the most unfeminine women are the ones clamouring for equal rights:

> You hear feminists talk, and the last ten, twenty years you hear women talking about fucking men rather than being fucked, to be crass about it. It's kind of unattractive, however liberated and emancipated it is. It kind of fights the whole wife role, the whole childbearing role. Sure you got your career and your success, but you are not fulfilled as a woman.

For his ideal of the 'feminine' woman, he points to his wife:

> My wife has never worked. She's the least ambitious person I've ever met. She's a terrific wife. She hasn't the slightest interest in doing a career. She kind of lives this with me, and it's a terrific feeling. I come home and she's there.

Michael Douglas harboured similar ill will for feminism and its effects. He told a reporter:

> If you want to know, I'm really tired of feminists, sick of them. They've really dug themselves into their own grave. Any man would be a fool who didn't agree with equal rights and pay but some women, now, juggling with career, lover, children,

wifehood, have spread themselves too thin and are very unhappy. It's time they looked at *themselves* and stopped attacking men. Guys are going through a terrible crisis right now because of women's unreasonable demands.

Even Dearden appears to have come around to Lyne's view of the single career woman. 'I think there are many women in New York who live like Alex Forrest,' Dearden says.

Maybe that thrusting career woman looks rather attractive for a brief fling, but in reality you don't want to spend your life with a woman like that. Because they have their careers and their careers would probably conflict with your career and there probably would be rivalry and it wouldn't be that kind of mutually supportive relationship.

Lyne's and Dearden's views on women alone did not shape the movie's ultimate message. Close consulted three psychiatrists, who assured her 'this kind of behaviour is totally possible'. And market research had the final cut. Originally, *Fatal Attraction* was supposed to end with Alex in deep despair over her unrequited love, committing suicide by slitting her throat to the music of *Madame Butterfly*. But when Paramount showed this initial version to test audiences, the response was disappointing. 'It was not cathartic,' Dearden recalls. 'They were all wound up to a pitch and then it all kind of went limp and there was no emotional payoff for them. They'd grown to hate this woman by this time, to the degree that they actually wanted him to have some retribution.' Suicide, apparently, was insufficient punishment.

The film's creators immediately decided to redraft the ending with an audience-pleasing climax – a last-minute revision that would cost them $1.3 million. Alex's death would be a murder, they decided – and the Light Woman would kill the Dark Woman. They set the climactic blowout in the home, 'the final sanctum', as Dearden describes it. The evil Alex invades, clutching a meat cleaver, and Dan grabs her by the throat, tries to drown her in the bath. But it is up to the dutiful wife to deliver the fatal shot, in the heart. The film ends with a slow pan of a framed family portrait, the family restored – the Gallagher family anyway. (For all their domestic sentimentality, the filmmakers gave no thought to the fact that Alex was pregnant when Beth shot her.)

What of Lansing's original objective – to make a feminist film? Lansing concedes that by the end of the film, 'Your allegiance is not with Alex. It's with the family.' But she contends that the film is on Alex's side to a point. 'I do sympathize with her up until she dumps the acid on the car,' Lansing says. She realizes, though, that most male viewers don't share her feelings. In one scene in the movie Alex sits on the floor in tears, compulsively switching a light on and off. 'I just found that tragic,' Lansing says. 'But in the screenings that often gets laughter. That surprised me.'

Still, Lansing maintains that this remains a story about 'the moral consequences of a man's actions'. For the straying husband, she says, 'his whole life turns into a horrendous nightmare'. That may be true, but it's a nightmare from which he wakes up – sobered, but unscathed. In the end, the attraction is fatal only for the single woman.

'I think the biggest mistake filmmakers can make is to say, OK, we're only going to show women who are together and stable and wonderful people,' Lansing says. In late eighties Hollywood, however, there didn't seem much danger of that. Asked to come up with some examples of 'together and stable and wonderful' single women in her films, Lansing says, 'Oh, I've made plenty.' Such as? 'I'm sure I've shown characters like this,' she repeats. Pressed once more to supply a specific example, she finally says, 'Well, Bonnie Bedelia in When the Time Comes [an ABC television movie] was just this functioning, terrific Rock of Gibraltar.' But then, Bedelia was playing a young woman dying of cancer – another Beth of Little Women. Lansing's example only underlines the point driven home in the final take of Fatal Attraction: the best single woman is a dead one.

The Seventies: Unmarried Women and Brilliant Careers

For a while in the 1970s, the film industry would have a brief infatuation with the feminist cause. Just as silent-era Hollywood gave the movement a short run – after a series of low-budget pro-suffrage films turned into big hits – movie studios in the late seventies finally woke up to the profit potential in the struggle for women's independence. In films like *Diary of a Mad Housewife*, *A Woman Under the Influence*, *An Unmarried Woman*, *Alice Doesn't Live Here Anymore*, *Up the Sandbox*, *Private Benjamin* and *The Turning Point*, housewives leave home, temporarily or permanently, to find their own voice. At the time, the female audience seemed to be on a similar quest. In New York cinemas in 1975, women were not sitting placidly in their seats. They were booing the final scene of the newly released *Sheila Levine Is Dead and Living in New York*, because the script rewrote the bestseller's ending to marry off the single woman – to a doctor, of course, who would presumably cure her of her singles' sickness.

Eventually, filmmakers came round to the boisterous audience's feminist point of view. The end of *Private Benjamin*, where the heroine rebuffs her domineering groom, is a case in point. 'It was very important to me that she walk out of that church,' recalls Nancy Meyers, who created the film with Charles Shyer. 'It was important to write about women's identity, and how easily it could be lost in marriage. That sounds almost old-fashioned now, I guess. But I know it mattered to many, many women.' After *Private Benjamin* came out Meyers was inundated with letters from women 'who saw themselves in her character'. It was a liberating event for the film's leading actress, too: Goldie Hawn had been typecast until then as a blonde bubblehead.

In *Private Benjamin* Hawn plays the single Judy, whose 'life's desire' – marriage – comes crashing down when her husband dies on their wedding night. 'If I'm not going to be married, I don't know what I'm supposed to do with myself,' she says. She winds up enlisting in the army, where basic training serves as a metaphorical crash course in emotional and economic independence. Over thirty but not panicking about her single status, Judy goes to work and lives on her own in Europe. Eventually she meets a French doctor and they are engaged, but when she discovers his philanderings she calls a halt to the wedding in mid-ceremony, flees the church and flings her bridal crown to the heavens. The scene recalls the famous ending of the 1967 *The Graduate*; but in the feminist version of this escape-from-the-altar scenario it was no longer necessary for a man to be on hand as the agent of liberation.

The women who go mad in the 1970s women's films are not over-thirty single women panicked by man shortages but suburban housewives driven batty by subordination, repression, drudgery and neglect. In the most extreme statement of this theme, *The Stepford Wives*, the housewives are literally turned into robots created by their husbands. In *Diary of a Mad Housewife* and *A Woman Under the Influence*, the wives' pill-popping habits and nervous breakdowns are presented as not-so-unreasonable responses to their crippling domestic condition – madness as a sign of their underlying sanity. What the male characters label lunacy in these films usually turns out to be a form of feminist resistance.

Women in these seventies films do not turn to male 'doctors' to cure them: in *Private Benjamin*, when her fiancé (who is, significantly, a gynaecologist) offers to give Judy a shot to help her 'calm down', she slaps his face. Instead these heroines seek counsel from other women, who dispense the opposite advice of traditional male clinicians: take action and speak up, they urge. The housewife in Paul Mazursky's *An Unmarried Woman* seeks advice from an independent female therapist, who tells her to go out, enjoy sex, and 'get into the stream of life'. In Martin Scorsese's *Alice Doesn't Live Here Anymore*, the housewife turns to a wise-cracking and foul-mouthed waitress for wisdom. 'Once you figure out what it is you want,' the waitress advises, 'you just jump in there with both feet and let the devil take the hindmost.'

Marriage, not the woman, is the patient under analysis in women's films of the seventies, and the dialogue probes the economic and social inequities of traditional wedlock. 'A woman like me works twice as hard and for what?' Barbra Streisand, the housewife Margaret in *Up the Sandbox*, demands of her husband, a history professor. 'Stretch marks and varicose veins, that's what. You've got one job; I've got ninety-seven. Maybe I should be on the cover of *Time*. Dust Mop of the Year! Queen of the Laundry Room! Expert on Tinker Toys!' Margaret's mother offers the most succinct summation of what, in the opinion of these films, lies at the core of marital distress: 'Remember, marriage is a 75–25 proposition. The woman gives 75.'

In these films the heroines are struggling to break out of the supporting-actress status that traditional marriage conferred on them; they are asking to be allowed, for once, to play a leading role in their own lives. 'This story is going to be all about me,' announces Judy Davis's Sybilla, in the first line of Gillian Armstrong's *My Brilliant Career*, an Australian film that was very successful in the late 1970s. The youthful heroine turns down a marriage proposal not because she doesn't care for her suitor, but because marriage would mean that her own story would never have a chance to develop. 'Maybe I'm ambitious, selfish,' she says apologetically. 'But I can't lose myself in somebody else's life when I haven't lived my own yet.'

Of course, according to the conventional 1980s analysis, these 1970s film heroines *were* selfish, their pursuit of self-discovery just a euphemism for self-involvement. But that reading misses a critical aspect of the female quest in these movies. The heroines did not withdraw into themselves; they struggled toward active engagement in affairs beyond the domestic circle. They raised their voices not simply for personal improvement but for humanitarian and political causes – human rights in *Julia*, workers' rights in *Norma Rae*, equal pay in *9 to 5*, and nuclear safety in *The China Syndrome*. They wished to transform not only themselves but the world around them. They were loud, belligerently loud, because speaking up was a social, as well as a private responsibility. 'Are you still as angry as you used to be?' Julia, the Second World War resistance fighter, asked Lillian Hellman in the biographical *Julia*. 'I like your anger. . . . Don't you let anyone talk you out of it.'

The Eighties: The Celluloid Woman's Surrender

If Vanessa Redgrave's Julia represented the kind of heroine that 1970s feminist cinema would single out for biographical study, then it fell to Redgrave's daughter, Natasha Richardson, to portray her counterpart for the late 1980s: Patty Hearst. As conceived in Paul Schrader's 1988 film, the bound and blindfolded heiress is all victim; her lack of identity is her leading personality trait. As

Schrader explained: '[E]ssentially the performance is like a two-hour reaction shot.'

The same might be said of the droves of passive and weary female characters filling the screen in the late 1980s. In so many of these movies, it is as if Hollywood has taken the feminist films and run the reels backwards. The women now flee the office and hammer at the homestead door. Their new quest is to return to traditional marriage, not challenge its construction; they want to escape the workplace, not remake it. The female characters who do have professional lives take little pleasure from them. They find their careers taxing and tedious, 'jobs' more than callings. While the liberated women of seventies films were writers, singers, performers, investigative reporters and political activists who challenged the system, the women of the late eighties are management consultants, investment advisers, corporate lawyers, behind-the-scenes production and literary assistants. They are the system's support staff.

Most women in the real contemporary labour force are, of course, relegated to ancillary, unsatisfying or degrading work, but these films aren't meant to be critiques of sex discrimination on the job or indictments of a demoralizing marketplace. They simply propose that women had a better deal when they stayed at home. The films stack the deck against working female characters: it's easier to rationalize a return to housekeeping when the job left behind is so lacking in rewards or meaning. It's hard to make the case that a woman misses out if she quits the typing pool – or that society suffers when an investment banker abandons Wall Street.

The career women of the late-1980s cinema are an unappealing lot. They rarely smile and their eyes are red-rimmed from over-work and exhaustion. 'I don't know what I'm doing any more,' Cher, an attorney, complains to a co-worker in *Suspect*; he's single, too, but, being male, immune to burn-out. She tells him:

> I don't have a life. The last time I went to the movies was like a year ago. The only time I listen to music is in my car. I don't date. I'd like to have a child but I don't even have a boyfriend so how can I have a child? . . . I don't think I can do it any more. You know, I'm tired. I'm really tired.

In *Surrender*, Sally Field's Daisy is an 'artist'. But her artistry is performed at an assembly-line factory, where she mass-produces landscape art for hotels. Her one stab at a personal statement is to brush a tiny female figure into one of the canvases; it is a picture of herself drowning. All she wants to do, understandably, is quit and devote her life to marriage and motherhood. 'If I'm not married again by the time I'm forty-one,' she moans, 'there's a 27 per cent chance I'll end up a lonely alcoholic.' Her 'biological clock' is practically a guest star in this film. She has a dream, she tells her enviably fertile friend, who is pregnant for the fourth time. 'This dream has a husband and baby in it.' The 'bottom line', says Daisy, is, 'I want a baby.' Although she claims to aspire to a career as a painter, after five minutes in front of the easel she is sidetracked by her more important marital mission. She hums the wedding march as she chases her prospective husband, a prolific and successful novelist.

The single Isabella in *Crossing Delancey* is another mirthless working woman. An assistant in a book shop, she serves the needs of successful male authors. Her leisure hours are not too gratifying either: in one painful scene in a Manhattan deli, she and other single women flutter like souls in limbo around the salad bar, their faces ghostly under the fluorescent lights. Clutching their Styrofoam food containers, they drift homeward – to consume their bland suppers curled solo on their beds.

Typical of 'post-feminist' fare, *Crossing Delancey* mouths sympathy for feminist aspirations, then promptly eats its words. The film's heroine takes a stand for self-determination only to undercut it. Isabella huffily tells her grandmother she has good friends and a full life, and doesn't 'need a man to be complete' – then admits to a nightmare she's just had about drowning. She claims she values her independence – then gathers with her girlfriends to bemoan the man shortage. She protests that she's really 'a happy person', that she doesn't need the matchmaker her grandmother has hired to save her from spinsterhood. But the film shows her bereft and alone on her birthday, eating a hot dog at a stall in Times Square – while a wild-eyed bag lady croons, 'Some Enchanted Evening' in her ear. 'A dog should live alone, not a woman,' her grandmother tells her. And in the end her words are the ones we're meant to believe. Isabella learns to 'settle' – in this case, for the pickle vendor in the old neighbourhood. He's dull but solid, a good provider for the little woman.

The professional women on screen who resist these nesting 'trends', who refuse to lower their expectations and their voices, pay a bitter price for their recalcitrance. In *Broadcast News*, Holly Hunter's Jane, a single network producer, fails to heed the cocooning call. She's not out there beating the bushes for a husband and she's passionate about her work. Her male co-worker, a single reporter, has the same traits; in him they are admirable, but in her they constitute neurosis. She is 'a basket case' and 'an obsessive', who dissolves into inexplicable racking sobs in the middle of the day and compulsively chatters directions. 'Except for socially,' a female colleague tells her, 'you're my role model.' While the two lead male characters wind up with brilliant careers and full private lives, Jane winds up alone. Her aggressiveness at work cancels out her chances of love. Her attempts to pull off a romantic encounter fail miserably every time. 'I've passed some line someplace,' she says. 'I'm beginning to repel people I'm trying to seduce.'

In these backlash films only the woman who buries her intelligence under a baby-doll exterior is granted a measure of professional success without having to forsake companionship. In *Working Girl* Melanie Griffith's Tess, an aspiring secretary with a child's voice, rises up the business ladder *and* gets the man – but she achieves both goals by playing the daffy and dependent girl. She succeeds in business only by combing the tabloid gossip columns for investment tips – and relying on far more powerful businessmen to make the key moves in her 'career'. She succeeds in love Sleeping Beauty-style, by passing out in a man's arms.

Tess is allowed to move up in the ranks of American business only by tearing another woman down; in 1980s cinema, as in America's real boardrooms, there's only room for one woman at a time. Female solidarity in this film is just a straw man to knock down. 'She takes me seriously,' the naïve Tess confides to her boyfriend about her new boss, Katharine. 'It's because she's a woman. She wants to be my mentor.' The rest of the narrative is devoted to disabusing Tess of that notion. Katharine, a cut-throat graduate of Harvard business school with a Filofax where her heart should be (the film's ads called her 'the boss from hell'), betrays Tess at the first opportunity. The film ends with a verbal cat fight between the Dark and Light Woman, a sort of comic version of *Fatal Attraction*'s final scene, in which Tess orders Katharine to get her 'bony ass' out of the office. Not only does Katharine *not* get the man; she doesn't even get to keep her job.

The incompatibility of career and personal happiness is preached in another prototypical woman's film of the eighties, *Baby Boom*. Like *Fatal Attraction*, it was a movie that the media repeatedly invoked as 'evidence' that babies and business don't mix. 'Remember the troubles that beset the high-powered Manhattan businesswoman played by Diane Keaton in the movie *Baby Boom* . . . ?' *Child* magazine prodded its readers. '[T]he talents needed to nurture a child are at odds with those demanded for a fast-paced career.'

As was the case in *Working Girl*, the male boss's hands in *Baby Boom* are clean. A benign patriarch, he reminds J. C. Wiatt, an aspiring management consultant with a messianic complex to match her initials, that she must choose between the corner office and the cradle. He's not being nasty, just realistic. 'Do you understand the sacrifices?' he asks as he offers her a chance to become one of the firm's partners. 'A man can be a success. My wife is there for me whenever I need her. I'm lucky. I can have it all.' *Baby Boom* was co-written by Nancy Meyers, creator of *Private Benjamin*, so one might expect that the film would set out to challenge this unjust arrangement – and argue that the corporation must learn to accommodate women, not the other way around. But this is a very different Nancy Meyers from the one who championed Private Benjamin's liberation seven years before.

In keeping with the decade's prevailing views, Meyers now envisages women as divided into two hostile camps. 'There are certain women who are very aggressive and great at business but who know nothing about babies and are intimidated by the thought of having kids,' she told the press. 'They want them but don't know how to go about settling down and having one out of fear of what it'll do to their careers. I feel bad for those women.'

'I don't see women having it all and achieving great things,' Meyers says later in an interview. She's sitting in her Studio City house with a baby in her arms. 'I don't see them in the corporate world.' Rather than protest against the lack of progress, Meyers has made adjustments. She says she has chosen to take a back seat to her creative partner and common-law husband, director Charles Shyer, so she can look after their two young children. Although Meyers was deeply involved in the creation of *Baby Boom*, Shyer got the directing credit. 'People ask me why I don't direct,' Meyers says. 'I've had directing offers and I've turned them down. It wouldn't be right for my family. It wouldn't be right for my children. The movie says "Directed by Charles Shyer" and people look at that and I guess they think, well . . . ' Her voice trails off. 'But that's just the way it is. I'm not saying it's fair; I'm not saying women should compromise, but they do have to compromise. I guess if more men would give up something . . . ' Meyer's voice trails off again. If this last remark is meant for Shyer, who is sitting across the table from her, he doesn't acknowledge it.

In cutting back her female characters' expectations, Meyers got plenty of encouragement from the Hollywood studios. When she and Shyer wrote *Protocol* they ran into heavy interference from the presiding studio, Warner Brothers. The story was supposed to be about a naïve waitress, again played by Goldie Hawn, who has her consciousness raised and becomes a politically wise diplomat. The studio insisted the producers rewrite the female character's development, Shyer recalls, removing Hawn's political evolution from the script. In the final version she winds up a scatterbrained national sweetheart, cheerleading for the American way. 'They were very nervous about the content of the movie, that it not have a political point of view,' Charles Shyer recalls. 'It was the beginning of the Reagan administration and they didn't want anything that might be seen as an anti-Reagan movie.' A woman who thinks for herself, apparently, could now be mistaken for a subversive.

By the time production rolled around for *Baby Boom* in the mid-eighties, Meyers and Shyer had internalized the studio's commands; no unseemly political outbursts sully Diane Keaton's performance. At the start of *Baby Boom*, J. C. Wiatt, the Tiger Lady of the boardroom, has 'chosen' career over marriage and maternity and in the process scoured away any trace of womanhood – or humanity. Diane Keaton's Wiatt is an efficient machine; even her sexual encounters are confined to passionless four-minute coup-lings. When a baby is forced into her unwilling arms by the death of a distant relative, she tries to explain about the zero-sum game of 'choice': 'I can't have a baby,' she says, 'because I have a twelve-thirty lunch meeting.' Because she has cast her lot in a man's world, she is also seemingly incapable of the simplest acts of childcare. Changing the baby's nappy becomes an impossible ordeal for this Ivy Leaguer. Eventually, in the female game of trade-offs, as her baby skills ascend, her career plummets. Devo-tion to the baby destroys her chances of a promotion; the partner-ship offer is retracted and she is demoted to the dog-food account.

It never occurs to the highly educated Tiger Lady that her treatment might constitute sex discrimination. Instead of proceed-ing to the courtroom, she quits and moves to the country. Ensconced in a bucolic estate, she soon softens up, learning to bake and redirecting her business skills to a more womanly vocation, making and marketing gourmet baby food. Ultimately, her truly feminine side is awakened by the local veterinarian, 'Cooper'. Like Tess, she finds love the old-fashioned way – by fainting. The doctor revives her on his examining table, and she falls in love.

Baby Boom's values are muddled: the film takes a feeble swipe at the corporate system before backing off completely. It pretends to reject the eighties money ethic without ever leaving its orbit. The Tiger Lady retreats to the country, but to an obscenely expen-sive farmhouse that she can afford only because of her prior Wall Street pay cheques. She turns up her nose at yuppie materialism, but supports herself by selling designer applesauce baby food to yuppie mothers. When one of her old corporate accounts at the firm offers to buy her baby-food company for $3 million in cash, she marches into the boardroom to reject the deal. 'Country Baby is not for sale,' she says piously. Her speech might have been an opportunity to take the firm to task for expelling its most valuable employee simply because she had a child. She could have spoken up for the rights of working mothers. But instead the former Tiger Lady's talk dribbles off into a dewy-eyed reverie about the joys of rural living. 'And anyway, I really think I'd miss my sixty-two-acre estate,' she explains. 'Elizabeth [her baby] is so happy there and well, you see, there's this veterinarian I'm seeing . . . ' The last shot shows her back at home in a rocking chair, baby in her arms, surrounded by curtain lace and floral upholstery.

Like *Fatal Attraction*'s creators, Meyers and Shyer defend the 'you-can't-have-it-all' message of the film by explaining that they based it on 'research'. To their credit, they did go to the trouble of interviewing an actual career woman. They modelled the Tiger Lady on a management consultant with a Harvard business degree. 'She was so torn by the whole thing,' Meyers says. 'It was so hard for her. She didn't know what to do.' What their model, Nadine Bron, didn't do, however, was give up work. She managed to find love and marry, too, despite the career. She's not even particularly 'torn', she says.

'Well, I know it's Hollywood and all,' Bron says diplomatically when asked later for her view of *Baby Boom*, 'but what bothered me is that the movie assumed that is the only way – to give it all up and move to the country.' Bron's life does not fit the you-can't-have-it-all thesis: she has worked for a large consulting firm and now runs her own money-management business – without abandoning a personal life. Her marriage, she says, is stronger because both she and her husband have 'full lives'. She has no desire to become a country housewife.

'My mother stayed home while my father ran the business,' she recalls. 'She was very frustrated.' Growing up, Bron was a pained witness to her mother's weight swings and bouts of depression. It is not a pattern she cares to repeat. 'For some women,' Bron says, 'staying home is preferable, but I could never do it. For me, it's very important to work.' The problem, as she sees it, is not women wanting to go home but the male business world refusing to admit the women on equal terms. 'Society has not been willing to adapt to these new patterns of women,' she says. 'Society punishes you.'

Bringing Up the Cinematic Baby

An unintentionally telling aspect of *Baby Boom* is its implication that working women must be strong-armed into motherhood. The

Date as postmark

Teachers of Students with Mental Health Problems

Training Session

WEDNESDAY 10 DECEMBER 1997

9.00am - 12.30

This is to confirm your place on the above training session.

Please let us know by 1 December if you do not require lunch.

Looking forward to meeting you then.

Jeremy Braund

film is not the first of its era to suggest that, at a time when 'baby fever' was supposedly raging in female brains, intense pressure, scoldings or a *deus ex machina* (like the Tiger Lady's improbable inheritance of a stranger's baby) are necessary to turn these reluctant modern women into mothers. Like the media, these movies aren't really reflecting women's return to total motherhood; they are marketing it. Sometimes, in fact, these films degenerate into undisguised advertising. In the last five minutes of *Parenthood*, the whole brood crowds into a maternity ward, with virtually every woman either rocking a newborn or resting a proud hand on a bulging tummy. As the camera pans over row upon row of gurgling babies in nappies, it's hard to remember that this is a feature film, not a commercial break for Pampers.

The backlash films struggle to make motherhood as alluring as possible. Cuddly babies in designer clothes displace older children on the 1980s screen; the well-dressed infants function in these films more as fashion accessories than people. The children of a decade earlier were talkative, unpredictable kids with minds of their own – like the precocious, cussing eleven-year-old boy who gives his mother both delight and lip in *Alice Doesn't Live Here Anymore*, or the seventeen-year-old girl who offers her mother both comfort and criticism in *An Unmarried Woman*. In the late 1980s, by contrast, the babies hardly cry.

Once again, women get sorted into two camps: the humble women who procreate, and their monied or careerist sisters who don't. *Overboard*'s haughty heiress refuses to reproduce. But by the end of the film – after she is humiliated, forced to scrub floors and cook meals, and at last finds happiness as a housewife – she tells her tyrannical new husband of her greatest goal in life: having 'his' baby. Women who resist baby fever, by controlling their fertility or postponing motherhood, are shamed and penalized. In *Immediate Family*, Glenn Close's career woman – an Ivy League-educated estate agent – delays and her biological clock expires. After a gruelling round of visits to the infertility doctors, she has to hire a teenage surrogate to have a baby for her.

In this sanctimonious climate, abortion becomes a moral litmus test to separate the good women from the bad. On the day the husband in *Parenthood* loses his job, his good wife announces she's pregnant with child number four; she recoils in horror from the mere mention of abortion. The options of her sister-in-law's pregnant teenage daughter are presented as similarly limited. She's just received her high SAT [Scholastic Aptitude Test] scores in the mail, but, of course, the movie assures us, she'll give up her college plans to have the baby and marry her deadbeat boyfriend – an unemployed dragstrip racer. Abortion is denounced in *Listen to Me*, which is supposedly an evenhanded debate on the issue, and demonized in *Criminal Law*, where the abortionist, Sybil, is a witchlike figure whose profession traumatizes her son and turns him into a psychopath. Even more intelligent films preach on this subject. In Woody Allen's *Another Woman*, the single scholar, a rigid unfeeling spinster, flashes back to a shameful youthful memory – her selfish decision to have an abortion. 'All you care about is your career, your life of the mind,' her lover charged at the time, and now she sees, too late, that he was right to castigate her.

Three Men and a Baby became the most popular of the pronatal films (later inspiring the sequel *Three Men and a Little Lady*) with its baby-girl heroine centre stage and its career woman expelled from nursery heaven. The premise – a single woman with career ambitions dumps her offspring on the doorstep of three bachelors – recalls the anti-suffrage films seventy years earlier. (In the 1912 *A Cure for Suffragettes*, for example, feminists flocking to a suffrage powwow abandon their prams on a street corner, leaving the policemen to look after the neglected babies.)

Three Men and a Cradle, the original French version of the film, was such a hit with American audiences that Paramount hastened to release its own version, and the revisions are illuminating. For the American story, Paramount inserted a new character, wretched Rebecca, a dour lawyer with perpetually pursed lips. The wet-blanket girlfriend of bachelor Peter, Rebecca recoils with disgust at their new bundle of joy. When the baby drools on Rebecca's fingers she can barely suppress her nausea. Peter pleads, 'Rebecca, please stay with me – help me take care of her,' but callous Rebecca refuses. She has no maternal juices, nor any romantic ones either. When Peter asks her to stay the night on his birthday, she refuses because she has a pre-trial court date in the morning – and that ranks higher on her in-tray priority list.

At first glance, *Three Men and a Baby* might seem like a film with feminist tendencies; after all, the men are taking care of the baby. But the movie does not propose that men take real responsibility for raising children. It derives all its humour from the reversal of what it deems the natural order: mother in charge of baby. Viewers are regaled with the myriad ways in which these carefree bachelors are not cut out for parenthood. The fact that one of them actually *is* the father is played for laughs. 'How do I know it's mine?' he says blithely. 'Boys Will Be Boys' is the song that plays incessantly throughout the film. Indeed, despite their upwardly mobile careers and advancing middle age, the three bachelors celebrate their arrested development inside a high-priced fraternity house. The three 'boys' gleefully adhere to an another night/another girl sexual philosophy. 'So many women, so little time,' they snort, slapping each other on the back like football teammates after another completed pass.

Unlike the French version, the American film keeps anxiously bolstering its male characters' masculinity. As if terrified that having a baby around the house might lower the testosterone level, the guys are forever lifting weights, sweating it out on the playing fields and jogging to the newsagent's for the latest issue of *Sports Illustrated* and *Popular Mechanics*. In the American remake, the straying mother will eventually learn to uphold the traditional 'feminine' role, too. In the final frame, remorseful mum not only reshoulders her maternal responsibilities but agrees to live under the men's roof. The baby, one of the bachelors asserts, 'needs a full-time mother' – and, one gets the impression, so do they.

Hollywood in the 1980s was simply not very welcoming to movie projects that portrayed independent women as healthy, lusty people without punishing them for their pleasure. Producer Gwen Field's experience with *Patti Rocks*, released soon after *Fatal Attraction*, is one measure of Hollywood's hostility to such themes during this decade. In Field's film, an opinionated single woman shuns marriage ('Marriage is fattening,' she jokes), enjoys sex, chooses to have a child on her own and yet pays no price for her behaviour. *Patti Rocks* received its share of good reviews from the critics, but generated nothing but animosity and rejection from the guardians of Hollywood. Field was turned away by one studio after another and always for the same reason: they told her the film's message was 'irresponsible' because it showed a single woman indulging in sex with whomever she pleased. (This same moral concern never surfaced over *Three Men and a Baby*, where the randy bachelors randomly scatter their seed.) The industry's ratings board tried to assign the film an X (18) rating, even though it featured no violence and no more sex than the average R movie (which requires that moviegoers under seventeen be accompanied by a parent). Field recalls that the board members disapproved not of the visual display but 'the language' – the same offence that brought down Mae West half a century earlier. As Field observes, 'It was very ironic that we had received an X rating for a film that is against what pornography depicts – the degradation of women.' It took three formal appeals before the board members finally approved an R rating. Ultimately *Patti Rock*'s chances for commercial success were slim anyway; as an independently produced film with out-of-the-mainstream content, it would get distributed to only a handful of cinemas.

The Celluloid Man Takes Charge

'Who am I?' the single female psychiatrist asks her male mentor, a small-time gambler and con artist, in David Mamet's 1987 *House of Games*. Although she's the one with the medical degree, he's playing doctor. Her hair shorn, her face severe and unsmiling, she clutches the book she has written, *Driven: Obsession and Compulsion in Everyday Life*, but its contents have no answers for her. Those must come from him. The consultation that follows recalls a therapy session from the last backlash cinema, between the male psychoanalyst and the driven single magazine editor in *Lady in the Dark*. That earlier film's dialogue:

> *He*: You've had to prove you were superior to all men: You had to dominate them.
> *She*: What's the answer?
> *He*: Perhaps some man who will dominate you.

After half a century of 'progress', the diagnosis remains the same in *House of Games*:

> *She*: What do I want?
> *He*: Somebody to come along. Somebody to possess you. Would you like that?
> *She*: Yes.

Offscreen, David Mamet was complaining bitterly about women in the entertainment business who apparently prefer to dominate and 'won't compromise'. In a 1988 essay on women entitled 'Bewitched, Bothered and Bewildered', he asserted, 'The coldest, cruellest, most arrogant behavior I have ever seen in my professional life has been – and *consistently* been – on the part of women producers in the movies and the theater'. In Mamet's *House of Games*, the stepped-on confidence man slips the cold careerist woman back under his thumb through his sleights of hand. And who is the actress Mamet cast in the demeaning female role? Lindsay Crouse, his own wife.

The 1980s backlash cinema embraces the Pygmalion tradition – men redefining women, men reclaiming women as their possessions and property. In the most explicit statement of this theme, the Wall Street tycoon in *Pretty Woman* remakes the loud, gum-smacking hooker into his soft-spoken and genteel appendage, fit for a Ralph Lauren ad. In film after film, men return to their roles of family potentate, provider and protector of female virtue. In films from *Moonstruck* to *The Family*, the celluloid neopatriarchs preside over 'old-fashioned' big ethnic families. In *The Untouchables*, when Eliot Ness goes into combat against the mob, he is as busy defending the traditional domestic circle as he is enforcing the law. In films like *Someone to Watch Over Me*, *Sea of Love* or *Look Who's Talking*, the backlash heroes play Big Daddy guardians to helpless women and families threatened by stalkers. In the real world, blue-collar men might be losing economic and domestic authority, but in these movies the cops and cabbies were commanding respect from cowering affluent women.

For all the sentimental tributes to the return of the all-American household – 'Nothing can take the place of the family!' the son toasts in *Moonstruck*, and 'Nice to be married, huh?' the men tell each other in *The Untouchables* – the late 1980s pro-family films are larded with male anger over female demands and male anxiety over women's progress. 'Stick it here, stick it there,' Al Pacino's divorced police officer says bitterly of his ex-wife in *Sea of Love*. 'I see eight women tonight, every one of them made more money than me,' his partner tells him. 'How come they're not married?' *She's Having a Baby* is supposed to celebrate a fifties-style sub-urban marriage, but most of the film is devoted to the husband's fantasies of escaping from under his nagging wife's thumb. In *Surrender*, the male protagonist, a twice-divorced author, suspects all women of malicious ulterior motives. 'We're all just meat to them,' he says of women, and vows to move to Kuwait 'because women don't vote there'. Standing in the lobby of his divorce lawyer's building, he faces a choice: entering one elevator with a leather-clad woman or another elevator with a snarling Doberman and street hood. He takes his chances with the canine-and-criminal duo.

The decade in family cinema ended not with a heartwarming salute to home's cosy comforts but with an explosion of hateful marital fireworks. The underbelly of the backlash finally surfaced on screen, as spouses lunged for each other's throats. In films like *The War of the Roses*, *She-Devil*, *I Love You to Death* and *Sleeping with the Enemy*, usually hidden fears about strong women's powers are on bold display.

In the 1970s women's liberation films and 1940s wartime movies, men and women struggled endlessly with each other, too, but they argued with good intentions – to understand and enlighten each other, to close rather than widen the gender gap. When the dust clears after the shouting match between Ellen Burstyn and Kris Kristofferson in *Alice Doesn't Live Here Any-more*, each comes to see the other's point of view, and they walk away from the struggle with stronger empathy and love. In *Adam's Rib*, Spencer Tracy's lawyer stomps from the house demanding divorce after his wife (Katharine Hepburn) wins her feminist case in court. 'I like two sexes,' he shouts at her. 'And another thing. All of a sudden I don't like being married to what is known as the New Woman.' She calls after him, 'You are not going to solve anything by running away,' and in the end, he agrees; they reunite and work out their differences. In *The War of the Roses*, by contrast, there's no hope for reconciliation, truce, or even escape from the marital battle – both spouses wind up dead, their bodies smashed in the familial foyer.

In many of these late-1980s films, men and women have not only given up trying to work things out, they don't even keep company on the same reel. Like the backlash cinema of the 1950s, independent women are finally silenced by pushing them off the screen. In the tough-guy films that proliferated at the end of the decade, male heroes head off to all-male war zones and the Wild West. In the escalating violence of an endless stream of war and action movies – *Predator*, *Die Hard*, *Die Harder*, *RoboCop*, *RoboCop 2*, *Lethal Weapon*, *Days of Thunder*, *Total Recall* – women are reduced to mute and incidental characters or banished altogether. In the man-boy body-swapping films that cropped up in the late eighties – *18 Again*, *Like Father, Like Son* and, the most memorable, *Big* – men seek refuge in female-free boyhoods. And male characters in another whole set of films retreat even further, to hallucinatory all-male fantasies of paternal renewal. In such films as *Field of Dreams*, *Indiana Jones and the Last Crusade*, *Dad* and *Star Trek V: The Final Frontier*, mother dies or disappears from the scene, leaving father (who is sometimes resurrected from the dead) and son to form a spiritually restorative bond.

Not surprisingly, when the Screen Actors Guild conducted a count of female roles in Hollywood in 1990, the organization discovered that women's numbers had sharply dropped in the previous two years. Men, the guild reported, were now receiving more than twice as many roles as women.

While men were drifting off into hypermasculine dreamland, the female characters who weren't already dead were subject to ever more violent ordeals. In 1988, all but one of the women nominated for the Academy Award's Best Actress played a victim. (The exception, fittingly, was Melanie Griffith's working 'girl'.) The award's winner that year, Jodie Foster, portrayed a rape victim in *The Accused*. The producer of that film was Sherry Lansing.

Lansing released *The Accused* a year after *Fatal Attraction*, and hoped that it would polish up her feminist credentials. The film told the story of a young working-class woman gang-raped at a local bar while a crowd of men stood by and let it happen – a tale based on a grisly real gang rape at Big Dan's tavern in New Bedford, Massachusetts. 'If anyone thinks this movie is anti-feminist, I give up,' Lansing told the press. 'Once you see this movie, I doubt that you will ever, ever think of rape the same way again. Those images will stick in your mind, and you will be more sympathetic the next time you hear of somebody being raped.'

Did people really need to be reminded that rape victims deserve sympathy? Apparently Lansing did: 'Until I saw this film, I didn't even know how horrible [rape] is,' she announced. Apparently many young men watching this film needed the reminder, too: they hooted and cheered the film's rape scene. And clearly a society in which rape rates were skyrocketing could stand some re-education on the subject.

Lansing said *The Accused* should be hailed as a breakthrough movie because it tells America a woman has the 'right' not to be raped. But it seems more reasonable that it should be mourned as a depressing artefact of the times – because it tells us only how much ground women have already lost. By the end of the 1980s a film that simply opposed the mauling of a young woman could be passed off as a daring feminist statement.

Chapter Six

Teen Angels and Unwed Witches: The Backlash on TV

'Under no circumstances is this going to be the return of "jiggle".
These aren't just girls who look good; they have actual personal-
ities.' Tony Shepherd, vice-president of talent for Aaron Spelling
Productions, puts his full weight behind each word, as if careful
enunciation might finally convince the remaining sceptics in the
Hollywood press corps. Thankfully, most of the reporters
assembled at the Fox Television Center for the announcement of
the network's new television series, *Angels '88*, see things
Shepherd's way; they reach across the buffet table's mountain of
pastries to shake his hand. 'Great work, Tony,' says one of the
guys from the tabloids, his mouth full of croissant. 'Great work
selecting the girls.'

This May morning in 1988 is the grand finale of Fox's two-
month quarter-million-dollar nationwide search for the four angels
– a quest the company publicists liken to 'the great search for
Scarlett O'Hara' and 'the glamour days of Old Hollywood'.
Shepherd has crossed the country four times ('I had to watch
Three Men and a Baby five times on the plane'), personally conducted open casting calls in twelve of the forty-four cities, and
eyeballed at least 6,000 of the 16,000 women who stood in half-
mile-long lines all day for one-and-a-half-minute interviews. Secretaries and housewives, he says, weathered 25-degree tempera-
tures just to see him; one woman even passed out from hypo-
thermia.

But a few journalists at this event can't resist asking: isn't *Angels*

'88 just a rerun of Spelling's *Charlie's Angels*, where three jiggle-prone private eyes took orders from invisible boss Charlie and bounced around in bikinis? 'No, no, no!' Shepherd, the chain-smoking great-grandson of Louis B. Mayer, exhales a fierce stream of smoke. '*They* didn't have distinct characters. They were just beauties.' The characters in *Angels '88*, he says, are more 'advanced', independent women who won't even necessarily be fashion plates. That's why the network interviewed so many real women for the leading roles. These new angels 'might not have perfect hair and be the perfect model types,' he says. 'In *Angels '88*, you're going to find these girls sometimes wearing no makeup at all. Particularly, you know, when they are running around on the beach.'

Just then, a Fox publicist takes the stage to announce the angels' imminent début. No interviews, he warns the media, until the photographers finish their 'beauty shots'. The angels file on stage and the cameramen begin shouting, 'Girls, over here, over here!' 'Oh, young ladies, right here!' The angels turn this way and that, well-coiffed hair swinging around flawlessly made-up faces. The idle reporters leaf through their press kits, which offer large photographs and brief biographies of each star – Tea Leoni, 'the 5'7" blonde beauty'; Karen Kopins, 'the 5'8" brunette beauty'; and so on. Of the four, only Leoni was actually picked from the nationwide casting call. The others are models with minor acting backgrounds.

The angels spend a carefully timed five minutes with the press before they are whisked off for a lengthy photo session for *Time*. The stage mike is turned over to Aaron Spelling, creator of some of the most lucrative programmes in television history. 'How's this show going to be different from *Charlie's Angels*?' a reporter asks. 'These young ladies are on their own; they do not report to any men,' Spelling says. 'It's an entire ladies' show without guidance. It's a young ladies' buddy-buddy show is what it is.' He turns a beseeching face on his audience. 'Why, why,' he wants to know, would anyone think that he wants to bring back 'the beautiful bimbos'? He shakes his head. 'It's going to be a show of today's young ladies of today [*sic*], and we'll go into their personal lives, we'll treat today's issues, we'll treat the problems of their dating and sex and safe sex and sex of our time. It's going to be a very attractive show.'

Later that same day in Santa Monica, screenwriter Brad Markowitz rolls his eyes as he hears the details of the press conference. A few months earlier Spelling had hired Markowitz and his writing partner to script the series pilot. 'Spelling made all these fine speeches to us about how "the girls" would be more real,' Markowitz recalls. 'He talked a good game about how the show would be more representative of how women really are, as opposed to that idealized, frosted look.' But when it came down to drafting a script, Markowitz says, Spelling instructed the screenwriters to open the episode with scantily clad angels wriggling to a rock video. Spelling was unhappy with their first draft, Markowitz recalls, because 'we didn't have enough girls in bikinis'; he ordered them to add more bathing-beauty scenes. Spelling also insisted that the thirty-two-year-old police-academy-trained detectives (their original status in *Charlie's Angels*) be demoted to unemployed actresses in their early twenties who just fall into police work and bungle the job. Spelling, who later denies demanding these changes – 'the script just wasn't good enough is all I know' – defended the alterations this way: 'That's what makes the show funny – that they are supposed to be doing it by themselves and they can't! They are incompetent!'

After various delays and script battles, *Angels '88* was put on hold, then reformatted as a 'telefilm', in which, Spelling says, the women will be even younger college 'co-eds'. Meanwhile, for the 1988–89 season, Spelling applied his 'young ladies' buddy-buddy show' concept to *Nightingales*, an NBC prime-time series about five jiggly student nurses who prance around the locker room in their underwear. While they aren't independent, their boss is a woman, Spelling says proudly – as if a female head nurse represents non-traditional casting.

Anyway, as Spelling pointed out at the *Angels* press conference, at least his shows have women in lead roles. 'Go and look at television today. Tell me how many shows outside of a few comedies are dominated by women. You'll find the answer is very few.'

True enough. In America in the 1987–88 season, the backlash's high-watermark on TV, only three of twenty-two new prime-time dramas featured female leads – and only two of them were adults. One was a co-ed and another a nubile private eye who spent much of her time posing and complaining about the dating scene. (The title of that show, *Leg Work*, speaks for itself.) In a sharp drop-off from previous seasons, 60 per cent of the shows launched as series in this season had either no regular female characters or included women only as minor background figures; 20 per cent had no women at all. And women over the age of consent were especially hard to find. Women were also losing ground in the one television genre they had always called their own: situation comedy. In a resurgence of the old *Odd Couple* format, bachelor buddies took up house together without adult women in one out of five new sitcoms, a list that included *Everything's Relative*, *My Two Dads*, *Trial and Error* and *Full House*. In Britain, the backlash on television was not so marked but even so, some of the most popular light entertainment programmes, like *Minder* and *Only Fools and Horses*, and dramas like *Inspector Morse*, relegated women to secondary status, with pairs of male buddies dominating the scene. On Australian television, network executives were less interested in reflecting social realism, in a country where 83 per cent of sole parents are women, than in promoting the comfortable image of fatherhood projected in *Hey Dad* – in which the only constant adult female is a dizzy secretary.

Women's disappearance from American prime-time television in the late 1980s repeats a programming pattern from the last backlash when, in the late 1950s and early 1960s, single dads ruled the TV roosts and female characters were suddenly erased from the set. By the 1960 season, only two of the top-ten rated shows had regular female characters – *Gunsmoke* and *Real McCoys* – and by 1962 the one woman on *Real McCoys* had been killed off, too. The vanishing act eventually spread to domestic dramas, where the single father took charge of the household on *Bachelor Father*, *My Three Sons*, *Family Affair* and *The Andy Griffith Show*.

In the 1980s women began to shrink and dwindle in the 1985–86 season, as a new breed of action-adventure series that included women only as victimized girls began crowding out more balanced fare. In this new crop of programmes, as uneasy critics commented at the time, the viciousness of the assaults on the young female characters rivalled slasher films. On *Lady Blue*, for example, teenage boys armed with scalpels eviscerate their female prey; on *Our Family Honor* a seventeen-year-old girl is slashed to death with a coat-hanger. And that season, female characters who weren't under attack were likely to be muzzled or missing from action: an analysis of prime-time American TV in 1987 found 66 per cent of the 882 speaking characters were male – about the same proportion as in the 1950s.

While the new male villains were busy pulverizing women, male heroes on continuing series were toughening their act. The 'return of the hard-boiled male,' *New York Times* television writer Peter Boyer dubbed it in an article on the phenomenon. In *St Elsewhere*, the affable Dr Caldwell was recast as an unapologetic womanizer. In *Moonlighting* the immature hireling of the elegantly confident Maddie Hayes now overshadowed his boss lady – and cut her down to size. Network executives even instructed Tom Selleck to get more masculine on *Magnum P.I.* And the networks continued to boost their macho output; of the ten new dramas unveiled in the autumn of 1989, five were about male cops or cowboys, with such self-explanatory titles as *Nasty Boys* and *Hardball*. The latter show's première made it clear who would be on the receiving – and losing – end of this game. In the début episode, a homicidal and evil female cop is beaten into submission by the male hero – a scene that re-enacts the climactic confrontation in *Fatal Attraction*. (He holds her head under water in the bathroom and tries to drown her.)

If TV programmers had their reasons for bringing on the hemen, popular demand wasn't among them. In audience surveys, TV viewers show the *least* interest in police dramas and westerns. Nonetheless, Brandon Tartikoff, president of entertainment at NBC, asserted in the *New York Times* that the TV men were turning brutish because 'the audience' was sick of male 'wimps' and 'Alan Alda-esque heroes who wore their sensitivity on their shirtsleeves'; as proof, he pointed not to real people but to the outpouring of macho movies – yet another case of the makers of one cultural medium invoking another's handiwork to reinforce the backlash. Glenn Gordon Caron, producer of *Moonlighting*, admitted to more personal motives in an interview in the *New York Times*: 'I very much wanted to see a *man* on television.' He complained that the last decade of social change had elbowed his sex off the screen. '[For] a long time, men just sort of went away,' he grumbled; one could only tell the gender of these ineffectual guys 'because their voices were lower and their chests were flatter'. Glen Charles, co-producer of *Cheers*, was even blunter: he turned his show's bartender Sam into a chauvinistic womanizer because 'he's a spokesman for a large group of people who thought that [the women's movement] was a bunch of bull and look with disdain upon people who don't think it was.'

The backlash on television would to a degree follow the film industry's lead. *Fatal Attraction* became ABC's *Obsessive Love* a year later; *Baby Boom* became a television series of the same name; *Working Girl*, *Parenthood* and *Look Who's Talking* all resurfaced as American TV series; the western returned to the big screen and the small set. The same backlash trends were recycled, from single women panicking at the man shortage to career women swooning with baby fever. But TV's counterassault on women would be, by necessity, more restrained than Hollywood's. Women have more influence in front of their sets than they do at the movies; women represent not only the majority of viewers but, more important, they represent the viewers that advertisers most want to reach.

As Sue Phipps pointed out in her 1991 paper, *A Woman's Place?*, for the UK's Advertising Association, 70 per cent of consumer spending is by women, and their purchasing influence is rapidly expanding into fields outside the conventionally female ones. Nevertheless, the advertising industry is still predominantly male, especially at a senior level. The emancipation of the housewife during the 1970s has led to some superficial changes in television advertising, including the arrival of the working mother – even if her hopeless brood are left to cook themselves a frozen dinner because she is late coming home. The most memorable working woman to appear in a recent British TV advert has been the star of the longrunning Nescafé saga, and in these ads the single 'career' woman – who, unlike her male counterpart, is rarely shown actually working – is arch, provocative, and ultimately available. In late 1991 her standoffishness disappeared, along with her power suit, and she breathed down the phone to her coffee-drinking sparring partner (who sat up naked from rumpled sheets to take the call), 'I want you . . . now.'

The majority of complaints to the Independent Television Commission about TV advertisements were again in 1991 about the representation of women: whether in stereotypical or traditional domestic roles, as being helpless or weak, sex objects, or the butts of misogynist jokes. A very small number of complaints were about the portrayal of men – and one of these was a protest at the overly macho image of men in the Castlemaine 'Four X' lager ad. A 1986 study of 175 evening adverts over a seven-day period underlined the stereotyping of British men and women, finding that male characters were much more likely to be authorities offering factual arguments in favour of the product (which was usually not domestic), and female characters were much more likely to be shown as consumers in family and domestic settings, associated with personal, household and food products. Women, too, were likely to be *visually* presented and to remain silent while men provided authoritative-sounding voiceovers. The ITC received a number of complaints about Prudential's 1991 'I want to be . . . ' advert, featuring female professional and personal aspirations, which closed with a male voiceover. A 1990 Broadcasting Standards Council survey found that twice as many men as women were featured in TV ads, and women were consistently shown in decorative rather than professional roles. The women shown were also younger than the men, with half being between twenty-one and thirty compared with only 30 per cent of men who were in that age group.

Perhaps the 1991 British Gas advert starring Burt Reynolds best illustrated the ways in which backlash thinking can employ humour to disguise its real agenda, and thus have it both ways. Burly Burt asks the blonde lying on the hearthrug to go and get more coal for the fire (which of course is not a real one), implying that she is stupid enough to be fooled. 'Yes, honey,' she simpers, but instead picks up the fire tongs and makes what looks like an assault on him from the rear. The slogan for the ad, delivered by a smug-looking Reynolds as he creates a flame with an easy flick of the thumb, is the half-ironic, 'Don't you just *love* being in control!' But despite the jokiness, he *is* in control – the woman's protest is limited to a wordless gesture of defiance with sexual overtones, while he remains the strong, macho central figure entitled to order her to do his bidding.

In the UK, unlike the US, women have been partly successful in fighting the backlash tide on television, with producers like Verity Lambert, Sarah Radclyffe, Philippa Giles (producer of *Oranges Are Not the Only Fruit*) and Sophie Balhetchet (producer of *The Manageress*) responsible for some of the most interesting and innovative programmes of the decade. Popular TV series such as *Widows* and *Making Out* (which starred Margi Clarke) offered strong roles for independent women. Towards the end of the 1980s, the American networks, too, admitted a couple of strong female leads to the prime-time scene. *Roseanne* and *Murphy Brown* both featured outspoken women and both – not coincidentally, created by women – became instant and massive hits: *Roseanne* was one of the most successful series launched in television history and held the number-one ratings slot in the US season after season. But two strong women were seen as two too many. Independent women were 'seizing control of prime time', *Newsweek* griped in a 1989 cover story. 'The video pendulum has swung too far from the blissfully domestic supermoms who once warmed the electronic hearth.' Behind the scenes, the network tried to make changes that amounted to 'taking all the stuffing out of Murphy,' the show's creator Diane English observed. The tart-tongued Roseanne Barr especially became a lightning rod for that rancour. While her penchant for mooning crowds and singing the national anthem off-key clearly warrants no Miss Congeniality prizes, the level of bile and hysteria directed at this comic seemed peculiarly out of proportion to her offences. The media declared her, just like the *Fatal Attraction* temptress, 'the most hated woman in America'; television executives savaged her in print; her former executive producer even took out a full-page ad in *Daily Variety* to deride the comedian; and, despite critical acclaim and spectacular ratings, *Roseanne* was shut out of the Emmys year after year after year. Outside the network suites, a chorus of male voices joined the Barr-bashing crusade. Sports writers, baseball players and news columnists damned her in print as a 'bitch' and a 'dog'. Even George Bush felt compelled to issue a condemnatory statement; he called her 'disgraceful'. (And later he told the troops in the Middle East that he would like to make her a secret weapon against Iraq.) Businessman James Rees, the son of the former congressman, launched a nationwide 'Bar Roseanne Club', soliciting members in the classified sections of *Rolling Stone* and *The National*. ('Hate Roseanne Barr?' the ad copy inquired. 'Join the club.') In a few weeks he had more than 600 responses, almost all from men who thoroughly agreed with Rees's assessment of 'old lard butt'. She's 'a nasty filthy ugly Jell-O-Bodied tasteless monster from the black lagoon,' wrote one man. Another proposed, 'Let's shish-Kebab [her].'

By the following season, prime time reverted to traditional feminine icons, as the new series filled the screen with teenage models, housewives, a nun and – that peculiar prototype of the last TV backlash – the good suburban housekeeper witch. An updated version of the tamed genie of *Bewitched* reappeared in the ironically named *Free Spirit*. By the next season women were shut out of so many new shows that even comic Jay Leno joked about it at the Emmys. TV critic Joyce Millman, observing that the new offerings were 'overloaded with adolescent boys and motherless households', asked 'Whatever happened to TV's "Year of the Woman"? . . . [I]t's back to "Boys' Night Out" for the upcoming fall season.' Only two of thirty-three new American shows were about women with jobs; on the rest they were housewives, little girls or invisible.

The lurching quality of television's backlash against independent women is the product of the industry's own deeply ambivalent affair with its female audience. TV prime-time programmers are both more dependent on women's approval than filmmakers and, because of their dependence, more resentful. Female viewers consistently give their highest ratings to non-traditional female characters, such as leaders, heroines and comedians. But to serve a female master is not why the TV men came west to Hollywood. (And most are men; more than 90 per cent of television writers, for example, are white males.) They say they want shows that draw a large audience, but when those shows feature autonomous women, they constantly interfere, undermine the independent female characters, or simply cancel the shows. In the US, *Designing Women* and *Kate and Allie*, both tremendously popular series, have fought back repeated network attempts to chase them off the set.

Even in countries like Britain where the backlash on television was not nearly so crudely enforced, women screenwriters still ran into difficulties when they tried to show women from a different perspective than the men with whom they generally had to work. *Tenko*, a top-rating BBC drama series about a group of British women interned by the Japanese during the Second World War, was conceived by a woman, Lavinia Warner, and represented, according to Jill Hyem who co-scripted it with Anne Valery, 'a heaven-sent chance for two women writers to explore a variety of female characters in depth and to dispel some of the clichés of past war dramas'. But the two producers, five directors and the original script editor appointed to the series were all male, as were the designers, the composer, and even the person in charge of publicity. It was not thought that a woman writer could 'handle the military side' and a man was commissioned to write the first two episodes which dealt with the fall of Singapore before the women reached the camp. *Tenko* was not expected – except by Lavinia Warner and the two screenwriters – to be a big success, as a group of mostly middle-aged women not looking their best was thought to have limited appeal. But *Tenko*'s impact was such that it ran for three series and a Christmas special, and was sold and repeated all over the world.

During the making of *Tenko* the women writers ran into 'unconscious male censorship of our work' and would find dialogue or scenes regarded as 'unfeminine' softened. A scene between two of the central characters set in the comparative privacy of the latrine was relocated to a more 'acceptable' environment – the cookhouse. Bad language or crude jokes were similarly edited out, and the writers had constantly to protest in order to save their lines. When Jill Hyem wanted to write in a story about a relationship developing between two of the younger women, 'the idea was rejected out of hand. I was told that if we introduced such a subject the characters concerned would lose audience sympathy.' Only after a struggle was Jill Hyem allowed to write her story, provided she never used the word 'lesbian'. Audience figures did not plummet; neither did the two characters lose popularity.

During another series that Jill Hyem wrote for, the BBC's *Howard's Way*, the all-male team with whom she was working 'saw the hero's "strength" (i.e. audience appeal) in terms of his physical superiority and his ability to "rule the roost". If I gave him an introspective scene I was told he was "spineless" or "wet". If he expressed the same sentiments while shouting and slamming his fist on the table he was showing "guts".' It is perhaps these differences in attitude, even where women *have* been given work in television drama series, that endanger women's progress in the industry. Hyem reports that Arline Whittacker's successful sitcom *Sharon and Elsie* was dropped because 'the new man up there didn't like it' – even though it had gone to two series, had impressive ratings, a good audience reaction and was expected to continue.

Even in so-called 'women's programmes' like the soaps – which in Britain, and to some extent Australia, attempt to reflect, unlike in America, a 'true' picture of day-to-day life, the ratio of women to men writers is not always favourable. A survey conducted by the Writers' Guild in 1985 showed that the long-running soap operas in the UK were still dominated by male writers: *Coronation Street* had seven men, no women; *Emmerdale Farm*, three men, no women; and *Crossroads*, three men and one woman. By contrast, *EastEnders* and *Brookside* both employed a consistently high number of women writers, which may explain, Hyem suggests, why some of the most 'truthful' female characters are to be found in these two serials.

A 1987 European Commission report on images of women in television programmes across the EEC found that in twenty-nine episodes of series or serials studied – which covered fifteen British productions including *All Creatures Great and Small* and *A Fine Romance*, as well as French, German, Dutch, Belgian, Danish and Italian programmes – two-thirds of the female characters were shown in a 'family' role and only one-sixth as engaged in any work. By contrast, almost half the male characters were shown at work. Over a third of all the female characters were seen in romantic roles, whereas the corresponding figure for men was 6.8 per cent.

Jane Aldridge at the Independent Television Commission in London has carried out research into the possible harmful effects television's portrayal of women may have on men's perceptions of real women in real life. Asked whether any of the following – adverts depicting women in seductive or domestic roles; sexist jokes by TV comics; short-skirted female assistants on game shows; dramas or thrillers where a woman is the victim of a sex attack or murder; and series where female characters are in subservient roles to men, for example as their secretaries – contribute to men viewing women in ways women do not like, the female respondents said that they did with markedly stronger emphasis, in all cases, than the male respondents. It may be a long time yet before the men who control television programming and advertising take these views into account.

As the eighties television backlash against independent women proceeded in fits and starts from season to season, a few shows managed to survive its periodic surges – *L.A. Law* and *The Golden Girls* are two examples. But overall, it succeeded in depopulating TV of its healthy independent women and replacing them with nostalgia-glazed portraits of apolitical 'family' women. This process worked its way through television entertainment in two stages. First, in the early 1980s it banished feminist issues. Then, in the mid-1980s, it reconstructed a 'traditional' female hierarchy, placing suburban housewives at the top, career women on the lower rungs and single women at the very bottom.

From Consciousness-Raising to Cheerleading

For a brief period in the mid-1970s America's prime-time television's domestic series tackled political issues – and with them, a whole range of feminist subjects. They weren't just restricted to single 'issue' episodes; discussions about women's rights were woven into the series' weekly fabric. The Bunkers argued about women's liberation constantly in *All in the Family*, Maude openly discussed abortion and, on *The Mary Tyler Moore Show*, Lou Grant's wife, Edie, went to consciousness-raising sessions and eventually left her husband.

By 1978, these programmes had all been cancelled; and the few programmers who tried to sell the networks programmes with feminist themes encountered fierce resistance. In 1980 Esther Shapiro, ABC's vice-president for mini-series (one of the few women ever to attain such a post), tried to interest her male colleagues in a script based on Marilyn French's novel *The Women's Room*. The script's author had come to Shapiro after CBS had turned her down. 'It was terrific,' Shapiro recalls. 'And I thought, this is something we have to get on television.' It also seemed like a guaranteed hit. The book was a huge bestseller; women had loved the story of the liberated housewife who leaves home.

But convincing the network turned into what Shapiro recalls as 'the most gruelling experience' of her career. The men were monolithic in their opposition. No matter what argument she used, 'all I got back was an absolute no,' she says. Not only would they personally stonewall the idea, they assured her, no advertiser would touch the feminist-tainted subject matter either. Shapiro launched a campaign on the show's behalf, sending telegrams to the most recalcitrant executives, even hanging signs on the men's lavatory door that read WOMEN'S ROOM. But the men just responded with the ratings argument: 'They said it wouldn't get more than an eleven share,' she says. 'They treated it like its audience was a minority, which seemed strange to me. I mean, women *are* fifty-four per cent of the population.'

Finally, she persuaded the network's executives to run *The Women's Room* simply to set off another show that they were very eager to air, a stock sexploitation number called *Dallas Cowboy Cheerleaders*. The network men agreed but instructed her to shrink *The Women's Room* from a mini-series to a one-night special. And the network's Standards and Practices division insisted that the programme should be aired with a disclaimer assuring viewers the show was set in the past and not meant to be relevant to current times. When such right-wing groups as Reverend Donald Wildmon's National Federation of Decency heard that ABC would be dramatizing this women's liberation drama, they inundated the network with boycott threats, and advertisers cancelled all but four minutes of the fourteen minutes' worth of commercial spots. Nonetheless, *The Women's Room* was finally aired, and it received a huge 45 share (the highest-rated movie on TV that week), prompted a flood of positive mail, and won an Emmy.

Feminist television writers Barbara Corday and Barbara Avedon got caught in the first waves of the backlash, too. They figured they had an original concept when they first drafted *Cagney and Lacey*: two strong, mature and fully formed female characters, one single, one married, who are partners on the police force. 'The original script was kind of an outrageous boisterous comedy; we even had a ring of male prostitutes,' Corday recalls. 'What we were trying to do was turn everything around to a feminist point of view.' But even after Corday toned down the script and brought on her husband, influential producer Barney Rosenzweig, to pitch it, *Cagney and Lacey* took six years to sell. They were turned down everywhere: movie studios, independent production companies, the networks.

Rosenzweig recalls hearing the same complaint wherever he went: 'These women aren't soft enough. These women aren't feminine enough.' The Hollywood executives were even upset that the women used 'dirty words', even though it was nothing more than a few damns and hells. As he struck out again and again, Rosenzweig recalls, '[Barbara] Corday said to me, "The women's movement is going to pass me by [before the show gets sold]."' She wasn't far wrong.

CBS executives finally decided to air *Cagney and Lacey* as a television movie in 1981. When it received a smash-hit 42 share, the network agreed to produce the series. Rosenzweig cast Meg Foster to play the single woman. After two episodes, CBS executives cancelled the show, claiming bad ratings. Rosenzweig convinced them to give the show another try – but they complained that the women were 'too tough' and Foster, especially, wasn't sufficiently genteel and would have to go. 'I said I can't review the show unless we have a casting change,' Harvey Shephard, then senior vice-president of programming, recalls. 'Meg Foster came across in this role as being masculine,' CBS vice-president Arnold Becker explains later. 'Mind you, they were policemen, and the notion of women policemen is not easily acceptable.' Rosenzweig replaced her with the blonde Sharon Gless.

Still the network programmers weren't satisfied. CBS executives were obsessed with the single-woman character, pestering the show's writers with endless demands to enhance her feminity, soften her rhetoric and appearance, make her more respectably 'high class'. An additional $15,000 was budgeted for 'classier clothes', her feminism muted, and a genteel Westchester County upbringing added to her family background.

The CBS executives were especially distressed by the character's varied romantic encounters. 'Cagney's sexual habits were constantly under scrutiny, not only by the network but by the head of programming,' Rosenzweig says. 'I would say, "You don't mind when Magnum P.I. has sex," and he would say, "That's different." That Cagney slept with someone cheapened her, he thought.' Shephard, CBS's programming chief, says he was worried that she would 'come off as promiscuous', which would be a problem because then she wouldn't be 'a positive role model'. CBS executive Becker explains the anxiety and interference over Cagney's behaviour in this way: 'Well [Lacey], she was married, and so they did have occasion to show her in her home being tender. But [Cagney] was single so that opportunity was not there, so it became more difficult to portray her as being vulnerable.' And why did she need to be portrayed as vulnerable? 'Because that's the way the vast majority of Americans feel women should be. . . . I wonder how many men there are in the US today who'd be anxious to marry a hard-boiled female cop.' Becker then notes, somewhat sheepishly, that 'my daughter might kill me for saying that.' She is a lawyer, he says, and such an 'extreme feminist' that she actually corrects him when he refers to grown women as 'girls'.

The network really clamped down on episodes that centred on feminist issues. On one segment that dealt with the Equal Rights Amendment, Rosenzweig wanted to ask feminist leader Gloria Steinem to play a bit part. As appalled as if the show's creators had selected Son of Sam for a cameo, executives in the network's Standards and Practices division barred her appearance. Then several affiliates cancelled the whole episode anyway, a few hours before air time, contending that the women's rights subject matter would offend female viewers.

An even greater furore erupted over an episode in which Cagney was to become pregnant and consider whether to have an abortion. The script provided that she would miscarry in the closing scene so she would never actually have to make the decision, but this was still too unsavoury for CBS programming executives. Finally, the show's writers reworked the script to duck the whole issue. In the final version, 'Choices', Cagney only mistakenly thinks she is pregnant. Lacey chastises her for not behaving more responsibly – and tells her that if she *had* been pregnant she should have got married. Abortion is never offered as a choice.

In a later episode, about the bombing of an abortion clinic, the network's broadcast standards officials sent Rosenzweig a three-page single-spaced memo 'filled with thou-shalt-nots,' he recalls. They were especially upset that both women on the show were supporting a woman's right to an abortion. Rosenzweig pointed out, to no avail, that the script was simply reflecting working women's views in the real world, where 70 per cent are pro-choice. Meanwhile outside the network, as soon as word leaked out about the upcoming episode, anti-abortion protestors mobilized and picketed local affiliates around the country. The controversy ended up on national talk shows and radio programmes.

The network's executives said they were meddling with the show's content only out of concern for female viewers, who might feel 'intimidated' by working women like Cagney and Lacey. Rosenzweig told them: "'I've got four thousand fan letters on my desk from women who don't seem intimidated. What's your research?" They didn't have any.' (In fact, the evidence in Becker's own living room pointed in the other direction. His wife, who had been a housewife for thirty-five years, was a 'big fan' of the show, he admits.) It was the CBS male programmers, not female viewers, who were uncomfortable with the two strong women of *Cagney and Lacey*. Becker complained at the time that the show's women were 'inordinately abrasive, loud, and lacking warmth'. Another CBS executive told *TV Guide* that the heroines 'were too harshly women's lib. . . . These women on *Cagney and Lacey* seemed more intent on fighting the system than doing police work. We perceived them as dykes.'

Ultimately, the show's staff tried to save the show by disavowing its own politics. For public consumption, they began denying that the show had any feminist content – even though the show regularly took feminist positions on employment discrimination, sexual harassment, domestic violence, women's health and prostitution. *Cagney and Lacey* producer April Smith assured the press that the show's crew had 'no desire to turn it into a women's lib vehicle'. On a talk show, the show's co-star, Sharon Gless, asserted that *Cagney and Lacey* was *not* a 'feminist' show because that label was too 'limiting'. When a women's studies scholar wrote in with some questions about the show's stance on women, she received a chilly letter from the show's appreciation club director, informing her, 'We do not wish to be involved in discussing our views on feminism.'

Recantation, however, wasn't enough to appease the network. In 1983, CBS cancelled *Cagney and Lacey*. After tens of thousands of letters poured in from loyal viewers (an avalanche outstripping the last leading fan-mail recall campaign, for *Lou Grant*, by ten to one), after Tyne Daly (Lacey) won the Emmy for best dramatic actress, and after the show scored number one in the ratings during summer *re-runs*, the network backed off and put the show back on the air. The programme went on to win five more Emmys, including best dramatic series. Nonetheless, in the autumn of 1987, CBS pulled *Cagney and Lacey* from its regular time and reassigned it to a doomed time slot. By the following season, *Cagney and Lacey* was gone for good.

Nesters and Patriarchs

'Nesting will be a crucial theme this year for returning shows,' America's *TV Guide* announced at the start of the 1988 autumn season, an observation that turned out to be something of an understatement. On prime-time series from *Cheers* to *Designing Women* to *L.A. Law*, dozens of female characters succumbed to 'baby craving', charged off to infertility clinics, and even gave birth on air. One show fed off another's fever. *Thirtysomething* devoted an entire episode to a delivery. Then, on the season première of *L.A. Law* the expectant mother discussed this *thirty-something* birth sequence in her Lamaze class. That same night, on *Cheers*, another mum went into labour. And that same week, on *The Cosby Show*, the men fantasized that *they* were pregnant.

The birthing festival itself was benign enough, if a little monotonous. But the networks weren't just bringing on the babies; they were bringing back regressive fantasies about motherhood and marriage. TV programmers began recycling their childhood memories of 1950s television; before long, 'retroprogramming', as it was dubbed, ruled the airwaves. The networks brought back 1950s television quite literally, with a deluge of re-runs and 'new' fare like *The New Leave It to Beaver*, *The New Newlywed Game*, and *The New Dating Game*, none of which exactly offered progressive views of womanhood. At the same time, the networks revived the fifties family shows more subtly, inside a modern shell. On a few of the programmes, the mothers ostensibly had jobs, but their employment is in title only. The wife in *The Cosby Show* may be the first attorney to hold down a full-time job without leaving home; when she does ply her trade, it's only to litigate domestic disputes in the family living room. These women are the same old TV housewives with their housecoats doffed, their 'careers' a hollow nod to the profound changes in women's lives.

The Cosby Show may present a black family, but it was the show's presentation of the nuclear family more than its racial make-up that network executives – and Ronald Reagan, one of its most loyal fans – found so appealing. 'Bill Cosby brought masculinity back to sitcoms,' NBC entertainment president Brandon Tartikoff told the press. In episode after episode, Cosby's Dr Heathcliff Huxtable – who is, appropriately, an obstetrician – reasserts his role as family potentate, quelling all insubordination with his genial but authoritarian voice. Political concerns are absent; teaching children to obey dad is the show's primary mission. Some typical 'issues' examined in this upper-middle-class family: a daughter's reluctance to change out of a party dress and a son's five-minute tardiness from basketball practice. 'I do believe in control,' Cosby told *Time*. He also believed in a 'traditional' division of domestic duties, judging by the advice he dispensed to men in his 1980s bestseller, *Fatherhood*. 'You see, the wives *pretend* to turn over the child-raising job to us fathers, but they don't really mean it,' Cosby assured male readers.

Other nesting shows escaped the world of working women by retreating to fantasy countrysides. In shows like *Blue Skies* and *Just the Ten of Us*, dad packs the family in the station wagon and heads for a 'better' life in rural America – where mum can stay at home with a full litter of children and dad can return to sole-earner status. More than one of these TV families heads to Amish country, where women don't work outside the home. Here the bad city women learn 'old-world' values. On *Aaron's Way*, for example, an Amish aunt gives a pregnant girl a stern lecture on the virtues of female sacrifice; the reluctant teenager finally faces up to her 'responsibilities' and agrees to have the baby. The men on these shows, meanwhile, regain their brawn: they are featured chopping wood, renovating old water mills, and joining other strapping country fellows to build a barn.

The pastoral retreat might be interpreted as a mild rebellion against the capitalist rat race – though the characters' homes are cluttered with enough consumer goods to assure advertisers that the revolt is not serious. But the march to the country is more forcefully a repudiation of American women's changed standing in the work force. And typically in the nesting shows, it's the housewife who serves as mouthpiece for the programmes' periodic anti-career-women tirades. Like late 1980s filmmakers, prime-time programmers resurrected the catfight. In *Just the Ten of Us* the stay-at-home wife blasts 'a rabble-rousing feminist'. She proves that she's more of a woman for having stayed at home, even if it does mean her poorly paid husband, a gym teacher at a Catholic school, must serve as solitary breadwinner for the overflowing household. A similar homage to the housewife at the career woman's expense occurs in *Family Man*. A nasty female lawyer asks the homemaking heroine how she can bear to stay at home all day; that evening in bed with her husband, the housewife dramatizes the sort of tongue-lashing she'd like to give that career woman: 'You are an idiot! You are a jerk! You big, fat yuppie phoney!' Then she bursts into tears and, gazing up at her husband's benevolent visage, whimpers, 'You don't care that I'm just a housewife?' He beams back. 'I love it, I love it,' he assures her.

At the same time that 1980s TV was busy saluting the domestic angels of 1950s TV, it was maligning mothers who dared step outside the family circle. The quest of the liberated wife who leaves home in *Raising Miranda* is reduced to a pathetic joke. Mum ran away after attending a 'self-improvement workshop', snickers Miranda, the superior daughter, an adolescent who becomes the dutiful surrogate mum to her macho blue-collar father. Her abundant housekeeping skills serve as a not-so-subtle rebuke of delinquent mum who, Miranda tells us disparagingly, 'couldn't do a load of laundry'. On *Blossom*, another deserted daughter is similarly disgusted with her indulgent mother. 'She's supposed to be in the kitchen, waiting for me after school,' she decrees, not 'on the road, fulfilling her needs.' Even in the UK, in *Coronation Street*, where some of the regular women characters were allowed to populate the local factory (albeit using the traditional female skill of running sewing machines), Deirdre Barlow became a progressively less sympathetic character and 'good mother' the more her interest in local council politics and activity outside the home grew. Ultimately she degenerated into a shrew, and her marriage disintegrated.

In America, even shows with a supposedly more enlightened mission couldn't resist slamming the working mother. When television producer Gary David Goldberg unveiled *Day by Day*, a series about a family-based childcare centre, he said the show would offer a rarity – a positive view of day care on prime-time television. Yet the show was unrelievedly contemptuous of its working mothers. Neurotic and inept, the show's career mums bumble into the centre each morning, thrusting their tots into the arms of its holier-than-thou directors – a husband and wife team who congratulate each other every five minutes for sacrificing *their* Wall Street careers to care for these negligent mothers' offspring.

The Single Lady Vanishes

'Single-woman leads don't work on hour-long dramatic television,' Scott Siegler, CBS vice-president for drama development, informed sociologist Todd Gitlin in the early 1980s. By the end of the decade American TV listings would suggest that the networks hardly believed single-woman leads worked at all.

The eviction of TV's single women repeats a pattern established in television's last backlash. Early television actually offered quite a number of single-woman shows, although most featured hapless schoolmistresses, maids and typists in such fare as *Private Secretary* and *Meet Millie*. By the mid-1950s, however, every programme with a single woman in the lead had been cancelled. And the unwed heroine would remain out of sight throughout the early and mid-1960s, appearing only as an incidental character, a reminder to female viewers of the woes of unwed life. On *The Dick Van Dyke Show*, single Sally Rogers served to throw into relief the good fortunes and greater femininity of Van Dyke's doted-upon housewife played by Mary Tyler Moore. In the many doctor and hospital shows of the 1960s single women surfaced only as patients, their illnesses typically caused by some 'selfish' act – getting an abortion, having an affair or, most popular, disobeying a doctor's orders.

But in 1970 Mary Tyler Moore traded in the Van Dyke doll's house for her own apartment and show. Moore's Mary Richards was not only unwed, she was more than thirty years old. Marriage panic did not afflict her. She had real male and female friends, enjoyed a healthy sex life, turned down men who didn't appeal to her, and even took the pill – without winding up in a hospital bed in the final scene. (She was, however, still the subordinated pseudo-schoolgirl to her boss; while her office mates called their chief 'Lou', she always said 'Mr Grant'.) Female viewers adored her. The programme maintained top ratings for its entire run, won twenty-five Emmys, and spun off two other successful sitcoms with independent female leads. Meanwhile, other programmers got the message and drafted their own shows about strong and independent unmarried women, from the realistic in *One Day at a Time*, to the superhuman in *The Bionic Woman*.

In 1986, a decade after her previous triumph, the networks returned Mary Tyler Moore to prime time – as a burned-out scowling divorcée whose career is only an object of derision. In *Mary*, she writes the consumer helpline column for a trashy tabloid. She has no confidantes on or off the job, a fact that heightens an already bleakly drawn existence. Next door, her earthy best friend Rhoda is replaced by a narcissistic single career woman, an ad executive who is desperate for a ring from any man. In one episode the neighbour meets a mobster – and announces her engagement the same day.

Moore's neighbour was not the only single television woman willing to lower her expectations in the quest for a marriage licence. Under pressure from the network, the creators of *Kate and Allie* married off divorced mother Allie to a colourless suitor she had known only a short time. That same season, on *Moonlighting*, a pregnant Maddie Hayes got hitched to a dishwater-dull accountant right after they met on a train. Cybill Shepherd, who played Maddie, was adamantly opposed to this plot twist, and viewers were similarly disgusted. The show was swamped with so many outraged letters that the producers finally had to annul the marriage.

Maddie's coerced matrimony was only the latest development in a long-running campaign to cow this independent female figure. David Addison, a carefree bachelor and Maddie's employer, ulti-mately tames his 'queen bee' boss the old-fashioned way; he slaps her, and she surrenders to his advances. Still not satisfied, the series' producers later have her grovel before the preening David, literally on her knees. The shaming of Maddie Hayes was no idle writing exercise. It mirrored a behind-the-scenes campaign, conducted by both executive producer Glenn Caron and actor Bruce Willis (who played David), to curb the single Shepherd's 'aggressive' personality. They told the press they didn't like the way she was always voicing her opinion when she disagreed with the show's direction. At Caron's behest, the network sent Shepherd a disciplinary letter. The memo ordered her, on penalty of legal action or the show's cancellation, to follow the director's orders, submit to timed breaks, and ask for permission before leaving the set. 'I felt ill when I received it,' Shepherd said at the time. 'It was like reform school.'

While TV generally presented single women's stampede to the altar as their 'choice', the story lines sometimes revealed their underlying agenda – to serve as wish-fulfilment for single men.

The show *Murder, She Wrote* (which, despite its name, had no female writers, producers or directors in 1987) offered one such transparent tale in a 1988 episode about the marital redemption of a single professional woman. Jilted by a female careerist, boyfriend Grady takes to the bar. Well, maybe it's for the best, he decides. 'I want a traditional girl.' A fellow drinker pipes up: 'Is she a career woman?' When Grady nods, the guy gives him a knowing look: 'Yeah, you give 'em a briefcase and they take your pants.' By the end of the episode the career woman (an accountant) recants and comes running to Grady for absolution. 'I don't want to be an accountant,' she cries. 'I just want to be your wife.' A pleased Grady concludes, 'I think everything's going to work out just fine.'

The matrimonial imperative was not limited to prime time; on daytime American soap operas, where wedding bells always rang frequently, the marriage rate climbed still higher, and the divorce rate fell. 'Ten years ago, we might have broken them up,' Mary Alice Dwyer-Dobbin, ABC's vice-president of daytime programming, says of soap opera's warring unmarried couples. 'Now the writers have been challenged to come up with new and inventive story lines that create conflict but don't break the core characters apart.' Why? 'Women are returning to the home,' she says. 'It's all part of the pendulum swinging back from the Superwoman era.'

Like the bedridden single patients of 1960s doctor shows, women on the 1980s soaps who resisted the wedding march risked death. In the real world in 1988, 8 per cent of AIDS victims were women. In daytime TV – 100 per cent. On *The Young and the Restless*, AIDS fells a former prostitute who abandons her child to follow her 'profession' – the ultimate in careerism. (She ends up infecting her daughter, too.) In *All My Children* AIDS strikes a divorcée and, her femininity apparently resuscitated on the sickbed, she decides to marry again. Is safe sex exercised in the nuptial bower? This 'socially responsible' soap doesn't say.

With the exception of *Murphy Brown*, the 1980s US prime-time line-up offered almost no shows centred on a single woman in the working world, much less one deriving pleasure or pride from her vocation. The occasional series that were about single women actively involved in their careers, like the lawyer of *Sara*, were typically cancelled after less than a season. The networks only seemed willing to support single-women shows when the heroines were confined to the home in non-threatening roles in a strictly all-female world – like the elderly widows in *The Golden Girls* or the home-based interior decorators of *Designing Women*.

Most of the single women who remained on television in this era were secondary and cautionary characters; like Sally Rogers on *The Dick Van Dyke Show*, their grim circumstances only underlined the good fortune of the leading wife. Relegated to incidental roles, the single women reverted to two stock types: the coldly calculating careerist or the deeply depressed spinster. Either she had no emotions or she was an emotional wreck. The single careerist belonged to the lowest order of females. She had traded in her humanity for a pay cheque, and spurned not only men but children. The mere sight of a baby could make her already frigid body temperature descend to arctic range. 'Oh, babies,' the single stockbroker on *Day by Day* gags as one trundles into her gunsights. 'Unappetizing and at the same time unappealing.' The tear-stained spinster, on the other hand, rated a bit higher on TV's backlash hierarchy of women. She was less intimidating than her professionally ambitious sister; she was too busy weeping to pursue that promotion. She deserved our pity, the shows suggested – though not our respect.

Thirtysomething: Stretch Marks and Stress Disorders

If all the 1980s trend stories about women were collated and fed into a television script machine, the result might be *thirtysomething*, ABC's celebrated 'realistic contemporary drama' about upwardly mobile baby boomers. The topics addressed in this prime-time programme, introduced in the autumn of 1987 to intense media attention, include cocooning, the mummy track, the man shortage and the biological clock. There's even an episode on the downside of no-fault divorce that could be straight out of Lenore Weitzman's *The Divorce Revolution*. In this segment, a nasty lawyer urges the estranged husband to use the new law to sell the house from under his wife and kids. The heartless attorney is, of course, a single career woman.

The creators of *thirtysomething* marketed the show as a thinking person's TV series. But, like the typical trend story, the show's scripts avoided any social or political analysis and pumped moralism into the vacuum. The cautionary tales were, in keeping with the media's trend tradition, aimed exclusively at women. The good mother, Hope Steadman, was bathed in a heavenly light as she floated about the kitchen, rapturous about breast-feeding. Meanwhile, the bad spinsters clutched their barren wombs and circled miserably around the happy Steadman homestead; like the single women of the *New York Times* article, they were 'coping with a void'. The scripts concealed their weekly sermons with progressive-sounding but hollow dialogue and an ironic stance that denied responsibility for its message. The characters mounted a feeble mock struggle against the domestic images of 1950s television, then gladly surrendered to them.

While the press greeted *Roseanne* with suspicion and fat jokes, it gave *thirtysomething* the red-carpet treatment. Talk shows even recruited Mel Harris, the actress who played the good wife, Hope, to instruct its viewers on mothering. Therapists hailed *thirtysomething* in the media and pestered the network for videotaped episodes that they could 'prescribe' to patients. The American Psychological Association gave the show its annual award for endorsing 'the notion of inner thinking'. (Their enthusiastic response made good business sense. As a professor reported in *Redbook*, a survey that he conducted showed that after viewers watch *thirtysomething*, they are more 'inclined to try therapy'.) Clergymen used the show to counsel singles at weekend retreats. Dating services offered *thirtysomething* matchmaking events and *The New Dating Game* promised male contestants with a 'real clean-cut *thirtysomething* look'. Even George Bush referred to the show in a campaign speech.

All this excitement was over a show that never ranked higher than twenty-fifth in the ratings – and slipped steadily in the charts its first season. But in this case, even advertisers didn't mind. They were willing to look the other way because the show rated high in 'quality demographics' – the term used by the television industry for upper-income viewers and the strategy the industry deployed for concealing a shrinking market share. The majority of *thirtysomething* viewers had household incomes that topped $60,000 a year – and, better yet, more than half had a child under the age of three. So businesses that stood to profit from the backlash jumped on the *thirtysomething* bandwagon. Jif peanut butter and Kool-Aid even presented ads with a '*thirtysomething* feel'. The creators of a Canada Dry commercial featuring cocooning couples justified their message by citing the show. How did the ad agency know it was a 'trend' that Americans were retreating to the home? 'Watching that show *thirtysomething*,' Marcia Grace, the ad's creative director at Wells Rich Greene, explains, 'that was real key.'

In *thirtysomething* a complete pantheon of backlash women is on display – from blissful homebound mother to neurotic spinster to ball-busting single career woman. The show even takes a direct shot at the women's movement: the most unsympathetic character is a feminist.

At the top of the *thirtysomething* female ladder, Hope enjoys the view. 'Hope is so hard to write for because she just exists in this glow,' Ann Hamilton, one of the show's writers, says. 'She never does anything, really.' When the show's producers, Ed Zwick and Marshall Herskovitz, drafted the original pilot, they drew up mini-biographies of each character. For the men they wrote down career goals, hobbies and convictions. For Hope Steadman they wrote: 'Hope is married to Michael.'

'I feel guilty,' Hope sighs to her single friends, 'because my life is so full.' Her biggest problem: she discovers her house has a 'borderline' case of radon contamination. Her darkest moment: Michael misplaces their dinner reservation and the movie they wanted to see is sold out. 'Michael,' she tells him, 'last night was the worst Saturday night of my life!'

A former 'overachiever', according to her biography, Hope has surrendered ambition in exchange for a happy family life. This was the right choice, the series hammers home in one episode after another. When Michael, an advertising executive, is having minor money troubles, Hope wonders if she should return to work. 'I earn the money now,' her husband assures her – and anyway, what of their two-year-old daughter, Janey? 'You love her. You don't want to go back to work now.' Apparently, it's not possible to work and still love your children.

Hope reaffirms her cocooning choice in a key episode, entitled 'Weaning', in which she returns part-time to her job as a magazine researcher. She's overwhelmed by the onerous burdens of part-time fact checking; we see her working until 3 a.m. every night. Her husband groans, 'We used to be madly in love.' She apologizes, 'It won't always be like this,' and he tells her, 'Yeah, it will probably be worse.' Hope suspects he's right. And she tells a friend, 'The only thing I've accomplished is being totally exhausted.'

On the job, Hope meets a grasping single career woman – in fact, she's grasping after Hope's job. Hope asks her if she wants to have kids. 'Oh, I don't know,' snaps the woman, 'I'd kind of like to get my game plan going first. . . . I mean I don't even have time for a relationship right now.' That does it; Hope flies from the office and into the arms of husband Michael. She can't do it any more, she tells him tearfully. 'I'm supposed to be able to do both. That's all I hear about.' With a sly smile, Michael confesses that, although he knows it's 'unliberated', he'd rather have her at home, too. Permission granted, Hope hurries homeward, sweeps baby Janey up in her arms and whirls around the nursery. Van Morrison croons 'She's an angel' as the credits roll.

Liberty Godshall wrote the 'Weaning' episode; she is the wife of the show's co-creator, Ed Zwick. A former actress with bit parts on television shows, including *Charlie's Angels*, Godshall grew frustrated with always having to play 'the blonde bimbo girlfriend' and switched to journalism. Then she had a baby and, like Hope, gave up work.

In writing 'Weaning', Godshall says she indeed intended to urge women to stay at home while their children were very young. In fact, Godshall says, the episode made the point *less* strongly than she would have liked. 'I think I probably wanted it to be more a celebration of staying home.' One day in the *thirtysomething* production offices in Studio City, she and her husband explain the development of that episode:

Godshall: 'I wanted to tell women, don't try it – unless, one, you really need to, or you really, really want to. Because, while the successes are there, the failures and the guilt are there, too.'
Zwick: 'What I loved about the episode was it was very deeply written from the inside. . . . It was hormonally written. The feelings had this rawness to them that pleased me. . . . This is a generation of women who, upon their adolescence, suddenly encountered Germaine Greer and Betty Friedan and they were told, "No, no, wrong, wrong. This way. Take a left turn." "Oh, OK," they said, and they did. And what they are discovering upon having the kid itself is there are some extraordinarily strong biological, and not just biological, attachments or bonding that supersede politics and rhetoric.'
Godshall: 'Raising a child is the most difficult thing in the world.'
Zwick: 'The days I've spent an entire day with my son . . . '
Godshall (shooting him a look): 'Not too many.'
Zwick: 'Well, more like taking a four-hour block of time so she could go out.'
Godshall: 'Fifty-fifty, I remember that concept. It was before I had my son. It doesn't seem to be a viable thing any more. . . . I call him [Zwick] Ward. It's like instant sex roles.'

For Melissa, the single and struggling freelance photographer in *thirtysomething*, no instant roles exist – only neurosis and the constant reminder that, as she puts it, 'my biological clock [is] going off.' Melissa is the tear-stained version of the 1980s spinster – more pitiable, and so more likeable, than her careerist single sister.

'Poor Melissa,' her married friends sigh all the time. 'If you were any closer to your feelings, you'd be molesting them,' says the single bachelor Gary, who is of course free of such afflictions himself. Stood up by a blind date on a Saturday night, Melissa tearfully takes a midnight oath by the full moon: 'I swear I will not idolize married people such as Hope and Michael who have their own problems even though I don't know what they are and want to kill them when they complain, especially Hope.'

Mostly Melissa mourns her barren womb. 'I want this baby,'

Melissa moans when in the presence of baby Janey. 'How am I ever going to have a baby?' Soon after, she falls for a gynaecologist, but he already has a child and won't have another, so she leaves him. 'Well, I guess me and my eggs will be moving on,' she says. Later she unsuccessfully recruits the carefree single Gary to play stud. In between, she has a nightmare in which she's trapped on a 'biological clock' game show.

Incredibly, the role as originally conceived by the show's creators was even more extreme. Actress Melanie Mayron, who played Melissa, recalls that when she first auditioned for the role, the producers explained her character this way: 'She was just described as "man-hungry".' Mayron asked them what kind of job she had. 'No one knew. I mean, a single woman in her thirties "man-hungry"? C'mon. That's what you do in your twenties. By your thirties you've got a career, you've got bills to pay; you've got better things to do than read the personals every day.'

Mayron came up with the photography career and pushed for fuller character development and fewer mental afflictions. 'I resent that message of, just because you're a single woman, you must be miserable,' says Mayron, who is single herself. 'That's not like me or any of my friends.'

At least Melissa gets some sympathy on the show. Ellyn, the hard-as-nails single career woman, gets none. Because she cares about her job as a City Hall official, she must forfeit a love life. In her biography, the show's creators describe her as 'a career woman whose career is ascending at the same rate as her sex life is descending'. Like Melissa, she started out as even more of a caricature, and was tempered only through repeated lobbying by Polly Draper, who played Ellyn. Draper recalls that when she auditioned for the role, the producers 'described [Ellyn] as the kind of person who was so irritating you would walk out of the room whenever she walked in. And they wanted her to worship Hope and to want to be exactly like her. And I said, "Wait a minute, can't she be OK in her own right?" '

In the show, Ellyn leads what the character herself describes as 'this faked rented existence'; her apartment makes the single woman's quarters in *Fatal Attraction* seem downright homey. 'Mine is rented,' Ellyn says of her surroundings. 'All of it. The couch. The artwork. Even the salt shaker.' Her career leaves little room for shopping – and none for companionship. She hasn't even had sex in fifteen months. 'Between work . . . and this exercise class,' she says, 'I don't even have time to have a relationship.' When a man does come into her life, she can barely stand it. She grumbles, 'My work is suffering.' When he tells her 'I love you,' she snarls, 'I can't handle that.'

Her work life doesn't sound too appealing, either. 'Man, I'm tired,' Ellyn tells Hope. 'I've been in the office till ten every night this week. Look at the bags under my eyes.' Serene Hope rocks her baby and asks, 'How's your stomach been?' Ellyn moans: 'Terrible. Stress. Total stress.' When Hope's baby begins to whimper, the unmaternal Ellyn snaps, 'Won't she just stop crying?'

Liberty Godshall had a strong hand in shaping Ellyn's unattractive personality, too. 'Yeah, Ellyn's a mess,' she says, laughing. 'In fact, she might get messier. We've been playing around with the idea of making her a drug abuser.' She even proposed adopting the pop tune 'Addicted' as Ellyn's theme song. Another fate she and her husband contemplated seriously for the career crone: a total nervous breakdown. Finally, as Zwick explains, 'We opted for a much more sophisticated event.' Ellyn develops a bleeding ulcer, collapses, and ends up in hospital. The boyfriend dumps her soon after, announcing, 'I feel sorry for you because you do such selfish, self-destructive things.' In the last scene Ellyn is back at her family's house, lying on her girlhood bed, surrounded by stuffed animals. Her womanly side reawakened, she does the right 'feminine' thing: she reaches for the phone and dials a psychiatrist.

It's hard to imagine a less flattering portrait of a single woman, but by the second season *thirtysomething* had, in fact, produced one: Susannah, the humourless feminist. Susannah is a social activist who works full time in a community-service centre in the city's ghetto, tending to homeless men and battered wives. Despite her selfless work, the show manages to portray her as inhumanly cold, a rigid and snarling ideologue with no friends. Everyone in the Steadman circle dislikes her and makes fun of her 'excessive' independence and unhip political commitment. Even the angelic Hope sneers at Susannah behind her back.

Finally the feminist shrew is tamed by bachelor Gary. When he impregnates her, she is determined to get an abortion. But then, at the clinic, she hears the biological clock ringing. 'I've always put things off,' she confesses to Gary, tearfully. 'I just can't make assumptions about the future any more.' He is triumphant, and she has the baby.

'When you look at the characters on this show,' *thirtysomething* staff writer Ann Hamilton observes, 'you get the sense that all single women are unhappy. You look at these women and you think, "God, I wouldn't want to be single now." . . . When I think of how seriously people out there seem to be taking this show, it's scary.' In production planning meetings Hamilton argued unsuccessfully against the 'Weaning' episode. Pregnant herself at the time, she had no plans to give up work after she had her baby. 'It made me feel awful because it was saying, "If you go back to work you are a bad mother."' And it made her angry because it slyly endorsed wifely obedience: 'It seemed that Hope made the decision Michael wanted her to make.'

The actresses on *thirtysomething* have been uncomfortable with the show's treatment of working mothers, too. After all, they have been putting *their* toddlers in day care so they can star in a programme exalting housewives. (The show's production company, like every studio but one in Hollywood, has no on-site childcare.) Mel Harris, who played Hope, returned to work nine months after having her son. 'I think I'm a better mother and a better person because I work,' she says. Patricia Wettig, who played Nancy, the show's other stay-at-home mother, has a career, marriage and children. (She's married to the actor who played Hope's husband, Michael.) She says, 'From my perspective all three things are extremely important and I'm not willing to give up any of them.' In the show, when Nancy makes tentative moves in the direction of a career as a children's book illustrator, she promptly falls ill with ovarian cancer – becoming, as Wettig put it, 'Queen for a Day'.

Even women watching the show were troubled by its attitude. ABC market research vice-president Henry Schafer, who surveyed *thirtysomething* viewers, reports that 'one of our key findings' was that female viewers didn't want Hope to stay at home. 'They said, "Move her out of the home, get her into other arenas." We tested different ways – having her do volunteer work, having her get a job. And the job won out.'

The show's female actors and viewers weren't clamouring for full-time nesters, but the show's male creators were. They were the ones distressed by the women's movement and its effect on *them*. 'I think this is a terrible time to be a man, maybe the worst time in history,' *thirtysomething* co-creator Marshall Herskovitz complained in a men's magazine. 'Men come into the world with certain biological imperatives,' he said, but they no longer have any 'acceptable channels' to express these needs. 'Manhood has simply been devalued in recent years and doesn't carry much weight any more.'

Chapter Seven

Dressing the Dolls: The Fashion Backlash

Just ten days after the October 19, 1987, stock market collapse, French fashion designer Christian Lacroix unveiled his 'Luxe' collection at a society gala on Wall Street. The setting, aptly for a post-crash event, was the ground floor of the towering World Financial Center. As brokers upstairs sorted through the shambles, hollow-cheeked models with crosses around their necks drifted down the courtyard's catwalk, their clothes-hanger bodies swaying under the weight of twenty pounds of crinoline and taffeta. The pushed-up breasts of 'Maria, Mounia, Veronica and Katoucha' blossomed with roses the size of cabbage heads; beneath their tightly laced waists, pumpkin-shaped skirts ballooned. Three layers of bustles brought up the rear. These were clothes, Lacroix said, for women who like to 'dress up like little girls'. The Lacroix price tags, however, were not so pint-sized; they ranged as high as $45,000 – among the costliest raiments ever to come out of Paris.

When the lights finally came up, the fashion writers leaped from their seats to litter the catwalk with pink carnations. Applause was deafening for the 'Messiah' of couture, as the fashion press had anointed him a year earlier, when he displayed his first 'Baby Doll' line in Paris. As fireworks burst outside in a Revlon-funded salute to the sartorial saviour, the well-heeled guests adjourned to a $500-a-plate meal in the Winter Garden atrium. There, surrounded by 3,000 votive candles, couture-industry boosters served up reverential testimonials in strategic earshot of the fashion press:

Lacroix's bubble skirts exuded 'independent strength and sensitivity'; it was like being 'in a room full of Picassos,' a designer told the *New York Times*.

The Luxe gowns went on sale at Bergdorf Goodman, and, with Lacroix on hand to sign autographs, seventy-nine society matrons hurried to place their orders for $330,000 worth in two days. Maybe the Messiah would convert women after all to the look of High Femininity – or 'frou-frou', as less worshipful observers dubbed the fashion world's sudden detour into frills and petticoats in the spring of 1987. At least designers and retailers hoped he had converted them. After Lacroix's July 1986 Paris 'fantasy fashion' début had won rave reviews from *Women's Wear Daily*, twenty-one of the twenty-four couture houses had rushed out their own versions of High Femininity; clothes manufacturers had begun promoting 'the idea of women as dressed-up dolls'; retailers had stocked up on puffball skirts, miniskirts, party-girl gowns and body-squeezing garments that reduced the waist by three inches. And the fashion press had smoothed the way, promoting 'the gamine look' and declaring 1987 'the Year of the Dress'. But all the preparation was for naught. That spring, women just stopped buying.

Lacroix's messianic appellation was more fitting than intended; by the end of the 1980s it would indeed have taken divine intervention to resurrect the US women's fashion market. Black Monday, which dampened enthusiasm for conspicuous displays of wealth, was only the latest blow to an industry staggering from foreign competition, massive merger debts, record costs for raw materials, a declining dollar overseas – and then that final indignity, rejection by American women.

That so-called feminine ardour for clothes shopping had been flagging for some time. Between 1980 and 1986, at the same time that women were buying more houses, cars, restaurant dinners and health care services, they were buying fewer pieces of clothing – from dresses to underwear. The shaky economy played a role, but mostly women just didn't seem to enjoy clothes shopping as much any more. In one poll, more than 80 per cent said they hated it, twice as many as a decade earlier.

Throughout the decade clothes manufacturers and retailers tried to make up for a shrinking shopper base with rapidly inflating clothes prices. But the more stores marked up the tags, the less likely women were to take them to the register. Then, in the High Femininity year of 1987, dress prices jumped as much as 30 per cent. Women took one look at the tickets, another at the thigh-high dresses – and fled the stores. That year, even with higher prices compensating for lower volume, total sales dollars of women's clothing fell for the first time in a decade. In the so-called Year of the Dress, dress sales alone dropped 4 per cent. Even during the height of the Christmas season, fashion sales fell; that hadn't even happened during the 1982 recession. And this was a one-gender phenomenon: that same year, sales of men's clothing rose by 2.1 per cent.

The women's 'fashion revolt' and 'sticker shock rebellion' of 1987, as the media came to call it, nearly ruined the American fashion industry. And the more the dress merchants tried to force frills on their reluctant customers, the more their profit margins plunged. In the spring of 1988, after another season of flounces, bubble skirts and minis, and another 40 per cent price rise, clothing retailers' stocks plunged and quarterly earnings fell by 50 and 75 per cent. Department stores – where clothing accounts for 75 per cent of sales – lost tens of millions of dollars in profits. By the second quarter of 1988 the clothing industry was drawing more than $4 billion less in annual women's clothes sales than in the period just before the High Femininity look was introduced.

Perhaps the designers should have expected it. They were pushing 'little-girl' dresses and 'slender silhouettes' at a time when the average American woman was thirty-two years old, weighed 143 pounds and wore a size 10 or 12 dress (equivalent to British size 12 or 14). Fewer than a quarter of American women were taller than 5′4″ or wore a size smaller than 14 (UK size 16) – but 95 per cent of the fashions were designed to fit these specifications. Of all the frilly and 'retro' fashions introduced in 1987, only one really caught on: the peplum, an extra layer of fabric that hung from the waist and concealed broadening hips.

How could the industry make such a marketing blunder? As Goldman Sachs's retail analyst Joseph Ellis pointed out a year later in his analysis, 'The Women's Apparel Retailing Debacle:

Why?', demographics 'have been warning of a strong population shift to older age categories for years now'. Yet designers, manufacturers and retailers went 'in exactly the wrong direction'. Ellis charitably concluded that the industry must have lacked the appropriate consumer research studies.

But the fashion world hardly needed a marketing expert to tell them baby boomers were ageing. The explosion of frills in 1987 wasn't simply a misunderstanding; it was an eruption of long-simmering frustration and resentment at the increasingly independent habits of the modern female shopper. 'What's the matter with American women?' a French fashion designer snapped at John Molloy, the author of *Dress for Success*, while he was touring design houses in the mid-1980s. 'They don't do as they're told any more. We tell them how to dress but they just don't listen.' Or, as Lacroix would complain later, '[W]ith the women's-lib movement at the turn of the 'sixties [and in the] 'seventies, women became less fashion conscious,' and so many affluent female customers deserted couture that 'Arabian princesses and classical dowagers remained the only customers.' High Femininity was an attempt to command liberated women's attention with a counter-attack. As fashion designer Arnold Scaasi, one of High Femininity's leading architects, explains it, the new fashion edict 'is a reaction to the feminist movement, which was kind of a war'.

The mission of Lacroix and his fellow designers was to win this war, to make women 'listen' and rein them in, sometimes quite literally. At a Lacroix fashion show, the designer trotted out his 'cowgirl' model, bound and harnessed in a bridle. It was not enough that women buy more clothes; they had to buy the clothes that the couturiers *told* them to buy. Designers wanted to be in charge of 'dressing women', as the Council of Fashion Designers of America phrased it in its 1987 tribute to Lacroix.

What happened in 1987 had happened before, almost identically, in the 1947 fashion war. Women who had discovered slacks, low-heeled shoes and loose sweaters during the Second World War were reluctant to give them up in peacetime. The fashion industry fell into a 'frightening slump', as *Time* described it at the time, with orders shrinking by as much as 60 per cent. And women only rebelled when French designer Christian Dior unveiled the

'New Look' – actually an old late-Victorian look – featuring crinolined rumps, corseted waists and long ballooning skirts. More than 300,000 women joined 'Little Below the Knee Clubs' to protest at the New Look, and, when Neiman Marcus gave its annual fashion award to Dior, women stood outside waving placards – DOWN WITH THE NEW LOOK – and booing the man who believed that waists wider than seventeen inches were 'repulsive' on a lady. 'Let the new look of today become the forgotten look of tomorrow,' labour lawyer Anna Rosenberg proclaimed, and her sentiments were widely shared. In a poll that summer, a majority of women denounced the Dior style.

The women's declarations, however, only strengthened the designer's resolve to silence them. 'The women who are loudest,' Dior retorted, ' . . . will soon be wearing the longest dresses. . . . You can never stop the fashions.' By the end of the 1940s, after a two-year promotional campaign by retailers and the fashion press, Dior won. Women were wearing the New Look, albeit a toned-down version. And they were obeying Dior's order that they wear corsets capable of shaving two inches from their waist; in fact, bustiers that reduced the waist by *three* inches were soon generating sales of $6 million a year.

In every backlash, the fashion industry has produced punitively restrictive clothing and the fashion press has demanded that women wear it. 'If you want a girl to grow up gentle and womanly in her ways and her feelings, lace her tight,' advised one of the many male testimonials to the corset in the late Victorian press. In the last half of the nineteenth century, clothing manufacturers crafted increasingly rib-crushing gowns with massive rear bustles. And ridicule from the press effectively crushed a women's dress-reform campaign for more comfortable, sports-oriented clothing. The influential *Godey's Lady's Book* sneered at such 'roomy and clownish apparel' and labelled its proponents dress 'deformers'.

When the fashion industry began issuing marching orders again in the 1980s its publicists advanced a promotional line that downplayed the domineering intent and pretended to serve women's needs. Like the other contributors to backlash culture, fashion merchants latched on to the idea that contemporary women must be suffering from an excess of equality that had depleted their femininity. In fashion terms, the backlash argument became: women's liberation has denied women the 'right' to feminine dressing; the professional work outfits of the 1970s shackled the female spirit. 'A lot of women took the tailored look too far and it became unattractive,' designer Bob Mackie says. 'Probably, psychologically, it hurt their femininity. You see a lot of it in New York, trotting down Wall Street.' While denying that the summer of 1987 would 'turn poised women of the 'Eighties back into the malleable dolly birds of the 'Sixties', a feature in British *Cosmopolitan* announced that fashion had 'shed its neurotic, aggressive overtones of recent years' and wondered if this betokened 'the calling of a truce between the sexes'.

In desperation the industry began to contradict its own time-honoured conventions. Fashion's promoters have long rhapsodized that femininity is 'eternal', rooted in women's very nature; yet at the same time they were telling women that simply wearing the wrong set of clothes could obliterate this timeless female essence. This became the party line, voiced by merchants peddling every garment from puffball skirts to panties. 'We were wearing pinstripes, we didn't know what our identity was any more!' cried Karen Bromley, spokeswoman for the Intimate Apparel Council. 'We were having this identity crisis and we were dressing like men.'

But the only 'identity crisis' that women faced when they looked inside their wardrobes was the one the eighties fashion industry had fabricated. The clothing manufacturers had good reason to try to induce this anxiety: personal insecurity is the great motivator to shop. Wells Rich Greene, which conducted one of the largest studies of women's fashion-shopping habits in the early 1980s, found that the more confident and independent women became, the less they liked to shop; and the more they enjoyed their work, the less they cared about their clothes. The agency could find only three groups of women who were loyal followers of fashion: the very young, the very social and the very anxious.

While the fashion industry's publicists helped provoke and aggravate anxiety in ageing baby-boomer women by their relentless promotion of 'youthful' fashions, they certainly weren't going to claim credit for it. Instead, they blamed the usual culprit –

feminism. The women's movement, they told fashion writers again and again, had generated women's sartorial 'identity crisis' – by inventing a 'dress-for-success' ideology and foisting it on to women. This was an accusation that meshed well with the decade's conventional wisdom on women, and the fashion press gladly bought it. But it was just another backlash myth. The leaders of the women's movement had about as much to do with pushing pinstripes as they did with burning bras.

From Household Rags to Grey-Flannel Stitches

'You must look as if you're working, not playing,' Henri Bendel's president instructed women readers in a 1978 *Harper's Bazaar* article entitled 'Self-Confident Dressing', one of many features at the time advising women to wear suits that projected 'confidence' and 'authority'. 'Dress for the job you want to have,' *Mademoiselle* told readers in its September 1977 issue. 'There's a clothing hierarchy paralleling the job hierarchy.' Its September 1979 cover story offered a 'Dress for Success Guide', promoting grey flannel suits and fitted tweed jackets for 'the woman who is doing something with her life'. The well-tailored suit, the late-1970s fashion press had uniformly decreed, was the ideal expression of women's rising economic and political aspirations.

The fashion press inherited these ideas not from the women's movement but from the writings of a male fashion consultant. John T. Molloy's *The Woman's Dress for Success Book* became an instant hit in 1977, remaining on the *New York Times* bestseller list for more than five months. The book offered simple tips on professional dressing for aspiring businesswomen, just as his first work, *Dress for Success*, had dispensed clothing advice to men. That earlier book, published in 1975, was hugely popular, too. But when the fashion media turned against 'dress for success' a decade later, they directed their verbal assault solely against the women's edition.

A former prep-school English teacher, Molloy turned to the study of women's business dressing in the mid-1970s for the money. Corporations like AT&T and US Steel, under government pressure to hire women, were funding research and seminars that made them look like good equal opportunity employers. Unlike the High Femininity merchants, who determined fashion trends based on 'feelings', Molloy actually surveyed hundreds of people in the work force. He even dispatched research assistants to spy on the dressing habits of corporate men and women and, in a four-year study, enlisted several hundred businesswomen to track changes in their dress and their career.

Based on his survey results, Molloy calculated that women who wore business suits were one and a half times more likely to feel they were being treated as executives – and a third less likely to have their authority challenged by men. Clothing that called attention to sexuality, on the other hand – women's or men's – lowered one's status at the office. 'Dressing to succeed in business and dressing to be sexually attractive are almost mutually exclusive.'

Molloy's motives were primarily commercial, but his book had a political subtext, as a primer for people disadvantaged by class and sex. A child of the lower middle class himself, Molloy addressed similarly situated readers, the 'American bootstrap types', as he called them, 'whose parents never went to college' and who were struggling to 'overcome socioeconomic barriers when they choose their clothes'. The author was also an advocate of women's rising expectations – and urged them to rely on their brains rather than their bodies to improve their station. 'Many women,' he wrote, 'still cling to the conscious or unconscious belief that the only feminine way of competing is to compete as a sex object and that following fashion trends is one of the best ways to win. It's not.'

When Molloy's book for women became a bestseller in the 1970s, publishers immediately rushed three imitations into print. Retailers began invoking Molloy's name and even claiming, usually falsely, that the clothing guru had personally selected their line of women's business wear. *Newsweek* declared dress-for-success a trend. And for the next three years, women's magazines recycled scores of fashion stories that endorsed not only the suits but the ambitions they represented – with headlines like YOUR GET-AHEAD WARDROBE, POWER! and WHAT TO WEAR WHEN YOU'RE DOING THE TALKING. At first fashion makers welcomed dress-for-success, too.

They issued new ads offering paeans to working women's aspirations – with, of course, the caveat that women could realize these objectives only in a suit. Clothing manufacturers had visions of exploiting a new and untapped market. 'The success of suits has made the fashion industry ecstatic,' *Newsweek* observed in 1979. They had good reason to feel that way: sales of women's suits had more than doubled that year.

But in their enthusiasm fashion merchants overlooked the bottom line of Molloy's book: dress-for-success could save women money and liberate them from fashion-victim status. Business suits weren't subject to wild swings in fashion and women could get away (as men always have) with wearing the same suit for several days and just varying the blouse and accessories – more economical than buying a dress for every day of the week. Once women made the initial investment in a set of suits, they could even take a breather from shopping.

Between 1980 and 1987 annual sales of women's suits in the US rose by almost 6 million units, while dresses declined by 29 million units. The $600 million gain in suit sales in these years was nice – but it couldn't make up for the *billions* of dollars the fashion industry could have been making in dress sales. Matters worsened when manufacturers raised their suit prices to make up for the shortfall – and women just started buying cheaper suits from foreign manufacturers. Between 1981 and 1986 imports of women's suits nearly tripled.

'When this uniform is accepted by large numbers of businesswomen,' Molloy's book predicted, ' . . . it will be attacked ferociously.' The fashion industry, the clothing consultant warned, may even yank the suits off the racks: 'They will see it as a threat to their domination over women. And they will be right.'

Requiem for the Little Bow Tie

In 1986 US clothing manufacturers cut their annual production of women's suits by 40 per cent; the following year, production dropped by another 40 per cent. Several large suit manufacturers shut down their women's lines altogether. The sudden cutback wasn't inspired by a lack of demand: in 1986 women's purchases of suits and blazers jumped by 5.3 per cent. And this reduction wasn't gender blind. In the same two years, output of men's suits stayed the same.

Soon department stores phased out the executive-dressing wings that they had opened for professional women in the late 1970s. Marshall's shut down its Careers department; Carson Pirie Scott closed its Corporate Level division for women; Neiman Marcus removed all coordinated women's business suits from many of its stores. Paul Harris Stores switched from women's career clothes to miniskirts (and promptly lost $5.6 million). And Alcott & Andrews, the store that billed itself as a female Brooks Brothers when it opened in 1984, began stocking ruffled dresses. When Molloy toured its New York store in 1987, he couldn't find a single suit. (Two years later, Alcott & Andrews went bankrupt.)

Fashion writers buried the dress-for-success concept as eagerly as they had once praised it. 'Bye-bye to the Little Bow Tie,' *Mademoiselle* eulogized in a 1987 article entitled 'The Death of Dress for Success'. It was one of many such media obituaries, among them THE DEATH OF THE DUMB BLUE SUIT and A UNIFORM FOR SUBMISSION IS FINALLY PUT TO REST. As the latter headline (from the *Chicago Tribune*) suggests, these articles were now proposing that business suits, not unequal business status, posed the greatest threat to women's opportunities. As a fashion consultant explained in a *Los Angeles Times* feature on the same subject, '[The suit] shows you aren't successful because you have no freedom of dress, and that means you don't have power.' 'Why intelligent women want to be sexy,' *Options* magazine told readers this side of the Atlantic in 1987. 'Times have changed. Now you can dress for sexcess . . . The last decade of flat shoes and harassment cases seemed to have kicked sex out of fashion and the office . . . Nowadays, sexiness can be born again.' *Cosmopolitan* agreed: 'Kiss goodbye to those blatant symbols of tough cookie authority . . . The new woman takes centre stage. A new Gigi in a swirl of pastels, her mood is cheeky, precocious, vulnerable.'

All the anti-dress-for-success crusade needed to be complete was a villain. John Molloy was the obvious choice. The fashion press soon served him with a three-count indictment; he was charged with promoting 'that dreadful little bow tie', pushing 'the boring navy blue suit', and making women look like 'imitation men'. When his book first came out, Molloy was so popular that newspapers fought to bid for his syndicated column, 'Making It'. But with Molloy's name on the fashion blacklist, newspapers cancelled their orders. A major daily paper, which had initially approached Molloy about publishing the column, pulled out with this explanation: 'The fashion people won't allow it.'

The charges against Molloy were largely trumped up. In fact, Molloy's book never mentioned the bow tie; it wasn't even on the market when the book was published. His book did not champion navy suits; it recommended grey, which he believed conveyed more authority. And a whole section of the book was specifically devoted to advising women how *not* to dress like an 'imitation man'. *Dress for Success* didn't even endorse suits exclusively, as many magazine stories maintained; it suggested women diversify their professional wardrobe with blazers, tailored skirts and dresses. The fashion press was attacking its own rigid version of dress-for-success, not Molloy's. As Molloy himself points out, a shrewder garment industry might have capitalized on his formula. 'My book recommended a wide variety of styles,' he says. 'My prescription was not that narrow. It was the fashion industry that narrowed women's choices. They became their own worst enemy.'

Lacroix: The Clown Who Would Be King

With the suits cleared from the racks and Molloy deposed, the American fashion industry moved to instal Lacroix as 'The King of Couture', an exalted title in keeping with 1980s fashion obsessions with class. While Molloy spoke to the 'American bootstrap types', Lacroix addressed only the élite. He concerned himself with a class of people who didn't have to dress for success. His female clientele, the ornamental ladies of American high society, had already acquired their upper-class status – through marriage or inheritance, not a weekly pay cheque.

Lacroix's preoccupation with the top rungs of the income ladder perfectly matched the upmarket sales policies of the decade's retailers. In the fashion equivalent of television's 'quality demographics', scores of retailers turned their backs on middle-class women and courted only the 'better-business' customers, as they euphemistically labelled the rich. Instead of offering a range of clothing choices and competitive pricing, they began to serve only the tastes and incomes of the most affluent. Instead of serving the needs of the many working women, they sponsored black-tie balls and provided afternoon tea service and high-priced facials for the idle few. 'We made a conscious decision as a store a few years back to deal primarily with better-quality, wealthy fashions,' explains Harold Nelson, general manager of Neiman Marcus's Washington, DC, store, where 90 per cent of the fashions were in couture or high-priced designer categories by 1988. 'Gradually, we've been removing the moderately priced merchandise.'

Lacroix's fashion gaze was ideally suited to the era in an even more fundamental way. For inspiration, he looked only backwards – 'I love the past much more than the future' – and primarily to the wardrobes of the late Victorian and postwar eras. In 1982, while chief designer at the House of Patou, he had even tried, unsuccessfully, to reintroduce the bustle. (As Lacroix explains this effort later, 'I must say, [the] bustle emphasizes the silhouette a way I like very much.') For the next three years, his five subsequent retro-tinged fashion shows fell flat, too; as he would say later of this period, he 'suffered from being considered the clown of couture'. Nonetheless, he clung to these more 'feminine' styles that had preoccupied him since childhood when, he recalled later, he had pored admiringly over late Victorian fashion magazines of corseted women and dreamed of being the world's next Dior, an aspiration he announced at the family dinner table one day. When he finally made it as an adult, he would dramatize this fantasy. He timed the grand opening of the House of Lacroix to coincide with the House of Dior's fortieth anniversary.

While the fashion press, of course, declares its 'trends' long before they reach the consumer, in Lacroix's case the leading trade paper in America, *Women's Wear Daily*, would take fashion forecasting to a new extreme. It declared Lacroix's first 'baby doll' line a hit two days *before* the designer even displayed the clothes at the Paris show in July 1986. As it turned out, the female audience that day was less than impressed by the onslaught of 'fantasy fashion' on the catwalk by Lacroix and fellow designers. As *Women's Wear Daily* remarked with more irritation than insight, reaction from the society women in attendance 'seemed cool'; even when one of the couturiers issued a 'call to a less self-important way of dressing', the front-row ladies 'failed to heed' him. But the lacklustre reception from the ladies didn't discourage the magazine, which hailed Lacroix and High Femininity in another front-page rave the next day. FASHION GOES MAD, the magazine's banner headline announced with self-induced brain fever. Lacroix has 'restored woman's right to outrageous, fun and high spirits'.

But was Lacroix offering women 'fun' – or just making fun of them? He dressed his catwalk models in dunce caps, clamped dogcollarlike discs around their necks, stuck cardboard cones on their breasts, positioned cabbage roses so they sprouted from their rear ends, and attached serving trays to their heads – the last touch suggesting its reverse, female heads on serving trays. Then he sent them down the catwalk to tunes with lyrics such as these: 'Down by the station, Early in the morning, See the little pufferbellies, All in a row.' *Women's Wear Daily* didn't celebrate Lacroix's High Femininity because it gave women the right to have 'fun' but because it presented them as unspoiled young maidens, ready and willing to be ravished. John Fairchild, the magazine's publisher and the industry's legendary 'Emperor of Fashion', said that what he really loved about the Lacroix gown was 'how you can see it in the middle of lavender fields worn by happy little virgins who don't want to be virgins'.

With Fairchild's backing, Lacroix was assured total adulation from the rest of the fashion world. The following July, three months before the stockmarket crash, he unveiled his first signature collection at a Paris show, to 'rhythmic applause' from fashion writers and merchants. Afterwards, retail executives stood in the aisles and worked the press into a lather with overwrought tributes. The president of Martha's predicted, 'It will change every woman's wardrobe.' The senior vice-president of Bloomingdale's pronounced it 'one of the most brilliant personal statements I've ever seen on the runway'. And Bergdorf Goodman's president offered the most candid assessment to reporters: 'He gave us what we were looking for.' Thus primed, the most influential fashion writers raced to spread the 'news'. Hebe Dorsey of the *International Herald Tribune* charged to the nearest telephone to advise her editors that this was a development warranting front-page coverage. The next day the *New York Times* fashion writer Bernadine Morris nominated Lacroix to 'fashion's hall of fame', declaring, 'Like Christian Dior exactly forty years ago, he has revived a failing institution.'

The rest of the press quickly fell into line. *Time* and *Newsweek* produced enthusiastic trend stories. *People* celebrated Lacroix's 'high jinks' and the way he 'jammed bustles up the backside'. And the mass media's infatuation with Lacroix involved not only his hyperfeminine clothes but the cult of his masculine personality. Lacroix, who stocked his own wardrobe with Ralph Lauren lord-of-the-manor wear, was eager to market an all-brawn self-image: 'Primitive people, sun and rough times,' he informed the press, 'this is my real side.' Stories on Lacroix were packed with approving allusions to his manly penchant for cowboys and matadors. *Time* offered this tribute from a fashion commentator: 'He looks like Brando; he is pantheroid, catlike. He is sexy in a way that is absolutely not effete.' His swagger, and the press's enthusiasm for it, indicated the real 'crisis' fuelling the backlash – not the concern that female professionalism and independence were defeminizing women but the fear that they were emasculating men. Worries about eclipsed manhood were particularly acute in the fashion world, where the perception of a widespread gay culture in the industry had collided in the 1980s with homophobia and rising anxieties about AIDS.

With Lacroix crowned as couture's king, rival designers competed fiercely to dethrone him. From Emanuel Ungaro to Karl Lagerfeld, they caked on even more layers of frills and pumped up skirts with still bigger bustles. If High Femininity was supposed to accent womanly curves, its frenetic baroque excrescences succeeded only in obscuring the female figure. It was hard to see body shape at all through the thicket of flounces and floral sprays. Dress-for-success's shoulder-pads were insignificant appendages compared with the foot-high satin roses Ungaro tacked to the shoulders of evening gowns.

While a few dozen rich American women had bought Lacroix's gowns from his 1987 Luxe collection, the designer was anxious to make his mark in the broader, real-world market of ready-to-wear clothes. His last effort while still at Patou in 1984 had failed miserably, after his designs proved too expensive for sale. This time he approached the market strategically. First, in the spring of 1988, he put the clothes 'on tour' at a select three stores: Martha's, Bergdorf Goodman and Saks Fifth Avenue. Then, that autumn, having tantalized women with this fashion tease, he would ship ready-to-wear clothes across the country.

In May 1988 big ads appeared in the *Washington Post*, courtesy of Saks Fifth Avenue, welcoming the Lacroix travelling show to town – and advising women to hurry down and place their special orders before the rush.

'I Guess They Don't Like Looking Superfluous'

The day the Lacroix dresses arrive at Saks, five men in dark suits hover around the designer salon, supervising four elderly saleswomen who are easing the gowns from their garment bags, blue-veined hands trembling slightly as they lift the heavy crinoline-encrusted costumes to the racks. 'Careful now, careful!' one of the suited men coaches whenever a hem threatens to touch the floor. A bell-shaped purple skirt is slipped out of its wrapper – $630. It comes with a top, $755.

About noon, a delivery man drops off a video of a Lacroix fashion show, to be screened for shoppers' viewing pleasure. The saleswomen gather around the TV set to watch the models teeter down the catwalk to the song the designer has selected for the occasion – 'My Way'. One of the models is covered, head to toe, in giant roses and bows. 'It's ridiculous,' mutters sales assistant Mimi Gott, who is wearing a grey tweed suit. 'Our customers are older people. They aren't going to buy this stuff.'

About 1 p.m., Pandora Gogos arrives at the salon, on the arm of her daughter Georgia. They are going to 'a black-tie dinner', and Gogos, who is 'around seventy', can find nothing in the shops to wear. 'I've been shopping here since they opened up in the 1950s,' she complains, lowering her aching back into a chair. 'Even in the fifties, I don't think they were crazy like this. I've gone all over town – Saks, Garfinckel's – and I can't find a dinner dress. There was one at Garfinckel's, a four-thousand-dollar jacket with a skirt up to here' – she raises her hands to her throat – 'nine thousand dollars!'

Soon later, a Mrs Barkin, a middle-aged woman, arrives at the designer salon to return a frilly dress concocted by one of Lacroix's imitators. It is studded with huge flowers and a back bustle. 'I just couldn't wear it,' she says apologetically. Sales assistant Venke Loehe, who is wearing a simple Diane Von Furstenberg wrap-around, gives her a sympathetic nod. 'It's the return to the fifties,' Loehe says. 'A lot of our clothes now are like that. . . . But the classic look is still what's selling best.' Mrs Barkin decides on an exchange – she has a cocktail party to attend – and starts rummaging through the racks. She settles reluctantly on a dress with a puffball skirt; it's the only evening outfit she can find with a lower hem. 'I don't know how I'll ever sit down in this,' she worries.

Back by the Lacroix racks, the only items that seem to be drawing interest are a plain overcoat and a tailored jacket. Mostly, women don't even stop to look; by mid-afternoon, the salon has had fewer than a dozen visitors. The men in suits are wondering what happened to all the customers. 'All that embellishment, the ruffles, lace and frills,' says a frustrated Lawrence Wilsman, Saks's buyer of European designer imports, 'women don't seem to want that much. They seem to want quieter, more realistic things. They want clothes to be taken seriously in. I guess they don't like looking superfluous.'

That autumn, Lacroix's full ready-to-wear collection arrived at Saks. A month later, markdown tags dangled from the sleeves. Department stores from Nordstrom to Dayton Hudson dropped Lacroix's clothes after one season. 'We needed to see a bit more that American women could relate to,' explained a Nordstrom spokesperson. And when *Women's Wear Daily* surveyed department stores, the Lacroix label ranked as one of the worst sellers. By 1989 Lacroix's design house was reporting a $9.3 million loss.

Flouncing into Work

Maybe Lacroix's puffballs hadn't won over the high-income shoppers who frequent designer salons, but clothing manufacturers and retailers were still hoping to woo the average female shopper with the habiliments of High Femininity. To this end, Bullock's converted 60 per cent of its women's apparel to a '1950s look' by spring 1987. And even more progressive designers like Donna Karan began parroting the couturier's retro edicts. 'There has been a shift in saying to a woman, "It's okay to show your derriere",' she told the *New York Times*. 'I questioned it at first. But women's bodies are in better shape.'

For High Femininity to succeed in the ready-to-wear market, working women had to accept the look – and wear it to the office. The clothing manufacturers could design all the evening gowns they pleased; it wouldn't change the fact that the vast majority of women's clothing purchases were for work wear. In 1987, for example, more than 70 per cent of the skirts purchased in the USA were for professional wardrobes. Pushing baby-doll fashions to working women was also going to be a trickier manoeuvre than marketing to socialites. Not only did the designers have to convince women that frills were appropriate on the job, the persuasion had to be subtler; high-handed commands wouldn't work on the less fashion-conscious working women. The designers and merchants had to present the new look as the career woman's 'choice'.

'This thing is not about designers dictating,' Calvin Klein proclaimed as he issued another round of miniskirts. 'We're taking our cues from what women want. They're ready.' 'Older women want to look sexy now on the job,' the head of Componix, a Los Angeles clothing company, insisted. 'They want men to look at them like they're women. Notice my legs first, not my appraisals.' One by one, the dressing authorities got behind this new fashion line. 'Gals like to show their legs,' designer Bill Blass asserted. 'Girls want to be girls again,' designer Dik Brandsma intoned. The lone dissenting voice came from veteran designer John Weitz, who said it was *Women's Wear Daily*, not women, clamouring for girlish frocks. 'Women change not at all, just journalism,' he said, dismissing High Femininity as 'a temporary derailment, based on widespread insecurity. Eventually it will go away and women will look like strong decisive human beings instead of Popsicles.' But then Weitz could afford to be honest; he made *his* money designing men's clothes.

Taking their cue from the designers, retailers unfurled the same 'choice' sales pitch – and draped it in seemingly feminist arguments, phrases and imagery. These constricting and uncomfortable clothes were actually a sign of women's advancement. As a publicist for Alcott & Andrews explained, 'Our woman has evolved to the point where she can really wear anything to the office that proclaims her femininity.' Bloomingdale's, which dubbed its latest dress department for women 'Bloomingdale's NOW', proposed that women try 'advancing at work with new credentials' – by buying the department's skimpy chemises and wearing them to the office. Like the designers, retailers claimed to speak for women, sometimes literally. 'Saks understands,' a mythical career woman murmured in the store's ad copy. 'They give me the options. . . . Showing me that "going soft" doesn't have to mean losing your edge.' What was she pictured wearing to work? Shorts.

The fashion press pitched in, too. *Cosmopolitan* in the UK dubbed them 'the charm-school designers' who were 'united in the fight against the hard-edged woman of seasons past'. Flowers were the key accessory, from hemlines to hair ornaments, 'introducing a fresher, frothy femininity'. The same publications that had urged working women to wear suits if they wanted to be taken seriously now began running fashion headlines like DRESSING CUTE EN ROUTE and THE NEW SUCCESS LOOKS: YOUNG AND EASY. Women could actually get ahead *faster* if they showed up for work in crinoline petticoats; DRESSING DOWN FOR SUCCESS, the *Los Angeles Times'* fashion editors called it. The fashion press also resorted to pseudo-feminist arguements to push pre-pubescent dressing: women should don party-doll frills, they argued, as an emblem of grown-up liberation – as a sort of feminist victory sash. Grasping for any angle, the fashion writers even tried invoking the Harvard–Yale marriage study. 'A man shortage? What man shortage?' *Mademmoiselle* crowed in its editorial for puffballs and minis. 'You'll be dated up till nexy July if you turn up in any of these ultrahot numbers.'

But no matter what argument the fashion promoters tried, American women, at least, weren't buying. Whereas the short-skirted suit and short, stretch clothes in (mostly black) Lycra, combined with leggings and flat shoes, took off in Britain – for reasons of comfort and ease of movement – a 1988 *New York Times*/CBS News poll found only a quarter of adult American women said they had worn a skirt above the knee even once in the past year. Some women were becoming as vocal in their resistance as the anti-Dior protesters a generation earlier. 'I will wear the new short skirts when men wear rompers to the office,' declared columnist Kathleen Fury in *Working Woman*. Nina Totenberg, legal affairs reporter for National Public Radio, exhorted female listeners from the airwaves, 'Hold the line. Don't buy. And the mini will die.'

The American retailers, saddled with millions of dollars of untouched miniskirts, were ready to surrender. The miniskirt has thrown the women's clothing market into 'confusion', worried a spokesperson for Liz Claiborne Inc., 'and we don't see any indication that it is going to pass soon'. But the high-fashion designers – who make their money more through licensing their names than through actual dress sales – could afford to continue the campaign. So when retail buyers flocked to market to inspect the designers' upcoming autumn fashions for 1988, they found – much to their amazement – yet another round of ruffled and rib-crunching styles.

'I think it's really a trend,' Yvette Crosby, fashion director of California Mart, is telling everyone at the 1988 Market Week in Los Angeles, as she hands out copies of this season's *Trend Report*. 'It's a more romantic and Victorian look, and I really believe it's right for this season,' says Crosby. She wears a suit.

The writers and buyers are crowding into the mart's auditorium for the morning show, entitled 'Thirty Something'. The programme notes advise that these clothes are designed 'for contemporary working women' – a necessary reminder, as it happens. As the models revolve in up to five tiers of frills, huge bows bursting from hips and shoulders, it's easy to forget that this is nine-to-five wear. To evoke a proper career mood, one designer has armed his models with briefcases. The gaunt young women trip down the catwalk in stiletto heels, hands snug in dainty white gloves. Their briefcases swing like Easter baskets, feather light; they are, after all, empty.

At last, the models retire backstage and the fashion buyers are herded to the buying services' suites upstairs. In the Bob Mallard showroom, the mart's largest buying service, manufacturing representatives scurry hopefully into place. Mallard, who joined the business in the 1950s as a garment manufacturer in the East Bronx, surveys the proceedings with grim resignation; he has the leathery, bruised face of a fighter who's been in the ring a while.

'Last year, the miniskirt was a disaster,' he says. 'Froufrou was no big hit either. Women still want suits. That's still the biggest seller.' But he knows his observations will fall on deaf ears back at the design houses. 'The average designer goes to the library and looks at pictures in a picture book. Maybe he worries about whether the dress is going to look good on the mannequin in the store window. That's it. I don't think he ever bothers to talk to a woman about it. The woman, she's the last to know.'

In the glass booths on either side of the long showroom corridor, Mallard's manufacturing reps are doing their best to pitch the 'new-romance' fashions to doubtful buyers. Teri Jon's rep, Ruth McLoughlin, pulls one dress after another off the racks and holds it up to buyers Jody Krogh and Carol Jameson of the Portland-based Jameson Ltd. 'Short didn't sell last year,' Krogh keeps saying. 'No, no, don't judge by what's on the hanger,' McLoughlin answers, a little peevishly. 'We can ship it long. Now how about this?' She holds up a dress with a plunging front, cinched waist and crinolines. 'I don't know,' Jameson says. 'Women will love it,' says McLoughlin. She is wearing a suit.

'This is my best reorder,' says Joe Castle, a fast-talking Cattiva salesman across the hall. He waggles a ruffle-decked gown in front of a buyer with a blank order form. 'It makes a great M.O.B. [mother of the bride] gown,' Castle wheedles. Sounding a bit like a *Newsweek* trend story, Castle tries this last argument: 'Everyone's looking for M.O.B.s. More and more people are getting married.'

At the fashion shows held in summer 1988 for the coming autumn season, designers made a few compromises – adding trouser suits and longer skirts to their collections – but these additions often featured a puerile or retaliatory underside. Jean-Paul Gaultier showed trousers and blazers – but they were skin-tight Lycra leotards and schoolgirl uniforms. Pierre Cardin produced capelike wraps that fitted so tightly even the *New York Times* fashion page found it 'fairly alarming because the models wearing them cannot move their arms'. Romeo Gigli dropped his hemlines but the skirts were so tight the models could only hobble down the catwalk. One of his models was doubly encumbered; he had tied her up in velvet ropes, straitjacket-style.

A year later, even the compromises were gone – as designers dressed up their women again in even shorter miniskirts, bone-crushing corsets, push-up cleavage and billows of transparent chiffon. The Lacroix brand of 'humour' returned to the catwalks: models wore costumes modelled on clown suits, 'court jester' jackets, moulded 'breastplates' and pinstriped suits with one arm and shoulder ripped to shreds. By 1990 Valentino was pushing 'baby dolls', Gianni Versace was featuring 'skirts that barely clear the buttocks', and the Lacroix collection was offering jumpsuits with 'gold-encrusted' corsets.

If the clothes manufacturers could not get women to wear puffball skirts, they would try dictating another humbling mode of fashion. The point was not so much the content of the style as its enforcement. There was a reason why their designs continued to regress into female infantilism, even in the face of a flood of market reports on ageing female consumers: minimizing the female form might be one way for designers to maximize their own authority over it. The woman who walks in tiny steps clutching a teddy bear – as so many did on the late eighties catwalks – is a child who follows instructions. The woman who steps down the aisle to George Michael's 'Father Figure' – the most popular cat-walk song in 1988 – is a daughter who minds her elders. Modern women 'won't do as they are told any more', the couturier had complained to Molloy. But just maybe they would – if only they could be persuaded to think of themselves as daddy's little girls.

Femininity, Undercover

The romantic refrain from a 1950s musical came up at the MK Club in New York, and the buyers and fashion writers, who had been downing drinks from the open bar for more than an hour, quietened as rose-coloured lights drenched the stage. Six models in satin panties and lace teddies drifted dreamily into view and took turns swooning on the main stage prop – a Victorian couch. The enervated ladies – 'Sophia', 'Desirée', 'Amapola' – languorously stroked their tresses with antique silver hairbrushes, stopping occasionally to lift limp hands to their brows, as if even this bit of grooming overtaxed their delicate constitutions.

The press release described the event as Bob Mackie's 'première collection' of fantasy lingerie. In fact, the Hollywood costume designer (author of *Dressing for Glamour*) had introduced a nearly identical line ten years before. It failed then in a matter of weeks – but the women of the late 1980s, Mackie believed, were different. 'I see it changing,' Mackie asserts. 'Women want to wear very feminine lingerie now.'

Mackie got this impression not from women but from the late 1980s lingerie industry, which claimed to be in the midst of an 'Intimate Apparel Explosion'. As usual, this was a marketing slogan, not a social trend. Frustrated by slackening sales, the Intimate Apparel Council – an all-male board of lingerie makers – established a special public relations committee in 1987. Its mission: stir up 'excitement'.

The committee immediately issued a press release proclaiming that 'cleavage is back' and that the average woman's bust had suddenly swelled from 34B to 36C. 'Bustiers, corsets, camisoles, knickers and petticoats,' the press kits declared, are now not only 'accepted' by women but actually represent 'a fashion statement'. A $10,000 focus-group study gathered information for the committee about the preferences of manufacturers and retail buyers. No female consumers were surveyed. 'It's not that we aren't interested in them,' Karen Bromley, the committee's spokesperson, explains. 'There's just limited dollars.'

In anticipation of the intimate apparel explosion, manufacturers boosted the production of undergarments to its highest level in a dozen years. In 1987, the same year the fashion industry slashed its output of women's suits, it doubled production of suspender belts. Again, it was the 'better-business' shopper that the fashion marketers were after; in one year, the industry nearly tripled its shipments of luxury lingerie. Du Pont, the largest maker of foundation fabrics, simultaneously began a nationwide 'education program', which included 'training videos' in stores, fitting-room posters and special 'training' tags on the clothes to teach women the virtues of underwired bras and girdles (or 'body shapers', as they now called them – garments that allow women 'a sense of control'). Once again a fashion regression was billed as a feminist breakthrough. 'Women have come a long way since the 1960s,' Du Pont's sales literature exulted. 'They now care about what they wear under clothes.'

The fashion press, as usual, was accommodating. 'Bra sales are booming,' the *New York Daily News* claimed. Its evidence: the Intimate Apparel Council's press release. Enlisting one fake backlash trend to promote another, the *New York Times* claimed that women were rushing out to buy $375 bustiers to use 'for cocooning'. *Life* dedicated its June 1989 cover to a hundredth-anniversary salute, HURRAH FOR THE BRA, and insisted, likewise without data, that women were eagerly investing in designer brassières and corsets. In an interview later, the article's author, Claudia Dowling, admits that she herself doesn't fit the trend; when asked, she can't even recall what brand of bra she wears: 'Your basic Warner whatever, I guess,' she says.

Hollywood also hastened to the aid of the intimate-apparel industry, with suspender belts in *Bull Durham*, push-up bras in *Dangerous Liaisons*, and merry-widow regalia galore in *Working Girl*. TV did its bit, too, as characters from *Dynasty* jumped into bustiers, and even the women of *thirtysomething* inspected teddies in one shopping episode.

The fashion press marketed the intimate apparel explosion as a symbol of modern women's new sexual freedom. 'The "Sexy" Revolution Ignites Intimate Apparel', *Body Fashions* announced in its October 1987 cover story. But the magazine was right to put quotes around 'sexy'. The cover model was encased in a full-body girdle, and the lingerie inside was mostly of Victorian vintage. Late 1980s lingerie celebrated the repression, not the flowering, of female sexuality. The ideal Victorian lady it had originally been designed for, after all, wasn't supposed to have any libido.

A few years before the intimate apparel explosion, Madonna gained notoriety by wearing a black bustier as a shirt. In her rebellious send-up of prim notions of feminine propriety, she paraded her sexuality and transformed underwear into an explicit ironic statement. This was not, however, the sort of 'sexy revolution' that the fashion designers had in mind. 'That Madonna look was vulgar,' Bob Mackie sniffs. 'It was overly sexually expressive. The slits and the clothes cut up and pulled all around; you couldn't tell the sluts from the schoolgirls.' The lingerie he advocated had 'a more ladylike feminine attitude'.

Late Victorian clothing retailers were the first to mass-market 'feminine' lingerie, turning corsets into a 'tight-lacing' fetish and weighing women down in thirty pounds of bustles and petticoats. It worked for them; by the turn of the century, they had ushered in 'the great epoch of underwear'. Lingerie publicists of the 1980s offered various sociological reasons for the Victorian underwear revival, from 'the return of marriage' to 'fear of AIDS' – though they never did explain how suspender belts ward off infection. But the real reason for the Victorian renaissance was strictly business. 'Whenever the romantic Victorian mood is in, we are going to do better,' explains Peter Velardi, chairman of the lingerie giant Vanity Fair and a member of the Intimate Apparel Council's executive committee.

In this decade's underwear campaign, the American intimate-apparel industry owed its heaviest promotional debt to the Limited, the fashion retailer that turned a Californian lingerie boutique named Victoria's Secret into a national chain with 346 shops in five years. 'I don't want to sound arrogant,' Howard Gross, president of Victoria's Secret, says, 'but . . . we caused the Intimate Apparel Explosion. We started it and a lot of people wanted to copy it.'

The designers of the Victoria's Secret shop, a Disneyland version of a nineteenth-century lady's dressing room, packed each outlet with 'antique' armoires and sepia photos of brides and mothers. Their blueprint was quickly copied by other retailers. Even Frederick's of Hollywood reverted to Victoriana, replacing fright wigs with lace chemises, repainting its walls in ladylike pinks and mauves and banning frontal nudity from its catalogues. 'You can put our catalogue on your coffee table now,' George Townson, president of Frederick's, says proudly.

The Limited bought Victoria's Secret in 1982 from its originator, Roy Raymond, who opened the first shop in a suburban mall in Palo Alto, California. A Stanford MBA and former marketing man for the Vicks company – where he developed such unsuccessful hygiene products as a post-defecation foam to dab on toilet paper – Raymond wanted to create a store that would cater for his gender. 'Part of the game was to make it more comfortable for men,' he says. 'I aimed it, I guess, at myself.' But Raymond didn't want his female customers to think a man was running the store; that might put them off. So he was careful to include in the store's catalogues a personal letter to subscribers from 'Victoria', the store's putative owner, who revealed her personal preferences in lingerie and urged readers to visit 'my boutique'. If customers called to inquire about Ms Victoria the sales assistants were instructed to say she was 'travelling in Europe'. As for the media, Raymond's wife handled all TV appearances.

Raymond settled on a Victorian theme both because he was renovating his own Victorian home in San Francisco at the time and because it seemed like 'a romantic happy time'. He explains: 'It's that Ralph Lauren image . . . that people were happier then. I don't know if that is really true. It's just the image in my mind, I guess created by all the media things I've seen. But it's real.'

Maybe the Victorian era wasn't the best of times for the female population, he acknowledges, but he came up with a marketing strategy to deal with that problem: women are now 'liberated' enough to choose corsets to please themselves, not their men. 'We had this whole pitch,' he recalls, 'that the woman bought this very romantic and sexy lingerie to feel good about herself, and the effect it had on a man was secondary. It allowed us to sell these garments without seeming sexist.' But was it true? He shrugs. 'It was just the philosophy we used. The media picked it up and called it a "trend", but I don't know. I've never seen any statistics.'

When the Limited took over Victoria's Secret, the new chief

continued the theme. Career women want to wear bustiers in the boardroom, Howard Gross says, so they can feel confident that, underneath it all, they are still anatomically correct. 'Women get a little pip, a little perk out of it,' he explains. 'It's like, "Here I am at this very serious business meeting and they really don't know that I'm wearing a garter belt!" ' Gross didn't have any statistics to support this theory, either: 'The company does no consumer or market research, absolutely none! I just don't believe in it.' Instead of asking the woman in the street what she wanted in underwear, Gross conducted in-house brainstorming sessions where top company managers sat around a table and revealed their 'romantic fantasies'. Some of them, Gross admits, were actually 'not so romantic' – like the male executive who imagined, 'I'm in bed with eighteen women.'

On a late afternoon in the summer of 1988, row after row of silk teddies hang, untouched, at the original Victoria's Secret shop in Palo Alto's Stanford Shopping Center. The shelves are stuffed with floral-scented teddy bears in tiny wedding gowns. At $18 to $34 each, these cuddly brides aren't exactly top sellers; dust has collected on their veils. But over at the bargains table, where basic cotton underwear is on sale, 'four for $16', it looks like a cyclone has touched down.

'Oh God, the panty table is a mess,' groans head 'proprietress' Becky Johnson. As she straightens it up for what she says must be the tenth time that day, two women walk in the door and charge the bargain knickers table. 'The prices on these panties are wonderful,' Bonnie Pearlman says, holding up a basic pair of briefs to show her friend. 'But will they shrink?' she wonders, pulling the elastic back and forth. Asked if they are here for the Victorian lingerie, they both shake their heads. Pearlman says, 'I look for what fits well.' Suzanne Ellis, another customer, surveys the racks of gossamer teddies and rolls her eyes. 'I've had a few of these things given to me,' she says. 'It was like, "Uh, gee, thanks." I mean, I really don't need to sit on snaps all day.' She holds up her purchase for the day: the four-for-$16 cotton knickers. Even proprietress Becky Johnson says she buys 'good ol' basic bras and panties' here. So who's buying the frilly Victorian stuff? Johnson: 'Men.'

While men represent 30 to 40 per cent of the shoppers at Victoria's Secret stores, they account for nearly half the dollar volume, company managers estimate. 'Men are great,' sighs one of the sales assistants at the Stanford store. 'They'll spend anything.'

One such specimen wanders into the shop just then. Jim Draeger, a thirty-five-year-old attorney, bypasses the basic knickers table and heads directly for the bustier racks. 'I've been coming here since 1980,' he says, scrutinizing a silky bodice. 'This type of clothes enhances a woman's sexuality. The laciness of it, the peekaboo quality of it. My only regret is that a lot of the stuff you see in the catalogue you can't buy in the store.' He settles on a tastefully dainty G-string.

The American intimate apparel explosion of 1987 never happened. That year, women's annual purchases of teddies actually fell 31 per cent. Women bought 40 million fewer pairs of knickers than a year earlier, and 9 million fewer bras. Sales of all chemises, slips and teddies fell by $4 million in two years. In the UK, *Company* magazine was forced to wonder, 'Why should a smalls renaissance take place now, not two years after that great foundation institution Berlei found itself in trouble?' A third of British women were reported to favour Marks & Spencer's cotton knickers; but market research by Mintel found that suspender-belt sales had risen by 150 per cent between 1982 and 1985. The revival of 'Janet Reger', the advent in 1986 of the shopping chain Knickerbox, and the evidence of an increase in popularity of camisoles, teddies and bodyshapers in British lingerie departments led *Company* to conclude only that it was a business 'fraught with contradictions'.

Alongside the 'glamour' displays, cotton, unisex briefs and unstructured short 'vest' tops were certainly enjoying more popularity. If American lingerie makers had leaped on this real trend, they might have made some real money. This business strategy occurred to one company, Jockey International, the nation's oldest manufacturer of premium men's underwear. In 1982 Jockey's new president stood up at a high-level marketing meeting and made a modest proposal: what if the company started selling women's underwear, with the same comfort and quality as the men's? After all, he pointed out, for years the company had received reams of letters from women asking them to do just that.

As Jockey president Howard Cooley recalls, grizzled company veterans responded with horror; he would turn Jockey into 'a woman's company', they sputtered. Executives in the company's ad agency were equally aghast: 'You are going to destroy your masculine image,' one of them told Cooley. And when the Jockey president put his proposal to retailers, every single one opposed it. Women won't buy underwear without lace, they told him, and they certainly won't buy briefs with the 'male' Jockey label on the waistband.

Cooley decided to try it anyway. In preparation, the company's market research department took another novel step – it actually solicited women's advice. Jockey's researchers invited scores of women to try on hundreds of pairs of knickers and say which they liked the best. The results: women want underwear that won't ride up, won't fall apart in the wash, and actually is the size promised on the label.

In 1983 the company introduced 'Jockey for Her' – with an advertising campaign featuring real women who actually wore and liked the underwear, women with a range of professions, ages and body types. They included a grandmother, an airline pilot, and a beautician who was even a little stocky. The brand became an instant success; within five years it was the most popular brand of women's underwear in America, with an extraordinary 40 per cent share of the market.

Jockey for Her inspired imitations from several large men's underwear manufacturers. But by and large, the women's underwear companies ignored Jockey's success, and headed even further in the opposite direction. Instead of comfortable briefs that don't ride up, the industry introduced this practical new undergarment – G-string-style 'thongs'. And on the rare occasion when women did get a chance to talk to lingerie makers, the companies simply disregarded their comments. Maidenform's ad agency, Levine Huntley Schmidt & Beaver, spent months interviewing focus groups of women about lingerie. 'The women complained that no one understood their needs,' creative director Jay Taub says. 'They wanted to be treated like real people.' But in the new Maidenform ad campaign that resulted, the only 'real people' featured were male celebrities and the only 'needs' the men addressed were their own. As Omar Sharif explained in one typical ad, he liked lingerie because it 'tells me how she feels about me'.

Guess Jeans and the Year of the Rear

For the most part, fashion-makers' efforts to regain control of the independent female consumer were veiled, tucked behind a flattering and hushed awe for that newly feminine lady of fashion. But this adoration was reserved for women who played by the backlash's rules, accepting casting as meek girls or virtuous Victorian ladies. For less malleable women, another fashion message began to surface – featuring the threat of discipline.

The beaten, bound or body-bagged woman became a staple of late-1980s fashion ads and editorial photo layouts. In the windows of major department stores female mannequins were suddenly being displayed as the battered conquests of leather-clad men and as corpses stuffed in rubbish bins. In *Vogue*, a fashion layout entitled HIDDEN DELIGHTS featured one model in a blindfold being pulled along by her corset ties, another woman with trussed legs, and still another with her arms and nude torso restrained in straps. Other mainstream fashion magazines offered fashion spreads with women in straitjackets, yanked by the neck with choke collars, and packed, nude, into a plastic rubbish sack. Fashion ads in the same vein proliferated in the US: a woman lying on an ironing board while a man applied an iron to her crotch (Esprit); a woman in a straitjacket (Seruchi); a woman dangling by her legs, chicken-style, from a man's fist (Cotler's – FOR THE RIGHT STANCE, the ad read); a woman knocked to the floor, her shirt ripped open (Foxy Lady); and a woman in a coffin (Michael Mann).

The girl with her rear end turned to the camera, as if ready for a spanking, was a particular favourite – just as it had been a century earlier, in late Victorian cartoons and popular art. By the late 1980s backside ads were so prevalent that they attracted editorial comment; one columnist even wondered if 1987 should be called 'The Year of the Rear'. *Company* magazine surveyed 1987's 'bottie-conscious' fashion look and argued that 'hi-thi swimsuits were on the point of losing their shock value . . . then *Crocodile Dundee*'s Linda Kozlowski gave us this scenic back view'. Adopting a sympathetic tone for the 'bottom heavy', the photo-feature acknowledged: 'Sadly, designers won't usually let you hide your bum . . . '

In the summer of 1987 in dozens of national magazines, American readers met yet another backside, this one attached to a girl in a bodysuit, crouched before an older man's trousered legs. Her gaze focused reverentially on his fly. On the following pages this same male figure loomed over other cowering girls, his lips curled in a condescending sneer. The ads' creator: Guess jeans.

Six years earlier, with the economy slipping into recession and the jeans market in its worst decline on record, Marseilles entrepreneur Georges Marciano had arrived in Bloomingdale's with a stack of skin-tight, stone-washed jeans. According to company lore, the buyer laughed at him and said, 'Nobody will wear these. They're uncomfortable and they look used.' They were also $60, nearly double the price of an average pair of jeans. But soon Guess would make, in the words of *Women's Wear Daily*, 'one of the biggest splashes in denim history'.

Georges and his brothers, Armand, Maurice and Paul, were chain-store merchants who set up shop in Los Angeles with an investment of only $100,000 and repackaged themselves as high-class jeans 'designers'; their élite jeans would be sold only in upmarket shops, they decided. Soon after they went into business, their small investment was yielding $250 million in annual revenue.

While Lacroix and his High Femininity succeeded only in littering the remainder racks with bubble skirts and puffballs, Guess found a way to use the backlash to sell clothes. Jeans, unlike party gowns, are affordable mass-market products, even at their overpriced extremes. And jeans are mostly bought by teenage girls, who are more vulnerable to fashion dictates than either the society women Lacroix initially targeted or the working women the industry hoped to sell on Lacroix's ideas.

Guess jeans weren't all that different from other designer jeans that flooded the 1980s market – except for the company's advertising. The Marciano brothers promoted their jeans with a $10 million annual campaign that never showed the product. The ads marketed instead what the company called 'The Guess Mystique': grainy shots of an American West peopled with tall cowboys on horseback and timorous women in wheat fields; a small-town 1950s America where the men cruise dusty country roads and girls wait passively at the diner, sipping milk shakes and swinging bobby-socked feet. The Guess ads generated media and public disapproval because some of the shots featured 'raunchy' sexuality; they lacked 'taste'. But in homing in on the question of sexual prurience, the company's critics missed the point; they overlooked the company's sexual politics.

'You should hear the things people say about the ads; it's hysterical,' says Lisa Hickey, Paul Marciano's personal assistant. The thin young woman in a puffball skirt leads the way into the front office of Guess's Los Angeles headquarters, a barbed-wire compound surrounded by a ghetto. 'What they don't understand is that Paul is very romantic. He looks at these things as love stories.' Hickey, a former journalism student, says she had been planning to get a master's degree, but Paul Marciano talked her out of it. 'Paul said, "Oh Lisa, you don't want to do that." He doesn't like it when we go to school.'

Paul saunters into the office just then, casual in a striped T-shirt and cotton trousers. Although the four brothers run the company as a team, Paul's post is the most crucial; he's in charge of advertising. Paul settles into a chair and dispatches Hickey to round up the portfolios of the company's past ad campaigns. 'When I came here, I fell in love with the American West,' the thirty-six-year-old Marciano says. 'I set the ads in the West because you will not see any change there. That seduced me tremendously.' Most appealing to him about this region is its women, who he believes remain untouched by feminist influence. In the American West, as Guess's coffee-table photobook on Texas observes, 'Women are treated with great respect, but it is assumed they know their place, which is supportive, and their function, which is often decorative.'

Aside from the West, Marciano says, he has another soft spot – for 1950s America – and for the same reason: 'I'm attracted to the femininity of the women in that era,' he says. 'The femininity like you find in Vargas drawings. That's what we want to bring back – everything that has been lost.' This isn't just what he wants, Marciano is quick to add. 'Women want to look the way they did in the 1950s,' he says. They feel cheated by liberation. 'The majority aren't getting married. . . . Their independence took over their private life, and their private life was tremendously damaged. They've passed thirty and they're still not married and they feel like they haven't accomplished what they wanted to as women.'

Hickey returns with the ad portfolios. Marciano opens one, the 'Louisiana campaign', and leafs slowly through the black-and-white stills. 'You see, each one is like a little theme film,' he says. The Louisiana campaign, for example, is based on one of his favourite American movies, *Baby Doll* – Elia Kazan's 1956 tale of a thumb-sucking child bride who sleeps in a crib. Marciano provides the soundtrack as he flips over the pages: 'This one girl is spying on the other one, who's with the man, and she's feeling a little bit envious' – he points to a photo of a fearful young woman hiding behind a tree – 'and now here she gets in a little bit of trouble with him' – the man grabs the woman's jaw and twists it – 'and here she's feeling a little sad . . .' – an anguished girl hides her face in her hands, her hair in knots and her clothes tattered.

He drops the portfolio and picks up another: the notorious 'Rome campaign' featuring the bodysuited bum. This one, he explains, is based on Fellini's *La Dolce Vita*. 'Some people objected to this campaign because he is so much older than her,' Marciano sighs, gesturing toward the leering gentleman. 'I guess he looks like he's in his fifties. But he could have just been the girl's father.' Marciano doesn't explain, then, why daughter is bouncing *shirtless* on dad's knee.

Marciano says he is proud that his ads use real men – real cowboys, ranchers, truck drivers, and an actual matador. 'My field is day-to-day street life,' he says. 'I don't want to create fake pictures.' Women, however, are another matter: 'We always use models. It's difficult to find real women who fit what we're trying to say. Real women, they aren't as cooperative as real men.' Marciano also favours relatively unknown models, with 'no identity':

'This way, we can make the Guess girl exactly who we want her to be.'

To capture her identity on film, Marciano hired fashion photographer Wayne Maser, who had shot the fashion photos with a quasi-bondage theme in *Vogue*. Maser also participated in selling another artefact of the backlash; he designed the promotional posters for *Fatal Attraction*. The film's director, Adrian Lyne, was a former colleague of Maser's in commercial photography. In 1988 Maser completed the circle, turning the former adman's movie back into advertising. Over four days that May, Maser shot the Guess version of *Fatal Attraction* in two white-picket-fence houses in Bedford, New York, the same homes Lyne had used for his set.

For the role of 'the other woman' in this ad's mini-movie script, Maser has cast a twenty-five-year-old French model, a Nastassia Kinski look-alike with pouting lips. Claudia, who is so uncomfortable with the way this ad campaign is shaping up that she asks that her last name not be used, keeps her distance from the crew – sitting by herself during breaks reading *Anna Karenina*. 'The only way I can do this,' she says, 'is because I have other aspects to my life.' She paints, brings up her two-year-old child, and works in a graphic design studio in Paris.

As the shoot progresses, Maser keeps scaling down the temptress's age and occupation – much the way TV producer Aaron Spelling shrank the status of his angels in subsequent rewrites. 'Let's put Claudia in a waitress uniform,' Maser proposes. 'No wait. Let's make her an au pair. You know, the little au pair seducing the husband? Brilliant, huh? Fucking brilliant.' Everyone agrees it is, and Maser instructs Claudia to change into a French maid's outfit. He orders the stylist to pin the skirt tighter. Then he positions Claudia in front of the kitchen stove, tells her to pretend she's cooking breakfast, and instructs, 'Arch your ass real good.'

'This is very cool,' Maser says, his Polaroid snapping. 'We need this dress tighter . . . it's got to look sexy.' Claudia complains, 'It's hurting me.' Maser ignores her and keeps shooting.

'The trouble with advertising today,' Maser says over a beer after the shoot is over, 'is everyone's afraid to take a stand on women. Everything's done to please the feminists because the feminists dominate these advertising positions. They've made women bland.' He sees his photographs as a challenge to the feminist cabal. 'My work is a reaction against feminist blandness,' he says. But, he wants to make clear, he isn't trying to restrict women, just endorse their new options. 'It's a post-feminist period,' he explains. 'Women can be women again. All my girls have a choice.'

Later, the Marciano brothers would set aside the *Fatal Attraction* ads – not because they were too demeaning or violent to women or too hostile to feminist 'blandness', but because they were too sexually graphic for mainstream presentation. Portraits of humiliated or battered young women passed muster with the Marciano censors, but depictions of adultery might disturb the sanctity of the family. Instead, that season, Guess substituted an ad campaign with cowgirls sucking their fingers. They gazed into the camera with startled and vulnerable doe eyes, Bambis before the hunters. It was the same message, really, as Maser's *Fatal Attraction* campaign, just more discreetly delivered – and ultimately more effective. In the eighties, fashion advertising often seemed to be one big woman-hunt. And by successfully camouflaging male anger, the Marciano brothers discovered, they could fire their best shots.

Chapter Eight

Beauty and the Backlash

With the aid of a metal rod, the first woman of the 'New Generation' stands in Robert Filoso's Los Angeles workshop, her feet dangling a few inches off the floor. Her clay arms are bandaged in gauze strips and her face hooded in a plastic bag, knotted at the neck to keep out dust motes. A single speck could cause a blemish.

'There are no imperfections in my models,' the thirty-eight-year-old mannequin sculptor explains. 'They all have to be taken out.' The dank environment inside the bag, however, has bred its own facial flaws. Between the woman's parted lips, a green mould is growing.

On this April morning in 1988 Filoso is at work on the model that will set the standard for the following year. Ever since he brought 'the new realism' to female mannequins – chiselling detailed vertebrae, toes and nipples – Filoso has led the $1.2 billion dummy industry, serving all the better retailers. This year he is making some major changes. His New Generation woman has shrunk in height, gained almost three inches on her breasts, shed an inch from her waist, and developed three sets of eyelashes. The new vital statistics, 34–23–36, are voluptuous by mannequin standards, but the Lacroix era of strapless gowns and bone-tight bodices requires bigger busts and wasp waists. 'Fashion,' Filoso says, 'determines the shape of my girls.'

The sculptor gingerly unwinds the cloth strips and hands them to his assistant and model, Laurie Rothey. 'It seems like so many of the girls are getting breast implants,' Rothey says as they work, and she isn't referring to the mannequins. 'It's the only way you can get jobs, because big breasts are all the [modelling] agencies are hiring now . . . '

Filoso interrupts her with a curse. The clay hasn't dried yet and the mannequin's arm has flopped off its metal bone. The sculptor tries to reattach the limb but now one arm is shorter than the other. 'Look at her now, she's a disaster,' Filoso cries, throwing his towel on the floor and departing in a huff.

Later that day, his composure regained, Filoso describes his vision of the New Generation. He pictures an in-shape upmarket Marilyn Monroe, a 'curvy but thin' society lady who can 'afford to go to Bergdorf Goodman's and buy anything'. Their poses, too, he says, will be 'more feminine, more contained. . . . In the 1970s, mannequins were always out there, reaching for something. Now they are pulling into themselves.' That's the way it is for real women in the eighties, too, he says: 'Now you can be yourself, you can be a lady. You don't have to be a powerhouse.'

In Filoso's opinion, these developments are a big improvement on the 1970s, when women 'didn't care' about their appearance. 'The stores didn't want beautiful mannequins, because they were afraid women customers would look at them and say, "God, I could never look like that in a million years." ' That era, Filoso is happy to report, has passed. 'Now, mannequins are really coming to life. They are going to start getting prettier again – more like the fashion photography you'd see in old magazines from the 1950s.' And what of female customers who might say, as he put it, 'God, I could never look like that in a million years'? But that's the good news, Filoso says. 'Today, women can look at a beautiful mannequin in a store and say, "I want to look like her," and they actually can! They can go to their doctor and say, "Doc, I want these cheekbones." "Doc, I want those breasts." '

He sighs. 'If I were smart, I would have become a plastic surgeon.'

During the 1980s mannequins set the beauty trends – and real women were expected to follow. The dummies were 'coming to life', while the ladies were breathing anaesthesia and going under the knife. The beauty industry promoted a 'return to femininity' as if it were a revival of natural womanhood – a flowering of all those innate female qualities supposedly suppressed in the feminist 1970s. Yet the 'feminine' traits the industry celebrated most were grossly unnatural – and achieved with increasingly harsh, unhealthy and punitive measures.

The beauty industry, of course, has never been an advocate of feminist aspirations. This is not to say that its promoters have a conscious political programme against women's rights, just a commercial mandate to improve on the bottom line. And the formula the industry has counted on for many years – aggravating women's low self-esteem and high anxiety about a 'feminine' appearance – has always served them well. The beauty makers' motives aren't particularly thought out or deep. But even so, in the 1980s the beauty industry belonged to the cultural loop that produced backlash feedback. Inevitably, publicists for the beauty companies would pick up the warning signals circulating about the toll of women's equality, too – and amplify them for their own purposes.

'Is your face paying the price of success?' worried a 1988 Nivea skin cream ad, in which a business-suited woman with a briefcase rushes a child to day care – and catches a glimpse of her career-pitted skin in a store window. If only she were less successful, her visage would be more radiant. 'The impact of work stress . . . can play havoc with your complexion,' *Mademoiselle* warned; it can cause 'a bad case of dandruff', 'an eventual loss of hair' and, worst of all, weight gain. Most at risk, the magazine claimed, are 'high-achieving women', whose comely appearance can be ravaged by 'executive stress'. In ad after ad, the beauty industry hammered home its version of the backlash thesis: women's professional progress had downgraded their looks; equality had created worry lines and cellulite. This message was barely updated from a century earlier, when the late Victorian beauty press had warned women that their quest for higher education and employment was causing 'a general lapse of attractiveness' and 'spoiling complexions'.

The beauty merchants incited fear about the cost of women's occupational success largely because they feared, rightly, what that success had cost *them* – in profits. Since the rise of the women's movement in the seventies, cosmetics and fragrance companies had suffered a decade of flat-to-declining sales, hair-product merchandisers had fallen into a prolonged slump, and hairdressers had watched helplessly as masses of female customers who were opting for simple low-cost cuts defected to discount unisex salons. In 1981 Revlon's earnings fell for the first time since 1968; by the following year, the company's profits had plunged a record 40 per cent. The industry aimed to restore its own economic health by persuading women that *they* were the ailing patients – and professionalism their ailment. Beauty became medicalized as its lab-coated army of promoters, and real doctors, prescribed medically endorsed potions, injections for the skin, chemical 'treatments' for the hair, plastic surgery for virtually every inch of the torso. (One doctor even promised to reduce women's height by sawing their leg bones.) In America dermatologists faced with a shrinking teen market switched from treating adolescent pimples to 'curing' adult female wrinkles. Gynaecologists and obstetricians frustrated with a sluggish birthrate and skyrocketing malpractice premiums traded their forceps for liposuction scrapers. Hospitals facing revenue shortfalls opened cosmetic-surgery divisions and sponsored extreme and costly liquid-protein diet programmes.

The beauty industry may seem the most superficial of the cultural institutions participating in the backlash, but its impact on women was, in many respects, the most intimately destructive – to both female bodies and minds. Following the orders of the 1980s beauty doctors made many women literally ill. Anti-wrinkle treatments exposed them to carcinogens. Acid face peels burned their skin. Silicone injections left painful deformities. 'Cosmetic' liposuction caused severe complications, infections, and even death. Internalized, the decade's beauty dictates played a role in exacerbating an epidemic of eating disorders. And the beauty industry helped to deepen the psychic isolation that so many women felt in the 1980s by reinforcing the representation of women's problems as purely personal ills, unrelated to social pressures and curable only to the degree that the individual woman succeeded in fitting the universal standard – by physically changing herself.

The emblems of pulchritude marketed in the eighties – frailty, pallor, puerility – were all beauty marks handed down by previous backlash eras. Historically, the backlash Venus has been an enervated invalid recovering on the *chaise-longue*, an ornamental and genteel lady sipping tea in the drawing room, a child bride shielded from the sun. During the late Victorian era the beauty industry glorified a cult of invalidism – and profited from it by promoting near-toxic potions that induced a chalky skin. The wasting-away look helped in part to unleash the first dieting mania and the emergence of anorexia in young women. In times of backlash, the beauty standard converges with the social campaign against wayward women, allying itself with 'traditional' morality; a porcelain and unblemished exterior becomes proof of a woman's internal purity, obedience and restraint. The beautiful backlash woman is controlled in both senses of the word. Her physique has been domesticated, her appearance as tamed and manicured as the grounds of a gentleman's estate.

By contrast, athleticism, health and vivid colour are the defining properties of female beauty during periods when the culture is more receptive to women's quest for independence. In the late 1910s and early 1920s female athletes began to eclipse movie stars as beauty archetypes; Coco Chanel's tan launched a vogue in ruddy outdoor looks; and Helena Rubinstein's brightly tinted cosmetics made loud and flamboyant colours acceptable. By the late 1920s and 1930s, however, the beauty press denounced women who tanned their faces and companies fired women who turned up at work sporting flashy make-up colours. Again, during the Second World War invigorated and suntanned beauties received all the praise. *Harper's Bazaar* described 'the New American Look of 1943' this way: 'Her face is out in the open and so is she. Her figure is lithe and strong. Its lines are lines of action. The glamour girl is no more.' With the war over, however, the beauty industry restored that girl – encouraged by a new breed of motivational research consultants who advised cosmetics companies to paint more passive images of femininity. Beauty publicists instructed women to inflate their breasts with padding or silicone, to frost their hair with carcinogenic dyes, to make themselves look paler by whitening their face and lips with titanium – to emulate, in short, that most bleached and medicalized glamour girl of them all, Marilyn Monroe.

Under the 1980s backlash the pattern would repeat itself, as

'Action Beauty', as it was labelled and exalted in 1970s women's magazines, gave way to a sickbed aesthetic. It was a comprehensive transformation carried out at every level of the beauty culture – from the most superficially applied scent to the most invasive and dangerous operations.

From Charlie to Ophelia

In the winter of 1973 Charles Revson called a high-level meeting of Revlon executives. He had a revolutionary concept, he told them: a fragrance that celebrated women's liberation. (It actually wasn't that revolutionary: in the 1910s, perfume companies like Shalimar replaced weak lavenders with strong musks and marketed them to liberated New Women.) The Revlon team code-named the plan 'Cosmo', and spent the next several months taking groups of women out to lunch and asking them what they wanted in a perfume.

The women told the Revlon interviewers that they were sick of hearing that fragrances were supposed to be defining them; they wanted a perfume that reflected the new self-image they had defined for themselves. The company's market researchers considered this and eventually came up with a fragrance called Charlie, which they represented in ads with a confident and single working woman who signs her own cheques, pops into nightclubs on her own, and even asks men to dance. Revlon introduced Charlie in 1973 – and sold out its stock within weeks. Less than a year into its launch, Charlie had become a bestselling fragrance.

'Charlie symbolized that new lifestyle,' Revlon executive vice-president Lawrence Wechsler recalls, 'that said, you can be anything you want to be, you can do anything you want to do, without any criticism being directed at you. If you want to wear pantsuits at the office instead of a skirt, fine.' The success of the Charlie ad campaign inspired nearly a dozen similar ones, from Max Factor's Maxi ('When I'm in the Mood, There's No Stopping Me') to Chanel's Cristalle ('Celebrate Yourself'), all featuring heroines who were brash, independent and sexually assertive. Super-athletes abounded, from Coty's ice-skating champion, Smitty, to Fabergé's roller-skating dynamo, Babe ('the fragrance for the fabulous new woman you're becoming') – in homage to Olympian Babe Didrikson Zaharias.

Suddenly in 1982, Revlon retired the old Charlie ad campaign and replaced her with a woman who was seeking marriage and a family. The change wasn't inspired by a decline in sales; Revlon's managers just 'sensed' that Charlie's time had passed. 'We had gone a little too far with the whole women's liberation thing,' Wechsler says. 'And it wasn't an issue any more, anyway. There were more important issues now, like drugs. And then there's the biological clock. There's a need now for a woman to be less striving.' But the cancellation of the Charlie ad campaign, he insists, is actually a sign of women's 'progress'. She has come so far, he says, 'she doesn't have to be so assertive any more. She can be more womanly.'

The new campaign, however, didn't appeal to female customers and Revlon had to replace it again in 1986. This time the company did away with the character of Charlie altogether and offered an assortment of anonymous women who were identified as 'very Charlie' types (in an ad campaign created by Malcolm MacDougall, the same ad executive who produced *Good Housekeeping*'s New Traditional woman). In a sense, the company had come full circle: once again the fragrance was defining the standard that women had to meet.

At least the 'very Charlie' women were still walking and showing signs of life. By the mid-1980s many of the fragrance ladies had turned into immobilized, chalky figurines. The perfume industry had decided to sell weaker fragrances to weaker women, and both the scent and the scented were toned down. 'In the past few years, many women have worn fragrances that were just as strong as their push for a vice-president position,' Jonathan King, marketing director for fragrance supplier Quest International, asserted in the press in 1987. But now more 'relaxed' fragrances with a more ladylike, restrained aura would take their place, restoring depleted feminine 'mystery'. A host of eighties perfume makers dispensed curative potions: 'aroma therapy' they were called, fragrance lines to induce a 'calming' mood in fretful careerist female wearers. These odours can 'relieve stress and depression without taking drugs,' International Flavors vice-president Craig Warren announced cheerfully. Avon marketers even insisted that their variety, Tranquil Moments, had a proven soothing effect on female brain waves. But it wasn't just the tranquillizing smells that symbolized the change. In a new round of perfume ad campaigns in the eighties, the female models on display were no longer 'pushing', either, as fragrance merchandisers focused their marketing drives on three stock 'feminine' types: the upper-class lady of leisure, the bride and the little girl.

In the first half of the 1980s 500 high-priced perfume brands claiming to offer an upper-class socialite scent flooded the market. (To reinforce the point, at least half a dozen lines added gold flecks to their high-society perfumes.) As couture designers sought lucrative fragrance licensing contracts for themselves, *their* names started showing up on perfume bottles instead of women's; Bill Blass replaced Babe Didrikson. The women who did make it into perfume ads were representatives of gentility or glamour, not independence or athleticism. To promote Passion, Parfums International deployed Elizabeth Taylor to play the aristocratic lady; she read poems in TV ads and hosted ladies' teas in department stores. Even middlebrow Avon tried to go upmarket, buying the rights to such perfume names as Giorgio, Oscar de la Renta and Perry Ellis and introducing Deneuve at $165 (about £89) an ounce.

As the fragrance industry geared up its second strategy, the marriage pitch, demure and alabaster brides soon proliferated in perfume ads, displacing the self-confident single women. In 1985, Estée Lauder unveiled Beautiful, the fragrance 'for all your beautiful moments'. But the only 'moment' the ads ever depicted was a wedding day. (The 'Beautiful Moments' campaign for women happened to coincide with Omega watches 'Significant Moments' campaign for men, making for an unintentionally instructive back-to-back contrast in many magazines: on one page, she lowered her veil; on the next, he raised his fist to celebrate 'the pure joy of victory'.)

Women in the fragrance ads who weren't having babies were being turned into them – as one company after another selected a pre-pubescent girl as the new icon of femininity. 'Perfume is one of the great pleasures of being a woman,' the caption read in *Vogue*, accompanying a photo of a baby-girl Lolita, her face heavily made up and blonde curls falling suggestively across cherubic cheeks. IN PRAISE OF WOMAN was the 1989 ad slogan for Lord & Taylor's perfume Krizia, but the only woman praised in this ad was a preschooler dressed in Victorian clothes, her eyes cast demurely downwards. 'You're a wholesome woman from the very beginning,' murmured still another perfume ad – of a ladylike five-year-old. Even one of Revlon's new 'very Charlie' types was under ten.

But none of these marketing strategies paid off. The flood of upmarket scents, in fact, caused fragrance sales to fall in 1986 – the first drop in years. At Avon, by 1988, quarterly earnings were dropping 57 per cent, less than half its beauty profits were coming from US sales, and the company had to fire one-third of its sales managers. By appealing to affluent 'ladies' that company had ignored its most loyal and numerous consumers: working-class women. Avon might have consulted its own research, which showed that its typical customer was a woman with a secondary-school education, blue-collar job and two children. How was she supposed to afford a vastly expensive 1-ounce bottle of perfume?

With the lures of wealth, marriage and infancy proving insufficient inducement, the perfume ad campaigns pushed idealization of weak and yielding women to its logical extreme – and wheeled out the female corpse. In Yves Saint Laurent's Opium ads a woman was stretched out as if on a bier, her eyes sealed shut, a funereal floral arrangement by her ashen face. In Jovan's Florals ads a modern-day Ophelia slipped into supreme repose, her naked body strewn with black and white orchids. The morbid scene sported this caption: EVERY WOMAN'S RIGHT TO A LITTLE INDULGENCE.

Keeping a Daily De-Ageing Diary

The cosmetics industry adopted a familiar Victorian maxim about children as its latest make-up 'trend' in the late 1980s. As a feature headline put it, THE MAKEUP MESSAGE FOR THE SUMMER: BE SEEN BUT NOT HEARD. The beautiful woman was the quiet one. *Mademoiselle*'s cosmetics articles praised the 'muted' look, warned against 'a mouth that roars', and reminded women that 'being a lady is better ... better than power, better than money'. *Vogue* placed a finger to women's lips and appealed for silence: 'There's a new sense of attractiveness in makeup. . . . [N]othing ever "shouts".' Ten years earlier, make-up, like fragrance, came in relentlessly 'spirited' and 'exuberant' colours with 'muscle'. The 'Outspoken Chanel' woman wore nail and face colour as loud as her new 'confidence' and 'witty voice'. Now cosmetics tiptoed, ghostly, across the skin. Partly, of course, this new beauty rule was just the by-product of that time-honoured sales strategy: create demand simply by reversing the dictates of style. But the selection of the muffled maiden as the new ideal was also a reveal-ing one, a more reassuring image for beauty merchants who were unnerved by women's desertion of the cosmetics counter.

The make-up marketers rolled out the refined upper-class lady, too; like the fragrance sellers, they hoped to make more money from fewer women by exhorting affluent baby-boom women to purchase aristocratic-sounding beauty products – with matching high-class prices. But again this marketing manoeuvre backfired. The heaviest users of make-up are teenagers and working-class women – and the formidable price tags on these new 'élite' make-ups just scared them off. The make-up companies' tactics only caused their earnings to fall more sharply; soon, leading securities analysts were warning investors to avoid all cosmetics stocks.

Finally, though, these companies came up with a more lucrative way to harness backlash attitudes to their sales needs. Many major cosmetics companies began peddling costly medicinal-sounding potions that claimed to revert older female skin to baby-pale youth and to shield women's 'sensitive' complexions from the ravages of environmental, and especially professional, exposure. By exploit-ing universal fears of mortality in the huge and ageing baby-boom population – exploiting it in women only, of course – the industry finally managed to improve its financial state. 'Time waits for no man (but it can for a woman),' promised Boots No. 7 in its ad for Replenish skin cream. 'With each daily application, you're helping slow down the ticking of the clock.' The accompanying photograph showed a woman desperately trying to hold back the minute hand on a giant clockface.

By the late 1980s, entering a cosmetics department was like stumbling into a stylish sanatorium. The sales assistants were wearing white nurses' uniforms, and the treatments were costly and time-consuming regimens with medicinal names and packages, accompanied by physicians' endorsements. Clarins's 'Biological Tightener' came in a twenty-day treatment rack lined with test-tube-shaped 'ampoules'. Glycel, an 'anti-ageing' cream, boasted the support of heart surgeon Dr Christiaan Barnard. La Prairie offered 'cellular therapy' from their 'world-renowned medical facility' in Switzerland – and its bottles of 'capsules' came with little spoons for proper dosage. Clinique's 'medically trained' staff urged women to exfoliate daily, chart their epidermal progress in a 'Daily De-Ageing Workbook', and monitor skin health on the company's 'computer' – a plastic board with sliding buttons that was closer to a Fisher-Price Busybox than a MacIntosh.

References to female fertility were abundant at the cosmetics counter, too, as the beauty industry moved to exploit the 'biologi-cal-clock' anxieties that popular culture had done so much to inflame. The labels of dozens of beauty treatments claimed remedial gynaecological ingredients: 'sheep placentas', 'bovine embryos', and even, bizarrely, 'human placental protein'. Also on display, in keeping with the demands of eighties backlash fashion, were 'breast creams' and 'bust firming lotions' to boost a woman's bra size – products not seen in department stores since the 1950s.

To promote their skin 'treatments' cosmetics companies employed traditional scare tactics about skin damage (PREMATURE AGEING: DON'T LET IT HAPPEN TO YOU. Ultima II ads warned – it's 'every skin-conscious woman's worst nightmare come true'), but they delivered these fear-inducing messages now with pseudo-feminist language about taking control. The ad agency that created Oil of Ulay's (Olay in the US) successful campaign in the 1980s – which shifted the company's focus from older women with real wrinkles to baby-boom women with imaginary ones – employed what its executives labelled 'the control concept'. Its age-terrorized but take-charge female model vowed in the product's American ads, 'I don't intend to grow old gracefully. . . . I intend to fight it every step of the way.' Chanel adverts even advised professional women to use anti-wrinkle creams to improve their work status; fighting wrinkles, they informed them, was 'a smart career move'.

While cosmetics companies used the vocabulary of women's

liberation for marketing purposes, they also claimed that the fruits of that liberation were eroding women's appearance. Career 'stress' was the real destroyer of feminine beauty, the cosmetics industry insisted. The fluorescent office lights and even daily commuting posed a greater threat to female skin than intensive tanning, Ultima II ads insisted. 'Dermatologists have agreed that you accumulate far more damage during the year going to and from work than in two weeks of concentrated sunbathing.'

The beauty companies fared better hawking anti-wrinkle potions than traditional scents and cosmetics because backlash appeals in this area were able to couple female awareness of ancient cultural fears of the older woman with modern realities of the baby-boom woman's ageing demographic. This was a most effective combination. By 1985 a cosmetics trade association survey of skin-care professionals found that 97 per cent had noticed that their clients were markedly more worried and upset about the threat of wrinkles than just a few years earlier. By 1986 skin-cream annual sales had doubled in five years to $1.9 billion. And for the first time many department-store cosmetics counters were selling more skin-treatment products than colour make-up.

The popularity of high-priced anti-wrinkle creams could hardly be attributed to improvements in the lotions' efficacy. The claims made on behalf of high-priced anti-ageing products were virtually all fraudulent, the promises of 'cell renewal', 'DNA repair' and age 'reversal' so ludicrous that even the Reagan-era US Food and Drug Administration issued cease and desist orders against twenty-three of the cosmetic firms. Promises to protect women's health by shielding their skin from the sun were similarly phoney. Skin-care companies cashed in with sunblocks claiming protection factors as high as 34; researchers and the FDA could find no effectiveness over 15. And while it would be nice to believe that beauty companies simply wanted to guard women's skin from carcinogenic rays, they showed no such vigilance against cancer when publicizing one of their most highly touted skin-treatment innovations of the decade: Retin-A.

A century earlier, women were encouraged to consume 'Fowler's Solution', an arsenic-laced acne cream, to revitalize ageing skin; it made them sick, some fatally. In the 1980s, beauty doctors in the USA dispensed a prescription acne ointment reputed to possess anti-ageing properties. Retin-A, however, is also suspected of causing cancer in mice and an oral version of the drug, Accutane, has been accused of producing birth defects. Moreover, Retin-A seemed more effective at burning women's faces than burnishing them. In the one study testing the cream's effect on wrinkles – sponsored by Retin-A's own Ortho Pharmaceutical Corporation – 73 per cent of the participants who took Retin-A needed topical steroids to reduce the painful swelling and 20 per cent developed such severe dermatitis that they had to drop out of the study. (On the other hand, the study found that Retin-A gave *one* of the participants a 'much improved' facial appearance.)

Despite the apparent medical risks involved with Retin-A the dermatologist who had conducted this lone study, John Voorhees (dermatology chairman from the University of Michigan), served as one of Ortho's promoters of Retin-A at a news conference in the Rainbow Room in Manhattan – a publicity event that caused Johnson & Johnson's stock price to leap eight points in two days. The media dubbed Voorhees the 1980s Ponce de Leon; *USA Today* declared his discovery 'a miracle'. In one year Retin-A sales rose 350 per cent to $67 million, chemists sold out of the $25 tubes, visits to dermatologists skyrocketed and doctors set up Retin-A shopping mall 'clinics' that drew hundreds of women. The FDA had not approved Retin-A's use for wrinkles, but dermatologists dispensed it for that purpose anyway, simply claiming on the prescription forms that their middle-aged female patients were suffering from outbreaks of adolescent acne. On paper at least, the doctors had succeeded in turning grown women back into pimply teenage girls.

Cosmetic Surgery: Cancer and Other 'Variations from the Ideal'

Starting in 1983, the American Society of Plastic and Reconstructive Surgeons launched a 'practice enhancement' campaign, issuing a flood of press releases, 'pre- and post-op photos', and patient 'education' brochures and videotapes. They billed 'body sculpturing' as safe, effective, affordable – and even essential to women's mental health. 'There is a body of medical information that these deformities [small breasts] are really a disease,' a statement issued by the society asserted; left uncorrected, flat-chestedness causes 'a total lack of well-being'. To fight this grave mental health hazard, the society was soon offering a financing plan for consumers – 'no down payment' and credit approval within twenty-four hours.

The inspiration for the society's PR blitzkrieg was the usual one – a little problem of supply and demand. While the ranks of plastic surgeons had quintupled since the 1960s, patient enthusiasm hadn't kept pace. By 1981 the flood of doctors into cosmetic surgery had made it the fastest-growing specialism in American medicine, and they simply needed more bodies. Plastic surgeons started seeking publicity in a systematic way. By the mid-1980s their appeals overran magazines and newspapers, offering 'low monthly payment plans', acceptance of all credit cards, convenient evening and Saturday surgery sessions. A single issue of *Los Angeles* magazine contained more than two dozen such ads.

The surgeons marketed their services as self-image enhancers for women – and as strategies for expanding women's opportunities. Cosmetic surgery can even help women 'pursue career goals', an ad in the *New York Times* promised. With liposuction, 'you can feel more confident about yourself', the Center for Aesthetic & Reconstructive Surgery said. 'Most important', you can exercise a 'choice' – although by that, the ad copy referred only to 'your choice of physician'.

From *Vogue* to *Time*, the media assisted the doctors, producing dozens of stories urging women to 'invest', as a *Wall Street Journal* article put it, in breast expansion and liposuction. 'Go curvy,' *Mademoiselle* exhorted. 'Add a bit above the waist'; it's easy and you can 'go back to work in five days, and to aerobics in six weeks'. 'Attention, front and center!' the magazine demanded again, three issues later. 'The lush bust is back' – and breast implants are the ideal way of 'getting a boost'. *Options* asked, 'If those are laughter lines . . . why are you crying?' and provided a 'top-to-bottom update on the cost and skill of cosmetic surgery'. Referring to the 'problem' of very small breasts, the article enthused: 'Augmentation [is] the most popular and widely practised operation in America and Europe today, and techniques to increase the size and improve the shape of the breasts have reached a new zenith of perfection in recent years.' American TV talk shows conducted contests for free cosmetic surgery; radio stations gave away breast implants as promotions. Even *Ms.* deemed plastic surgery a way of 'reinventing' yourself – a strategy for women who 'dare to take control of their lives'.

Soon the propaganda circle was complete: cosmetic surgeons quoted from these articles in their advertisements, as if media publicity were proof of their own professional excellence. 'Dr Gaynor is often called "the King of Liposuction",' an ad for dermatologist Dr Alan Gaynor boasted. 'He has appeared as a liposuction expert on TV dozens of times, as well as in *Time* magazine and the *Wall Street Journal*, and most local newspapers.' In Britain surgeons are not allowed to advertise but clinics can, with the result that 'cowboy' operators and suspect private clinics and advisory services have proliferated; increasing women's risk of encountering insufficient check-ups, perfunctory consultation and scant post-operative care.

The American campaign worked. By 1988 the cosmetic surgeons' caseload had more than doubled, to 750,000 annually. And that was counting only the doctors certified in plastic surgery; the total annual figure was estimated to be in excess of 1.5 million. More than 2 million women, or one in sixty, were sporting the $2,000 to $4,000 breast implants – making breast enlargement the most common cosmetic operation. More than 100,000 had undergone the $4,000-plus liposuction surgery, a procedure that was unknown a decade ago. (By 1987 the average plastic surgeon in America made a *profit* of $180,000 a year.) About 85 per cent of the patients were women – and they weren't spoiled dowagers. A 1987 survey by a plastic surgery association found that about half their patients earned less than $25,000 a year; these women took out loans and even mortgaged homes to pay the surgery bill.

Publicity, not breakthroughs in medical technology, had made all the difference. Plastic surgery was as dangerous as ever; in fact, the operations would become even riskier as the big profits lured droves of untrained practitioners away from other specialisms. In 1988 a congressional investigation revealed widespread charlatanry, ill-equipped facilities, major injuries, and even deaths from botched operations. Other studies found that at least 15 per cent of cosmetic surgery caused haemorrhages, facial nerve damage, bad scars, or complications from anaesthesia. Follow-up operations to correct mistakes filled a two-volume, 1,134-page reference manual, *The Unfortunate Result in Plastic Surgery*. Plastic surgeons were devoting as much as a quarter of their practices to correcting their colleagues' errors.

For breast implants, in at least 20 per cent of the cases repeat surgery was required to remedy the ensuing pain, infection, blood clots or implant ruptures. A 1987 study in the *Annals of Plastic Surgery* reported that the implants failed as much as 50 per cent of the time and had to be removed. In 1988 investigators at the FDA's Product Surveillance division found that the failure rate of breast implants was among the highest of any surgery-related procedure under their purview. But rather than take action, the FDA stopped monitoring failure rates altogether – because consulting doctors couldn't decide what constituted 'failure'.

Contracture of scar tissue around the implant, separation from the breast tissue and painful hardening of the breasts occurred in one-third of women who had the operation. The medical literature reported that 75 per cent of women had some degree of contracture, 20 per cent of it severe. Implants also caused scarring, infection, skin necrosis and blood clots. And if the implants ruptured, the leaking could cause toxicity, lupus, rheumatoid arthritis and autoimmune diseases such as scleroderma. The implants could also interfere with nursing, prevent cancer detection, and numb sensitivity. In 1989 a Florida woman died during breast enlargement surgery. While the cause, an overdose of anaesthetic, was only indirectly related to the procedure, it's still fair to describe her as a backlash victim: a model with two children, she had the operation because the modelling agencies were demanding women with big breasts.

In 1982 the FDA declared breast implants 'a potentially unreasonable risk of injury'. Yet the federal agency did not pursue further research. And when a 1988 study by Dow Corning Corporation found that silicone gel implants caused cancer in more than 23 per cent of rats tested, the FDA dismissed the findings. 'The risk to humans, if it exists at all, would be low,' FDA commissioner Dr Frank Young said. Not until April 1991, after still more federal research linking foam-coated implants to cancer surfaced and after a congressional subcommittee intervened, did the FDA finally break down and give the implant manufacturers ninety days to demonstrate that their devices were safe or take them off the market. A nervous Bristol-Myers Squibb Co. wasted no time yanking its two brands from the shelves. In January 1992, after an FDA advisory panel called for a forty-five-day halt to breast-implant operations, Dow Corning also announced that, at least temporarily, it would suspend sales. The news prompted several well-known British women to reveal that they, too, were having physical problems as a result of breast-implant operations. Former *Howard's Way* star Sally Farmiloe spoke of the discomfort and pain that she suffered after an implant operation which she had at the behest of her boyfriend – who told her that 'looking like Raquel Welch' would help her acting career.

The American Society of Plastic and Reconstructive Surgeons responded to the myriad complaints over implants with a 'position statement', written as a press release, which offered 'reassurance to the nearly 94,000 women who undergo breast enlargement every year'. Women with breast implants 'are at no increased risk of delayed cancer diagnosis', the statement soothed, without offering any medical evidence to back its claim. It did, however, propose that 'the real causes of late diagnosis are ignorance, complacency, neglect, and denial.' In other words, the woman's fault.

The track record of liposuction – the scraping and vacuuming of fat deposits – was no better. Between 1984 and 1986 the number of liposuction operations rose 78 per cent – but the procedure barely worked. Liposuction removed only one to two pounds of fat, had no mitigating effect on the unseemly 'dimpling' effect of cellulite, and, in fact, often made it worse. The procedure could also produce permanent bagginess in the skin and oedema, just two of the 'variations from the ideal' that the plastic surgery society catalogued in its own report. Another 'variation' on the list: 'pain'.

Furthermore, the plastic surgery society's survey of its members discovered several other unfortunate incidents. A liposuction patient lay down to have stomach fat removed and woke up with a perforated bowel and faecal matter leaking through the abdominal cavity. Three patients developed pulmonary infections and two had massive infections. Three suffered pulmonary fat embolism syndrome, a life-threatening condition in which fat can lodge in the heart, lungs and eyes. And 'numerous patients' required, as the survey delicately put it, 'unplanned transfusions'.

On March 30, 1987, Patsy Howell died of massive infections three days after a liposuction operation performed by Dr Hugo Ramirez, a gynaecologist who ran a plastic surgery clinic in Pasadena, Texas. The same day Howell had her operation, Ramirez performed liposuction on Patricia Rogers; she also developed massive infections, was hospitalized in critical condition, and eventually had to have all her skin from below her chest to the top of her thighs removed.

Howell, a thirty-nine-year-old floral shop manager and the mother of two sons, submitted to liposuction to remove a small paunch on her 5' 1" frame. She weighed only 120 pounds (8st. 8lb). 'This literature she got at a shopping mall said the procedure was so simple,' her friend Rheba Downey told a reporter. 'She said, "Why not?" ' She made up her mind after reading Ramirez's newspaper advert, which called the surgery 'the revolutionary technique for reduction of fat without dieting'. No one told her about the dangers. Ramirez operated on more than 200 women, causing numerous injuries and two deaths before his licence was finally revoked.

By 1987, only five years after the fat-scraping technique was introduced in the United States, the plastic surgery society had counted eleven deaths from liposuction. A 1988 congressional subcommittee placed the death toll at twenty. And the figure is probably higher, because patients' families are often reluctant to report that the cause of death is this 'vanity' procedure. A woman in San Francisco, for example, who was not on the surgery society's or Congress's list, died in 1989 from an infection caused by liposuction to her stomach; the infection spread to her brain, her lungs collapsed, and she finally had a massive stroke. But her family was too ashamed about the procedure to bring it to public attention.

The society's 1987 report on liposuction, however, seemed less

concerned with safety than with 'the reputation of suction lipectomy', which its authors feared had been 'marred by avoidable
deaths and preventable complications'. It concluded that all problems with liposuction could easily be solved with 'guidelines gov-
erning who is permitted to perform and advertise surgical procedures'. In other words, just get rid of the gynaecologists and
dermatologists and leave the surgery to them.

Yet some of the liposuction patients had died at the hands of
plastic surgeons. The most common cause of death was the release
of fat emboli into the heart, lungs and brain – a risk whenever
inner layers of epidermis are scraped, no matter how proficient
the scraper. As even the report acknowledged: '[Liposuction] is
by its nature a tissue-crush phenomenon. Therefore, fat embolism
is a realistic possibility.'

Surgeons also marketed the injection of liquid silicone straight
into the face. *Vogue* described it this way: 'Plastic surgery used
to be a dramatic process, but new techniques now allow doctors
to make smaller, sculptural facial changes.' This 'new' technique
was actually an old practice that had been used by doctors in the
last backlash era to expand breasts – and abandoned as too dangerous. It was no better the second time round; thousands of women
who tried it developed severe facial pain, numbing ulcerations and
hideous deformities. One Los Angeles plastic surgeon, Dr Jack
Startz, devastated the faces of hundreds of the 2,000 women he
injected with liquid silicone. He later committed suicide.

For the most part, these doctors were not operating on women
who might actually benefit from plastic surgery. In fact the
number of reconstructive operations to aid burn victims and breast
cancer patients declined in the late 1980s. For many plastic surgeons, helping to boost women's self-esteem wasn't the main
appeal of their profession. Despite the ads, the doctors were less
interested in improving their patients' sense of 'control' than they
were in improving their own control over their patients. 'To me,'
said plastic surgeon Kurt Wagner, who operated on his wife's
physique nine times, 'surgery is like being in the arena where
decisions are made and no one can tell me what to do.' Women
under anaesthesia don't talk back.

Part Three
Origins of a Reaction:
Backlash Movers, Shakers
and Thinkers

Chapter Nine

The Politics of Resentment: The New Right's War on Women

'*The politics of despair in America has typically been the politics of backlash.*'

SEYMOUR MARTIN LIPSET AND EARL RAAB

'I have hope for the first time in a long time,' declares Paul Weyrich. The 'Father of the New Right' gazes out the window at the squalor surrounding his Washington, DC, office. Homeless families huddle on the pavements; half a block from Weyrich's Free Congress Research and Education Foundation, sirens wail and gunshots ring out.

The good cheer of the New Right leader would seem as inappropriate to the times as it is to his location. Isn't the winter of 1988, after all, a little late for the founder of the Heritage Foundation to be feeling good about America? Wasn't the New Right movement's time of hope at the start of the decade, when its leaders drove liberal senators from office, rewrote the Republican party's platform, and marched triumphantly into Washington? Hasn't it all been downhill since then?

Weyrich, who has just returned from a college lecture tour, reads the signs differently. 'I see great hope because there's a new receptivity out there for the first time. Ten years ago, when I talked on campuses about the lie of women's liberation, about withholding sexual gratification, I got an absolutely hostile reaction. People hissed and booed. Now I get great interest. Now at Kent State – Kent State! – I get a nineteen-year-old girl coming up to me afterward with grateful tears in her eyes, and she says, "Thank you. Thank you very much." '

Not only are some college girls listening, the 'liberal media' seem to be coming round to Weyrich's point of view on women. This encourages him the most: 'At last the lie of feminism is being understood. Women are discovering they can't have it all. They are discovering that if they have careers, their children will suffer, their family life will be destroyed. It used to be we were the only ones who were saying it. Now, I read about it everywhere. Even *Ms.* magazine. *Ms.*!'

While the New Right movement failed to enact many of the specific legislative measures on its list, it made great strides in the wider – and, in the Reagan and Bush years, increasingly more important – realm of public relations. By the end of the 1980s men like Weyrich no longer appeared to loom large on the Washington political landscape, but then that's not where they had intended to end up. As a New Right minister put it to his fellows at an early strategy session at the Heritage Foundation: 'We're not here to get into politics. We're here to turn the clock back to 1954 in this country. And once we've done it, we're gonna clear out of this stinking town.' In the final years of the decade, when men like Weyrich picked up their newspapers, it seemed to them that, as their sentiments began to seep into mainstream culture, the hands of time were indeed starting to inch counterclockwise.

If the contemporary backlash had a birthplace, it was here within the ranks of the New Right, where it first took shape as a movement with a clear ideological agenda. The New Right leaders were among the first to articulate the central argument of the backlash – that women's equality is responsible for women's unhappiness. They were also the first to lambaste the women's movement for what would become its two most popularly cited, and contradictory, sins: promoting materialism over moral values (i.e., turning women into greedy yuppies) and dismantling the traditional familial support system (i.e., turning women into welfare mothers). The mainstream would reject their fevered rhetoric and hellfire imagery, but the heart of their political message survived – to be transubstantiated into the media's 'trends'.

The leaders of the New Right in the USA were rural fundamentalist ministers whose congregations were shrinking, and electronic preachers whose audience was declining. In the countryside, the steady migration of evangelicals to the suburbs and cities and the indifference of a younger generation were emptying their pews. On the airwaves between 1977 and 1980, at the very time of the 'rise' of the New Right, the TV preachers' audience fell by 1 million viewers. By November 1980 nine of the ten most popular TV preachers had fewer viewers than in February of that same year; Oral Roberts had lost 22 per cent of his TV audience, and the PTL [Praise the Lord] Club had lost 11 per cent. Even at the peak of Moral Majority's national prominence in the media, less than 7 per cent of Americans surveyed said the organization represented their views. A Harris poll found that no more than 14 per cent of the electorate followed the TV evangelists – and half of the followers told pollsters they were considering withdrawing their support.

'Backlash politics,' political scientists Seymour Martin Lipset and Earl Raab observed in their study of this periodic phenomenon in modern public life, 'may be defined as the reaction by groups which are declining in a felt sense of importance, influence, and power.' Unlike classic conservatives, these 'pseudoconservatives' – as Theodore Adorno dubbed the constituents of such modern right-wing movements – perceive themselves as social outcasts rather than guardians of the status quo. They are not so much defending a prevailing order as resurrecting an outmoded or imagined one. 'America has largely been taken away from them and their kind,' historian Richard Hofstadter wrote, 'though they are determined to try to repossess it and to prevent the final destructive act of subversion.' As Weyrich himself observed of his liberal opponents: 'They have already succeeded. We are not in power. They are.'

The New Right movement has its counterparts in other countries and in other backlash eras: in the USA, the American Protective Association of the late nineteenth century comes to mind, the Ku Klux Klan revival and Father Coughlin's right-wing movement in the 1920s and 1930s, the John Birch Society's anti-communist campaign in the postwar years. The constituents of these crusades were failing farmers who could no longer live off the land, lower-middle-class workers who could not support their families or rural fundamentalists in a secular urban nation. They found their most basic human aspirations thwarted – the yearning to be recognized and valued by their society, the desire to find a firm footing on an unstable economic ladder. If they couldn't satisfy these fundamental needs, they could at least seek the bitter solace of retribution. As Conservative Caucus founder Howard Phillips declared, 'We must prove our ability to get revenge on people who go against us.' The New Right's prime fund-raiser Richard Viguerie vowed to 'do an awful lot of punishing'. If they weren't going to be rewarded in this life, they could at least penalize the people who they suspected had robbed them of good fortune. Every backlash movement has had its preferred scapegoat: for the American Protective Association, Catholics filled the bill. For Father Coughlin's 'social justice' movement, Jews. For the Ku Klux Klan, of course, blacks. And for the New Right, a prime enemy would be feminist women.

In 1980 Weyrich was among the first of many New Right leaders to identify the culprit. In the *Conservative Digest* he alerted followers to the feminist threat:

> [T]here are people who want a different political order, who are not necessarily Marxists. Symbolized by the women's liberation movement, they believe that the future for their political power lies in the restructuring of the traditional family, and particularly in the downgrading of the male or father role in the traditional family.

That same year, Moral Majority's Reverend Jerry Falwell issued the same warning. 'The Equal Rights Amendment strikes at the foundation of our entire social structure,' he concluded in *Listen, America!*, a treatise that devotes page after page to the devastation wreaked by the women's movement. The feminists had launched a 'satanic attack on the home,' Falwell said. And his top priority was crushing these women, starting with the execution of the

ERA. 'With all my heart,' he vowed, 'I want to bury the Equal Rights Amendment once and for all in a deep, dark grave.'

One New Right group after another lined up behind this agenda. The Conservative Caucus deemed the ERA one of 'the most destructive pieces of legislation to ever pass Congress', and to determine which candidates deserved funding, the Committee for the Survival of a Free Congress made each politician's stance on the ERA the deciding factor. The depiction of feminists as malevolent spirits capable of great evil and national destruction was also a refrain. The opening of the American Christian Cause's fund-raising newsletter warned, 'Satan has taken the reins of the "women's liberation" movement and will stop at nothing.' The Christian Voice held that 'America's rapid decline as a world power is a direct result' of the feminist campaign for equal rights and reproductive freedom. Feminists, the Voice's literature advised, are 'moral perverts' and 'enemies of every decent society'. Feminists are a deadly force, as the commentators on the evangelical 700 Club explained it, precisely because they threatened a transfer of gender power; they 'would turn the country over to women'. That the New Right fastened on feminism, not communism or race, was in itself a testament to the strength and standing of the women's movement in the last decade. As scholar Rosalind Pollack Petchesky observed, 'The women's liberation movement in the 1970s had become the most dynamic force for social change in the country, the one most directly threatening not only to conservative values and interest, but also to significant groups whose "way of life" is challenged by ideas of sexual liberation.' Significantly, the critical New Right groups all got under way within two years after the two biggest victories for women's rights – Congress's approval of the ERA in 1972 and the US Supreme Court's legalization of abortion in 1973.

For the New Right preachers, the force of feminist ideas was also threatening their professional status. Like the late Victorian ministers who led their era's vanguard against the nineteenth-century women's movement, the New Right clergy depended on a mostly female flock of worshippers for their livelihood – and that flock was not only diminishing but becoming increasingly disobedient. In a 1989 survey of about 18,000 Christian-identified

263

women in the United States, only 3 per cent said they turned to their minister for moral guidance. Frustrated, the pastors tried to at least keep these women quiet. When a researcher tried to conduct a survey of evangelical women, one preacher after another refused to give her access to their female congregations. In their sermons, the New Right ministers invoked one particular biblical passage with such frequency that it even merited press attention: Ephesians 5:22–24 – 'The husband is the head of the wife, even as Christ is the head of the church' – became an almost weekly mantra in many pulpits. In their domestic life, too, much as the fundamentalist men tried to seal shut the doors, feminist ideas persisted in slipping through the cracks. 'Wife beating is on the rise because men are no longer leaders in their homes,' an evangelical minister told a sociologist. 'I tell the women they must go back home and be more submissive.'

To the New Right ministers, feminism and the sweeping political forces they associated with it seemed too powerful to rein in, but individual women closer to home made for more convenient and vulnerable whipping girls. Disappointed and embittered with the Carter administration for ignoring their demands for government-legislated school prayer, federally funded religious education, and a host of other objectives that they had hoped a Baptist president would back, fundamentalist leaders went after his sister Ruth Carter Stapleton with the most wrath. In a smear campaign that produced anti-Stapleton tapes, radio sermons, even a book, these men denounced the woman they dubbed 'Queen of the Witches'. (Sorcery and sex equality were never far removed in New Right rhetoric.) 'They really came after me,' Stapleton would recall later. ' . . . They were against women evangelists. Really, they were against women altogether. They said every woman had to be in total submission to the male.'

When the New Right men entered national politics, they brought their feminist witch-hunts with them. Howard Phillips charged that feminists had overrun the capital and were behind 'the conscious policy of government to liberate the wife from the leadership of the husband'. Jerry Falwell seemed to see strident feminists everywhere he looked in Washington: even a federal Health and Education advisory committee on women's needs was 'made up of twelve very aggressive, self-proclaimed feminists,' he observed ominously. 'Need I say that it is time that moral Americans became informed and involved in helping to preserve family values in our nation? . . . [W]e cannot wait. The twilight of our nation could well be at hand.' Not just the domestic cabinet was in jeopardy, Falwell advised. Feminists were undermining the military and now advancing on international affairs. In *Listen, America!*, Falwell outlined a global feminist conspiracy – a sinister female web of front organizations spreading its tentacles across the free world. Even the 1979 International Year of the Child had 'a darker side', he maintained: the event was a back door through which scheming socialist-minded women's rights activists had 'gained access to a worldwide network of governments'.

Mandate for Leadership, the Heritage Foundation's 1981 master plan for the Reagan administration, warned of the 'increasing political leverage of feminist interests' and the infiltration of a 'feminist network' into government agencies; it called for a slew of countermeasures to minimize feminist power. *Mandate for Leadership II*, three years later, was equally preoccupied with conquering the women's rights campaign; its authors asserted, 'The fight against comparable worth must become a top priority for the next administration.' And *Cultural Conservatism*, another basic tract in the New Right library, wasted no time singling out 'radical forms of feminism' as the source of a long list of social ills, from fractious youth to anti-American sentiments. Feminism's radical operatives had made deep inroads into our government and schools, *Cultural Conservatism* warned. 'One need not wander over to the Women's Studies Department' any more to encounter the 'liberationists', the book's authors observed; now these pernicious ideas were deeply embedded in college literature departments, law school classes, TV talk shows, and 'many a rock video'. Even when the New Right turned to 'secular humanism' they found feminism lurking between the lines. The schoolbooks that incensed them most were the texts portraying women in independent roles. The publications list of the Rockford Institute's Center for the Family in America, a New Right think-tank, read like a rap sheet against independent, single, professional and, of course, feminist, women. In fact, only two of the twenty-one titles on its

1989 list *didn't* deal with female crimes. Some typical offerings: *Perilous Parallel: Working Wives, Suicidal Husbands, Why More Women Working Means Lower Pay for Men, The Frightening Growth of the Mother–State–Child Family*, and *The Link Between Mother-Dominated Families and Drug Use.*

'Feminism kind of became the focus of everything,' Edmund Haislmaier, a Heritage Foundation research fellow, recalls. As an economic conservative who did not share his colleagues' desire for a regressive social revolution, Haislmaier came to observe the in-house anti-feminist furore with an uneasy detachment.

In retrospect, I'd have to say they blamed the feminists for an awful lot more than they actually deserved. The women's movement didn't really cause the high divorce rate, which had already started before women's liberation started up. The femin-ists certainly didn't have anything to do with disastrous econ-omic policies. But the feminists became this very identifiable target. Ellie Smeal [former president of the National Organiz-ation for Women] was a recognizable target; hyperinflation and tax bracketing were not.

Setting the Anti-Feminist Agenda

Soon after the New Right scored its first set of surprise victories in Congress, an ebullient Paul Weyrich assembled his most trusted advisers at the Heritage Foundation. Their mission: draft a single bill that they could use as a blueprint for the New Right pro-gramme. It would be their first legislative initiative and an emblem of their cause. They would call it the Family Protection Act. But the Bill they eventually introduced to Congress in 1981 had little to do with helping households. In fact, it really had only one objective: dismantling nearly every legal achievement of the women's movement.

The Act's proposals: eliminate federal laws supporting equal education; forbid 'intermingling of the sexes in any sport or other school-related activities'; require marriage and motherhood to be taught as the proper career for girls; deny federal funding to any school using textbooks portraying women in non-traditional roles;

repeal all federal laws protecting battered wives from their husbands; and ban federally funded legal aid for any woman seeking abortion counselling or a divorce. The Bill was largely written in the negative; in its long list of federal programmes to rescind, the Act offered only one real initiative of its own – new tax incentives to induce married women to have babies and stay at home. Under this provision of the Bill, a husband could set up a tax-deductible retirement fund if his wife earned *no* money at all that year. Evidently even a Tupperware-hawking housewife was suspect.

Other 'family' legislative proposals from the New Right would follow in the USA in the next several years, and they were virtually all aimed at slapping down female independence wherever it showed its face: a complete ban on abortion, even if it meant the woman's death; censorship of all birth-control information until marriage; a 'chastity' Bill; revocation of the Equal Pay Act and other equal employment laws; and, of course, defeat of the Equal Rights Amendment.

In the 1980 election, the New Right would figure in the national presidential campaign almost exclusively on the basis of its opposition to women's rights. Their most substantial effect on the Republican party was in forcing its leaders to draft a platform that opposed legal abortion and the Equal Rights Amendment – the first time since 1940 that the ERA failed to receive the Republican party's endorsement. The Republican convention's acceptance of the New Right's anti-feminist agenda that year, in fact, carved one of the only clear dividing lines between two national party platforms whose boundaries were blurring on so many other fronts, from foreign policy to law and order. And their candidate for top office distinguished himself most clearly from his predecessors by his views on women's rights: Reagan was the first president to oppose the ERA since Congress passed it – and the first ever to back a 'Human Life Amendment' banning abortion and even some types of birth control.

Yet strangely, most chroniclers of the New Right's errand into the capital – supporters and opponents alike – characterized feminism as a 'fringe' issue. Press accounts, even those emanating from liberal and leftist journals, generally presented the right-wing movement's opposition to abortion and the ERA as distracting sidelights to the meatier, more 'important' policy aims – decreasing government regulation, cutting the budget, bolstering defence. The first round of history books on the movement were no better. Richard G. Hutcheson, Jr's *God in the White House*, a typical account, allotted only two pages to the ERA and explored every possible cause for the right wing's mobilization except feminism, from Watergate to the 'new narcissism'. '[T]he "hearth and home" issues' on the New Right agenda, Alan Crawford concluded in *Thunder on the Right*, were merely 'nonpolitical, fringe issues at best'.

But while these commentators judged the New Right's attack on the women's movement to be a sideshow, the players in the right-wing fundamentalist drama knew better. For them, public punishment of autonomous feminist women was no less than the main event.

The War of Words

'We are different from previous generations of conservatives,' Weyrich said in a speech in 1980. 'We are no longer working to preserve the status quo. We are radicals, working to overturn the present power structure of the country.' Margaret Thatcher and her followers would adopt this language in Britain, with her new kind of Toryism and its 'radical', 'reforming' agenda. In the US, these 'radicals' were also the 'new macho preachers', as they were soon dubbed, swaggering and spouting a tough line from the TV screen. Reverend James Robison, 'God's Angry Man', boasted of his past violent exploits (including the claim that he 'planned rapes'); Reverend Tim LaHaye liked to tell the press about his days as a military man when he would 'punch anyone's lights out'. As they emphasized repeatedly in their texts and speeches, they were 'warriors', marching into enemy territory behind a barrel-chested Christ holding high the flag. 'Jesus was not a pacifist,' Falwell liked to say. 'He was not a sissy.'

Yet the fundamentalist soldiers had trooped to Washington precisely because they feared they had already become the 'weak men' that Falwell's writings repeatedly and anxiously derided. As much as the New Right warriors billed themselves as aggressive and free agents of change, their manoeuvres were all reactions against what they saw as the dominant enemy – the proponents of women's rights. Despite the verbal bravado, the New Right was wholly dependent on another movement for its identity. This is, of course, the situation for any conservative group attempting to preserve or resurrect a threatened way of life. 'Paradoxically, conservatism requires liberalism for its meaning,' political writer Sidney Blumenthal observed in *The Rise of the Counter-Establishment*. 'Though [conservatives] have a sense of mission, they have difficulty rising above the adversarial stance.' But the New Right men found themselves in a position of dependency that was doubly demeaning: not only were they reacting rather than acting, they were reacting against women. At least John Birchers could picture themselves beating back the advances of communist thugs. The New Right preachers faced the embarrassing task of fending off the ladies.

There seemed no escape from this posture of passivity built into a backlash movement. But the New Right men finally found a way. 'For twenty years, the most important battle in the civil rights field has been for control of the language,' *Mandate for Leadership II* asserted – especially, such words as 'equality' and 'opportunity'. 'The secret to victory, whether in court or in congress, has been to control the definition of these terms.' By relabelling the terms of the debate over equality, they discovered, they might verbally finesse their way into command. By switching the lines of power through a sort of semantic reversal, they might pull off a coup by euphemism. And in this case, words would speak louder than actions.

Under this linguistic strategy, the New Right relabelled its resistance to women's newly acquired reproductive rights as 'pro-life'; its opposition to women's newly embraced sexual freedom became 'pro-chastity'; and its hostility to women's mass entry into the work force became 'pro-motherhood'. Finally, the New Right renamed itself – its regressive and negative stance against the progress of women's rights became 'pro-family'. Earlier, the anti-ERA group Eagle Forum had formally dubbed itself 'An Alternative to Women's Lib'. After the 1980 election it changed its motto to 'Leading the Pro-Family Movement Since 1972'. Before, Weyrich had no choice but to describe his enemy as 'women's liberation'. Now Weyrich could refer to his nemesis as 'the anti-family movement'. Now he was in charge – and the feminists would have to react to *his* programme.

This Orwellian wordplay not only painted the New Right leaders out of their passive corner; it also served to conceal their anger at women's rising independence. This was a fruitful marketing tool, as they would draw more sympathy from the press and more followers from the public if they marched under the banner of traditional family values. In the 1920s the Ku Klux Klan had built up support with a similar rhetorical manoeuvre, downplaying their racism and recasting it as patriotism; they weren't lynching blacks, they were moral reformers defending the flag.

The New Right leaders' language was, in many respects, as hollow as the Klan's. These 'pro-life' advocates set fire to inhabited family-planning clinics, championed the death penalty, and called the atom bomb 'a marvellous gift that was given to our country by a wise God'. These 'pro-motherhood' crusaders campaigned against virtually every federal programme that assisted mothers, from pre-natal services to infant feeding programmes. Under the banner of 'family rights' these spokesmen lobbied only for every man's right to rule supreme at home – to exercise what Falwell called the husband's 'God-given responsibility to lead his family'.

Ladies in Retirement

While the 'pro-family' strategy allowed the New Right men to launch an indirect attack on women's rights, they also went for the direct hit – using female intermediaries. When they wanted to lob an especially large verbal stone at feminists, they ducked behind a New Right woman. 'Women's liberationists operate as Typhoid Marys carrying a germ,' said their most famous spokeswoman, Phyllis Schlafly. 'Feminism is more than an illness,' asserted Beverly LaHaye, founder of the New Right's Concerned Women for America. 'It is a philosophy of death.' In time-honoured fashion, anti-feminist male leaders had enlisted women to handle the heavy lifting in the campaign against their own rights.

Yet in mounting their attack on a public stage, the New Right women had to speak up and display independent strength – exhibitions that revealed them to be anything but the ideal models of passive and sequestered womanhood that they were supposedly saluting. These female leaders who relayed the movement's most noxious anti-feminist sentiments to public ears embraced far more of the feminist platform than either they or their male leaders let on – or perhaps realized.

Schlafly was only the earliest, most well known, and extreme, example. The woman who opposed the ERA because it 'would take away the marvellous legal rights of a woman to be a full-time wife and mother in the house supported by her husband' was a Harvard-educated lawyer, author of nine books and twice a congressional candidate. And she was far more favourably disposed to the agenda of the women's movement than her public reputation suggested. In her anti-feminist treatise, *The Power of the Positive Woman*, she actually gives an approving nod to feminist-inspired equal-rights legislation and seventies-era federal sex discrimination suits that paved the way for 'a future in which [the American woman's] educational and employment options are unlimited'. All the women her book points to as positive role models are, in fact, stereotypical Superwomen: Olympic athletes, powerful political leaders and ambitious business executives. To her mind, Margaret Thatcher is 'surely one of the outstanding Positive Women in the world'. At times, Schlafly almost sounds as if she is lauding the other side's accomplishments. 'The Positive Woman in America today,' she writes gleefully, 'has a near-infinite opportunity to control her own destiny, to reach new heights of achievement, and to motivate and influence others.'

The New Right women's organizations that emerged in the late 1970s and early 1980s weren't mere adjuncts to the male-led lobby. In fact, they often modelled the structure of their 'auxiliary' groups more on women's rights organizations than on the male New Right hierarchies. And they borrowed political tactics and rhetoric, too, from feminist events, speeches and literature. It was the 1977 International Women's Year in Houston, which endorsed an essentially feminist platform, that first provoked the New Right women who attended to speak up and organize. Out of the conference, a host of New Right women's groups sprang up and eventually consolidated into the National Pro-Family Coalition. President Carter's 1979 White House Conference on Families, another feminist-minded gathering, served as the coalition's springboard into national politics. This time, when the feminist agenda dominated the conference, the New Right women produced a shadow conference with a similar format – and they staged a walkout, formed an 'alternative' assembly and set their own agenda.

For many of these women, the experience was an exhilarating first brush with political activism, a liberating discovery of their public voice. 'IWY was our "boot camp",' Rosemary Thomson, author of *The Price of Liberty* and coordinator of the Eagle Forum's contingent at the White House Conference on Families, proudly told a sociologist after the showdown. 'Now we're ready for the offensive in the battle for our families and our faith.' A national organizer for the Eagle Forum explained, 'I had never given a speech, written a speech, testified, never been on radio, never been on television. . . . [Y]ou start getting some self-confidence. You beat a lawyer in a debate a couple of times and you start thinking, "Well, gee, that's pretty good. I didn't know I could do that."'

Ultimately, however, the New Right turned the rising confidence and aspirations of these women to its own ends. The movement needed both articulate intellectuals to occupy the podiums and adroit organizers to fill the stands; the New Right women provided both. Two women in particular, Connaught 'Connie' Marshner, the highest-level woman in the Heritage Foundation, and Beverly LaHaye, the director of Concerned Women of America, the largest female New Right group, would take on the direction of these respective missions.

The Heritage Foundation's Superwoman

A woman's nature is, simply, other-oriented. . . . Women are ordained by their nature to spend themselves in meeting the needs of others.

CONNAUGHT C. MARSHNER, *The New Traditional Woman*

'If anywhere along the line, from 1979 to 1984, someone had

said to me, "You should spend more time with your kids," I would have been highly offended.'

CONNAUGHT C. MARSHNER, INTERVIEW, 1988

'Oh yeah, the Family Protection Act,' Connie Marshner is recalling. 'I wrote the fact sheet on it. I sold it. I became its chief marketer.' Just after supper one evening in the spring of 1988, Marshner is sitting in the living room of her home in a suburb of Washington, DC. Her husband, Bill, clears the table and then retreats to the kitchen to wash the dishes. She was too busy working today to cook, she explains, so it was takeaway Chinese food for dinner again. While she balances her newborn in one hand and a pile of research papers in the other, she recalls the first heady days when she sat down to write the Family Protection Act.

'I was becoming so caught up in politics. I remember, I was in this neighbourhood [childcare] co-op at the time, but it quickly became clear I was never going to repay the favour. I was just too busy. Finally, well, the other mothers basically asked me to leave.'

Marshner's political career began in 1971, at the University of South Carolina; undergraduate Connie Coyne was reading English and secondary education, but spending all her time at the campus chapter of Young Americans for Freedom, a conservative political organization. Right after college, she became an assistant to the editor of YAF's magazine, the *New Guard*. When her boss moved to YAF's Capitol Hill office, he offered her a job as his secretary. She quickly accepted, but she had no intention of staying in the clerical pool. Soon after her arrival the boss gave her a paper, an attack on a childcare Bill, to type; she took it home instead and wrote, as she recalls, 'the definitive analysis of what was wrong with it'. Her paper 'became the conservative critique of Mondale's Child Development Bill that eventually led to its defeat'.

By Connie Marshner's own analysis, aspects of her youthful conservatism – like her insistence that she attend Sunday school regularly – began as 'child rebellion', a desire to irk her more liberal and only nominally Catholic parents. But at the same time that she was fighting her elders, she was absorbing their advice for future use. Her mother, a frustrated housewife married to a navy officer, told her two daughters not to follow in her footsteps. 'Mother read Friedan's *Feminine Mystique* when it first came out,' Marshner says, 'and I remember her saying, "You won't understand how awful married life is until you read it." Mother was always saying to me, "You don't want to marry and ruin your life. Be independent." '

Her father, too, urged Connie and her older sister, who would become a lawyer, to get a good education and steer clear of low-paying 'women's work'. She recalls, 'My father was very wise. He told me, "Don't learn shorthand." ' The Coynes encouraged their daughters to appreciate the value of self-sufficiency – a lesson Connie would carry into adulthood. 'It never occurred to me to be helpless,' she says. 'I guess someone who is taught to be helpless needs to be liberated. But I was never taught that.'

As a young woman, she was so set on maintaining her independence that 'I was determined never to marry.' But then she met Bill Marshner at a church service in the early 1970s. They were wed in 1973. That same year, the Heritage Foundation was established as the New Right's first think-tank. Connie Marshner's former boss at YAF, and a Heritage founder, recommended her to the foundation's organizers. She accepted their offer – a researcher's job – and she and Bill moved to a Washington apartment convenient to her office.

Again, Connie Marshner quickly transformed her lowly assignment into a more influential position. When her superiors saw 'how good I was at handling reporters' phone calls' they promoted the twenty-two-year-old to education director. She began generating a steady stream of articles and monographs opposing government subsidies for childcare, decrying the baleful influence of feminism in textbooks, and advocating government policies that would discourage women from seeking fulfilment outside the home. Both cerebral and pragmatic, Marshner fortified her writings with scholarly references – among them, infant mortality rates in eighteenth-century Paris and the limits of Malthusian theory – and then used hardheaded business logic to win points with corporate leaders. Abortion, for example, was bad for commerce; one in five fewer babies, she told a group of executives, meant they would sell 'five fewer *Star Wars* toy sets – which translates to fifty or more individual *Star Wars* action figures'.

In the winter of 1974, she discovered she was pregnant. 'I assumed I would give it [the job] all up, but then we were dirt poor so I didn't.' Bill was in graduate school and she had no maternity medical benefits; her emergency delivery and seven-day hospital stay nearly wiped out their savings. In 1976, she was pregnant again. By then she was holding down two jobs – as a research consultant for the Heritage Foundation and a field co-ordinator for the Committee for Survival of a Free Congress. And she had just accepted a publisher's advance to write a book on education. Bill, meanwhile, had enrolled on a divinity graduate course in Texas. Rather than move west and sacrifice her work, Marshner stayed on in Washington and sent her one-year-old son to her mother's house in Baltimore. In the final months of the pregnancy she rejoined her family in Texas, so that her husband could handle the childcare and cooking – 'thank goodness for Bill' – while she finished the book, writing into the night. 'I was typing the final draft when I went into labour,' she recalls.

After Bill's graduation they moved back to Washington. Her career was prospering. 'The book really changed my status in the conservative movement,' she says, and when Weyrich decided, after the 1978 election, to organize a major conference for new congressmen, he put her in charge. At the opening session she delivered a speech that would, as she points out, prove 'prophetic'. The topic: 'Why social issues are going to be important in the 1980s'. Marshner smiles as she recalls the moment: 'It was a case of "You heard it here first." '

Also prominent in her memories of the conference is a small but telling incident:

> At the conference breakfast, I was sitting at the table with Paul and the other newly elected congressmen. And one of them asks for everyone's opinion on a particular subject, but he skips over me. Then he picks up the schedule and sees my name as the next speaker and he looks at me strangely, and all of a sudden, I realize, Oh, he thought I was Weyrich's secretary.

A decade later, that moment is still sharp in her mind, yet she says the congressman's slight barely bothered her. 'I mean, I wasn't pleased. It did teach me a lesson that men in politics, they think of girls as something to take orders. But I guess I have a funny mind; I forget people like that. I'm not one to hold a grudge.'

Marshner is able, if not exactly to forget the insult, then at least to salve its personal sting – by not counting herself as one of the 'girls'. She seems to picture herself seated on the other side of the table, one of the honorary men, dispatching those 'orders' to women. She got there out of sheer talent. 'My experience in the job market was not anything that made me feel discriminated against. Everything I've got has been through merit.' She is the 'exception' that proves the rule: her gender lacks ability, not opportunity, to make it in public life.

Campaigns for women's rights, therefore, are 'silly', she says, because merit will always win in the end. If most women haven't made it, that's because most women don't have what it takes. Judging by her writings and speeches, Marshner takes a dim and often disdainful view of her sex, a perspective she shares with Schlafly, who addresses housewives in her books as a camp counsellor might lecture sulky Guides. Just quit whining and be 'cheerful' even if you don't feel like it, she orders them in *The Power of the Positive Woman*. When Marshner refers to women, she uses a distancing second or third person, as if she doesn't include herself in their numbers. 'Women need to know that somebody will have the authority and make the decision' – and 'your job,' she lectures women, 'is to be happy with it.' When Marshner and Schlafly trained women for the protest rally at the White House Conference on Families, Marshner recalls that she was most impressed by Schlafly's ability to 'control the women. . . . When she said jump, they did.' Women need that direction from above, Marshner says: 'You know, it's very hard to organize women because they tend to be catty. They get all sidetracked on who will get what title. They just waste a lot of time.'

By 1979 Marshner had become director of the Free Congress Foundation's 'family policy' division and founding executive editor of the *Family Protection Report*. Then, the year of President Reagan's election, Weyrich appointed Marshner to the 'team of four', an élite group that travelled across the country, hand-picking and training state leaders to foment grassroots action. 'In 1980 I was on ninety-nine airplanes,' she says. 'I kept track.'

Meanwhile, her husband had found a job at a small college in Front Royal, Virginia. Connie didn't want to move there, so she rented an apartment for herself in Washington. Then she persuaded an aunt in California to move to Front Royal to help Bill look after the kids. She visited at weekends. 'Bill saw more of them than I did,' she says. 'We had not only a commuter marriage but a commuter motherhood. And this was before it was fashionable! I guess I was ahead of my time.'

After the 1980 election, Marshner chaired half a dozen advisory panels, directed a staff of five employees, continued giving speeches around the country, and debated with everyone from abortion-rights activist Kate Michelman to former Senator George McGovern. In 1982 the local county chairman asked her to run for the Virginia House of Delegates. She turned this down, but not out of a sense of feminine propriety. 'I was intrigued but I was too busy saving the country to worry about one district in Virginia,' she says. Her third child was born the following year – and Weyrich, concerned that she might take time off, proposed that she set up a nursery in a spare office. 'Paul was very accommodating,' recalls Marshner.

That year, with her career approaching its zenith – she bought a car phone to field all her business calls – Marshner spoke before the Family Forum conference in Washington, DC. Her subject: 'Who Is the New Traditional Woman?' Her answer sounded a lot like the New Traditionalist advertising copy that *Good Housekeeping* would later script: 'She is new,' Marshner said of this feminine icon, 'because she is of the current era, with all its pressures and fast pace and rapid change. She is traditional because, in the face of unremitting cultural change, she is oriented around the eternal truths of faith and family.' Marshner made no connection between the positive, 'new' aspects of women's lives and the fruits of feminism. In fact, Marshner told her listeners that the women's rights movement was the enemy of the New Traditionalist. It had unleashed 'a new image of women: a drab, macho feminism of hard-faced women who were bound and determined to carve their place in the world, no matter whose bodies they have to climb over to do it'. The archetypal macho feminist, she said, was the bad mother in the film *Kramer vs. Kramer* who put her husband in charge of their child and went off to find herself. 'Macho feminism has deceived women,' she said, 'in that it convinced them that they would be happy only if they were treated like men, and that included treating themselves like men.'

Marshner delivered similar rallying calls for the traditional family at the 1984 Family Forums II and III in San Francisco and in Dallas, deliveries timed to coincide with the presidential political conventions in these cities. Then she flew back to the office – to accept the title of executive vice-president of the Free Congress Foundation, making her the highest-ranking woman in the New Right Washington establishment.

Marshner's own interest in the housewifely duties of traditional family life, as she freely admits, remains limited. 'I'm no good with little kids and I'm a terrible housekeeper,' she says. 'To me, it's very unrewarding, unfulfilling work. By contrast, what I'm doing in Washington has real tangible rewards, accomplishments.' Yet neither she nor her husband believes this makes her a 'macho feminist'.

In 1987, pregnant with her fourth child, it looked as if Marshner might finally take her own advice: she decided to take a break from Washington politics. Weyrich again tried to talk her out of it; by now, the foundation depended heavily on her literary and speaking talents. But this time she turned him down. The harrowing death in 1984 of her infant daughter, born with a congenital heart defect, haunted her. She wanted to be at home for the new baby.

'Marshner's out of it now,' Weyrich says, when asked about her in early 1988, waving a dismissive hand in the air. 'She just left to have her fourth child. OK, she's still executive editor of the *Family Protection Report*. But basically she's out of it. She's a classic example of what I'm talking about – women just can't do it all. . . . Every single one of the girls I've had here who've had children has left.' As he speaks, four women are hard at work in their offices down the hall – from his finance manager to his vice-president of operations to his secretary. All of them have children; several are even single mothers.

Nor did Marshner take time off to devote herself to traditional housekeeping. She immediately set up an office at the house, accepted a post as general editor for a Christian publishing house, began freelancing numerous articles and landed a contract for her fourth book – this one against day care. 'I'm going to look at the data on the effects of day care,' she says, 'and talk to mothers who use it about why they regret it.' Now that she is home, she seems quick to judge women who aren't. 'When you have a child, that has got to be your priority. If you don't, sooner or later you will pay the price, either in maladjustment or your own consciousness.'

The woman she judges most harshly, and unfairly, is herself; the backlash ideas she helped unleash have come back to roost in her own psyche. She wonders now if her preoccupation with her career might have 'caused' her daughter's heart defect. 'I think the boys would probably have been happier if I stayed home,' she says.

The boys, however, who are listening from the living room couch, disagree. 'Those were great days,' sighs Mike, who is twelve. 'I liked it when you worked.'

A Spirit-Controlled Woman . . . or a Control-Seeking Spirit?

The woman who is truly Spirit-filled will want to be totally submissive to her husband . . . This is a truly liberated woman. Submission is God's design for women.

BEVERLY LAHAYE, *The Spirit-Controlled Woman*

'God didn't make me to be a nobody.'

BEVERLY LAHAYE, INTERVIEW

The founder of Concerned Women for America always tells the press the same story of her anti-feminist 'awakening': one evening in 1978 in her San Diego living room, Beverly LaHaye was nestled at the side of her husband, Moral Majority co-founder Tim LaHaye; they were watching the evening news. Barbara Walters was interviewing Betty Friedan, and when the feminist leader suggested that she represented many women in America, LaHaye leapt to her stockinged feet and declared, 'Betty Friedan doesn't speak for me and I bet she doesn't speak for the majority of women in this country.' She vowed then and there to rally other 'submissive' women who believe, like her, that 'the women's liberation movement is destroying the family and threatening the survival of our nation.'

Shortly, thereafter, she chaired a meeting for this purpose at a local church. 'I didn't know if anyone would even show up,' she says, 'but twelve hundred women filled that room. I couldn't believe it! The only way I could explain it is that the majority of women out there do not agree with Betty Friedan and the ERA.' There was, however, a more likely explanation for the big turnout: by 1978, Beverly LaHaye's name guaranteed a crowd in the evangelical community – and not because of her opposition to feminism.

The real awakening of Beverly LaHaye had occurred two decades before this electronic encounter with Betty Friedan, at a 1965 motivational conference for Sunday-school teachers. At the time, LaHaye was a 'fearful, introverted' housewife who clung to her husband's side and was so shy that 'it was difficult for me to entertain in our home,' much less venture outside it. She was the Submissive Woman she would later celebrate, and she did not enjoy it. 'I refused most invitations to speak to women's groups because I felt very inadequate and questioned if I really had anything to say to them,' she wrote in *The Spirit-Controlled Woman*, in a chapter entitled, 'The Missing Dimension'. Its contents could as easily have belonged to the famous chapter in Friedan's *Feminine Mystique*, 'The Problem That Has No Name':

One very well-meaning lady said to me in the early days of our ministry, 'Mrs LaHaye, our last pastor's wife was an author; what do you do?' That was a heavy question for a fearful twenty-seven-year-old woman to cope with. And I began to wonder, 'What did I do?' Oh yes, I was a good mother to my four children, I could keep house reasonably well, my husband adored me, but what could I do that would be eternally effective in the lives of other women? The answer seemed to come back to me. 'Very little!' There was something missing in my life.

Likewise, LaHaye's analysis of housework might sound familiar to early readers of *Ms*. She wrote:

> In my case it was not the major problems that succeeded in wearing me down; it was the smoldering resentment caused from the endless little tasks that had to be repeated over and over again and seemed so futile. Day after day I would perform the same routine procedures: picking up dirty socks, hanging up wet towels, closing closet doors, turning off lights that had been left on, creating a path through the clutter of toys.

When her youngest child was still in nappies, LaHaye went back to work, full time, as a teletype operator for Merrill Lynch. 'Thirty years ago, ministers didn't get paid very much. We couldn't survive, so I had to go to work,' she explains. But that wasn't the only reason. 'I liked working there. It was kind of exciting. You had to get there at 6 a.m. because that's when the stock market opened in New York. They paid well. And I enjoyed it.' She hired a 'housekeeper', as she calls her nanny, a black single mother who 'couldn't find work because she lacked job skills'.

The teletype job helped build her confidence, but it was the changes triggered by the 1965 Sunday-school conference that finally supplied 'the missing dimension' in her life. The speaker, the popular Christian psychologist Henry Brandt, talked to the teachers about every human being's basic need for self-improvement and expression. The words stirred dormant passions within the young preacher's wife. 'Down deep in my heart, I felt I would like to stand up and express myself,' she says later. 'And I never thought that would change.'

The psychologist's words got her thinking about a way to overcome her fears. So did a biblical passage that he alluded to – a line from Timothy that promised the Holy Spirit would deliver disciples not only love but 'power'. 'This is what I needed!' LaHaye said to herself, as she later wrote. If she had 'a new power within', she reasoned, maybe she could combat her timidity and develop 'confidence'. In the months that followed, LaHaye began to cobble together a self-improvement plan that was part pop psychology and part religion, founded on the principles of assertiveness training and buttressed by Christian dogma. As she diagnosed the problem later in a self-help book for Christian women, she and many other housewives suffered from 'a rather poor self-image', 'passivity' and a 'sense of inferiority'. She wanted to assert herself and exert 'strength', but she wanted to do it without challenging the church or threatening her husband. And she found she could, if she made it clear that she was seeking only 'spiritual power'. It was acceptable to crave authority by framing it as a desire for 'access to the power of the Holy Spirit'. No one in the evangelical community could object to her ambitions, as long as they were holy.

Although LaHaye was quick to label her desire to take charge a 'spiritual submission to God', the steps she outlined in her writings about it later were suspiciously action oriented. Her semantic strategy was the opposite of that of her New Right male peers; while they concealed their feelings of weakness in active-sounding terminology, LaHaye hid her newly assertive self behind a screen of passive-sounding rhetoric. The New Right male leaders protested too loudly that they *were* in command; she protested too much that she had no interest in taking the helm.

By tapping 'spiritual power', LaHaye wrote in *The Spirit-Controlled Woman*, a fundamentalist woman could 'step forth in all confidence', 'overcome her passivity', and become 'a capable person'. In LaHaye's version of spiritual growth, self-confidence was next to godliness and timidity a black mark on the soul. A spirit-controlled woman must 'recognize her fearfulness as a sin and cope with it accordingly'. Through such inversions of religious tenets, she could dare to concentrate on building self-esteem, an independent identity and a public voice – all the while claiming to be doing it only through, and for, Jesus.

LaHaye's journey toward spiritually mediated liberation began in earnest the day she forced herself to accept an invitation to talk before a woman's church club. She told them about her confidence-boosting ideas, and to her amazement the women applauded and crowded around afterwards, seeking her advice. She agreed to talk to other women's groups. Her popularity grew quickly on the Christian speaking circuit. With her husband, she began directing 'Family Life Seminars', hosting a weekly cable television programme and a live phone-in radio chat show on family living.

Soon a publisher approached her with a proposal to write a self-help book for Christian women. 'I said, "Oh no, I'm not a writer," ' she recalls. 'Then I thought, wait a minute. I can do that.' *The Spirit-Controlled Woman*, published in 1976, sold more than half a million copies. In the next decade LaHaye wrote five more books for Christian women, self-development tracts with chapter titles like 'You Can Help Yourself' and 'Can a Courageous Woman Be Silenced?'

At the same time that she was busy writing *The Spirit-Controlled Woman*, LaHaye was finishing a long-term book project with her husband, Tim. In 1976, against the advice of all their fellow Christian marriage counsellors, the LaHayes finally published *The Act of Marriage*, a sex manual. The book instantly became the evangelical equivalent of *The Joy of Sex*; it was read by millions. *The Act of Marriage: The Beauty of Sexual Love* was a revolutionary document for evangelical readers, both for its frank and graphic content (it covered foreplay, lubrication and multiple orgasms – in remarkable detail) and for its female perspective on sexual pleasure. Not only did the book teach Christian men how to gratify their wives in bed, it informed them in no uncertain terms that an orgasm is every woman's right: 'Modern research has made it abundantly clear that all married women are capable of orgasmic ecstasy. No Christian woman should settle for less.' The book's observations often suggested that a female hand was wielding the authorial pen: 'Regrettably some husbands are carryovers from the Dark Ages, like the one who told his frustrated wife, "Nice girls aren't supposed to climax." Today's wife knows better.' The manual urged women to forget their submissive behaviour at the bedroom door: 'Many women are much too passive in lovemaking. . . . Lovemaking is a contact sport that requires two active people.' The LaHayes even declared the vaginal orgasm a myth, sang the praises of clitoral stimulation – 'Your heavenly Father placed [your clitoris] there for your enjoyment' – and referred dubious readers to a biblical passage that they said justified their enthusiasm (Song of Solomon 2:6: 'Let his left hand be under my head and his right hand embrace me'). As if all this weren't enough, the authors actually endorsed birth control, and for this reason: to maximize women's enjoyment of sex.

The Act of Marriage may have read as if Beverly LaHaye were on the verge of a feminist conversion. And, indeed, in other arenas, too, she seemed to be endorsing basic feminist tenets. She declared herself a supporter of equal rights for women, said she was 'totally in favour' of pay equality, and called herself a firm believer in 'a woman's right to be free from sexual harassment on the job'. Yet she was never prepared to take the final steps, which had the potential of separating her from her church, husband and social universe. Instead, in the years following the book's publication, she wound up leading a countercharge against the women's movement. Having introduced equal rights to the evangelical bedroom, she now moved to fight it on all other fronts. Having attracted a huge following by telling women to 'step forth in all confidence', she now mobilized her female army for a campaign to chase themselves home.

In drawing women to her new cause, LaHaye played on both traditionalist fears and feminist aspirations. She emphasized how changes in women's status might threaten their traditional marriages and leave them 'unprotected'. At the same time, she gave hundreds of thousands of Christian women an acceptable outlet for the assertiveness that she had recognized as fundamental to human growth and that she had helped foster. 'I discovered an organization where I could think, use my brain,' said Cheryl Hook, a Chicago housewife who was spending thirty hours a week on CWA activities. By working for Concerned Women for America, women could be vocal and forceful – without setting off any alarms at home or in the pews. They were, after all, only speaking up for their sex's right to stay quietly at home.

After founding Concerned Women for America in 1979, LaHaye set up a national network that could dispatch hundreds of thousands of women at short notice. She organized what she claimed was the nation's largest women's group (estimates range from 150,000 to half a million members) into 2,000 'prayer/action chapters' – with the accent on action. Even the prayers were notably this-worldly in sentiment. 'Father, we pray that money being considered by the legislature is not used for teenage pregnancy,' began one, served up at a 1986 breakfast prayer meeting in a Maryland hotel. 'We ask that You confuse the plans of our enemy, particularly our enemy Planned Parenthood.' LaHaye used her network to swamp Congress with bags of letters and to detail hundreds of out-of-state women to 'local' anti-abortion protests around the nation. In 1986 her rapid-response team descended on Vermont and, with the aid of a $350,000 war chest, helped defeat the state's Equal Rights Amendment.

In the press, Concerned Women for America was often described as the Moral majority's ladies' club, a sort of Daughters of the New-Right Revolution. The characterization wasn't entirely unjust; the CWA women were certainly treated like auxiliaries by the New Right and the Reagan administration, who often deployed them tactically as fund-raising and letter-writing foot soldiers. New Right leaders, in fact, originally funded Concerned Women for America in hopes that the organization would generate reinforcement troops. Tim LaHaye offered his wife as a safe figurehead; the board members of Moral Majority packed CWA's board of directors with their wives, who, they assumed, would do their bidding.

But as time went by, Concerned Women for America evolved from a spousal service society into a one-woman fiefdom. Beverly LaHaye's unchallenged authority became the envy of men like Paul Weyrich. 'She has the kind of loyalty from her people,' he said, 'where literally she can call them up and say, "Don't do that," and they'll drop it.' Much to their chagrin, the New Right male leaders were unable to command the same kind of obedience from LaHaye herself. She refused to support candidates as they specified. When Falwell, Ed McAteer of the Religious Roundtable and the other top men of the New Right endorsed Bush, LaHaye broke the united front and backed Jack Kemp. Later, she abruptly removed her endorsement after Kemp annoyed her. His offence: he sent a letter to CWA members over her signature, calling him the 'only true conservative', without asking her permission first.

In 1983 LaHaye moved her office from San Diego to Washington, DC, where she built up a twenty-six-person Capitol Hill staff, launched a five-attorney legal division to take on the courts and wielded a $6 million annual budget. She began jetting around the country, then the world. One year she went to Costa Rica nine times. While on the road, LaHaye dispatched orders via her new car phone. And she made it clear that she would have no successors; by 1987, she had become president for life.

'I think the women's movement really hurt women because it taught them to put the value on the career instead of the family,' Beverly LaHaye says. She has granted an interview in her Washington, DC, office. It is her sixth today, she reports.

As might be expected, the business cards on the desk of this champion of femininity are pink. So are her nails, the chairs arranged around her boardroom table and the frilly curtains. Yet she wears a well-tailored suit. On the wall behind her hangs a framed photograph of Ronald Reagan and herself, clasping hands. Some of her other decorative choices lean to the presidential, too: an Oval-Office-sized desk and a large American flag stationed at its side. A large mirror hangs at a strange angle on the opposite wall – but it's not for applying pink lipstick. 'Mrs LaHaye had that mirror put up there like that,' Rebecca Hagelin, spokeswoman for Concerned Women for America, explains, 'so she can look at it from her desk and see Capitol Hill.'

'Feminism really blotted out motherhood,' LaHaye asserts from behind her desk. 'Family must come first for a woman; it's just not natural any other way.' Just then, LaHaye's personal assistant slips into the office, bearing a Filofax. Apologizing for the interruption, the assistant proceeds to review LaHaye's travelling schedule: 'This weekend you're out of town till Sunday,' she says, reading from the Filofax. 'On the 5th, it's your National Day of Prayer speech, then the 6th is St Louis, the 7th through the 8th is Florida, the 9th through the 17th Costa Rica, the 18th that speech in New Jersey, the 19th Washington again, the 27th and the 28th Massachusetts . . . '

LaHaye approves the itinerary, the assistant departs, and the director of Concerned Women for America returns to her defence of traditional motherhood. 'Women must put family as their top priority. If that means giving up the career, then so be it. It's just the natural way. It's built into us as women.' What of her own long bouts away from home? 'Oh well, my children are grown.

When my children were growing up, it was another matter,' she says, her early-morning work shifts at Merrill Lynch conveniently forgotten.

'These career women, what's happening to them is their biological clocks are going off,' she says, supporting her anti-feminist precepts with evidence from popular culture rather than the Bible. By the late 1980s the backlash was so widespread that LaHaye could find as many useful media buzzwords as scriptural quotations. (Her latest anti-feminist book, *The Restless Woman*, would invoke the all-popular trends of 'post-feminism' and 'baby hunger', footnoting not Heritage Foundation tracts but the *New York Times* and *Glamour*.) Career women, she continues in the same vein, 'looked up one day from their desks and they realized they couldn't have it all. . . . That's why the trend is that more and more women are leaving the work force.' Asked for evidence to support this 'trend' she says, 'I don't have the statistics in front of me, but I read about it in the paper. . . . Look at the movies. They're all about having babies now. Like *Three Men and a Baby*.'

LaHaye excuses herself: she has a 'management meeting' she must attend. She grants permission to talk to a few women on the staff; no one is allowed to speak without clearance from the top. Elizabeth Kepler, director of legislative affairs, is one of the women on the approved list, and she has just breezed in from 'the Hill', where she's been lobbying all week against federally funded day care.

'I just love it, absolutely love it,' Kepler says, flopping into a chair. She furtively pokes some pesky shoulder-pads back into place as she talks. 'I was drawn to Washington for the excitement. You know, power. How people come into power, how they use that power.'

How did she end up at Concerned Women for America? 'To be honest, I was more interested in the general process of Washington politics than this organization itself.' She hastens to add that she is in 'total agreement' with the organization's goals of restoring women's traditional roles. But would she personally like to go back to the roles women were limited to in her mother's day? She shakes her head. 'It would be frustrating. I'm glad I live in the time I do.'

At twenty-seven, Kepler is single, and describes herself as 'very content' and in 'no rush' to wed. Unlike some of her more liberal counterparts in mainstream professional careers, she finds the talk of man shortages and biological clocks 'pretty silly'. If she does have children, she's not sure she would give up her job. Although she is lobbying this week against federally supported childcare, she says she would not be averse to leaving her own child in day care, though she prefers a 'family-based' centre. Her explanation is couched in pseudo-feminist terms. 'I just think that the federal government shouldn't tell us what kind of day care our children should have. I believe women should have a choice.'

Down the hall, Susan Larson, director of management, is reviewing office reports. Recently wed, she advocates a return to traditional marriage. But accepting the CWA post meant putting her career before her husband's; he followed her to Washington – without any job prospects. And in her house, she adds, 'I change the car oil and my husband does the laundry.'

In another room, publicity director Rebecca Hagelin is on the phone to her husband. 'Now, let's see, the carpet needs to be vacuumed,' she instructs. 'And if you could straighten up the living room a bit.' It's past 6 p.m. and Hagelin is still at the office. Her husband is at home making dinner, taking care of their baby and preparing the house for guests that evening. The Hagelins might have found the blueprint for their domestic arrangement in an early-1970s manual for liberated couples: they divide up the chores and trade off childcare. 'See, I really wanted to have a baby, but I really wanted to work,' Hagelin says. 'I love to work.' She likes the fifty-fifty arrangement. 'That's the way it is in the eighties, it's not an either–or situation. It really is possible to have it all.'

The New Right women were, in some respects, the reverse image of their more progressive 'yuppie' sisters who got trapped in the backlash eddies. While mainstream professional women were more likely to voice feminist principles while struggling internally with the self-doubts and recriminations that the backlash generated, the New Right women were voicing anti-feminist views – while internalizing the message of the women's movement and quietly incorporating its tenets of self-determination, equality and free-dom of choice into their private behaviour.

If the right-wing activists at Concerned Women for America seemed less anxiety ridden about the 'price' of their own liberation than the average liberal career woman, maybe that's because these New Right women were, ironically, facing less resistance in their world. As long as these women raised their voices only to parrot the Moral Majority line, as long as they divided up the chores only so that they could have more time to fight equal rights legislation, the New Right male leaders (and their New Right husbands) were happy to applaud and encourage the women's mock 'independence'. The women always played by their men's rules, and for that they enjoyed the esteem and blessings of their subculture. On the other hand, working and single women in the mainstream, who were more authentically independent, had no such cheering squad to buoy their spirits; they were undermined daily by a popular culture that parodied their lifestyle, heaped pity and ridicule on their choices, and berated their feminist 'mistakes'.

The activists of Concerned Women for America, like New Right women activists elsewhere, could report to their offices in their suits, issue press releases demanding that women return to the home, and never see a contradiction. By divorcing their personal liberation from their public stands on sexual politics, they could privately take advantage of feminism while publicly deploring its influence. They could indeed 'have it all' – by working to prevent all other women from having that same opportunity.

Chapter Ten

Ms Smith Leaves Washington: The Backlash in Politics

Having committed their intellects and numbers to installing their man in office, the New Right women anticipated new opportunities for themselves in the post-1980 White House. Instead, with Ronald Reagan's election, women began disappearing from federal office.

On the bench, new female judicial appointments fell from 15 per cent under Carter to 8 per cent. The number of female appointees requiring Senate confirmation plunged, too, making Reagan the first president in more than a decade not to better his predecessor's record. On the White House staff, the number of women appointed dropped from 123 in 1980 to 62 in 1981. In fact, even 62 was an inflated figure; the Reagan administration padded the numbers by suddenly labelling women in lower-ranking government career jobs – such as third-level assistant secretary posts – 'political appointments'.

The ironies were even more legion in Britain, where the champion of the New Right successfully elected (and re-elected) to office was herself a woman. But as Joan Smith pointed out in her book *Misogynies*, Mrs Thatcher's success was built on other women's failure, and she had a vested interest in keeping them in their place. As Prime Minister, she once wrote to the 300 Group, set up in 1980 with the aim of getting at least 300 women MPs into Parliament (there were only 44 in 1991), 'Progress is being made but at a slow pace. We want lots more women coming forward, lots more chosen.' But she showed herself to be remarkably resistant to the idea of promoting them once they *had* made it into the House of Commons. In her eleven years in office, Britain's first woman Prime Minister failed to put another woman in her Cabinet of twenty or so males, with the short-lived exception of Baroness Young. Her ministerial appointments amounted to only eight women, only one of whom rose higher than the ranks of junior minister.

At the start of Ronald Reagan's second term, without re-election pressures to inspire even nominal equal opportunity efforts, the administration immediately discontinued both the Coalition on Women's Appointments and the Working Group on Women. The numbers of women appointed fell even more steeply, and for the first time since 1977 not one woman ranked high enough to attend the daily senior staff meetings or report to the president. At the Justice Department in 1986, Ed Meese had yet to hire a woman as a senior policy-maker two years after taking office – in spite of federal regulations requiring the department to set such hiring goals. The Federal Women's Program, established in 1967 to recruit women to government agencies, was essentially disbanded: its recruitment coordinators at the various federal agencies were either assigned other duties, stripped of their budgets, or quietly laid off. 'Each year, our budget has been cut and it was cut again this year,' Betty Fleming, the personnel management specialist who was second in command in the Federal Women's Program central office in 1991, explains. But, she says, she wasn't complaining; they didn't need the funds, because 'We're just going to meet and talk.' Finally, as part of Reagan's Paperwork Reduction Act, the federal government gave up collecting most recruitment statistics on women altogether. Now the federal government could give up seeking women – and no one would be any the wiser. In Australia, some of the government agencies that concentrated on advancing women's rights – such as the Women's Bureau in the Department of Employment and the Women's Directorate in New South Wales – have been swallowed up by larger bureaucracies that have no specific interest in gender equality.

The few women who did slip past the no-girls-allowed sign on the White House lawn didn't exactly feel at home. UN ambassador Jeane Kirkpatrick had a revelation one day while sitting in the Situation Room, surrounded by a sea of white male faces. Out of the corner of her eye, she saw a rodent scurry across the floor. 'I thought to myself,' as she later told the *Wall Street Journal*, 'that the mouse was no more surprising a creature to see in the Situation Room than I.' She left government with this conclusion: 'Sexism is alive.'

Faith Whittlesey received the 'highest' female post on the Reagan White House staff: assistant to the president for public liaison, paying lip service to women's and children's issues. The Reagan administration, she asserted, would aid women by seeing to it that *men* earned a higher 'family' wage, so that 'all those women can go home and look after their own children.' In her 1984 address on women's status, Whittlesey assured her audience that women's rights were in good hands in Washington: 'I know the president is deeply committed to providing women with the broadest range of options in exercising their choice.' But working at the White House, Whittlesey soon developed doubts about Reagan's deep commitment – doubts that probably deepened after Don Regan became chief of staff and demoted her post. Like Kirkpatrick, she eventually bailed out. As she headed for the car park with her packing boxes on the last day, 'all I saw was a sea of men coming and going in those cars,' she recalled. 'I began to think, "Maybe they're right. Women aren't welcome in the White House." '

The New Right women who received political appointments typically landed in posts that either came with inflated titles but no authority or required them to carry out the administration's most punitive anti-feminist policies. Women like Beverley LaHaye ended up in the first group, shunted to such powerless panels as the Family Advisory Board. On the other hand, a series of women were assigned to the Office of Population Affairs to do the administration's dirty work against emancipated girls and women. First, anti-abortion activist Marjory Mecklenburg was charged with promoting the 'squeal rule', a Reagan policy proposal to make clinics blow the whistle on teenage girls who were seeking birth control without parental permission. Jo Ann Gasper, *Conservative Digest* columnist and editor of *The Right Woman*, inherited Mecklen-burg's job (Mecklenburg, ironically, was forced out of office after rumours circulated that she was having an extramarital affair with a staff member). Gasper was given the thankless task of shutting down domestic violence programmes. She, in turn, was replaced by Nabers Cabaniss, who got to promote a Reagan plan to retract federal funding from any clinic staff that so much as mentioned the word abortion.

Out with the Feminists . . .

If the Reagan climate in Washington was chilly for New Right women, it was poisonous for feminists: they became targets of a purge incited by the New Right. When the Heritage Foundation's 1981 *Mandate for Leadership* itemized the federal programmes it wanted cut or eliminated, on its top priority list was an agency 'dominated' by feminists. Of the dozens of government services targeted by the Heritage Foundation, the Women's Educational Equity Act programme was singled out for a uniquely fierce, personal and sustained assault. *Mandate for Leadership* demanded the dismemberment of WEEA for one reason only: as its authors explained, WEEA represented an 'important resource for the prac-tice of feminist policies and politics'. It was a 'top priority item for the feminist network' and espoused 'extreme feminist ideology'.

WEEA's director, Leslie Wolfe, a ten-year civil service veteran who had pioneered government programmes to promote women's education, enraged the New Right like no other government figure. 'I was a "known feminist",' Wolfe says later. 'And because WEEA was seen as a "feminist group", it got treated very differ-ently from other government programmes that the New Right disliked.' She was one of the only directors of a federal programme that the New Right lobby bothered to single out by name. In a flurry of internal memos, public magazine articles and radio talks, New Right leaders denounced Wolfe as a 'radical feminist', spread slanderous tales about her professional behaviour, and called for her 'swift dethronement'.

At the centre of all this fury was a tiny and underfunded office in the Education Department – the only federal programme to promote equal education for girls. WEEA offered small grants to projects supporting non-sexist education and combating sex discrimination in the schools. It had been hailed as 'one of the most cost-effective programs in government' by the Association of American Colleges. The woman who first proposed WEEA wasn't even one of those 'radical feminists' from NOW; Arlene Horwitz was a clerical worker in a congressional office, a working woman who understood from personal experience – trying to live on her skimpy salary – that unequal schooling could have painful and long-term economic consequences. The projects WEEA funded were hardly radical either: a guide to help teenage handi-capped girls; a programme to enforce equal education laws in rural school districts; a maths counselling service for older minority women returning to community college.

Nonetheless, to the men of the Heritage Foundation, WEEA was 'the feminist network feeding at the federal trough'. Charles Heatherly, Heritage Foundation fellow and the *Mandate* editor who made this charge at August 1983 hearings before the House Education and Labour Committee and attacked Wolfe most vigor-ously, later admits that he never dealt 'with her personally'. But he had made up his mind about the WEEA director. 'She was widely perceived to be a radical feminist,' he explains. And his campaign against Wolfe and WEEA only intensified with Reagan's election: the new president appointed Heatherly deputy under-secretary of management in the Education Department, putting him in charge of the programme.

Heatherly recruited his New Right colleagues, some on staff, others, like Conservative Caucus founder Howard Phillips, as consultants to review the programme's budget. Their mission: to wipe out WEEA. They found a sympathetic ear in the White House; soon after his inauguration Reagan proposed an immediate 25 per cent cut of its already approved budget, with total defund-ing the following year. In Congress, WEEA's supporters fought back. Led by Republican Representative Margaret Heckler, the programme won a reprieve, though not without a 40 per cent budget cut.

The New Right leaders weren't ready to give up after this first round. In the winter and spring of 1982 they pursued a months-long media and letter-writing campaign against Wolfe. *Human Events: National Conservative Weekly* claimed it had 'uncovered' such apparently offensive WEEA grants as an award to the Council on Interracial Books for Children. *Conservative Digest*, the publication of the Conservative Caucus, attacked Wolfe personally in an anonymously written article by a 'concerned employee in the Education Department'. She was guilty, the author asserted, of 'twisting the grant approval process', exercising 'near total control', and using WEEA as a slush fund for NOW and a 'money machine for a network of openly radical feminist groups'. Leslie Wolfe was a 'monarch', who was 'imperiously guarding her fiefdom'. Again, on a talk show, Howard Phillips accused her of underhandedly funnelling money to women's rights organizations. He complained, too, that she was guilty of insubordination; Wolfe, he said indignantly, once referred to the Education Secretary as 'His Wimpiness'.

Just a week after the *Conservative Digest* broadside, Wolfe was demoted – by memo. WEEA would henceforth be run by a Heatherly appointee, and Wolfe would 'serve in an advisory capacity', the memo informed her. Wolfe wrote back, protesting against the decision. She got no response. Finally, three weeks later, Wolfe was summoned to the office of Acting Assistant Secretary Jean Benish – a woman had been picked once again to deliver the bad news to a feminist woman. 'You are being temporarily reassigned as of Monday morning to a task force on fraud, waste and abuse,' Wolfe recalls Benish telling her. 'I said, "I'm not the right person for that kind of job. My background is education, not fraud." ' The assistant secretary told her she had no choice; this was an emergency and the department needed a 'high-level manager' with 'outstanding management skills' to handle this important project. She told Wolfe to leave her key on the desk by the end of the day.

When Wolfe reported to her new assignment, however, she found no emergency and no request for a high-level manager. Her new boss did, however, point out that she was lucky to land where she did; Heatherly's men had considered transferring her to the 'Secretarial Certification Program'. Again, WEEA's congressional supporters protested against the administration's heavy-handed tactics. Finally, three months later, Wolfe was told she could reclaim her old job. But when she returned she found the halls filled with strangers.

Every year, the programme must hire 150 outside field readers to review grant applications – and under the WEEA Act the readers must understand and support educational equality laws and have some educational expertise. In Wolfe's absence – just one day, in fact, after she was reassigned – Heatherly had thrown out her field readers and installed his own: a group of women from Phyllis Schlafly's Eagle Forum. 'There was a general feeling that there had been too much inbreeding,' Heatherly explains later of the wholesale dismissal. 'New faces were needed.' These readers weren't picked for their enthusiasm for WEEA's goals. As one of them explained at the time to her hometown paper, the *Tulsa World*, she was on her way to Washington to help curb a 'feminist agency' that Reagan wanted abolished.

The new field readers, for the most part, neither understood nor supported educational equality. One reader, whose job was to review applications that would help enforce Title IX, asked the panel's moderator plaintively, 'What *is* Title Nine?' Another woman, who was supposed to be reviewing applications to help disabled women, wanted to know if being a Native American qualified as a 'disability'. The field reader considering applications for educational equality projects for minority women was on loan from the infamously discriminatory Bob Jones University. They repeatedly rejected grant proposals to alleviate sex discrimination on the grounds that discrimination never existed. 'Do not see the need in project,' wrote one field reader in her evaluation. 'Most girls and boys go into fields,' she explained, because 'it is [the] way parents bring them up and mostly they are born with certain desires. . . . [I] just disagree with whole approach.' Another wrote of one grant application, 'The title of program concerns me.' Why? It 'encourages women not to stay in low-paying jobs but to move up if they desire'. Finally, the General Accounting Office investigated and found that 20 per cent of the field readers did not meet a single qualification for their WEEA jobs and most only barely qualified. And the numbers of minority field readers, the GAO noted, had been cut by 75 per cent. The auditors' findings, however, did not discourage the administration from continuing its campaign against WEEA.

A year later, Wolfe was ushered into her boss's office one last time. Her job had been abolished, she was told, and she would be laid off unless she cared to accept a new assignment: clerk-typist in the Office of Compensatory Education. Wolfe resigned. All five other women on the WEEA staff were fired or reassigned – while all five male employees were retained. With Wolfe gone, the Education Department immediately demoted the office to the bottom of the bureaucracy – and the director's post to 'section chief', a low-authority classification. The job went to a career civil servant, who herself was demoted two grades to fill the post. 'Dethronement', while not swift, had at last succeeded.

... And in with the Fathers

The Department of Education, which had starred in the campaign to oust the feminists, now directed the effort towards crowning the fathers. If the 'pro-family' movement was 'pro' anything, it was paternal power.

The White House based the 'family policy' office in the Education Department, a logical enough choice for an administration that viewed 'family policy' as a series of didactic lectures, not a programme offering the family economic, medical or legal assistance. As Gary Bauer, who would become the department's family-policy czar, told civil-rights leaders: 'The values taught on the "Cosby" show would do more to help low-income and minority children than a bevy of new federal programs. . . . [A] lot of research indicates that values are much more important, say, than the level of welfare payments.' The values he had in mind weren't simply familial love and understanding. What Bauer found most edifying about *The Cosby Show* was its depiction of a household where, as he puts it in a later interview, 'children respect their father'.

Bauer was having some trouble himself mustering respect from the governmental family he joined in 1981. He entered public service as deputy under-secretary for education with visions of launching a 'social revolution' from his desk. But he was ignored by senior Reagan officials, and even his staff paid no attention to him; Bauer spent his first two years trying to silence the Education Department's remaining 'moderates', who insisted on talking to the press without his permission. Bauer finally advanced to director of the Office of Policy Development, only to discover that the office's purposes primarily involved public relations. When the administration handed him yet another window-dressing assignment, chairman of the 1986 task force on the family, Bauer exploded. His petulantly worded fifty-two-page report was, as Senator Daniel P. Moynihan remarked at the time, 'less a policy statement than a tantrum'.

'The Family: Preserving America's Future' opens, aptly enough, with a quote from that late Victorian champion of endangered masculinity, Teddy Roosevelt: 'If the mother does not do her duty, there will either be no next generation, or a next generation that is worse than none at all.' Bauer's report proceeds to excoriate all manner of independent women who aren't doing their duty: women who work, women who use day care, women who divorce, women who have babies out of wedlock. In the world according to Bauer, wives are forever abandoning their husbands and children, throwing away their marriages 'like paper towels'. The report justifies this position not with statistics but with a newspaper cartoon, in which a bride tells her groom, 'I'm sorry, Sam, I just met my dream man in the reception line.' Even female poverty is the woman's fault; 'more and more,' he writes, female financial problems 'result from personal choices' like seeking a divorce or bearing illegitimate children. Of the offspring of these broken homes, Bauer concerns himself only with the fate of the sons (a one-gender fixation typical of New Right writings on the subject). He decries the 'far more detrimental effects of divorce on boys than on girls' – as if divorce would matter less if it were the girls who suffered more.

Bauer's 'recommendations' to save the family read more like a list of punishments for girls and mothers: bar young single mothers from public housing; revive old divorce laws to make it harder for women to break the wedding vows; deny contraceptives to young women. On the other hand, he proposes prizes for women who follow his dictates. Mothers who stay at home, he suggests, should get tax concessions; the more babies, the more credits.

'We're running at 1.8 children per woman in this country,' Bauer says darkly, on a spring afternoon in the final year of Reagan's tenure. He is seated in his cramped suite in the White House's west wing; if square footage is any indicator of federal priorities, saving the family ranks low on this administration's list.

'That's below replacement level,' Bauer warns of the impending birth dearth. 'There are going to be serious consequences for free society if we continue down this path.' Who's to blame? 'Militant feminists who seemed to hold sway ten years ago couldn't help but have a negative influence on the family.' The evidence? 'Take *Kramer vs. Kramer*. There's that poignant letter the mother leaves behind addressed to her son, where she says, "That's not all there is in life. Mommy has to do some other things." I think that was a real symbol of the times. An excuse for women to run out on their responsibilities.'

Other than the 'irresponsible' behaviour of the celluloid Mrs Kramer – who never actually declared herself a feminist – does Bauer have any other proof that feminism hurt the family? 'Look at textbooks,' he offers. 'Twenty years ago, women in textbooks were housewives and in the home. Now, you look at a textbook and what's missing is any sign of women in a nurturing role in the family. Now our daughters are being taught that life is not full unless they're stewardesses, reporters, etc.'

Bauer says 'most women' in America have come to share his views; they 'are discovering you can't have it all. There's some statistical evidence that women who decided early on to establish a career, and now are getting close to the end of the time they can start a family, feel cheated. Their clock is running out.' Asked to provide this 'statistical' evidence, he says that, alas, it isn't handy.

Even working women whose biological clocks are in working order, Bauer says, 'are realizing they'd rather be at home with their children. Most women work only because they have to.' Mothers should stay at home for the sake of the children, he says. Children in day care, which he characterizes as 'Marxist', suffer long-term damaging effects – according to 'many studies', he adds.

It comes then as a bit of a surprise to learn that Bauer has subjected his own children to this leftist institution – for nine years.

He can explain it, he says. His use of day care was 'different' and 'better' because he placed his children in 'home-based' day care – that is, an unlicensed centre run in a woman's living room. (It's unclear how this is better: a national review of child abuse statistics at day care centres finds that the most incidents of abuse have occurred at such unlicensed sites.) At any rate, Bauer says, a bit defensively, it's not as if his kids went directly from the maternity ward to the nursery. His wife, Carol, waited 'at least three, four months' before she returned to work. 'For my wife, it's been a slow process of concluding you can't have it all.'

Carol Bauer, however, remembers events differently. 'Actually, I went back to work six weeks after Elyse was born,' she says, sitting at their dining-room table on a spring morning in 1988, picking absentmindedly at breadcrumbs on the tablecloth. The children are out – the older ones at school, the youngest at a 'mother's day off' scheme.

At the time of her daughter Elyse's birth in 1977, Carol Bauer explains, she was a top assistant to Congresswoman Margaret Heckler; she couldn't just leave. A lack of federal assistance programmes for mothers also played a role in her decision: 'There's no set leave policy on the Hill,' she points out. Financial considerations entered into it, too: 'We had bought a house and we had a mortgage.' And then there was that other impulse that she just couldn't seem to squelch: 'It wasn't just economics. I enjoyed the intellectual stimulation of the work. I loved work.' She laughs. 'I mean, when I had Elyse, I literally took my work with me. After I got out of the hospital, I was working the next day at home.'

For years, at eight o'clock every morning the Bauers dropped off Elyse, and eventually their second daughter, Sarah, at childcare, put in a full day of work, and then picked up the girls on the way home, usually after six o'clock. The children spent so much time at day care, in fact, Carol Bauer says, that when it was time for Elyse to go to nursery school, they enrolled her in the one in the centre's neighbourhood rather than their own. How did the girls feel about childcare? 'Oh, fine,' Carol Bauer says. 'They were very happy there. For them it was normal.'

What has been harder is Carol Bauer's own adaptation to becoming a full-time housewife. National politics had been her obsession since childhood, when she kept scrapbooks of the presidential elections and proudly wore her Republican campaign badges to school. At Muskingum College in Ohio she read political science and had the *Washington Post* mailed to her dormitory. 'I had Potomac fever,' she recalls. 'I just couldn't wait to get to Washington. I wanted a career. You know, I guess I wanted a family, too, eventually, but what I was really dreaming of was a career in politics.'

After graduation, she headed for the capital and moved from research assistant in the Republican National Committee to an appointment in Heckler's congressional office, where she rose quickly to the top executive post. She was especially pleased to be on the staff of one of the few congress*women*. 'There was something about working for a woman who had managed to do it all,' she says. When Heckler took charge of the Department of Health and Human Services, Carol Bauer came with her in a part-time position. But then the Reagan administration forced Heckler from office. The new HHS Secretary, Otis Bowen, asked Bauer to stay and help with the transition. She agreed – but with her role model and her power base gone, the job soon lost its appeal. 'That was the most difficult part of my career,' she says. 'One day you're the top aide to the secretary, the next day you're not part of the in-crowd any more. I felt like something akin to a fifth wheel.' He also refused to give her the flexible schedule she had had under Heckler. Finally, she left in the late autumn of 1986 – announcing that her children needed her at home.

But nesting, she has discovered, has its trials. 'It was a long winter,' she says of her first season at home. 'It was quite an adjustment.' She pauses. 'It still is.' The first months were the worst: 'I felt rather isolated. I was so used to going to Washington.' She tried to make the best of her new circumstances. 'By last spring I decided if I'm going to be home, I would have to get involved in other things. So this school year, I'm in the Mantua Women's Club; I'm on the board of the baby-sitting co-op, I do PTA work. It gives me some satisfaction.' She shrugs. 'Also, I still talk to my office. And I pump Gary for information every night at dinner.'

This year, she says, her eldest daughter, Elyse, is running for president of her student council. And the other day, Sarah came home from first grade, modelling what Carol Bauer calls 'my dream T-shirt'. Her daughter had inscribed it in art class with her life's goals: 'Go to college. Practice. Get a job.'

Just Not Enough Good Women

Gary Bauer never made much headway with his legislative programme to promote homemaking. The $5,000 personal tax exemption he envisaged for families with housewives would have cost the deficit-stricken government about $20 billion a year in lost tax revenue. But while New Right men like Bauer lost many of their bureaucratic battles, they would eventually win the war for the national political agenda. In that struggle, the 1984 presidential election figured as a crucial turning point – the Democratic party's last stand for women's rights.

By nominating Representative Geraldine Ferraro to the vice-presidential spot on the ticket, the Democrats boldly advertised to women the clear differences between the parties. The measure did not go unappreciated; it earned the Democrats new support from millions of female voters, who contributed more money to Ferraro's campaign fund than women had ever donated to any candidate's coffers. For the first time a Democratic vice-presidential candidate received as much in political contributions as the candidate at the top of the ticket. The Democratic National Committee added 26,000 new names to its rolls, the largest campaign-year increase ever spurred by a single candidate. And Ferraro's presence encouraged other aspiring female politicians. The number of women running for Senate more than tripled and the number of female congressional candidates jumped to a record high.

Ferraro's nomination also inspired instantaneous backlash from the New Right Reaganites, who attacked her not as a politician but as a woman – and, more specifically, as a 'radical left-wing feminist'. Before the TV cameras, they repeatedly suggested that her gender would render her incapable of defending the nation.

Behind the scenes they launched a series of whispering campaigns, all focused on her sexuality. 'There were rumours about me being involved in lesbianism,' Ferraro recalls, 'about me having affairs, about me having an abortion.' The leaders of the anti-abortion movement pursued her with vindictiveness. They even followed her around in an airship.

Though many political candidates in the 1980s were subjected to harsh attacks and close scrutiny, the assault on Ferraro was unprecedented: it wasn't her behaviour that was on trial, but her husband John Zaccaro's; she was to be punished for his management of some muddy New York property deals. Ferraro herself was no promoter of that profession – in fact, the Realtors Association had given her an 88 per cent disapproval rating. She was excoriated for her husband's reluctance to disclose his tax returns – while Bush was unscathed after placing his own assets in a blind trust, thus avoiding having to reveal his tax returns. Rumours about Zaccaro's improprieties were floated first by the New Right magazine *Human Events* and the right-wing Accuracy in Media organization. The Washington press corps probed the business practices of this small-time landlord as if he would soon be managing the White House budget. And reporters applied themselves with a perseverance that was to be notably absent four years later in the reporting on George Bush's role in the Iran-Contra affair. The *Philadelphia Inquirer* assigned *thirty* reporters to the Zaccaro story. Even after Ferraro released her family's tax returns and reviewed them in excruciating detail at a one-and-a-half-hour nationally televised news conference, investigations of 'her' finances persisted, ranging far from her bank account. The press even looked into long-ago business associations of Ferraro's father (dead since she was eight) and Ferraro's husband's *father*. As columnist Richard Reeves, one of the few journalists to step back from the fray, remarked at the time, 'The stoning of Geraldine Ferraro in the public square goes on and on, and no one steps forward to help or protest – not even one of her kind.'

In the end, as myriad post-election polls demonstrated, neither the scandal over Zaccaro's business affairs nor Ferraro's presence on the ticket contributed to the Democrats' defeat. A recovering economy returned the White House to Republican hands. Nearly

80 per cent of voters polled by *Newsweek* said the flap over Ferraro's husband did not figure in their voting decision. Voters weren't rejecting the possibility of a woman in high office either. In fact, a national survey after the 1984 election found that having seen Ferraro on the campaign trail, one-quarter of the electorate was now *more* inclined to vote for a female candidate. Moreover, exit polls found that among voters who cast their ballot on the basis of the *second* person on the ticket, *Ferraro* had the edge over Vice-President Bush.

But history has a way of rewriting itself: 'Polling indicated that she detracted from, rather than added to, Mondale's electoral strength,' an article in the *National Review* decreed a year after the campaign. It did not cite these mystery polls. Other political analysts in the media characterized Ferraro's appearance on the ticket as the Democratic 'surrender' to feminists – and they blamed these feminists for making Mondale look 'weak' to the electorate. Democratic party leaders charged that women were responsible for the party's poor showing and women had had too much influence in the campaign and were driving away white men. Writer Nicholas Davidson asserted that Mondale 'was under the gun from feminists – far more so than from other constituencies. Such was the feminist stick'. *Washington Post* columnist Richard Cohen complained that Mondale had been 'henpecked' and had succumbed to 'the hectoring and – yes – threats of the organized women's movement'. He has been reduced to 'a stock American wimp' and 'might as well sit out the campaign in an easy chair, munching a Dagwood sandwich'.

Eventually Ferraro would internalize much of this revisionist history, too – and turn on herself. In subsequent press interviews, Ferraro said that if she had it to do again, she wouldn't have run for office. Accepting the nomination wasn't 'fair' to her husband, she said. And she backed off from plans to run for the Senate in 1986.

'[T]he defeat of one woman is often read as a judgment on all women,' Ferraro wrote in her memoirs. And indeed, her rough experience during the campaign and her much publicized regrets later translated similarly in the minds of many American women. In 1984, 53 per cent of women in a national poll said they believed a woman would be president by the year 2000; in 1987, only 40 per cent expected it. Women who aspired to a career in politics were even more demoralized by Ferraro's public drubbing. By 1988, recruiters from both parties suddenly encountered difficulties finding women willing to run for office. The bipartisan Women's Campaign Fund had trouble giving away its seed money. Ruth Mandel, director of the Center for the American Woman and Politics, kept hearing potential women candidates beg off with the same reason; they feared 'the Ferraro factor'. The popular California secretary of state, March Fong Eu, backed away from a US Senate bid that year on the Democratic ticket. Her reason: her husband didn't want to have to disclose his finances like Ferraro's husband.

On election day, only two women (both Republicans) were on the ballot in the 1988 US Senate race, down from ten in 1984. It was the smallest number of women running for Senate in a decade. On the House side, the number of female candidates slipped, too. And in every category of statewide executive races – from governor to lieutenant governor to secretary of state to state treasurer to state auditor – women's numbers plunged. Female gubernatorial candidates, for example, dropped to two, from eight just two years earlier. Only in state legislative races did the number of women running increase slightly – and even here the growth rate had dropped substantially from previous years.

When the election results came in for 1988, both women who ran for US Senate had lost, leaving the Senate with its usual two women. (The last time women broke out of that holding pattern was in 1953 – when the Senate boasted a grand total of three women.) On the House side, only two new women were elected in 1988, down from four in 1986. Overall, the percentage of women in both the US Congress and state legislatures had stalled, and the proportion of women in statewide elective office had shrunk to 12 per cent from 15 per cent just a year earlier – the first decline in eleven years.

On a bitterly cold morning in January 1988 in Des Moines, Iowa, more than a thousand delegates gathered in the city's convention centre for the Women's Agenda Conference. The women were there to make their wishes known to the presidential hopefuls. But candidates were scarce. Not one of the six men in the Republican presidential primary showed up for the conference's central event, the Presidential Forum; and only two even bothered to decline their invitations. Two of the Democrats were also absent: Gary Hart and Albert Gore. It wasn't that this was a 'radical feminist' event: the bipartisan conference was sponsored by the National Federation of Business and Professional Women's Clubs, a national association with a 'moderate' reputation and a majority Republican membership. It wasn't that the timing or location was bad: the candidates were all milling about Iowa in January for the primary, desperate for publicity. It wasn't that they hadn't been given enough notice: the invitations had been sent out the previous June. It wasn't that the candidates had more pressing commitments: one of them even went fishing that day. That left only one explanation. As the organization's executive director, Republican Linda Dorian, reluctantly concluded, 'There is something deeply troubling about the way Republican candidates view women.'

Mostly, the 1988 Republican candidates preferred not to view women at all. They represented a growing Republican problem that the party's leaders would just as soon not spotlight. The 'gender gap' appeared in the 1980 election, when for the first time more women than men favoured the Democrats (by a 5 to 7 per cent margin), and Gallup polls began reporting that the Democratic party was enjoying as much as a 19 per cent edge among women. On the top of the ticket on election day, exit polls found, men and women parted company: a majority of men (55 per cent) cast their vote for Reagan, but only a minority of women (47 per cent). The split along gender lines was greater than in any previous presidential election – and striking enough to inspire Reagan to commission pollster Richard Wirthlin to investigate how to combat it in the next election.

That same year, in an unprecedented fissure that went unnoted in the press, a feminist gap also emerged. Women's rights, in fact, would become the only issue on which Carter led Reagan in the polls. The first substantial feminist vote surfaced – and, as political scientist Ethel Klein observed in her study of national voting patterns, it was a vote that surfaced only among women. It was 'the first election,' Klein noted, 'in which there was a group of voters having a preferred candidate on women's rights issues that could be mobilized around a feminist vote.' By 1988, in fact, a remarkable 40 per cent of women who favoured equal rights said in a poll that they would like to have a 'feminist party'. The greatest fear of suffrage's opponents sixty years earlier was finally threatening to come true: a significant number of women were beginning to constitute a bloc of voters who cast their ballots independently of men.

As the decade progressed, the gender gap widened – for Reagan, at times, by as much as 17 per cent – and, with it, women's power to sway elections. By 1984 female votes decided more elections than men's. By 1986 the gender gap returned the Senate to Democratic control; in nine critical Senate races, women favoured the Democrat who won, men the Republicans who lost. In 1988 the gender gap would be a factor in over forty state elections. The gender gap's effect was further strengthened by women's increasingly large numerical edge at the polls. Female voters outnumbered men in 1980 by 5.5 million votes; by 1984, for the first time a higher proportion of women than men voted; by 1988, women were casting 10 million more ballots than men.

In Britain, too, the effect of years of Conservative policies that ignored childcare and equal rights and undermined women's position in regard to health and welfare services had been to close the gender gap. The tendency for more women than men to vote Conservative was at an end for the first time in years, and a Fabian Society report by Patricia Hewitt of the Institute of Public Policy Research predicted that it was likely to go into reverse. A 1989 MORI poll showed that young women, particularly, were deserting the Conservative party in droves because of the Government's refusal to listen to them or to take their needs seriously.

By 1988 the voting preferences of American men and women had diverged so much that at one point in the presidential race, polls picked up a 24 per cent gender gap in favour of Democratic candidate Michael Dukakis. It was single women, whether unwed, divorced or widowed, who contributed most dramatically to the gap, along with working, educated, professional, young and black women. In other words, Dukakis's supporters who gave him this

huge female advantage were women who most supported a feminist agenda of pay equity, social equality and reproductive rights.

Republican leaders weren't oblivious to this threat: chairman
Frank Fahrenkopf, Jr, warned his colleagues during the 1988 presidential race, 'We are particularly vulnerable, if I can use that word,
among young women between the ages of eighteen and thirty-five
who work outside the home and particularly within that subgroup,
those young women who are single parents.' This shouldn't have
come as a surprise: female-headed households had suffered disproportionately from Reagan domestic policy, losing billions of dollars in desperately needed childcare assistance, medical aid, legal
services, nutritional supplements and subsidized housing.

One solution, of course, would have been for the Republicans
to try to win over this expanding female, and feminist, vote by
pursuing progressive social policies – policies that the majority of
American women clearly supported. Instead, Republican leaders
cold-shouldered women and chased twice as desperately after men.
None took positions that the majority of women support – from
the right to abortion to social welfare funding to the Equal Rights
Amendment. And those who once did take such stances were busy
recanting them. Bush, Robert Dole and Pete Du Pont all backed
away from previous, more pro-feminist postures. Bush used to
support the ERA, legal abortion and federally funded birth-control services. The very federal contraceptive programme he would
attack in the 1980s, in fact, was the one he had co-sponsored as a
congressman in 1970 – with the pronouncement then, 'No one
has to feel timid about discussing birth control any more.' Now,
though, Bush and Republican party officials shied away from all
but the most symbolic, and empty, expressions of support for
women. At the 1988 Republican National Convention, the party's
officers paid homage to women in one respect only: they gave
out plaques to four good mothers, including Representative Jack
Kemp's wife Joanne, who had put their careers on hold when they
had children.

Rather than meeting the demands of women, the Republican
men struck macho stances that they hoped would impress their
own sex. Bush hoped especially to prove his manly mettle to
members of the press corps, who seemed as obsessed with the

'wimp factor' as the male politicians they were covering. 'I get furious,' Bush assured them. 'I go ballistic. I really do and I bawl people out. Of course, everyone's running for cover.' He even predicted, more wistfully than assertively, 'Maybe I'll turn out to be a Teddy Roosevelt.'

During the race, Bush's campaign managers dismissed questions about women's rights; they were too trivial to warrant comment, they said. 'We're not running around and dealing with a lot of so-called women's issues,' Bush's press secretary indignantly told the *New York Times*. When Bush summoned a group of elected officials to advise him during the campaign, only one was a woman. While the candidate claimed that opposition to abortion was a cornerstone of his campaign, he didn't give this critical concern of women's much apparent thought. When asked in a televised debate if he was 'prepared to brand a woman a criminal for this decision,' he said, 'I haven't sorted out the penalties.' His one seeming nod in the direction of working women's needs during the campaign was a penny-ante childcare proposal that would give the poorest working families about $20 a week in tax concessions. This small change was supposed to pay for basic childcare that, on average, costs four times as much. In the end, the Bush campaign's only real gesture to women was, incredibly, the selection of Dan Quayle. His youthful blond looks, Republican leaders told journalists, would surely charm the ladies.

The Democrats would seem the obvious beneficiaries of women's deepening alienation from the Republican party. (Indeed, the 1988 *Los Angeles Times Mirror* survey on the electorate found that the biggest proportion of women defined themselves as 1960s-style Democrats, identifying with 1960s-era peace and civil rights movements; the *smallest* proportion of men, by contrast, identified with this group.) Yet by 1988 Democratic candidates and leaders were so preoccupied with proving *their* macho credentials and adopting *their* 'pro-family' strategy that they nearly wiped women's rights off the party slate. Paul Kirk, chairman of the Democratic National Committee, announced that such 'narrow' issues as the Equal Rights Amendment and the right to abortion – both supported by large majorities of American voters – had no place on the party platform. Then he tried to disband the party's women's caucuses – after explicitly promising during his campaign for chairman that he wouldn't. Meanwhile, the Democratic Leadership Council quietly omitted abortion rights from its agenda.

In 1984, when women were still being courted by the Democrats, the Democratic National Committee held a gala dinner party to honour its women, and every presidential candidate spoke before the national women's caucuses. In 1988, the party for Democratic women was literally over. Not only was there no honorary banquet that year, during the four days of the women's caucuses, no presidential candidates turned up. Dukakis sent his wife; and his running mate, Senator Lloyd Bentsen, was the only prominent male figure to address the women. In Dukakis's acceptance speech at the Democratic convention, he did not once mention reproductive freedom. Nor, for that matter, did he take a position on sex discrimination, pay equality or the ERA. He didn't offer even a vague endorsement of women's rights. The closest he came was an allusion to the importance of childcare. Like his Republican fellows, he could envisage women only when they were tucked snugly into the family unit.

By turning his back on women, Dukakis managed to turn off his greatest source of support. The 24 per cent gender gap that he enjoyed that summer quickly shrivelled to less than 8 per cent by election day. Only then, after the votes had all been counted, did Bush's men talk about the gap – to claim Dukakis's failure as their success. 'The major accomplishment of Bush/Quayle was the closing of the gender gap,' Bush's polling consultant, Vince Breglio, crowed later. 'It was critical to winning.' Breglio claimed the Republicans won women over by playing up childcare and a 'kinder, gentler' agenda. But the exit polls show this victory to be a less than resounding one; Bush got 49 to 50 per cent of the female vote, not a real majority, and women's affiliation with the Republican party actually fell an additional four percentage points in 1988. (Only 26 per cent of women were calling themselves Republicans in the polls that year.) The Republican party only 'won' the battle over the gender gap by default. Dukakis, for all his muscle-man flexing, never once summoned the courage to punch through Bush's family-values façade. Donna Brazile, the one member of Dukakis's campaign staff who dared to comment in public about the possible hypocrisy lurking behind Bush's family-man show, was fired for her frankness – and a nervous Dukakis hastily apologized to Bush for his aide's indiscretion.

Far from protesting at their candidate's desertion of the female population, most women in the Democratic party seemed to be studying to be ladies, by suffering in silence. When a few women at the caucuses dared to challenge Bentsen for his poor record on women's issues, their inquiries were immediately shushed – by other women in the room. When feminist writer Barbara Ehrenreich approached a prominent female politician about sponsoring a Bill on women's economic rights, she was told to forget it. 'We're not doing "women's issues" any more,' the politician's aide told Ehrenreich – before she even had a chance to describe the proposal. 'We're doing "family issues".'

Such traditional 'feminine' protestations recall the demurrals of second-generation suffragists in the early twentieth century. They, too, tried the ladylike strategy; they gave up speaking of the need for equality and began claiming that they only wanted to be the guardians of motherhood and domesticity, the 'housekeepers' of national politics. Nearly a century later, their counterparts in Washington politics would wrap themselves once more in the family flag. Women's political groups began billing themselves, first and foremost, as maternal champions; they launched a Great American Family Tour and a 'Family Matters' survey, kicked off by a TV special featuring *thirtysomething*'s maternal goddess, Hope Steadman. In a final press mailing a few days before the election, the National Women's Political Caucus and the Women's Vote Project issued a thick packet that focused with virtual exclusivity on 'family' issues. Women should go to the polls, the enclosures instructed, because 'America's Families Need Our Votes'. What about what American women needed? The packet didn't say.

Protecting the interests of families and children, of course, belongs in any comprehensive vision of social welfare. And the efforts of women's groups to aid the family were legitimate, necessary – and far more sincere than the 'save the family' cant recited by so many disingenuous presidential candidates. ('I do hope we can move on to matters of importance, and stop playing games with this parental leave and childcare,' Senate Republican leader Bob Dole griped in Congress – the same year he was running for president under a pro-family banner.) But by allowing themselves to be restricted to family issues alone, women in politics wound up hamstrung and pigeonholed. By 'choosing' to neglect women's issues for the sake of the family cause, female politicians succumbed to yet another of the backlash's you-can't-have-it-all axioms. Women could only ask for childcare and parental leave by not asking for educational opportunities, pay equality and reproductive freedom. Not only was this unfair, the half-a-loaf strategy didn't even work. All the childcare and parental leave Bills that year were defeated.

As the 'pro-family' ideology expanded into the heart of right-wing politics, it pushed women to the fringes. By the end of the decade the vanishing act had become so accepted that it barely attracted notice. While women's status in politics received a tangible amount of press coverage in early-1980s election news, the media's interest evaporated by the decade's final presidential race. The day after the election, the *Washington Post* ran a fourteen-page special election section; it included nothing on women. In the week after the 1988 election, the *New York Times* devoted more than thirty pages to reviewing and analysing the electoral results. Only two paragraphs, in the last column of a general story on political trends, mentioned the gender gap – even though the gap decided at least five House seats, evicted several Republican congressmen, and split voting patterns in congressional elections overall (with a majority of women voting for Democrats, a majority of men for Republicans). While a raft of articles probed the election results from the viewpoint of every conceivable interest group, no story focused on the fate of female candidates. So, not only did the numbers of women elected to national political offices shrink, the public was never informed of this serious setback to women in politics.

In January 1989, days after Bush's inauguration and exactly a year after the first Women's Agenda Conference, female politicians and activists assembled for the conference's second session. Even though Bush hadn't bothered to turn up last year, the delegates were still hopeful. Prominent women in politics predicted that Bush would now drop the campaign's opportunistic anti-feminist veneer and show his true colours as a champion of women. But Bush turned down his invitation to speak yet again, sending a videotape this time. On it, he promised 'to keep talking' to the women. Of course, on tape he'd never hear their side of the conversation.

Chapter Eleven

The Backlash Brains Trust: From Neocons to Neofems

The New Right's leaders could never have marketed the backlash alone. They may have enjoyed unlimited airtime on Jerry Falwell's *Old-Time Gospel Hour*, but their thundering oratory would never go over on breakfast television. Their anti-feminist tracts may have made the evangelical bestseller lists, but the big publishing houses weren't exactly clamouring for paperback rights. Entrée to centre stage awaited cooler talking heads, intermediaries with the proper media polish and academic credentials to translate fiery tirades against women's independence into tempered sound bites and acclaimed hardcovers.

The backlash's emissaries reported from all scholarly outposts; they were philosophers invoking the classics, social scientists brandishing maths scores, and anthropologists claiming Aboriginal evidence of women's proper place. But they weren't just academic authorities. They were also popular writers and speakers; they were mentors in the men's and even women's movements. These middlemen and women did not ally themselves with any single ideological camp, either; indeed, their endorsements helped spread anti-feminist sentiments across the political spectrum. While at the start of the decade the most celebrated of them were neoconservative commentators, by the decade's end, theoreticians who identified with liberal and leftist causes crowded on to the backlash dais, too. By the early 1990s, Reaganite author George Gilder ceded the platform to leftist intellectual Christopher Lasch, who was castigating pro-choice women and calling for a constitutional ban on divorce for couples with children.

While a few of these thinkers openly denounced women's demand for equality, most professed neutrality. They were engaged in a philosophical, not a personal, discourse over female independence. When *they* said feminism had wounded women, they were speaking only as informed and concerned bystanders, surveying the feminist crime scene from an objective distance. The public could trust their judgements. Unlike the New Right, they had no brief against the feminist movement. They just wanted what was best for women.

In fact, some of the backlash experts were even women who claimed to be feminists. Some classified themselves as second-generation 'neofeminists', speaking up for 'mothers' rights'. Others brandished membership cards from the early days of the women's movement; they were feminist writers of the 1970s now issuing revisionist texts. And then there were the unwitting and unwilling messengers – feminist scholars, who watched in dismay as their studies of gender difference were distorted by the backlash's burgeoning staff of zealous interpreters.

The experts who delivered the backlash to the public were a diverse and unrelated clan who defied political or social generalization – but they all carried personal baggage when they stepped up to the mike. Their interest in examining women's status may have been genuine, their intellectual curiosity keen enough. But they were also moved by private yearnings and animosities and vanities that they barely recognized or understood themselves. Like the men and women of the New Right, they, too, struggled in their domestic and professional lives with the wrenching social transformations that the last two decades had brought. And, as seems inevitable in such stressful periods between the sexes, personal anxiety and intellectual inquiry would eventually fuse to make women a 'problem' demanding feverish and microscopic study, a blight on the landscape worthy of endless beard-pulling and pontification. In their own lives, women may or may not have been the source of trouble, but in their writings and speeches, 'Woman' became the all-purpose screen on which so many private apprehensions and apparitions might be projected.

The donnish robes of many of these backlash thinkers cloaked impulses that were less than scholarly. Some of them were academics who believed that feminists had cost them in advancement, tenure and honours; they found the creation of women's studies not just professionally but personally disturbing and invasive, a trespasser trampling across *their* campus lawns. Some of them were writers who believed feminist authors and editors had overshadowed their literary careers or monopolized the publishing industry. Others were theorists trying to come to terms with very untheoretical changes in their own domiciles and marriages. Still others were political tacticians fighting unresolved, decade-old personal battles with women's rights organizations or brooding over real and imagined slights from feminist leaders. And many others were simply publicity seekers, looking to restore former fame that they had originally won by taking a stand in favour of women's rights.

It would be neither feasible nor advisable here to attempt to psychoanalyse these individual men and women. Nor would it be fair; they took on the women's movement for a tangled set of reasons – of which private circumstance is but one. The point is not to reduce the backlash theorists to psychological case studies but to widen the consideration of their ideas to include some less recognized factors – from professional grievances to domestic role strains – that played important contributory roles in shaping these thinkers' attitudes toward feminism.

The brief cameos that follow are not meant, either, to represent a comprehensive catalogue of the many scholars, writers and speakers in different countries who stirred the backlash stew. There were simply too many cooks – from brand names to mere media blips – who helped make the backlash palatable for public consumption. The succeeding pages offer instead a sampler of anointed spokespersons – thumbnail sketches of some lofty experts who could also be frightened or confused people, bluffing or blustering or bullying their way through a trying and bewildering time of change.

George Gilder: 'America's Number-One Anti-feminist'

When the United States invaded Cambodia in 1970, a twenty-nine-year-old George Gilder, then a spokesman for the liberal Republican Senator Charles McC. Mathias, found himself 'besieged' by anti-war protesters who demanded to know how the congressman could claim both to oppose the invasion and support the president. They derided Gilder, too. 'In their view, I might be against the war,' he recalled, 'but I was part of the "system".' One evening, having squeezed his way through a sea of shouting demonstrators, Gilder sat at home and brooded. His feelings of 'uneasiness' that night, as he would write later, 'reached beyond the dilemmas of my job. I also had qualms about my virility.'

> Not only was I avoiding enemy fire in Southeast Asia, I was also shunning full commitment in Washington. Thousands of young men and women would be marching the next day full of moral fervor, while I would be worrying about violence, about affronting powerful senators who might vote for peace.
>
> In a way, I knew my commitment was deeper, more practical, professional. But it didn't allow a fusion of physical and emotional engagement: a delivery of myself to the group and the cause.

After much soul-searching, he settled on a solution – jogging. 'A good run could give me a sense of manliness and moral sufficiency often lasting several hours.' As Gilder was puffing up the hill to the Washington Monument, an object fell from the sky and suddenly he was 'bowled to the ground in the darkness, as if by a bullet in the gut or a noose at the neck'. The police had mistaken him for a protester and lobbed a tear-gas canister in his direction. It hadn't actually hit him, but it was 'baptism by fire' nonetheless. 'As I stood there on the hill . . . I was not exactly pensive or philosophical,' he writes. 'I was surprised by a surge of elation. It might not be history but it had made me part of the flow of events. I saw that I must have been one of the very first demonstration casualties. Perhaps *the* first.'

The following year, Gilder moved back to Harvard Square with hopes of launching a career as a 'famous writer', a family tradition

– among the women anyway. An exceptional number of his female relatives, as he notes, had been successful and even distinguished authors and playwrights. (Gilder was also raised by the Rockefellers after his father, David Rockefeller's college room-mate, was killed in the Second World War – an environment that no doubt contributed to greater expectations.) As he recalls later, he had hoped to become *the* social commentator of the era's turbulent national scene – a literary figure of the order of Joan Didion, his designated role model. In the meantime, however, he was editing the *Ripon Forum*, the newspaper of the liberal Republican Ripon Society.

At the offices of this Republican newsletter, he would face another, more directly political, threat of eviction from his own turf. After he wrote an article praising President Nixon's veto of a day care Bill, the 'feminists' at the *Ripon Forum* ganged up on him, he says, and tried to get rid of him. Even worse, they got media attention by bad-mouthing him. 'Several of them got on the *Today* show with Barbara Walters,' he recalls. 'I mean, here was this obscure magazine that had virtually no subscribers and yet these female officers could get on TV, on the *Today* show no less, to protest [against] my views.'

Then he discovered that the TV hosts were even more interested in his counterattack. 'I was on *Firing Line* with all these congressmen and leading professors and feminists, just because of this article I wrote.' And he got the attention of a long-sought-after audience: 'After the program, virtually all the women rushed forward to argue with me. All these years I'd been looking for a way to arouse the passionate interest of women, and it was clear I had reached pay dirt.' It was then that the notion struck him: he could make a national name for himself another way – as 'America's number-one anti-feminist'.

Until then Gilder had, in fact, described himself as a feminist. He maintains now that he had no choice; back then, 'women's libbers' forced men to mouth the words. 'In Cambridge, the feminists just dominated the scene,' he says. 'Really, everybody was a feminist. It was like a rhetorical requirement.' But by becoming 'the nation's number-one male chauvinist', yet another title he, half-jokingly, conferred upon himself, he saw a way to escape that dominance and build a literary career at the same time. Immediately after the showdown with the Ripon feminists, Gilder gave up his editing job, moved to New Orleans and began writing *Sexual Suicide*. It was to be the first of four Gilder books on the ravages of feminism: *Naked Nomads*, *Visible Man* and *Men and Marriage* followed. (The last, published in 1986, was really just a revised version of *Sexual Suicide*, reissued in hopes of capitalizing on feminism's 'serious setbacks', as Gilder put it, in the backlash eighties.) In each of them he would write of women who are 'displacing more and more men at work', and of men – even 'many conservative men' – who are 'lacking the guts to rebuff the upper-class feminist ladies'. Feminists are turning to 'coercion' to have their way, his books warned: in business, they 'menace not only the sex roles on which the family is founded but also the freedoms at the very heart of free enterprise'; in Washington, they are trying to 'emasculate the political order itself'.

'Let us dream a dream of liberation, a dream of young women,' begins Gilder's fable, 'The Princess' Problem'. Like a media trend story, Gilder's tale for single career girls is a cautionary one. The princess is the unhappily liberated Susan, an associate editor at 'Rancour House'. Her 'problem': she's single and pushing thirty. She's having an affair with Simon, Rancour's married editor-in-chief.

'Why are there no single men?' Susan sighs to herself in her office, as she 'lets her eyes rest on her small but privileged view of the East River'. She considers, simultaneously, the Statue of Liberty and the downside of women's liberation.

> What does Liberty ask in 1986? Bring me your associate editors yearning to breathe free, your girl executives weary of the office air, your young lady lawyers with brisk efficient smiles and medicated wombs, your tired and hungry heiresses with advanced degrees – all your single women moving upward behind the glowing unopenable glass windows, who gaze at the brown river and ponder the passage of time, the promise of freedom.

Susan could solve her 'problem', Gilder writes, if she would only lower her standards and marry Arnold, an unsuccessful writer and bachelor. Arnold is a persistent, if somewhat pathetic, suitor, but Susan considers Arnold barely worthy of her Rolodex. His latest manuscript gathers dust on her desk.

Susan will pay for spurning Arnold, Gilder writes. Simon won't leave his wife and Susan will end up 'well into her thirties, without a husband'. She 'will have to marry whoever happens to be available as her thirties pass by. . . . If she waits too long, she may well find that even Arnold is no longer interested, particularly if he has at last managed to succeed in his career. He may reject her with regret. But reject her he will, in favour of a woman in her twenties.' Wimpy Arnold will have the last laugh. And she will become a spinster who 'all too often . . . gives herself to drugs and the bottle'.

Why must Susan marry Arnold? Women 'have to bet on the Arnolds of the world,' Gilder writes, because 'by choosing them and loving them and bearing their children, the young women greatly enhance the likelihood that struggling young single men will in fact become successful men like Simon.' In other words, Susan must marry Arnold for *Arnold's* sake. The princess's 'problem', it turns out, is the prince's.

In the 1970s, the struggling author and frustrated bachelor was having his own Arnold-like difficulties. He was past thirty, unwed and, by his own account, extremely unhappy about it. Gilder's 'single man's predicament', as he calls it, is a constant complaint in his works of this decade. Of his five boyhood friends, he writes worriedly, every one of them is married except for 'P.J.', a marine who recently shot himself in the head. Eager to avoid a similar fate, Gilder 'was very aggressively pursuing women' – but none would marry him.

Gilder's books lament the oversupply and shaky emotional status of contemporary single *men*. 'The single man is caught on a reef and the tide is running out,' he writes. 'He is being biologically stranded and he has a hopeless dream.' Unlike some other backlash writers, he is at least honest about the advantages marriage offers his sex and about the real ratio of single men to single women. (Even so, when he issued *Men and Marriage* in the 1980s, he couldn't resist citing the Harvard–Yale marriage study in the introduction as evidence of feminism's damaging effect on women.) Wherever one looks, single women today are far better off than single men, Gilder asserts, pointing dispiritedly to a study that finds single women even have more than twice as much sex as single men. 'As in the case of poverty, crime, mental illness, depression and mortality,' he writes, 'it is single men who are the casualties of the Sexual Revolution.' And he points out that single men *need* to get married a lot more than women: 'Although they may make claims to the contrary, women, in fact, can often do without marriage; single women at least can live to a stable and productive old age. . . . Men without women frequently become the "single menace",' and they are 'often destined to a Hobbesian life – solitary, poor, nasty, brutish and short.'

A man also must marry so he can support a family – the acid test of manhood. '[V]irile masculinity,' he writes, ' . . . is reserved chiefly for the married.' And how can a single man prove himself as a 'provider', Gilder asks, 'in a society where he cannot earn more money than the females eligible to him'? Like the Yankelovich researchers, Gilder has stumbled across America's still largely unchallenged social prerequisite to masculinity: a real man pays the family bills – all of them. Gilder parts company with these social scientists, however, by claiming that this economic definition of manhood is basic to human biology.

Gilder's version of young underemployed single men is far gloomier than the Yankelovich's 'Contenders'. To Gilder, single men in general are an inordinately unsavoury breed, 'a baboon troop' of 'naked nomads' who are far more likely than married men to become drug addicts, alcoholics, compulsive gamblers, criminals and murderers. '[T]he older a man gets without marrying,' he writes, 'the more likely he is to kill himself.' Only a wedding ring, Gilder warns, can 'tame the barbarians'. But if the typical single man is this unappealing, what woman would consider a date with him, much less marriage? Gilder's answer to women: you have no choice – wed or prepare to die. '[T]he peripheral men are not powerless,' he advises ominously. 'They can buy knives and guns, drugs and alcohol, and thus achieve a brief and predatory dominance.' They will 'rape and pillage,

debauch and despoil'. Better to march down the aisle with them
– than to meet them in a dark alley.

Gilder's early books won him a niche as an anti-feminist media
pundit, but not the readership he craved. The sales figures declined
through the 1970s: 12,000 for *Sexual Suicide*, 7,000 for *Naked
Nomads*, and a whopping 600 for *Visible Man*. 'It's the world's
leading loser for a career move,' Gilder sighs. (*Men and Marriage*,
on the other hand, printed in the midst of the backlash, sold more
than 30,000 copies – even though the book was only available by
mail order.)

But in 1981 Gilder finally became a literary success by harness-
ing his career to Ronald Reagan's. Throwing away his liberal
Republican leanings with his feminist past (as a young Ripon
charter member, he had co-authored a book mocking this 'Class-
B' movie star), Gilder became a Reagan speechwriter, helped script
Reagan's acceptance address, and, most famously, produced a
book that would be the blueprint for the new administration's
supply-side economics and budget-cutting scheme – a scheme that,
notably, hit female heads of household disproportionately hard.
While *Wealth and Poverty* was most widely characterized at the
time as a broadside against liberals and their legacy, what was less
recognized was the book's attack on members of another political
group: this Gilder work delivered more than a few kicks in the
pants to feminists and their handiwork, too.

Overnight, the unheralded and unwealthy freelance writer
became the intellectual darling of the Reagan administration – and
went from poverty to wealth. Reagan's men acted as indefatigable
patrons and publicity agents for *Wealth and Poverty*: Reagan
campaign chairman William Casey supplied financial support
during the writing stages and Reagan's budget director David
Stockman peddled the book and even proposed handing it out to
cabinet members in front of the press. All the promotion paid off:
Wealth and Poverty sold more than a million copies.

While the book critics at the time focused exclusively on *Wealth
and Poverty*'s economic message, Gilder continued his war on
independent women in its pages. In fact, he widened it. *Wealth
and Poverty* blames the women's movement not only for single

men's failure to marry but for married men's failure to prosper. When wives march purposefully to work, the book charges, they reduce their husbands to useless cripples: 'The man has the gradually sinking feeling that his role as provider, the definitive male activity from the primal days of the hunt through the industrial revolution and on into modern life, has been largely seized from him.' The women's movement, in Gilder's view, has undercut the male provider twice – first, directly, by encouraging women to work, and then, indirectly, by championing social welfare programmes that allow wives to survive without their husbands. First, feminists homed in on men's role as breadwinners, he writes, then they saw to it that men were 'cuckolded by the compassionate state'.

At the same time that Gilder was bemoaning the loss of traditional manhood in society at large, he was finally laying claim to a version of it for himself. At last, he had scored in the marriage game and found a wife. Nini was, as he described her, a traditional-minded woman who earned a smaller salary than he, and Gilder hoped to keep it that way. As he asserted in *Men and Marriage*, he didn't want his wife 'to feel she is unequal to me if she earns less money than I do, or unequal to the careerist women I meet in my work'. To be sure, she didn't quite live up to his helpmate ideal. When they met, he concedes later, she had a career as an architectural historian. And even after they wed, she remained active in her field, writing several books. But maybe this ageing prince had considered *his* marital odds – and decided he'd better settle for what he could get.

Allan Bloom: A Refugee from the Feminist Occupation

Ostensibly about the decline in American education, Allan Bloom's *The Closing of the American Mind* dedicates page after page to an assault on the women's movement. Whether he is deploring the state of scholarship, the emasculating tendencies of music or the transience of student relationships, the baleful influence he identifies is always the same: the feminist transformation of society that has filled women with demands and desires and depleted men of vim and vigour. 'The latest enemy of the vitality of the classic texts is feminism,' he writes; concerted attacks on the literary canon from 1960s student radicals and minorities pale in comparison, he says. Even the sexual revolution, Bloom's other *bête noire*, is cast as a mere warm-up exercise to the 'grimmer' rule of feminist tyranny. 'The July 14 of the sexual revolution,' he writes, 'was really only a day between the overthrow of the Ancient Regime and the onset of the Terror.'

Very little in Bloom's treatise actually pertains to slipping educational standards; very much space, on the other hand, is devoted to a prolonged rant against the rising female Terror. 'The feminist project,' he warns, has unleashed 'a multitude of properly indignant censors equipped with loudspeakers and inquisitional tribunals' and 'a man pays a high price' for violating their edicts. 'Feminism has triumphed over the family', led to 'the suppression of modesty', rearranged sex roles 'using force', made it so that a woman 'can easily satisfy her desires and does not invest her emotions in exclusive relationships', and enabled women to bear children 'on the female's terms with or without fathers'. In short, feminism has freed women from the dictates of the male will 'so that [women] can live as they please' – a development that this scholar deems a serious problem.

Bloom's was only the most notorious of many 'decline of America' tomes that hit the book shops in the late eighties. Like the producers of a similar outpouring in the late nineteenth century, the learned authors of these alarmist texts wrote darkly of America's dropping educational standards, deteriorating moral values and flagging economic prowess – and, one way or another, they found a way to blame feminism, at least partially, for these national tribulations. In *The True and Only Heaven*, Christopher Lasch sees 'the unwholesomeness . . . of our way of life' highlighted in the feminist insistence on 'freedom of choice', the feminist challenge to traditional marriage, and the feminist 'propaganda for unlimited abortion'. In *Tenured Radicals: How Politics Has Corrupted Our Higher Education*, Roger Kimball indicts the women's movement on the very first page. 'Radical feminism,' he warns, is 'the single biggest challenge to the canon'. Feminist studies has become 'the dominant voice in the humanities departments of many of our best colleges and universities', to the grave detriment of American intellectual life. Feminist scholars are intimidating universities into hiring other feminists, and 'their object is nothing less than the destruction of the values, methods, and goals of traditional humanistic study.' By 1991 in California, about one hundred professors who shared this view had formed the California Association of Scholars; the group railed against women's studies programmes, claimed that efforts to enrol and hire women and minorities were destroying academic standards, and rallied round University of California anthropology professor Vincent Sarich, who had incensed female and minority students with his denunciations of positive discrimination and his 'scholarly' speculation that women had smaller brains than men.

A few years after *The Closing of the American Mind*'s publication, Bloom not only stands by his indictment of feminism, he now says his celebrated 1987 bestseller 'underestimated' the problem. Feminism 'has become infinitely more powerful', he maintains. And nowhere are the feminists ruling with more iron-fisted authority than the American campus, where their views have become 'really a kind of orthodoxy' and those who don't toe their line are liable to 'get shut down'.

The fifty-seven-year-old Plato scholar teaches at the University of Chicago, where he has retreated to the conservative, and practically all-male, bunker of the Committee on Social Thought (which had only one woman on its faculty): 'I'm protected in my eccentric ivory tower,' he says. 'It's worse in the departments.' When venturing outside the committee's demilitarized zone, he treads warily. 'It's hard to explain to people who aren't in the universities how extraordinary it is,' he says, comparing his lot to a shell-shocked refugee bearing atrocity stories: 'I'm like one of the first people out of Cambodia.'

According to Bloom's report from the front, feminists have invaded every academic sanctuary – a view shared by the many male scholars denouncing 'political correctness' in the early 1990s. 'One finds it in all the various departments. They have made tremendous changes in courses. But more than that, in the old established courses with traditionalist books, a huge number [of professors] are teaching from that point of view. You study American history now, and what is America but the history of the enslavement of women! There's no question but it's become the doctrine.'

The feminists rule because they have the numbers. 'This terrific attack on the curriculum is fundamentally by the feminists because the feminists have been the most successful,' Bloom says. 'There was this great push to hire women no matter what, and women have really achieved and they're there now. And the simple fact is, you get a majority with a certain interpretive opinion and they think everybody is incompetent and they hire their own.'

Bloom's conviction that most faculty jobs and publication rights are now reserved for feminist women is shared by many of his conservative, as well as liberal, male colleagues on campus. But it is a conviction based on fear, not fact. Women, feminist or otherwise, account for a mere 10 per cent of the tenured staff at all four-year American institutions (and a mere 3 to 4 per cent at Ivy League colleges) – a rise of only 6 per cent since the 1960s. Five times more women with PhDs are unemployed than men. Nor are feminist professorships overrunning campuses; only twelve women's studies chairs exist in the USA. As for dominance in academic publications, a census taken of the roughly 1,500 articles published annually in journals of history, literature, education, philosophy and anthropology found that only 7.4 per cent of them dealt with women or women's issues, a tiny 5 per cent increase since the 1960s. In Bloom's field, philosophy, the proportion of women's issues articles was the tiniest of all, 2.7 per cent – and had actually *declined* from a 1974 'peak' of 5.4 per cent. If scholars like Bloom had fewer opportunities in their fields, financially motivated shifts in university priorities were more to blame than feminist studies. In the 1980s, one university after another cut liberal-arts budgets and poured their funds instead into the decade's two on-campus growth industries: medical and business schools.

Perhaps what troubled Bloom was not so much that the feminist-tainted American mind was closing – but that it was closing against him. In 1970 Bloom felt compelled to flee his Ivy League haven for Canada. 'The guns at Cornell', as he characterized the student uprising, drove him out. While only a very few of the guns were in women's hands, they are the ones he most vividly recalls – and resents. 'That's when I began encountering the feminists,' he recalls of Cornell, which was one of the first college campuses to establish a women's studies programme. 'The feminists started speaking very strongly. . . . Some of them are students who have since become well known. They were mostly women doing comparative literature who got a lot of attention.'

While these women were building their careers and collecting their kudos, he felt exiled for ten bitter years at the University of Toronto. 'I was lost,' he told a reporter later. Two years into his expatriate post, at the relatively young age of forty-one, he suffered a heart attack. Finally, after two years of negotiations, he received a faculty appointment at the University of Chicago. But even there he remained, in his word, a 'nobody'. He even had great trouble getting *The Closing of the American Mind* published. Finally, he had to settle for a $10,000 advance.

As Bloom sees it, the faculty feminists barred him from his rightful place of honour. 'There's a certain kind of ostracism if you don't follow the doctrine'; and, because he dared to write that 'the women's movement is not founded on nature', he says, he has been punished. 'For *that*, I don't get invited a lot of places. I can have none of the ordinary academic honours.'

Even his female students don't respect him. 'I went to a theology class at a major theological school. . . . I came in just to discuss these issues and the entire class, which was eleven people, nine of them women, started calling [the presiding professor] a liar and a cheat for bringing me in.' He adds, 'But that's nothing, it really gets violent.' For example, he says, once he lectured at 'a very important college' and the women in the audience actually got mad because he didn't call on them during the question-and-answer period. One even accused him of 'excluding women'.

To Bloom's way of thinking, it's men like him who have been excluded. In *The Closing of the American Mind*, his lament about the 'decay of the family' is, like the New Right's, really a lament over lost traditional male authority in the home and in public life, an authority that he believes is violently under attack. He writes wistfully of the days when it was still believed that 'the family is a sort of miniature body politic in which the husband's will is the will of the whole.' He is upset about wives who cavalierly ditch their husbands under the liberalized divorce laws, and daughters who are under 'less supervision in their relations with boys than at any time in history'.

At times Bloom sounds almost nostalgic for the days when men were free to have their way with women against fear of censure. He suggests that talk of violence against women is . . . just talk. 'Women, it is said,' he writes in *Commentary*, in a tone of high scepticism, ' . . . are raped by their husbands as well as by strangers, they are sexually harassed by professors and employers at school and work.' And feminists, he writes with mounting irritation, want all these so-called crimes to be 'legislated against and punished'. There is one place, at least, where the traditional balance of sexual power is still preserved – pornographic magazines. Feminists are against pornography, he writes, not because they object to its humiliating and violent depictions of women but only 'because it is a reminiscence of the old love relationship, which involved differentiated sexual roles'.

A bachelor himself, Bloom harangues against women most vigorously for their failure to marry; he repeatedly underlines the 'inharmoniousness' of the 'female career' and marriage. He writes that women are unhappy and 'dogged by doubt' because their liberation has denied them love and marriage. It is the standard paradoxical backlash analysis he is offering, albeit in high-flown prose: young women's battles have all 'been won', he writes, and they have emerged the loveless losers. 'All our reforms have helped to strip the teeth of our gears, which therefore can no longer mesh.'

But while Bloom suggests that feminism has cheated women, he soon reveals his underlying suspicion – that the women's movement's greatest victims are men. 'And here is where the business turns nasty,' he writes, turning to what he calls the most 'tyrannical' demand of feminism: that men should change, too (or rather, as Bloom's book describes it, that 'the souls of men . . . must be dismantled'). The consequence, he reports, is universal emasculation. When he surveys the modern-day campus, he sees only 'spiritually detumescent' schoolboys and scholarly men who have become 'old maid librarians'. When he contemplates modern-day society, he sees only the ruins of a male golden age: 'There is nothing left of the reverence toward the father as the symbol of the divine on earth, the unquestioned bearer of authority.' He peers inside the crumbling male castle and beholds that even its innermost sanctum – the connubial bedroom – houses a hobbled stud. Modern men are beset with 'nervousness about their sexual performance', he writes. 'In the past a man could hope to be admired for what he brought.' But now 'he could be pretty sure that he was being compared and judged', a 'daunting' state of affairs that makes it 'difficult for him to perform'.

Feminism, Bloom argues, has not only denied men erections, it has destroyed their basic identity, by dismantling the foundation on which that identity rests – the traditional family. The spectre of the 'decline of the family' appears to trouble Bloom not so much because he wants to preserve the cosy domestic joys but because he sees the family as central to a male sense of self. '[A] man without family lands, or a family tradition for whose continuation he is responsible,' Bloom writes, invoking Tocqueville, is a man who will have trouble 'seeing himself as an integral part of a past and a future, rather than an anonymous atom in a merely changing continuum.'

The Closing of the American Mind is so packed with erudite and classical allusions that its critique of feminism appears to be grounded in Plato, not personal umbrage. But weed the Bloomian garden of its overcultivated metaphors, polysyllabic flourishes and profuse quotations from the ancient Greek philosophers, Rousseau, Flaubert and Shakespeare, and you're left with a scholarly wasteland: no research, no evidence, not even a single quotation from a single living human being to support Bloom's analysis of the contemporary situation between the sexes. The closest he comes is one reference to 'overhearing' conversations between couples in restaurants. If scholarship is, in fact, in decline, then Bloom's work isn't going to save it.

Michael and Margarita Levin: Boys Don't Cook and Girls Don't Do Long Division

In his 1988 book, *Feminism and Freedom*, philosophy professor Michael Levin characterizes feminism as an 'antidemocratic, if not totalitarian, ideology' without a single redeeming feature. 'Surely no body of ideas is wrong about *everything*, as I imply feminism is,' he writes. 'Yet while feminism may have accomplished some good *per accidens*, I would no more pander to the reader by straining to praise rape crisis centers than I would strain to praise the punctuality of trains under Mussolini were I discussing fascism.' His motives for writing this work are purely high-minded, he assures the reader. 'I have felt compelled by conscience to present feminism as I see it.'

Levin's work sets forth the standard tenets of 1980s backlash 'scholarship'. He makes the following key assertions: (1) women with successful careers sacrifice marriage and motherhood; (2) sex roles are innate: women naturally prefer to cook and keep house, and men naturally don't; (3) men are better at maths.

He supports these propositions with dense, footnoted passages about !Kung boys and girls, hermaphrodites, hypogonadics (men with shrivelled testicles), and castrated rhesus monkeys. For example: 'The Hier-Crowley study of nineteen male idiopathic hypogonadics supplies further physiological evidence of the innateness of spatial ability in males.' Or: '!Kung juvenile play-groups are single-sex; boys spend far more time than girls in exploring technology (e.g., digging up termite mounds with arrows), and play rough-and-tumble play.'

Plodding through these pages, one can't help but wonder why they feature so many eunuched monkeys and idiopathic hypogonadics – yet no contemporary men and women. A visit to Levin's house clears up the mystery.

'If you want to interview Michael tomorrow, you can't,' his wife, Margarita Levin, is explaining over the telephone, a few days before the visit. 'That's my teaching day and he has to watch the boys.' This, it turns out, is no isolated occasion. Despite his position in *Feminism and Freedom* that, genetically, 'women prefer to care for children more than men do', in the Levins' dual-career household, childcare duties are routinely divided in half. Margarita Levin has her career to consider. She's a professor at Yeshiva University, teaching philosophy – and, her speciality, the philosophy of maths.

'My wife does the cuddling; all I'm good for with the boys is roughhousing,' Michael Levin emphasizes a few days later, leading the way into his living room in the family's apartment in Manhattan. He picks his way through the clutter of children's toys and settles in an armchair. Sure, he looks after the boys, aged five and eight, when his wife is away, he says, 'but there are certain things that are out. . . . Cleaning up and food preparation are still my wife's job. I don't like to cook. That's just the way men are.' Men find they lose 'tremendous status if they start adopting things that women do', he explains. In fact, 'I feel I've lost a lot of status just talking about [feminism].' But he feels he must address it – to 'reclaim my genitalia and my masculinity'.

Levin recalls that he was first moved to take a stand against the women's movement many years earlier, when some feminist-minded women he knew began calling on men to alter their behaviour. 'I won't forget' one particular incident, he says: a friend's liberated girlfriend was talking about women's rights, 'and she gave me this look and said, "Men will have to change." It was very totalitarian. I found myself really stewing about it.'

As he's speaking, his son Mark races across the room, clambers on his father's knee, and demands 'a hug'. Levin gives him one, then, seemingly mindful of his no-cuddling posture just a minute earlier, shoos his son in the direction of mother. But the little boy will have none of it; throughout the conversation, he makes periodic leaps into his father's lap.

'Did you see Michael on *Geraldo*?' Margarita, who has joined them in the living room, asks. Talk-show host Geraldo Rivera recently asked Levin to serve as an expert on an episode about why men prefer women who aren't their equals. 'If a man does not feel dominant, he won't feel sexually aroused,' Levin recalls telling them. 'It diminishes his masculinity. That's why we are seeing the growth of impotency among younger men.' But how does he know there's a 'growth of impotency'? Levin shrugs good-naturedly. 'It's just my impression.' A pause. 'I suspect it.' Another pause. 'I think I saw a magazine article once about it.'

Michael Levin's marriage does not exactly fit his ideal domestic model. 'My wife is smarter than I am,' he says flatly. She is not only a philosophy scholar but a gifted mathematician. And she is even an intellectual partner in his anti-feminist writings. But Levin has managed to reconceptualize their relationship in terms that restore, at least in his mind, the traditional balance between man and wife. He maintains that he is actually the dominant one because, 'when we met, I was the teacher and she was the student.' Lest the point be missed, he takes pain to repeat it, several times: 'She was a former student of mine, so I don't feel threatened by it,' he assures me.

As Levin is speaking, his other son Eric appears in the living room, clutching a frying pan. He wants to know if his father will help him cook rice. Maybe later, he's told. Michael Levin confesses that cooking is currently his son's 'favourite activity'. Mark, meanwhile, has fallen down and is crying, and Michael goes into the other room to comfort him. Margarita seats herself in the patriarchal armchair – to tell the story of how she became a maths whiz.

She discovered her aptitude in grammar school in the early 1960s – when girls were not typically pushed in the direction of algebra. Margarita, however, says she was fortunate enough to fall into the hands of a few enlightened teachers who recognized her talents: 'No one ever said to me, "don't do it," so I just kept going.' She graduated in maths at City College of New York, where Michael teaches. Then she moved on to the University of Minnesota's graduate programme, where she got her PhD in the philosophy of mathematics. (The summer she wrote her dissertation, Michael stayed at home to look after the kids.) 'I think I'm better at math than the majority of men,' she says.

But the example of her own intellectual abilities has not led Margarita Levin to reject her husband's biological argument about the sexes – only to define herself, as Connie Marshner did, as 'an exception'. The hard sciences, she says, just have 'very few female worthies'. Not only does she endorse her husband's views on women, she is, as Michael points out, 'even a bigger anti-feminist'. She says her opposition to the women's movement began on campus, where university women were questioning their underrepresentation in certain male enclaves. 'It was the feminists' attack on science that really lit the fuse under my rockets,' she says. 'I just don't tolerate fools.' In a 1988 article in the *American Scholar*, she struck back, warning that if feminists were granted admission to the science departments, a host of unreasonable demands would surely follow – preferential treatment for female students or even extra space in scientific journals for 'non-masculinist' writing.

Margarita Levin soon expanded her anti-feminist crusade beyond the sciences. She found a welcoming forum in *Newsweek*, which published her essay deploring the 'feminist excesses' of children's books that depict a 'unisex' world of female doctors, traffic wardens and car mechanics. These books, her article contended, 'clash so blatantly with real life'. If these writers keep this up, 'our children may find themselves confronted with Long Jane Silver and a Wendy who fights Captain Hook while Peter Pan stays home to care for the boys.' . . . Or maybe, one can't help thinking, even a maths professor named Margarita, who fights faculty feminists while husband Mike stays at home to look after the kids.

Rejoining the conversation, Michael Levin complains that, until recently, it's been hard to get the mass media's attention. He sees promising signs – asked for an example, he cites Beautiful perfume's bridal ads – but still, he says, it's tough going for anti-feminists. 'The feminists have a lockup on the media,' he says, and the tone in his voice suddenly turns rancorous. 'They control advertising. They have taken over the universities – it's occupied territory for feminists.' Once Levin gets going in this vein, there's no stopping him. The affable professor is suddenly red in the face. 'A guy gets a PhD in philosophy,' he says, 'and even if he's the best, he's going to lose out to a woman. Feminist headquarters is the women's studies department on every campus. It's command central. And what they produce, it's faecal matter. Maybe a little urine mixed in, but mostly faecal matter.' His scholarly geniality has given way, though not his scholarly diction.

Just then, Eric interrupts the conversation. He still wields the frying pan, and again seeks his father's assistance. Levin, his temperature returning to normal, follows his son into the kitchen. Margarita continues to hold forth from the armchair on her career's development. At the end of the interview, Michael Levin emerges from the kitchen to say goodbye. He looks a little chagrined – he's wearing an apron.

Warren Farrell: The Liberated Man Recants

'Men are hurting more than women – that is, men are, in many ways, actually more powerless than women now.' Warren Farrell pauses to sip from the coffee mug that his female housekeeper has just handed him. In another room his female secretary is busy typing and tidying his files. 'The women's movement has turned out not to be a movement for equality but a movement for women's maximization of opportunities,' he says.

This morning Farrell is on his way to teach a 'men's issues' class at the University of California School of Medicine at San Diego. The subject: 'male powerlessness'. The text they will be using: Farrell's new *Why Men Are the Way They Are*, a book that, among other things, takes feminism to task for 'blaming' men for inequality and for encouraging women to focus excessively on their own independence. Feminism may have improved female lives, he asserts, but for some women 'the deeper the feminism, the more closed the women were to men'. So far, Farrell says, the book has sold more than 100,000 copies in hardcover. 'We are in an era now where men don't feel understood by women,' he says. It's got so bad that middle-aged women seeking husbands might even benefit from the shortage of sensitive young ladies. 'Older women who are looking to get married could really compensate for their loss of looks by understanding men.'

Farrell picks up his leather jacket and heads for his leather-upholstered Maserati. The sports car's vanity plate reads Y MEN R. He slides behind the wheel and guns the engine; the tyres screech as he rounds the suburban street corners of Leucadia, California.

In a medical school classroom, he takes a seat before fifteen pupils. 'OK, so as we discussed last week, until the sixties, women were economically secure in marriage. As long as it was a lifetime arrangement, the system worked. This has been true in almost every society. . . . It was not a bad system. It helped survival for thousands of years. The women were getting the men who were the best protectors and hunters, and the men competed for the most beautiful women.'

A young woman raises her hand. In some societies, she tells the teacher, 'the females did the gathering and provided for the

334

offspring. Hunting was a minor part of their diets.' That, Farrell explains, was just a 'deviation from sex roles'. She tries again: 'No, the point I'm trying to make is, in many cases it wasn't so much that the men were "the providers" as that they were controlling women's access to food and land.' Farrell frowns slightly. 'That would be a pejorative interpretation,' he tells her, and quickly moves the history lesson forward to the 1970s.

'Now it all broke down the moment divorce made that system insecure. . . . And then, once that got started, the anger carried inside the woman added another level of distance from her goal of marriage,' he explains. 'The anger drove men away.'

Again, a hand shoots up. 'But I thought the anger of women came from their feeling that the *old* system had worked against them,' a student says, looking confused. Farrell shakes his head. 'No,' he corrects. 'The system was built for the benefit of both men and women, and worked most to the advantage of women. Men were slaves to the work force, in some respects more enslaved than women.'

This was not exactly the conclusion that Farrell had reached a decade earlier. In the early 1970s, in fact, he had been drawn to the feminist movement precisely because he had been troubled by the effect that 'system' had on women trapped in claustrophobic or destructive traditional marriages. In particular, he witnessed the system's toll on one woman he knew well – his mother. 'I had seen her move in and out of depression,' he would later write. 'Into depression when she was not working, out of depression when she was working. The jobs were just temporary, but, she would tell me, "I don't have to ask Dad for every penny when I'm working".' When her jobs came to an end, the gloom returned and deepened. She took prescription drugs to control it, but the medication only gave her dizzy spells that made her stumble and fall. One day, when she was only forty-nine, she fell to her death. As Farrell recalls:

Soon after my mother's death, the women's movement surfaced. Perhaps because of her death, it made sense to me in an instant. I could not miss the sense of self that I saw in my mother when her work brought her both income and adult human communication, when it brought her a sense of purpose and a feeling of having some rights.

As a young graduate student in New York, Farrell heard other college men mock the goals of the women's movement. 'I was surprised when I saw men trivialize the intent of what women were struggling to articulate. I soon found myself at the homes of emerging feminist friends in Manhattan, plopped in front of their husbands with instructions to "tell him what you told me".'

Eventually, Farrell's devotion to the cause expanded to his professional life. He changed his dissertation to a feminist examination of changing sex roles, gave up his job as an assistant to the president of New York University, and began writing what would become a celebrated male feminist tome, *The Liberated Man*. He organized hundreds of men's groups, counterparts to women's consciousness-raising sessions, in which men were encouraged 'to listen [to women] rather than dominate', to explore the political underpinnings of their marriages and relationships, and to expose links between machismo and violence. And he encouraged the men's and women's groups to meet regularly and seek common ground. Feminism, he said, would free men, too: from the economic burden of supporting a family alone and from the physical and mental strain of constantly proving masculinity and repressing 'feminine' emotions. 'A boy who is not taught to fight to display his manhood is psychologically much freer to walk away from a potential fight,' he wrote in a 1971 op-ed piece in the *New York Times*. 'As an adolescent man he is freer to drive a car carefully rather than "peel out" and display the "horsepower" of his car – a vicarious display of his own power.'

This message was repeated in popular books by male feminist writers in the 1970s, works that questioned the precepts of American manhood. 'The truth is that men are not very happy with the world they have created,' Michael Korda wrote in his 1973 *Male Chauvinism*. Neither sex profits from the traditional masculine ideal of 'obsessive competitiveness' and 'invulnerability', Marc Feigen Fasteau proposed in his 1974 *The Male Machine*; not only is it bad for women, it unhealthily restricts men, too, to 'all but a narrow range of human contact'. Within this literary camp of men's liberation, Farrell presided as the undisputed leader. He founded sixty 'men's liberation' chapters of the National Organization for Women, was elected three times to NOW's New York City board, and was hailed in the *Chicago Tribune* as 'the Gloria Steinem of Men's Liberation'. A flattering four-page profile and photo layout in *People* featured Farrell and his wife, Ursie, a mathematician – a *Love Story* couple tossing a football in Central Park and whipping up an omelette in their West Side apartment. He mingled with media luminaries like Barbara Walters, dined with Gloria Steinem, and played tennis with fellow male feminist icons Alan Alda and Phil Donahue. He appeared on Donahue's show, he says, seven times.

But as feminism lost its media glitter, Farrell's enthusiasm seemed to fade, too. Perhaps the changes he said he had made in himself were superficial, little more than cosmetic touch-ups to enhance his stardom in the short-lived seventies liberation drama. Or perhaps mounting a challenge to traditional manhood, a monumental project in the best of circumstances, seemed a thankless and impossible task to Farrell once the cultural supports were yanked out. As Farrell himself warned in his 1971 *New York Times* essay, 'the image of masculinity is so all-pervasive' that 'it is easier to use surgery' to change a man's sex than it is 'to undo the social and cultural conditioning'.

In any event, by the mid-1980s he decided it was time to start standing up for men, the new downtrodden. Independent women were venting too much anger at men; they were criticizing men's behaviour just to 'confirm their number-one status', he grumbles in *Why Men Are the Way They Are*. Soon he was running workshops that emphasized *female* re-education, sensitivity training sessions to teach women to hear, and heed, men's grievances against them. In *Why Men Are the Way They Are*, Farrell reverses the feminist picture; he depicts a world of gender where women exert 'enormous leverage' over slavish men, who have been reduced to 'success objects' by achievement-obsessed women. Men who want to be secretaries, he charges, are now the ones who face discrimination from these haughty female professionals, who use their male typists for one-night stands and then rebuff their pleas for long-term commitment. In Farrell's new cosmos of oppressed and oppressors, the most domineering are the independent women with good careers. 'Executive women have begun to discriminate against non-executive men,' he says. 'Successful women, I find, are often married to their career. Many men don't feel they are getting the devotion of the women.'

As the ranks of career women have grown, the situation has only become worse for men, Farrell says. Unlike many of the neoconservative men, he at least doesn't pretend that women are the ones who feel crippled by the new female professionalism. 'I know millions of men who don't feel sought after,' he says. 'From their perspective, there is no man shortage.' For Farrell, the career woman's brush-off is also no abstract affair: his wife, a Harvard-educated, fast-rising IBM executive, left him and eventually married another IBM manager. Farrell sees a direct link between her professional success and their marital dissolution. 'My ex-wife is a vice-president at IBM,' the now single Farrell tells one of his classes. 'She makes a quarter-million dollars a year. A woman can be successful or not successful and still get love. But a man who's only good-looking but not successful, what happens to him?'

By the mid-1980s Farrell's male comrades in the men's liberation movement had abandoned him, too. The tennis games with Alda ended and Donahue 'stopped calling me'. Then, with the publication of Farrell's latest book, some female feminist friends started avoiding him as well. Worse, many paid him no attention at all. '*Ms.* magazine's basic reaction has been to ignore the book and ignore me,' he says. Farrell's office filing cabinets are now crammed with grateful letters from men. His phone rings regularly for invitations to address men's clubs and men's rights associations. His book is selling well and he says he already has a contract to write another two on the same theme, *The Disposable Sex* and *The Myths of Male Equality*. But these anti-feminist fans may not be the audience that Farrell most wanted to reach.

After teaching two classes on men's issues, lunching with a like-minded male teacher of men's studies, and checking on his book's sales at a university book shop, Farrell adjourns to a bar on the edge of San Diego. He orders a beer but barely touches it. Staring into the glass, he becomes grave, mournful. 'I see now that the ideologues of the feminist movement don't want to listen,' he says, returning to the subject of *Ms.*'s failure to acknowledge his book. 'Gloria Steinem didn't return my phone calls, and she used to.' He studies his glass some more, then says: 'It affected me a lot to see my popularity waning among people who saw me as an idol. When Gloria Steinem distanced from me, that hurt.'

Robert Bly: Turning 'Yoghurt Eaters' into 'Wild Men'

> It is a massive
> masculine shadow,
> fifty males sitting together
> in hall or crowded room,
> lifting something indistinct
> up into the resonating night.
>
> ROBERT BLY, 'FIFTY MALES SITTING TOGETHER'

'All of you men who are going to the men's weekend tomorrow, remember to bring a large stone.' Shepherd Bliss, a stern-faced man with rounded shoulders, is standing in front of the crowded back room at the Black Oak book shop in Berkeley. So many have showed up for the evening's event that scores must be turned away; they linger out front, listening via wall speakers. Inside, more than a hundred people are elbowing each other for a closer view of the dais, where poet Robert Bly will soon appear, 'coming out of hibernation', as Bliss puts it, to read his latest works.

Bliss, whose recent transformation includes changing his first name from Walter to Shepherd and his profession from army officer to psychologist, is one of Bly's chief spokesmen in the New Age masculinist community. But at the moment, he is being a bit close-mouthed about the stones. They will be using them to build a 'monument to Hermes', but that's all he'll say. He doesn't want to get too specific because there are ladies in the room.

Suddenly, the men on stage begin to beat on conga drums. The hibernating bear himself, roused from his great sleep in the 'far north' – Moose Lake, Minnesota, to be exact – lumbers down the aisle. Just turned sixty, Bly, with his tangled white mane and rounded belly, looks a little like Father Christmas. His heritage, as he will tell listeners several times that evening, is Norse, and something in his pose – perhaps the way he plants his feet as if manning a storm-swept deck – suggests that he intends his audience to take him for a Viking.

We no longer have images of 'real men', Bly says, as the men continue the drum beat. Stereotypical sissies have replaced macho men. 'Woody Allen is just as bad – a negative John Wayne,' he says, raising his voice to a nasal squeak in imitation. 'Men used to make models for what a man is from the *Iliad* and the *Odyssey* and places like that.' On the all-male weekend, he promises, he will bring back these role models for male edification: 'One of the things we do is go back to the very old stories, five thousand years ago, where the view of a man, what a man is, is more healthy.'

Two decades earlier Bly was a Berkeley hero for another reason: a sixties peace activist, the poet gained fame for his literary stand against the Vietnam War. When he won the National Book Award in 1967 for his poetry collection *The Light Around the Body*, he gave the money to a draft-resistance group and blasted American literary smugness at the awards ceremony: 'Since we are murdering a culture in Vietnam at least as fine as our own, have we the right to congratulate ourselves on our cultural magnificence?'

Back then, Bly lauded women who encouraged draft-age young men to resist the war and flee to Canada. To bring peace into the world, Bly argued, men and women both should embrace their feminine principle; the life-preserving nature, he maintained, resided in both sexes but was unhealthily repressed in men. In the 'Great Mother' conferences he conducted in the 1970s, gatherings open to both sexes, Bly tried to foster that 'feminine' peace-loving spirit.

But as the peace movement sputtered and the years passed, Bly was no longer commanding crowds – nor receiving national awards he could reject. By the early 1980s he was even, he confessed, starting to feel less than manly. 'I began to feel diminished,' Bly writes, 'by my lack of embodiment of the fruitful male – or the moist male.' It wasn't his loss of early prominence, however, that he identified as the problem. It was his 'missing contact with men' and his overexposure to strong and angry women, including his own mother, who were speaking out about the mistreatment they had endured from men in their lives. (In his family's case, as Bly recalls, his mother was reacting to his father, a remote and chilly alcoholic.) He feared that he and men like him had allied themselves *too* closely with such women, and consequently taken 'a female view' of their fathers and their own masculinity. He decided he'd made a mistake with his earlier recommendation: 'If someone says to me now, "There is something missing on your feminine side," I say, "No, what is missing is the masculine," ' Bly told *Whole Earth* magazine in 1988. He worried that he was only 'superficially' manly. Men had awakened their feminine principle only to be consumed by it. They had gone 'soft'.

To remedy this latest imbalance, Bly began running all-male workshops to reintroduce men to 'the deep masculine'. Soon he was leading wilderness weekend retreats where men dressed in tribal masks and wild-animal costumes, beat drums and redis-covered 'the beast within'. While Warren Farrell and even neocon-servative men like George Gilder at least sought to be heard by women, Bly believed strict separatism was the soft male's only salvation.

By the mid-1980s Bly was drawing crowds again; hundreds of men were paying $55 for a single lecture, $300 for a two-day retreat. By the end of the decade Bly was back on the media throne, too, meriting a ninety-minute TV special with Bill Moyers, feature treatment in the *New York Times Magazine*, and tributes from traditional men's magazines and New Age periodicals. He was lionized in both *Gentleman's Quarterly* and *Yoga Journal*. Mainstream newspapers hailed him as the 'Father Figure to the New, New Man'. By 1990 his self-published pamphlets on the masculinity crisis had been compiled and reissued in hardcover by a leading publisher – and the book, *Iron John*, quickly climbed the *New York Times* bestseller list.

Bly's success inspired scores of imitators; by the late eighties the men's movement had turned into a cottage industry complete with lecture series ('Moist Earthy Masculinity, for Men Only'), books (*Phallos: Sacred Image of the Masculine*), newsletters (*New Warrior News*), tapes (*The Naive Male*), radio shows (*Man-to-Man with Jerry Johnson*), and even board games ('A Game of Insights for Men Only'). This new men's movement wasn't just another California curiosity. 'Brotherhood lodges' sprang up in Tulsa, Oklahoma; Washington, DC, supported six men's organizations offering 'wild man' rituals; *The Talking Stick: A Newsletter About Men* issued from Frederick, Maryland; the Austin, Texas, 'Wild Man Gatherings' got booked up months in advance; and the Men's Center in Minneapolis drew enough men to keep up a daily schedule of 'playshops'. In New York City and Oakland, California, the Sterling Institute of Relationships' $400 'Men, Sex and Power' weekends taught 'wimps' to become 'real men', dressing up like gorillas, beating their chests, and staging fistfights. These seminars alone enrolled more than 10,000 men in the 1980s. Bly's weekend retreats logged 50,000 men in the last half of the 1980s alone. Nor were those who attended marginalized drifters. On Bly's retreat roster were lawyers, judges, doctors, accountants and corporate executives; at one wilderness experience the group included several vice-presidents of Fortune 500 companies and two television-station owners.

The New Age masculinists claimed to bear no ill-will towards the women's movement. The two movements were running on 'parallel tracks', as Bly's disciples liked to emphasize. When a woman asked Bly at the Black Oak poetry reading for his view of feminism, the poet assured her, 'I support tremendously the work of that movement.' The only reason he doesn't invite women to most of the events, he explained, is because men 'can be more honest when women aren't around'. But Bly's writings and speeches suggest other reasons, too, for the poet's ban on women.

'I remember a bumper sticker [advocating draft-dodging] during the 60s that read WOMEN SAY YES TO MEN WHO SAY NO,' he writes in *The Pillow & the Key*, his 1987 manifesto of New Age masculinism. ' . . . The women were definitely saying that they preferred the softer receptive male, and they would reward him for being soft: "We will sleep with you if you are not too aggressive and macho".' That, Bly suggests, was the first of many female jabs that would deflate the male psyche. 'The development of men was disturbed a little there,' he writes, 'interfered with.'

The arrival of the women's movement in the early seventies increased the interference. *What Men Really Want*, a written 'dialogue' between Bly and fellow New Age masculinist Keith Thompson, outlines the problem:

> *Bly:* I see the phenomenon of what I would call the 'soft male' all over the country today. Sometimes when I look out at my audiences, perhaps half the young males are what I'd call soft. . . . Many of these men are unhappy. There's not much energy in them. They are life-preserving but not exactly life-giving. And why is it you often see these men with strong women who positively radiate energy?
> *Thompson:* Perhaps it's because back in the sixties, when we looked to the women's movement for leads as how we should be, the message we got was that the new strong women *wanted* soft men.
> *Bly:* I agree. That's how it felt.

In short, the Great Mother's authority has become too great. 'Men's societies are disappearing, partly under pressure from women with hurt feelings,' he writes. Too many women are 'raising boys with no man in the house'. The single mother's son has become 'a nice boy who now not only pleases his mother but also the young woman he is living with'.

To restore the nice boy's male identity, Bly proposes, he must stop taking cue from mother and 'go down into the psyche and accept what's dark down there'. As a key guide to the journey, Bly offers 'The Story of Iron John', borrowed from a fairy tale by the Brothers Grimm. In the story, a hairy 'wild man' is locked up in an iron cage near the royal castle; the key to the cage is under the queen's pillow. One day the young prince loses his prized 'golden ball' when it rolls into an abandoned pond, and he can only retrieve it by stealing the key from mother and freeing the wild man. The young man, in the words of Bly's sidekick Keith Thompson, 'has to take back the power he has given to his mother and get away from the force field of her bed. He must direct his energies away from pleasing Mommy.'

At Bly's all-male 'mythopoetic' weekends, the not-so-young princes reclaim their golden balls, with a few adjustments for modern times. At one such weekend – located at a Bible camp in Mound, Minnesota – the 'wild men' build their lairs with plastic lounge chairs. Journalist Jon Tevlin, who attended the event, recalls a typical wild-man encounter that weekend, led by the omnipresent Shepherd Bliss.

As he [Bliss] spoke of recovering the 'wild man within' that first night, Shepherd slowly dropped to his knees. 'Some of you may want to temporarily leave the world of the two-leggeds, and join me in the world of the four-leggeds,' he said. One by one, we slid from our orange Naugahyde chairs onto an orange shag carpet ripped straight out of the 1960s. 'You may find yourself behaving like these four-leggeds; you may be scratching the earth, getting in contact with the dirt and the world around you.'

As he spoke, people began pawing at the ground.... 'You may find yourself behaving like the most masculine of all animals – the ram,' Shepherd said in a coaxing voice.... 'You may find unfamiliar noises emerging from your throats!' ... There were gurgles and bleats, a few wolf calls.... Out of the corner of my eye, I saw Shepherd coming toward me, head down, tufts of white hair ringing a bald spot.... Meanwhile, I felt a slight presence at my rear, and turned to see a man beginning to sniff my buttocks.

'Woof!' he said.

The question of how to improve relations with women, in or out of bed, gets remarkably short shrift on these weekends. 'In two full days women were hardly mentioned,' Trip Gabriel writes of a 'Wild-Man Gathering' in Texas. Writers Steve Chapple and David Talbot, who attended Bly's 'Love, Sex and Intimate Relationships' weekend in California, report that none of these three billed topics was on the agenda:

Men young and old are beating drums and wailing about the fathers they never knew. They are laying bare their deepest shame and, more than a little bit, heaping scorn on the dominating women in their lives. Surprisingly, though, sex is not at all a hot topic at these gatherings. The New Man seems infinitely more fascinated with himself than with the ladies.

When one of the men is asked to draw his 'ideal mate', Chapple and Talbot note, he draws himself in bed alone, 'whacking off', as he puts it.

But maybe the lack of relationship-talk shouldn't have been so surprising. The true subject of Bly's weekends, after all, is not love and sex, but power – how to wrest it from women and how to mobilize it for men. Indeed, the Bly retreat that Chapple and Talbot attended opened with a display of 'power objects', which each man was instructed to bring from home. On this weekend, the trophies included a .380-calibre automatic pistol. Bly may be an advocate of world peace, but as the general of the men's movement, he is overseeing a battle on the domestic front – and he withholds his dovish sentiments from the family-circle conflict. At a 1987 seminar, attended by a thousand men, a man in the audience told Bly, 'Robert, when we tell women our desires, they tell us we're wrong.' Bly instructed, 'So, then you bust them in the mouth.' After someone pointed out that this statement seemed to advocate violence against women, Bly amended it, 'Yes. I meant, hit those women verbally!'

'What's the matter? Too much yoghurt?' Bly is shouting. He is midway through a two-day lecture at the Jung Center in San Francisco – one of the rare events to which he will admit women. He is back in his sea captain's pose, hands on hips, scowling at this audience of more than 400. 'There's too much passivity and naïveté in American men today,' he says, as he begins to pace the stage. 'There's a disease going around, and women have been spreading it. Starting in the sixties, the women have really invaded men's areas and treated them like boys.'

A woman in the audience asks if he's saying that the women's movement is to blame. 'The men's movement is not a response to the women's movement,' he says. A few moments later, though, he is back to warning men in the audience to beware of 'the force-field of women'. When another woman in the crowd points out the contradiction, he gets mad. He picks up the microphone and marches over to the troublemaker, a frail elderly woman clutching a flowered tote bag. He sticks his face in hers and yells into the microphone, 'It's women like you who are turning men into yoghurt eaters.' Embarrassed, the woman tries to appease the fuming poet; in a quavery voice, she asks if he has 'any suggestions' about how she can improve her relationship with her emotionally distant husband. 'Why don't you stop making demands and leave him alone,' Bly shouts. 'Just leave him alone.'

Sylvia Ann Hewlett: The Neofeminist's Lesser Work

'I grew to understand why Phyllis Schlafly was appealing,' Sylvia Ann Hewlett, a member of the Council of Foreign Relations and other think-tanks, says. The author of *A Lesser Life: The Myth of Women's Liberation in America* is seated at the highly polished boardroom table in the council's Upper East Side office. 'I realized that the ERA, though it might appeal to élite and chic career women who belong to NOW, might actually get in the way of helping ordinary women.'

Hewlett explains how she reached her revisionist view of feminism. 'I used to be quite active in the women's movement,' she says. She recalls attending a consciousness-raising group in the 1970s and helping occasionally to canvass for the Equal Rights Amendment. 'But slowly I came to see that the ERA would take away special protective labour legislation for women. If the ERA were around today, I would not vote for it because it could really backfire.' Ordinary women have convinced her, she says. As she writes in her book, 'In a profound way, feminists have failed to connect with the needs and aspirations of ordinary American women.' They failed to understand that 'many homemakers did not want to be treated equally'. And finally, she says, 'When you add in the legitimate fears of blue-collar women that they would lose their hard-won protective benefits, you have a powerful constituency ranged against the ERA.'

When did Hewlett, who was living at the time at a fashionable Manhattan address with her investment banker husband, come into contact with these ordinary women? In *A Lesser Life*, she gives a few examples – a very few. In one case, she quotes an anonymous millworker getting off her shift at a textile plant; the woman tells her that she's against equal rights because 'us girls get an extra break in the shift'. Hewlett says that she was so shaken by the woman's remark that she never canvassed for the ERA again.

Here is another 'ordinary' female example that Hewlett cites: an anonymous woman, one of the 'traditional women of Middle America', who complains, 'Women's liberation wants to liberate us from the very institution that is most indispensable to overcoming our present social crisis: the family.' Her footnote attributes these words to a woman quoted in George Gilder's *Sexual Suicide*. But if you look up the original reference, you find that Hewlett has altered the quote – adding the 'us', among other things – to make it read as if a woman were saying it. In fact, the words are Gilder's own. This 'traditional woman' is an anti-feminist man. Asked about it later, Hewlett will say only, 'I don't have much of a sense of [how] that happened. It's not clear to me.'

Based on these informative encounters with the average woman in the street, Hewlett concludes that feminism has cheated her sex. 'The American [women's] movement has defined the problem of womenkind as that of acquiring a full set of legal, political and economic rights, and achieving control over one's body.' But most American women, she asserts, don't want equality, personal or sexual freedom; they 'want to strengthen, not weaken the traditional family structure'. By concentrating on equality instead of maternity, feminists made 'one gigantic mistake'. The women's movement actually created 'a lesser life' for women by failing to champion the needs of working mothers and their children. Feminism 'threw the baby out with the bathwater'.

Playing up this 'mistake', especially with her supposedly 'feminist' credentials, guaranteed Hewlett immediate attention from the backlash mass media. Hewlett's book proposal sparked a bidding war between eleven eager publishing companies and a six-figure advance. The publishers were mistaken about female readers' interest in this thesis. *A Lesser Life* did not become a major seller. But they weren't wrong to anticipate huge press enthusiasm for such revisionist fare; the book became an instant media event. As a *Washington Post* reviewer cheered, 'SING HOSANNAS! Someone reputable has finally said it in print.' As Hewlett observes in an afterword to the paperback edition a year later, she was besieged with talk show requests – 'all one hundred ten of them!' And she immediately became a national authority on family policy – 'Senator Moynihan, Governor Cuomo, and Representative Oakar have sought my counsel' – the governor of Arizona appointed her to a family-welfare panel and the Woman's National Democratic Club invited her to give the keynote address.

For the next several years, hundreds of journalists, newscasters and columnists would invoke Hewlett's work whenever they wanted to underline the tragic consequences of feminism. Her attack on the women's movement earned her a showcase in every press outlet from the *New York Times* to *People* to *Donahue*. Even the *National Enquirer* was intrigued; the tabloid featured the book's incredible findings under the headline GALS ARE BEING HURT – NOT HELPED – BY WOMEN'S LIB.

Hewlett indicts the women's movement on three counts. Feminists failed women by (1) promoting the Equal Rights Amendment; (2) pushing for no-fault divorce laws; and (3) ignoring motherhood. Maybe the *Enquirer* coverage should have been a clue; her 'facts' were often closer to tabloid fare.

'It is sobering to realize that the ERA was defeated not by Barry Goldwater, Jerry Falwell, or any combination of male chauvinist pigs, but by women who were alienated from a feminist movement the values of which seemed elitist and disconnected from the lives of ordinary people,' she writes. The majority of women opposed the ERA, she says, because it would have eliminated housewives' right to be supported by their husbands and working women's right to 'hard-won protective benefits', such as 'extra rest periods and better rest rooms'.

To support these assertions, Hewlett quotes almost exclusively from one source: Eagle Forum's Phyllis Schlafly, who directed the Stop ERA campaign. The only other authority Hewlett quotes on the ERA is 'a prominent labor and civil-rights lawyer', never identified, who assures Hewlett that the ERA is unnecessary. Hewlett does not explain how she knows that the majority of women opposed the ERA at the time. If she had checked the national polls then, she would have found nearly 60 per cent of women favouring the ERA. (The proportion has increased since then – to more than 70 per cent.) And 'ordinary' women weren't exactly hostile to ERA. According to a 1982 Gallup poll, clerical and saleswomen were even a bit more enthusiastic about the ERA than professional women – and low-income women favoured extending the deadline to ratify the amendment more than upper-income women.

Hewlett says women opposed the ERA because they knew it would cost them in marital support and 'protective labor benefits'. But the ERA would have had no effect on these supports other than to make them sex blind, as most state laws had already stipulated anyway. Half the states didn't require husbands to support their wives – and, as any abandoned wife could have told her, the states that did have such provisions hardly enforced them. As for protective labour benefits, the courts had already eliminated them – having found them to be in violation of women's civil rights. These laws had served historically to protect not women but men's jobs, by shutting women out of higher-paying occupations. And it was blue-collar women who petitioned the courts to overturn these 'benefits'.

Ultimately, the people who defeated the ERA were not ordinary women but a handful of very powerful men in three key state legislatures. These were men who opposed the ERA not because it would hurt women's traditional protections but because it challenged their own belief that, as one of the key state legislators put it, 'a woman should serve her husband'.

Hewlett's second charge – that feminist advocates hurt traditional housewives by promoting no-fault divorce – is based on a backlash myth. Hewlett's evidence is drawn from Lenore Weitzman's flawed *The Divorce Revolution*.

Hewlett's final allegation is the most widely quoted. The women's movement, she charges, 'revile' and 'rage at' mothers and children; 1970s feminists gave 'bottom' priority to childcare and failed even to take up the cause of maternity leave. The 'anti-children' and 'anti-motherhood' stance, she says, has discredited the women's movement today in the eyes of most ordinary women. This negligence she contrasts with Western European 'social feminists', whom she credits for the availability of government-supported childcare and maternity leave benefits, such as they are.

But in fact the European policies she praises were drafted not by social feminists but, decades earlier, by governments trying to reverse falling birthrates and replenish war-devastated populations. And, in America, the 'equal rights' feminists' record on childcare and maternity leave is hardly blank. While the women's liberation movement certainly, and rightly, criticized American society for offering mothers hollow sentiments as a substitute for legal rights and genuine respect, its leaders also pressed for a wide range of rights that would benefit mothers. In the early 1970s feminists campaigned for *five* day care bills in Congress. Three of the eight points of NOW's original 1967 'Bill of Rights for Women' dealt specifically with childcare, maternity leave and other benefits. In the following years, NOW and other women's groups repeatedly lobbied Congress, staged national protests and filed class-action suits to combat discrimination against pregnant women and mothers. And, a key point that Hewlett and like-minded critics overlook, when feminists pushed for women's rights in other areas – employment opportunities, pay equality, credit rights, women's health – mothers and their children benefited, too.

Anyway, Hewlett is just wrong when she says most ordinary women see the feminist movement as 'anti-family'. When the Yankelovich pollsters in 1989 specifically asked, 'Is the women's movement anti-family?' the vast majority of women, in every age group, said no.

On the national front, the real 'anti-motherhood' crusaders weren't feminists, either; they were New Right leaders, conservative politicians and corporate executives, who not only ignored mothers' rights but attacked them. It was, after all, Phyllis Schlafly, not Gloria Steinem, who led the opposition to congressional childcare and maternity leave Bills for two decades. It was the Chamber of Commerce, not the National Organization for Women, that was the single most effective force behind the defeat of the 1988 Family and Medical Leave Act. (The Chamber triumphed largely by claiming that the legislation would cost businesses at least $24 billion a year; the General Accounting Office later put the cost at about $500 million.)

Governmental and corporate indifference to the rights of working mothers would eventually become painfully apparent to Hewlett, too, when she tried to organize a family policy panel at the

Economics Policy Council, a New York think-tank. Hoping to bring government and business leaders together to draft a benefit plan for working mothers, she approached big names like Atlantic Richfield's chairman Robert Anderson, Warner Communications' chairman Steven Ross, and even former president Gerald Ford. But she found that once the men realized the panel's subject matter, they usually bailed out. 'It became this sort of revolving door,' Hewlett recalls. 'It was a real disappointment.' The men would stay for one session, fidgeting and checking their watches, then disappear. 'There was this real sense that they'd be contaminated, that people would think they were wimps,' Hewlett recalls. Some requested that they be switched to another panel that didn't deal with 'women's stuff'. 'Why don't I send my head of human resources?' one chief executive told Hewlett when she approached him. 'She's a woman; she'd be interested.'

Nonetheless, Hewlett kept the panel going, and the group finally issued a set of recommendations, released with much fanfare at a black-tie dinner on Capitol Hill. The recommendations themselves, however, were little different from those contained in dozens of feminist reports in the last two decades. The document proposed the usual solutions for working mothers: government-assisted childcare, maternity leave, maternal and child health care, and flexible work schedules. Policy-makers received them and, no doubt, filed them in the usual place.

Betty Friedan: Revisionism as a Marketing Tool

When Hewlett organized her family policy panel, she had included two women from 'the feminist establishment', as she called it. One of them was Betty Friedan. Like some of the men, Friedan attended only one meeting and then vanished. She would later publicly criticize Hewlett's work as a 'deceptive backlash book'. The attack surprised Hewlett, who had assumed after reading Friedan's latest work that they were kindred spirits. 'I specifically invited Friedan to sit on the panel because she seemed to be thinking along the same lines as me in her new book, *The Second Stage*.'

Indeed, in *The Second Stage*, published in 1981, Friedan issued many of the same charges against the women's movement. Its leaders had ignored the maternal call: 'Our failure was our blind spot about the family.' Not only that, Friedan's book alleged, the feminist campaign often mistakenly concentrated on 'direct' and 'confrontational' political tactics – tactics she herself had pioneered but which she now found too 'masculine' – when they should be trying volunteerism and taking up a more genteel 'Beta style'.

Friedan was not the only famous feminist yanking out the stitches in her own handiwork. A handful of authors whose bestselling books helped popularize the women's liberation movement in the 1970s were busy issuing retractions. To the New Right, the new words of the old-line feminists were almost too good to be true. 'Feminism, which once helped open windows of opportunity for women, has turned against itself,' rejoiced Reagan aide Dinesh D'Souza, managing editor of the neoconservative *Policy Review*. After the *New York Times Magazine* featured an excerpt from *The Second Stage* on its cover, Phyllis Schlafly exulted in her newsletter that Friedan had 'just put another nail in the coffin of feminism'.

By the mid-1980s the voices of feminist recantation became a din, as the media picked up the words of a few symbolically important feminists and broadcast them nationwide. Many of these new books read like extended and hastily thrown together press releases. For the most part, these 'leaders' ' moment under the camera lights had actually long since passed; but, like the retiring male feminist Warren Farrell, they hoped to reclaim centre stage.

While there were plenty of feminist thinkers – new and old, famous and obscure – who stood firm in their political beliefs, they were invisible to the media's roving eye. The one new self-proclaimed 'feminist' theoretician that the press did pluck from obscurity was actually an embittered anti-feminist academic. Literary scholar Camille Paglia became an overnight celebrity, landing on the cover of both *New York* and *Harper's* the same month, soon after launching a vitriolic attack on 'whining' feminists in her 1990 book, *Sexual Personae: Art and Decadence from Nefertiti to Emily Dickinson*. The press assiduously recycled her anti-female and anti-feminist zingers ('If civilization had been left in female hands, we would still be living in grass huts,' and, '[Feminist scholars] can't think their way out of a wet paper bag'); *Newsday* featured her dismissal of date rape as feminist nonsense; and television producers raced to option her book. And what was Paglia's motive – freely admitted – for assailing feminists? Simple spite. Rival literary scholars who were feminists, she complained, had grabbed all the 'acclaim' and failed to be 'respectful' of her prodigious talents, a situation that consigned her to the non-tenure track at the unsung Philadelphia University of the Arts and allowed her book to be snubbed by seven publishers. It was then, as she told a *New York* writer later, that she began 'preparing my revenge' against feminist academics.

In 1984, feminist Germaine Greer followed up *The Female Eunuch*, her 1970 smash-hit celebration of female independence and sexuality, with the dour and deterministic *Sex and Destiny*. Formerly the media's favourite as a flamboyant advocate of sexual emancipation – a 'saucy feminist that even men like', a *Life* cover story had declared at the time – Greer now championed arranged marriages, chastity and the chador, and named as her new role model the old-fashioned peasant wife, happily confined to kitchen and nursery and happily concealed under her chador. Greer herself billed the book an 'attack upon the ideology of sexual freedom'. Ironically, just as Concerned Women of America's Beverly LaHaye was endorsing birth control, sex for fun and clitoral orgasms, Greer was signalling her opposition to all three. The best form of contraception, she asserted, was abstinence. Clitoral orgasms are too 'one-dimensional' and 'masculine', she wrote.

By 1986, anti-feminist spokesmen were also making much of the revisionist murmurings of feminist activist Susan Brownmiller, author of the 1975 landmark work on rape, *Against Our Will*, who was now saying the women's movement may have overlooked 'profound biological and psychological differences' between the sexes. The author of a meticulously documented historical analysis of sexual violence, Brownmiller now produced a footnoteless and fuzzy look at feminine behaviour through the ages. *Femininity* pondered such pressing issues as whether a hair on Brownmiller's face was the result of 'unholy ambition' – or, perhaps, 'some dormant source of testosterone within my system' – and whether she should pluck it. The answer to that last question: yes.

As the decade progressed, these famous feminists of the seventies would continue to churn out increasingly retrograde fare. In her 1989 memoir about her weak-willed father, *Daddy, We Hardly Knew You*, Greer nearly outdid Philip Wylie's 'Momism' in her demonization of mother – 'the mad dog in the kitchen', as she called her, a literalized bitch who was always 'foaming at the mouth' and emasculating dad. Meanwhile, Brownmiller turned her literary gun sights on a *victim* of domestic violence; on the *New York Times* op-ed page and in *Waverly Place*, a fictionalized and hurriedly issued account of the celebrated case of Lisa Steinberg (the New York City child beaten to death by her adoptive father), Brownmiller reserved her harshest words for the failings of the battered wife. (She finished the book before the court verdict even came in.)

And celebrated feminist author Erica Jong quickly joined the recanters. (Her support for feminism had actually always been rather equivocal, despite a public reputation as a leading 'libber', bestowed upon her by the press after *Fear of Flying* became a hit.) Not only did her liberated characters eat their words, she disavowed the cause herself – in *Ms.*, of course. Women of 'my generation', she wrote, 'look longingly at the marriages of our parents and grandparents. . . . Alone in our single-parent families, still searching for the one great love, we begin to smell a rat.'

But of all the declarations of apostasy, *The Second Stage* had the potential to be the most damaging to the feminist cause. Betty Friedan was the household name, synonymous in the minds of millions of Americans with the women's liberation movement. She was 'the mother of the modern women's movement', as hundreds of newspaper articles had called her, ever since her 1963 classic, *The Feminine Mystique*, first gave voice to 'the problem that has no name' and helped catalyse a movement for social change. That book was Friedan's labour of love; she spent years researching and writing in an annexe of the dusty New York Public Library. Yet here she was, two decades later, attacking the 'feminist mystique' and accusing the women's movement of 'breeding a new "problem that has no name" ' – in a thinly

THE BACKLASH BRAINS TRUST

documented book that often reads as if it were dictated into a tape recorder. What happened?

One gets few insights directly from Friedan herself. 'I don't use the term "feminist mystique" in my book,' Friedan says in an interview, sounding indignant. Reminded that she, in fact, uses that term *twice* in the first fifty pages, she responds, 'Well, there was some extremism in the seventies. The radical feminists started a reactive feminism that was limited and wrong and distorted.' Anyone who disagrees with her is simply dismissed as one of those radical feminists who is 'still locked into first-stage thinking themselves' and 'threatened by my attempt to reconceptualize the movement'.

The 'radical feminists' of the 1970s have executed many serious strategic mis-steps, according to Friedan's book. Feminists, she says, were so caught up seeking access to the men's world that they failed to 'affirm the differences between men and women' and celebrate the 'female sensitivities to life'. They shouldn't have devoted their energies to protesting against rape (a problem that 88 per cent of women cited in a 1989 Yankelovich poll as the 'most important issue for women today'); in her view, marching against sexual violence is a 'kind of wallowing in that victim-state' that 'dissipates our own well-springs of generative power'. (Her words recall George Gilder's in *Men and Marriage*; he, too, complained of feminists 'palavering endlessly' about rape.) They lost the ERA by being 'co-opted by "masculine" political power'. They focused too much on issues like abortion rights, which are 'surely', she sniffs, 'not the main problems in America today'. In fact, the movement's continued emphasis on women's rights itself is misguided. 'I do not think,' Friedan writes, 'women's rights are the most urgent business for American women.'

Why was Friedan stomping on a movement that she did so much to create and lead? Perhaps under the backlash the tendency to turn and bite one's tail is inevitable. As feminist scholar Judith Stacey writes: 'Aging, in the right-wing and "postfeminist" climate of the 1980s, has been a traumatic experience for many Second Wave feminists, and we lack convenient scapegoats for our distress. . . . Perhaps this accounts for the strident and unmodulatd quality of recantation in the new pro-family feminism.' But in Friedan's case, another possibility presents itself as well. A closer reading of *The Second Stage* suggests that the prime mistake the 'radical feminists' made was in not following her orders. Friedan may say she 'easily related' to the 'Beta style' of leaderless, co-operative and 'relational' organization that her book expounds. Yet her book is punctuated with the tantrums of a fallen leader who is clearly distressed and angry that she wasn't allowed to be the Alpha wolf as long as she would have liked.

Much of the book is insistently self-referential, devoted to rehashing power struggles she lost at long-forgotten feminist conferences, reprints of her old speeches, and complaints that other feminists kept ignoring her proposals. Friedan's penchant for imperial decrees and self-dramatization is longstanding. In 1970 she retired as president of NOW with the words, 'I have led you into history. I leave you now – to make new history.'

Her departure was an embattled one – Friedan versus the 'radical feminists' was how she cast it at the time – and ever since, her accounts of political infighting have featured the same subtext: she was unfairly locked out of the feminist power structure. While the general public may have been under the impression that she was the movement's leading 'mother', she felt that she had been too quickly relegated to the media sidelines, shoved aside in favour of younger and more photogenic leaders. She may have been dubbed feminism's 'mother', but the media had designated Gloria Steinem, literally, the movement's 'glamour girl' – and Friedan well knew which was the more prized honorific in America.

Rather than understanding the media bias as the press's typical preference for youthful blondes, she came to suspect that feminist women themselves were plotting to depose her. While philosophical differences certainly existed, sometimes sharply, within the women's liberation movement (as they do within every political movement), Friedan seemed to believe all the internal debates added up to, in her words, a 'scheme', a cabal that excluded her. She lashed back in the press in 1972, accusing Steinem of 'ripping off the movement for private profit' and announcing 'No one should mistake [Steinem] for a leader.' Years later, in Marcia Cohen's *The Sisterhood*, the 1988 chronicle of the women's movement, Friedan was still fixated on this theme. 'Gloria [Steinem] wanted me to disappear,' she told the author. 'She just wanted to *disappear* me.'

The 'new history' Friedan's book scripts for feminism is a 'second-stage solution', a call for a murkily defined new order that is heavy on old Victorian rhetorical flourishes. In this new stage she envisages, women will rediscover the family circle 'as the base of their identity and human control'. Like the nineteenth-century proponents of separate spheres, Friedan proposes that women can exert influence from the home front: 'The power of "women's sphere" in shaping political as well as personal consciousness has clearly been underestimated by feminists today,' she asserts – a strange statement from a woman who eagerly broke out of that sphere and has since chosen to live almost exclusively, and with great relish, in the public realm. This solution puts the burden on women; the need for men to change barely figures in Friedan's new plan. In fact, she blithely dismisses feminists' observations that men have been loath to shoulder their share of household and childcare responsibilities. If men haven't changed, she writes, then 'why, in 1981, do three out of every four gourmet dinners suddenly seem to be cooked, soup to mousse, by men?' Where does this 'statistic' come from? She invented it – based on some off-the-cuff remarks from 'a number of my women colleagues'.

The book also borrows some points of style and substance from Reaganism. In the 'second stage', she proposes, feminists should stop pressing corporations, legislatures and the 'tired welfare state' to expand women's rights – and get involved in voluntary and neighbourhood work instead. 'Individual' responsibility and 'voluntary pooling of community resources', she writes, will be the second-stage's watchwords. To liberate themselves, she proposes, women should become Girl Scout leaders. Friedan is convinced that the women's movement has made a big error in overlooking the potential of such institutions, which 'may be as important' as political-action groups in advancing women's rights. In one of the book's more bewildering passages – the writing is often jumbled – Friedan assails NOW for encouraging women 'to volunteer only for social change and feminist groups, and not in community service where their labor was exploited. . . . I myself never liked that stand on volunteerism – though we should indeed have opposed the exploitation of women in volunteer work as in office and home . . . '

The rhetoric of the New Right in refurbished form is strewn throughout the book. Connie Marshner's phrase for overambitious career women: 'macho feminists'. Betty Friedan's: 'Female machismo'. Friedan sketches a grim scenario indeed of what could happen to the young liberated woman who succumbs to 'the insatiable demands of female machismo':

> What if, in reaction, she strips her life clean of all these unmeasured, unvalued feminine tasks and frills – stops baking cookies altogether, cuts her hair like a monk, decides not to have children, installs a computer console in her bedroom? She suffers finally a new 'crisis of confidence.' She does not feel grounded in life. She shivers inside. She is depleted by female machismo.

By accepting the New Right language, Friedan has walked right into the New Right's 'pro-family' semantics trap. She is reacting to the backlash rather than setting her own agenda, even referring to the women's movement now as 'the feminist reaction'.

In the end, the language and logic of *The Second Stage* is so muddled that it's ultimately impossible to say what Friedan really believes in today. At times in the book she seems to be retreating into a domestic haze, but at other points she seems simply to be restating fundamental feminist principles – as when she writes that the 'second stage' is all about 'the restructuring of our institutions on a basis of real equality for women and men'. Maybe Friedan actually meant to recant many of the tenets of *The Feminine Mystique*. Or maybe she just got tangled in her own words.

Carol Gilligan: Different Voices or Victorian Echoes?

Friedan's elevation of the 'relational' Beta mode and other distinctively 'feminine' traits didn't occur in a vacuum. In the 1980s, popular works praising 'women's ways' and 'women's special nature' began to crowd out other fare in the women's sections of American book shops, works that ranged from Sara Ruddick's *Maternal Thinking* to Sally Helgesen's *The Female Advantage*. The authors wrote, sometimes in starry-eyed terms, of women's inordinate capacity for kindness, service to others, and co-operation. Soon, 'feminine caring' became the all-purpose tag to sum up the female psyche. And by the decade's end, some of the authors of this genre (who were largely women) even seemed at times to be actively joining the backlash. Suzanne Gordon, in her 1990 *Prisoners of Men's Dreams: Striking Out for a New Feminine Future*, blamed much of the unkind 1980s on 'equal opportunity feminists', who encouraged women 'to devalue caring work' and 'exacerbated a widespread societal crisis in caring'.

While these works passed along such ideas to the general public, the theories on which they were based had germinated in the world of feminist scholarship. In the late 1970s a new school of 'relational' feminist thought arose, focusing on a separate 'women's culture' and women's special 'difference'. By the 1980s feminist scholarship conferences would be awash in papers on women's special virtues: their 'nurturing qualities', their 'caring ethic', their 'contextual thinking'. In this decade, just as a fascination with gender differences had flowered in late Victorian academia, a preoccupation with women's distinctive nature spread quickly to nearly every discipline. By 1987 the American Educational Research Association's annual conference was offering twenty-five sessions on sex differences.

Most of the feminist scholars originally set out to investigate the origins of men's and women's differences, not to glorify them. They wanted to challenge the longstanding convention of defining male behaviour as the norm, female behaviour as deviant. And they hoped to find in women's 'difference' a more humane model for public life – one that both men and women might adopt. Psychiatrist Dr Jean Baker Miller's classic 1976 work, *Toward a New Psychology of Women*, is an early and successful example of that effort. 'The task,' as she wrote later, in the 1986 fore-word to the second edition, 'was to begin a description of women's strengths and to account for the reasons that they went unrecognized. . . . Out of this can follow a new framework for understanding women – and men.'

But by the 1980s the task of building a new framework had largely been abandoned; while many relational scholars sought to give long overdue recognition to women's accomplishments in the home, in the process they often lost sight of the larger context – and offered dewy-eyed visions of female domestic confinement instead. As feminist scholar Ellen DuBois warned her peers in an essay in a women's studies journal, '[T]he dominant tendency in the study of women's culture has not been to relate it to feminism, but to look at it in isolation and to romanticize what it meant for women.' Sometimes the academics seemed to forget the force of socialization altogether and presented women's and men's roles as biologically predetermined and intractable. The eminent feminist scholar Alice Rossi even proposed that men might refuse to cook dinner or take care of the children at home simply for anatomical reasons: they just don't have the same finger dexterity as those fine-boned women, she wrote.

Examining gender differences can be an opportunity to explore a whole network of power relations – but so often it becomes just another invitation to justify them. Whenever the 'specialness' of women is saluted (or any population group's, for that matter), the recognition is bound to be double-edged. Women are willing to forgo some legal equality for 'special rights' that suit their special place as mothers, Elizabeth Wolgast argues in her 1980 *Equality and the Rights of Women*; in fact, she says, equality can actually serve to discriminate against them because it doesn't meet their special needs. Marking women as 'special' slips easily into placing limits on them. 'Special' may sound like superior, but it is also a euphemism for handicapped.

Most relational scholars no doubt believed they could bring back the cult of domesticity on their own terms. These academics hoped to push for women's 'special rights' without jeopardizing fundamental civil rights and opportunities. All the same, in their tributes to the 'domestic arts', their sometimes self-righteous homages to female moral superiority, and their denigration of 'simple-minded equality', they risked clothing old Victorian conceits in modern academic dress. And in the end, legislators would not be influenced to enact 'special' rights for women. Instead, in the wider backlash era in which relational feminists were writing, their words would be used and misused – by anti-feminist authors and, worse, corporate lawyers fighting sex discrimination suits. The women who would pay for the relational scholars' miscalculation were, as we shall see in a later chapter, working-class women who had never heard of them.

Under the backlash, the proponents of women's 'difference' found that they were rewarded with approving critical and media attention. 'Difference' became the new magic word uttered to defuse the feminist campaign for equality. And any author who made use of it, even one who could hardly be considered anti-feminist, was in danger of being dragooned into the backlash's service.

Carol Gilligan's 1982 *In a Different Voice*, one of the most widely quoted and influential feminist works of the eighties, became the most famous emblem of scholarship on women's 'difference'. As one commentator noted, '[T]he very name Gilligan has become a buzzword in academic and feminist circles.' The book was cited in psychology papers, legal briefs and public policy proposals. Beyond academia, the adult-education industry turned Gilligan's idea into a sales tool for workshops with names like 'Men's and Women's Reality – Making the Differences Count'. Advice writers plugged it into self-help manuals. Even *Vogue* invoked the scholar's work in its meditations on High Femininity wear: Gilligan, the magazine mused, 'may well have anticipated this season's fashion references'. In the media, *Ms.* named Gilligan 'Woman of the Year' and the *New York Times Magazine* put Gilligan on its cover. And when Radcliffe convened its 1989 political conference, 'Meeting the Challenge: Women as Leaders', college president Matina Horner told the assembly in her opening remarks, 'The question for the twenty-first century is whether or not women can bring a different voice to the table than men.' She did not ask what would seem a more pressing question – why that table still had so few women at it.

Gilligan's work grew out of her discovery as a teacher of psychological development that virtually wherever she looked in the research, the studies drew exclusively on groups of men. 'It was like a first-year graduate had conducted all these studies – and left out half the sample!' Gilligan recalls. And worse, women teaching in her field 'weren't even seeing this omission of ourselves'. One day in 1975 she sat down at her dining-room table and wrote a short essay on this omission, which would eventually become *In a Different Voice*. 'It never occurred to me that anyone would be interested but a few people in my little world, in the underground [of academic psychology].'

In her book, Gilligan aims to show how women's moral development has been devalued and misrepresented by male psychological researchers, how ethics has been defined only in male terms. Since at least the 1950s, Gilligan observes, researchers have evaluated women's and men's ability to make moral judgements on the basis of one all-male study. Psychologist Lawrence Kohlberg had used this study to devise his widely used scale of moral judgements, a six-stage ladder in which helping and pleasing others ranks only as the third stage, while a preference for abstract principles of justice over relationships rates as the top rung. Gilligan proposes that women are more likely to make moral choices within the context of particular situations and out of concern for specific individuals – rather than on the basis of impersonal rules of fairness and rights. This does not make women morally 'immature', she says – just different.

At the book's outset she also stresses that this different voice does not belong naturally to women only. 'The different voice I describe is characterized not by gender but theme. . . . The contrasts between male and female voices are presented here to highlight a distinction between two modes of thought and to focus a problem of interpretation rather than to represent a generalization about either sex,' she writes. Nor does she attribute the differences to genes alone. 'Clearly, these differences arise in a social context,' she says, in which 'factors of social status and power' play a role, too.

Despite these initial statements, however, Gilligan may have left herself wide open to misinterpretation – and so to the likelihood that feminism's opponents would harness her arguments for their own ends. After disavowing generalizations about either sex, she seems to make them herself in the three main studies she provides as the foundation of her argument.

In the first 'rights and responsibilities' study, she focuses almost exclusively on two eleven-year-olds, whom she calls Jake and Amy. The two come to serve as near archetypes of gender behaviour – based largely on their responses to a hypothetical question. The moral dilemma they are asked to resolve: a man must decide whether to steal a drug he can't afford so that he can save his wife's life. Jake says to steal it because 'a human life is worth more than money'. Amy waffles and wonders if the man could 'borrow the money or make a loan or something' because otherwise he might have to go to jail later and then what if his wife got sick again? Judging by these answers, it would seem that the ailing wife had better survival odds under Jake's care than Amy's, but this is not the issue that interests Gilligan. Jake, Gilligan writes, is 'constructing the dilemma, as Kohlberg did, as a conflict between the values of property and life'. Amy's reasoning, on the other hand, is founded on a vision of 'a world comprised of relationships rather than people standing alone, a world that coheres through human connection rather than systems of rules'. Gilligan goes on to expand this case study into two distinct moral systems, with Jake representing 'an ideal of perfection' and Amy signifying an 'ideal of care'. The difference between these stereotypical male and female voices is repeatedly emphasized without reference to those 'factors of social status and power' that she had originally suggested should be taken into account. Is Jake preoccupied with perfection partly because that's how boys are brought up? Is Amy more concerned with relationships partly because girls are taught that achievement in this arena will bring them the greatest applause? These questions are never explored.

Gilligan's 'studies' aren't exactly drawn from ideal demographic samples. The 'college student study' bases its findings on twenty-five Harvard undergraduates who chose to take a class on moral and political choices – hardly a representative slice of American society. And the evidence that Gilligan offers in the 'rights and responsibilities' study – based on a sample of eight boys and eight girls from different age groups – boils down to anonymous quotes from two eight-year-olds and two eleven-year-olds. Most frustrating is *In a Different Voice*'s final study, which examines how twenty-nine young women decide whether or not to have abortions. 'No effort was made to select a representative sample of the clinic or counseling service population,' Gilligan writes, but the problem with *this* case study is even more basic than its data base. The choice of issue for the study seems self-defeating in a book that supposedly examines the different ways men and women approach moral dilemmas. Obviously, for abortion there was no male control group. (Gilligan argues that a control group in this case is not necessary; rather, the abortion study illustrates how women's perceptions of moral choices sometimes vary from men's simply because women's situations are different.)

To be fair, Gilligan doesn't hold out her studies as scientific research efforts. 'I would never want to say this is an exhaustive group of people,' she says. 'It was a very small piece of work with three little pilot studies.' In a written defence of her work later, she supports her approach by saying that her argument was 'not statistical' but 'interpretive', and by observing that 'data alone do not tell us anything.' But even so, Gilligan doesn't give readers the basic data they do need to evaluate her case studies: she says almost nothing about the backgrounds, education or income of the children she interviewed. Nor does she make allowances for the difference between what people *say* about their own moral behaviour and how they really act. While the young women in her interviews may have talked more than the young men about compassion and caring, in the many observational studies in which the two sexes are actually called on to help someone in need, women are consistently no more altruistic than men.

The differences in moral reasoning that social science researchers *have* been able to find are most often linked not with sex but with class and education – that is, those very social and economic forces that relational feminists, Gilligan included, have given such a wide berth. 'If there is one statement to be clearly and loudly stated to the public by students of sex differences,' Zella Luria writes, 'it is that overlap of scores by males and females is always far greater than the differences in those scores, particularly on psychological measures. We are not two species; we are two sexes.'

Zella Luria's voice, however, would not be heard over the roar of acclaim for *In a Different Voice*, which had sold 360,000 copies by 1989. The *New York Times Magazine*'s cover story on Gilligan swept aside dissenters in a single paragraph, claiming that they suffered from 'murky academic psychologese'.

In large part, the popularity of Gilligan's book was due to its elegant prose and its many literary allusions to Chekhov, Tolstoy and George Eliot. Maybe her statistics were dubious, but the lyrical writing, a rarity in psychological texts, seemed to more than compensate. As Stanford psychological researchers Catherine Greeno and Eleanor Maccoby observe in their analysis of the book, 'It seems almost philistine to challenge the nature of her evidence.'

But *In a Different Voice* had another sort of appeal in the eighties, too. Under the backlash, it became easy to appropriate Gilligan's theories on behalf of discriminatory arguments that could cause real harm to women. Very much against her will, Gilligan became the expert that backlash mass media loved to cite. *Newsweek* used her book to support its contention that career women pay 'a psychic price' for professional success. Retrograde pop psychology books, including both *Smart Women/Foolish Choices* and *Being a Woman*, invoked Gilligan's work to bolster their arguments that independence was an unnatural and unhealthy state for women. Anti-feminist scholars such as Michael Levin abused Gilligan's scholarship even further, characterizing it as a reaffirmation of traditional Freudian analysis of the female psyche – and gleefully insisting that Gilligan had circled back to what *they* had been saying all along. As anti-feminist writer Nicholas Davidson wrote of Gilligan in his 1988 work, *The Failure of Feminism*: 'Was it really necessary to pass through all the storm and stress of the Feminist Era in order to arrive at ideas that were generally available forty years ago . . . ?'

Gilligan could and did object to such representations of her work. 'I am well aware that reports of sex differences can be used to rationalize oppression, and I deplore any use of my work for this purpose,' she wrote in the scholarly feminist journal *Signs*. And she now says privately that if she had it to do again, she would cast some of her ideas differently; in particular, she would refine her argument 'so that Jake and Amy wouldn't be presented so starkly "male" and "female".' But her regrets don't really matter. The general public does not subscribe to *Signs*. And the damage has already been done.

Part Four

Backlashings:
The Effects on Women's
Minds, Jobs and Bodies

Chapter Twelve

It's All in Your Mind: Popular Psychology Joins the Backlash

Inside the Center for Relationship Studies, a small medical office near Hollywood, celebrated self-help authors Melvyn Kinder and Connell Cowan are working their way through the morning's business. First on the agenda: contract negotiations with ABC for a 'Movie of the Week' version of *Smart Women/Foolish Choices*. Next, deliberations on whether to appear on *Oprah* or *Donahue*. ('You can't do both,' Kinder sighs.) Now, time for another media interview, another opportunity to air their analysis of the contemporary female malady.

> *Kinder*: 'The women's movement pulled women away from caring about relationships.'
> *Cowan*: 'The women's movement tended to suppress women's interest in relationships and refocused women on careers.'
> *Kinder*: 'The smarter the women were, the more likely they were to have these illusory notions. They thought they could hold out. I know loads of women in their thirties and forties who could have had scores of husbands, by virtue of how many men they rejected.'

The two advice experts hardly needed to explain their diagnosis to the press; by the late 1980s their advice manuals, *Smart Women/ Foolish Choices* and *Women Men Love/Women Men Leave*, had become media classics and record-breaking bestsellers. (*Smart*

Women became the second-longest-running book on the *New York Times* non-fiction bestseller list, after Lee Iacocca's autobiography.) Both of these books drove the same point home: women's independence had made women think they were too 'smart' for just any man – and so made women act too 'foolish', postponing marriage for personal, educational or professional pursuits. Feminism gave women swollen, and consequently sick, heads.

But, strangely enough, towards the end of the decade Kinder and Cowan were marketing a contradictory diagnosis. Women's psychological problem, they now said, wasn't the result of women caring too little about relationships – but of caring too much.

> *Cowan*: 'A lot of women are obsessed now with getting married.'
> *Kinder*: 'It's all they talk about! When you put off your needs, you create personality disorders – and all these women in their late thirties, they are getting very anxious, very upset. . . . I mean, the best-selling book now is *How to Marry the Man of Your Choice!*' [Margaret Kent's book that came with a money-back guarantee for unsuccessful spinsters.]

Indeed, this most recent female neurosis has become such a 'trend', Kinder says, that he and his partner are considering writing a third book to address it.

Could this new marital 'disorder' be, perchance, related to the protracted scolding of single women that preceded it – a chastisement to which popular psychologists such as themselves amply contributed? Certainly not, the self-help authors retort. 'We're not goading them on,' Kinder says. 'We're providing information.' Who, then, induced this latest psychic disturbance? 'If anyone's to blame for women's obsessive behaviour,' Kinder volunteers, 'it's the women's movement.'

But in the 1980s, advice writers like Cowan and Kinder did play a role in the development of such 'obsessive behaviour' – a highly instrumental and, for the writers at least, profitable one. Via popular psychology, the backlash insinuated itself into the most intimate front lines, impressing its discouraging and moralistic message most effectively, and destructively, on the millions of women seeking help from therapy books and counselling – women who were already feeling insecure and vulnerable, already bunkered in isolated private trenches.

To the vast female readership of self-help manuals, the advice experts delivered a one-two punch. First they knocked down the liberated woman, commanding that she surrender her 'excessive' independence, a mentally unhealthy state that had turned her into a voracious narcissist, a sterile cuckoo. Then, having brought the 'victim' of feminism to her more feminine knees, the advice writers reaped the benefits – by nursing the backlash victim. In the first half of the 1980s the advice experts told women they suffered from bloated egos and a 'fear of intimacy'; in the second half, they informed women that atrophied egos and 'co-dependency' were now their problems. In the decade's war on women, these popular psychologists helped fire the opening shots – then rushed to the battlefield to bandage the many wounds.

In the quietist eighties, the advice book and therapy couch may have been the only sources of relief left to women who were feeling demoralized. In an era that offered little hope of real social or political change, the possibility of changing oneself was the one remaining way held out to women to improve their lot. And there *was* much that these advice writers and counsellors could have done, even more so under the backlash, to bolster bombarded female egos and provide solace and support for women who were feeling increasingly alone and overwhelmed. Certainly, many counsellors in the 1980s provided useful and much-needed aid and comfort. But the advice experts with the highest media profiles in the decade were not among them. These representatives of the psychology profession managed to reinforce female isolation more than relieve it. They helped to inflame anxieties women already had about their worth and place in the world. In the guise of self-help, the experts issued only demands and dictates about how women should behave to win a man, rather than dispensing therapeutic tools and encouragement that women could have used to help themselves.

Instead of assisting women to override the backlash, the advice experts helped to lock it in female minds and hearts – by urging women to interpret all of the backlash's pressures as simply 'their' problem. While of course many of the psychological problems that women (and men) struggle with are highly individualized and idiosyncratic – people seek counselling for many reasons, of which socialization of women is, obviously, only one – the counsellors who dominated eighties advice bookshelves recognized *no* outside factors in their analysis and treatment of women. Backlash psychology turned a blind eye to all the social forces that had converged on women in the last decade – all the put-downs from mass media and Hollywood, all the verbal attacks from moral crusaders and political leaders, all the frightening reports from scholars and 'experts', and all the rage, whether in the form of firebombings of women's clinics or sexual harassment or rape. These popular psychologists failed to take account of or even to acknowledge the sort of psychic damage that a prolonged cultural onslaught was capable of inflicting on its targets. Nor, needless to say, did they contemplate the psychological difficulties that the *other* sex might be having in this decade, adjusting to the changes in women's roles. Advice books directed at men just weren't marketable enough to make that therapeutic enterprise worthwhile.

The abuse that women had experienced in the 1980s, the advice manuals decreed by the end of the decade, must be self-inflicted. Rather than ask why so many women had become the object of rising male wrath, they concluded that these women must simply be courting punishment. One popular psychology tome after another unveiled an updated version of the masochistic female psyche – couched, of course, in the language of women's liberation. And while many of the works were trivial – the product of pop-therapy trends that come and go like fashions in the book shops – the regressive vision of the female mind that these books endorsed would ultimately surface in a far more damaging context: in the most important reference manual of professional psychiatry.

Stage One: Feminist-Taming Therapy

Get 'power' by 'surrendering' and 'submitting' to your man's every whim, a leading eighties self-help manual advises in typical feminist-sounding rhetoric. Don't talk back, because a ladylike silence will 'enhance' your 'self-respect' and 'feeling of mastery'. 'Take charge . . . of your courtship,' suggests another popular text. 'Overcome obstacles' so you can get married. The pseudo-feminist title of one 1989 advice book puts it most succinctly: *Women Who Marry Down and End Up Having It All.*

While the backlash therapy books may be written in feminist ink, they blot out the most basic precept of feminist therapy – that both social and personal growth are important, necessary and mutually reinforcing. This is a view that was supported, albeit in a rather degraded, commercialized form, in the leading self-help manuals of the seventies; in 1975 *The New Assertive Woman* issued an 'Everywoman's Bill of Rights' that called for 'the right to be treated with respect' and 'the right to be listened to and taken seriously'. The 1980s advice writers, by contrast, seemed to go out of their way to urge women to *stop* challenging social constraints and to keep their thoughts to themselves – to learn to fit the mould rather than break it.

On no group of women did the self-help authors impress this message more strongly than the ones without wedding rings. The diagnosis was, underneath it all, little changed from the postwar era, when that era's leading advice book – Marynia Farnham and Ferdinand Lundberg's *Modern Women: The Lost Sex* – declared all single women neurotics and proposed subsidized psycho-therapy to get them married. In the 1980s even advice experts more sympathetic to single women and the pressures they faced touted the same marital party line. In the popular 1988 advice book, *If I'm So Wonderful, Why Am I Still Single?*, counsellor Susan Page acknowledges in her introduction that unwed women are contending with a social climate that is especially rough on them now; they are burdened by 'the specific problems that our times have spawned, such as misogyny', she writes. But she's not interested in helping single women develop the self-confidence and internal strength they need to bear up under these antagonistic conditions. Nor does she propose that single women even question the culture's marital marching orders. 'I want to accept certain sociological and psychological factors as *given* [her emphasis],' she writes. 'In this book we will not discuss *why* [her emphasis] these conditions are as they are, and we will not lament them.' What then should single women do to ease what Page calls the 'Great Emotional Depression' that she says has descended on millions of them? Just change your single status, she proposes. She dispenses 'strategies' only to make women more marketable for marriage.

The backlash therapists of the 1980s firmly rejected another fundamental feminist principle – that men can, and should, change, too. '[L]ately it seems there is a rising tide of utter frustration among women concerning men,' *Smart Women/Foolish Choices* observes, and a lot of women 'always end up feeling disappointed by men'. But Cowan and Kinder do not go on to consider what men might be doing to inspire such an outpouring of frustration, nor how men might change their behaviour to make women feel better. Instead, the psychologists conclude that men are fine and any disappointment women feel is wholly self-generated. It's not the men who are 'inadequate', the authors write; it's just that the women's 'expectations are distorted'. Women are just 'hypercritical' of men. All would be well if women only learned to 'truly understand men' and their 'need for mastery and career success'. Women would be happy if they only stopped 'pushing' the opposite sex to change and learned to 'compromise.'

Asked later what sort of compromises he had in mind, Kinder says: 'Women could have their kids while they are still in college, and then, if they still want a career, they can do that after the kids are grown. You do have to make some sacrifices.' What about fathers 'sacrificing' by taking some responsibility for their children? Kinder, whose wife stayed at home to raise their children, mulls it over. 'Yeah, well that would solve the problem,' he says. 'But men won't do it. And it's not our place to be saying things like that. We're not social engineers.' Not, anyway, when it comes to men.

Confronted with the anti-feminist implications of their message, the backlash therapists almost always issue a denial. 'We're talking about broadening expectations, not settling for less, and that's not just a play on words,' Cowan says. But it is exactly that – unless Cowan has already forgotten his own 'Rules for Finding the Right Man' in *Smart Women*. Rule number 8: 'Fewer expectations lead to greater aliveness.'

Some of the therapists attacking women's liberation most forcefully claimed, in fact, to be proponents themselves. As many media-conscious therapists in the 1980s discovered, feminist-bashing 'feminists' garnered the most airtime. Susan and Stephen Price, authors of the popular *No More Lonely Nights: Overcoming the Hidden Fears That Keep You from Getting Married*, were one such 'feminist' husband-and-wife therapy team who got a lot of mileage in the American press plugging this backlash diagnosis of modern single women: 'androphobia'. This 'problem without a name', they wrote, shamelessly stealing Friedan's phrase, was a 'deep-rooted intense fear of men' shared by most unmarried women over thirty, especially professional women. The cause: 'You have been deeply influenced by feminism.'

'These obsessive androphobic fears are a major ingredient in women's resistance to marriage today,' Stephen Price is saying in his Manhattan office, a few weeks after his appearance on the *Today* show. 'Now that we've reached the end of the women's movement, which is where our culture is today . . . ' Here he hesitates, then says, 'We both, of course, feel very *pro* the gains of the women's movement.'

His wife, Susan, seated in the office's other therapeutic armchair, nods vigorously. 'We're both feminists,' she says. 'In fact, it was almost me being a feminist that kept me from seeing these hidden fears developing. As a therapist I encouraged women to pursue careers. But what happened is, women escaped into their careers and they didn't put their energy into their relationships. Their feminist viewpoint became a trap.' But if careers hurt women psychologically, then why do professional women consistently rank highest, as we've seen, in virtually all measures of mental health? The Prices have no answer.

In spite of their pro-feminist claims, the Prices seem to oppose every feminist tenet, from economic independence to sexual freedom. In their book and in their counselling sessions, they advise women to refrain not only from initiating sex but from having sex at all before marriage. 'If the woman is sexually aggressive, the man might put her in the category of someone to go to bed with, period,' Susan Price says. Evidence? '*Fatal Attraction* may be overdrawn in some ways, but you can really see that operating there,' she says.

Unlike authentically feminist therapists, the Prices don't consider, much less confront, other forces at work in women's lives. They reinforce the era's isolation of single women by encouraging their female readers to see themselves as defective units, alone and isolated only by their own aberrant behaviour. They advise women to 'deal with your own personal crisis: What might *you* [their emphasis] be doing to make intimacy with a man impossible? What attitudes are keeping *you* [their emphasis] unavailable for marriage?' The primary offending attitude that the book singles out: an insistence on respect and equal treatment from one's mate. 'The desire to avoid a submissive status in relationship to men can lead you into a loveless life,' they assert. Again, there is no analysis of the attitudes of men, much less proposals for altering them. If a man mistreats a woman, she probably asked for it. 'A resistant woman picks a resistant man,' Susan Price says. 'What we help single women to see is how what they think is a problem with the man is really something inside them.' Don't men play *any* role in difficult relationships? 'Probably it is a fifty-fifty proposition,' Stephen Price concedes, shrugging. 'But this book is focused on women – for the purpose of clarity.'

While they don't actually support a feminist vision, the Prices are happy to appropriate the movement's activist language to promote their own agenda. They urge women to 'take control' of their love lives by playing down their career aspirations and to 'gain power' over potential husbands by remaining celibate. 'It's Up to You to Get Married', the manual instructs, this being the only arena, apparently, in which it's OK for women to take the initiative.

Androphobia may have a scientific ring, but it's not based on scientific research – or any research at all. 'We just knew it was a phobia,' Stephen Price says flatly. How? 'Well, because there's an avoidance there.' Pressed to explain what that means, Stephen Price falls silent. Finally, he says: 'A lot of the dynamics of phobia are hidden. That's how we know it's a phobia. It's very hidden.'

This invisible phobia turned the Prices into very visible 'marriage gurus', as they now call themselves. 'We are inundated,'

Susan Price says happily. 'We've been doing three radio shows a week. Women are calling up saying, what's your [marriage] success rate? We do sessions by phone. We have women flying in from out west. And we get so many letters from women saying they read our book and they realize now how they did it to themselves. They are grateful.'

It turns out that Susan Price does actually support feminist principles in one way – for herself. 'When we first married, Steve couldn't understand my need for my own career and not wanting to be a homemaker,' she recalls. 'I got jobs [to support him] while he was in graduate school. He was being groomed for a career and what was I doing?' First she became a schoolteacher, but she didn't find it fulfilling enough. 'I decided I wanted to be a therapist. So I went back to graduate school. The kids were still babies at the time. We hired a lot of babysitters and put them in a lot of nursery schools.' Was any of this a mistake? 'Oh, no. I love what I do.'

Stage Two: Therapy for the Overly Feminine Woman

On an unusually sunny day in San Francisco, sixty women are huddled inside a shuttered half-lit shopfront, curled on sagging armchairs and sofas. Yellowed oil paintings hang cockeyed on the walls; dustballs drift like tumbleweed across the floor. In an attempt at cheer, someone has set a rose on the chipped coffee table, but the lone flower only highlights the gloom.

At one time, only Alcoholics Anonymous met in these dreary quarters. But in 1986, a group trying to conquer another 'addiction' began convening every Saturday. And soon, fifty, sometimes a hundred, 'women who love too much' were reporting regularly to the room. Like thousands of women in identical meetings around the country, they were flocking to contemplate the written word of Robin Norwood, therapist and author of *Women Who Love Too Much: When You Keep Wishing and Hoping He'll Change*.

On this particular Saturday in 1987, the group leader rises and locks the front door, giving the knob a few sharp rattles. 'We are all here,' she says, 'because we share one thing in common. We all have basically miserable relationships.' A list of Norwood's 'Characteristics of Women Who Love Too Much' is passed around, and each woman reads one line aloud. 'Number one: you come from a dysfunctional home in which your emotional needs were not met' . . . 'Number eleven: you are addicted to men and emotional pain.' . . . 'Number fourteen: you have a tendency toward episodes of depression.' Women sip decaffeinated coffee from a carafe on the counter; no stimulants are allowed at these meetings. On one sofa, women take turns cradling a teddy bear.

The group leader reminds attendees of two ground rules for Women Who Love Too Much support groups: no advising each other and no talking about 'him'. Remember, she stresses, this is *your* problem, not his.

Then the 'sharing portion' of the meeting begins.

'Hi, my name is Sandra [names have been changed] and I'm a Woman Who Loves Too Much. I got married to a man who became addicted to liquor. . . . What is it about me that attracted a sick, dependent alcoholic?'

'Hi, my name is Nancy and I'm a Woman Who Loves Too Much. I'm involved with a man who is very sexually rejecting. I think I am attracted to him because when he rejects me, that allows me to play the hurt, angry one and close down.'

And so it goes for the next hour and a half, each speaker ticking off her troubles and pointing an accusatory finger at herself. One woman tells the group that she is 'tired all the time' and doesn't know why. Another cries 'for no reason', sometimes twice a day, huddled in the bedroom cupboard. The confidences are offered up to an unresponsive audience. Since no one is permitted to comment on anyone else's troubles, authentic 'sharing' is absent; the women seem more like children in a sandpit, engaged in parallel play.

When the personal accounting is done, the women finish as they do every week. They rise from their seats, clasp hands in a circle, and chant the Serenity Prayer, asking God to help improve their relationships with their men. Then the leader unlocks the door and the women wander out, one by one, to face the sun-drenched streets alone.

*

First published in 1985, Norwood's book on female 'relationship addiction' became the guiding light to more than 20 million readers. More than a year in the number-one spot on the *New York Times* bestseller list, *Women Who Love Too Much* was America's number-one 1986 bestseller in mass-market paperbacks nationwide. A year and a half after the book's publication, cities from Philadelphia to Atlanta to Los Angeles supported scores of Women Who Love Too Much groups. In 1987, when the *New York Daily News* ran a small item that simply mentioned a Women Who Love Too Much group, the leaders of the group received several hundred calls by the end of the day.

When the book was published in Britain in 1986 it initially had only a moderate impact. Then excerpts from a second book, *Letters from Women Who Love Too Much*, were published in the national press and, according to a report in the *Guardian*, 'the hype really began'. British women, too, clamoured to confess their shortcomings in personal relationships, in several waves of letters to the Sunday press. One of them wrote: 'I have had a horrendous life, establishing in me from a very early age – four – the need to love much too much.'

There plainly were great numbers of women who were locked in destructive relationships and in desperate need of help. And surely there were many women who found comfort in Norwood's book and the meetings that the text inspired. But the book's cover promised women more practical help than it delivered; the underlying Women Who Love Too Much message was a quasi-mystical one that advocated a childlike and passive acceptance more than grown-up and active change. To borrow from the wording of the Serenity Prayer, Norwood's text offered women more serenity to accept things they couldn't change than courage to change the things they could.

Like so many therapists in the decade, Norwood had an opportunity to observe at close hand the increasing toll of emotional and sexual violence amongst women. She puzzled over the evidence of millions of women suffering verbal and physical abuse from husbands and lovers. Yet, in the end, she proposed an explanation that entirely ignored the social dimensions of these developments and turned the problem inward. Women today, she writes, are literally 'addicted' to men who hurt them. 'Many, many of us have been "man junkies",' she writes, 'and, like any other addict, we need to admit the severity of our problem.' While many women, of course, do follow such self-destructive patterns, Norwood's ahistorical analysis doesn't help to explain why the problem is so acute now – or why the violence directed at women is rising so dramatically. Nor does it ever turn the tables: her book asks why so many women 'choose' abusive men, but not why there are so many abusive men to choose from.

Norwood's self-help plan, modelled on Alcoholics Anonymous's twelve-step programme, advises women seeking the source of their pain to refrain from looking beyond themselves, a habit she calls 'blaming'. Instead of encouraging women to develop stronger egos, get feistier, and challenge men to change, Norwood recommends that her readers 'build your willingness to surrender', steer clear of 'passion', and 'let go of self-will'. Only by 'getting in touch with your higher power' can a man-addicted woman escape from emotional pain. 'Spiritual practice calms you,' she writes. It doesn't actually help you to change your circumstances or yourself, but it 'helps change your perspective from being victimized to being uplifted'; simply by saying, silently and to herself, 'I no longer suffer', a woman can get relief. Taking the initiative to improve one's situation is not part of the Norwood plan. Instead she advises 'letting go' of 'the determination to make things happen'. She explains, 'You must accept the fact that you may not know what is best in a given situation.' In fact, the reader should regard self-assertion itself as a 'character defect'.

Real personal growth and mental health are also excluded from Norwood's treatment programme. There are no cured Women Who Love Too Much, she warns, only 'recovered' ones. 'Man junkies', like chronic drinkers, are hooked for life. The women can only work to 'control' the illness, which will always linger in their systems. To keep the sickness in check, she prescribes only one thing: regular attendance at Women Who Love Too Much 'support groups'.

The meaning of 'addiction' itself – 'the giving of oneself to a desire' – nicely matches the traditional Victorian vision of feminine passivity. The Women Who Love Too Much treatment strategy trades one form of passivity for another, more glorified one, the giving of oneself to a 'higher power'. The students of Women Who Love Too Much don't learn to direct their lives but only to credit a mysterious force for directing it for them. They learn not to fortify and harness power inside themselves but only to submit to its delivery from on high. In a way, Norwood's cure is the reverse image of the personal transformation plan of the New Right's Concerned Women for America's Beverly LaHaye. LaHaye concealed her drive for self-determination and authority under the cover of 'spiritual submission'; Norwood tries to pass off a true form of surrender as an active way of taking charge of one's life.

Norwood cast herself, too, as a mere spiritual medium rather than an actor in her own life. Even her book, she says, was written by a 'higher power', not her. 'I feel it was really guided from the beginning,' she says later. Even the title was whispered in her ear while she was driving on the highway. In defining herself in these terms, as a passive recipient of divine wisdom, she recalls the Victorian Verena Tarrant in Henry James's *The Bostonians*, the childlike heroine who explained away her talent for public speaking by saying, 'Oh, it isn't me, you know; it's something outside! . . . I suppose it is a power.'

In late 1980s America, with the rise of 'co-dependency', the addiction or disease model of female neurosis quickly spread to other forms of therapy. It helped to double membership in self-help counselling organizations, spawning an endless variety of 'support' groups for co-dependents from Women for Sobriety to Women with Multiple Addictions. There was even a group of Formerly Employed Mothers at Loose Ends, or FEMALE. Aparently now even a poor job market was seen as an individual woman's personal psychosis. The professional medical journals supported this illness metaphor, defining co-dependency as 'a disease of relationships' in which the individual '*selects* a life partner who is chemically dependent or who is otherwise dysfunctional'. (The individual they had in mind was almost always a woman; the co-dependency market was about 85 per cent female. Co-dependency was even defined in female terms – its original model the alcoholic's wife.)

The leaders of the co-dependency movement exhorted their female patients to picture and even treat themselves like little girls. One self-help strategy that these gurus widely recommended to their patients: a doll to cuddle, and carry it at all times. 'Reclaiming the inner child' was the movement's mantra, and co-dependent initiates were encouraged to call themselves 'adult children'. While this concept may well have begun with good intentions – to revisit the crimes of one's abused and victimized childhood in order to transcend them – too often the excavation of the buried injured child became the all-consuming central drama, and the effort to reject victim status and move towards maturity was largely side-lined. In many co-dependency groups women waded into the quagmires of childhood to 'rescue' their hurting little-girl selves – only to sink deeper in the mud.

Despite their infantilizing methods and their distaste for 'self-will', co-dependency's creators and practitioners claimed to have a feminist outlook. The co-directors of the National Self-Help Clearinghouse declared, 'The codependency movement may well be the psychological arm of the women's movement.' Norwood herself compared her Women Who Love Too Much groups to the consciousness-raising sessions of the early 1970s.

But by sequestering women in dimly lit, locked and caffeine-free meeting rooms and instructing them to swap adult assertiveness for an unpassionate, passive and peurile tranquillity, Norwood's regimen comes closer in spirit to the late nineteenth-century 'rest cure' than to early-seventies feminist rap sessions. The hundred-year-old cure, which also involved confinement in darkened rooms, diets of unstimulating foods, and a denial of self-expression, succeeded more often in accelerating the deterioration of its patients than in curing them. As feminist writer Charlotte Perkins Gilman observed most famously of her 1887 rest cure, she had tried to follow the doctor's orders to put down her pen and 'live as domestic a life as possible' – and 'came perilously near to losing my mind'.

The consciousness-raising movement of the 1970s, by contrast, whatever its foibles, at least called on its participants to act, speak out and grow up. Its meetings were envisaged as sort of weekly pit stops in a social revolution. As *Ms.*'s 1972 guide to the consciousness-raising described it, the groups were intended to provide emotional refuelling, companionship and confidence building, 'when we come back battered or ridiculed from trying to change our worlds'. The sessions were free – so that women of all incomes could join – and leaderless – so that no one would become the authority figure and each member would be encouraged to think and speak for herself.

The women who flocked to the Women Who Love Too Much groups in the 1980s were battered and ridiculed, too, from trying to change their world. But if they were hoping to pursue such social change further, they weren't likely to find much encouragement at these counselling sessions. 'Most of the women who come to our workshops have spent years trying to change and reform their partners,' said one British psychotherapist who ran day and weekend workshops to help women with 'relationship addiction'. 'What they have to realize is that this is impossible – that the only person you can ever hope to change is yourself.' Working in pairs, with role-play, and encouraging women to help one another, these British workshops at least aimed to build women's self-esteem and 'make them more self-reliant'. Even so, one woman who attended a workshop, Alison, the wife of a heavy drinker, said that the experience was extremely difficult and painful at first: 'The worst thing was facing up to inadequacies and problems in myself – I got used to blaming Bill and his drink for everything.'

Research by research psychologist Bernice Andrews led her to believe that the mushrooming of self-help groups and profit-making 'therapeutic' organizations might be doing already-depressed women, with a tendency to self-blame, more harm than good. Reinforcing the belief in women that they had character defects was potentially very dangerous. Writing in the *Guardian*, she pointed out: 'Both the research I have been involved in and studies in the United States have shown that objective material dependency is by far the most important factor binding women to abusive men. Furthermore, my study has shown that it is not primarily unhappy childhoods that make women more likely to experience violence from their partners, but marrying before the age of twenty, and being pregnant before marriage.'

In many of the American Women Who Love Too Much groups,

the counsellors were running the show – and not *pro bono*, despite Norwood's original proposal that the groups be free and leader-less. At the regular Friday session of the Women Who Love Too Much group at the California Family Therapy Institute, the women are seated in a circle, the blinds drawn, the lights low. They have paid the group's therapist leader $30 to $40 a week – on top of her $80 fee for individual counselling.

'I'm like a mother to them all,' the therapist says, surveying her brood of 'adult children'. Of herself, she says, 'I am definitely a Woman Who Loves Too Much.' She was a full-time housewive, she relates, until her husband ran off with her best friend after twenty-three years of marriage. Then she went back to school at forty and became a therapist. Now she's 'in recovery', having figured out what went wrong in her marriage. 'I let myself go. I don't blame him. He's a man just like any other man. If I had done all this work on me before, maybe he would have stuck around.'

Each of the women in this group had good reasons for seeking help when the sessions started ten months earlier. One woman was living with a man who had barely spoken to her since she had embarked on a career. Another woman was living with a man who called her at work, screaming, when she failed to iron his favourite shirt. Another woman's husband, who launched periodic tirades about dust in the carpet, was having an affair, which he said was 'her fault'.

Asked why they originally joined, the women offer variations on the same answer. 'I wanted to be tougher,' says one. 'Not be such an emotional bimbo,' sys another. 'I wanted to be strong,' says a third. But asked what they learned in the group, their replies are very different: 'I learned how I was a little girl within,' says a middle-aged businesswoman. 'I realized I'm a little child,' says a forty-year-old teacher. 'And I learned how to get in touch with that child.' At her therapist's request, she purchased a doll and it is now her constant companion; in the car, she says, she is always careful to put on its seat belt. 'You'll notice,' the therapist says, 'how in the group my girls' little voices just get smaller and smaller.'

Presumably the point of retreating to a childhood state is to make a new start. But here, the women seem to regress and get stuck. Rather than change their lives, they seem, at best, to have learned how to adjust to intolerable situations. One woman, a housewife who had recently gone back to work as an estate agent, originally joined Women Who Love Too Much so she could have some support while divorcing her husband. He was seeing another woman, but that was the least of it. Ever since she had returned to work, his anger had mounted; eventually, it became intolerable. 'If I didn't vacuum the house every day, he'd scream,' she says. 'If I forgot to lay out his clothes one morning, I'd hear about it. If the fish wasn't fresh or if I said we were having fish and then I served steak, he would go into a rage. He would take away all my money and credit cards and my car and push me out of the house and tell me to try living on my own.' But after ten months in Women Who Love Too Much, she decided to move back in with him. 'See, the thing I learned in the group is, it wasn't really his fault. I allowed it to happen.'

For more than a year, the publicity department at Pocket Books was getting virtually daily calls from women desperate to talk to Robin Norwood. 'She's the only one who can help me,' they would say. Some women even flew out to Santa Barbara, Norwood's residence, in hopes of an on-the-spot session with her. They hoped to join the list of the man-addicts that Norwood had helped, the dozens of real women who had been featured in *Women Who Love Too Much*. Norwood's own much advertised recovery also played a major role in attracting hordes of supplicants. As Judith Staples, a San Francisco addiction counsellor who organized Norwood's last public appearance, observes, 'Robin is a symbol of hope for so many women in pain. Because Robin did it, you know. She pulled herself out of relationship addiction and into recovery.'

For a year and a half after the book was published, Norwood told the story of her recovery to thousands of women in marathon six-hour-long speeches she delivered around the country. Her lecture fee was $2,500; an admission ticket was $40. When Norwood spoke in San Francisco in 1987, her sponsors were besieged by more than a thousand women applicants within a week. The meeting eventually had to be moved to a cavernous church, and even these quarters weren't spacious enough. Norwood's congregants, the event's organizer recalls, were 'hanging from the choir loft'.

Norwood's all-day lecture concerned her life story, but it was an oral biography that omitted all events except the particulars of various dead-end relationships. She covered each failed affair in microscopic detail, starting with the story of the boy who snubbed her on the playground – at nursery school. And she closed each anecdote with the same conclusion. 'It was an inside job,' she told her audience. 'For a long time I thought, "Why are all these bad things happening to me?" It's because I *chose* them. We choose alcoholics. We choose men who are incapable of being faithful to us.'

Her second husband was an alcoholic, prone to binges, and his periodic desertions eventually took a toll on her job – she worked as an alcohol-addiction counsellor in a hospital. 'Every morning after a while I was showing up at work and starting to cry,' she recalls. 'And then one day I couldn't stop crying. . . . So they took me by the arm and said, "Robin, why don't you go home and why don't you stay there?" And I went home and I just stayed there. For almost three months.'

Out of work, Norwood went downhill fast. 'Part of that time, I could not function. I had a very hard time talking. I couldn't move. It was as though I was in very heavy wet cement. I lived in my bathrobe. We ate Springfield chili almost every night. It was a big deal if I could make it to the mailbox and back. That was the highlight of the day.' Finally, her husband reappeared and vowed to reform; she returned to work and the depression receded. But soon he was back to bingeing and she slipped back into despair. Her skin, she says, began breaking out in 'great big bruises', which she believes was a sign that her 'connective tissue' was dissolving. She said, 'I knew I was dying.'

Norwood at last turned to an Al-Anon meeting. It was here, she says, that she discovered the merits of surrender. 'For me, recovery meant leaning on something much larger than myself.' She 'turned the whole thing over to God' and 'found myself praying'. She prayed especially for a 'nice man'. Her prayers were answered; a divine power, she says, caused her to meet her third husband. He was 'real boring', she says, but now that she was in recovery she realized that this was for the best. Passion was only 'suffering', a drug that 'kills'.

Readers of *Women Who Love Too Much* who attended Norwood's lectures might have been struck by the remarkable resemblance between her own story and the case histories of the patients featured in her book. Just like 'Pam', Norwood's first marriage was to a high-school dropout; just like 'Jill', Norwood met her second husband at a dance club; just like 'Trudi', her final marriage was to a boring nice guy. This is no coincidence. As Norwood let slip to a few colleagues, many of her 'patients' in the book are really just her. The grand finale of the book – a long and detailed final therapy session between Norwood and the grateful, 'recovered' Trudi (in which the therapist rhapsodizes about her client's 'warm brown eyes shining and the beautiful cloud of softly waved reddish brown hair longer and fuller than I remember') – is only the therapist talking to and about herself.

Asked later why she misrepresented herself as her patients in the book, Norwood says, 'I never claimed those were case studies. Some are really fictional. The point is not which parts are me and which aren't.' But regrettably this distinction *is* very much the point. Norwood originally proposed to spark a 'raising of consciousness' by sharing diverse intimate female experience; her book ushered readers into her therapy office to listen, and take heart from, the voices of many women. But inside this confessional one can hear the regrets of just one woman, a stricken and solitary figure who sees only her reflection in her lonely hall of mirrors.

Norwood's own 'recovery' – through marriage to the 'right' man – proved short-lived. In the spring of 1987 Norwood abruptly gave up making speeches. She could no longer market her experience as a successful case study: being married to the nice boring husband turned out to be not so nice after all, and soon she divorced him.

Following the breakup of her marriage, Norwood chose a path that would seem more likely to promote, not mitigate, her isolation. She gave up her practice, moved to a cottage by the sea, and retreated into a shell-like existence. Her daily life there, she reports, involves 'absolutely no social life'. She no longer reads or even watches TV. 'I never look at the newspaper.' In fact, she does nothing. 'I just hold still.' Wouldn't contact with other people be comforting? 'I don't want to be involved with other people's lives,' she says. Doesn't she at least wonder what's going on in the world? 'I don't want to know,' she says. 'It's just a distraction from staying in touch with myself.'

This self-help programme of Norwood's was no consciousness-raising cure; it was closer to solitary confinement. 'The heart of [consciousness-raising],' as historian Hester Eisenstein writes, 'was the discovery that one was not alone, that other women had comparable feelings and experiences.' But Norwood was very much alone – more alone, in fact, than when she began her treatment. So, too, were some of the 'co-dependent' women in treatment who took their dolls home and slammed the doors behind them. As long as these female patients continued to be convinced that unhappy domestic affairs were a woman's problem only, they would each end up in a room talking to themselves. They would end up like Norwood, sitting in a house by the sea, ears plugged from the noises of the outer world, eyes, like Verena Tarrant's, turned towards heaven.

Feminine Masochism, Eighties Style

The psychiatric diagnosis of masochism first formulated in the late Victorian era described people who derive sexual pleasure from pain. It soon, however, degenerated into a sort of all-purpose definition of the female psyche; so many women got abused because so many women preferred it that way – an early statement, in some respects, of Robin Norwood's thesis.

But masochism as a therapeutic diagnosis eventually fell into disrepute. As psychoanalyst Karen Horney first pointed out in the 1920s, so-called 'natural' female masochism was more likely to be the unnatural product of a sexist social system of rewards and punishments that induced many women to adopt submissive behaviour. Horney's Freudian male colleagues didn't appreciate her observations – they forced her out of the New York Psychoanalytic Society. But eventually most mental health professionals came round to her point of view, and by the 1970s the notion of an innate female masochism seemed a quaint relic, more a jocular buzzword than a defensible psychoanalytic theory.

Then, in 1985, some psychoanalysts at the American Psychiatric Association (APA) decided it was time for masochism to make a comeback, as a 'new' disorder in the professional *Diagnostic and Statistical Manual of Mental Disorders*, or *DSM*, the Bible of American psychiatry. This was no arcane matter of classification. The *DSM* is the standard reference book that mental health professionals rely on to diagnose patients, researchers use to study mental illness, private and public insurers require to determine compensation for therapy, and courts turn to when ruling on insanity pleas and child custody decisions.

That year, Dr Teresa Bernardez was chairing the APA's Committee on Women, which is supposed to be consulted on all proposed new *DSM* diagnoses affecting women. But the APA panel drafting the new diagnoses never bothered to inform her or anyone else on the committee. By chance, as the APA was nearing a vote on the diagnosis, Bernardez heard about it from a friend across the country. She investigated further – and discovered that the APA panel planned to add not one but *three* diagnoses affecting women, all in troubling ways. 'Premenstrual dysphoric disorder' was another one, a diagnosis that revived the long-discredited notion that PMS was a mental illness rather than a simple matter of endocrinology. 'Paraphiliac rapism disorder' was the third, a diagnosis that the APA panel intended to apply to any man (or, theroetically, woman) who reported repeated fantasies about rape or sexual molestation and 'repeatedly acts on these urges or is markedly distressed by them'. If approved, this vague definition could prove a handy insanity plea for any rapist or child molester with an enterprising lawyer. This was obvious enough to the US Attorney General's office which, once alerted, even issued an objection.

In some ways the 'masochistic personality disorder' may have been the most regressive, and peculiar, of the three proposed diagnoses. The APA panel had come up with nine characteristics to define masochism – and they were strangely broad indeed. They included anyone who 'rejects help, gifts, or favors so as not to be a burden on others' or 'worries excessively' about troubling others or 'responds to success or positive events by feeling undeserving'. Included in this list was even the undergraduate who puts aside her homework to help fellow students write their essays. None of the nine characteristics of this new 'masochism' mentioned taking pleasure in pain. Instead, they described only the self-sacrificing and self-denigrating sort of behaviour that is supposed to typify ideal femininity. The APA panel had neatly summed up female socialization – and stamped it a private, psychiatric malfunction. In fact the APA panel went even further, dubbing this problem not only a pathological imbalance but a 'personality disorder', a category of mental illness that psychiatry defines as *least* related to social conditions and most rooted in the underlying structure of an individual's personality from early childhood – and so most difficult to change.

Worst of all, the diagnosis threatened to invite a return to treating battered women as masochists who court domestic violence. The APA panel included these traits in its definition of the new masochists: 'choosing' people who 'disappointed' or 'mistreat' them and remaining 'in relationships in which others exploit, abuse, or take advantage'. The panel illustrated these traits with an example of a masochist who sounded more like the male perspective on the backlash than a description of mental illness: a spouse who criticizes a mate, thus 'provoking an angry counterattack'.

Once again under the backlash, attention was deflected from the causes of that 'counterattack': male anger at women's increasing demands and male fear of women's growing autonomy. Once again, each female target of the backlash's fury was redefined as her own, and only, assailant. And while the pop-psychology books that told women to blame themselves would come and go in American book shops during the 1980s, the *DSM* was a permanent fixture. If the APA inscribed this definition of masochism on its pages, it would institutionalize the psychological message of the backlash for years to come.

Alarmed by the news of the proposed masochism diagnosis, Dr Teresa Bernardez sent a letter detailing her concerns to Dr Robert

Spitzer, a psychiatrist at Columbia University and chairman of the APA panel in charge of revising the *DSM*. The panel was dominated by psychoanalysts, the subspeciality most partial to traditional Freudian psychiatry and a group of professionals who were still brooding over the last round of *DSM* revisions five years earlier, when vestiges of more outdated Freudian terminology were finally removed. The masochism disorder's backers at the APA also seemed to resent the rise of the 'female-dominated' psychology profession, which had been cutting into the psychiatry business since the 1970s with its lower-cost and shorter-term treatments. As APA vice-president Dr Paul Fink groused in 1987, some psychologists 'won't be happy until there is no more psychoanalysis'.

In the course of the battle over the APA's masochism diagnosis, many of these simmering animosities would surface – and eventually boil over – as female therapists refused to back down and accept the ruling of the psychoanalysts. 'The anger we saw was unbelievable to me,' recalls Bernardez, an Argentinian émigré who had previously seen her share as a citizen under the repressive Perón regime. 'It was really just lying there and when women pressed and didn't give up, it just all came up.'

Initially, Bernardez got nowhere lodging protests on her own, nor did the APA panel respond to repeated appeals from other women's committees in the profession. It wasn't until the Feminist Therapy Institute threatened legal action that Spitzer and his fellow panellists even agreed to grant the women a hearing. And the mostly male panel – the only woman on it was Spitzer's wife, a social worker – advised the female critics in advance that only six of them would be allowed to speak.

At the hearing in November 1985 Spitzer opened by explaining the purpose of revising the *DSM*: to make diagnoses more 'scientific'. Then he revealed the scientific data: a study, which he had directed, of eight patients who were all clients of psychiatrists in his department at Columbia. Only two of the patients were men. The study was supposed to demonstrate that masochism existed because the psychiatrists had 'independently' diagnosed these eight patients as masochists. This was an 'excellent' sample, Spitzer said, because the patients had been observed in analysis over a long period of time. One of the feminist therapists in the audience asked him how many of these eight 'masochistic' patients were battered women or victims of violence. Spitzer couldn't answer: none of the psychiatrists had bothered to find that out – despite having counselled these 'masochists' for a year and a half.

The APA panel's 'data' rolled on, with a historical overview, written by Dr Richard Simons, president of the American Psychoanalytic Association, who argued that masochism must be a legitimate diagnosis because a 1950s European psychiatrist had described a depressive personality disorder 'that had almost identical features'. Simons seemed to believe that psychiatry, like law, was a field where one could rely on precedent alone. Spitzer also had the results of a questionnaire about masochism he had sent to APA members interested in personality disorders. The poll, however, had a rather imposing bias built into it. The first question asked its readers: Do you support including the masochistic disorder in the *DSM*? If the answer was no, they were instructed *not* to fill in the rest of the questionnaire. This method, Spitzer conceded, managed to eliminate half of the people polled.

With the psychoanalysts' data entered into evidence, the six female therapists had a chance to present their side. They argued that the masochistic diagnosis put all the blame on the patients' shoulders, without also taking into account social conditioning and real-life circumstances. Displays of deference and martyrdom are not necessarily evidence of masochism, the female therapists told the panel; they are also the culture's traditional badges of female honour, billed as bringing women social approval and love.

Next, psychological researcher Lenore Walker told the panel how domestic violence often produces the very behavioural traits that the panel had included in its definition of masochism – opening the door to misdiagnosis and mistreatment of female patients and to the opportunity for battering husbands and courts to define the spouses' violence as the wives' problem. In her studies of battered women, Walker had found that the victims often don't strike back – not because they want to be beaten but because they have learned that responding only inflames the batterer. These women often remain with their abuser, too, not because they enjoy torment but because they realistically fear worse violence if they walk out; the majority of murdered battered women are killed by their abusers *after* they leave home. Finally Walker presented her study of hundreds of battered women, which could locate no connection between childhood-developed personality disorders and adulthood battering. The real problem, she told the panel, is simply that violence against women is *so* widespread. As many as 50 per cent of women report being abused at some point in their lives. Clearly not all of them are masochists.

In response, the members of the panel told the women that they had never looked at any of their studies – and they didn't intend to. 'It's irrelevant,' Spitzer says later of all the domestic-violence research presented. He scoffs at the statistics. He says he can recall treating only two abused women in his career, and he doubts that the rate of abuse is 'anywhere near' 50 per cent.

The hearing was supposed to last all day, but at noon Spitzer announced that they had heard enough from the women; in the afternoon the panel would start drafting diagnoses and the women should leave. The female therapists protested and finally they were told they could stay, but only under the condition that they must 'not speak'. This stipulation would be repeated at a subsequent hearing chaired by Fink. Later, Fink (now APA president) explains the reasons for the gag order: 'I didn't think it was worth a whole day's discussion. . . . I controlled the meeting.' He didn't care for the women's rude behaviour either: 'Certain of the women were absolutely unwilling to listen to anything we said or understand anything we were saying. . . . I really felt under attack.'

After the hearing, a flood of critical letters, a formal protest from the American Psychological Association and petitions signed by thousands of mental health practitioners nudged the APA panel to offer this 'compromise': they would change the names of some of the offending diagnoses. 'Masochistic personality disorder' became 'self-defeating personality disorder'; 'premenstrual dysphoric disorder' became 'late luteal-phase dysphoric disorder'; and 'paraphiliac rapism' became 'paraphiliac coercive disorder'. The definitions, however, remained the same.

In December 1985 an ad hoc committee of the APA's board of trustees agreed to a final hearing on the masochism/self-defeating diagnosis. The female therapists again came and protested, and the psychiatrists again dismissed the women after a few hours. Then they sequestered themselves in 'the Freud Room' – and voted in favour of the masochism diagnosis.

That spring, the feminist opponents continued protesting and organizing. But women's efforts only seemed to stiffen the male panellists' resolve. As a senior APA official said later, board members who wanted to throw out the new disorders were accused of 'giving in to the women'. Just before the APA's trustees took a final vote, Dr Teresa Bernardez appeared before them to make a last plea. 'I began to speak and they would not let me continue,' she recalls. 'I had to fight to be heard.' Finally she said her piece, but she suspected her words had barely registered. Her unladylike outspokenness, however, was noted – and later punished. When Bernardez's term on the APA women's committee came up for renewal, she was not invited back. She wasn't the only member of the women's committee to be penalized for speaking out against the new disorders; within a year the APA's women committee had been purged of all the feminists.

In the end, the APA's trustees approved both the masochism and the PMS diagnoses. (The rapism disorder was temporarily shelved, pending further study.) The APA officers made one concession to all the protests over these two diagnoses: they listed both of them in the *DSM*'s appendix – supposedly a section for provisional disorders.

But even this qualification was a ruse. Ordinarily, disorders in the appendix don't have the code numbers that medical insurance companies require for reimbursement. The APA leaves them uncoded purposely – to discourage mental health professionals from applying such controversial diagnoses in their practice. In this case, however, following Dr Spitzer's recommendations, the APA trustees made an exception. They assigned code numbers to both masochism and PMS. The new female ailments were on the books.

Chapter Thirteen

The Wages of the Backlash:
The Toll on Working Women

The backlash against women's rights would be just one of several powerful forces creating a harsh and painful climate for women at work. Reaganomics, Thatcherism, other variants of economic 'rationalism', the recession, and the expansion of a low-paid service economy also helped, in no small measure, to slow and even undermine women's momentum in the job market.

But the backlash did more than impede women's opportunities for employment, promotion and better pay. Its spokesmen kept the news of many of these setbacks from women. Not only did the backlash do grievous damage to working women – it did it on the sly. The Reagan administration downplayed or simply shelved reports that revealed the extent of working women's declining status. Corporations claimed women's numbers and promotions were at record highs. And the press didn't seem to mind. As the situation of working women fell into increasing peril in the 1980s, the backlash media issued ever more upbeat reports – assuring that women's only problem at work was that they would rather be at home.

Many myths about working women's 'improving' circumstances made the rounds in the eighties – while some discouraging and *real* trends that working women faced didn't get much press. Here are just a few examples.

The trend story we all read about women's wages:
PAY GAP BETWEEN THE SEXES CLOSING!

The difference between the average man's and woman's pay cheque, we learned in 1986, had suddenly narrowed. Women who worked full time in the USA were now said to make an unprecedented 70 cents to a man's dollar. Newspaper editorials applauded and advised feminists to retire their 'obsolete' badges protesting that female pay was only 59 cents to a man's dollar.

The trend story we should have seen:

IT'S BACK! THE 1950S PAY GAP

The pay gap in America did *not* suddenly improve to 70 cents in 1986. Women working full time made only 64 cents to a man's dollar that year, actually slightly *worse* than the year before – and exactly the same gap that working women had faced in *1955*.

The press got the 70-cent figure from a one-off Census Bureau report that was actually based on data from another year and that departed from the bureau's standard method for computing the gap. This report artificially inflated women's earnings by using weekly instead of the standard yearly wages – thus grossly exaggerating the salary of part-time workers, a predominantly female group, who don't work a full year. Later, the Census Bureau calculated the pay gap for 1986 using its standard formula and came up with 64 cents. This report, however, managed to elude media notice.

By that year, in fact, the pay gap had only 'improved' for women by less than five percentage points since 1979. And as much as half of that improvement was due to men's falling wages, not women's improving earnings. Take out men's declining pay as a factor and the gap had closed only three percentage points.

By 1988 women with a college diploma could still wear the famous 59-cent badges. They were still making 59 cents to their male counterparts' dollar. In fact, the pay gap for them was now a bit worse than five years earlier. Black women, who had made almost no progress in the decade, could wear the 59-cent badges, too. Older and Hispanic women couldn't – but only because their pay gap was even worse now than 59 cents. Older working women had actually fared better in *1968*, when they had made hourly wages of 61 cents to a man's dollar; by 1986, they were down to 58 cents. And Hispanic women, by 1988, found their wages backsliding; they were now making an abysmal 54 cents to a white man's dollar.

In Britain, according to figures from the Low Pay Unit, the overall pay gap in 1991 stood at £42.44 billion. A fair distribution of pay between men and women would require the transfer of £21.22 billion in earned income from men to women. Full-time women still earn only around 70 per cent of male earnings. Women's average hourly earnings (excluding overtime) as a percentage of men's actually fell in 1987, and the slow rate of increase since then still leaves them at only 78.3 per cent of men's. Between 1979 and 1991 women's average hourly earnings increased by only 5.3 per cent, compared to a 9.1 per cent increase between 1970 and 1979. And the official New Earnings Survey figures do not even include over 3 million people whose pay is below the PAYE threshold – most of whom are women. The Conservative government undermined women's pay still further by gutting the powers of industry-based wages councils, which had guaranteed a structure of minimum rates of pay, as well as overtime and holiday pay, for women in menial occupations from clothing piecework to hairdressing. Three-quarters of the workers under the age of twenty-one who lost the protection of the wages councils were women.

Equal pay legislation was introduced in New Zealand in 1972 and during the implementation period (1972–8) the earnings gap narrowed by six to seven percentage points, from 72.1 to 78.5 per cent. But over the next decade the rate of change slowed dramatically, with a narrowing in the ratio of only about three percentage points. In Australia, where the pay gap is the lowest of any of the Western countries, the signs of the backlash are already ominous. Legislation to remove the centralized wage-fixing system, which favours women, has already been passed in New South Wales and looks likely to be adopted nationally. The pay gap will undoubtedly widen if a system of industry-by-industry bargaining is introduced, and women's wages will fall – undermining the efforts of women's organizations ever since trade unionist Muriel Heagney set up the Council of Action for Equal Pay in 1937.

*

The trend story we all read about integrating the workplace:
WOMEN INVADE MAN'S WORLD!

Women, we learned, charged into traditional 'male' occupations. A sea of women in their dress-for-success suits and stride-to-work trainers abandoned the 'pink-collar' ghettos and descended on Wall Street, law firms and corporate office suites. Still other women laced up army boots, slapped on hard hats, and barged into the all-male military and blue-collar factories.

The trend story we should have seen:
MORE AND MORE, WOMEN STUCK IN SECRETARIAL POOL

While the level of occupational segregation between the sexes in the USA eased by 9 per cent in the 1970s – the first time it had improved in the century – that progress stalled in the 1980s. The Bureau of Labor Statistics soon began projecting a more sex-segregated work force. This was a bitter financial pill for women: as much as 45 per cent of the pay gap is caused by sex segregation. A resegregating work force was one reason why women's wages fell in the eighties; by 1986 more working women would be taking home poverty-level wages than in 1973.

Women were pouring into many low-paid female work ghettos. The already huge proportion of working women holding menial clerical jobs climbed to nearly 40 per cent by the early 1980s, higher than it had been in 1970. By the late 1980s the proportion of women consigned to the traditionally female service industries had grown, too. A long list of traditionally 'female' jobs became *more* female-dominated, including sales assistanting, cleaning services, food preparation, and secretarial, administrative and reception work. In Britain, according to Labour Force Survey figures, women remain segregated in a narrower range of lower-paid, lower-status jobs. The worst-paying occupations for women include hairdressing, bar work, jobs as launderers and dry cleaners, and waitressing – all ghetto areas where women heavily outnumber men. Australia has a highly segregated work force: in 1911 84 per cent of female labour worked in disproportionately female occupations, and by 1985 the figure, at 82 per cent, had barely changed. In New Zealand, too, 80 per cent of working women in 1990 were employed in service industries, particularly community, social and personal services, and the wholesale and retail trade.

In the US, black women, especially, were resegregated into such traditional female jobs as nursing, teaching and secretarial and social work. And the story was the same at the office of the nation's largest employer, the federal government. Between 1976 and 1986 the lowest job rungs in the civil service ladder went from 67 to 71 per cent female. (At the same time at the top of the ladder, the proportion of women in senior executive services had not improved since 1979 – it was still a paltry 8 per cent.)

The breathless reports about droves of female 'careerists' crashing the legal, medical and other élite professions were inflated. In 1988 in the UK, more than nine out of ten appointments made by the Ministry of Defence, the Department of Energy and the Inland Revenue were men. And even though, in the law profession, there are, according to Helena Kennedy QC, 'very able, bright women who could be made judges tomorrow, such QCs as Barbara Mills, Head of the Serious Fraud Office [since appointed Director of Public Prosecutions], Mary Arden in Family Law, criminal lawyers Ann Curnow and Ann Mallalieu, and civil lawyer Barbara Dohmann', none has at the time of writing been appointed to the bench. There are only two female high-court judges out of 83, and only 19 female circuit-court judges out of 426.

Much was made in the media of John Major's backing of Opportunity 2000, Business in the Community's 1991 initiative to employ and promote more women. But speculation that a large number of British companies would now be setting themselves targets for the employment of women was ill-founded. In the end, the *Guardian* reported, only eight companies set themselves numerical targets and the sixty-one who ultimately participated outlined their plans for 'cultural change' rather than opting for a formal commitment to 'equality of opportunity'. Britain seems to remain reluctant to support any legislative action to fight the inequities of the system. Lady Elspeth Howe, former chair of the Equal Opportunities Commission and now chair of Business in the Community, thinks legislation is unnecessary at the moment, believing that the recognition that women are a valuable source of labour will do the trick and trigger companies into action. The figures, however, seem to make this voluntary transformation unlikely. A 1991 survey showed that fewer than 2 per cent of the directors of companies in the FTSE 100 Index of top firms are women – because of multiple directorships this works out at around only *eighteen* women. In 1991, Australia's 100 biggest publicly listed companies had only three women in their lists of directors. And in New Zealand in 1990 women comprised just 3 per cent of all directors in the country's top twenty companies.

In the few cases where working women did make substantial inroads into male enclaves, they were only admitted by default. As a job-integration study by sociologist Barbara Reskin found, in the dozen occupations where women had made the most progress entering 'male' jobs in the USA – a list that ranged from typesetting to insurance adjustment to pharmaceuticals – women succeeded only because the pay and status of these jobs had fallen dramatically and men were bailing out. Computerization, for example, had demoted male typesetters to typists; the retail chaining of drugstores had turned independent pharmacists into poorly paid clerks. Other studies of women's 'progress' in bank management found that women were largely just inheriting branch-manager jobs that men didn't want any more because their pay, power and status had declined dramatically. And still another analysis of occupational shifts concluded that one-third of the growth of female employment in transportation and half of the growth in financial services could be attributed simply to a loss of status in the jobs that women were getting in these two professions.

In many of the higher-paying white-collar occupations, where women's successes have been most heavily publicized, the rate of progress slowed to a trickle or stopped altogether by the end of the decade. The proportion of women in some of the more élite or glamorous fields actually shrank slightly in the last half of the 1980s. Professional athletes, screenwriters, commercial voice-overs, producers and musicians in orchestras, economists, geologists, biological and life scientists were all a little *less* likely to be female by the late 1980s than earlier in the decade.

Under Reagan, women's progress in the US military soon came under fire. In the mid-1970s, after quota ceilings on female recruits had been lifted and combat classifications rewritten to open more jobs to women, women's ranks in the armed services had soared – by 800 per cent by 1980. But shortly after Reagan's election, the new army chief of staff declared, 'I have called a pause to further increases in the number of army women' – and by 1982 the army had revised combat classifications to bar women from an additional twenty-three career occupations. All the services reined in their recruitment efforts, subsequently slowing female employment growth in the military throughout the 1980s.

The blue-collar working world offered no better news. After 1983, as a Labor Department study quietly reported to no fanfare, women made *no* progress breaking into the blue-collar work force with its better salaries. By 1988 the tiny proportions of women who had squeezed into the trades were shrinking in a long list of job categories from electricians and plumbers to mechanics and machine operators.

The trend story we all read about equal opportunity:
DISCRIMINATION ON THE JOB: FADING FAST!
Corporations, we read, were now welcoming women. 'Virtually all large employers are now on [women's] side,' *Working Woman* assured female readers in 1986. Discrimination was dropping, mistreatment of female workers was on the wane – and any reports to the contrary were just 'propaganda from self-interested parties', as *Forbes* asserted in 1989 – in its story on the 'decline' of sexual harassment on the job.

The trend story we should have seen:
NOW MORE THAN EVER! INEQUITY AND INTIMIDATION
The well-publicized Anita Hill/Judge Clarence Thomas case elicited an enormous response worldwide from women who had until then kept silent about harassment they had suffered at work. Even before Hill's testimony, reports of sex discrimination and sexual harassment in the USA had reached record highs in the decade – by both private and federal employees. Women's sex discrimination complaints to the Equal Employment Opportunity Commission climbed by nearly 25 per cent in the Reagan years – and by 40 per cent among federally employed women just in the first half of the 1980s. Complaints of exclusion, demotions, and discharges on the basis of sex rose 30 per cent. General harassment of women, excluding sexual harassment, more than doubled. And while the EEOC's public relations office issued statements claim-

ing that sexual harassment in corporate America was falling, its own figures showed that annual charges of sexual harassment nearly doubled between 1981 and 1989.

Australia's Sex Discrimination Commissioner, Quentin Bryce, reported in 1990 that she had been concerned for some time about the increasing numbers of complaints about sexual harassment in the workplace – not all of which had been the subject of formal proceedings at the Human Rights and Equal Opportunity Commission. Complaints lodged in Australia under the Sex Discrimination Act have risen each year, particularly regarding discrimination on the ground of pregnancy (13.9 per cent of all complaints in 1989–90, compared with only 9 per cent the year before). Case studies, Bryce says, 'show that discrimination on the grounds of sex is alive and well. Women continue to be denied access to a full range of occupations and continue to encounter sexual harassment in the workplace. And indeed there are still some situations where women are denied the right to work at all.'

In Britain, as journalist Angela Phillips has pointed out, it is not possible for a whole group to act together, nor is it possible for the Equal Opportunities Commission to start legal proceedings against a company, even if it is clear that their pay system is discriminatory. It is up to an individual woman to take action against her employer. 'Most of the cases so far taken under the legislation have been test cases. Many go on for years and applicants need stamina, support and resources to attempt a challenge. Not surprisingly, few stay the course.' Frank Spencer, deputy director of the EOC's Pay Policy Unit, would like to see a single Equal Treatment Act which would allow organizations such as trade unions to take action on behalf of their members.

The 'equal pay for work of equal value' amendment to the Equal Pay Act that the British government was forced to adopt by the European Court will be even harder to enforce. Individual women must be able to describe in detail the job of a named individual man with whom she claims equality. Angela Phillips reported in December 1991: 'Comparing one group of workers with another can run into incredible legal barriers if employers decide to resist. Lloyds Bank are fighting tooth and nail against a judgement that it is unreasonable to pay typists £4,500 less per year than messengers.' But even with all the discouragements to women that the system offers, the number of cases brought to industrial tribunals in Britain on the grounds of sex discrimination leapt from 691 in 1987–8 to 935 in 1988–9, and rose again in 1989–90 to 1,046.

If Americans heard less about discrimination in the 1980s workplace, that was partly because the federal government had muzzled, or fired, its equal employment investigators. At the same time that the EEOC's sex discrimination files were overflowing, the Reagan administration was cutting the agency's budget in half and jettisoning its caseload. The year Reagan came to office, the EEOC had twenty-five active class-action cases; a year later, it had none. The agency cut back the number of suits it pursued by more than 300 per cent. A House Education and Labor Committee report found that in the first half of the 1980s the number of discrimination victims receiving compensation fell by two-thirds. By 1987, a General Accounting Office study found that EEOC district offices and state equal employment agencies were closing 40 to 80 per cent of their cases without proper, or any, investigation.

An exhaustive study of women's occupational patterns in the 1980s would be outside the scope of this book. But it is possible to tell the stories of some women in key representative employment areas – from the white-collar media to the pink-collar sales force to the most embattled blue-collar universe. These are women who, one way or another, set themselves against the backlash in the work force and, in the process, ran up against the barriers built by employers, male peers, judges, government officials, and even 'feminist' scholars. They had to face ridicule, ostracism, threats, and even physical assaults – as they simply tried to make a living.

Women in the Media

Women's employment in the press and broadcasting is worth special attention because of the media's central role in propagating the myths of the backlash. If newspapers, magazines and television stations had managements and staffs that more nearly reflected the proportion of women in the general population – or, for that matter, in their audiences – maybe they would have reported all the backlash trends of the 1980s exactly the same way. But maybe, just maybe, they would have told a different story.

In the early 1970s, US federal legislation enacted under intense lobbying efforts by the National Organization for Women culminated in the Equal Employment Opportunity Act of 1972. This Act first cleared the way for women to enter broadcasting and print journalism in significant numbers. As a result, a group of women who were to become the most prominent female newscasters of their generation joined the networks around the same time. Under the Carter administration, women's numbers in broadcasting and print continued to rise because of the Federal Communications Commission's strict enforcement of positive discrimination and the many legal actions taken by female journalists themselves. This litigation led to a series of court-supervised 'consent decrees' that required news employers to take steps to recruit and promote women and equalize wages.

But Reagan's new FCC commissioner, Mark Fowler, like so many Reagan appointees, sought to abolish his agency's own regulations. Under his tenure, the FCC severely cut back on the information it compiled on women and minority employees, making it virtually impossible to document discrimination in class-action suits. And the information the FCC did still make available was misleading, often ludicrously so. 'Eighty per cent of TV employees can't all be decision-makers,' a five-year study of the broadcasting industry's hiring practices wryly observed of a particularly absurd case of statistic-doctoring.

With government pressure gone, the little progress that women had made at the networks began unravelling. The networks took a string of 'ageing' women anchors and put them out to pasture, replacing them with either much older men or much younger – and much less well paid – women. In 1989, at the ripe old age of thirty-nine, the popular Jane Pauley was pushed out of her co-anchor slot on the *Today* show, in a very public and humiliating campaign, and replaced by the younger and blonder Deborah Norville (who was later sacked and replaced by another youthful model, Katie Couric, at half her salary). This wasn't a decision made with viewers in mind: Pauley's ratings were much higher than those of her male co-host, Bryant Gumbel, and her expulsion caused the show to torpedo to the very bottom of the morning ratings, even below the cartoons. At CBS, Kathleen Sullivan was yanked from the morning news show to make way for the younger and blonder Paula Zahn, whom the network's male brass deemed both a more comely and upstanding model of true womanhood than the divorced Sullivan. 'Paula's married with a child; Kathleen is a single woman' was how CBS executive producer Erik Sorenson explained it to the press. 'You get some differences in how settled a person feels.' (Ironically, Sullivan was the same anchor who had so gamely hosted the network's patronizing series on the psychic ills of single women a few years earlier.) By 1983, the number of female anchors was falling at commercial TV stations nationwide, a national survey by the Radio-Television News Directors Association reported. By 1989 only eight women were among the one hundred most frequently seen correspondents – down from fifteen just a year earlier.

In the UK, female newsreaders and reporters have made an impact, and often 'front' news bulletins. But according to Gillian Dyer, co-editor of *Boxed In: Women and Television*, news and current affairs are still the preserve of men, on and off the screen. *Skill Search*, a 1989 Institute of Manpower Studies report, disclosed that 74 per cent of broadcast employees were male, and in some key grades, such as camera, sound and light, more than 86 per cent were men. Overall, 73 per cent of freelance producers, directors and producer-directors as a group were male. Although women make up a third of all television journalists, only 13 per cent of editors and 8 per cent of correspondents are female. European Commission research across the EC shows that three out of five women who work in television hold secretarial or clerical jobs. Despite initiatives like JOBFIT, which has a 50 per cent female intake on its training scheme, fewer than one in ten senior production staff is a woman. And all but a tiny minority of policy-making posts are held by men. Margaret Gallagher, coordinator of the EC's steering committee for equal opportunities in broadcasting, believes: 'The last ten years have seen very little change in employment patterns in the industry. With all the other changes taking place in television this decade has not been the most auspicious period for pushing ahead with equal opportunities.'

The *Today* newspaper reported in October 1990 that out of 28,000 employees at the BBC, 11,500 were female but 'the Director-General Michael Checkland admits the vast majority of these women are clerical and cleaning staff'. Only one woman, Jane Drabble, has been appointed to senior management to date, despite the BBC's announcement of gender targets for 1996, designed to raise the number of women in senior management from 10 per cent to 30 per cent, and in middle management from 18 per cent to 40 per cent. The outlook in the commercial sector is no less bleak, despite Section 38 of the Broadcasting Act which required bidders for the ITV franchises to 'make arrangements for promoting . . . equality of opportunity between men and women'. A very small number of applicants committed themselves to setting equal opportunities targets; and even those that did, like Sunrise, one of the successful newcomers, seem to have a different approach when it comes to applying the policy to programme content. *Broadcast* magazine reported that after 9 a.m., when its audience is predominantly female, Sunrise proposes to 're-define news values', giving as examples of lead stories for the new audience, 'the campaign to raise money for a small child's vital operation, a dangerous toy, or the value of the Duchess of York's new diet'. Carlton, which succeeds Thames TV, does not mention employment targets at all, and only says that independents will be 'encouraged within their resources' to pursue equal opportunities policies. Overall, in the twenty-two terrestrial TV companies operating in Britain, ony one-twelfth of all board members are female.

Meanwhile at major newspapers in the US, the court-negotiated decrees won by women which obliged employers to recruit and promote female journalists were running out by the mid-1980s and the media corporation's enthusiasm for equal opportunity expired with them. Progress in improving newsrooms' sex ratios stalled after 1982, a survey conducted by Ohio State University researchers found. At the *Washington Post*, a guild study finds, the pay gap between the sexes worsened after 1985 – the final effective year of the *Post*'s conciliation agreement to settle a sex-discrimination suit. By 1987, Newspaper Guild records show, white women at the *Post* were making an average of $204 less a week than men, and the gap for black female reporters had doubled in five years. While the *New York Times*'s consent decree was in effect, the wage gap at the paper had slowly improved – and, again, once the decree expired, the gap quickly began to widen once more. By 1989 women's representation in the *New York Times* newsroom hadn't improved much either. The total number of women employed as reporters, critics and correspondents was fifty-four, only fourteen more than in 1972. The *New York Times* sports department had no female reporters in 1972; in 1989, it had one.

After 1982, newspaper managements' efforts to promote women to top newspaper posts fell off, too. After having reached a 'high' of 2 per cent in 1982, the annual gain women made in becoming directing editors slipped to 0.5 per cent by 1984, and barely improved for the rest of the decade. Nearly 90 per cent of directing editor jobs were held by men. By the late 1980s, 76 per cent of newspaper dailies had no female associate editors, executive editors, managing editors, editors, editorial chiefs, or any women in variations of these job titles, according to a national survey conducted for the American Society of Newspaper Editors. Despite this pathetic record, at an ASNE panel on women's status in 1988 *Washington Post* executive editor Ben Bradlee pronounced from the podium that women's presence in media management has 'changed radically in the last ten years'.

The problem wasn't on the supply end. Women's desire to enter media jobs was at an all-time high. The numbers of women entering journalism schools climbed steeply, and throughout the decade two-thirds of all journalism school graduates were women. A 1989 ASNE survey found these female journalists had even higher grades and expressed more ambition than their male colleagues. Yet in this same period newsrooms remained 65 per cent male and continued to hire far more men than women. At large daily papers, women made up less than a third of the staff. In fact, women were only in the majority at small suburban papers with substandard pay.

Remarkably, at the same time that women's status in journalism was being eroded on almost every front, complaints began surfacing in newsrooms and broadcasting crews that the field now had 'too many women'. However, the real problem for media men was that there were too few jobs. Corporate mergers, falling ad lineage, declining circulation, collapsing afternoon newspapers and a shrinking market share for network news – all of these forces helped to cut into employment in print journalism and, at the networks, to provoke mass layoffs in the 1980s, layoffs that, despite male complaints, hurt women more than men.

Under the economically contracting, backlash-influenced climate of 1980s newsrooms, female journalists started backing away from the more aggressive tactics that a previous generation of women had exercised to claim their rights. Dangled instructively before this younger generation of women were the fates of former female activists at their companies. At NBC, two female producers who had played key roles in a sex-discrimination suit against the network were forced out and replaced by inexperienced young white men – at the same salary. At the *New York Times*, all the named plaintiffs in the sex-discrimination suit suffered major career setbacks, and most had to leave the paper. These stories did not inspire those who remained to stage a repeat performance. 'There's apparently a smell of cordite that we give off that terrifies the younger women,' observed Betsy Wade, a central figure in the *New York Times* suit, who was herself shunted to late-night duty.

Not surprisingly, women became increasingly reluctant to fight discrimination collectively the way they had in the seventies. At a meeting in 1986 of the Journalists' Trade Group of the National Writers Union, a journalist reviewed the erosion of women's progress in the media and proposed forming a women's caucus. As she wrote later: 'The group's response was informative, if depressingly predictable. Every woman who spoke after me agreed with my assessment of the situation, and each had a story of sexist treatment to tell. At the same time, every woman in the group made a point of saying that she was not a feminist and was not interested in forming a women's caucus.'

Two efforts to organize women in the 1980s, at NBC and ABC, were hastily abandoned in the face of management resistance. At

NBC, women organized a grievance committee and began to talk about launching a legal challenge. Soon afterwards, in September 1984, the network announced a new round of staff cuts that hit women hardest; when NBC handed out pink slips to employees in its news documentary unit, for example, nine of the ten fired were women. The grievance committee quickly disavowed any litigious intentions and began referring to its gatherings as mere 'support' sessions. After a while, the obsequious nature of the group became so obvious that the members themselves began to joke bleakly about their 'Ladies Sewing Circle'.

In the mid-1980s ABC was most notorious in the industry for its poor showing on women's employment. It had the worst record of the networks in hiring and promoting women; by 1986 it had no female executive producers and only one female bureau chief. Women that year had reported only 12 per cent of the evening news spots. The network also boasted a 30 per cent pay gap and several egregious cases of sexual harassment.

In 1983 Rita Flynn arrived at ABC's Washington bureau, a seasoned newswoman from CBS with ten years of broadcasting experience. But her new employer, she recalls, treated her and the other female broadcasters like cub reporters, begrudging them serious assignments and airtime. After a while she began to feel as if she had tumbled into 'a time warp'. It felt, she says, 'like 1969 all over again'.

Finally, the women in the bureau met for dinner one night to discuss the problem. 'None of us could ever get on prime time so it was no problem getting together,' Flynn observes wryly. When the women compared stories, they realized they had the makings of a discrimination lawsuit. They started collecting network statistics on women's employment and pay. Flynn had a meeting with a labour lawyer.

A decade ago such rumblings would have prompted management to offer a settlement to fend off damaging and embarrassing legal action. But in the present environment, corporate executives were more inclined to dig in their heels. It took months of appeals from the women just to get a brief hearing with ABC News president Roone Arledge. At the session, they presented their numbers and grievances; the executives disputed them, and the meeting was over. ABC management made only one concession: promoting one woman, a company loyalist, to vice-president of public relations. As company cheerleader in this traditional female job, she served the network's, not the women's, cause, by defending the network's treatment of women to the press.

Then discouragement came from another quarter of ABC, as the treatment of one woman served as a bitterly instructive lesson for many others. Cecily Coleman, the executive director of ABC's Advisory Committee on Voter Education, had filed a confidential complaint of sex harassment against James Abernathy, vice-president for corporate affairs. Coleman said that he had repeatedly harassed her – cornering her in his office to grab and fondle her, trying to force his way into her hotel room on business trips and implying that she would lose her job if she didn't succumb to his advances. Instead of investigating her complaint, the network fired her at once – while she was away on a business trip – then rifled through her office.

As a woman on the committee said later, its members 'backed off fast' after Cecily Coleman's firing. 'It was like someone threw a snake in a barnful of horses and everybody jumped.' The number of committee members dropped to half a dozen and the group dropped its demands. Soon the committee's spokeswoman was describing its grievances as 'challenges rather than problems'.

Rita Flynn, one of the most outspoken committee members, found her career suddenly on the skids. First she was shifted to weekend hours – and told it was a 'promotion'. Then she was shunted from the White House beat to 'the parade route'. Soon she was no longer invited to the bureau's social functions and was ostracized by nervous colleagues. Because she had been the one to consult discrimination lawyers and speak to the press, 'I was seen as the real bad gal.'

After a while, the experience wore her down. When Flynn's husband was offered a job at a Portland, Oregon, newspaper, she left ABC and moved with him, confident she could find a job in the more enlightened West. When she arrived in Oregon, however, she found that her reputation had preceded her. The general manager at one of the network affiliates there told her that he had heard she was 'a big-time feminist troublemaker'. No TV station in Oregon would touch her. After Flynn's husband left her, she ended up working at a bank and taking freelance jobs in public relations to support herself.

In the end, she came away from the experience with only one conclusion: 'I'm more convinced than ever that it's a man's world.'

The Sears Case

Most working women, of course, aren't fortunate enough to land a job in a middle-class profession like journalism. This was even more true in the 1980s, when real job growth was occurring in the lowest levels of the service sector. While 146,000 American women were editors and reporters by the end of the decade, 4.2 million were sales assistants, the lowest paid of all the major occupations.

American saleswomen suffer the largest pay gap of women in any field (51 to 53 cents to a man's dollar in the last decade) and they earn less than men in any other occupation, including labourers. The average female sales assistant earns $226 a week; her male counterpart makes $431. In retail, that's largely because the average department store is still set up like the traditional family household, with the women dusting the cosmetics counters and straightening the dress racks in the minimum-wage 'ladies' departments, while the men adjust television sets and manoeuvre hot-water heaters in the 'big-ticket' departments – and clock up big commissions on these sales. The result: women selling clothing (and about 83 per cent are women) get an average wage of about $170 a week; men selling cars and boats (and about 93 per cent are men) earn about $400.

In 1973, the Equal Employment Opportunities Commission began investigating such employment practices at Sears, Roebuck & Company. The Commission had received hundreds of sex-discrimination complaints about the giant retailer, the nation's largest private employer of women. And EEOC investigators had found evidence of major disparities between the sexes at Sears in pay, recruitment and promotion. The average salesman on commission at Sears in his first year on the job, the EEOC estimated, was earning twice as much as the average 'non-commission' female saleswoman, no matter how many years she had worked for the retailer. The agency calculated that about 60 per cent of Sears's job applicants were women and at least 40 per cent of the applicants who met all the requirements for commission sales were women. Yet, in the five years before the EEOC launched its investigation, less than 10 per cent of the high-paying commission sales jobs had gone to women each year.

By the end of the 1970s the EEOC had negotiated multimillion-dollar settlements from every other corporate defendant it had targeted through class-action litigation. In 1973, for example, AT&T paid $50 million in settlement fees and, after claiming for years that it could find no women interested in technical work, it met 90 per cent of its hiring goals within a year, quickly signing on 10,000 women to climb telephone poles, crawl into cable tunnels, and install equipment. In the next ten years, behemoth corporations from General Electric to General Motors hastened to negotiate with the EEOC, and each eventually shelled out tens of millions of dollars for compensation, back pay and training programmes rather than face what they feared would be much higher costs in the courts.

The Sears suit, however, would take a different course. The EEOC and women's rights organizations had hoped it might extend the gains women were making in other fields to the vast retail sales force. But the Sears case came in last to bat; the EEOC filed suit in 1979, and as the national climate shifted and the leadership in Washington changed, the case's prospects dimmed. Seeing no need to settle in such an environment, Sears vowed to fight the government in the courtroom. In 1986, the company won – with help from a judge who had trouble believing that any working woman had ever faced discrimination, from a women's history scholar who provided 'evidence' that women just preferred lower-paying jobs, and from the government itself.

In court, Sears's defence was largely based on portraying the typical saleswoman as a shrinking violet – a timid and dependent homebody who works for pin money and doesn't like to muss her skirts. Women, as Sears's attorneys repeatedly and euphemistically put it, simply had different 'interests' from men; they just weren't interested in higher-paying, more 'demanding' jobs. This in-court argument wasn't exactly in accordance with the in-store developments that followed news of the EEOC's investigation. As soon as Sears found out that it was the subject of an EEOC probe, the retailer's personnel office had managed to find plenty of interested women in a hurry – enough to double the proportion of women in commission sales by the following year, and even triple and quadruple the ranks of women in such 'male' departments as car parts, plumbing, heating and fencing.

Nonetheless, during the ten-month trial of 1984–5, Sears stuck to its 'interest' argument about women. A Sears personnel manager named, aptly enough, Rex Rambo explained to the court that saleswomen were 'more interested in the idea of dressing up the home and that sort of thing'. Women wouldn't want to sell tyres because they might have to go out 'if it's snowing or raining or whatever it is'. They wouldn't want to sell household equipment because women 'did not like the idea of going into strangers' homes'. Sears salesman Ed Michaels testified that women couldn't cope with selling fences: 'It does require walking through the yards,' he said. 'You have to have boots with you.' And Ray Graham, Sears's director of equal opportunity, offered only this piece of evidence to support his theory that women recoiled from big-ticket sales work: when he was a store manager back in 1965, he recalled, he once assigned three women to sell kitchen stoves; two left within months and one asked for a transfer. Under cross-examination, he admitted there might be another reason for the women's dissatisfaction: at the time, employees of both sexes considered the stoves division one of the least desirable assignments.

The company's hiring procedures codified the idea that only the manliest could stomach what one Sears witness called the 'rough and tumble' of commission sales. All applicants for commission jobs at Sears had to take a 'vigour' test that asked questions like: 'Do you have a low-pitched voice?' 'Have you played on a football team?' 'Have you ever done any hunting?' 'Do you swear often?' Though Sears told the court that by the 1970s it no longer paid much attention to the test results, the company continued to administer the exam – even after an in-house study actually linked higher 'vigour' scores with poorer salesmanship.

To make its case that women were simply uninterested in commission jobs, Sears needed an expert with more credibility and less partiality than its own managers. The company found a key witness in Rosalind Rosenberg, a women's history professor at Barnard College. And she came with a big bonus: she was a feminist. Rosenberg might have seemed an odd choice. Her 1982 book, *Beyond Separate Spheres: Intellectual Roots of Modern Feminism*, focused on the success of feminist social scientists in the early 1900s in challenging the late-Victorian view of sex differences as iron-clad and biologically determined. One might assume that she would make a similar argument about the sex roles assigned to modern-day saleswomen. But in Rosenberg's testimony for Sears, the scholar argued that the tiny number of women in commission sales reflected only 'the natural effect' of women's special 'differences'. To regard these natural disparities as evidence of sex bias at Sears, she told the court, was 'naïve'.

A lot of saleswomen simply prefer low-paying sales jobs, Rosenberg maintained. They tend to be less competitive than men, she said, and less eager to work full-time or night and weekend shifts, which could interfere with their child-rearing duties. These were, of course, the same arguments as Rex Rambo's, but Rosenberg delivered them in loftier lingo. 'Many women choose jobs that complement their family obligations over jobs that might increase and enhance their earning potential,' was how Rosenberg put it. Or, women 'are less likely to make the same educational investments as men'.

Rosenberg didn't explain what 'educational investments' are necessary to sell Sears sofas. Nor did her theory that women would rather not work at evenings and weekends make sense: Sears's 'non-commission' sales assistants have no choice but to work evenings and weekends, too, and some lower-income working mothers who can't afford high-priced childcare prefer such shifts anyway, because their husbands are more likely to be at home to look after the children. Finally, by arguing that saleswomen prefer part-time work, Rosenberg assumed that they don't bear major responsibility for supporting their households. But at

Sears, a 1982 survey found that almost a third of the saleswomen were married to unemployed husbands, another 25 per cent had husbands who earned less than $15,000 a year, and 75 per cent had husbands who made less than $25,000 a year.

Rosenberg was initially drawn into the Sear case for personal reasons; she was friendly with Sears's chief defence lawyer, Charles Morgan, Jr, employer of her former husband. But when Morgan first asked her to testify, she was reluctant. 'My gut personal feeling was EEOC were the good guys and private employers weren't,' she recalls. 'I suggested some other names.' Besides, as she told Morgan at the time, labour history wasn't even her field. But when the labour historians that Sears approached refused to testify, Morgan asked her again, and this time she consented.

Rosenberg says that in part she decided to testify after hearing of the EEOC's plan to rely on statistical evidence – which she maintains is insufficient to prove discrimination. But the scholar also says her decision to participate was influenced by the new relational feminist scholarship that had emerged on women's 'difference'. These academic ideas, she says, inspired her to rethink her attitudes about feminism and to regard the demand for simple gender equality in a new light – as 'old seventies feminism' and 'simpleminded androgyny'.

In forming her opinions on this case, Rosenberg didn't conduct any independent research. She didn't talk to any actual saleswomen or interview any female employees at Sears: 'I just pretty much relied on what [the Sears legal team] gave me.' To help the Sears lawyers, she culled evidence from other scholars' books, evidence that she said showed that women traditionally prefer 'different', more female types of job. She handed over this material to the Sears lawyers. They wrote her court statement for her, she says – then handed her the completed brief to sign.

In her historical survey Rosenberg relied on the texts of several labour scholars, most extensively the writings of Alice Kessler-Harris, a feminist labour historian at Hofstra University and author of *Out to Work: A History of Wage-Earning Women in the United States*, a historical study of wage-earning women. When the EEOC lawyers received a copy of the written testimony, they passed it on to Kessler-Harris for her comments. She read it, with increasing disbelief. 'This is not an argument that any reasonable historian would make,' Kessler-Harris recalls thinking at the time. She was sure Rosenberg wouldn't actually testify to it. Moreover, she felt that Rosenberg's statement had misrepresented her work. When Rosenberg did proceed to court, Kessler-Harris agreed to testify for the EEOC to correct the record on her own writings.

In court, Kessler-Harris pointed out where Rosenberg had twisted the meaning of her work, mostly through the creative use of ellipses. For example, Rosenberg had quoted Kessler-Harris as saying that women left industrial jobs in droves after the Second World War – as historical evidence that women have 'chosen' not to hold traditional male jobs. But she skipped over the part where Kessler-Harris said that women hadn't willingly abandoned their posts, but had been forced out to make way for returning soldiers. Evidence came out in court that Rosenberg appeared to have taken similar liberties with the work of at least one other scholar. One of the distortions, of Phyllis Wallace's study of the AT&T case, was so egregious that when she was challenged in court Rosenberg retracted it and asked that it be expunged from the record. 'It was a mistake,' she says now, made in the rush of compiling her evidence for Sears.

If claiming support from feminist scholars was one cornerstone of the Sears defence, hunting down feminist infiltration of the EEOC was the other. It was here that the backlash mentality surfaced most blatantly, as Sears attorney Charles Morgan twice tried to have the suit dismissed on the grounds that he had heard that some of the EEOC's employees were members of women's rights groups. Throughout the litigation, Morgan and his legal team harped on this 'conflict of interest', embarking on a kind of feminist witch-hunt that became increasingly extravagant in its accusations and its rhetoric. With words that could have been lifted from a Jerry Falwell tract, the Sears attorneys charged that the National Organization for Women and other women's groups had created 'a female underground within the EEOC' that had orchestrated the 'usurpation' of the agency and was now plotting to 'injure' Sears. In other words, the company's attorney held,

Sears wasn't hurting women's rights; advocates of women's rights were hurting Sears. 'There was no victim here except one,' Charles Morgan proclaimed in court, 'and that one victim is Sears, Roebuck and Company.'

Eager to support their claim of a feminist invasion, the Sears attorneys hauled in dozens of EEOC employees for depositions and demanded lists of EEOC colleagues who were members of women's rights groups or who had so much as 'communicated' with any of twenty-six women's organizations or thirty-nine feminist leaders. An elderly saleswoman, who was suing Sears independently, was called before the Sears inquisitors. Isn't it true, they demanded, that her daughter was a member of a group called Stewardesses for Women's Rights? The Sears defence even grilled one EEOC employee for having capitalized the word 'now' in a memo. Perhaps, the lawyers insinuated, the adverb was a covert reference to the women's organization.

The NOW connection proved almost entirely insubstantial. When Sears's lawyers demanded that Isabelle Capello, the EEOC assistant counsel who had originally proposed the Sears suit, reveal her links with feminist groups, it turned out she had none. The whole fishing expedition netted only one potential conflict of interest: David Copus, former acting director of the EEOC's National Programs Division, had served on the board of NOW's Legal and Education Defense Fund for less than a year. The question was murky, since Copus played no role in the EEOC's decision to file the Sears suit and, at the EEOC chairman's request, had stepped down from the NOW board a decade before the case came to trial. The Sears legal team tried to discredit Copus anyway, by raising questions about his relationship with a NOW activist. Sears even submitted deposition testimony that the couple had been observed 'walking in the halls . . . together'.

Finally, the presiding judge called a halt to Sears's inquisition. But if Morgan hadn't proved any of his charges, they nonetheless lingered to affect the case's outcome. The trial judge and the appeals court judges who reviewed the case all accepted the 'conflict of interest' allegation as valid; although they didn't consider it grounds to dismiss the suit, they took it seriously, chastising

the EEOC and devoting extensive space to the 'female underground' threat in their written decisions.

In the end, these legal manoeuvrings would be almost irrelevant
to the outcome of the case. The simple fact was that the government itself had changed sides. Far from desiring to prosecute Sears,
the EEOC leadership that came in with the Reagan administration
was desperate to back out; they tried twice to settle with Sears,
mid-trial, without demanding any fines or back-pay compensation. A high-ranking Justice Department official described the
Sears suit to the press as a 'straw man we would like to have beaten
to death to prevent future class-action cases'. EEOC chairman and
Reagan appointee Clarence Thomas told the *Washington Post* in
1985, as his own litigators were arguing the case in court, 'I've
been trying to get out of this since I've been here.' Thomas maintained that all the pay, hiring and promotional inequities in the
Sears docket could easily be explained by such factors as education
and, curiously, commuting patterns. Thomas was, in fact, so outspoken that the Sears lawyers at one point even considered calling
him as their own witness.

As it turned out, the trial judge, Reagan-appointee John A.
Nordberg, didn't stand far from Thomas on the issues in the Sears
case. At one point in the trial Nordberg actually demanded that
EEOC attorneys demonstrate that American women had ever
faced employment discrimination; he was sceptical. 'It was very
bizarre,' Karen Baker, one of the three EEOC attorneys on the
case, recalls. 'We actually had to go through and explain the
history to him.'

Nordberg's decision, which was upheld on appeal, threw out
the EEOC case. The judge agreed with Sears that the jobs women
naturally 'prefer' happen to be lower-paying ones. His vision of
the squeamish Sears saleswoman was close to Rex Rambo's. If
women weren't working in men's clothing departments, he opined
in his decision, it was probably 'because it sometimes involved
taking personal measurements of men'.

The EEOC drew the most criticism, from Nordberg and also
from the press, for relying on statistics alone. Where were the
actual victims? the media demanded. The EEOC attorneys said
they stuck to the numbers because in the past they found that

THE WAGES OF THE BACKLASH

putting individual women on the stand just sidetracked the case into debates about personal character. But in criticizing the EEOC for this omission, the press overlooked a crucial fact of the Sears trial: the EEOC *did* put women on the stand.

During the trial, Sears attorneys kept alluding to the vast numbers of female job applicants who weren't interested in commission sales work. The EEOC attorneys pressed them to produce some names from this reputedly voluminous list. After much stalling, Sears offered only three. Through social security records, the EEOC's attorneys were able to track down two of them and both agreed to testify – for the EEOC.

'I was after commission work,' Lura Lee Nader recalls a few years after her Sears testimony. A soft-spoken woman nearing sixty, she nurses a cup of tea in a Columbus, Ohio, coffee shop by her home. 'I don't really like office work.' Nader had been working for years before she applied to Sears. In 1965, when she was pregnant with her fifth child, her husband fell off a ladder and died. The very first job Nader took as a widow was making curtains on commission. The only aspect of the job she disliked: it involved working at home. As she told the court later, 'I needed to get out into the world, where there were adults to talk to.' So she went to work as a supermarket meat buyer; to supplement her income, she took a second evening job selling jewellery – on straight commission. She liked it and soon started to work full-time. Later, she switched to cosmetics, also on commission; she spent half her job on the road. Then she applied to Sears 'because of the volume of sales you could do' at a big retailer. When she did not get the job, she went to work for a spectacles firm, again on commission.

Nader was hardly the helpless damsel that Sears officials had described as the store's typical female applicant. A national roller-skating champion, she also built the garage for her house, installed the shingles on her roof and repaired her own car. And throughout her life she was the sole provider for her five children. Alice Howland, the other woman who took the stand, was also a sole provider when she applied to Sears. Years earlier in the 1950s, this straight-A student had given up college – she 'panicked', she recalls, after a sociology teacher told the class, 'Women who don't get married by the time they are twenty-five are old maids' – and married a man she met in a car park. At first she had stayed at home because her husband, a department-store salesman, told her, 'No wife of mine is going to work.' But when he fell behind on the mortgage payments he allowed her to accept a job as a translator. (A Second World War refugee who fled Russia as a little girl, Howland spoke several languages.) The longer she worked, the less he liked it. In 1971, they divorced. He never paid any child support. So Howland brought up their five children by herself.

After the divorce, she took a tough commission job with the US Chamber of Commerce: straight commission, cold-call, door-to-door sales of chamber memberships. There was no product to sell, only a subscription to the chamber newsletter. She was on the road for weeks at a time. 'I was out all hours because some people you couldn't reach except evenings,' she remembers. 'I called on dairy farmers out in the country. I would be out in the winter with the wind blowing, the snow all around my ankles. I'd walk into dirty machine shops; sometimes the men would yell lewd things.' But she remained unfazed. 'I'd just try to stay as professional as I could. I just kept going. I don't give up very easily.' Each subscription was $40, from which she took a 50 per cent commission. In her first six months she made $10,000, a company record. She held the job for three years.

When Howland applied to Sears, she marked on the form that she preferred full-time work. By then she had remarried and, with the children from her new husband's first marriage, they now had ten mouths to feed. She, too, was hoping for commission work. 'I like the idea of my income depending on the amount I choose to put out.' She wanted a job selling appliances. 'I find selling women's clothing boring, and you can't make as much money.' When Sears turned her down, she took her first and last 'woman's' job, as an office clerk. She hated it. 'My boss would say, "If my coffee cup needs cleaning, I will put it on this side of the desk; if my pencils need sharpening, I will put them in the outbox." I don't like that in an office you are dependent on someone to say, "OK, you are doing a good job, I guess you can have a ten-cent raise."' In 1982 she left the office job and she and her husband purchased a run-down marina in Erie, Pennsylvania. He was still working full time at AT&T, so she managed the marina's operations, supervised the mechanics, and sold the 42-foot boats, motor parts and bilge pumps.

'For Sears to say that I wasn't interested in commission sales, it was just so—' Howland stops, speechless. She looks around the house that she largely designed and built herself. 'I just couldn't believe it.'

In all the years of government investigation, multimillion-dollar litigation and intensive media coverage, no one – from the lawyers to the reporters – ever asked any actual Sears saleswomen what *their* 'interests' were. In an admittedly unscientific experiment, I wandered into the Sears outlet in San Francisco one day and walked up to the first sales assistant by the door, an elderly woman in the clothing department, wearing a pink sweater and lace-collared dress. She seemed a likely spokeswoman for traditional 'women's work'. But it turned out she had just been moved, against her will, from the camera section to the dress department. She was fuming.

'I've been in cameras since 1964,' she said. 'I liked it because I learned all about photography, films, projectors. Now, all of a sudden my manager comes over and says, "You're in dresses from now on." No explanation, no nothing.' She hates the dress department: 'Here it's just: they try on the dresses, you hang them up again, they try them on again, you hang them up again. Then it's tear off the tags, ring it up, tear off more tags.'

Told of Sears's contention that women don't have the same interests as men, she waves a gnarled dismissive hand in the air. 'That's a bunch of baloney. I had two kids to raise. If they would have offered me commission sales, I would have taken it. I needed the job.' What about women preferring to work days, as Rosenberg had maintained. The hand sails in the air once more. 'The lady in personnel said to me, "Either you come to work the hours we give you or you stay home." There was no choice. When I started out, I worked all nights and Saturdays. I didn't have a babysitter, so my kids just stayed home by themselves.'

In another section of the ladies' department, Ann Sirni is ringing up sales. She says she remembers the EEOC suit because all of a sudden, store managers were running around, 'asking all of us women if we wanted to sell big-ticket items'. She adds, 'They had no trouble getting women to take those jobs. A lot of them liked it because there's more money in big-ticket items.'

Charlotte Mayfield, a saleswoman in the jewellery department, remembers the suit, too; she was one of the women who signed up when the recruiters came round. 'They wanted minority women to get into management when that suit came out,' recalls Mayfield, who is black. 'They invited me into this management training programme, but I was a little disappointed, if you want to know the truth. We went to this classroom and they gave us a manual and a diploma and everything, but they never did offer us management jobs.'

She would have taken a commission sales job if they had offered it, she says. 'The pay is better.' Would she have been afraid of the 'competition', as the Sears officials said in court? She thought about it. 'I probably would have been a little scared at first, but I was scared when I came here and got put on the registers, because I'd never worked a register before. Even if I was nervous, I would have taken the job. I would have challenged myself to do it.'

But with the pressure off retailers to uphold equal employment laws, women like Charlotte Mayfield would have fewer opportunities to challenge themselves outside of the 'ladies'' departments. In the backlash decade, as Labor Department data chronicle, the ranks of women relegated to sales-counter jobs climbed still higher – and the small proportions of women in such 'men's' departments as hardware, building supplies, parts and furniture began to shrink once more.

Diane Joyce: Women in the Blue-Collar World

It would take Diane Joyce nearly ten years of battles to become the first female skilled crafts worker ever in Santa Clara County history. It would take another seven years of litigation, pursued all the way to the US Supreme Court, before she could actually start work. And then the real fight would begin.

For blue-collar women, there was no honeymoon period on the job; the backlash began the first day they reported to work – and intensified as the Reagan economy put more than a million blue-collar men out of work, reduced wages, and spread mounting fear. While the white-collar world seemed capable of absorbing countless lawyers and bankers in the 1980s, the trades and crafts had no room for expansion. 'Women are far more economically threatening in blue-collar work, because there are a finite number of jobs from which to choose,' Mary Ellen Boyd, executive director of No-Traditional Employment for Women, observes. 'An MBA can do anything. But a plumber is only a plumber.' While women never represented more than a few percentage points of the blue-collar work force, in this powder-keg situation it only took a few female faces to trigger a violent explosion.

Diane Joyce arrived in California in 1970, a thirty-three-year-old widow with four children, born and raised in Chicago. Her father was a tool-and-die maker, her mother a returned-goods clerk at a pharmaceuticals warehouse. At eighteen, she married Donald Joyce, a tool-and-die maker's apprentice at her father's plant. Fifteen years later, after working knee-deep in printed circuit boards for years, he died suddenly of a rare form of liver cancer.

After her husband's death, Joyce taught herself to drive, packed her children in a 1966 Chrysler station wagon and headed west to San Jose, California, where a lone relative lived. Joyce was an experienced bookkeeper and she soon found work as a clerk in the county Office of Education, at $506 a month. A year later, she heard that the county's transportation department had a senior account clerk job vacant that paid $50 more a month. She applied in March 1972.

'You know, we wanted a man,' the interviewer told her as soon as she walked through the door. But the account clerk jobs had all taken a pay cut recently, and sixteen women and no men had applied for the job. So he sent her on to the second interview. 'This guy was a little politer,' Joyce recalls. 'First, he said, "Nice day, isn't it?" before he tells me, "You know, we wanted a man." I wanted to say, "Yeah, and where's my man? I am the man in my house." But I'm sitting there with four kids to feed and all I can see is dollar signs, so I kept my mouth shut.'

She got the job. Three months later, Joyce saw a posting for a 'road maintenance man'. An education up to age thirteen and one year's work experience was all that was required, and the pay was $723 a month. Her current job required a high-school education, bookkeeping skills and four years' experience – and paid $150 less a month. 'I saw that flier and I said, "Oh wow, I can do that." Everyone in the office laughed. They thought it was a riot. . . . I let it drop.'

But later that same year, every county worker got a 2 to 5 per cent pay rise except for the seventy female account clerks. 'Oh now, what do you girls need a raise for?' the director of personnel told Joyce and some other women who went before the board of supervisors to object. 'All you'd do is spend the money on trips to Europe.' Joyce was shocked. 'Every account clerk I knew was supporting a family through death or divorce. I'd never seen Mexico, let alone Europe.' Joyce decided to apply for the next better-paying 'male' job that came up. In the meantime, she became active in the union; a skilful writer and one of the best-educated representatives there, Joyce ended up composing the safety language in the master contract and negotiating what became the most powerful county agreement protecting seniority rights.

In 1974 a road dispatcher retired, and both Joyce and a man named Paul Johnson, a former oil-fields roustabout, applied for the post. The supervisors told Joyce she needed to work on the road crew first and handed back her application. Johnson didn't have any road crew experience either, but his application was accepted. In the end, the job went to another man.

Joyce set out to get road crew experience. As she was filling in her application for the next road crew job that came up, in 1975, her supervisor walked in, asked what she was doing, and turned red. 'You're taking a man's job away!' he shouted. Joyce sat silently for a minute, thinking. Then she said, 'No, I'm not. Because a man can sit right here where I'm sitting.'

In the evenings, she took courses in road maintenance and truck and light equipment operation. She came in third out of eighty-seven applicants on the job test; there were ten openings on the road crew, and she got one of them.

For the next four years Joyce carried pots of tar on her shoulder, pulled rubbish from the median strip, and manoeuvred trucks up the mountains to clear mud slides. 'Working outdoors was great,' she says. 'You know, women pay fifty dollars a month to join a health club, and here I was getting paid to get in shape.'

The road men didn't exactly welcome her arrival. When they trained her to drive the pick-up trucks, she says, they kept changing instructions; one gave her driving tips that nearly blew up the engine. Her supervisor wouldn't issue her a pair of overalls; she had to file a formal grievance to get them. In the yard, the men kept the ladies' room locked, and on the road they wouldn't stop to let her use the lavatory. 'You wanted a man's job, you learn to pee like a man,' her supervisor told her.

Obscene graffiti about Joyce appeared on the sides of trucks. Men threw darts at union notices she pinned on the noticeboard. One day, the stockroom storekeeper, Tony Laramie, who says later he liked to call her 'the piglet', called a general meeting in the depot's Ready Room. 'I hate the day you came here,' Laramie started screaming at Joyce as the other men looked on, many nodding. 'We don't want you here. You don't belong here. Why don't you go the hell away?'

Joyce's experience was typical of the forthright and often violent backlash within the blue-collar work force, an assault undisguised by decorous homage to women's 'difference'. At a construction site in New York, for example, where only a few female hard-hats had found work, the men took a woman's work boots and hacked them into bits. Another woman was injured by a male co-worker; he hit her on the head with a piece of plywood. In Santa Clara County, where Joyce worked, the county's equal opportunity office files were stuffed with reports of ostracism, sexual harassment, threats, verbal and physical abuse. 'It's pervasive in some of the shops,' says John Longabaugh, the county's equal employment officer at the time. 'They mess up their tools, leave pornography on their desks. Safety equipment is made difficult to get, or unavailable.' A maintenance worker greeted the first woman in his department with these words: 'I know someone who would break your arm or leg for a price.' Another new woman was ordered to clean a transit bus by her supervisor – only to find when she climbed aboard that the men had left a little gift for her: faeces smeared across the seats.

In 1980 another dispatcher job became vacant. Joyce and Johnson both applied. They got similarly high scores on the written exam. Joyce now had four years' experience on the road crew; Paul Johnson only had a year and a half. The three interviewers, one of whom later referred to Joyce in court as 'rabble-rousing' and 'not a lady', gave the job to Johnson. Joyce decided to complain to the county affirmative action office.

The decision fell to James Graebner, the new director of the transportation department, an engineer who believed that it was about time the county hired its first woman for its 238 skilled-crafts jobs. Graebner confronted the roads director, Ron Shields. 'What's wrong with the woman?' Graebner asked. 'I hate her,' Shields said, according to other people in the room. 'I just said I thought Johnson was more qualified,' is how Shields remembers it. 'She didn't have the proficiency with heavy equipment.' Neither, of course, did Johnson. Not that it was relevant anyway: dispatch is an office job that doesn't require lifting anything heavier than a microphone.

Graebner told Shields he was being overruled; Joyce had the job. Later that day, Joyce recalls, her supervisor called her into the conference room. 'Well, you got the job,' he told her. 'But you're not qualified.' Johnson, meanwhile, sat by the phone, dialling the chain of command. 'I felt like tearing something up,' he recalls later. He demanded a meeting with the affirmative action office. 'The affirmative action man walks in,' Johnson says, 'and he's this big black guy. He can't tell me anything. He brings in this minority who can barely speak English. . . . I told them, "You haven't heard the last of me".' Within days, he had hired a lawyer and set his reverse discrimination suit in motion, contending that the county had given the job to a 'less qualified' woman.

In 1987, the Supreme Court ruled against Johnson. The decision was hailed by women's and civil rights groups. But victory in Washington was not the same as triumph in the transportation yard. For Joyce and the road men, the backlash was just warming up. 'Something like this is going to hurt me one day,' Gerald Pourroy, a foreman in Joyce's office, says of the court's ruling, his voice low and bitter. He stares at the concrete wall above his desk. 'I look down the tracks and I see the train coming toward me.'

The day after the Supreme Court decision, a woman in the county office sent Joyce a congratulatory bouquet, two dozen carnations. Joyce arranged the flowers in a vase on her desk. The next day they were gone. She found them finally, crushed in a rubbish bin. A road foreman told her, 'I drop-kicked them across the yard.'

Several months after the court's verdict, on a late summer afternoon, the county trucks groan into the depot yard, lifting the dust in slow, tired circles. The men file in, and Joyce takes their keys and signs them out. Four men in one-way sunglasses lean as far as they can over the counter.

'Well, well, well. Diii-ane. How the hell are you?'

'Hey, Diane, how the fuck are you?'

'Oh, don't ask her. She don't know that.'

'Yeah, Diane, she don't know nothing.'

Diane Joyce continues to smile, thinly, as she collects the keys. Some of the men drift over to the Ready Room. They leaf through dog-eared copies of *Guns* magazine and kick an uncooperative vending machine. When asked about Diane Joyce, they respond with put-downs and bitterness.

'She thinks she is high class now that she's got her face on TV,' one of the men says. 'Like we are dirt or something.'

'Now all a girl has got to do is say, Hey, they're discriminating, and she gets a job. You tell me how a man's supposed to get a promotion against something like that.'

'She's not qualified for ninety-nine per cent of the jobs, I'll tell you that right now. I bet next foreman's job opens up, she'll get it just because she's female. I've been a road maintenance worker sixteen years. Now you tell me what's fair?'

Paul Johnson has since retired to the tiny fishing town of Sequim, Washington. From there, he dispatches an 'Open Letter to the White Males of America' to newspaper offices across the country: 'Fellow men,' he writes, 'I believe it is time for us to object to OUR suppression.' His wife Betty, Johnson explains, helped compose and typed the letter. Her job at a bank also helped pay the bills – and underwrote much of his reverse discrimination lawsuit.

Women's numbers in the Santa Clara County's skilled-crafts jobs, after the Supreme Court ruling, increased by a paltry two to three a year. By the end of 1988, while the total number of available craft jobs had grown from 238 to 460, the number of women rose only to 12. This was not because women had lost interest in these jobs. They were enrolling in union craft apprenticeship programmes in the area in record numbers. And a county survey of its own female employees (who were still overwhelmingly relegated to the clerical pool) found that 85 per cent of these women were interested in higher-paying 'men's' jobs. Moreover, 90 per cent of the women surveyed said they believed they knew the reason why they weren't getting these higher-paying positions: discrimination.

Lady Bench-Hands and Gentlemen Testers

The Supreme Court would ultimately undercut Diane Joyce's legal victory, too – only two years after she 'won' in Washington. Within ten days in June 1989, the US Supreme Court rolled back two decades of landmark civil rights decisions in four separate rulings. The court opened the way for men to challenge positive discrimination, set up new barriers that made it far more difficult to demonstrate discrimination in court with statistics, and ruled that an 1866 civil rights statute doesn't protect employees from discrimination that occurs after they are hired.

One of the four cases that summer, *Lorance* v. *AT&T Technologies*, dealt a particularly hard blow to blue-collar women. The court ruled that women at AT&T's electronics plant in Illinois couldn't challenge a 1979 seniority system that union and company officials had openly devised to lock out women. The reason: the women had missed the 180-day federal filing deadline for lodging unfair employment practices. The court made this ruling even though five past court rulings had all allowed employees to file such challenges after the deadline had passed. And ironically enough, that very same day the court ruled that a group of white male firefighters were not too late to file *their* reverse discrimination suit – against a settlement of an affirmative action case filed in *1974*.

In the economically depressed town of Montgomery, Illinois, forty miles outside Chicago, nearly all the jobs pay the minimum wage – except at the Western Electric plant, where circuit boards are assembled and tested for AT&T. As long as anyone at the plant can remember, the factory had been rigidly divided by sex: the women had virtually all the lowly 'bench-hand' jobs (assembling and wiring switching systems by hand) and the men had virtually all the high-paying 'testing' jobs (checking the circuit boards). So it had remained until 1976, when three women decided, without so much as a nudge from positive discrimination recruiters, to cross the gender line.

Pat Lorance was one of the first to ford the divide. She had been working since adolescence, ever since her father had deserted the family and left her mother with no job and five children to bring up. She joined the plant in 1970 as a bench-hand; after nine years she was weary of the tedious work and even wearier of the low pay. When she heard that the local community college was offering courses to qualify as a tester, Lorance decided to give it a try. She brought two women, both bench-hands, with her.

'In the beginning, it was a little intimidating because the teacher, who was from Western Electric, told us, "You know, women don't usually finish." But by the fourth course, we won his respect.' She eventually completed sixteen courses, including electronic circuitry, computer programming and 'AC/DC fundamentals'. To fit it all in, Lorance worked the 5 a.m. – or sometimes even the 3 a.m. – shift, studied in the afternoon, and attended class until 9.30 at night.

Officials at Western Electric–AT&T were closely, and uneasily, following the women's efforts. At the time, the EEOC was pursuing its highly visible round of class-action suits against industrial employers, including other divisions of AT&T, and the company's managers knew that if the women at the plant began raising questions publicly about the company's equal employment record, they could well be the next target. In 1976, as employees at the time recall, the personnel office suddenly began calling in some of the female bench-hands, one by one, and offering them a deal. As several women who got the summons remember, a personnel manager informed them that the company had 'mistakenly' over-looked them for some job openings. They could now receive a cheque of several hundred dollars as 'compensation'; all they had to do in return was sign a statement promising never to sue the company for discrimination. The women say they were also instructed not to discuss the matter with their co-workers. 'Some of the girls wanted to know what the jobs were,' recalls one woman, a bench-hand, who, like the others, asked that her name not be used for fear she will lose her job. 'Some didn't want to take the money. But it was like, "Take the money or you are out the door." I got over $600.' (Company officials say they have no record of these sessions in the personnel office. 'We have found no facts to support such claims,' the company's attorney Charles Jackson says.)

By autumn 1978 Lorance had all the academic credentials she needed and she applied for the first vacancy in testing. Company officials accepted her for the job – then, a week later, told her the job had been eliminated. Then she heard that the company had hired three men as testers that same week. She protested to the union and, after a struggle, finally became the company's first female tester.

By the end of 1978 about 15 of the 200 testers were women. To the men in the shops, that was 15 too many. 'They made these comments about how women were dumb and couldn't do the job,' Lorance recalls. 'I have a pretty good personality and I just shrugged it off, figured they'd get over it.' But as the number of women rose, so did the men's resentment.

Some of the men began sabotaging women's test sets, hooking up the wires the wrong way while the women were on their breaks or spilling ink on their schematic notebooks. They tacked up a series of humiliating posters around the plant. A typical example: a picture of a grotesquely fat woman standing on a table with her stockings down around her calves and money spilling out of her shoes. The men wrote on it: 'Yesterday I couldn't spell tester. Today I are a tester.'

In 1980 Jan King joined the second round of women to break into the tester ranks. She had worked at the company as a bench-hand since 1966, starting at $1.97 an hour. King desperately needed the extra money: her husband, a violent alcoholic, spent most of the money he earned on drink and gambling, and she had a child to support. 'I looked around at the plant one day and I realized I had just accepted what I saw there,' she says. 'I thought I wasn't any good in math because that's what they said about women. But part of my brain said, Wait a minute, if they can do it, I can. Just because I was brought up to be a certain way, that doesn't mean I have to stay that way.'

King had to fight for the job on two fronts, work and home. 'My husband said, "You are not going to go to school for this. It's a waste of time." ' First he threatened her. Then, when she went to classes anyway, 'he'd do stuff like five minutes before it was time for me to leave, he'd announce that he wasn't going to babysit. But I just kept at it because there was this little voice in the back of my mind saying, "You are going to end up taking care of your daughter by yourself." I knew if he left, he was the kind of guy who was not going to be paying child support.'

The company officials weren't any more helpful. As King recalls, 'The whole attitude at the company was, women can't do it. Women can't do math, women can't do electronics.' As women began applying to become testers, the company suddenly issued a new set of training and examination requirements. Some of the tactics were peculiar. One of the top managers tried to require that female testers be sent home if they didn't carry see-through handbags, a strategy supposedly to discourage thieving.

When some of the men who were testers heard that twelve more female bench-hands had signed up for training at the community college, they decided matters had gone far enough. The younger men were the most upset; because they had the least seniority, they knew that the bench-hand women who had worked at the plant for years would be ahead of them for advancement – and behind them for layoffs. In the winter of 1978 the men organized a secret union meeting; when Lorance heard about it, she and a female co-worker made a surprise appearance.

'They weren't real happy to see us,' she recalls. Lorance sat in the union hall and listened. She discovered they were drafting a new seniority system that would prevent women from counting their years as bench-hands in calculating their length of employment. If approved, it would mean that women would take the brunt of any layoff in the testing department. Lorance and her friend went back and spread the word to the other female testers.

At the union meeting to vote on the new seniority proposal, ninety men gathered on one side of the hall, fifteen women on the other. One man after another stood up to speak on behalf of the proposed seniority plan: 'I have a family to feed. Do you know how much a loaf of bread costs now?' Then the women stood up, to say that many of them were divorced mothers with families to feed, too; their ex-husbands weren't paying any child support. 'This is a man's job,' one of the men yelled. 'Yes, but this is a woman's factory,' a woman retorted, pointing out that more women than men were on the company payroll; he just didn't notice them because they were tucked away in the lowest-paying jobs.

In the end, the men won the vote; in the testing universe, anyway, they still had numbers on their side. The union official-dom assured Lorance and the other women at the time that the seniority plan would have no effect on downgrades or layoffs, just advancement. Company officials, who had helped design the new seniority system and quickly approved it, made similar promises about layoffs. The women accepted their guarantees – and didn't file suit. As Lorance points out, no one was being laid off in 1978, so 'why cause trouble when you don't have to?' None of the women wanted to risk losing the jobs they had fought so hard to get.

Jan King, for one, needed her pay cheque more than ever; she was facing even more problems at home. 'It was like every step I took toward improving myself, every step forward, he saw it as a rejection of him,' she says of her husband. 'As long as he could keep me dependent on him, then he could think that I would stay.' Her husband turned even more violent; he began dragging her out of bed by the hair, beating and, ultimately, raping her. Whenever she made a move towards divorce, he would threaten murder. 'If you leave me, you're dead,' he told her. 'If I can't have you, no one can.'

When the recession hit in 1982, the women discovered that the union and company officials had misled them; the seniority plan *did* apply to layoffs, and the women were the first ones out of the door. Eventually, women with nearly twenty years' experience would lose their jobs. Even women who weren't let go were downgraded and shunted back to the bench-hand side of the plant, a demotion that cost some women more than $10,000 in yearly wages.

Lorance was downgraded immediately. She went to a superior she trusted and asked for an explanation. He spoke to his bosses, then came back and told her, 'I'm sorry, Patty, but they told me I have to write you up [for a reprimand].' But what, she asked, had she done? He explained that she had 'asked a question'. Then he took her aside and said he suspected the real reason was that they hoped this would discourage her from taking legal action. 'Well, you know what that made me do,' Lorance says. The next day she pulled out the Yellow Pages and started dialling lawyers.

Ultimately, Lorance and three other female testers filed suit against the company. (One of the women later dropped out, after her husband forbade her to pursue the litigation.) Bridget Arimond, a Chicago attorney who specializes in sex-discrimination law, took the case, which was promptly derailed in the courts over a technical debate about the filing deadline for unfair employment practices. The company contended that the clock started running in 1978, when the seniority system was first adopted, and their complaints constituted 'stale claims'. 'The ladies hadn't exercised their legal rights at the appropriate time,' Charles Jackson, Western Electric's counsel on the case, asserts later. 'It was really their fault.' The women maintained the clock started when they were fired; how could they have known until then that the policy was unfair? 'The irony of it all,' Arimond says, 'was that the whole

fight in court came down to whether women who had no background in the law didn't file on time. Yet, the judge [in the lower
court] waited over a year to rule on the motion.' That judge: John
Nordberg of the Sears case.

Meanwhile, Pat Lorance kept getting laid off and rehired.
Finally, on March 31, 1989, she was laid off for good. She had to
take a job as a bartender. Two months later, when she turned on
the television set one night to watch the news, she learned that
she had lost the ruling. 'I was very disappointed,' she says. 'I don't
think the court gave it a fair look. None of us were screaming.
We just wanted to right a wrong, that's all.'

King wasn't surprised by the decision. 'You could see, the way
the court had been going, we weren't in good water.' The ruling
was a financial disaster for King, who was now a single mother.
Her violent husband had been killed in a street brawl in 1983.
After his death, she took a leave of absence to pull herself together. While she was away the company fired her, maintaining
she had failed to notify the personnel office at the appropriate
time of her return date. Desperate for work to support her two
children, King cleaned houses, then took a job as a waitress. She
lost all her benefits. 'Today I cleaned the venetian blinds at work,'
she says. 'I make $2.01 an hour and that's it, top pay. It's
demeaning, degrading. It makes you feel like you are not worthwhile.'

As she scrapes gravy from diners' plates, King replays the scenes
that led her to this dismal point. 'Whenever I'm thinking about
it, the feeling I get is of all these barricades, the ones with the
yellow lights, and every time you try to take a step, they throw
another barricade at you.' But in spite of everything, she says –
the legal defeat, her late husband's reign of terror, the humiliating
descent to dish-washer – she has never regretted her decision to
ask for more. 'If it gets someone fired up enough to say, "We've
got to turn this thing around," then it's been worth it,' she says.

The newspapers that year may have been full of quotes from
middle-class and professional women, feverishly recanting their
feminist convictions, but Jan King – who likes to say, 'Just call
me one of those women's libbers' – would probably find such
remarks alien – even shameful. She hasn't lost sight of what she

and many other economically deprived women want, and she is still willing to rush the backlash barricades to get it. 'I don't believe you have to accept things the way they are,' she says. 'I'll never change my mind about that.'

Chapter Fourteen

Reproductive Rights Under the Backlash: The Invasion of Women's Bodies

'Don't kill me, mommy!' A grown man clutching a crucifix shouts these words over and over, as he tries fruitlessly to push through a line of women guarding the Sacramento Pregnancy Consultation Center. He is just one of the many 'warriors' in Operation Rescue's 'National Day of Rescue II' – the title that the anti-abortion group chose for its dramatic sequel, an April 1989 nationwide siege of family-planning clinics.

But the spear carriers on location here have been outflanked by feminists. Operation Rescue's northern California caravan set out for the clinic at dawn, only to find the doors barred and the centre's defenders circled around the building, their arms linked in a human chain. Frustrated, the Operation Rescue men resort to force, twisting wrists, kicking shins. As they push, they praise the Lord but they also curse the women; mingled among the 'amens', the words 'whore' and 'dyke' can be heard more than once. A man in a baseball cap presses his face up to a woman hoisting a pro-choice sign. 'I'll smash you through the window,' he says, making a fist. But the press is watching; he keeps his clenched hands at his side.

Down the block, Operation Rescue's 'Prayer Support Column', a largely female auxiliary, is lined up in neat rows along the pavement. The wives and daughters of the 'warriors' stand very still, their lips whispering 'Jesus loves the little children', their palms raised towards heaven. 'We're not allowed to speak', one of the women says when approached for an interview.

Across the street, Russell Walden III takes a break from the skirmish. A stocky man with sad eyes, he mops his brow as he offers some personal history. Waldens I and II, he says, were both city tax assessors, community pillars; he's the first to fall from the family line. Muddling along in a series of odd jobs, mortuary assistant and wild-animal caretaker among them, Walden III joined Operation Rescue after he met some of the group's members – in a county jail cell. They were there for trespassing on clinic property; he was there on a drunk-driving charge. When they offered him some paralegal work, he accepted and joined their campaign.

'My wife almost had an abortion a few years ago but I stopped her,' he says. 'I said, "No, no, no." ' They had four kids and his wife didn't want another; when she went to the clinic anyway, he followed her into the examination room, where she was lying in a hospital gown. 'I came in and snatched her and I said, "Let's get out of here. Now!" I'm not going to let her be anywhere where I'm not.' She had the baby, but later she left him. Tears fill his eyes as he says this. He wipes them away and explains, 'I'm crying for the unborn babies.'

While he's talking, Don Grundemann, a gaunt young chiropractor in an army jacket, joins the conversation. His girlfriend had an abortion without even asking him, he says. 'What I think is, the woman didn't want a child like me.' Abortion, Grundemann says, is women's way of getting even: 'In a subliminal way, it's revenge against men. Men have treated women shabbily and now the women's movement has struck back in overkill.'

In 1986, Randall Terry, a twenty-six-year-old used-car salesman from upstate New York, launched Operation Rescue. His mission: to padlock the doors of the nation's family-planning clinics. Like the 'anti-vice' crusade against contraception and abortion in late Victorian America – also led by an underemployed New York salesman, Anthony Comstock, who also raided women's health clinics – Operation Rescue attracted thousands of young men who, one way or another, felt locked out themselves by a world that no longer seemed to have a productive place for them. Contrary to the popular image of the anti-abortion lobby as a group of grizzled Christian elders, the Operation Rescue men (and the majority were men) most often resembled the youthful and angry 'Contenders' that the Yankelovich researchers had identified. Virtually all of Operation Rescue's leaders and about half its active participants were in their early twenties to mid-thirties, and the vast majority belonged to the lower income brackets. These were men who belonged to the second half of the baby boom, who had not only missed the political engagement of the 1960s but had been cheated out of that affluent era's bounty. They were downwardly mobile sons, condemned by the 1980s economy to earn less than their fathers, unable to afford the ballooning mortgages or to put food on the table without their wives' help.

Operation Rescue has sent its full-time organizers to countries like Britain to extend its 'direct action' methods against abortion clinics. They call it 'Operation Rescue Outreach'. Twenty-two American Rescuers arrived in 1989, and soon after invaded a Lancashire clinic's operating theatre on two occasions as well as organizing daily pickets and demonstrations in London. Although the Catholic Church's Society for the Protection of Unborn Children (SPUC) and the non-denominational lobby group Life have both distanced themselves from these actions, leaflets proffered by protesters outside clinics have carried Life phone numbers, and SPUC placards have been seen at Rescue demonstrations. In Australia, anti-abortion groups regularly picket clinics and harass staff, visitors and patients. One Sydney clinic experienced an arson attempt, two episodes of firebombing, and had its front windows smashed. New Zealand saw clashes in 1989 outside a Wellington clinic when a Rescue squad arrived to find thirty women already there and intent on allowing women in. Fifteen of the sixteen people arrested that day were Operation Rescue members, but nevertheless the press managed to give the impression that it was the pro-choice women who were violent.

The media generally would define the struggle over abortion as a moral and a biological debate – when does life begin? Doubtless for many uneasy about abortion, that was the central issue. But the peculiarly fierce animosity that the Rescuers brought to the battle over women's reproductive freedom was fuelled by passions other than philosophy or science. While they may well have been 'crying for the unborn babies', these men were also hurting from severe economic and social dislocations in their lives – changes that they so often blamed on the rise of independent and professional women. As they lost financial strength at work and private authority at home, they saw women gaining ground in the office, challenging their control of the family at home, and even taking the initiative in the bedroom. As resentment over women's increasing levels of professional progress became mixed with anxiety over the sexual freedoms women had begun to exercise, they developed a rhetoric of puritanical outrage to castigate their opponents.

For public consumption, the spokesmen of the militant anti-abortion movement called feminists 'child-killers' and berated them for triggering 'breakneck' abortion rates. But more revealing was what they said under their breath: their whispered 'whores' and 'dykes' were perhaps their more telling epithets. Sexual independence, not murder, may have been the feminists' greater crime.

To men like John Willke, president of the National Right to Life Committee, legal abortion assailed not only the foetus but the primacy of male family control. Pro-choice women, he charged, 'do violence to marriage', because they 'remove the right of a husband to protect the life of the child he has fathered in his wife's womb'. 'God didn't create women independently,' Father Michael Carey, the keynote speaker at the National Day of Rescue II rally in San Jose, declared, a point that he would hammer home throughout his address. What was most distasteful about these abortion rights activists, he said, was their insistence that women be free to make reproductive choices without consulting their husbands. If these 'feminist-infected' women have their way, he warned his audience, men 'won't be allowed to decide about abortion'. In his 1986 *Men and Marriage*, George Gilder most forthrightly expressed the fear underlying much of the male anxiety about female reproductive freedom. The feminists' successful campaign for birth control and abortion, he wrote, 'shifts the balance of sexual power further in favour of women', depletes male patriarchal 'potency', and reduces the penis to 'an empty plaything'.

So often in the battle over the foetus's 'right to life' in the 1980s, the patriarch's eclipsed ability to make the family decisions figured as a bitter subtext, the unspoken but pressing agenda of the anti-abortion campaign. The desire to defend traditional paternal authority surfaced again and again in the many 'father's rights' lawsuits filed to stop abortions in the decade, where plaintiffs were typically husbands struggling with wives who wouldn't listen or wouldn't comply with their commands or had recently filed for divorce. In the case of Eric Conn of Indiana, his wife sued him for divorce only hours before he lodged his complaint on behalf of the foetus. 'I just didn't like being theatened and told what to do,' David Ostreicher, a Levittown dentist and another 'father's rights' litigant, told the court. Not only did his wife seek an abortion against his wishes, he said, but she was also challenging the premarital agreement he had insisted that she sign – an agreement that would leave him with most of the marital assets. In upstate New York, the twenty-six-year-old sailor who sued to stop his fiancée's abortion in 1988 was also trying to stop a separate decision she had just made – not to marry him.

The men of the anti-abortion movement may have said they were just trying to staunch the runaway pace of abortions, but the rate wasn't really escalating. In fact, women have been terminating about one in three pregnancies for at least the last hundred years; the only real difference in countries like the USA post-*Roe v. Wade* and Britain after the 1967 Abortion Act was that women were now able to abort unwanted pregnancies legally – and safely. While the number of abortions performed on residents of the UK rose in the early 1970s, it dipped again between 1973 and 1977. The rise between 1978 and 1981 was followed by another decline in 1982–3. The increases in 1984 and 1985 may well, says the Family Planning Association, have been associated with the 'pill scare' of 1983 when publicity given to reported links between pill use and some forms of cancer led to women suddenly giving up the pill and risking unintended pregnancies. The number of legal abortions in 1990 involving resident women in England and Wales stood at 173,900. Given that estimates of the numbers of abortions carried out illegally before the 1967 Act range upwards to 250,000 per year, this total does not seem to represent an avalanche. According to Margaret McDonald, chief executive officer of Australia's FPA, there has been 'a small but steady increase' in the number of Australian abortions, 'but the rates have remained fairly constant'. Despite an annual increase in New Zealand from 1985 to 1988, abortion rates there are still low by international standards.

The real change was women's new ability to regulate their fertility without danger or fear – a new freedom that in turn had contributed to dramatic changes not so much in the abortion rate as in female sexual behaviour and attitudes. Having secured first the mass availability of contraceptive devices and then the option of medically sound abortions, women were at last at liberty to have sex, like men, on their own terms. As a result, in the half-century after birth control was legalized, women doubled their rate of pre-marital sexual activity, until it nearly converged with men's by the end of the 1970s. (At the same time, men's premarital sexual encounters increased much more slowly, at about half the pace of women's.) By 1980, a landmark sex survey of 106,000 women conducted for *Cosmopolitan* found that 41 per cent of women had extramarital affairs, up from 8 per cent in 1948. In fact, women's sexual behaviour and attitudes had changed so much that they were now close to mirroring men's. 'The woman we're profiling,' *Cosmopolitan* observed in its introduction to the survey, 'is an extraordinarily sexually free human being' whose new bedroom expressiveness constitutes a 'break with the old double standard'.

Women also became far more independent in their decisions about when to have children, in what marital circumstances, and when to stop. In these decisions the biological father increasingly didn't have the final say – or much of a say at all. Women's support for motherhood out of wedlock rose dramatically in the 1980s. The 1987 Women's View Survey found that 87 per cent of single women believed it was perfectly acceptable for women to bear and raise children without getting married – up to 14 per cent from just four years earlier. Nearly 40 per cent of the women in the 1990 Virginia Slims poll said that in making a decision about whether to have an abortion, the man involved should not even be consulted.

The Abortion Act in the UK was one of the most popular pieces of legislation enacted in recent years. A National Opinion Poll in

1976 showed that 55 per cent of the public favoured abortion on request – i.e. much easier abortion than that provided for by the 1967 Act. A Marplan poll conducted in 1987 for the Abortion Law Reform Association found that 79 per cent of those questioned thought that the decision as to whether or not a woman should continue her pregnancy should be left to the woman in consultation with her doctors. Despite attempts in Parliament to restrict abortion, the British Attitudes Survey reveals that in the 1980s public attitudes became significantly more liberal towards the social and medical grounds for abortion.

To many men in the anti-abortion movement, the speed with which women embraced sexual and reproductive freedom could be frightening. And unlike the rise of the gender voting gap or the increasing number of women at work, this revolution in female behaviour had invaded their most intimate domain. 'Males have almost completely lost control of procreative activity,' Gilder wrote; it is 'now dependent, to a degree unprecedented in history, on the active pleasure of women'. No wonder, he observed, so many men 'resist abortion on demand'. Men who found these changes distressing couldn't halt the pace of women's bedroom liberation directly, but banning abortion might be one way to apply the brakes. If they couldn't stop growing numbers of women from climbing into the sexual driver's seat, they could at least make the women's drive more dangerous – by jamming the reproductive controls.

The political imagery of the 1980s anti-abortion movement bore all the hallmarks of the New Right ideology that had preceded it. In its war-torn psychological landscape, the enemy was feminism, the weapon was aggressively moralistic rhetoric, and the strategy for reclaiming the offensive was largely semantic. Like the New Right men, anti-abortion leaders saw feminists as figures of frightening size and power. 'The harridans', anti-abortion advocate Tom Bethell called them in the *American Spectator* – women who 'howled' and 'scream[ed] with awesome ferocity'. In his 1988 anti-abortion work, *Grand Illusions*, George Grant portrayed pro-choice women and clinic counsellors as 'contorted, wildeyed' Furies guarding the 'Altar of Convenience' with a 'frenzied rage'.

Planned Parenthood, he said, is an institution that dwarfs the Pentagon; its mighty force 'has muscled into virtually every facet of modern life'. Anti-abortion leader Father Norman Weslin felt the same way. He said he had served as a paratrooper and 'commander in charge of nuclear weapons' in the US Army for twenty years, but 'that was bush league' compared with the feminist foes he faced now.

To stake out the commanding position, to remake themselves into true 'activists', the anti-abortion men resorted to the verbal tactics pioneered by the New Right. In Joseph Scheidler's *Closed: 99 Ways to Stop Abortion*, a primary text of the militant anti-abortion movement, the Pro-Life Action League director stressed the importance of 'controlling' the language on abortion. When speaking to the press, his manual instructed, '[R]arely use the word "fetus." Use "baby" or "unborn child." . . . You don't have to surrender to their vocabulary. . . . They will start using your terms if you use them.' The Willkes' *Abortion: Questions and Answers*, which became the bible of anti-abortion activists, stressed the same objective: 'Let's be positive, if possible,' the book asserted. 'We are *for* protection for the unborn, the handicapped, and the aged. If possible, don't accept the negative label "anti-abortion".'

In their battle for verbal control, anti-abortion activists also co-opted their enemy's vocabulary and images. The Willke handbook urged followers to borrow the 'feminist credo' of 'right to her own body' and apply it instead to aborted female foetuses. At anti-abortion demonstrations, 'The baby has to have a choice!' became a favourite chant. 'Little Ones', an Operation Rescue protest song, called for 'Equal rights/Equal time/For the unborn children.' Women didn't choose to have abortions; they were 'Women Exploited By Abortion', the name of the American anti-abortion group that promised to counsel the 'victims' of abortion. Anti-abortion literature portrayed abortion providers as quasi-rapists who subjected young women to untold horrors, then snatched their money and drove off in limousines. One Australian leaflet issued by 'Life Lobby' accused the Family Planning Association of having 'abortionists and others in the lucrative abortion industry high in their ranks'. By identifying women as victims of their own right to an abortion, the anti-abortion movement did more than debase the rhetoric – it reinforced the backlash thesis. The cause of women's liberty was once again defined as the cause of women's pain. Women who were unhappy, the movement's spokespersons contended, were probably suffering the residual effects of 'post-abortion syndrome', the new ailment that the anti-abortion movement claimed plagued the female population.

By and large, anti-abortion leaders denied that they were hostile to women's rights, but their actions spoke louder. National Right to Life leader John Willke said he supported equality – while opposing the Equal Rights Amendment; soon the National Right to Life board recanted its once neutral position on the amendment. Pro-Life Action League director Joseph Scheidler said, 'I have no problem with women's rights'; he just wanted to make women's lives 'less painful' by sparing them the physical and mental agony of abortion. Yet at a 1986 anti-abortion conference, he vowed to inflict 'a year of pain and fear' on any woman who disagreed with him.

The leading figure of the decade's militant anti-abortion crusade, Operation Rescue founder Randall Terry, was likewise careful to skirt the issue of women's equality in his many public speeches. Restricting women's freedom wasn't part of his agenda, he assured the press; he was only trying 'to save the mothers and their unborn babies'. But the story of Terry's political evolution suggests a more complex and personal set of motives – in which the campaign for women's rights figured prominently.

Randall Terry: Who Was He Rescuing?

'I was conceived out of wedlock. I could've been aborted. I hope and think that my parents wouldn't have, but I'm just real glad they didn't even have the choice.'   RANDALL TERRY

Randall Terry grew up in the suburbs of Rochester, New York, birthplace of Susan B. Anthony and launch-pad for the nation's first wave of feminism 150 years ago. But his relationship to feminist activism would involve more than the coincidence of geography and history. Terry was the eldest son in a family that, on his mother's side, had produced politically vocal and self-determined women for three generations. From the start of the century, when his maternal great-grandmother disobeyed a parish priest and abandoned the Catholic church, the DiPasquale women had been outspoken, progressive and feminist. 'Randy Terry's backlash against women's rights may be more intimate than people realize,' says Dawn Marvin, former communications director of the Rochester chapter of Planned Parenthood – and Randall Terry's aunt. 'He was raised at the knee of feminists.'

Terry's three aunts, Diane, Dawn and Dale, agitated for civil rights, peace and, especially, women's equality. During the 1970s the sisters on the close-knit maternal side of the family launched a women's welfare-rights programme, the first women's studies programme at Buffalo State University, a women's arts collective, a women's talk show, a women's consciousness-raising group and a women's health clinic. But more than any feminist issue, their cause was reproductive freedom. Diane wrote and spoke on campuses in favour of legal and safe abortions. Dawn stood in the rain for hours seeking signatures for a petition to legalize abortion in New York State. Dale put her picture on a citywide bus ad campaign for birth-control education.

The sisters' activism was grounded in painful personal experience. Each of the four sisters had an unplanned pregnancy as an unmarried teenager before abortion was legal; Randy, in fact, was the product of one of them. In one case, a condom failed. In another, a boyfriend said he'd pull out and didn't. Whatever the 'mistake', the women paid. Dawn gave up a college scholarship and an arts career to marry a man she did not love, a man who smashed her jaw with his fists during her pregnancy. Diane gave up plans for an Ivy League education and spent the final months of her senior year in high school searching for an illegal abortion; she was five months pregnant by the time she found a willing 'doctor' who took her $500, injected her with saline, and abandoned her in a stranger's house. She nearly bled to death.

'Our diehard enemies are almost totally feminist,' Terry says. A young man of twenty-nine with a baby face and gangly limbs, he is hunched on the kerb outside Operation Rescue's Binghamton,

New York, headquarters. Behind him is 'command-central', a musty three-room suite with walls covered with water stains and photos of bloody foetuses. Inside one office cabinet, 'Baby Choice' floats in a jar. This embalmed foetus often accompanies Terry to press conferences, dressed in swaddling clothes and laid out in a tiny shoe-box 'coffin'.

'Radical feminism gave birth to child killing,' he says. 'They were the ones out in the streets demanding their rights – NARAL (National Abortion Rights Action League), NOW (National Organization for Women), with their lies and their false propaganda that the media lapped up obediently and spewed back out to the American people. Lies.' But then, most reporters are 'tools of NOW', too, he says. 'Radical feminism, of course, has vowed to destroy the traditional family unit, hates motherhood, hates children for the most part, promotes lesbian activity.' He offers an example: Margaret Sanger, birth-control pioneer and founder of Planned Parenthood. She was a 'whore', he says. 'She was an adulteress, and slept all over the place, all over the world, with all kinds of people.' It's not just abortion he opposes; Terry says he would like to ban all contraception – and, of course, call a halt to all premarital sex. He says he intends to deliver his own daughter to the wedding altar with her virginity intact.

A few hours later, Terry heads home. His wife, Cindy, a thin woman with almost translucent skin, meets him at the door, their three-year-old daughter, Faith, clinging to her side. 'I told her you don't talk,' Terry tells his wife, jerking his thumb at me. She reports that the lawn mower won't start. He gives the ignition cord a few yanks and, when the motor kicks in, turns the job over to her. He retires to the living-room couch and, propping up his feet, recalls with a nostalgic sigh that it was this very day a year ago that he reached his media zenith: 'I would have been in a hotel resting, getting ready for the limo to pick us up and take us to the *Morton Downey, Jr* show.'

His rise to 'national media star', as he puts it, was meteoric; a few years before the Downey limo arrived, he was selling jalopies in an upstate second-hand car lot. As the lawn mower bellows outside, Terry recounts the critical events in his young life that led to sudden fame.

At sixteen, he headed for California to 'find' himself and become 'a rock and roll star'. A talented pianist and guitarist, an honours student just four months from graduation, he dropped out in the winter of 1976 and hitchhiked west. 'I was a young rebel,' he recalls. 'I was born out of time, almost', a throwback from the 1960s.

He was also fleeing a tension-filled home. His father, Michael Terry, was an unhappy schoolteacher, a gifted classical vocalist whose singing career had evaporated after he dropped out of music college and then entered a shotgun wedding at twenty. The marriage was a difficult one and Michael Terry often turned his violent temper on his eldest son. The night before Randy left home, his father beat him up.

Terry never reached California and the trip was a disappointment; 1976 turned out to be a little late for the quintessential 'on-the-road' experience. 'I wanted to know answers,' he says. But 'in the '70s, people just wanted to get high.' He got as far as Galveston, Texas, where he camped out on the beach, smoking dope and playing air guitar, until a vagrant stole his backpack and all his possessions. He returned home, clutching a Gideon bible he had acquired on the way.

Back in a suburb of Rochester, he took the only job he could find, scooping ice cream at the Three Sisters, a local food-stall. From time to time, a lay minister from the nearby Elim Bible Institute would stop in to testify about Christ. Finally one night, Terry was converted. Vowing to become a religious leader, he gave up the ice-cream stand and enrolled at Elim to train for the ministry.

But his diploma from Elim, an unaccredited school, didn't help him in his search for even a decent job. He sold tyres and flipped burgers at McDonald's. During the recession he was laid off twice. Married by then, he couldn't afford a home – he and Cindy had to live, like charity cases, in a vacant church caravan. When he needed to pay medical and sometimes even grocery bills, he had to borrow money from Cindy's mother. While Terry would later blame working women for 'the destruction of the traditional family unit', it was his wife's job at a florist's shop that helped the young Terry family through this lean period. It was not until

Terry started Operation Rescue, and hundreds of thousands of dollars in donations began rolling in, that he was able to make a living wage – and send his wife home.

The 'vision' of Operation Rescue, he recalls, came to him in a prayer meeting in autumn 1983. It was a 'three-point plan': blockade clinics, counsel women against abortion, and provide homes for unmarried mothers. He led several clinic raids, but his campaign didn't register on the media monitors until July 1988, when he descended on Atlanta and a captive national press corps, which was in town for the Democratic National Convention. In the week-long siege that followed, 134 protesters were arrested, Terry 'made the networks', and his star status was all but guaranteed.

As Terry arrives at the apex of his story, Cindy returns to the house, her mowing finished, to prepare the family supper. After a while, she wanders into the living room. 'I told her you don't like media people, so she shouldn't expect to get any comment from you,' Terry tells his wife. But Cindy seems willing enough to talk. She tells how she met Randy at Elim, where she was 'just studying to be a better Christian'. She wasn't attracted to him at first, she says, but she had learned in her Christian Womanhood class that 'blind love' can lead to 'bad marriages'. Randy, on the other hand, says he was drawn to Cindy at once – he liked it that 'she was quiet'.

Cindy Dean grew up in Manchester, a small town in upstate New York. She worked as a waitress and barmaid at the local Sheraton Hotel, but she yearned for more. 'I didn't want my life to be a total failure,' she says. So at twenty-three, she enrolled in the Culinary Institute of America at Hyde Park, 'one of the best cooking schools in the United States', she points out. She was one of a few female students in training to be chefs; she was breaking into 'a male-dominated profession', she says proudly. 'I was really into it. I had real excellent grades because, you know, I wanted to make something of my life.' She began working at a French restaurant in Rochester, creating fancy pastries and soon managing the entire kitchen staff. Then she met a group of born-again Christians. They eventually converted her – and convinced her she should give up her cookery training.

'We need to wrap it up,' Randy says, interrupting her story. 'I want to eat.' They move to the dining room, where he sits at the head of the table and Cindy serves. He lectures her for having 'burned the beans'. After supper, he retires to the living room with a video of the TV movie about Lieutenant-Colonel Oliver North, *Guts and Glory*. As Cindy clears the dishes, she confides that it was she who first had the idea to picket the clinics. She had great difficulty getting pregnant – it took five years – and she came to resent women who so effortlessly conceived yet aborted. By herself, she took to marching in front of the Southern Tier Women's Services, the local family-planning clinic in Binghamton. With a home-made placard in her hands, she called out to women, 'Don't kill your baby. I'll take it. I can't have a baby.' Alex Aitken, a clinic employee at the time, recalls of Cindy, 'In the beginning, she was a fairly strong personality. She would approach anyone.'

One day, though, Randy appeared at her side. Soon, Aitken recalls, Cindy 'just disappeared from the scene'. In her place, Terry patrolled the parking lot, literally throwing his weight against car doors to stop women from entering the clinic. Once he found out the identity of a patient and burst into the waiting room, screaming her name over and over like the hero in *The Graduate*. Another time, clinic workers recall, he posed as a clinic 'counsellor' and led a sixteen-year-old girl to what he claimed was 'our other office', actually his own office suite. There, she later told clinic workers, he showed her gory films about the supposed aftermath of abortion – infertility, madness and death – until the frightened girl fled.

By 1985 Terry had organized a group of church supporters, and they were making daily visits to the clinic. They sprayed the door locks with Krazy Glue and followed the employees to and from work. One day they stormed the clinic, smashed the furniture, ripped out the phones and locked themselves in the counselling room. The police had to break the door down with a crowbar. During still another protest, one of the Operation Rescue activists, a young man, leaped in a window and punched a five-months-pregnant woman in the stomach. She was taken to hospital in an ambulance – and miscarried three weeks later.

Terry never got very far with the other two points in his 'three-point plan'. By 1989, Operation Rescue had set up only one counselling service for young and needy pregnant women, the Crisis Pregnancy Center. It showed intimidating anti-abortion films to the teenagers it lured with a Yellow Pages ad promising free pregnancy tests. The day I visited, the only real service it offered needy mothers was a few packets of powdered milk and two hand-me-down cots. As for the homes for unmarried mothers, Terry set up only one, the House of Life in Pennsylvania. It took in only four pregnant girls before shutting down. The reason? The couple operating the home announced that they were too busy preparing for their own baby's birth.

The Legacy of the Anti-Abortion Movement

The anti-abortion warriors were the backlash's most blatant and violent agents. At their instigation, between 1977 and 1989 seventy-seven family-planning clincs in the USA were torched or bombed (in at least seven instances, during working hours, with employees and patients inside), 117 were targets of arson, 250 received bomb threats, 231 were invaded and 224 vandalized. With time, the attacks only accelerated. In April 1991 the numbers of bombings and arson attacks had already exceeded the figure for the full year of 1990. Clinic patients were harassed and even kidnapped; staff members received death threats at sixty-seven family-planning centres and endured assault and battery attacks at forty-seven centres. Anti-abortion arsonists blinded a clinic technician with chemicals before setting fire to the Concerned Women's Clinic in Cleveland, Ohio. A staff doctor at another clinic was maimed when her morning newspaper was booby-trapped. The executive director of Planned Parenthood in Minnesota was struck repeatedly and choked. At a Youngstown, Ohio, clinic, a worker suffered concussion when twenty-five anti-abortion picketers stampeded the building. The employees of still other clinics were beaten, taken hostage, hit by protestors' cars and, in one case, even the clinic director's dog was poisoned.

In 1880, abortion was legal in every American state and popular opinion on it largely neutral. It was only after the midcentury rise of the women's rights movement that abortion became a battleground. As women pressed for such simple family-planning reliefs as 'voluntary motherhood' – which proposed that wives be free to refuse sex occasionally for health reasons – doctors, legislators, journalists and clergymen countered with a far more extreme campaign against all forms of birth control. Suddenly, the *New York Times* was crammed with stories deploring abortion as 'the evil of the age'. Suddenly, the American Medical Association (then a fledgling organization that was trying to establish its credentials by putting midwives and other female abortion providers out of business) was launching a massive public relations campaign against this 'criminal' and 'irresponsible' practice, even offering an annual prize for the best anti-abortion book. Suddenly, clergymen were declaring abortion a grave sin. Suddenly, 'purity' crusaders were storming abortion clinics and dragging their mostly female operators to court. By the end of the nineteenth century this backlash against reproductive rights would result in a federal ban on all birth-control distribution (upheld until well into this century) and the outlawing of abortion (except to save a woman's life) in every state.

Perhaps it is inevitable that even the most modest efforts by women to control their fertility spark a storm of opposition. All of women's aspirations – whether for education, work or any form of self-determination – ultimately rest on their ability to decide whether and when to bear children. For this reason, reproductive freedom has always been the most popular item in each of the successive feminist agendas – and the most heavily assaulted target of each backlash. During the feminist revival of the early twentieth century, the birth-control movement that Margaret Sanger launched enjoyed far broader appeal than any other plank of the women's rights campaign, cutting across class and race lines. As women's rights and peace activist Crystal Eastman wrote in 1918 of her feminist contemporaries, 'Whether we are the special followers of Alice Paul, or Ruth Law, or Ellen Key, or Olive Schreiner, we must all be followers of Margaret Sanger.'

Like its nineteenth-century precursor, the 1980s anti-abortion campaign would exhibit signs of punitive excess, as once again the achievement of modest reproductive liberties for women was greeted with an outpouring of repressive outrage. In the hundreds of legislative initiatives and referenda that followed, opponents of women's reproductive freedom often seemed intent on forcing far more than the repeal of *Roe v. Wade*, the landmark US Supreme Court decision recognizing women's constitutional right to an abortion. Some proposed outlawing abortion even when a woman's life was in danger, an extreme stance that was hardly part of the pre-*Roe* laws restricting abortion. Others wanted to require that the woman get her husband's permission before she proceed; still others wanted her to submit to a mandatory lecture from her doctor, too. Other proposals included forbidding any birth-control device that might possibly work after fertilization, banning basic birth-control information even from public libraries, and allowing total strangers to file a court order prohibiting a woman from having an abortion. In Utah, lawmakers wanted abortion providers to be sentenced to up to five years in prison; in Louisiana the legislature called for a mandatory ten years of hard labour; in Massachusetts, a twice-introduced state bill demanded the electric chair.

There have been several attacks on abortion legislation in Britain during the backlash years. In 1979 John Corrie introduced a Private Member's Bill to restrict the grounds for abortion to 'grave risk to the life of the pregnant woman; or substantial risk of serious injury', and to reduce the upper time limit from 28 to 20 weeks. It received its second reading but failed to get a third. Then Lord Robertson of Oakridge, in the House of Lords, tried to restrict the grounds to 'serious risk . . . substantially greater than if the pregnancy were terminated'. His Bill's aim was to take social factors out of medical decision-making. Its reading was delayed for six months, which removed any chance of further progress. Enoch Powell then introduced another unsuccessful Bill, on experimentation on embryos, which also threatened a woman's right to choice in the matter of abortion. The backlash had a more effective spokesman in David Alton, whose Private Member's Bill aimed to reduce the time limit to 18 weeks, except 'where a woman's life was in danger or where the baby would be born dead or unable to survive'. But his Bill, too, ran out of time. Finally, the 1967 Act was successfully amended – by Section 37 of the Human Fertilization and Embryology Act 1990. Although the amendments do not alter the basis of access to abortion, there is now an upper time limit of 24 weeks, except in cases of risk of grave permanent injury to, or risk to the life of, the mother, or risk of severe foetal handicap.

Restrictions on the availability of abortion have been economic as well as parliamentary. The *Guardian* reported in November 1991 that a health district in Kent, Medway, was cutting by two-thirds the number of abortions available on the National Health Service and was deleting 'poverty' and 'severe social deprivation' from its criteria for a free termination. The proportion of abortions performed on the NHS in Medway will fall from 40 per cent in 1990 to between 12 and 15 per cent in future as a result of the new restrictions. Members of 'Doctors for a Woman's Choice on Abortion' wrote to the newspaper, protesting at the cut in services and pointing out that it will most likely 'affect the poorest women most as they will not be able to raise the money for a non-NHS abortion'. What the knock-on effects in welfare spending will be if these women decide to continue with their unwanted pregnancies, neither Medway health district nor the government seems to have calculated.

Australia has seen numerous attempts to restrict access to abortion over the past ten to fifteen years, notably by 'Call to Australia' members the Rev. Fred Nile and his wife Elaine. Nile's unsuccessful Bill in 1988-9 included a proposal that consent for an abortion should be given by the father of a foetus. The legislation on abortion is complex in Australia, with eight sets of laws – one each for the six states and the two territories. In some states, like New South Wales, abortion is still technically part of the Crimes Act, and there is no guarantee that the law will always be interpreted as liberally as it has been in recent years. Indeed, on occasion, anti-abortion laws *have* been enforced strictly. In 1985 two clinics in Queensland were raided by state police and 47,000 private documents seized. Two doctors were prosecuted for unlawful abortion as a result. Although they were acquitted by jury, the case caused Australian women much disquiet. Even in Victoria, the first state in which the law was liberally applied, a doctor was prosecuted in 1987. The charges were ultimately dismissed, but the very fact that restrictive laws still exist under which they could be pressed indicates the potential danger facing

women in Australia in periods of backlash. The apparently powerful influence of the Catholic bishops on the Australian Labor
Party has been cited as an explanation of the party's failure to
ensure the right to abortion in law. With the fall of Bob Hawke
and the prospect of a new, more conservative government, the
outlook for Australian women's ability to choose is not very
bright.

As the reproductive rights backlash deepened in the USA,
journalists, clergymen and lawyers joined it. In the last two years
of the 1980s alone, more than 1,500 articles on abortion appeared
in the major dailies, and the news weeklies devoted more space to
abortion than to any other social policy issue. (These articles rarely
explored the needs or views of the millions of women hurt by the
attack on abortion; instead, they moralized, wondered if female
reporters should even be allowed to cover the abortion debate,
and worried about how the abortion battle might 'hurt' various
politicians.) The American Bar Association voted to rescind its
pro-choice policy in 1990, only seven months after it had approved
it. Even moderate religious denominations – the American Baptist,
Presbyterian, United Methodist and Episcopal churches among
them – backed away from formerly pro-choice positions. The
Catholic bishops pulled out all the stops, hiring Hill & Knowlton,
the nation's largest public relations firm, to launch a $5 million
publicity drive against abortion. The New York archdiocese proposed a new order of nuns, the Sisters of Life, that would be
devoted exclusively to opposing abortion. New York's John Cardinal O'Connor issued a twelve-page statement notifying Roman
Catholic politicians that they risked excommunication if they supported a woman's right to an abortion. New Jersey bishop James
McHugh declared that, from now on, Catholic politicians who
disagreed with the church's stance would be barred from speaking
at church events or holding church office. The Archbishop of
Guam vowed to excommunicate any senator who opposed an
extreme bill that outlawed virtually all abortions on the island.
And Bishop Rene Gracida of Corpus Christi, Texas, excommuni-
cated the director of a family planning center in town, and promised a similar fate for a worker at another clinic if she didn't leave
her job.

By the end of the decade, the anti-abortion campaign hadn't overturned *Roe*, draconian legislative proposals had been mostly defeated or reversed, and public support for legal abortion had risen. Nonetheless, the relentless publicity, litigation, harassment and violence had gone far toward a de facto elimination of access to abortion for much of the female population.

The climate of fear discouraged an already reluctant medical establishment from offering the procedure. By 1987, 85 per cent of American counties had no abortion services. According to a nationwide survey, the number of rural abortion providers dropped by more than 50 per cent between 1977 and 1988 – and 20 per cent of the decline occurred after 1985. And the pool of doctors trained or seeking training to perform abortions was drying up. North Dakota and South Dakota had only one abortion provider each, and in at least a dozen states, from Mississippi to Maryland, women had to cross state lines to get an abortion. In Missouri, women seeking abortions were travelling all day across the state and camping in the car park of the lone family planning clinic in St Louis that performs second-trimester abortions.

For the tens of millions of women who depended on publicly financed health care, even the few abortion clinics that were still operating were beyond reach. Federal funding was no longer available to the more than a quarter of a million women on Medicaid who sought abortions each year. And all but a dozen states had banned abortions funded from their coffers, too, by the close of the decade. (Moreover, eight states passed laws in the early 1980s restricting even private insurance coverage of abortions.) In Michigan, a state ban on Medicaid-funded abortions that came into effect in 1988 caused the number of abortions to plunge by 10,300, or 23 per cent, by the following year. It was as if *Roe* had never existed.

The handful of private agencies that dispensed minimal abortion funding were overwhelmed with appeals from desperate women; the Chicago Abortion Fund had to turn away hundreds of women each year. Rosie Jimenez, a twenty-seven-year-old single mother on a college scholarship, had six months to go before completing her teaching credentials when she discovered she was pregnant. She had to cross the border to Mexico to find abortion services she could afford. The cheap, illegal operation killed her. When Spring Adams, a thirteen-year-old Idaho girl on welfare, was raped and impregnated by her father in 1989, her mother could find only one doctor in the entire state willing to perform the second-trimester abortion – and he refused to waive the cost. Unable to afford his fees (Idaho banned the use of Medicaid funds for all abortions unless the mother's life was threatened), Spring's mother went on a desperate nationwide search. She finally found a clinic in Portland, Oregon, that agreed to take on her daughter's case and waive all but $200. But two days before Spring was due to board the Greyhound bus to Portland, her father – who opposed abortion – shot and killed her with an assault rifle.

The anti-abortion movement also made it harder to learn about the few clinics performing abortions that were still in business. The high court's 1991 ruling muzzled women's health providers who received federal funds. Federally funded sex-education classes under the Adolescent Family Life Act withheld all information on abortion and birth control from students. And meanwhile public school administrators, fearful of threats from anti-abortion groups, shut down courses that did provide such information. In Minnesota by 1989, less than half of the city's high schools offered any sex education – a direct response to pressure from the state's strong anti-abortion lobby. Anti-abortion lobbies put pressure on the media to reject family-planning clinic ads and cancel public-service programming on abortion services, too. Whether as a direct response to such pressure or simply to head off controversy, dozens of newspapers, radio stations, television networks, college and high-school publications, yearbooks and even football pro-grammes began rejecting or banning outright notices and advertise-ments for family-planning services and even basic informaton announcements from pro-choice groups.

A NOW ad that simply offered the time and place of a national march for reproductive rights was rejected as 'too controversial' by twenty-six radio stations in five of the nation's largest media markets. The *Los Angeles Times* and the *Washington Post* refused to run the Fund for Feminist Majority's ad for a pro-choice film, *Abortion for Survival*. (And women who wrote to the *Los Angeles Times* to protest against the decision received a letter from its advertising department, advising them they were just puppets of a 'certain orchestration' by feminist interests.) On the other hand, *USA Today* was willing to run a huge advertisement for the American Life League that called on raped women not to have abortions. And the networks had no problems airing segments of the controversial, and misleading, anti-abortion film *The Silent Scream* (shown around the world), which purported to show a foetus at twelve weeks. The media's corporate advertisers, fearful of anti-abortion boycott threats, didn't make it any easier for broadcasters to offer news programming on abortion. An ABC radio special on abortion, hosted by Barbara Walters, couldn't find a single sponsor.

The anti-abortion movement also succeeded in inspiring massive cutbacks in public and private support and funding for birth-control clinics and other family-planning services besides abortion. Under pressure from the 'right-to-life' lobby, many corporations, charities and foundations withdrew their financial assistance to family planning, too. In 1988 United Way stopped funding Planned Parenthood, and in 1990, under pressure from the Christian Action Council, AT&T cut off its contributions, too (after twenty-five years), claiming that shareholders had objected to the agency's association with abortion – even though 94 per cent of its shareholders had voted in favour of funding Planned Parenthood.

The curtailment of family-planning funds led, ironically, to more abortions among younger and poor women, as the lack of birth-control services drove up the numbers of unwanted and teenage pregnancies. By 1990, the National Center for Health Statistics was reporting an increase in the teenage birthrate, reversing an eighteen-year decline. England, too, saw a substantial rise in teenage births outside marriage: according to OPCS figures, from 24 per thousand in girls under twenty in 1979 to 43.5 per thousand in 1989. Pressure from campaigners of the moral Right, like Mary Whitehouse, Valerie Riches, founder of the Responsible Society, and Victoria Gillick, who focused on under-sixteens, put providers of contraception on the defensive and gained the ear of government. Even Establishment groups opposed to Gillick's attempt to end patient confidentiality for underage girls took on the language of the Right; and the FPA moved its position to extol the ideal of sex within a 'loving, caring, responsible and lasting relationship'. Most of the direct provision of contraceptives had passed from the FPA to NHS family doctors by the end of 1976, potentially discouraging many teenage girls from seeking advice. This was later confirmed; a report from the Policy Studies Institute in 1991 revealed that young people were failing to seek contraceptive advice from family doctors, because they feared their parents would be told or because they found their GPs unsympathetic or disapproving.

The anti-abortion crusade in the USA also diminished women's reproductive options for the future, by virtually closing down federal and private research on birth control. By the end of the decade, only one corporation was still funding research on contraception – down from two dozen in the 1960s and 1970s. Insurance companies retreated, too, and by 1990 none of them was willing to cover clinical testing of most contraceptives. A 1990 Institute of Medicine study found that the United States, which had once been a world leader in contraceptive research, had fallen critically behind the rest of the industrialized world in birth-control development and was now endangering the future of 'contraceptive choice' in the country.

Anti-abortion threats also halted research on abortifacients. Sterling Drug, which had one abortion drug under development in 1986, hastily dropped it. Upjohn Company cancelled its abortion drug and closed its contraceptive research programme in 1985, after right-to-life groups launched a boycott. And the Population Council discontinued its research on the French abortion pill RU-486, which was finally given its licence in Britain in July 1991, despite opposition from Life and SPUC. In 1989, the Food and Drug Administration banned importation of RU-486 for private use, under pressure from such congressional abortion opponents as senators Jesse Helms, Henry Hyde and Robert Dornan. In 1990 the makers of the abortion pill, Roussel-Uclaf, stopped supplying it to the only US clinical research team ever to test it. And these researchers, at the University of Southern California, found support from their medical peers evaporating, too; although most doctors they approached originally expressed interest, soon the physicians were calling back to say the study was 'too controversial' for their participation. Meanwhile, when a shareholder proposed that the pharmaceutical giant Eli Lilly and Co. simply *study* the possibility of making RU-486, the drug company's executives hastened to the Securities and Exchange Commission to have the proposal excised from the company's proxy statement. They succeeded and shareholders never even had a chance to vote on it. Only one American company, the tiny New Jersey firm Gyno-Pharma, admitted, for less than twenty-four hours, that it might consider marketing RU-486; and after threats of boycotts rumbled from the anti-abortion lobby, company officials immediately disavowed any interest in the drug. RU-486 is not available in Australia, either: a trial was started, but after considerable pressure from 'right-to-life' groups, it was discontinued.

Foetal Rights: Mother Versus Foetus

The anti-abortion iconography in the last decade featured the foetus but never the mother. In the movement's literature, photographs, films and other props, the whole 'unborn child' floats in a disembodied womb. The foetus is a conscious, even rumbustious tyke, the mother a passive, formless and inanimate 'environment'. The foetus is the occupant, the mother its temporary living quarters. One right-to-life committee even produced an 'unborn child's diary', in which a precocious foetus penned ruminations about flowers and confided, 'I want to be called Kathy.' The Willkes' manual instructs the movement's participants to make a point of using 'humanizing terms . . . such as "this little guy",' when referring to the foetus – and phrases like 'place of residence' when talking about the mother. Dr Bernard Nathanson, creator of *The Silent Scream* – a film in which the truly silent cast member is the mother – describes the foetus in *The Abortion Papers* as 'the little aquanaut', a child in 'intrauterine exile' who is 'bricked in, as it were, behind what seemed an impenetrable wall of flesh, muscle, bone and blood'. At least the pregnant woman is envisaged as an occupied house; the anti-abortion metaphor for the woman who aborts is a bombed-out shell: 'Her body is a haunted house where the tragic death of a child took place,' Joseph Scheidler writes.

To a remarkable degree, the anti-abortion movement succeeded by the end of the 1980s in bringing much of the medical and legal establishment round to its vision of the foetus and mother. The foetus would become the primary patient in the antenatal operating room, the full citizen in the lawbooks, and the lead plaintiff in the courtroom. In fact, by the close of the 1980s a foetus actually had more legal rights in some areas than a live child.

Doctors drafted the first lines in the foetal declaration of independence. In 1982 a group of obstetricians and geneticists met in California and agreed that they had made sufficient medical advances in the still highly experimental practice of foetal surgery to treat the foetus as an independent 'patient'. At the same time, in the equally experimental field of infertility treatment, doctors were also treating the foetus as if it were a baby with a separate existence from the mother. In the waiting rooms of in-vitro fertilization (IVF) centres, doctors posted 'baby pictures' of their embryos – 'Our Katy', read the caption of one of the many murky sonograms plastered on the walls of the Pacific Fertility Center in San Francisco. Some infertility specialists even offered videotapes of 'our children' – footage of barely fertilized eggs – and enthused about how 'the sonographic voyeur, spying on the unwary foetus, finds him or her a surprisingly active little creature.' In fact, some infertility doctors were beginning to act as if the foetus really were *their* baby. At the Jones Institute of Reproductive Medicine, Dr Howard Jones claimed custody of a patient's embryo; the woman had to sue him in federal court to force him to release it.

In Britain and Australia, much of the agitation around foetal rights has centred on IVF provision. In Australia there have been restrictions on embryo research, especially in the state of Victoria where IVF programmes were most advanced. In New South Wales a young girl successfully sued her mother for damage sustained in the womb when the mother had a car accident. The verdict was hailed as a victory for foetal rights. In the UK the Whittington Hospital in north London allowed an Anglican chaplain to conduct funeral services for aborted foetuses, put into baby-sized caskets, often several to one casket, at East Finchley crematorium – without the knowledge or permission of the mothers, many of whom were not even of Christian background. And there was a right-wing and media outcry when the news broke in early 1991 that artificially inseminated 'virgin births' were being made possible by infertility clinics. Seasoned anti-abortion campaigners like Ann Winterton and Dame Jill Knight, both Conservative MPs, joined those in the press who condemned women who had never had sex but wanted a child.

The *Observer* commented that at the heart of the protest lay 'a defence of the traditional family and a fear that donor insemination will lead women to reject men'. 'Whose body is it anyway?' asked Roger Scruton, commentator of the New Right in the *Sunday Telegraph*, accusing a supporter of women's right to bring up children on their own of 'feminist claptrap'. The *Daily Mail* spoke of 'a scheme which strikes at the very heart of family life', under the headline: STORM OVER VIRGIN BIRTHS. Another alarmist *Mail* headline read: NIGHTMARE VISION OF BABY PRODUCTION LINE. Virginia Bottomley, the Health Minister, was reported in the *Independent* as saying that the new Human Fertilization and Embryology Act provided the social safeguards, 'including the child's need for a father'. It is now much less likely that infertility clinics will offer IVF treatment to single women who are not in 'a stable union'.

Lawmakers and judges in the USA were also moving to elect the foetus to citizenship. For the first time in history, legislators and state courts began to define the foetus as a legally independent 'person' rather than an entity whose interests were inseparable from its mother's. A New Hampshire court even deemed the foetus a 'household resident' who could collect on a homeowner's insurance policy. By the mid-1980s a majority of states had passed 'foeticide' laws that extended wrongful death statutes to the foetus. Some states went even further. A Louisiana law defined fertilized eggs as fully formed humans. Courts, too, were pushing the bounds of personhood to pre-foetal stages. In a 1989 divorce case, a Tennessee circuit judge ruled that a couple's frozen pre-embryonic clusters of four to eight cells were legally their children and couldn't be destroyed.

While these early foeticide laws primarily defended the foetus from an intruding third party – a drunken driver or mugger who accosted the mother – the laws and court rulings that arose in the second half of the decade were directed with increasing exclusivity, and wrath, at the mother herself. If the early legislative and judicial decisions separated mother and foetus, then the later ones set mother and foetus against each other.

By the late 1980s state legislators were seeking to apply child abuse laws to the foetus to protect it from an offending mother. On the federal level, California's US Senator Pete Wilson crusaded for the Child Abuse During Pregnancy Prevention Act. 'Surely the most sordid and terrifying story is that of exploding child abuse through the umbilical cord,' he told his fellow lawmakers. Meanwhile, in the states, a raft of 'foetal neglect' bills flooded the legislatures. The proposals called for the prosecution of women whose behaviour during pregnancy was deemed negligent of their foetuses – behaviour that included everything from not following doctors' orders to eating the wrong foods to giving birth at home. Other legislative initiatives sought to criminalize alcohol use by pregnant women and to imprison repeat pregnant offenders for as much as twenty-five years. In many states it became routine for juvenile courts to claim 'custody' of the foetuses of low-income pregnant women whose antenatal practices might constitute harm; then, at birth, the children were declared state wards and whisked away.

The general public eventually joined the campaign. By 1988, half of the people surveyed in a Gallup poll agreed that pregnant women who drank, smoked or refused obstetrical surgery should be held legally liable. Shops, restaurants and even subways posted lecturing signs about proper consumption. Medical and legal scholars proposed mandatory breathalyser tests for seemingly tipsy pregnant women, mandatory screenings of the foetus (with criminal penalties for those who resisted), and arrests for those who didn't follow nutritious diets. In this environment, total strangers felt free to approach pregnant women in public places and accost them for buying a six-pack at the grocery store or ordering a single glass of wine at dinner. In Seattle in 1991, a pregnant woman who ordered a single drink in a bar was hounded and lectured by two waiters – so vigorously that she sued. The local newspaper columnist, however, applauded the waiters' vigilance. That same year, a Seattle health club ordered a pregnant bus driver with sore muscles out of its jacuzzi. She needed written permission from her doctor, the club's officers insisted. (The woman had, in fact, checked beforehand with her doctor, who had approved the regimen.)

As the foetus's rights increased, the mother's just kept diminishing. Poor pregnant women were hauled into court by male prosecutors, physicians and husbands. Their blood was tested for drug traces without their consent or even notification, their confidentiality rights were routinely violated in the state's zeal to compile a case against them, and they were forced into obstetrical surgery for the 'good' of the foetus, even at risk of their own lives.

Here are just a few of the many cases from the decade's pregnancy police blotter and court docket:

• In Michigan, a juvenile court took custody of a newborn because the mother took a few Valium pills while pregnant, to ease pain caused by a car accident injury. The mother of three had no history of drug absue or parental neglect. It took more than a year for her to get her child back.

• In California, a young woman was brought up on foetal neglect charges under a law that, ironically, was meant to force negligent fathers to pay child support. Her offences included failing to heed a doctor's advice (a doctor who had failed to follow up on her treatment), not getting to the hospital with due haste, and having sex with her husband. The husband, a batterer whose brutal outbursts had summoned the police to their apartment more than a dozen times in one year alone, was not charged – or even investigated.

• In Iowa, the state took a woman's baby away at birth even though no real harm to the infant was evident – because she had, among other alleged offences, 'paid no attention to the nutritional value of the food she ate during her pregnancy', as an AP story later characterized the Juvenile Court testimony. '[S]he simply picked the foods that tasted good to her.'

• In Wyoming, a woman was charged with felony child abuse for allegedly drinking while pregnant. A battered wife, she had been arrested on this charge after she sought police protection from her abusive husband.

• In Illinois, a woman was summoned to court after her husband accused her of damaging their daughter's intestine in a car accident during her pregnancy. She wasn't even the driver.

• In Michigan, another husband hauled his wife into court to accuse her of taking tetracycline during her pregnancy; the drug, prescribed by her physician, allegedly discoloured their son's teeth, he charged. The state's appellate court ruled that the husband did indeed have the right to sue for this 'pre-natal negligence'.

• In Maryland, a woman lost custody of her foetus (in other words, state officials took away her infant at birth) when she refused to transfer to a hospital in another city, a move she resisted because it would have meant stranding her nineteen-month-old son.

• In South Carolina, an eighteen-year-old pregnant woman was arrested before she had even given birth, on the suspicion that she might have passed cocaine to her foetus. The charge, based on a single urine test, didn't hold up; she delivered a healthy drug-free baby. Even so, and even though the Department of Social Services found no evidence of abuse or neglect, state prosecutors announced that they intended to pursue the case anyway.

• In Wisconsin, a sixteen-year-old pregnant girl was confined in a secure detention facility because of her alleged tendencies 'to be on the run' and 'to lack motivation' to seek antenatal care.

Certainly society has a compelling interest in bringing healthy children into the world, both a moral and practical obligation to help women take care of themselves while they're pregnant. But the punitive and vindictive treatment mothers were beginning to receive from legislators, police, prosecutors and judges in 1980s America suggests that more than simple concern for children's welfare was at work. Police loaded their suspects, still bleeding from labour, into paddy wagons; prosecutors barged into maternity wards to conduct their interrogations. Judges threw pregnant women with drug problems into jail for months at a time, even though, as the federal General Accounting Office and other investigative agencies have found, the antenatal care offered to pregnant women in American prisons is scandalously deficient or nonexistent (many prisons don't even have gynaecologists) – and has caused numerous incarcerated women to give birth to critically ill and damaged babies. Police were eager to throw the book at erring pregnant women. In the case of Pamela Rae Stewart of San Diego – the battered woman charged with having sex against her doctor's orders – the officer who headed the investigation wanted her tried for manslaughter. 'In my mind, I didn't see any difference between born and unborn,' Lieutenant Ray Narramore explained later. 'The only question I had was why they didn't go for a murder charge. I would have been satisfied with murder. That wouldn't have been off-base. I mean, we have a lady here who was not following doctor's orders.'

Lawmakers' claims that they just wanted to improve conditions for future children rang especially false. At the same time that legislators were assailing low-income mothers for failing to take care of their foetuses, they were making devastating cuts in the very services that poor pregnant women needed to meet the law-makers' demands. How was an impoverished woman supposed to deliver a healthy foetus when she was denied antenatal care, nutrition supplements, welfare payments and housing assistance? In the District of Columbia, Marion Barry declared infant health a top priority of his mayoral campaign – then cut health-care funding, forcing antenatal clinics to scale back drastically and eliminate outright their evening hours needed by the many working women. Doctors increasingly berated low-income mothers, but they also increasingly refused to treat them. By the end of the decade more than a quarter of all counties in America lacked any clinic where poor women could get antenatal care, and a third of doctors wouldn't treat pregnant women who were Medicaid patients. In New York State, a health department study found that seven of the state's counties had no comprehensive antenatal care for poor women whatsoever; several of these counties, not so coincidentally, had infant mortality rates that were more than double the national average. In California in 1986, twelve counties didn't have a single doctor willing to accept the state's low-income Medi-Cal patients; in fact, the National Health Law Program concluded that the situation in California was so bad that poor pregnant women are 'essentially cut off from access to care'.

Scalpels and Caesareans: Intruders in the Womb

Doctors, who had first defined the foetus as an independent patient with a right to treatment, now began to define the pregnant woman as an ancillary party with no right to refuse treatment. First the doctors had issued a list of prohibitions, telling pregnant women what they couldn't do with their own bodies. Then the doctors went on the offensive, telling pregnant women that physicians would now be free to operate on their bodies – with or without their consent. In a 1986 survey of directors of US maternal-foetal medicine fellowship programmes, nearly half the doctors said they supported court orders that forced pregnant women to submit to obstetrical procedures – and favoured involuntary detention of pregnant women whose failure to submit they believed might pose a risk to the foetus. Less than a quarter consistently supported a competent pregnant woman's right to refuse her doctor's orders. In the professional medical literature, physicians and medical school professors were proposing increasingly harsh and punitive methods of dealing with pregnant women who wouldn't comply with doctors' orders. Their recommendations included arresting women for 'refusal to accept genetic counseling' or for choosing to deliver their baby by midwife against the recommendations of a physician.

The judges supported the doctors. When the physicians asked for judicial muscle to enforce their will, the courts almost always delivered. The men on the bench, too, while crusading for foetal rights, often seemed to have trouble envisaging the women as full and live persons. A Washington, DC, Superior Court judge ordered a Caesarean section against the wishes of a nineteen-year-old pregnant woman, Ayesha Madyun, with this decree: 'All that stood between the Madyun foetus and its independent existence, separate from its mother, was, put simply, a doctor's scalpel.'

A review of medical institutions in eighteen states between 1981 and 1986 identified thirty-six cases where doctors had gone to court to force an unwilling woman to submit to obstetrical intervention – most times within a day after they first heard of the woman's refusal. Judges granted all but three of the requested court orders – 88 per cent within six hours, 20 per cent within an hour or less. At times, consent was conveniently granted over the phone. The women's wishes were ignored in these cases even though in no instance had they been found to be mentally incompetent. And most of these situations weren't even emergencies; in only two cases did doctors demand a Caesarean section because they believed the foetus was in serious medical danger. And these doctors' judgements were often wrong. Their predictions of harm proved false in six of the fifteen cases involving court-ordered Caesareans. In a 1981 court order involving a Georgia woman, doctors testified that without the procedure, the chances of the foetus's demise were 99 per cent. After the court granted the order, the woman went into hiding – and delivered a healthy baby without the operation.

At a time when the right of patients to refuse treatment in all other areas was gaining legal ground, pregnant women were increasingly losing battles to exercise their right of refusal in the obstetrical ward. The doctors, hospitals and courts involved in these forced obstetrical surgeries often seemed contemptuous of pregnant women's rights. In Chicago, a woman expecting triplets was tied down to her hospital bed with wrist and ankle cuffs after she refused to consent ahead of time to a Caesarean. Instead of allowing her to seek care elsewhere, the hospital obtained custody of the unborn triplets and got a court order to force her to have the procedure. In at least two instances, the doctors didn't even bother to get a court order before wheeling their protesting patients into the operating room. In a 1982 Michigan case, the judge didn't just order a woman to undergo a Caesarean against her will; he told her that if she didn't comply, he would send the police to her house to drag her to the hospital. (She, too, fled and gave birth to a healthy baby.)

In ordering these operations, judges went far beyond the case law on parental duties to live children. The courts have long held that parents cannot be compelled to take actions to benefit their children's health. In two key cases, the courts refused to force a father to donate a kidney to his dying child and declined even to make parents move to a new climate to aid their ailing child. 'To compel the defendant to submit to an intrusion of his body would change every concept and principle upon which our society is founded,' the judge wrote in one such decision. 'To do so, would defeat the sanctity of the individual.' It was apparently less of a legal leap to intrude upon the body of a pregnant woman.

The proponents of forced obstetrical surgery argued that protecting the foetus didn't interfere with pregnant women's rights in any serious way; even if the mother didn't want a Caesarean, the procedure was unlikely to hurt her. But when it came down to a choice between the health of the mother and the rights of the foetus, the foetus began to win out. This coercive ranking of maternal and foetal rights was nowhere more brutally spelled out than in the case of 'A.C.' – the impersonal I.D. the court would assign to Angela Carder in her final dehumanizing days.

On a June day in 1987, Angela Carder lay in a hospital bed at George Washington University Hospital in Washington, DC. A twenty-eight-year-old secretary, twenty-six weeks pregnant, she was missing a leg, a casualty of her lifelong war with bone cancer. Doctors had told her twice before to be prepared for imminent death. Both times they had been wrong. She was, in fact, one of the first children to survive Ewing's sarcoma, cancer of the connective tissue.

In 1984 Carder had married and decided she wanted to have a baby. She asked her doctor's advice. Her cancer had been in remission for several years and her obstetrician told her to go ahead and get pregnant. But midway through her pregnancy, the disease returned with a vengeance. In her sixth month, an inoperable tumour engulfed her lung. She was hospitalized at George Washington and the doctors there issued a terminal prognosis. Her long-time oncologist, who had witnessed Carder pull through before and did not consider her to be a terminal case, recommended radiation and chemotherapy – treatment which Carder wanted, too. 'She told the doctor in the beginning she wanted her health to come first,' her mother Nettie Stoner recalls. 'Angie had been through too much in her life struggling to survive to give up her life.'

But the doctors at the hospital, who had just entered the case and were giving Carder only days to live, wouldn't prescribe chemotherapy because they feared it would endanger the foetus. At twenty-six weeks, it was unlikely to survive, but if they could prolong Carder's life for a couple of weeks – rather than attempting to save it – the foetus would have a better chance. So instead of treating her cancer, they jammed a tube down her throat and pumped her with sedatives, a strategy to delay the hour of death. Carder tried to fight this 'treatment', her mother says, remembering how her daughter thrashed and twisted on the bed, fending off the doctors. 'She said, "No, no, no. Don't do that to me".' But Carder lost the battle and was, quite literally, silenced. With the tube in place, she couldn't speak.

Word of the Carder case quickly travelled to the hospital's executive and then legal departments. George Washington Hospital's lawyers were not oblivious to the current climate on foetal rights. They had seen other hospitals dragged into court by anti-abortion activists for failing to pursue heroic measures to save severely compromised foetuses. They began to worry: what if the foetus were 'viable'? The hospital could be held liable for its death. The administration proposed that the doctors try to rescue the foetus with immediate intervention – a Caesarean section.

In Carder's fragile state, performing major surgery would probably kill her. Even the hospital's doctors, who wanted to save the foetus, opposed it. As for the opinion of the patient herself, she was said to be 'unconscious' from the sedatives and unavailable for consultation. Rather than waiting a few hours for the drug-induced haze to clear so they could ask Carder's permission – and without ever seeking the advice of her family – the hospital administration called in a judge.

Superior Court judge Emmet Sullivan came that very afternoon and set up court in a hospital conference room. On one side: the hospital's legal team, two city attorneys, and the lawyer for the foetus. On the other: a lone court-appointed attorney representing Carder, appointed half an hour before the hearing.

Carder's family was invited to the session, but no one apprised them beforehand that it was a hearing to decide their daughter's fate. While visiting her daughter in the intensive care unit earlier that day, Nettie Stoner recalls a social worker drawing her aside and simply telling her she was needed for a 'short meeting' down the hall. 'No one told me what was wrong,' Stoner says, and the atmosphere in the conference room only confused her further. 'I walked in and they were having lunch catered like a party. They were saying, "Have a sandwich! Have a soda!" '

The judge asked for a medical opinion. Each of the physicians in the hospital's obstetrical department came out against the operation. Then the foetus's lawyer, Barbara Mishkin, spoke up. 'Well, I suppose it will hasten her death,' she said, but Carder was probably going to die in a few hours anyway. Her rights should be put aside. To support her argument, Mishkin related a story she had heard at second hand. Carder, she told the court, had reportedly said the previous evening that she had 'had enough of the pain'. Mishkin concluded from this hearsay evidence that Carder might not have wanted to live anyway, so the foetus's interests should prevail.

The judge's questions to Mishkin and the others focused almost exclusively on the foetus. He wanted to know how a Caesarean section would affect the foetus's health – but not how it would affect Carder's. He championed the foetus's right to live – but characterized Carder's struggle to survive as an almost selfish concern for 'her own comfort'. Not once did the judge explore or challenge the assumption that Carder was all but dead. Her long-time oncologist was not even invited to the hearing. When Carder's attorney observed that performing a Caesarean on Carder 'would in effect be terminating her life', he was cut off in mid-sentence by the judge, who said, 'She's going to die.' Hearing this, Carder's anguished father cried out, 'Who is to say she's going to die?' His question was ignored.

Although Carder lay just down the hall, neither the judge nor the attorneys engaged in this life-and-death proceeding bothered to take the short walk to her room. Later, everyone would have their reasons. 'If I wanted to go, then everybody would want to,' is the explanation that Mishkin offers. 'I didn't want to intrude.' She adds, 'It was the end of an exhausting day. We couldn't take any more.'

The judge took a brief recess, then reconvened the hearing.

'There's been some testimony that the performance of a Caesarean section may very well hasten the death of Angela,' he told them. 'There's also been testimony that delay in performing the Caesarean section greatly increases the risk to the foetus. . . . Given the choices, the court is of the view the foetus should be given an opportunity to live.' Then he said, 'I have ruled' – and told the doctors to operate immediately.

Dr Louis Hamner from the obstetrical unit returned to Carder's room to deliver the news. The sedatives were just beginning to wear off and Carder was still foggy. He asked her if she wanted the surgery and she mouthed the word 'yes'. Half an hour later, he returned to her room. This time, she told him, 'I don't want it done, I don't want it done' – unambiguously and repeatedly. It was, Hamner said, 'quite clear to me'.

But when the doctor hastened to the conference room to tell the others still assembled there, they were dubious. The judge said, 'The court is still not clear what her intent is.' And one of the city's lawyers, Richard Love, thought that Carder's opinion didn't matter anyway, because the court had originally made the decision on the assumption that it was to be an operation performed without her consent. The judge agreed and, once more, told the doctors to start the operation.

In a last-ditch effort, Carder's court-appointed attorney Robert Sylvester called the American Civil Liberties Union Reproductive Freedom Project; the ACLU attorneys filed an emergency appeal for a stay. Within the hour, the case was heard via a conference phone call, with a hastily assembled three-man panel from the appeals court. The judges, told that the operation had to begin at once, agreed to hear all the evidence and make a decision in 'sixteen minutes'.

Almost immediately doubts were raised about Carder's ability to make a decision. Was her 'mental frame of mind' impaired? the judges wanted to know. 'Does this woman seem to be ambivalent?' Judge Frank Nebecker pressed. 'Changed her mind at least twice, is that correct?' The foetus's attorney Barbara Mishkin told the judges that the operation's threat to Carder's life was 'insignificant' because she was a terminal cancer patient. It was 'not a question of choosing between the life of the mother and the life of the foetus because the mother cannot be restored to normal life expectancy'. The 'right of the foetus' to live in this case, she said, 'overrides any interest in the mother's continued very short life'.

Because the attorneys had all been appointed at the last minute, none was well informed of reproductive rights law. The only one attending this telephonic hearing who was familiar with the legal case history in this area was Elizabeth Symonds, the ACLU attorney. The law 'is quite clear', she told the judges. 'The Supreme Court unequivocally ruled a woman's life and health must always prevail over the foetus's life and health, direct quote 439 US 379, 400.' Judge Nebecker asked her one question, interrupted her midway through the first sentence of her answer, then said, 'With the time constraints, we don't have time to start reading.' Instead, with the sixteen minutes up, the judges ordered the hospital to perform the operation.

A short while later, the doctors delivered a girl. She was said to have 'lived' two hours, although it's unclear how: repeated efforts to inflate her lungs with a respirator were unsuccessful. It was 'like trying to ventilate a rock', Dr Hamner told a *Washington Post* reporter later. Nettie Stoner was invited up to see the baby; she recalls the hospital staff handing her a tiny stiff corpse, dressed in a nappy, T-shirt and cap. A nurse told her that the baby had lived briefly, but Stoner didn't believe her. 'They wanted a live product,' she says bitterly. 'They wanted a live product so they could justify what they had done.'

Carder awoke a few hours later. When she was told the baby was dead, she cried. Her mother held her hand and told her it would be OK, that they all loved her and maybe one day she would have another baby. Soon after, Carder slipped into a coma. Two days later, she was dead. An autopsy report determined that the operation was a contributing cause of her death.

Five months later the Court of Appeals finally issued its written opinion in support of its sixteen-minute decision. 'We well know,' the unapologetic opinion said, 'that we may have shortened A.C.'s life span.' Carder's parents would later appeal against the order, on the grounds that their daughter had not consented to the operation and that the surgery had violated her right to live. Three years later, the DC Court of Appeals finally agreed and ruled the judicial decision in error. But that was three years too late to matter to Angela Carder.

After Carder's story hit the papers, it entered the popular culture's feedback loop and soon became grist for an episode of *L.A. Law*. But in the TV version the judge makes the 'right' choice. Foetal rights are vindicated: the mother dies but the baby survives. For Carder's mother, the show was the final indignity. First the hospital sought to invade her daughter's body against her will. Then the courts knowingly hastened her daughter's death. And now Hollywood was going to cover up these crimes. When NBC aired that script, Stoner says, 'They took Angela's story away from her.'

On the Job: The Rise of Foetal Protection

At least in the 'foetal-neglect' cases that reached the courts in the 1980s the doctors and judges were dealing with *real* foetuses. When corporate America started championing the foetal rights cause, the 'unborn children' they proposed saving hadn't even been conceived.

Starting in the late 1970s and accelerating in the 1980s, at least fifteen of the nation's largest corporations, from Du Pont to Dow to General Motors, began drafting 'foetal protection policies' that limited or barred women from traditionally 'male' higher-paying jobs that involved exposure to chemicals or radiation – exposure that the companies said might cause birth defects. By mid-decade, hundreds of thousands of employment opportunities had been closed to women in this way. And a survey of chemical companies found unanimous support for the exclusion of women from these work settings.

On the surface, these policies looked like enlightened corporate concern for employees. But they were motivated by liability fears, not compassion. And they were uniformly crafted by companies whose histories suggest that they would welcome an excuse to exclude women. Passed off as progressive efforts by health-conscious corporations, foetal protection policies actually had more in common with the backward 'protective labour policies' that had proliferated at the turn of the century, policies that restricted the hours, pay and type of work women could do – and cost women at least 60,000 jobs. The proponents of these policies likewise professed benevolent interest in women's prospective children, but many of these proponents were male union leaders and legislators patrolling all-male turf. As Cigarmakers International stated forthrightly in its 1879 annual report, 'We cannot drive the females out of the trade, but we can restrict their daily quota of labor through factory laws.'

In the 1980s, neither corporate America nor the US government made reproductive safety a real priority. In fact, the corporate desire to guard female fertility vanished mysteriously for women who worked outside the high-paid circle of the 'male' workplace. Working women were exposed to proven reproductive risks and many of the same chemicals and radiation in clothing sweatshops, hospitals, dental offices, dry cleaners and beauty parlours, but no one was calling for their protection. (Pregnant beauticians suffer a higher rate of toxaemia, miscarriage and premature deliveries; pregnant nurses and hospital technicians are exposed to anaesthetic gases, which have been shown to provoke spontaneous abortion.) These companies banned women from their production lines but not their clerical staff – even though exposure to video display units (VDUs) was suspected at the time of causing higher miscarriage rates, birth defects and other fertility problems. The Reagan administration demonstrated the same double standard over on-the-job reproductive threats. While encouraging foetal protection policies for the 1.4 million women who worked in traditional 'men's' industries, the White House thwarted investigations into the threat that VDU work might pose to 11 million women. When the National Institute for Occupational Safety and Health (NIOSH) tried to probe the causes behind the higher rates of reproductive problems among Southern Bell VDU operators, the Office of Management and Budget demanded that the agency drop all the survey questions on fertility and stress – claiming that such inquiries had 'no practical utility'.

The companies that passed foetal protection policies in the 1980s virtually all belonged to male-dominated industries that had faced intensive federal pressure to hire women a decade earlier. AT&T, for example, which banned women from its computer chip production-line jobs in 1986, was one of the prime EEOC targets in the 1970s. Officials at Allied Chemical were still stewing about laws that 'dictate we must use women' when they moved to lay off some female plant packagers – claiming that these women needed protection from the chemical fluorocarbon 22. After two of the women got sterilized so they could keep their jobs, Allied officials admitted that fluorocarbon wasn't really a foetal hazard after all. And these companies were eager to bar women from more than simply the jobs that involved chemical exposure. Johnson Controls, the nation's largest car battery maker, even banned women from the career path *leading* to these higher-paying jobs. Any slot that might conceivably, through transfer or promotion, advance a worker one day to a lead-exposing job was out of bounds for Johnson Controls' working women.

In making the case for foetal protection, the industries restated the anti-abortion movement's view: foetuses were independent people, women were mere holding units. In a federal survey of industry attitudes towards regulating reproductive hazards, corporate officials and industry lobbyists described the foetus as the 'uninvited visitor' who needed protection – and the woman as the 'room and board', who needed to maintain a 'safe and healthy environment' for her foetus. One industry group described 'the unborn child' as 'a member of the public involuntarily brought into controlled areas'.

The companies also repeated judicial priorities on women's rights in the 1980s – foetuses first, mothers second. In a federal suvey on foetal protection policies, company spokesmen consistently said they believed the rights of the prospective foetus should take precedence over the employment rights of women. To the Synthetic Organic Chemical Manufacturers Association, the exclusion of women was a minor inconvenience, 'a small price for mothers, potential mothers, and society to pay'.

These same companies weren't worried enough about unborn children, however, to ban their fathers from the factory floor – in spite of substantial evidence linking birth defects to men's contact with industrial toxins. A study by the OSHA (the federal Occupational Safety and Health Administration) found that twenty-one of the twenty-six chemicals currently covered by foetal protection policies also caused male infertility or genetic damage. Johnson Controls barred women from its battery-making plants because of the danger of lead exposure, but it didn't bar men – even though lead is a well-known reproductive hazard to both sexes. A 1989 survey of 198 large chemical and electronics companies in Massachusetts found that 20 per cent had foetal policies restricting women's employment; none restricted men's – even though all but one of the chemicals in question were known to pose reproductive hazards for men, too.

Nor was the sudden burst of interest in female reproductive health the result of newly available research. On the rare occasions when the companies bothered to produce data to support their foetal protection policies, they generally relied on a few antiquated studies. Du Pont based its foetal protection policy on a single animal study, later disproven. More often, the 'research' didn't exist. Of the tens of thousands of occupational chemicals in use, only about 6 per cent had been subject to scientific review for reproductive effects. And neither corporate nor federal foetal protectors were rushing to finance new studies. In fact, the Reagan administration severely cut federal funds to support research into occupational and reproductive hazards.

Working women filed suit against Johnson Controls over its extreme foetal-protection policy, which the company had first adopted in 1982. The case inched its way through the judicial system. A federal appeals court upheld the company's policy. The Bush administration allied itself with the company's interests, arguing that such bans on women were perfectly acceptable as long as the employer demonstrated that they were necessary. Finally, in 1991, the Johnson Controls' female workers triumphed in the Supreme Court; the justices found that the company's foetal-protection plan violated the 1978 Pregnancy Discrimination Act. The court could not, however, recompense these women for nine years of lost wages and missed employment opportunities. Nor were the corporations touting foetal-protection policies discouraged; they simply shifted to subtler and more sophisticated tactics, 'counselling' women in new, required-training sessions about foetal threats on the job, or demanding that women get letters from their doctors permitting them to work, or requiring them to sign legal waivers.

In much the way that Victorian medical manuals had categorized women as 'mental' or 'uterine', corporate foetal protection policies of the 1980s divided women into two opposing camps. As these companies would have it, women could choose to be procreators who stayed home – or workers who were sterilized. Take your pick, they told their female employees: lose your job or lose your womb.

In the case of American Cyanamid, some women would lose both.

The commercial message of the eighties backlash received a warm welcome, and an additional boost, from the American Cyanamid's beauty division. Marching under its return-to-femininity banner, the Fortune 500 company's strategists sought a comeback for their ailing Breck Shampoo and hiked sales of their La Prairie skin-'treatment' line. They even hired trend specialist Faith Popcorn to help them to promote 'retro' buying habits. But American Cyanamid did more than profit from the backlash; the company pitched in.

Behind the retouched faces in their beauty-product ads ranged the belching smokestacks of the many chemical and paint plants belonging to this diversified conglomerate. And, like virtually every company in the chemical industry in the early 1970s, American Cyanamid employed a factory work force that was solidly male. When the federal government began to push for integration on the factory floor, American Cyanamid was one of the first chemical companies to feel the pressure. Its Willow Island, West Virginia, plant, in particular, drew the federal investigators' attention.

Since the 1940s American Cyanamid had operated this sprawling chemical-based production factory in Pleasant County, in what had quickly become an unpleasing swathe of polluted land along the Ohio River. The Willow Island plant was (and still is) the only show in town, its assembly line the only workplace for miles offering a living wage. Set in the heart of a state with the highest unemployment rate in the nation, the plant had at its disposal one of America's most desperate labour pools in the country. Few residents here, male or female, would have passed up the opportunity to work at American Cyanamid.

Yet when federal investigators visited Willow Island in 1973, they found the company had never hired a woman to work on its production lines. The federal government soon put American Cyanamid on notice to open its factory doors to women or face legal action. By 1974 Willow Island's plant manager got the word from New Jersey headquarters to start seeking female prospects. Within days after the news reached Pleasant County, women were pouring into the plant's personnel office. 'After we interviewed a couple,' Glenn Mercer, director of industrial relations at the plant, recalled later, 'we had no need to recruit. We had an ample supply of applications.'

At the time, Betty Riggs was a young mother and clerk at the Farm Fresh Market in nearby Belmont. One day early in 1974, some of the men from the plant stopped at the store for sandwiches. The company might start hiring women, she heard them complaining. When Riggs pressed for details, they told her the plant was 'hard work' and 'no place for a woman'.

In Riggs's experience, men had always talked about a 'woman's place' but wives and mothers had always worked. When she was growing up, the women in her family had put food on the table for the eight children; and when they couldn't afford groceries, they hunted. 'We'd either eat wild meat or we didn't eat,' Riggs recalls. By the time she was eleven years old, she was holding down a job. After her marriage at fifteen, an unhappy shotgun wedding, she 'mostly did the providing'. Her husband drank steadily and worked sporadically. Riggs supported her son, husband and both parents from her poverty wages at a series of 'women's' jobs: 75 cents an hour as a waitress at the Parkette Truck Stop, $1 an hour as a cashier at Hammet's Dairy Bar, $2 at Farm Fresh.

When Riggs heard that American Cyanamid was hiring women, she wasted no time applying. When she got no response, she just kept showing up at the company's personnel office. 'I went down about every other day,' she remembers. But even under orders to hire women, the company's officials proved reluctant equal opportunity employers. As a number of women who applied later reported, the personnel officers either told them they were too feminine for a man's plant or not feminine enough. Some were told they were 'too pretty' to work in a factory; others were advised they were 'too fat'. Riggs recalls that the personnel manager told her he wouldn't hire her because he thought she was overweight and he wasn't 'running a diet clinic'. Riggs shed the pounds, then reapplied. He still wouldn't hire her.

After a year of nearly daily pilgrimages, Riggs finally got a job offer from American Cyanamid – but it was for a position as a cafeteria worker, paying the same salary as she was drawing at Farm Fresh. She turned it down and kept applying for factory work. Finally, in December 1975, American Cyanamid hired her as a janitor. A few months later she managed to get a transfer to the lead pigments department – where the pay was six times higher then her Farm Fresh wages.

In the pigments department Riggs worked as a 'cake breaker' and a 'blue bagger'. All day, she hoisted 50 pound pans of solid baked paint from an industrial oven, slid the paint cakes into a grinder, and collected and bagged the blue dust at the other end. 'I liked the work a lot,' she recalls. 'It was real hard work, real exercise.' In the course of the year, several other women joined Riggs in the department.

Donna Lee Martin was unemployed and desperately searching for work when she heard that American Cyanamid was hiring. She had been looking for work ever since she lost her $4-an-hour position at a fibre plant that had shut down. When she went over to Cyanamid for an interview, the personnel supervisor 'asked me about my family and about having to work shift work and having responsible babysitters and how I would handle it if my kids were sick'. She told him she could manage it. In October 1974, she accepted a job at the plant as a 'helper' in the catalyst department. Six weeks later she transferred to the pigments department, because she heard the chances for advancement were better there.

Barbara Cantwell Christman was in her late twenties, recently divorced, supporting her two boys. She was taking whatever jobs she could find: hostess at the North Bend State Park diner, clerk at a clothing factory, receptionist in a doctor's office. In April 1974 she, too, applied to work at Cyanamid. In her job interviews, the personnel officers warned her that she would have to 'work midnights with a bunch of horny men'. One of them said she 'would possibly have to shovel coal in a coal car' and wondered whether she could really manage it. 'I told him yes,' she recalled later in a court deposition. 'I had worked in a hayfield and I could do that. He told me I was awfully pretty to want a job like that and I told him I wanted the job. . . . I needed the job.'

All told, thirty-six women were hired for production work between 1974 and 1976. In the pigments department, in the first year that the women joined, both the quality and quantity of production increased dramatically – a fact begrudgingly noted at the plant's annual banquet that year. Riggs wasn't surprised that output had improved. She took the company-required quota of twelve completed 'centre feeds' a night seriously, much to the irritation of her male work partner, who had become used to a more leisurely pace of ten. 'You screwed up a good thing,' he told her. She ignored him. 'I was hired to do a job,' she says, 'and I was going to do it.'

Riggs's partner wasn't the only man in the pigments department put out by the female invasion. 'Women shouldn't be in here working, taking jobs away from men,' was a popular refrain. 'One guy,' Riggs recalls, 'told Barb [Christman], "If you were my wife, you'd be home darning my socks and making my dinner".' She had to laugh; his wife worked. The foreman was fixated on another 'problem' posed by the women's presence. He complained that they were a safety risk because they could 'get [a] teat caught in the centre feed' or 'get their breasts caught in the pan'.

As the women's numbers mounted, so did the reprisals. One day the women arrived at work to find this greeting stencilled into a beam over the production floor: SHOOT A WOMAN, SAVE A JOB. Another day, the women found signs tacked on their lockers, calling them 'whores'. Riggs found a violent pornographic centre-fold stuffed into her locker; the note attached said, 'This is what I want to do to you.' In two separate incidents, women fended off sexual assaults in the ladies' locker room and showers.

For Riggs, the most bitter opposition came from her first husband. He had never been reluctant to use his fists to keep her in line. One year, he had beaten her up so many times that her friends at Farm Fresh gave her an eye-patch for Christmas. (It was tragically appropriate; the day she unwrapped the present, she recalls, she had two black eyes.) Before her job at American Cyanamid, Riggs says, she had endured the beatings because her husband owned the house and, when he was working, brought home the larger pay cheque – money she badly needed to feed their son and take care of her parents. But now that she was making a decent wage, she had the means to leave him. 'That's why the job at Cyanamid meant so much to me,' she says. 'Because I knew one day I had to be on my own.'

Initially, her husband relied on euphemism to deal with his wife's new financial strength. 'When I first started working at the plant, all of it was "his money",' Riggs recalls. 'Whenever payday came, he'd make me sign over the cheque and then he'd say, "This is how much you get for the week." He said, "Don't tell anyone how much you make".' He also fought the domestic shift in earning power by refusing to take care of their son while she worked. Even when he was unemployed, she had to hire help. And, Riggs recalls, 'I had to keep getting new babysitters because he couldn't keep his hands off of them.'

Eventually, he resorted to more direct and brutal strategies. He locked her in the house or beat her until she was too bruised to appear in public. One day, after he had smashed her head against the kitchen floor until she had passed out, she made her move. She left and filed for divorce. Her exodus only accelerated his violence. Soon after the separation, he sought out a job at the plant and continued the harassment there, in increasingly frightening ways. One night she came out to the parking lot to find her car on fire. Another night on the graveyard shift, he slipped into the pigments department, sneaked up behind her, and flung her to the ground. He pummelled her face until her glasses broke. 'There was another guy there,' Riggs recalls, 'and he just stood and watched. The foreman . . . just ran out of the room. He didn't want to be a witness.' She reported the attack to the company's safety officer, who agreed only to give her husband a 'verbal warning'.

The women at the Willow Island plant were determined to stay no matter what the men did. But, starting in the late 1970s, a bigger opponent than their blue-collar male colleagues loomed: the company's top management. In 1976 the plant abruptly stopped hiring women. That same year back at headquarters, company executives decided to develop a foetal protection policy. American Cyanamid had never demonstrated a strong desire to protect factory workers in the past – employees at the explosion-prone Willow Island plant had worked for years in dirty and dangerous conditions. Suddenly, though, management was worried about reproductive hazards in the factory. American Cyanamid's corporate medical director, Dr Robert Clyne, quickly drafted a policy statement that would prohibit all women of childbearing age from working in production jobs that exposed them to any of twenty-nine chemicals.

The protection plan wasn't a response to complaints from female employees; as Clyne himself conceded, there had been none he was aware of, and he never had doctors at the plant survey workers about possible reproductive problems, anyway. Nor was the move inspired by scientific research. The company's medical department neither reviewed the literature nor conducted any independent research on the reproductive risks of the chemicals that it had singled out. As Clyne explained later, the twenty-nine chemicals were 'compiled as a result of a quick review of computer sheets'. In fact, only one of the selected toxins, lead, was actually known to cause reproductive damage. And while lead is a risk to both sexes, Clyne didn't consider reproductive hazards for men. 'We just did not have enough information to incorporate that facet of it at that time,' he said later in a court deposition. In a radio interview, he said that if it were determined that men's reproductive abilities were being threatened by conditions at the plant, he wouldn't call for men's removal: 'Other steps will be taken to protect the man; either possibly discontinuing the manufacture of the product or using personal protective garments, or respirators.' Nor did the company consider another solution – reducing the level of toxins in the workplace instead of banishing the women. The company later claimed that there was 'no technology available' that was up to the task. A government inspection, however, had found that some changes in engineering controls could have lowered lead exposure to federally acceptable levels for both sexes. But the price tag – $700,000 – apparently didn't appeal to Cyanamid management.

In 1978 the company unveiled the first draft of its foetal protection policy. 'We recognize that this may infringe on the scope of jobs available to the individual woman,' the company's executive committee stated in an in-house memo, 'but in our judgment this is certainly the lesser of the two evils.'

The policy wasn't official yet, but Willow Island's managers decided to enforce it at once. In a series of meetings in January and February 1978, industrial relations director Glenn Mercer summoned women to the plant medical office to lay down the new ground rules. After May 1, he told them, no fertile woman under fifty would be allowed to work in eight of ten departments – a ruling that eliminated all but seven factory jobs for women – unless they were surgically sterilized. As Mercer put it to the women, the company was 'getting the jump on OSHA', which, he assured them, would be passing similar regulations any day now. Riggs recalls: 'He told us it was going to be worldwide. He said there was going to be a time in the future when women wouldn't work at any chemical plant unless they were sterile.'

The women began asking questions. Was he going to lay off the younger men to make way for displaced women with more seniority? No, he answered, just women. What if they took birth-control pills? Not good enough, Mercer said, because they might 'forget'. What if they agreed to take monthly pregnancy tests? Mercer shook his head again. What if their husbands already had a vasectomy? No, Mercer said. It was the women who had to have the operation.

The women asked for a list of the chemicals in question. Mercer said he didn't have it handy but that there were 'hundreds of them', with more being added 'almost on a daily basis'. Then a company nurse and doctor stepped forward to explain to the women that sterilization was simple and could be obtained locally. With that, the meeting was adjourned and the women filed out, most too shaken to speak.

Donna Martin listened to Mercer's speech with mounting horror.

She knew she didn't have enough seniority to get one of the seven remaining jobs. How was she going to support her five children? Her husband was out of work, and they were already beset by financial problems. For weeks she agonized, and the more she turned it over in her mind, the more depressed she became: 'Mentally, I couldn't handle the pressure of having to choose between losing my job and never having more children.' She had some painkillers left over from an old neck injury; in February she took an overdose and ended up in hospital for a month.

Within a week after her release from the hospital she had decided to have the surgery 'so I would quit worrying about losing my job'. She went to Dr George Gevas, a local obstetrician, signed a consent form for the operation that same day and scheduled surgery the following week – because she wanted to be sure she met the company's May Day deadline for sterilization. Afterwards, frightened that she could lose her job if she stayed away too long, Martin allowed herself only three weeks of recuperation – 'that was the shortest time he [Gevas] would agree to me being off,' she said.

When Martin returned to work, she discovered that the plant management had postponed the deadline for surgery in her absence; the corporation's medical department was redrafting the foetal protection policy. Deadlines were set, then extended, throughout the summer. Finally, that September, the plant's officials made a final announcement: the list of chemicals had been reduced from twenty-nine to one, lead, and only the women working in the lead pigments department would be affected. These women, he said, had until October 2 to choose between sterilization and termination of their employment.

Barbara Christman wanted to have more children, but she also desperately needed her job. Like Martin, the more she pondered the alternatives, the more she got 'all messed up worrying about it'. Finally, she, too, went to Dr Gevas. He scheduled surgery for the very next day. When Christman surfaced from the anaesthesia she found herself in an inappropriate locale. The hospital had considerately assigned her a bed in the maternity ward.

Betty Riggs and Lola Rymer also made appointments with Dr Gevas. The doctor, Rymer recalled, gave each of them a lecture;

he said it was 'a poor way to hold on to a job' but 'if you want it done, I'll do it'. Both said yes, and he scheduled their operations for the same day. As Riggs says later, she just didn't see any other option: 'I did what I did because I was more or less the sole supporter for a lot of people who were depending on me. I couldn't let them down. I was up against a brick wall and there was no place to go but forward.'

In the end, five of the seven women in the pigments department were sterilized. The company moved the remaining two to the janitorial staff.

Back at corporate headquarters the news of the sterilizations would eventually reach the company physician who had drafted the foetal protection policy. Dr Clyne heard about it from a woman during an office meeting, but the news didn't seem to trouble – or even much interest – him. Questioned about it later during a deposition, he responded this way:

Q: Did she tell you anything else?
Clyne: No.
Q: Did you ask her any questions?
Clyne: It was more or less of a brief aside. . . . It was just a piece of information that was delivered to me.

Riggs returned to work depressed – and frightened. 'I wondered . . . if they didn't get rid of us this way, what would be next?' Her first week back, she recalls, Mercer called her into his office and proposed that, even though she had been sterilized, maybe she would like to transfer out of the pigments department anyway. He warned her that if she stayed she would be 'branded' by the men. She told him, 'I've never done anything that I'm ashamed of.' Mercer had a similar talk with Christman. When she took two or three days to think about it, he complained. She told him that 'it was a hard decision and I needed some time to think. And he said he needed to really know because he had a lot of scheduling and things to do and by my not deciding he didn't know how to work his work schedule.'

Both women decided to stay in the pigments department. It wasn't the easy route; as Mercer predicted, they were branded. Soon after Donna Martin returned from her operation, one of the guards handed her an insurance pamphlet on maternity coverage. The men in the department jeered that the women had been 'spayed'. 'You're one of the boys now' and 'The veterinarian's having a special' were two favourite lines. The management's attitude was little better: its own literature referred to the women as 'neutered'.

In early 1979 OSHA conducted an inspection of the Willow Island plant. As news of the investigation spread, along with rumours that the company was considering layoffs or cutbacks in the pigments department, tension rose even higher. 'You women are going to get this place closed down,' men in the pigments department began shouting. 'You're the ones who got us into all this trouble.' That October, OSHA ruled that American Cyanamid had violated the Occupational Safety and Health Act and ordered the company to pay a $10,000 fine. The policy constituted a 'hazard' of employment, OSHA found, because it had essentially coerced women into sterilization. In addition, OSHA noted that the lead exposure was equally dangerous to men, and should be cleaned up. American Cyanamid responded by shutting down the pigments department. The jobs the five women had sacrificed their wombs to keep were gone.

In 1980 American Cyanamid contested the government ruling and an OSHA review commission agreed to set aside the citation, concluding that the violation was not covered by the OSHA Act because the hazard it posed did not 'operate directly upon employees'. The Labor Department began preparing an appeal against that decision, but just then the Reagan administration took over, and the appeal was dropped.

Meanwhile, the women were seeking legal relief themselves – first from the state civil rights commission, then the local office of the EEOC. After officials at both agencies made it clear that it would take years for a government ruling, the women turned to the union and legal services. The Oil, Chemical and Atomic Workers International agreed to pursue the legal appeal that the Labor Department had abandoned. And, in a separate action, thirteen women from the plant also filed suit against the company, charging violations of the federal Civil Rights Act.

The union's case came up before federal appeals court Judge

Robert Bork, and in 1984 he ruled in favour of the company. The foetal protection policy wasn't hazardous, he wrote, because the women had 'the option' of surgical sterilization: 'The company was charged only because if offered the women a choice.' The women's civil rights action would peter out after three and a half years of pre-trial proceedings. The company outspent them by millions of dollars. In 1983 they accepted the company's small settlement offer – $200,000 to be divided between the remaining eleven plaintiffs.

The women who participated in the suit would be among the first to be laid off in the 1980s. And when they went looking for work elsewhere they found that their reputations as troublemakers had preceded them. Betty Riggs, the most outspoken, had the hardest time. She finally had to settle for a minimum-wage job at a state park – as a maid. It was back to women's work.

One day in 1987, Betty Riggs was sitting with some friends in the gloomy Sunshine Club near the plant, watching Judge Bork's Supreme Court confirmation hearings on television. Much to her surprise, one of the congressmen on the panel asked about the American Cyanamid decision. She listened carefully as Bork explained his thinking on the case: 'I suppose the five women who chose to stay on the job and chose sterilization, I suppose they were glad to have the choice.' Stunned, Riggs jumped up from her seat and found herself addressing the room. 'Did you hear that? That lying, lying man.' Desperate 'to do something', Riggs sent a telegram to the Senate Judiciary Committee:

> I cannot believe that Judge Bork thinks we were glad to have the choice of getting sterilized or getting fired. Only a judge who knows nothing about women who need to work could say that. I was only twenty-six years old, but I had to work, so I had no choice. . . . This was the most awful thing that ever happened to me. I still believe that it was against the law, whatever Bork says.

The letter inspired only two responses. An aide to one of the senators called to say he found the letter too well written – he wanted to know whether an attorney had 'put her up to it'. And at the hearings, Senator Alan Simpson said that he found Riggs's telegram 'offensive'.

By the end of the decade Bork's rhetoric had travelled the backlash circuit, from the court record to the press accounts and finally back to Pleasant County, West Virginia, where it would be invoked, time and again, to dismiss the women's plight.

On a spring morning in 1988, Steve Tice and a friend, both former Cyanamid plant workers recently laid off at the plant, are lounging against one of the many shuttered shop fronts down the road from the factory. Asked about the case of the Willow Island women, Tice shrugs and says: 'Everybody had a choice. They shouldn't have went ahead and done it [got sterilized] and then raised hell about it. It just got too easy for the women to complain about every little thing.'

In nearby Parkersburg, on a tree-lined street in the older section of town, Dr Gevas maintains a thriving private practice. He offers a similar analysis. 'I feel these women had a choice,' he says. 'If they had a rope around their neck or a gun to their head, then the women would have had a good case. But they had a choice.'

The company's industrial relations manager, Glenn Mercer, lives on another well-groomed street; in the garden, rose bushes are in full and fecund bloom. Mercer plants his legs on the wide porch and folds his arms. 'I don't care to talk about it,' is the only answer he offers to each question put to him. Finally, asked if he has any regrets about his instructions to the women, he says: 'None whatsoever. That's all I'll say. I have no regrets.' Then he retreats inside, slamming the door.

With all avenues for public redress closed, the women's anguish turned inward. In the years since the operations, each of the five sterilized women of Cyanamid has come to think of herself as 'unfeminine' and 'incomplete'. Some say they have stopped sleeping with their husbands – they don't feel 'woman enough'. All have suffered crippling bouts of depression. And when they have sought help, from therapists or doctors, their despair has only been treated, or in some cases deepened, with prescriptions for mind-numbing drugs. They were medicated with tranquillizers, anti-depressants and lithium.

For a long time after the operation Betty Riggs simply withdrew from the world around her. 'I became cold and very unloving to a lot of the needs of other people,' she recalls. On the street, just seeing a woman with a child filled her with envy and shame. At home, 'any TV show that had anything to do with family life just tore me apart'. It was as if, Riggs says, 'I just couldn't get my mind and my body and my heart together. . . . I was less than a person. I was lacking something. It's like your sole individuality just went right down the drain. Like you gave up your only right.'

It was, moreover, the one 'right' that the backlash era was supposed to be championing. The women at American Cyanamid, like women in every area, class and occupation across the United States in the 1980s, had been on the receiving end of a relentless cultural barrage. It told them motherhood was their highest calling. It told them they could restore their femininity by giving up their jobs. It told them they could only make economic and public progress by forsaking domestic and private happiness. While this programme had little bearing on or practical relevance to the hard-pressed lives that Betty Riggs and her co-workers were leading, it could still make them feel 'lacking' in the most deeply personal and agonizing ways.

The 'choice' American Cyanamid gave these employees, like so many of the other options the backlash magnanimously granted women, was framed as a clear-cut and forward-looking development – it represented progress for women. Feminism had opened up choices for women, and now the corporations, the courts and the rest of the society claimed they were doing the same. The American Cyanamid case shows, through the very extremity and horror of what happened to the women caught up in it, how much of a lie the backlash's language of 'choice' really was. There was never anything straightforward, helpful or enlightened about the options presented to the Cyanamid women. Their alternatives were paradoxical, harmful and regressive – and rigged against them from the start.

These were women who had no choice in the matter of their working: it was both a necessity – required by the economy they lived in and the unreliable men in their lives – and a basic source of self-sufficiency and self-respect. They had to work and they wanted to work; yet no one else wanted them to, neither the employers they had to deal with nor the male workers they had to work beside nor the men whose beds they shared. If they kept working, they were humiliated at the office, assailed in the showers and beaten at home; if they tried to obey the social signals and go home, they would starve.

These were the 'choices' the women already faced when American Cyanamid gave them the ultimatum built into the foetal-protection policy. Now they could choose to give up the jobs that they needed to survive or become sterilized and give up what they had been told was their most glorious reason for living. The backlash told women they must choose between a womanly existence and an independent one, and it made the choice for them; it told women that if they gave up the unnatural struggle for self-determination, they could regain their natural femininity. But the women at Cyanamid weren't even offered this pre-selected option. First the company's foetal-protection policy defined the women by their wombs, then it forced them to make the decision themselves to cut their wombs from their bodies. And having compelled the choice, the company ultimately revoked all options – the working women were sent home anyway, without their uteruses.

The distress these women felt was, in large measure, the result of the signals they picked up from their culture and the way these signals conflicted with the real circumstances of their lives. It was a predicament that, to one degree or another, women in many countries and cultures faced during the 1980s. The particular tragedy for the women at American Cyanamid was that these signals conflicted and pushed them to make 'choices' in irrevocable, starkly physical ways.

The backlash could never mould a nation into the backward-looking, dad-hailing, nuclear family fantasy it promoted. But it could implant that image in many women's minds and set up a nagging, even tormenting, dissonance. If women were miserable in the 1980s – and no doubt many were, more so as the backlash deepened – it was not for the reason most widely offered. In the end, feminism and the freedoms that came with it had little part in making women unhappy. It was rather that women's desire for equality, an impulse that refused to disappear throughout the decade, kept clashing with the backlash's agenda, spurring women to batter against the walls of self-doubt and recrimination that the backlash helped to build.

The backlash gave women a prescription for happiness that wouldn't and couldn't be effective. It split women's lives into two half-lives, work and home, and then billed the latter as a full, fulfilled existence. When women resisted the prescription, they were made miserable through psychological and material punishments; when they tried to follow it, they found that it was a faulty cure – half-fantasy, half-punishment – that had no place in their contemporary lives. In fact, it had never been effective; it was always a poor substitute. It could never meet the basic human needs and desires that women have brought forward time and again throughout the centuries – and that society has always sought to turn back.

Epilogue

The backlash decade produced one long, painful and unremitting campaign to thwart women's progress. And yet, for all the forces the backlash mustered – the blistering denunciations from the 'radical' Right, the legal setbacks, the powerful resistance of big business, the self-perpetuating myth machines of the media and Hollywood, the 'neotraditional' marketing drive of the glossy magazines – women never really surrendered, and continued to enter the work force in growing numbers each year. News-stands and airwaves may have been awash with frightening misinformation on spinster booms, birth dearths and deadly childcare – yet women continued to postpone their wedding dates, limit their family size and combine work with having children. Television sets and cinema screens may have been filled with nesting good-wives, but female viewers still gave their highest ratings to programmes with strong-willed and independent heroines. Backlash fashion designers couldn't even get women to follow the most trivial of fashion prescriptions; while retailers crammed their racks with puffball skirts and flower-strewn dresses, women just kept reaching for the suits and leggings.

'I was up against a brick wall,' Betty Riggs said of her terrible predicament at American Cyanamid. Yet in the end she decided, like so many other women in this decade, 'there was no place to go but forward.' No matter how bruising and discouraging her collisions with the backlash wall, each woman in her own way persisted in pushing against it. This quiet female resistance was the uncelebrated counterpoint to the anti-feminist campaign of the eighties, a common thread in the narrative of so many women's lives, no matter where they belonged on the ideological spectrum, no matter what their rung on the class ladder. Even those women who helped build the backlash levees were simultaneously trying to surge over them – whether it was Heritage Foundation's Connie Marshner typing her right-wing treatise the day she went into labour, or ex-TV producer Maeve Haran writing her bestseller while participating in a back-to-the-home 'trend'. Concerned Women for America's president Beverly LaHaye may have said she was trying to resurrect 'traditional' family life, but she was also demanding equal time in the bedroom.

The backlash did manage to infiltrate the thoughts of women, broadcasting on these private channels its sound waves of shame and reproach. But it never quite silenced what factory worker Jan King had called 'this little voice in the back of my mind', the whisper of self-determination that spurred on so many nearly defeated women. It was this voice, so long held in check, so desperate to be heard, that kept dispatcher Diane Joyce in her job, long after the mockery, threats and ostracism from the men around her had become intolerable. It was this voice that finally provoked Beverly LaHaye to throw off her housecoat and paralysing timidity, to write her many books and deliver her many speeches. 'Down deep in my heart,' as she said, 'I felt I would like to stand up and express myself.' It was this voice, barely audible but still unsilenced, that murmured even in the heart of Operation Rescue's goodwife Cindy Terry, who confessed to wanting 'to make something of my life'. No matter how many times women have been told to sit down and keep quiet, they have struggled to their feet. No matter how often they have heard that they would be happier in the shadows, they have continued to seek a sunnier public stage, where their performance, whatever its form or lyrics, will be acknowledged – even applauded.

Women have always fought the periodic efforts to force them back behind the curtain. The important question to ask about the current backlash, then, is not *whether* women are resisting, but how effectively. Millions of individual women, each in her own way, spent the last decade kicking against the backlash barricades. But much of that effort proved fruitless. While women didn't succumb to the backlash agenda, they didn't gain sufficient momentum to crash its steel-reinforced gates, either. Instead, when women tried to drive privately against the anti-feminist forces of the 1980s, they most often found their wheels spinning, frustration and disappointment building as they sank deeper into the same old ruts.

There are so many ways to rebel that pose no real or useful challenge to the system – like the proverbial exploited worker who screws the bolts in backwards or the dutiful daughter chronically late for Sunday dinner. Some women tried to slip by the backlash checkpoint by mouthing the backlash passwords or trying to tailor the 'pro-family' agenda to their own ends or by insisting that *they* were certainly not feminists. Still others resorted to the old 'feminine' strategy – just be good and patient; the world will eventually take pity on women who wait.

While the 1980s was an era that trumpeted the 'one person can make a difference' credo, this strategy proved a blind alley on the road to equal rights. To remove the backlash wall rather than to thrash continually against it, women needed to be armed with more than their privately held grievances and goals. Indeed, to instruct each woman to struggle alone was to set each woman up, yet again, for defeat.

In the past, women have proven that they can resist in a meaningful way, when they have had a clear agenda that is unsanitized and unapologetic, a mobilized mass that is forceful and public, and a conviction that is uncompromising and relentless. On the rare occasions when these three elements have coalesced in the last two centuries, women have won their battles. The suffrage campaign faltered when its leaders resorted to accommodation and deception – daintily claiming they just viewed the vote as a form of 'enlarged housekeeping'. The British government did not give women over thirty the vote in 1918 solely as a reward for their patriotic warwork. Between 1914 and 1918 women poured into industry, and in the post-war atmosphere of widespread industrial militancy, feminist consciousness was very strong. The pre-war years had seen escalating attacks on property, arson, and imprisonment of suffragettes. After the war women had a new cultural confidence, and the government knew it. Ultimately, it was the combination of a forthright agenda, mass action and sheer physical resistance that won the day.

Likewise, the women's liberation movement had many false starts. As political scientist Ethel Klein has observed, despite individual women's repeated efforts only 10 of the 884 women's rights Bills introduced in the US Congress in the 1960s ever passed. It took a sheer display of numbers and determination for the women's movement to force its way into public consciousness. The 1970 Women's Strike for Equality, then the largest demonstration for women's rights in history, turned the tide – inspiring a vast growth in feminist organization membership and a flood of legal victories. Before the strike, the politicians ignored feminists. Afterwards, seventy-one women's rights Bills were signed into law in a matter of a few years – nearly 40 per cent of all the legislation on women's rights passed in the century.

It was in this period that favourable attitudes toward women's rights experienced their greatest growth among men, too. While many women in the backlash eras have feared 'offending men' with feminist demands, women in the 1970s who were assertive and persistent discovered that they could begin to change men's views. By vigorously challenging the conventional definition of masculinity, these women allowed men to start to question it, too. After all, to a great extent so many men have clung to sole-provider status as their proof of manhood because so many women have expected it of them. (In the Yankelovich poll, it's not just men who have consistently identified the breadwinner role as the leading masculine trait; it has also consistently been women's first choice.) As much as men fought the female challenge in the 1970s, they also absorbed and incorporated it into their private experience; and when they saw that women wouldn't back down, many men started to make accommodations to keep the women they loved in their lives. Even blatant anti-feminists like Michael Levin, while vocally decrying the equal rights campaign, were quietly making domestic deals with their wives. For what has largely been forgotten in the backlash era – when women are encouraged to please men by their demeanour or appearance rather than persuade them by the force of their argument – is that men don't hold all the emotional cards. Men need women as much as women need men. The bonds between the sexes can chafe, and they can be, and have been, used to constrain women. But they also can promote mutually beneficial growth and change.

Under the 1980s backlash, in the very few instances where women have tried such a vocal and unapologetic strategy, they *have* managed to transform the public climate, set the agenda on their own terms, and change the minds of many individual men. The spectacular turnaround in American abortion politics, pulled off by a rejuvenated pro-choice movement in 1989, is a textbook case in point. It happened when women who believed in the right to control their own bodies finally made a mighty showing of those bodies in 1989 – half a million marched on the Capitol on April 9, Washington, DC's largest demonstration ever – and confronted the anti-abortion protesters at the clinic doors. Among female students, too, pro-choice protests drew more under-graduates than came to the anti-war marches of the 1960s. Their vast numbers steamrolled over an anti-abortion crusade that seemed, only weeks earlier, on the verge of wiping out women's reproductive rights. The mass mobilization of a pro-choice coalition defused all but a few of the hundreds of anti-abortion Bills introduced in the state legislatures in 1989, swept pro-choice candidates into gubernatorial and congressional office and even scared Republican National Committee chairman Lee Atwater enough for him to relabel the Republican party 'an umbrella party' on the abortion question. In Idaho in 1990, one of the nation's most restrictive abortion Bills was vetoed by Cecil Andrus, the state's 'pro-life' governor – after pro-choice women declared a boycott of Idaho potatoes. Some feminist leaders argued against such forceful tactics. 'Let the governor make his decision based on the seriousness of this issue and the Constitution, not potatoes,' National Abortion Rights Action League's executive director Kate Michelman advised. But it was the boycott that clinched it. 'Any time someone threatens one of our major cash crops,' Governor Andrus explained, 'it becomes significant.'

For most of the decade, however, the increasingly reinforced fortress of an anti-feminist culture daunted women more than it galvanized them. The backlash watchtowers flashed their warning signals without cease, and like high-security floodlights, they served to blind women to their own prodigious strengths. Women of the 1980s were the majority in the general population, on the college campuses, at the voting booths, the book shops, at the news-stands, and in front of the television sets. They represented nearly half the workers in offices and were responsible for nearly 80 per cent of consumer spending in the shops. Yet so often in this era, women seemed unaware of the weight and dynamism of their own formidable presence.

'Women are not taking advantage of the power they already have,' Kate Rand Lloyd, editor of *Working Woman*, told a women's rights conference in 1988. 'There are a great many men who know their backs are up against the wall . . . What is regrettable to me is we don't yet see what it is we have done, how badly we are needed, how we really do have tools for changing our own future in our own hands.'

That women have in their possession a vast and untapped vitality also explains one of the more baffling phenomena of the backlash – the seeming 'over-reation' with which some men have greeted even the tiniest steps toward women's advancement. Maybe these men weren't over-reacting after all. In the 1980s male politicians saw the widening gender gap figures. Male policy-makers saw the polls indicating huge and rising majorities of women demanding economic equality, reproductive freedom, a real participation in the political process, as well as a real governmental investment in social services and a real commitment to peace. (A record gender gap of 25 per cent divided the sexes on the 1991 Gulf war; on the eve of battle, a majority of US women opposed military intervention, while a majority of men supported it.) Male corporate heads saw the massive female consensus on childcare and family-leave policies and the vast female resentment over indecent pay and minimal promotions. Male evangelical leaders saw the huge numbers of 'traditional' wives who were ignoring their teachings or heading for the office. All of these men understood the profound force that a women's movement could exert if it got half a chance. It was women, tragically, who were still in the dark.

'The reason men "overreact" is *they* get it,' Eleanor Smeal, founder of the Fund for the Feminist Majority, says. 'If women all got together on the same day, on the same hour, we would go over the top.' That day could have been any one of the 3,650 days in the last backlash decade. But women never did capitalize on the historic advantage they enjoyed; and as the attack on equal rights gathered momentum, women's energies were diverted and ultimately exhausted in fending off anti-feminism's punishing blows. What is perhaps most depressing to contemplate is what might have been. The 1980s could have become women's great leap forward.

At the start of the 1990s some forecasters – most of them advertisers and political publicists – began declaring that the next ten years was going to be 'the Decade of Women'. What they meant by this prognosis was not entirely clear. Were they divining a real phenomenon or just inventing another 'trend'? Were they suggesting that women would wield more authority in the 1990s, or were they simply envisaging another nostalgia-drenched epoch in which women would adopt a softer, more 'feminine' pose?

In any event, when the media set out to report this story, they had the usual trouble rounding up evidence. 'I get press calls every election season,' Ruth Mandel, director of the Center for the American Woman and Politics, wearily told a reporter. 'But the answer is no, this isn't the year [for women] – it wasn't the year in 1986 or 1988, and it won't be in '90 or '92.'

One might hope, or dream, that mandel's gloomy prediction is proved wrong. But more productively, women can act. Because there really is no good reason why the 1990s can't be their decade. Because the demographics and the opinion polls are on women's side. Because women's hour on the stage is long, long overdue. Because, whatever new obstacles are mounted against the future march toward equality, whatever new myths invented, penalties levied, opportunities rescinded or degradations imposed, no one can ever take from women the justness of their cause.

Notes

Notes

Chapter One. Introduction: Blame It on Feminism

1   **Women's fight for**: Nancy Gibbs, 'The Dreams of Youth,' *Time*, Special Issue: 'Women: The Road Ahead,' Fall 1990, p. 12.

1   **The battle for women's rights**: Margaret Thatcher, quoted by Eileen Fairweather, 'The Feminist Backlash,' *Cosmopolitan*, Jan. 1985, p. 88.

1   **The *New York Times* reports**: Georgia Dullea, 'Women Reconsider Childbearing Over 30,' *New York Times*, Feb. 25, 1982, p. C1.

2   ***Newsweek* says: unwed women**: Eloise Salholz, 'The Marriage Crunch,' *Newsweek*, June 2, 1986, p. 55.

2   **The health advice manuals**: see, for example, Dr Herbert J. Freudenberger and Gail North, *Women's Burnout* (New York: Viking Penguin, 1985); Marjorie Hansen Shaevitz, *The Superwoman Syndrome* (London: Fontana Books, 1986); Harriet Braiker, *The Type E Woman* (New York: Dodd, Mead, 1986); Donald Morse and M. Lawrence Furst, *Women Under Stress* (New York: Van Nostrand Reinhold, 1982); Georgia Witkin-Lanoil, *The Female Stress Syndrome* (New York: Newmarket Press, 1984).

2   **The psychology books**: Dr Stephen and Susan Price, *No More Lonely Nights: Overcoming the Hidden Fears That Keep You from Getting Married* (New York: G.P. Putnam's Sons, 1988) p. 19.

2   **Even founding feminist Betty Friedan**: Betty Friedan, *The Second Stage* (London: Michael Joseph, 1982), p. 9.

2   **'In dispensing its spoils'**: Mona Charen, 'The Feminist Mistake,' *National Review*, March 23, 1984, p. 24.

2   **'Our generation was the human sacrifice'**: Claudia Wallis, 'Women Face the '90s,' *Time*, Dec. 4, 1989, p. 82.

2   **In *Cosmopolitan*, writer**: Erica Jong, 'I *Am* Having It All – So Why Do I Feel Terminally Exhausted?', *Cosmopolitan*, March 1985, p. 108.

3   **In *Newsweek*, writer**: Kay Ebeling, 'The Failure of Feminism,' *Newsweek*, Nov. 19, 1990, p. 9.

3   **Even the beauty magazines**: Marilyn Webb, 'His Fault Divorce,' *Harper's Bazaar*, Aug. 1988, p. 156.

3   **In the last decade**: Mary Anne Dolan, 'When Feminism Failed,' *The New York Times Magazine*, June 26, 1988, p. 21; Erica Jong 'The Awful Truth about Women's Liberation,' *Vanity Fair*, April 1986, p. 92.

3   **The *Today* show**: Jane Birnbaum, 'The Dark Side of Women's Liberation,' *Los Angeles Herald Examiner*, May 24, 1986.

3   **A guest columnist**: Robert J. Hooper, 'Slasher Movies Owe Success to Abortion'

(originally printed in the *Baltimore Sun*), *Minneapolis Star Tribune*, Feb. 1, 1990, p. 17A.

3 **In popular novels**: Gail Parent, *A Sign of the Eighties* (London: Grafton Books, 1988); Stephen King, *Misery* (London: Hodder & Stoughton, 1987).

3 **We 'blew it by waiting'**: Freda Bright, *Singular Women* (London: Michael Joseph, 1988), p. 12.

4 **Even Erica Jong's**: Erica Jong, *Any Woman's Blues* (London: Chatto & Windus, 1990), pp. 2–3. A new generation of young 'post-feminist' female writers, such as Mary Gaitskill and Susan Minot, also produced a bumper crop of grim-faced unwed heroines. These passive and masochistic 'girls' wandered the city, zombie-like; they came alive and took action only in seeking out male abuse. For a good analysis of this genre, see James Wolcott, 'The Good-Bad Girls', *Vanity Fair*, Dec. 1988, p. 43.

4 **'Feminism, having promised her'**: Dr Toni Grant, *Being a Woman: Fulfilling Your Femininity and Finding Love* (New York: Random House, 1988) p. 25.

4 **The authors of**: Dr Connell Cowan and Dr Melvyn Kinder, *Smart Women/Foolish Choices* (London: Bantam Books, 1986), p. 16.

4 **Reagan spokeswoman Faith**: Faith Whittlesey, 'Radical Feminism in Retreat,' Dec. 8, 1984, speech at the Center for the Study of the Presidency, 15th Annual Leadership Conference, St Louis, Mo., p. 7.

4 **As a California sheriff**: Don Martinez, 'More Women Ending Up in Prisons,' *San Francisco Examiner*, Sept. 4, 1990, p. A1. Judges have blamed women's increasing economic independence for increasing *male* crime, too: 'What do we do [about crowded prisons]?' Texas District Judge John McKellips asked, rhetorically. 'Well, we can start in our homes. Mothers can stay home and raise their children during the formative years.' See 'For the Record,' *Ms.*, May 1988, p. 69.

4 **The US Attorney-General's**: Attorney General's Commission on Pornography, Final Report, July 1986, p. 144. The commissioner's report goes on to undermine its own logic, conceding that since women raped by acquaintances are the least likely to report the crime, it might be difficult to attribute a rise in reported rape rates to them, after all.

4 **On American news**: Sylvia Ann Hewlett, *A Lesser Life: The Myth of Women's Liberation in America* (London: Sphere Books, 1988).

5 **Legal scholars have**: Mary Ann Mason, *The Equality Trap* (New York: Simon & Schuster, 1988).

5 **Economists have argued**: James P. Smith and Michael Ward, 'Women in the Labor Market and in the Family,' *The Journal of Economic Perspectives*, Winter 1989, 3, no. 1: 9–23.

5 **In *The Cost of Loving***: Megan Marshall, *The Cost of Loving: Women and the New Fear of Intimacy* (New York: G. P. Putnam's Sons, 1984) p. 218.

5 **Other diaries of**: Hilary Cosell, *Woman on a Seesaw: The Ups and Downs of Making It* (New York: G. P. Putnam's Sons, 1985); Deborah Fallows, *A Mother's Work* (Boston: Houghton Mifflin, 1985); Carol Orsborn, *Enough is Enough* (New York: Pocket Books, 1986); Susan Bakos, *This Wasn't Supposed to Happen* (New York: Continuum, 1985). Even when the women aren't really renouncing their liberation, their publishers promote the texts as if they were. Mary Kay Blakely's *Wake Me When It's Over* (New York: Random House, 1989), an account of the author's diabetes-induced coma, is billed on the dust jacket as 'a chilling memoir in which a working supermom exceeds her limit and discovers the thin line between sanity and lunacy and between life and death'.

5 **If women are now so equal**: 'A new future for women,' Labour Party, 1991; 'Putting Equality into Practice, A Shadow Ministry of Women Consultation Document,' Labour Party, 1991; Anne Caborn, 'Why Women Must Ask For More,' *Options*, Mar. 1989, p. 64.

5 **If women have 'made it'**: 'A New Ministry for Women,' Labour Party, 1991; Lesley Abdela, letter to Jane Hill, Nov. 1991; Melissa Benn, 'Brace yourself for

the backlash', *Cosmopolitan*, Feb. 1992, p. 12; Joanna Foster, Plenary Address to the 1989 Human Rights Congress, Melbourne.

6   **If women 'have it all'**: 'Women and Europe, a Briefing Note Prepared by Jo Richardson,' Labour Party, 1991; Lesley Abdela, *Independent*, Sept. 25, 1991; *Labour Research*, Jan. 1992, vol. 81, no. 1, p. 11.

6   **Even in Australia**: Quentin Bryce AO, Federal Sex Discrimination Commissioner, Occasional Paper no. 3; Marian Sawer, University of Canberra, paper for the XVth World Congress of the Political Science Association, 1991.

6   **The Equal Pay Act of 1972 in New Zealand**: *Women in New Zealand*, Department of Statistics and Ministry of Women's Affairs (Wellington, 1990), p. 73; Lesley Haynes, Ministry of Women's Affairs, letter to Jane Hill, Jan. 1992.

7   **In September 1991**: Lesley Abdela, *Independent*, Sept. 25, 1991.

7   **Why do women who want**: Data from Alan Guttmacher Institute.

7   **Nor is women's struggle for equal education**: *The American Woman 1990–91: A Status Report*, ed Sara. E. Rix (New York: W. W. Norton, 1990), p. 63; 'Feminization of Power Campaign Extends to the Campus,' Eleanor Smeal Report, 6, no. 1, Aug. 31, 1988; Project on Equal Education Rights, National Organization for Women's Legal Defense and Education Fund, 1987; Sharon Maxwell, 'No More Educating Rita,' *Cosmopolitan*, Feb. 1985, p. 4.

7   **Nor do women**: Deborah L. Rhode, 'Perspectives on Professional Women,' *Stanford Law Review*, 40, no. 5 (May 1988), p. 1183; 'The Family Today,' Family Policy Studies Centre, 1991, p. 10; Mark Clements Research Inc.'s Annual Study of Women's Attitudes, 1987; Arlie Hochschild, *The Second Shift: Working Parents and the Revolution at Home* (New York: Viking, 1989), p. 227. In fact, Hochschild's twelve-year survey, from 1976 to 1988, found that the men who said they were helping tended to be the ones who did the least.

8   **Furthermore, in thirty states**: Statistics from National Center on Women and Family Law, 1987; National Woman Abuse Prevention Project; Cynthia Diehm and Margo Ross, 'Battered Women,' *The American Woman 1988–89: A Status Report*, ed. Sara E. Rix (New York: W. W. Norton, 1989) p. 292.

8   **In Canada in 1991**: David Vienneau, *Toronto Star*, Aug. 23, 1991, p. 1.

8   **Federal funding**: 'Unlocking the Door: An Action Program for Meeting the Housing Needs of Women,' Women and Housing Task Force, 1988, National Low-Income Housing Coalition, pp. 6, 8.

8   **In the 1980s, almost half of all homeless**: Katha Pollitt, 'Georgie Porgie Is a Bully,' *Time*, Fall 1990, special issue, p. 24. A survey in New York City found as many as 40 per cent of all homeless people are battered women: 'Understanding Domestic Violence Fact Sheets,' National Woman Abuse Prevention Project.

8   **Nearly 70 per cent**: E. J. Dionne, Jr, 'Struggle for Work and Family Fueling Women's Movement,' *New York Times*, Aug. 22, 1989, p. A1. The Yankelovich Clancy Shulman poll (Oct. 23–25, 1989, for *Time*/CNN) and the 1990 Virginia Slims opinion poll (The Roper Organization Inc., 1990) found similarly large majorities of women who said that they needed a strong women's movement to keep pushing for change.

8   **A clear majority of women**: *Guardian* survey of 11,000 women, Mar. 7, 1991.

8   **In poll after poll**: The Louis Harris poll, 1984, found 64 per cent of women wanted the Equal Rights Amendment and 65 per cent favoured affirmative action. Similar results emerged from the national *Woman's Day* poll (Feb. 17, 1984) by *Woman's Day* and Wellesley College Center for Research on Women, which emphasized middle-American conventional women (80 per cent were mothers and 30 per cent were full-time housewives). The *Woman's Day* poll found a majority of women, from all economic classes, seeking a wide range of women's rights. For instance, 68 per cent of the women said they wanted the ERA, 79 per cent supported a woman's right to choose an abortion, and 61 per cent favoured a federally subsidized national childcare programme. Mark Clements Research Inc.'s Annual Study of Women's Attitudes found in 1987 that 87 per cent of women wanted a federal law guaranteeing maternity leave

and about 94 per cent said that more childcare should be available. (In addition, 86 per cent wanted a federal law enforcing the payment of child support.) The Louis Harris poll found 80 per cent of women calling for the creation of more day care centres. See *The Eleanor Smeal Report*, June 28, 1984, p. 3; Warren T. Brookes, 'Day Care: Is It a Real Crisis or a War Over Political Turf?' *San Francisco Chronicle*, April 27, 1988, p. 6; Louis Harris, *Inside America* (New York: Vintage Books, 1987), p. 96.

9   **To the contrary**: In the 1989 *Time*/CNN poll, 94 per cent of women polled said the movement made them more independent; 82 per cent said it is still improving women's lives. Only 8 per cent said it may have made their lives worse. A 1986 *Newsweek* Gallup poll found that 56 per cent of women identified themselves as 'feminists', and only 4 per cent described themselves as 'antifeminists'.

9   **In public opinion**: In the Annual Study of Women's Attitudes (1988, Mark Clements Research), when women were asked, 'What makes you angry?' they picked three items as their top concerns: poverty, crime and their own inequality. In the 1989 *New York Times* poll, when women were asked what was the most important problem facing women today, job inequality ranked first.

9   **The Roper Organization's**: Bickley Townsend and Kathleen O'Neil, 'American Women Get Mad,' *American Demographics*, Aug. 1990, p. 26.

9   **When the *New York Times***: Dionne, 'Struggle for Work and Family,' p. A14.

9   **In the 1990**: 1990 Virginia Slims Opinion Poll, pp. 29–30, 32.

9   **In US polls**: Data from Roper Organization and Louis Harris polls. The 1990 Roper survey found most women reporting that things had 'gotten worse' in the home and that men were more eager 'to keep women down': see 1990 Virginia Slims opinion poll, pp. 18, 21, 54. The Gallup Organization polls charted an 8 per cent increase in job discrimination complaints from women between 1975 and 1982. Mark Clements Research's 1987 Women's Views Survey (commissioned by *Glamour* magazine) found that on the matter of women's inequality, 'more women feel there is a problem today.' Reports of wage discrimination, the survey noted, had jumped from 76 per cent in 1982 to 85 per cent in 1988. (See 'How Women's Minds Have Changed in the Last Five Years,' *Glamour*, Jan. 1987, p. 168.) The annual surveys by Mark Clements Research also find huge and increasing majorities of women complaining of unequal treatment in hiring, advancement and opportunities in both corporate and political life. (In 1987 only 30 per cent of women believed they got equal treatment with men when being considered for financial credit.) A *Time* 1989 poll found 94 per cent of women complaining of unequal pay, 82 per cent of job discrimination.

10   **In the home, a much increased**: Townsend and O'Neil, 'American Women Get Mad,' p. 28.

10   **And outside their homes**: 1990 Virginia Slims opinion poll, p. 38.

10   **Government and private surveys**: Economic trends from US Bureau of Labor Statistics, US Equal Employment Opportunity Commission, Office of Federal Contract Compliance, National Committee on Pay Equity, National Commission on Working Women. See Chapter 12 for a closer look at the deteriorating status of women in the work force.

10   **The status of women**: In the first six years of the Reagan administration, $50 billion was cut from these social programmes, while at the same time defence spending rose $142 billion. See 'Inequality of Sacrifice: The Impact of the Reagan Budget on Women,' Coalition on Women and the Budget, Washington, DC, 1986, pp. 5, 7; Sara E. Rix and Anne J. Stone, 'Reductions and Realities: How the Federal Budget Affects Women,' Women's Research and Education Institute, Washington, DC, 1983, pp. 4–5.

11   **In Britain, over**: 'The Family Today,' Family Policy Studies Centre, 1991; Consultation Paper from Michael Meacher, MP, 'Lone Parent Families and Maintenance: Labour's Approach,' 1989.

11   **In US politics**: Data from Center for the American Woman and Politics, Eagleton Institute of Politics. See Chapter 9 on women in politics.

11   **In private life**: National Audit Office Report, *Department of Social Security: Support for One Parent Families*, HC 328, 1989–90. Reference supplied by Mary Walker, Researcher to Michael Meacher, MP.

11   **Domestic-violence shelters**: 'Unlocking the Door,' p. 8.

11   **Reported rapes more than**: Statistics are from the US Department of Justice's Bureau of Justice Statistics; the Sourcebook of Criminal Justice Statistics, 1984, p. 380; Uniform Crime Reports, FBI, 'Crime in the United States,' 1986; 'Sexual Assault: An Overview,' National Victims Resource Center, Nov. 1987, p. 1. While rape rates between 1960 and 1970 rose 95 per cent, this increase – unlike that of the 1980s – was part of a 126 per cent increase in violent crime in that era. (Crime statisticians have widely rejected the argument that the increase in the 1980s might simply be the result of an increasing tendency for women to report sexual assaults. The National Crime Survey found no significant change in the percentage of rapes reported to police in the periods between 1973–77 and 1978–82.) Scattered indicators suggest a sharp rise in the rate of rapes committed by young men, too. Between 1983 and 1987, rape arrests of boys under 18 years old rose 15 per cent. In New York City between 1987 and 1989, according to data from the district attorney's office, rape arrests of boys under the age of 13 rose 200 per cent. In Alaska, according to the state Division of Youth and Family Services, sexual abuse and assaults by young men increased ninefold in the course of the 1980s, the fastest-growing juvenile problem in the state. See Larry Campbell, 'Sexually Abusive Juveniles,' *Anchorage Daily News*, Jan. 9, 1981, p. 1.

11   **They believed they were facing**: 1990 Virginia Slims opinion poll, p. 16.

12   **In the 1989 *New York Times***: Lisa Belkin, 'Bars to Equality of Sexes Seen as Eroding, Slowly,' *New York Times*, Aug. 20, 1989, p. 16.

13   **Just when women's quest**: 'Inequality of Sacrifice,' p. 23.

14   **Just when record numbers**: A 1986 Gallup poll conducted for *Newsweek* found a majority of women described themselves as feminists and only 4 per cent said they were 'antifeminists'. While large majorities of women throughout the 1980s kept on favouring the full feminist agenda (from the ERA to legal abortion), the proportion of women who were willing publicly to call themselves feminists dropped off suddenly in the late eighties, after the mass media declared feminism the 'F-word'. By 1989 only one in three women were calling themselves feminists in the polls. Nonetheless, the pattern of younger women espousing the most pro-feminist sentiments continued throughout the decade. In the 1989 Yankelovich poll for *Time*/CNN, for example, 76 per cent of women in their teens and 71 per cent of women in their twenties said they believed feminists spoke for the average American woman, compared with 59 per cent of women in their thirties. Asked the same question about the National Organization for Women, the gap appeared again: 83 per cent of women in their teens and 72 per cent of women in their twenties said NOW was in touch with the average woman, compared with 65 per cent of women in their thirties. See Susanna Downie, 'Decade of Achievement, 1977–1987,' The National Women's Conference Center, May 1988, p. 1; 1986 Gallup/*Newsweek* poll; 1989 Yankelovich/*Time*/CNN poll.

14   **'A backlash may be an indication that'**: Dr Jean Baker Miller, *Toward a New Psychology of Women* (Boston: Beacon Press, 1976), pp. xv–xvi.

14   **Some women now**: Kate Michelman, '20 Years Defending Choice, 1969–1988,' National Abortion Rights Action League, p. 4.

14   **Some women can now**: 'Employment and Earnings,' Current Population Survey, Table 22, Bureau of Labor Statistics, US Department of Labor.

14   **(Contrary to popular myth)**: Cheryl Russell, *100 Predictions for the Baby Boom* (New York: Plenum Press, 1987), p. 64.

14   **Longtime activist Jane Fonda**: Priscilla Painton, *Time*, Jan. 11, 1992.

14   **While a very few**: Maeve Haran, 'Can You Have It All, Or Is It All a Con?',

She, July 1991; 'Facts on Working Women,' Aug. 1989, Women's Bureau, US Department of Labor, no. 89–2; and data from the Coalition of Labor Union Women and Amalgamated Clothing and Textile Workers Union. The surge of women joining unions in the late 1980s was so great that it single-handedly halted the ten-year decline in union membership. Black women joined unions at the greatest rate. Women led strikes around the country, from the Yale University administrative staff to the Daughters of Mother Jones in Virginia (who were instrumental in the Pittston coal labour battle) to the Delta Pride catfish plant processors in Mississippi (where women organized the largest strike by black workers ever in the state, lodging a protest against a plant that paid its mostly female employees poverty wages, punished them if they skinned less than 24,000 fish a day, and limited them to six timed bathroom breaks a week). See Tony Freemantle, 'Weary Strikers Hold Out in Battle of Pay Principle,' *Houston Chronicle*, Dec. 2, 1990, p. 1A; Peter T. Kilborn, 'Labor Fight on a Catfish "Plantation," ' *The News and Observer*, Dec. 16, 1990, p. J2.

15   **In 1986, while**: 1986 Gallup Poll; Barbara Ehrenreich, 'The Next Wave,' *Ms*, July/Aug. 1987, p. 166; Sarah Harder, 'Flourishing in the Mainstream: The US Women's Movement Today,' *The American Woman 1990–91*, p. 281. Also see 1989 Yankelovich poll: 71 per cent of black women said feminists have been helpful to women, compared with 61 per cent of white women. A 1987 poll by the National Women's Conference Commission found that 65 per cent of black women called themselves feminists, compared with 56 per cent of white women.

15   **As Brenda Polan put it**: 'The Feminine Fiction,' *Guardian*, Aug. 18, 1988.

15   **Other signs of**: For increase in violent pornography, see, for example, April 1986 study in the Attorney General's Commission on Pornography, Final Report, pp. 1402–3.

16   **More subtle indicators**: Sally Steenland, 'Women Out of View: An Analysis of Female Characters on 1987–88 TV Programs,' National Commission on Working Women, Nov. 1987. Mystery fiction survey was conducted by Sisters In Crime and presented at the 1988 Mystery Writers of America conference; additional information comes from personal interview in May 1988 with the group's director, mystery writer Sara Paretsky. On popular music: Alice Kahn, 'Macho – the Second Wave,' *San Francisco Chronicle*, Sept. 16, 1990, Sunday Punch section, p. 2. On American Women in radio & TV: Betsy Sharkey, 'The Invisible Woman,' *Adweek*, July 6, 1987, p. 4.

17   **The backlash line claims**: Data from Children's Defense Fund. See also Ellen Wojahm, 'Who's Minding the Kids?' *Savvy*, Oct. 1987, p. 16; 'Child Care: The Time is Now,' Children's Defense Fund, 1987, pp. 8–10.

17   **'I myself'**: Rebecca West, *The Clarion*, Nov. 14, 1913, cited in Cheris Kramarae and Paula A. Treichler, *A Feminist Dictionary* (London: Pandora Press, 1985) p. 160.

18   **The meaning of the word 'feminist'**: *The Feminist Papers: From Adams to de Beauvoir*, ed. Alice S. Rossi (New York: Bantam Books, 1973) p. xiii. For discussion of historical origins of the term feminism, see Karen Offen, 'Defining Feminism: A Comparative Historical Approach,' in *Signs: Journal of Women in Culture and Society*, 1988, 14, no. 1, pp. 119–57.

18   **I AM NOT A BARBIE DOLL**: Carol Hymowitz and Michaele Weissman, *A History of Women in America* (New York: Bantam Books, 1978) p. 341.

Chapter Two. Man Shortages and Barren Wombs

22   **'The picture that has emerged'**: Bill Barol, 'Men Aren't Her Only Problem,' *Newsweek*, Nov. 23, 1987, p. 76.

22   **Four-fifths of them**: Shere Hite, *Women and Love: A Cultural Revolution in Progress* (London: Viking, 1988), pp. 41–2.

23   The *Washington Post* even: 'Things Getting Worse for Hite,' *San Francisco Chronicle*, Nov. 14, 1987, p. C9.

23   **'Characteristically grandiose'**: Claudia Wallis, 'Back Off, Buddy,' *Time*, Oct. 12, 1987, p. 68.

23   **And Hite specifically**: Hite, *Women and Love*, pp. 774–8.

24   **'I have given heart'**: *Ibid.*, pp. 79, 12, 96, 99, 39.

24   **Maybe it was easier**: Tom Hibbert, 'My Sex Life Is Like a Rocket Ship,' *Options*, Feb. 1989, pp. 42–4.

25   **Psychologist Dr Srully**: Dan Collins, 'Is He Handing Readers a Line?' *New York Daily News*, July 19, 1987, p. 4.

25   **His conclusion**: Dr Srully Blotnick, *Otherwise Engaged: The Private Lives of Successful Women* (New York: Penguin Books, 1985), p. 316.

25   **In his 1985 book**: *Ibid.*, pp. viii, xi, 265, 278, 323.

25   **'In fact,' he wrote**: *Ibid.*, p. 278.

25   **He took some swipes**: *Ibid.*, pp. 323–4.

25   **None doubted his methodology**: *Ibid.*, p. xiii.

25   **After his interview, Collins**: Personal interview with Dan Collins, Nov. 1989.

26   **'People I've dealt with'**: Personal interview with Martin O'Connell, 1988.

26   **And results that didn't**: Marilyn Power, 'Women, the State and the Family in the US: Reaganomics and the Experience of Women,' *Women and Recession*, ed. Jill Rubery (New York: Routledge & Kegan Paul, 1988) p. 153.

26   **The Public Health Service**: Michael Specter, 'Panel Claims Censorship on Abortion,' *San Francisco Chronicle*, Dec. 11, 1989, p. A1.

27   **'Most social research'**: Kingsley Davis, *Human Society* (New York: Macmillan, 161 edition [original edn: 1948]) p. 393.

27   **Her 'angle'**: Personal interview with Lisa Marie Petersen, Nov. 1989.

27   **'The marriage market'**: Lisa Marie Petersen, 'They're Falling in Love Again, Say Marriage Counselors,' *Stamford* (Conn.) *Advocate*, Feb. 14, 1986, p. A1.

28   **In no time**: Personal interview with Neil Bennett, June 1986.

28   **At the very time**: By 1987, just a year later, the gap was down to 1.7 years, compared with 2.2 years in 1963. See 'Advance Report of Final Marriage Statistics,' 1986, 1987, National Center of Health Statistics. In 1986, nearly a quarter of brides were older than their grooms, up from 16 per cent in 1970. National Center of Health Statistics, Unpublished table, 1986. On the 'age gap' in England and Wales, 'Key Population and Vital Statistics, England and Wales, 1986,' OPCS.

29   **That study, an October**: Robert Schoen and John Baj, 'Impact of the Marriage Squeeze in Five Western Countries,' *Sociology and Social Research*, Oct. 1985, 70: no. 1, pp. 8–19.

29   **Princeton professors**: Susan Faludi, 'That Marriage Trap,' *Ms*, July/Aug. 1987, p. 62.

29   **Coale, asked about it later**: Personal interview with Ansley Coale, June 1986.

29   **She decided to**: Personal interviews with Jeanne Moorman, June 1986, May 1988, Sept. 1989.

29   **The results**: Jeanne E. Moorman, 'The History and the Future of the Relationship Between Education and Marriage,' US Bureau of the Census, Dec. 1, 1986.

30   **In June 1986, Moorman wrote**: Letter to Neil Bennett from Jeanne Moorman, June 20, 1986.

30   **Then, in August**: Ben Wattenberg, 'New Data on Women, Marriage,' Newspaper Enterprise Association, Aug. 27, 1986.

30   **'I understand from Ben'**: Letter from Neil Bennett to Jeanne Moorman, Aug. 29, 1986.

30   **(Bennett refuses to discuss)**: Personal interview, Nov. 1989. Bloom also declined to comment.

31   **At the same time, in an op-ed piece**: Neil G. Bennett and David E. Bloom, 'Why Fewer Women Marry,' *Advertising Age*, Jan. 12, 1987, p. 18.

31 **'I believe this reanalysis'**: Letter from Robert Fay to Neil Bennett, March 2, 1987.

32 **'Things have gotten'**: Letter from Neil Bennett to Jeanne Moorman, March 3, 1987.

32 **Three and a half years**: Felicity Barringer, 'Study on Marriage Patterns Revised, Omitting Impact on Women's Careers,' *New York Times*, Nov. 11, 1989, p. 9.

32 **As a simple check**: 'Marital Status and Living Arrangements,' US Bureau of the Census, Series P-20, no. 410, March 1985. In addition, in the broader not-currently-married population (a classification that includes divorced and widowed people as well), there were 1.2 million more men than women between the ages of twenty-five and thirty-four. 'Key Population and Vital Statistics, England and Wales, 1986,' OPCS.

32 **If anyone faced**: 'Marital Status and Living Arrangements.' Still-younger men faced a similar problem: between the ages of fifteen and twenty-four, there were 112 single men for every 100 women. Also, William Foster, 'How To Meet Your Match,' *Woman's Journal*, Nov. 1991, p. 94.

32 **The proportion of never-married women**: US Bureau of the Census, Sept. 1975, Series A-160–171, and Sept. 1988, Table 3. Also, Anthony Clare, 'High Monogamy,' *Cosmopolitan*, Feb. 1988, p. 94.

33 **If one looks at never-married**: Current Population Reports, Series P-20, no. 410, Table 1, US Bureau of the Census; 'Special Report: Marital Characteristics,' Table 1, 1950 Census of the Population, US Bureau of the Census; Ellen Kay Trimberger, 'Single Women and Feminism in the 1980s,' June 1987 paper, National Women's Studies Association.

33 **In fact, the only place**: 'Marital Status and Living Arrangements,' March 1985.

33 **A massive study**: *The Cosmopolitan Report: The Changing Life Course of American Women*, Battelle Memorial Institute, Human Affairs Research Center (Seattle: The Hearst Corporation, 1986).

33 **The 1985 Virginia Slims**: The 1985 Virginia Slims American Women's Opinion Poll, The Roper Organization, Inc., p. 13.

33 **In the 1989 'New Diversity'**: 'New Diversity,' Significance Inc. and Langer Associates, 1989.

33 *Cosmopolitan* **reported**: 'Results of Our Singles Survey,' *Cosmopolitan*, Oct. 1988, p. 12.

33 **And a 1989 Louis Harris Poll**: ' "Mad Housewives" No Longer,' *San Jose Mercury News*, Feb. 10, 1989, p. C5.

33 **A review of fourteen years**: Norval D. Glenn and Charles N. Weaver, 'The Changing Relationship of Marital Status to Reported Happiness,' *Journal of Marriage and the Family*, 50 (May 1988): 317–24.

33 **The cohabitation rate**: *Social Trends*, 1991 edition, Central Statistical Office; Peter McDonald, Australian Institute of Family Studies, Melbourne; *Women in New Zealand*, Department of Statistics and Ministry of Women's Affairs, 1990, p. 38; 'Marriage, Cohabitation and Divorce,' Family Planning Information Service Fact Sheet, Jan. 1989.

34 **Single-person households**: *The Times*, Jan. 23, 1992.

34 **A 1982 study of 3,000**: Jacqueline Simenauer and David Carroll, *Singles: The New Americans* (New York: Simon & Schuster, 1982) p. 15.

34 **'What is going to happen'**: Alan T. Otten, 'Deceptive Picture: If You See Families Staging a Comeback, It's Probably a Mirage,' *The Wall Street Journal*, Sept. 25, 1986, p. 1.

34 **In the mid-eighties**: Personal interviews with dating and matchmaking service organizations in New York, San Jose, San Francisco and Chicago, June 1986.

34 **In an analysis of 1,200 ads**: Keay Davidson, 'Sexual Freedom Will Survive Bush, Researchers Say,' *San Francisco Examiner*, Nov. 13, 1988, p. A2.

35 **'Being married,' the**: Jessie Bernard, *The Future of Marriage* (New Haven: Yale University Press, 1982 edn) p. 25.

35 **'There are few findings'**: *Ibid.*, pp. 16–17.

35   **'All this business'**: Personal interview with Ronald G. Kessler, 1988.

35   **The mental health data**; See, for example, the following: Bernard, *Future of Marriage*, pp. 306, 308; Joseph Veroff, Richard A. Kulka and Elizabeth Douvan, *The Inner American: A Self-Portrait from 1957 to 1976* (New York: Basic Books, 1981); Walter R. Gove, 'The Relationship Between Sex Roles, Marital Status, and Mental Illness,' *Social Forces*, 51 (Sept. 1972): 34–44; Walter R. Gove, 'Sex, Marital Status and Psychiatric Treatment: A Research Note,' *Social Forces*, 58 (Sept. 1979): 80–93; Ronald C. Kessler, R. L. Brown and C. L. Broman, 'Sex Differences in Psychiatric Help-Seeking: Evidence from Four Large-scale Surveys,' *Journal of Health and Social Behavior*, 22 (March 1981): 49–63; Kay F. Schaffer, *Sex-Role Issues in Mental Health* (Reading, Mass.: Addison-Wesley, 1980) pp. 132–59; Blayne Cutler, 'Bachelor Party,' *American Demographics*, Feb. 1989, pp. 22–6.

36   **In 1987 news surfaced**: Judith Waldrop, 'The Fashionable Family,' *American Demographics*, March 1988, pp. 23–6.

36   **'A new traditionalism'**: Jib Fowles, 'Coming Soon: More Men than Women,' *New York Times*, June 5, 1988, III, p. 3.

36   **'There's not even going'**: Personal interview with Jib Fowles, June 1988.

37   **In the 1980s, these 'feminist-inspired'**: Marcia Cohen, *The Sisterhood: The True Story of the Women Who Changed the World* (New York: Simon & Schuster, 1988) p. 365.

37   **The Lord Chancellor**: *Family Policy Bulletin*, Dec. 1991, Family Policy Studies Centre, pp. 1, 8.

37   **At present**: *Guardian*, Nov. 30, 1991.

37   **The government's backtracking**: *Daily Mail*, Dec. 2, 1991.

37   **As seven out of ten**: *Family Policy Bulletin*, Dec. 1991, p. 16.

37   **Mrs Valerie Riches**: *Daily Mail*, Dec. 2, 1991, p. 2.

37   **According to Lord Mackay**: *Family Policy Bulletin*, Dec. 1991, p. 8.

37   **Dr Jack Dominian**: *Daily Mail*, Dec. 2, 1991, p. 2.

38   **Elsewhere in the world**: *The Macquarie Book of Events*, Macquarie Library Pty Ltd, Sydney, 1983, p. 371; *Women in New Zealand*, Department of Statistics and Ministry of Women's Affairs (Wellington, 1990), p. 39.

38   **Until her study**: Lenore J. Weitzman, *The Divorce Revolution: The Unexpected Social and Economic Consequences for Women and Children in America* (New York: Free Press, 1985) p. 362.

38   **'The major economic result'**: *Ibid.*, pp. xiv, 13, 365.

38   **Weitzman's work does not**: *Ibid.*, pp. 364, 487.

39   **The Divorce Revolution, Time**: Wallis, 'Women Face the 90s,' p. 85.

39   **'The impact of the divorce revolution'**: Mason, *The Equality Trap*, pp. 68, 53. Other examples include Diane Medved, *The Case Against Divorce* (New York: Donald L. Fine, 1989) and Mary Ann Glendon, *Abortion and Divorce in Western Law* (Cambridge, Mass.: Harvard University Press, 1987).

39   **The 1970 California no-fault law**: Weitzman, *Divorce Revolution*, pp. 364–5, 41–2.

39   **Weitzman argued that**: *Ibid.*, pp. 358–62.

39   **'The research shows'**: *Ibid.*, p. xii.

40   **In the summer of 1986**: Personal interviews with Saul Hoffman, Greg Duncan, 1988, 1989, 1991. The '5000 Families' study, or the Panel Study of Income Dynamics, has been following a group of families since 1967. See Greg J. Duncan and Saul D. Hoffman, 'Economic Consequences of Marital Instability,' *Horizontal Equity, Uncertainty and Economic Well-Being* (Chicago: University of Chicago Press, 1985) pp. 427–71.

40   **Five years after**: The average living standard five years later is even better than during the marriage largely because so many women remarry men with higher incomes. For women who remain single, the living standard improves more slowly. Greg J. Duncan and Saul D. Hoffman, 'A Reconsideration of the Economic Consequences of Marital Dissolution,' *Demography*, 22 (1985), 485.

40 **'Weitzman's highly publicized'**: Greg J. Duncan and Saul D. Hoffman, 'What Are the Economic Consequences of Divorce?' *Demography*, 25, no. 4 (Nov. 1988), 641.

40 **The *Wall Street Journal***: Alan J. Otten, 'People Patterns,' *Wall Street Journal*, Dec. 12, 1988, p. B1.

40 **'They are just wrong'**: Personal interview, Dec. 1988.

41 **Confirmation of Duncan**: Suzanne Bianchi, 'Family Disruption and Economic Hardship,' Survey of Income and Program Participation, US Bureau of the Census, March 1991, Series P-70, no. 23.

41 **'[Weitzman's] numbers are'**: Personal interview with Suzanne Bianchi, March 1991.

41 **'We were amazed'**: Weitzman, *Divorce Revolution*, p. 409.

41 **And she strongly**: *Ibid.*, p. 383.

42 **(A later 1990)**: David L. Kirp, 'Divorce, California-Style,' *San Francisco Examiner*, Dec. 12, 1990, p. A19.

42 **National data**: 'Child Support and Alimony, 1983,' US Bureau of the Census, Series P-32, no. 14. The Census Bureau stopped collecting alimony data in the 1920s, then resumed in 1978.

42 **Yet her own data**: Weitzman, *Divorce Revolution*, p. 177.

42 **Her other point**: *Ibid.*, pp. xii, 358.

43 **Between 1978 and 1985**: Philip Robins, 'Why Are Child Support Award Amounts Declining?' June 1989, Institute for Research on Poverty Discussion Paper no. 885–89, pp. 6–7; Saul Hoffman, 'Divorce and Economic Well Being: The Effects on Men, Women and Children,' *Delaware Lawyer*, Spring 1987, p. 21.

43 **Divorced men are now more**: Hewlett, *A Lesser Life*, p. 63; Deborah L. Rhode, 'Rhode on Research,' Institute for Research on Women and Gender Newsletter, Stanford University, 13, no. 4 (Summer 1989), 4.

43 **A survey in the UK**: Jonathan Bradshaw and Jane Millar, *Lone-Parent Families in the UK* (London: HMSO, 1991), cited in 'Supporting our Children: The Family Impact of Child Maintenance,' Family Policy Studies Centre, 1991, p. 24.

43 **Although the number**: Michael Meacher, MP, press release, July 31, 1991.

43 **As sociologist Arlie**: Hochschild, *Second Shift*, pp. 250–1.

43 **A 1988 US audit**: Pat Wingert, 'And What of Deadbeat Dads?' *Newsweek*, Dec. 19, 1988, p. 66.

43 **Instead, surveys in several**: Weitzman, *Divorce Revolution*, pp. 48, 106; Allan R. Gold, 'Sex Bias Is Found Pervading Courts,' *New York Times*, July 2, 1989, p. 14.

43 **'The concept of "equality" '**: Weitzman, *Divorce Revolution*, p. 366.

44 **If the wage gap**: Marian Lief Palley, 'The Women's Movement in Recent American Poltics,' *The American Woman 1987–88* (New York: Norton, 1987), p. 174; Greg J. Duncan and Willard Rodgers, 'Lone Parents: The Economic Challenge of Changing Family Structures,' Organization for Economic Co-operation and Development, Nov. 1987. Further, there would be fewer divorces if there was less poverty: the likelihood of divorce is three to five times higher among couples who live in poverty. As Jessie Bernard observed, 'We could do more to stabilize marriage by providing this income than by any other single measure.' See Bernard, *The Future of Marriage*, pp. 168–9.

44 **'The dramatic increase'**: Personal interview with Greg Duncan, 1988.

44 **In 1984, demographers**: Ronald C. Kessler and James A. McRae, Jr, 'Note on the Relationships of Sex and Marital Status to Psychological Distress,' in *Research in Community and Mental Health* (Greenwich, Conn.: JAI Press, 1984), pp. 109–30.

44 **From the start, men**: Gallup Poll, May 1989: 31 per cent of men said they were the spouse who wanted the divorce versus 55 per cent of women. In only 20 per cent of the cases did both spouses want the divorce. The 1985 *Cosmopolitan/Battelle* report also found that women were more approving than men of divorce

for unhappily married couples with young children: 43 per cent versus 31 per cent. See Judith S. Wallerstein and Sandra Blakeslee, *Second Chances: Men, Women and Children a Decade After Divorce* (New York: Ticknor & Fields, 1989) p. 39.

44   **A 1982 survey**: Simenauer and Carroll, *Singles*, pp. 379–80.

44   **America's largest study**: Wallerstein, *Second Chances*, pp. xvii, 40, 41. Weitzman, too, had trouble finding divorced women who regret their decision. She notes: '[E]ven the longer-married older housewives who suffer the greatest financial hardships after divorce (and who feel most economically deprived, most angry, and most "cheated" by the divorce settlement) say they are "personally" better off than they were during marriage. . . . They also report improved self-esteem, more pride in their appearance and greater competence in all aspects of their lives.' When Weitzman asked divorced men and women to describe what they missed most from the marriage, the men said they missed having a lover and partner in life, while women said they missed only their husband's income. See Weitzman, *Divorce Revolution*, p. 346.

45   **'Indeed, when such'**: Wallerstein, *Second Chances*, p. 41.

45   **Nonetheless, in her much-publicized**: 'Lasting Pain,' *The Family in America* newsletter, June 1989, p. 1; Judith S. Wallerstein, 'Children after Divorce: Wounds That Don't Heal,' *The New York Times Magazine*, Jan. 22, 1989, p. 18.

45   **'Because so little was'**: Wallerstein, *Second Chances*, p. 319.

45   **'It's not at all'**: Personal interview with Judith Wallerstein, Feb. 1991.

46   **Public support for**: General Social Survey, National Opinion Research Center, University of Chicago. See also Arland Thornton, 'Changing Attitudes Toward Separation and Divorce: Causes and Consequences,' *American Journal of Sociology*, 90, no. 4, 857.

46   **On February 18**: Fédération des Centres d'Etude et de Conservation du Sperme Humain, D. Schwartz and M. J. Mayaux, 'Female Fecundity as a Function of Age,' *The New England Journal of Medicine*, 306, no. 7 (Feb. 18, 1982), 404–6.

46   **The supposedly neutral**: Alan H. DeCherney and Gertrud S. Berkowitz, 'Female Fecundity and Age,' *The New England Journal of Medicine*, 306, no. 7 (Feb. 18, 1982), 424–6.

46   **The New York Times**: Bayard Webster, 'Study Shows Female Fertility Drops Sharply After Age of 30,' *New York Times*, Feb. 18, 1982, p. A1; Peter Watson, 'New Study Shows Risk of Delay in Starting a Family,' *The Times*, Feb. 19, 1982, p. 24.

46   **A self-help book**: Price and Price, *No More Lonely Nights*, pp. 19–20.

47   **In fact, in an earlier study**: D. Schwartz, P. D. M. MacDonald and V. Heuchel, 'Fecundability, Coital Frequency and the Viability of Ova,' *Population Studies*, 34 (1980), 397.

47   **The one-year cutoff is widely**: Infertility: Medical and Social Choices, US Congress, Office of Technology Assessment, May 1988, p. 35; Jane Menken, James Trussell and Ulla Larsen, 'Age and Infertility,' *Science*, Sept. 26, 1986, 1389–94; John Bongaarts, 'Infertility After Age 30: A False Alarm,' *Family Planning Perspectives*, 14, no. 2 (March/April 1982), 75.

47   **In a British**: Bongaarts, 'Infertility,' pp. 76–7.

47   **John Bongaarts**: *Ibid.*, p. 75.

47   **Three statisticians**: Menken *et al.* 'Age and Infertility,' p. 1391.

47   **Three years later**: The 1982 National Survey of Family Growth Cycle III, National Center for Health Statistics; W. D. Mosher, 'Infertility: Why Business is Booming,' *American Demographics*, July 1987, pp. 42–3. Five years later, the 1988 update of the Family Growth Survey found that infertility had decreased still further to 7.9 per cent.

48   **'No, none at all'**: Personal interview with Alan DeCherney, March 1989.

48   **A New York Times columnist**: Anne Taylor Fleming, 'The Infertile Sisterhood: When the Last Hope Fails,' *New York Times*, March 15, 1988, p. B1.

48   **Writer Molly McKaughan**: Molly McKaughan, *The Biological Clock* (New York: Doubleday, 1987) pp. 123, ff.

48   **It afflicts women who**: Christopher Norwood, 'The Baby Blues: How Late Should You Wait to Have a Child?' *Mademoiselle*, Oct. 1985, p. 236.

48   **(In fact, epidemiologists find)**: Data from American Fertility Society, the Endometriosis Association, Centers for Disease Control and Family Growth Survey Branch of the National Center for Health Statistics, 1989.

49   **(In fact, professional women)**: Norwood, 'The Baby Blues,' p. 238.

49   **(In fact, a 1990 study)**: 'Older Mothers, Healthy Babies,' *Working Woman*, Aug. 1990, p. 93; Diane Calkins, 'New Perspective on Pregnancy after 35,' *McCalls*, Jan. 1987, p. 107; Stephanie J. Ventura, 'Trends in First Births to Older Mothers,' *Monthly Vital Statistics Report*, 31, no. 2, National Center for Health Statistics (May 27, 1982), 5.

49   **More than 150**: Carol J. Rowland Hogue, Willard Cates, Jr and Christopher Tietze, 'Impact of Vacuum Aspiration Abortion on Future Childbearing: A Review,' *Family Planning Perspectives*, 15, no. 3 (May–June 1983): 119–25; Carol J. Rowland Hogue, Willard Cates, Jr and Christopher Tietze, 'The Effects of Induced Abortion on Subsequent Reproduction,' *Epidemiologic Review*, 4 (1982), 66.

49   **But, as a research**: Hogue *et al.*, 'Impact of Vacuum Aspiration Abortion', pp. 120, 125.

49   **Dr Jack Glatt**: Interview with Jane Hill, Dec. 2, 1991.

49   **Statistics show**: Sevgi O. Aral and Dr Willard Cates, Jr, 'The Increasing Concern with Infertility: Why Now?' *Journal of American Medical Association*, 250, no. 17 (1983), 2327. Infertility: Medical and Social Choices, p. 51; William D. Mosher, 'Fertility and Family Planning in the United States,' *Family Planning Perspectives*, 20, no. 5 (Sept./Oct. 1988), 207–17; Charles F. Westoff, 'Fertility in the United States,' *Science*, 234 (Oct. 31, 1986), 554–9.

49   **The same White House that**: Infertility: Medical and Social Choices, p. 17.

49   **In the US the infertility rates**: 'Fecundity, Infertility and Reproductive Health in the United States, 1982,' Data from the National Survey of Family Growth, Series 23, no. 14, National Center for Health Statistics, Hyattsville, Maryland, May 1987; Infertility: Medical and Social Choices, p. 52.

50   **This epidemic**: Julius Schachter, 'Why We Need a Program for the Control of Chlamydia Trachomatis,' *The New England Journal of Medicine*, 320, no. 12 (March 21, 1989), 802–3; A. Eugene Washington, Robert E. Johnson and Lawrence L. Sanders, 'Chlamydia Trachomatis Infections in the United States: What Are They Costing Us?' *Journal of American Medical Association*, 257, no. 15 (April 17, 1987), 2070–4; Infertility: Medical and Social Choices, pp. 61–2. Pharmaceutical manufacturers helped to spread PID, too, through gross negligence – by dispensing IUDs long after their managements were aware of the infection-inducing effects. IUDs increased women's odds of contracting PID by 9 per cent; women who used the infamous Dalkon Shields were six times more likely to develop PID. See Morton Mintz, 'The Selling of an IUD: Behind the Scenes at G.D. Searle During the Rise and Fall of the Copper-7,' *Washington Post*, Health section, Aug. 9, 1988, p. Z12; Pamela Rohland, 'Prof Continues Battle over Defective IUDs,' *Reading Eagle*, Nov. 18, 1990, p. A20; William Ruberry, 'Tragic Dalkon Story Finally at an End,' *Richmond Times-Dispatch*, Jan. 21, 1990, p. F1; The Boston Women's Health Collective, *The New Our Bodies, Ourselves* (London: Penguin Books, 1989), pp. 423, 493.

50   **By the mid- to late 1980s as many as**: David G. Addiss, Michael L. Vaughn, Margi A. Holzheuter, Lori L. Bakken and Jeffrey P. Davis, 'Selective Screening for Chlamydia Trachomatis Infection in Nonurban Family Planning Clinics in Wisconsin,' *Family Planning Perspectives*, 19, no. 6 (Nov.–Dec. 1987), 252–6; Julius Schachter, Dr Moses Grossman, Dr Richard L. Sweet, Jane Holt, Carol Jordan and Ellen Bishop, 'Prospective Study of Perinatal Transmission of Chlamydia Trachomatis,' *Journal of the American Medical Association*, 255, no. 24

(June 27, 1986), 3374–7; personal interview with Julius Schachter of the University of California at San Francisco, March 1989.

50   **F. M. Graham:** 'The Social Relevance of Infertility' by F. M. Graham and J. Ellis, National Women's Hospital, Auckland, New Zealand, summer 1987.

50   **A 1987 *British Medical Journal*:** Editorial, *BMJ* 1987, 294, no. 6576, 853.

50   **Dr Glatt's experience:** Interview with Jane Hill, Dec. 2, 1991.

51   **If women go to the:** Information from John Dixon, Director of Issue (formerly the National Association for the Childless), Birmingham, Jan. 1992.

51   **Men's sperm count:** Amy Linn, 'Male Infertility: From Taboo to Treatment,' *Philadelphia Inquirer*, May 31, 1987, p. A1.

51   **(Poor semen quality is):** Infertility: Medical and Social Choices, p. 85.

51   **The alarming depletion:** *Ibid.*, p. 121.

52   **A 1988 congressional study:** *Ibid.*, p. 29.

52   **'Why don't we do':** Personal interview with William D. Mosher, March 1989.

52   **'Most of this small book is':** Ben J. Wattenberg, *The Birth Dearth* (New York: Pharos Books, 1987) pp. 1, 127.

52   **Harvard psychologist:** Richard J. Herrnstein, 'IQ and Falling Birth Rates,' *The Atlantic*, May 1989, p. 73; 'A Confederacy of Dunces,' *Newsweek*, May 22, 1989, pp. 80–1.

52   **'Sex comes first':** Herrnstein, 'IQ and Falling Birth Rates,' pp. 76, 79, 73.

53   **His inflammatory tactics:** Ben J. Wattenberg, *The Real America: A Surprising Examination of the State of the Union* (Garden City, NY: Doubleday, 1974) pp. 152, 168–71; Wattenberg, *The Birth Dearth*, p. 179. For an excellent analysis, and debunking, of Wattenberg's birth-dearth theory, see Tony Kaye, 'The Birth Dearth', *The New Republic*, Jan. 19, 1987, pp. 20–3.

53   **Just ten years later:** Wattenberg, *Birth Dearth*, pp. 14, 97–8.

53   **According to Wattenberg's:** *Ibid.*, pp. 9, 57, 95, 115.

53   **For generating what:** *Ibid.*, pp. 119–28, 159.

54   **'I believe that *The Birth Dearth*':** *Ibid.*, p. 204.

54   **Illegitimate births to:** Data from National Center for Health Statistics, Children's Defense Fund's Clearinghouse on Adolescent Pregnancy, and Alan Guttmacher Institute.

54   **The fertility rate in the USA:** Data from National Center for Health Statistics, US Bureau of the Census.

54   **Similarly, the number:** 'Compendium of Health Statistics,' Office of Health Economics, 1989; 'On the State of the Public Health for the Year 1990,' Department of Health report.

54   **In other words, he was speculating:** Kaye, 'Birth Dearth,' p. 22.

55   **They failed to:** Frank Furstenberg, 'The State of Marriage,' *Science*, 239 (March 1988), 1434.

55   **In the mid-1980s several:** See, for example, 'The Age of Youthful Melancholia: Depression and the Baby Boomers,' *USA Today Magazine*, July 1986, pp. 69–71; Martin E. P. Seligman, 'Boomer Blues,' *Psychology Today*, Oct. 1988, pp. 50–5; 'Depression,' *Newsweek*, May 4, 1987; Susan Squire, 'The Big Chill,' *Gentlemen's Quarterly*, Nov. 1987, p. 137; Mark MacNamara, 'The Big Chill Syndrome,' *Los Angeles*, Aug. 1988, p. 71.

55   **The rising mental distress:** Elizabeth Mehren, 'Frustrated by the Odds, Single Women over 30 Seeking Answers in Therapy,' *Los Angeles Times*, Nov. 30, 1986, VI, p. 1.

55   **A 1988 article in *New York Woman*:** Meryl Gordon, 'Rough Times,' *New York Woman*, March 1988, p. 80.

55   **In fact, no one:** Personal interviews with Ben Z. Locke, chief of epidemiology and psychopathology research, National Institute of Mental Health; Dr Myrna M. Weissman, psychiatry professor at Columbia University and former director of the Yale University Depression Research Unit; Dr Gerald L. Klerman, associate chairman for research and professor of psychiatry at Columbia University; Jane Murphy, associate professor of anthropology, department of psychiatry, at

Harvard Medical School and Chief of Psychiatric Epidemiology, Massachusetts General Hospital, 1988, 1989.

56 **As psychological researcher Lynn L. Gigy**: Lynn L. Gigy, 'Self-Concept of Single Women,' *Psychology of Women Quarterly*, 5, no. 2 (Winter 1980), 321–40.

56 **But the lack of data**: Elaine Showalter, *The Female Malady: Women, Madness and English Culture, 1830–1980* (New York: Pantheon Books, 1985) pp. 61, 134.

56 **The 1983 landmark 'Lifeprints' study**: Grace Baruch, Rosalind Barnett and Caryl Rivers, *Lifeprints: New patterns of Love and Work for Today's Women* (New York: Signet Books, 1983) pp. 261, 279.

56 **Researchers from the**: Lois M. Verbrugge and Jennifer H. Madans, 'Women's Roles and Health,' *American Demographics*, March 1985, p. 36. The 1990 Virginia Slims opinion poll also finds a direct link between self-image and employment. See The 1990 Virginia Slims Opinion Poll, p. 28.

56 **Finally, in a rare**: Baruch *et al.*, *Lifeprints*, p. 281.

56 **The warning issued by**: Susan Faludi, 'Marry, Marry? On the Contrary!' *West Magazine, San Jose Mercury News*, Aug. 10, 1986, p. 6.

57 **The psychological indicators**: See, for example, Carol Tavris and Carole Offir, *The Longest War: Sex Differences in Perspective* (New York: Harcourt Brace Jovanovich, 1977) p. 221; Bernard, *The Future of Marriage*, pp. 30–2, 312–13; *Women and Mental Health*, ed. Elizabeth Howell and Marjorie Bayes (New York: Basic Books, 1981) pp. 182–3; Kay F. Schaffer, *Sex-Role Issues in Mental Health* (Reading, Mass.: Addison-Wesley, 1980) pp. 136–67; D. Nevill and S. Damico, 'Developmental Components of Role Conflict in Women,' *Journal of Psychology*, 95 (1977), 195–8; Walter R. Gove, 'Sex Differences in Mental Illness Among Adult Men and Women,' *Social Science & Medicine*, 12B (1978), 187–98; Mary Roth Walsh, *The Psychology of Women: Ongoing Debates* (New Haven: Yale University Press, 1987) p. 111.

57 **A twenty-five-year longitudinal**: Judith Birnbaum, 'Life Patterns and Self-Esteem in Gifted Family-Oriented and Career-Committed Women' (1975), in *Women and Achievement: Social and Motivational Analyses*, ed. M. Mednick, S. Tangri and L. Hoffman (New York: Halsted Press, 1975) pp. 396–419.

57 **A 1980 study**: Gigy, 'Self-Concept,' pp. 321–39.

57 **The Mills Longitudinal**: Scott Winokur, 'Women Pay a Price,' *San Francisco Examiner*, Dec. 16, 1990, p. E1.

57 **A *Cosmopolitan* survey**: Linda Wolfe, 'The Sexual Profile of the Cosmopolitan Girl,' *Cosmopolitan*, Sept. 1990, p. 254.

57 **Finally, when noted mental**: Walter R. Gove, 'Mental Illness and Psychiatric Treatment,' in *The Psychology of Women*, ed. Mary Roth Walsh (New Haven: Yale University Press, 1987) p. 11.

57 **'Women's burnout has'**: Freudenberger and North, *Women's Burnout*, p. xiv.

58 **'More and more'**: Shaevitz, *Superwoman Syndrome*, p. 17.

58 **'A surprising number'**: Susan Agrest, 'Just a Harmless Little Habit,' *Savvy*, Oct. 1987, p. 52.

58 **As *The Type E***: Braiker, *Type E Woman*, p. 5.

58 **'Women are freeing themselves'**: personal interview with James Lynch, March 1988.

58 **'The women's liberation'**: Morse and Furst, *Women Under Stress*, pp. 275, 305.

58 **Ex-hippie writer**: Richard Neville, 'Pasta Glories revisited', *Evening Standard*, Aug. 23, 1991, p. 9.

58 **'Although being a full-time homemaker'**: Witkin-Lanoil, *Female Stress*, p. 119.

58 **Psychotherapist Vera Diamond**: 'Stress: A Sign of the Times,' *She*, Mar. 1989, p. 84.

59 **Yet the actual evidence**: 'Basic Data on Depressive Symptomatology, 1974–75,' US National Health Survey, Public Health Service, April 1980, p. 3; S. Haynes and M. Feinleib, 'Women, Work and Coronary Heart Disease: Prospective Findings from the Framingham Heart Study,' *American Journal of Public Health*, 1980, pp. 133–41; Lois Wladis Hoffman, 'Effects of Maternal Employment in the Two-parent Family,' *American Psychologist*, Feb. 1989, pp. 283–92; Baruch

et al., *Lifeprints*, pp. 179–80. A Metropolitan Life Insurance survey found that women in executive jobs have a 29 per cent higher life expectancy than women in clerical and low-status jobs; they also have a lower rate of heart disease. See 'Gender Health,' *Women/Scope*, 2, no. 7 (April 1989), 4. The 1988 Gallup Poll found that women's sense of worth and satisfaction is 'strongly conditioned by educational, occupational and financial status': 81 per cent of the women making more than $35,000 were satisfied with themselves, compared with 62 per cent of women who made between $15,000 and $34,999, and 42 per cent of the women who made less than $15,000. See 'Personal Goals of Women,' Sept. 25, 1988. The Gallup Organization, pp. 164–5.

59 **They are less**: Ruth Cooperstock, 'A Review of Women's Psychotropic Drug Use,' in *Women and Mental Health*, p. 135.

59 **'Inactivity,' as a study**: Verbrugge and Madans, 'Women's Roles and Health,' p. 38.

59 **Career women in the 1980s**: David Alexander Leaf, 'A Woman's Heart: An Update of Coronary Artery Disease Risk in Women,' *Western Journal of Medicine*, 149 (Dec. 1988), 751–7; Bonnie R. Strickland, 'Sex-Related Differences in Health and Illness,' *Psychology of Women Quarterly*, 12 (1988), 381–99.

59 **In fact, there was no**: Professor D. G. Julian and Claire Marley, *Coronary Heart Disease: the Facts* (Oxford: Oxford University Press, 1991), p. 26.

59 **Only the lung cancer rate**: Strickland, 'Sex-Related Differences,' p. 387.

59 **The proportion of adult**: 'Lung Cancer and Smoking,' Factsheet 11.2, Cancer Research Campaign, 1989.

59 **Even in the 'feminine mystique'**: William H. Chafe, *The American Woman: Her Changing Social, Economic and Political Roles, 1920–1970* (New York: Oxford University Press, 1972) p. 220.

59 **In the 1980s 87 per cent**: Hochschild, *Second Shift*, pp. 241–2.

59 **In short, as one**: Lois Verbrugge, 'A Life and Death Paradox,' *American Demographics*, July 1988, pp. 34–7.

60 **By helping to widen**: Ronald C. Kessler and James A. McRae, Jr, 'Trends in the Relationship Between Sex and Psychological Distress: 1957–1976,' *American Sociological Review*, 46 (Aug. 1981), 443–52; J. M. Murphy, 'Trends in Depression and Anxiety: Men and Women,' *Acta Psychiatr. Scand.*, 1986, 73, pp. 113–27; Leo Srole, 'The Midtown Manhattan Longitudinal Study vs. "The Mental Paradise Lost" Doctrine,' *Archives of General Psychiatry*, 37 (Feb. 1980), 220; Jane M. Murphy, Richard R. Monson, Donald C. Olivier, Arthur M. Sobol and Alexander H. Leighton, 'Affective Disorders and Mortality,' *Archives of General Psychiatry*, 44 (May 1987), 473–80; Jane M. Murphy, Arthur M. Sobol, Raymond K. Neff, Donald C. Olivier and Alexander H. Leighton, 'Stability of Prevalence: Depression and Anxiety Disorders,' *Archives of General Psychiatry*, 41 (Oct. 1984), 990–7.

60 **The changes**: Srole, 'Midtown Manhattan,' p. 220.

60 **'There is a direct link'**: Witkin-Lanoil, *Female Stress*, p. 124.

60 **In a review**: Ronald C. Kessler and James A. McRae, Jr, 'Trends in Relationships between Sex and Attempted Suicide,' *Journal of Health and Social Behavior*, 24 (June 1983), p. 106. The researchers also found that husbands who were the most resistant or hostile to their wives' employment were the most likely to report higher rates of psychological distress. On the other hand, husbands who willingly participated in childcare seemed to be weathering the social changes with far less psychological disruption.

60 **The role changes that**: Kessler and McRae, 'Trends in Sex and Psychological Distress,' p. 450.

61 **'Have changes in'**: Murphy, 'Stability of Prevalence,' p. 996.

61 **As Kessler says**: Personal interview with Ronald Kessler, March 1988.

61 **A 1980 study finds**: S. Rosenfield, 'Sex Differences in Depression: Do Women Always Have Higher Rates?' *Journal of Health and Social Behavior*, 21 (1980), 33–42.

61   **A 1982 study:** Ronald C. Kessler and James A. McRae, Jr, 'The Effect of Wives' Employment on the Mental Health of Married Men and Women,' *American Sociological Review*, 47 (1982), 216–27.

61   **A 1986 analysis:** Sandra C. Stanley, Janet G. Hunt and Larry L. Hunt, 'The Relative Deprivation of Husbands in Dual-Earner Households,' *Journal of Family Issues*, 7 (March 1986), no. 1, 3–20.

61   **A 1987 study:** Niall Bolger, Anita DeLongis, Ronald C. Kessler and Elaine Wethington, 'The Microstructure of Daily Role-related Stress in Married Couples,' to be published in *Cross the Boundaries: The Transmission of Stress Between Work and Family*, ed. John Eckenrode and Susan Gore (New York: Plenum) pp. 16, 25. Numerous other studies have come up with similar findings. See G. L. Staines, K. J. Pottick and D. A Fudge, 'Wives' Employment and Husbands' Attitudes toward Work and Life,' *Journal of Applied Psychology*, 71 (1986), no. 1, 118–28; P. J. Stein, 'Men in Families,' *Marriage and Family Review*, 7 (1984), no. 3/4, 143–59.

61   **When *Newsweek* produced:** David Gelman, 'Depression,' *Newsweek*, May 4, 1987, p. 48.

62   **The anti-childcare:** Deborah Fallows, ' "Mommy Don't Leave Me Here!" The Day Care parents Don't See,' *Redbook*, Oct. 1985, p. 160; J. L. Dautremont, Jr, 'Day Care Can Be Dangerous to Your Child's Health,' *San Francisco Examiner*, Jan. 20, 1990, p. A25; 'When Child Care Becomes Child Molesting,' *Good Housekeeping*, July 1984, p. 16; 'Creeping Child Care . . . Creepy,' Connaught Marshner, *National Review*, May 13, 1988, p.28.

62   **The spokesmen of the New Right:** For 'Thalidomide of the '80s,' see Richard A. Vaughan's solicitation letter for *Family in America*, a New Right publication, 1989, p. 3.

62   **'American mothers who work':** 'End-of-Year Issue,' *Eleanor Smeal Report*, 1987, p. 4. See also, Alexander Cockburn, 'Looking for Satan in the Sandbox,' *San Francisco Examiner*, Feb. 7, 1990, p. A21.

62   **In 1984 a *Newsweek*:** Melinda Beck, 'An Epidemic of Child Abuse,' *Newsweek*, Aug. 29, 1984, p. 44.

62   **Just in case:** Russell Watson, 'What Price Day Care?' *Newsweek*, Sept. 10, 1984, p. 14.

62   **'I had to admit':** *Ibid.*, p. 18.

62   **Still later, in a:** Pat Wingert and Barbara Kantrowitz, 'The Day Care Generation,' *Newsweek*, special issue, Winter/Spring 1990, pp. 86–92. The only new 'evidence' that the story offered was a study of third-graders (eight- or nine-year-olds) in Texas, which found that the children with more than thirty hours of day care during infancy were more likely to become discipline problems. But the study's researcher herself concluded that poverty, not day care, was the more important underlying factor, and that problems with day care in Texas had far more to do with the state's poor record of day care regulation than with the nature of day care itself.

63   **But the *New York Times*:** Warren E. Leary, 'Risk of Sex Abuse in Day Care Seen as Lower Than at Home,' *New York Times*, March 28, 1988, p. A20.

63   **The study concluded:** David Finkelhor, Linda Meyer Williams, Nanci Burns and Michael Kalinowski, 'Sexual Abuse in Day Care: A National Study,' March 1988, Family Research Laboratory, p. 18.

63   **In fact, if there:** *Ibid.*, pp. vii, xvii. Data also from National Committee for the Prevention of Child Abuse, which reported in 1986 that 72 per cent of all sexual abuse was perpetrated by fathers and stepfathers. Ironically, the press *had* cast doubt on reports of a child-molestation epidemic in the home; a spate of stories in the mid-1980s proposed that the problem was actually fabricated by conniving ex-wives who were angling for sole custody of the children. Although there undoubtedly were women who stooped to this tactic, they were the exception. In the 1980s only 2 per cent of divorce and child-custody disputes even involved allegations of sexual abuse.

63   **'Day care is not'**: *Ibid.*, Finkelhor *et al.*, 'Sexual Abuse in Day Care,' pp. 18–19.

63   **Research over the last two decades**: *Children of Working Parents: Experiences and Outcomes*, ed. Cheryl D. Hayes and Sheila B. Kamerman (Washington, DC: National Academy Press, 1983); Lois Wladis Hoffman, 'Effects of Maternal Employment in the Two-parent Family,' *American Psychologist*, Feb. 1989, pp. 283–92; Kathleen McCartney, Sandra Scarr, Deborah Phillips, Susan Grajek and J. Conrad Schwarz, 'Environmental Differences Among Day Care Centers and Their Effects on Children's Development,' *Day Care: Scientific and Social Policy Issues*, ed. E. Zigler and E. Gordon (Boston: Auburn House, 1982) pp. 126–51; Barbara J. Berg, *The Crisis of the Working Mother* (New York: Summit Books, 1986) pp. 58–60; Ellen Galinsky, 'The Impact of Parental Employment on Children: New Directions For Research,' Work and Family Life Studies, Bank Street College of Education, unpublished paper: Hochschild, *The Second Shift*, pp. 235–6. See also Susan Faludi, 'Are the Kids Alright?' *Mother Jones*, Nov. 1988, pp. 15–18.

64   **The actual studies**: Data from Child Care Law Center and Children's Defense Fund. See also Carolyn Jabs, 'Reassuring Answers to 10 Myths About Day Care,' *Child-Care Referral & Education*, July–Aug. 1985 edition, p. 2.

64   **But the research offers**: Sandra Scarr, *Mother Care/Other Care* (New York: Basic Books, 1984) pp. 100–4; Michael Rutter, 'Social-Emotional Consequences of Day Care for Preschool Children,' *Day Care: Scientific and Social Policy Issues*, pp. 5–9; Kathleen McCartney and Deborah Phillips, 'Motherhood and Child Care,' in *The Different Faces of Motherhood*, ed. Beverly Birns and Dale F. Hay (New York: Plenum Press, 1988) pp. 170–2, 176–7; Hoffman, 'Effects of Maternal Employment in the Two-Parent Family,' p. 288.

64   **Their evidence, however**: The data most widely relied on in making these claims come from British psychologist John Bowlby's studies of orphaned children after the Second World War. See John Bowlby, *Attachment and Loss*, 2 vols (New York: Basic Books, 1969); Scarr, pp. 207–8.

64   **Psychologist Harry Harlow**: Michael Rutter, *Maternal Deprivation Reassessed* (Harmondsworth: Penguin Books, 1972) pp. 36–7.

64   **Up until this point**: Jay Belsky, 'Two Waves of Day Care Research: Developmental Effects and Conditions of Quality,' *The Child and the Day Care Setting*, ed. R. Ainslie (New York: Praeger, 1984); J. Belsky and L. Steinberg, 'The Effects of Day Care: A Critical Review,' *Child Development*, 49, 929–49.

64   **Then, in the September**: Jay Belsky, 'Infant Day Care: A Cause for Concern?' *Zero to Three*, 6, no. 5 (Sept. 1986), 1–7.

64   **Soon Belsky found himself**: Personal interviews with Jay Belsky, 1991.

65   **Belsky peppered his report**: Belsky, 'Infant Day Care,' pp. 4, 6.

65   **Finally, in every press interview**: Personal interview with Jay Belsky, 1991. (Subsequent quotes from Belsky are from interview unless otherwise noted.)

65   **But that person**: Ann C. Crouter, Maureen Perry-Jenkins, Ted. L. Huston and Susan M. McHale, 'Processes Underlying Father Involvement in Dual-Earner and Single-Earner Families,' *Developmental Psychology*, 23, 431–40.

Chapter Three. Backlashes Then and Now

66   **'The progress of women's rights'**: Ann Douglas, *The Feminization of American Culture* (New York: Avon Books, 1977) p. 199.

66   **Women's studies historians**: Deirdre English, 'What Do Which Women Really Want,' *The New York Times Book Review*, Sept. 4, 1988, p. 20; Ethel Klein, *Gender Politics* (Cambridge, Mass.: Harvard University Press, 1984) p. 9; Juliet Mitchell, 'Reflections on Twenty Years of Feminism,' in *What Is Feminism? A Re-Examination*, ed. Juliet Mitchell and Ann Oakley (New York: Pantheon Books, 1986), p. 36.

66   'While men proceed': *Feminist Theorists: Three Centuries of Key Women Thinkers*, ed. Dale Spender (New York: Pantheon Books, 1983) p. 4.

66   It is, as poet: Adrienne Rich, *On Lies, Secrets and Silence* (New York: W. W. Norton, 1979) pp. 9–10.

67   'At the opening of the twentieth': Lois W. Banner, *Women in Modern America: A Brief History*, 2nd edn (New York: Harcourt Brace Jovanovich, 1984) p. 1.

67   Soon the country would have to: Nancy F. Cott, *The Grounding of Modern Feminism* (New Haven: Yale University Press, 1987) p. 39.

67   'The old theory that': Chafe, *The American Woman*, p. 179.

67   Different kinds of backlash: Vern L. Bullough, Brenda Shelton and Sarah Slavin, *The Subordinated Sex: A History of Attitudes Toward Women* (Athens, Georgia: The University of Georgia Press, 1988) pp. 73–82; Mary R. Beard, *Women as Force in History: A Study in Traditions and Realities* (New York: Octagon Books, 1976); Elaine Pagels, *The Gnostic Gospels* (New York: Random House, 1979) and *Adam, Eve and the Serpent* (New York: Random House, 1988); Barbara Ehrenreich and Deirdre English, *Witches, Midwives and Nurses: A History of Women Healers* (New York: The Feminist Press, 1973); Simone de Beauvoir, *The Second Sex* (London: Penguin Books, 1972), p. 22.

68   White European women: Bullough *et al.*, *The Subordinated Sex*, p. 261.

68   This transaction was billed: Eleanor Flexner, *Century of Struggle: The Woman's Rights Movement in the United States* (New York: Atheneum, 1974) p. 1.

68   'It may be said that she': Page Smith, *Daughters of the Promised Land: Women in American History* (Boston: Little, Brown 1970) p. 91.

68   As scholar Cynthia: Cynthia D. Kinnard (ed.) *Antifeminism in American Thought: An Annotated Bibliography* (Boston: G. K. Hall, 1986) p. xv.

69   Educated women of this era: *Ibid.*, p. 307; Barbara Ehrenreich and Deirdre English, *For Her Own Good: 150 Years of the Experts' Advice to Women* (Garden City, NY: Anchor Books, 1978) p. 128; Lee Virginia Chambers-Schiller, *Liberty, A Better Husband: Single Women in America – The Generations of 1780–1840* (New Haven: Yale University Press) pp. 32–3.

69   They, too, faced: Ehrenreich and English, *For Her Own Good*, pp. 125–31.

69   And Victorian women: Nancy Sahli, 'Smashing: Women's Relationships Before the Fall,' *Chrysalis*, no. 8 (Summer 1979), 17–27.

69   Then as now, late: Linda Gordon, *Woman's Body, Woman's Right: Birth Control in America* (New York: Penguin Books, 1977) pp. 137, 138–42.

69   The media and the: *Ibid.*, pp. 49–71; William L. O'Neill, *Divorce in the Progressive Era* (New Haven: Yale University Press, 1967) pp. 33–56; Elaine Tyler May, *Great Expectations: Marriage and Divorce in Post-Victorian America* (Chicago: University of Chicago Press, 1980) p. 4.

69   By the late 1800s: Gordon, *Woman's Body*, p. 57.

70   The word 'feminism': Nancy F. Cott, *The Grounding of Modern Feminism* (New Haven: Yale University Press, 1987) p. 13.

70   The International Ladies': Banner, *Women in Modern America*, p. 71.

70   And Heterodoxy: Cott, *Modern Feminism*, pp. 38–9.

70   The US War Department: *Ibid.*, pp. 241–60; Banner, *Women in Modern America*, pp. 152–3; Carol Hymowitz and Michaele Weissman, *A History of Women in America* (New York: Bantam Books, 1978) p. 233.

70   The media maligned: Cott, *Modern Feminism*, pp. 272, 362; Kinnard, *Antifeminism*, p. 183.

70   Young women: Jessie Bernard, *The Female World* (New York: Free Press, 1981) p. 146.

70   Post-feminist sentiments: Cott, *Modern Feminism*, pp. 271–6.

70   'Ex-feminists' began: *Ibid.*, p. 276. 'For us to even use the word feminist is to invite from the extremists a challenge to our authority,' explained Ethel M. Smith, a top officer in the Women's Trade Union League – an explanation that would be largely restated in the 1980s, in that decade's near elimination of 'the F-word'. See *ibid.*, p. 134.

70   **In place of equal rights**: Alice Kessler-Harris, *Out to Work: A History of Wage-Earning Women in the United States* (New York: Oxford University Press, 1982) pp. 204–14.

71   **The 1920s eroded**: O'Neill, *Everyone Was Brave: The Rise and Fall of Feminism in America* (Chicago: Quadrangle Books, 1969), p. 305.

71   **When the Depression**: Hymowitz and Weissman, *A History of Women in America*, pp. 306–7.

71   **'All about us we see'**: Whilliam O'Neill, *Everyone Was Brave*, pp. 292–3.

71   **'It looks sometimes as if'**: Margaret Culkin Banning, 'They Raise Their Hats,' *Harper's*, Aug. 1935, p. 354.

71   **As political science scholar**: Klein, *Gender Politics*, p. 17.

71   **The spiral swung**: The federal government's support for day care, however, was more verbal than financial: it provided day care programmes for only 10 per cent of the children who needed them. See Banner, *Women in Modern America*, p. 221; Carl N. Degler, *At Odds: Women and Family in America from the Revolution to the Present* (New York: Oxford University Press, 1980) p. 420.

71   **Women welcomed their**: Kessler-Harris, *Out to Work*, p. 276; Hymowitz and Weissman, *A History of Women in America*, p. 312; Degler, *At Odds*, p. 420.

71   **Seventy-five per cent reported**: Hymowitz and Weissman, *A History of Women in America*, p. 314; Chafe, *The American Woman*, pp. 178–9.

71   **Women's political energies**: Kessler-Harris, *Out to Work*, pp. 290–1, 296.

72   **This time, the amendment**: Cynthia Harrison, *On Account of Sex: The Politics of Women's Issues, 1945–1968* (Berkeley: University of California Press, 1988) pp. 15–16, 19, 21.

72   **In a record outpouring**: Klein, *Gender Politics*, p. 18.

72   **Two months after**: Hymowitz and Weissman, *A History of Women in America*, p. 314; Kessler-Harris, *Out to Work*, p. 287.

72   **Employers revived prohibitions**: Hymowitz and Weissman, *A History of Women in America*, pp. 314, 316, 323; Kessler-Harris, *Out to Work*, p. 309; Chafe, *The American Woman*, p. 190; Banner, *Women in Modern America*, pp. 222–4.

72   **An anti-ERA coalition**: Harrison, *On Account*, p. 20.

72   **When the United Nations**: Chafe, *The American Woman*, pp. 306–7.

72   **Employers who had**: Harrison, *On Account*, p. 5.

72   **Advice experts**: Chafe, *The American Woman*, pp. 176–7, 187.

73   **Better watch out**: *This Week*, cited in Catherine Johnson's 'Exploding the Male Shortage Myth, *New Woman*, Sept. 1986, p. 48.

73   **Feminism was 'a deep'**: Marynia Farnham and Ferdinand Lundberg, *Modern Woman: The Lost Sex* (New York: Harper & Row, 1947), cited in Betty Friedan, *The Feminine Mystique* (London: Pelican Books, 1982 edn), p. 107.

73   **Independent-minded women**: Chafe, *The American Woman*, p. 176.

73   **The rise in female autonomy**: Kessler-Harris, *Out to Work*, p. 304; Banner, *Women in Modern America*, p. 234.

73   **Advertisers reversed their**: Maureen Honey, *Creating Rosie the Riveter: Class, Gender, and Propaganda During World War II* (Amherst, Mass.: University of Massachusetts Press, 1984) p. 122.

73   **As a survey of**: Harrison, *On Account*, p. 6; Susan M. Hartmann, *The Home Front and Beyond: American Women in the 1940s* (Boston: Twayne Publishers, 1982) p. 200.

73   **On the comics pages**: Hartmann, *Home Front*, p. 202; *Pronatalism: The Myth of Mom and Apple Pie*, ed. Ellen Peck and Judith Senderowitz (New York: Thomas Y. Crowell, 1974) p. 69.

73   **In 1948 Susan B. Anthony**: Chafe, *The American Woman*, p. 184.

73   **Margaret Hickey**: *Ibid.*, p. 185.

73   **Soon Hickey herself**: Harrison, *On Account*, p. ix.

73   **Their age at first marriage**: Degler, *At Odds*, p. 429; Jessie Bernard, 'The Status of Women in Modern Patterns of Culture,' in *The Other Half: Roads to Women's*

Equality, ed. Cynthia Fuchs Epstein and William J. Goode (Englewood Cliffs, NJ: Prentice-Hall, 1971) p. 17.

74 **As literary scholars Sandra M. Gilbert**: Sandra M. Gilbert and Susan Gubar, *No Man's Land: The Place of the Woman Writer in the Twentieth Century*, Vol. I: *The War of the Words* (New Haven: Yale University Press, 1988) p. 47.

74 **These cultural images notwithstanding**: Degler, *At Odds*, p. 418; Hymowitz and Weissman, *A History of Women in America*, p. 314; Kessler-Harris, *Out to Work*, p. 301.

74 **While 3.25 million**: Harrison, *On Account*, p. 5.

74 **Two years after**: *Ibid.*, p. 181; Hymowitz and Weissman, *A History of Women in America*, p. 314; Chafe, *The American Woman*, p. 181.

74 **By 1955 the *average***: Married women doubled their representation in the labour force, from 15 per cent in 1940 to 30 per cent by 1960. Hymowitz and Weissman, *A History of Women in America*, p. 314; Harrison, *On Account*, p. 5; Sara M. Evans and Barbara J. Nelson, *Wage Justice* (Chicago: University of Chicago Press, 1989) p. 23.

74 **The backlash of the**: Chafe, *The American Woman*, p. 181; Kessler-Harris, *Out to Work*, p. 309.

75 **The ranks of working women**: O'Neill, *Everyone Was Brave*, p. 305; Dean D. Knudsen, 'The Declining Status of Women: Popular Myths and the Failure of Functionalist Thought,' in *The Other Half: Roads to Women's Equality*, ed. Cynthia Fuchs Epstein and William J. Goode (Englewood Cliffs, NJ: Prentice-Hall, 1971) pp. 98–108; Hymowitz and Weissman, *A History of Women in America*, p. 315; Bernard, 'Status of Women,' p. 16; Kessler-Harris, *Out to Work*, p. 305. The proportion of women who were working as professionals fell from 45 per cent in 1940 to 38 per cent in 1966, while at the same time the proportion employed as clerical workers climbed from 53 per cent in 1940 to 73 per cent by 1968. M. P. Ryan, *Womanhood in America: From Colonial Times to the Present* (New York: Franklin Watts, 1983) p. 281.

75 **At the turn of the century**: William L. O'Neill, 'The Fight for Suffrage,' *The Wilson Quarterly*, 10, no. 4 (Autumn 1986), 104; *Sisterhood Is Powerful*, ed. Robin Morgan (New York: Vintage Books, 1970) p. 21.

75 **As a 1985 AFL-CIO report**: 'The AFL-CIO and Civil Rights,' Report of the Executive Council to the 16th Constitutional Convention of the AFL-CIO, Anaheim, Calif., Oct. 28–31, 1985.

76 **As Henry Adams**: Henry Adams, *The Education of Henry Adams* (Boston: Houghton Mifflin, 1973 edn) p. 447.

76 **With the exception of**: Data from US Bureau of Census, Fertility Statistics Branch.

77 **The media have circulated**: See Chapter 13 on women in the work force.

77 **It maps the road**: Henrietta Rodman, *New York Times*, Jan. 24, 1915, cited in *Feminist Quotations: Voices of Rebels, Reformers, and Visionaries*, ed. Carol McPhee and Ann Fitzgerald (New York: Thomas Y. Crowell, 1979) p. 239.

78 **Feminist-minded institutions**: Michael deCourcy Hinds, 'Feminist Businesses See the Future,' *New York Times*, Nov. 12, 1988, p. 16.

78 **Millions of women**: See Chapter 12 on backlash psychology.

79 **In Wendy Wasserstein's**: Phillip Lopate, 'Christine Lahti Tries to Fashion a Spunky "Heidi," ' *New York Times*, Sept. 3, 1989, Arts and Leisure section, p. 5.

79 **'I'm alone'**: Caroline Knapp, 'Whatever Happened to Sisterhood?' *The Boston Phoenix*, April 7, 1989, p. 13.

79 **'I feel abandoned'**: Angela Brown, 'Throwing in the Towel' Letter to the editor, *Ms*, Jan. 1988, p. 10.

80 **'In a state of'**: Susan Griffin, 'The Way of All Ideology,' in *Feminist Theory: A Critique of Ideology*, ed. Nannerl O. Keohane, Michelle Z. Rosaldo and Barbara C. Gelpi (Chicago: University of Chicago Press, 1982) p. 279.

80 **'If I were to overcome the conventions'**: Virginia Woolf, 'The Pargiters,' cited

in Michelle Cliff, 'The Resonance of Interruption,' *Chrysalis*, 8 (Summer 1979), 29–37.

80 **By 1989 almost:** Belkin, 'Bars to Equality,' p. A16. By 1990, the Virginia Slims poll also found that the 'increasing strains, pressures, and demands' placed on 1980s women had taken its toll. While the overwhelming majority of working women still wanted a marriage where both spouses worked and equally shared familial duties, the share of working women who wanted to go back to 'traditional' marital arrangements had risen by five percentage points since 1985 – the first increase in decades. See Virginia Slims Opinion Poll, 1990, p. 46.

80 **'And when women do not':** Betty Friedan, *The Feminine Mystique*, p. 331.

80 **'I am sure the emancipated':** Cott, *Modern Feminism*, p. 45.

80 **'There has been much':** Banning, 'Raise Their Hats,' p. 358.

81 **When author:** Anthony Astrachan, *How Men Feel: Their Response to Women's Demands for Equality and Power* (Garden City, NY: Anchor Books, 1986) p. 402.

81 **In 1988 the American:** Significance Inc., 'The American Male Opinion Index,' I (New York: Condé Nast Publications, 1988) p. 2.

81 **Other studies examining:** Klein, *Gender Politics*, pp. 126, 136–8, 163; Andrew Cherlin and Pamela Barnhouse Walters, 'Trends in United States Men's and Women's Sex Roles Attitudes: 1972 to 1978,' *American Sociological Review*, 46 (1981), 453–60; Richard G. Niemi, John Mueller and Tom W. Smith, *Trends in Public Opinion: A Compendium of Survey Data* (New York: Greenwood Press, 1989).

81 **As the American Male:** 'The American Male Opinion Index,' I, p. 26.

81 **At the same time that:** *Trends in Public Opinion*; The Gallup Poll; Roper Organization's Virginia Slims Opinion Poll; Townsend and O'Neil, 'American Women Get Mad,' p. 26.

82 **This was especially:** 'Women and Men: Is Realignment Under Way?' *Public Opinion*, 5 (April–May, 1982) 2, 21; Karlyn H. Keene and Everett Carll Ladd, 'American College Women: Educational Interests, Career Expectations, Social Outlook and Values,' unpublished paper for Women's College Coalition, American Enterprise Institute/Roper Center for Public Opinion Research, Sept. 1990; personal interviews with Karlyn H. Keene and William Schneider, research fellows with the American Enterprise Institute, 1991.

82 **A national survey:** Craver Matthews Smith Donor Survey, 1990; personal interview with Roger Craver of Craver Matthews Smith, 1991.

82 **For the first time in American:** Klein, *Gender Politics*, p. 6.

82 **For the first time, polls:** *Ibid.*, pp. 158–9; Doris L. Walsh, 'What Women Want,' *American Demographics*, June 1986, p. 60; 1985 Virginia Slims American Women's Opinion Poll.

82 **A national poll found:** *Trends in Public Opinion*, 1986, 1988 surveys.

82 **By the end of the decade:** 1988 National Opinion Research Poll.

82 **In 1989, while:** Belkin, 'Bars to Equality,' p. A1.

83 **'Violating sex roles':** Joseph H. Pleck, *The Myth of Masculinity* (Cambridge, Mass.: MIT Press, 1981) p. 9.

83 **'[M]aleness in America':** Margaret Mead, *Male and Female* (New York: William & Morrow, 1949) p. 318.

83 **'Men view':** William J. Goode, 'Why Men Resist,' in *Rethinking the Family*, ed. Barrie Thorne with Marilyn Yalom (New York: Longman, 1982) p. 137.

83 **'Women have become so powerful':** Tavris and Offir, *Longest War*, p. 10; Smith, *Promised Land*, p. 12; Bullough *et al.*, *The Subordinated Sex*, p. 74.

83 **In the sixteenth century:** Bullough *et al.*, *The Subordinated Sex*, p. 171.

84 **As Edward Bok:** Kinnard, *Antifeminism*, p. 308.

84 **In the late 1800s:** Theodore Roszak, 'The Hard and the Soft: The Force of Feminism in Modern Times,' in *Masculine/Feminine: Readings in Sexual Mythology and the Liberation of Women*, ed. Betty and Theodore Roszak (New York: Harper & Row, 1969), pp. 87–104; Joe L. Dubbert, 'Progressivism and

the Masculinity Crisis,' in *The American Man*, ed. Elizabeth H. and Joseph H. Pleck (Englewood Cliffs, NJ: Prentice-Hall, 1980), pp. 303–19.

84   **'The whole generation is womanized'**: Henry James, *The Bostonians*, (Harmondsworth: Penguin Books [1886], 1979 edn) p. 290.

84   **Child-rearing manuals**: Michael S. Kimmel, 'Men's Responses to Feminism at the Turn of the Century,' *Gender & Society*, 1, no. 3 (Sept. 1987), 269–70; Allen Warren, 'Pop Manliness: Baden Powell, Scouting and the Development of Manly Character,' in *Manliness and Morality: Middle-Class Masculinity in Britain and America, 1880–1940*, ed. J. A. Mangan and James Wadvin (Manchester: Manchester University Press, 1987) pp. 200–4; Douglas, *Feminization*, p.327.

84   **Billy Sunday**: Douglas, *Feminization*, p. 397.

84   **Theodore Roosevelt**: Kimmel, 'Men's Responses,' p. 243.

84   **'The period'**: Roszak, 'Hard and the Soft,' p. 92.

84   **The fledgling Boy**: Kimmel, 'Men's Responses,' p. 272; Jeffrey P. Hantover, 'The Boy Scouts and the Validation of Masculinity,' in *The American Man*, ed. Elizabeth and Joseph H. Pleck (Englewood Cliffs, NJ: Prentice-Hall, 1980). p. 294.

85   **At home, 'momism'**; Philip Wylie, *Generation of Vipers* (New York: Holt, Rinehart & Winston, 1942); Philip Wylie, 'Common Women,' in *Women's Liberation in the Twentieth Century*, ed. Mary C. Lynn (New York: John Wiley & Sons, 1975) p. 60.

85   **In what was supposed**: Lynn, *Women's Liberation*, p. 72.

85   **In the business**: Chafe, *The American Woman*, p. 182.

85   ***Look* decried**: Barbara Ehrenreich, *The Hearts of Men: American Dreams and the Flight from Commitment* (Garden City, NY: Anchor Books, 1983), p. 37.

85   **In the UK, *Punch***: David Thomas, 'Men Have Feelings Too: Exploding the Myth of Feminism,' *Daily Express*, Dec. 13, 1990.

85   **In a prominent *Sunday Times***: Neil Lyndon, 'Badmouthing,' *Sunday Times Magazine*, Sept. 12, 1990, p. 48.

85   ***Harper's* editor**: Lewis Lapham 'La Différence,' *New York Times*, March 4, 1983, cited in Kimmel, 'Men's Responses,' p. 279.

86   **In films and television**: 'The Female in Focus: In Whose Image? A Statistical Survey of the Status of Women in Film, Television & Commercials,' Screen Actors Guild, Aug. 1, 1990; Meryl Streep, 'When Women Were in the Movies,' *Screen Actor*, Fall 1990, p. 15; Steenland, 'Women Out of View.'

86   **In fiction, violent macho**: Elizabeth Mehren, 'Macho Books: Flip Side of Romances,' *Los Angeles Times*, reprinted in *San Francisco Chronicle*, Aug. 2, 1988, p. B4.

86   **In apparel**: Jennet Conant, 'The High-Priced Call of the Wild,' *Newsweek*, Feb. 1, 1988, p. 56.

86   **'I'm not squishy soft'**: Doyle McManus and Bob Drogin, 'Democrats and Foreign Policy: Test of Toughness,' *Los Angeles Times*, Feb. 28, 1988, I, p. 1.

86   **George Bush, whose**: Margaret Garrard Warner, 'Fighting the Wimp Factor,' *Newsweek*, Oct. 19, 1987, p. 28.

86   **'At Columbia'**: Carolyn Helibrun, *Reinventing Womanhood* (New York: W. W. Norton, 1979) p. 203.

86   **At Boston University**: 'Tenure and Loose Talk,' *Washington Post*, June 26, 1990, p. A20.

86   **Feminists have 'complete control'**: Jerry Falwell, *Listen, America!* (Garden City, NY: Doubleday-Galilee, 1980) pp. 158–9.

87   **A little-noted finding**: *The Yankelovich Monitor*, 1989 edn; personal interview with Susan Hayward, senior vice-president of Yankelovich Clancy Shulman, Sept. 1989. The largest share of men (37 per cent) defined masculinity in the 1989 Monitor survey as the ability to be the good family breadwinner. Nearly as large a share of women (32 per cent) defined masculinity in the same way, giving men all the more reason to continue to define themselves in this way.

87 **In this period**: Kevin Phillips, *The Politics of Rich and Poor* (New York: Random House, 1990) p. 18.
87 **That the ruling definition**: For polling evidence that hostility toward feminism was most concentrated in these two groups, see Astrachan, *How Men Feel*, pp. 367–8, 371–5; 'The American Male Opinion Index,' I, pp. 17, 19, 26.
87 **The 1980s was the decade**: Barbara Ehrenreich, *Fear of Falling: The Inner Life of the Middle Class* (New York: Pantheon Books, 1989) p. 207; Barbara Ehrenreich, 'Marginal Men,' *New York Woman*, Sept. 1989, p. 91.
87 **It was a time when**: Phillips, *Rich and Poor*, pp. 19, 204; 'What's Really Squeezing the Middle Class,' *The Wall Street Journal*, July 26, 1989, p. A12.
87 **Inevitably, these losses**: Louis Harris, *Inside America* (New York: Vintage Books, 1987) pp. 33–7.
88 **When analysts at**: Personal interview with Susan Hayward, 1989. In the Yankelovich surveys, 'The Contenders' give substantially less support to women's rights and express far more doubt that women can do as well as men in high-level jobs. They are also deeply unhappy with their work life: while only 30 per cent of the people in the total sample say they don't expect to get much pleasure from their work, 74 per cent of the Contenders felt that way.
88 **'It's these downscale men'**: *Ibid.*
88 **By the late 1980s**: 'The American Male Opinion Index,' I, pp. 17, 19, 29.
89 **They are men like**: Fox Butterfield, 'Suspicions Came Too Late in Boston,' *New York Times*, Jan. 21, 1990, p. 17; Richard Lingeman, 'Another American Tragedy,' *New York Times*, Jan. 22, 1990, p. A19.
89 **They are young men with little**: Joan Didion, 'New York: Sentimental Journeys,' *The New York Review of Books*, Jan. 17, 1991, p. 45.
89 **They are men like George**: Richard Woodbury, 'Ten Minutes in Hell', *Time*, Oct. 28, 1991, p. 31.
89 **And they are men like**: Elizabeth Kastor, 'When Shooting Stopped, Canada Had Changed,' *Washington Post*, Dec. 10, 1989, p. A3.
89 **It was a moment**: William B. Johnston and Arnold H. Packer, *Workforce 2000: Work and Workers for the 21st Century* (Indianapolis, Indiana: Hudson Institute, June 1987) p. 85; Evans and Nelson, *Wage Justice*, p. 23; Nancy Barrett, 'Women and the Economy,' in *The American Woman: 1987–88*, p. 107; Bernard, *The Future of Marriage*, p. 298–9; Digest of Education Statistics, 1987, US Department of Education.
90 **'Part of the unemployment'**: Susan Faludi, 'Why Women May Be Better Off Unwed,' *West Magazine, San Jose Mercury News*, Aug. 10, 1986, p. 9.
90 **In reality**: Phillips, *Rich and Poor*, p. 202.
90 **About a third**: Lawrence Mishel and David M. Frankel, *The State of Working America* (Armonk, NY: M. E. Sharpe, 1991) pp. 83–5, 105.
90 **The eighties economy**: Philips, *Rich and Poor*, p. 12.
91 **'There had to be'**: Mary Anne Dolan, 'When Feminism Failed,' *The New York Times Magazine*, June 26, 1988, p. 23.
91 **'FATS'**: Steven F. Schwartz, 'FATS and Happy,' *Barron's*, July 6, 1987, p. 27.
91 **When the *New York***: Jane Gross, 'Against the Odds: A Woman's Ascent on Wall Street,' *The New York Times Magazine*, Jan. 6, 1985, p. 16; Ellen Hopkins, 'The Media Murder of Karen Valenstein's Career,' *Working Woman*, March 1991, p. 70.
91 **She was dubbed**: Harry Waters, 'Rhymes with Rich,' *Newsweek*, Aug. 21, 1989, p. 46; Mark Hosenball, 'The Friends of Michael Milken,' *The New Republic*, Aug. 28, 1989, p. 23. Howard Kurtz, 'Leona Helmsley Convicted of $1.2 Million Tax Evasion,' *San Francisco Chronicle*, Aug. 31, 1989, A1; Scot J. Paltrow, 'Helmsley Gets Four Years,' *San Francisco Chronicle*, Dec. 13, 1989, p. A1.
92 **Beset by corruption**: Brian Mitchell, *The Weak Link: The Feminization of the American Military* (Washington, DC: Regnery Gateway, 1989); David Evans, 'The Navy's 5000 Pregnant Sailors,' *San Francisco Examiner*, Aug. 15, 1989, p. A19; Falwell, *Listen, America!*, pp. 158–9.

92   **Mayor Marion Barry**: Tom Shales, 'The Year of Roseanne, Saddam, Bart and PBS' Civil War,' *Washington Post*, Dec. 30, 1990, p. G3; Scott Rosenberg, 'No Soothing for this "Savage" Beast,' *San Francisco Examiner*, Aug. 28, 1990, p. D1.

92   **Joel Steinberg's**: Erika Munk, 'Short Eyes: The Joel Steinberg We Never Saw,' *The Village Voice*, Feb. 21, 1989, p. 20.

92   **And even errant**: Rich Jaroslovsky, 'Washington Wire,' *The Wall Street Journal*, Feb. 2, 1990, p. A1.

93   **She is Laura Palmer**: 'Women We Love,' *Esquire*, Aug. 1990, p. 108.

93   **Bush promised 'empowerment'**: Alan Murray and David Wessel, 'Modest Proposals: Faced with Gulf War, Bush's Budget Avoids Bold Moves at Home,' *The Wall Street Journal*, Feb. 5, 1991, p. A1.

94   **Even *Playboy***: Alan Carter, 'Transformer,' *TV Guide*, Aug. 27, 1988, p. 20.

94   **Criticized for targeting**: Peter Waldman, 'Tobacco Firms Try Soft, Feminine Sell,' *The Wall Street Journal*, Dec. 19, 1989, p. B1.

94   **As Christopher Lasch**: Christopher Lasch, *The Culture of Narcissism* (London: Abacus Books, 1980), pp. 139–40.

Chapter Four. The 'Trends' of Anti-feminism

99   **The first action of the**: Klein, *Gender Politics* pp. 23–4.

99   **(The only two such)**: Joanna Foley Martin, 'Confessions of a Non-Bra-Burner,' *Chicago Journalism Review*, July 1971, 4, 11.

99   **The 'grand press blitz'**: Jo Freeman, *The Politics of Women's Liberation: A Case Study of an Emerging Social Movement and Its Relation to the Policy Process* (New York: David McKay, 1975) p. 148; Edith Hoshino Altbach, *Women in America* (Lexington, Mass.: D. C. Heath, 1974) pp. 157–8. For an example of the media using the 'bra-burning' myth to invalidate the women's movement, see Judy Klemesrud, 'In Small Town USA, Women's Liberation Is Either a Joke or a Bore,' *New York Times*, March 22, 1972, p. 54.

100   **At *Newsday*, a male**: Sandie North, 'Reporting the Movement,' *The Atlantic*, March 1970, p. 105.

100   **At *Newsweek*, Lynn**: *Ibid.*

100   **(This tactic backfired)**: 'Women in Revolt,' *Newsweek*, March 23, 1970, p. 78. Helen Dudar, the *Newsweek* editor's wife, confessed that after having 'spent years rejecting feminists without bothering to look too closely at their charges', she had become a convert and wrote that she now felt a 'sense of pride and kinship with all those women who have been asking all the hard questions. I thank them and so, I think, will a lot of other women.'

100   **Prestige launched a**: Christine Dann, *Up From Under: Women and Liberation in New Zealand 1970–1985* (Wellington: Allen & Unwin/Port Nicholson Press, 1985), p. 100.

100   UP THE LADDER: 'Up the Ladder, Finally,' *Business Week*, Nov. 24, 1975, p. 58.

101   **Feminism is 'dead'**: See, for example, Sally Ogle Davis, 'Is Feminism Dead?' *Los Angeles*, Feb. 1989. p. 114.

101   **'The women's movement is over'**: Betty Friedan, 'Feminism's Next Step,' *The New York Times Magazine*, July 5, 1981, p. 14.

101   **In case readers**: Susan Bolotin, 'Voices from the Post-Feminist Generation,' *The New York Times Magazine*, Oct. 17, 1982, p. 29.

102   **'The *Daily Mail*'s**: June Tarlin, 'Femail', *Daily Mail*, June 10, 1975, p. 10.

102   **'What has happened to'**: 'After the Sexual Revolution,' *ABC News Closeup*, July 30, 1986.

102   ***Newsweek* raised**: Eloise Salholz, 'Feminism's Identity Crisis,' *Newsweek*, March 31, 1986, p. 58.

102   **(This happens to be)**: *Newsweek*, March 7, 1960, cited in Friedan, *Feminine Mystique*, p. 22.

102   **The first article sneering**: 'Superwoman,' *Independent*, Feb. 21, 1907, cited in Kinnard, *Antifeminism*, p. 214.

102   **Feminists, according to the**: *Ibid.*, pp. 55–61, xiii–ix.

104   **And repetition**: In 1982, fifty corporations controlled over half the media business; by the end of 1987 the number was down to twenty-six. See Ben H. Bagdikian, *The Media Monopoly* (Boston: Beacon Press, 1990) pp. xix, 3–4; *Media Report to Women*, Sept. 1987, p. 4.

104   **Fear was also driving**: After 1985, profit margins fell steadily at papers owned by publicly traded communications companies. Women, who make up the majority of newspaper readers and network news viewers, were turning to specialized publications and cable news programmes in mass numbers, taking mass advertising dollars with them. See Alex S. Jones, 'Rethinking Newspapers,' *New York Times*, Jan. 6, 1991, III, p. 1; 'Marketing Newspapers to Women,' *Women Scope Surveys of Women*, 2, no. 7 (April 1989), 1–2.

104   **Anxiety-ridden**: In a typical media strategy of the decade, Knight-Ridder Newspapers launched a 'customer-obsession' campaign to give readers what management imagined they wanted, rather than what was simply news.

104   **'News organizations are'**: Bill Kovach, 'Too Much Opinion, at the Expense of Fact,' *New York Times*, Sept. 13, 1989, p. A31.

104   **NBC, for instance**: 'Bad Girls,' *NBC News*, Aug. 30, 1989.

105   **'The media are having'**: 'The Next Trend: Here Comes the Bribe,' *Advertising Age*, June 16, 1986, p. 40.

106   **THE UNDECLARED WAR**: Carol Pogash, 'The Undeclared War,' *San Francisco Examiner*, Feb. 5, 1989, p. E1.

106   ***Child* magazine offered**: Sue Woodman, 'The Mommy Wars,' *Child*, Sept.–Oct. 1989, p. 139; Barbara J. Berg, 'Women at Odds,' *Savvy*, Dec. 1985, p. 24.

106   **IS HE SEPARABLE?**: Kate White, 'Is He Separable?' *Newsday*, May 15, 1988, p. 25.

106   **The ABC report**: Transcript, *After the Sexual Revolution*.

107   **'MANY YOUNG WOMEN NOW SAY'**: Dena Kleiman, 'Many Young Women Now Say They'd Pick Family Over Career,' *New York Times*, Dec. 28, 1980, p. 1. See also 'I'm Sick of Work: The Back to the Home Movement,' *Ladies' Home Journal*, cover story, Sept. 1984.

107   **BrainReserve, which had one**: 'The BrainReserve Mission Statement,' press packet, and promotional literature, 1988; 'Her ideas on Tomorrow Pop Up Today,' *USA Today*, Oct. 5, 1987, p. 1; Tim Golden, 'In, Out and Over: Looking Back at the 90's,' *New York Times*, Jan. 16, 1990, p. B1.

107   **The word 'just popped'**: Personal interview with Faith Popcorn, Nov. 1989.

107   **'We're becoming a nation of nesters'**: Gay Hanauer, 'Faith Popcorn: Kernels of Truth', *American Way*, July 1, 1987.

107   **As one enthusiastic**: 'Putting Faith in Trends,' *Newsweek*, June 15, 1987, pp. 46–7.

107   **'Fewer women will work'**: Elizabeth Mehren, 'Life Style in the '90s, According to Popcorn,' *Los Angeles Times*, Jan. 16, 1987, p. 1.

107   **'Little in-home wombs'**: *Ibid.*

108   **Women steadily increased**: *The American Woman 1990–91*, Table 14, p. 376.

108   **Opinion polls didn't support**: Harris, *Inside America*, pp. 94, 96.

108   **'I'm hooked on my work'**: Personal interview with Faith Popcorn. (Subsequent quotes are from personal interviews with Popcorn unless otherwise noted.)

108   **In the press, she cited**: See, for example, William E. Geist, 'One Step Ahead of Us: Trend Expert's View,' *New York Times*, Oct. 15, 1986, p. B4.

109   **Popcorn borrowed**: Alex Taylor III, 'Why Women Are Bailing Out,' *Fortune*, Aug. 18, 1986, p. 16.

109   **The article about**: *USA Today*'s story was, in fact, a report on the *Fortune* 'findings': '1 in 3 Management Women Drop Out,' *USA Today*, July 31, 1986, p. 1.

109   **A year later at Stanford**: Personal interviews with a group of female Stanford MBA students, Summer 1988.

110   **The year after** *Fortune*: Laurie Baum, 'For Women, the Bloom Might Be Off the MBA,' *Business Week*, March 14, 1988, p. 30.

110   **Witham is 'happier'**: Taylor, 'Bailing Out,' pp. 16–23.

110   **'He had this anecdotal evidence'**: Personal interview with Alex Taylor III, 1988.

110   **'I told him'**: Personal interview with Mary Anne Devanna, 1988.

111   **'The evidence is'**: Personal interview with Taylor, 1988. (Subsequent quotes are from personal interview with Taylor unless otherwise noted.)

111   **'A woman who wants marriage'**: Stratford P. Sherman, 'The Party May Be Ending,' *Fortune*, Nov. 24, 1986, p. 29.

112   **In fact, in 1987**: F. S. Chapman, 'Executive Guilt: Who's Taking Care of the Children?' *Fortune*, Feb. 16, 1987. A later review of the graduate records at Columbia University's Graduate School of Business for the class of '76 (the same class that Taylor's story focused on) found no significant female defection from the corporate world and no differences in the proportion of men and women leaving to start their own businesses. See Mary Anne Devanna, 'Women in Management: Progress and Promise,' *Human Resource Management*, 26, no. 4 (Winter 1987), 469.

112   **The national pollsters were**: The 1986 Virginia Slims Opinion Poll; Walsh, 'What Women Want,' p. 60. A survey conducted jointly by *Working Woman* and *Success* magazines also found that men were more concerned about family life than women and less concerned about career success than women. See Carol Sonenklar, 'Women and Their Magazines,' *American Demographics*, June 1986, p. 44.

112   **A 1989 survey**: Margaret King, 'An Alumni Survey Dispels Some Popular Myths About MBA Graduates,' *Stanford Business School Magazine*, March 1989, p. 23.

112   **Finally** *Fortune*: Julie Connelly, 'The CEO's Second Wife,' *Fortune*, Aug. 28, 1989, p. 52.

112   *Esquire*, **a periodical**: 'The Secret Life of the American Wife,' special issue, *Esquire*, June 1990.

112   **WHY 90S WOMEN**: Anne Barrowclough, 'Femail,' *Daily Mail*, Jan. 1, 1990, p. 12.

113   *Options* **asked**: Caroline St John-Brooks, *Options*, Jan. 1985, p. 70.

113   *Company* **said**: Julia Orange, *Company*, June 1986, p. 44.

113   **Kathy Gyngell**: 'Femail,' *Daily Mail*, June 22, 1991, p. 25.

114   **After a hotly contested**: Maeve Haran, 'A Write to a Happy Ending,' *Observer*, July 8, 1990.

114   **'Maeve Haran has broken**: Justine Picardie, book review, *Independent*, July 22, 1991.

114   **Angela Neustatter**: 'To Have and To Hold Forth', *Guardian*, July 11, 1991.

114   **The** *Daily Mail*: Polly Samson, 'Knives out for a Frill Seeker', *Daily Mail*, June 27, 1991.

114   **Libby Purves**: 'Which Way to the Promised Land?' *The Times*, June 19, 1991.

114   **The media jumped when**: Felice N. Schwartz, 'Management Women and the New Facts of Life,' *Harvard Business Review*, Jan.–Feb. 1989, pp. 65–76.

114   **The 'mommy-tracking' trend**: The *New York Times*, not Schwartz, came up with the phrase. The interview count comes from a personal interview with Schwartz's media relations director, Vivian Todini, Nov. 1989.

115   **'Across the country'**: Elizabeth Ehrlich, 'The Mommy Track,' *Business Week*, March 20, 1989, p. 126.

115   **The media in other**: Christopher Reed, *Guardian*, April 6, 1989.

115   **In fact, at a conference**: Ellen Hopkins, 'Who Is Felice Schwartz?' *Working Woman*, Oct. 1990, p. 116.

115   **Women with this**: *The Newsweek Research Report on Women Who Work: A National Survey* (Princeton, NJ: Mathematica Policy Research, 1984), p. 32.

115   **And a year after**: The 1990 Virginia Slims Opinion Poll, pp. 79–81.

116   **Only in 1989 did the company**: Personal interview June 1991.

116   **'I was not writing'**: Personal interview with Felice Schwartz.

116   **Statistics that have compared**: Data from division of Health Interview Statistics, National Center for Health Statistics.

116   **In an about-turn**: Felice N. Schwartz, *HBR In Retrospect*, pamphlet published by Catalyst, June 1989.

116   **'She speaks with a tone'**: Barbara Ehrenreich and Deirdre English, 'Blowing the Whistle on the "Mommy Track," ' *Ms.*, July–Aug. 1989, p. 56.

116   **Later that spring**: Alan M. Webber, 'Is the American Way of Life Over?' *New York Times*, April 9, 1989, p. 25.

117   **The New Traditionalist Woman wasn't**: The same year, the *New York Times* began running 'I Read It My Way' ads, in which such women as 'Lesley Cooke – Housewife/Mother' recounted the joys of reading the *Times*'s interior decorating and parenting columns while nestled in her 1920s Colonial home. *Country Living* issued a similarly pointed ad campaign entitled 'Traditions Renew'.

117   **The *New York Times* even**: Patricia Leigh Brown, 'The First Lady-Elect: What She Is and Isn't,' *New York Times*, Dec. 11, 1988, p. 22.

117   **The accompanying**: 'The New Traditionalist,' *Good Housekeeping* ad tear sheets, 1988, 1989.

117   **As *Good Housekeeping* publisher**: Carla Marinucci, 'The New Woman,' *San Francisco Examiner*, Dec. 4, 1988, p. D1.

118   **After all, even**: Personal interviews with *Good Housekeeping* circulation staff, 1989.

118   **'The problem'**: Personal interview with Malcolm MacDougall, Oct. 1989. (Subsequent quotes are from personal interview with MacDougall unless otherwise noted.)

118   **'I cheerfully disavow'**: Personal interview with Susan Hayward, 1989.

118   **The British *Good Housekeeping***: See, for example, 'Traditional Crafts: the Charm of the Old,' *Good Housekeeping*, Nov. 1989.

119   **Brenda Polan**: 'The Feminine Fiction,' *Guardian*, Aug. 18, 1988.

119   **'In all respects, young'**: Philip H. Dougherty, 'Women's Self Esteem Up,' *New York Times*, May 15, 1974, p. 71.

119   **'Within just'**: 'Games Singles Play,' *Newsweek*, July 16, 1973, p. 52.

120   **The stereotype got so bad**: Susan Jacoby, '49 Million Singles Can't All Be Right,' *The New York Times Magazine*, Feb. 17, 1974, p. 12.

120   **DROPOUT WIVES**: Enid Nemy, 'Dropout Wives – Their Number Is Growing,' *New York Times*, Feb. 16, 1973, p. 44.

120   **According to *Newseek***: 'Games Singles Play,' p. 52.

120   ***Newsweek* was now**: Eloise Salholz, 'The Marriage Crunch: If You're a Single Woman, Here Are Your Chances of Getting Married,' *Newsweek*, p. 54; Jane Gross, 'Single Women: Coping With a Void,' *New York Times*, April 28, 1987, p. 1.

120   **TOO LATE FOR**: Salholz, 'Marriage Crunch,' p. 54.

120   **On the front page**: Gross, 'Single Women,' p. 1.

121   ***New York* magazine's**: Patricia Morrisroe, 'Born Too Late? Expect Too Much? You May Be Forever Single,' *New York*, Aug. 20, 1984, p. 24.

121   **LOVELESS, MANLESS**: 'Loveless, Manless: The High Cost of Independence,' *Chatelaine*, Sept. 1984, p. 60.

121   **'Feminism became a new form'**: Tricia Crane, 'Are You Turning Men Off? Desperate and Demanding,' *Harper's Bazaar*, Sept. 1987, p. 300.

121   **An *Options* feature**: Stephanie Calman, 'The Single Woman's Lament,' *Options*, Oct. 1989, p. 93.

121   ***New York*'s story**: Morrisroe, 'Born Too Late?' p. 30.

121   **ABC's 1986 special**: ABC News, *After the Sexual Revolution*.

122   **Between 1980 and 1982**: Trimberger, 'Single Women and Feminism in the 1980s.'

122   **The headlines spoke**: 'The Sad Plight of Single Women,' *Philadelphia Inquirer*, Nov. 30, 1980; Kiki Olson, 'Sex and the Terminally Single Woman (There Just Aren't Any Good Men Around),' *Philadelphia Magazine*, April 1984, p. 122.

122   *McCall's* **described**: Peter Filichia, 'The Lois Lane Syndrome: Waiting for Superman,' *McCall's*, Aug. 1985, p. 55.

122   **In the late Victorian**: Kinnard, *Antifeminism*, p. 202.

123   **'May not some'**: Kessler-Harris, *Out to Work*, p. 255.

123   **'Why Is Single Life'**: 'Why Is Single Life Becoming More General?' *The Nation*, March 5, 1868, pp. 190–1.

123   **The ratio was so bad**: 'Wives at Discount,' *Harper's Bazaar*, Jan. 31, 1874, p. 74.

123   **By the mid-1980s**: Billie Samkoff, 'How to Attract Men Like Crazy,' *Cosmopolitan*, Feb. 1989, p. 168.

124   **'The traumatic news'**: Salholz, 'Marriage Crunch,' p. 25.

124   **A few months later**: David Gates, 'Second Opinion,' Update, *Newsweek*, Oct. 13, 1986, p. 10.

124   **'We all knew'**: Personal interview with Eloise Salholz, July 1986.

124   **The *New York Times***: William R. Greer, 'The Changing Women's Marriage Market,' *New York Times*, Feb. 22, 1986, p. 48.

124   **But when it came time**: AP, 'More Women Postponing Marriage,' *New York Times*, Dec. 10, 1986, p. A22.

124   **And almost a year after**: Gross, 'Single Women,' p. 1.

124   **'It was untimely'**: Personal interview with Jane Gross, 1988.

124   **The article dealt with**: Gross, 'Single Women,' p. 1.

124   **The *Newsweek* story**: Salholz, 'Marriage Crunch,' p. 55.

124   **'Do you know that'**: Promotional letter from Dell Publishing Co., from Carol Tavoularis, Dell publicist, Dec. 5, 1986.

125   **A former *Newsweek* bureau**: Personal interview, Oct. 1986.

125   ***Newsweek*'s preachers**: Salholz, 'Marriage Crunch,' pp. 61, 57.

125   **'For many economically'**: *Ibid.*, pp. 61, 55.

125   **'Susan Cohen wishes'**: *Ibid.*, p. 57.

126   *CBS Morning News* **devoted**: *CBS Morning News, What Do Single Women Want*, Nov. 2–6, 1987.

126   **ABC took television**: ABC News, *After the Sexual Revolution*.

126   **Apparently still not**: ABC, *Good Morning America, Single in America*, May 4–7, 1987.

127   **'There wasn't any time'**: Personal interview with Richard Threlkeld, 1988.

127   WHY WED?: Trip Gabriel, 'Why Wed?: The Ambivalent American Bachelor,' *The New York Times Magazine*, Nov. 15, 1987, p. 24.

128   **Having whipped**: Brenda Lane Richardson, 'Dreaming Someone Else's Dreams,' *The New York Times Magazine*, Jan. 28, 1990, p. 14.

128   **In what amounted to**: See, for example, Barbara Kantrowitz, 'The New Mating Games,' *Newsweek*, June 2, 1986, p. 58; James Hirsch, 'Modern Matchmaking: Money's Allure in Marketing Mates and Marriage,' *New York Times*, Sept. 19, 1988, p. B4; Ruthe Stein, 'New Strategies for Singles,' *San Francisco Chronicle*, March 29, 1988, p. B1.

128   **'Time is running out'**: Gerald Nachman, 'Going Out of Business Sale on Singles,' *San Francisco Chronicle*, Dec. 1, 1987, p. B3.

128   **'When they really decided'**: Barbara Lovenheim, 'Brides at Last: Women Over 40 Who Beat the Odds,' *New York*, Aug. 3, 1987, p. 20.

128   *USA Today* **even**: Marlene J. Perrin, 'What Do Women Today Really Want?' *USA Today*, July 10, 1986, pp. D1, D5; Karen S. Peterson, 'Men Bare Their Souls, Air Their Gripes,' *USA Today*, July 14, 1986, p. D1. And the women who called weren't all pleading for a man: 'How do you get people to stop asking why I'm not married yet?' was the question posed by one thirty-two-

year-old woman from Virginia. See Karen S. Peterson, 'Stop Asking Why I'm Not Married,' *USA Today*, July 9, 1986, p. D4.

128   **Options offered**: Victoria McKee, 'Love Forty,' *Options*, Sept. 1989, p. 56.

128   **She gave advice**: Alexandra Campbell, 'How To Get Married in a Year,' *She*, May 1988, p. 54.

129   **Cosmopolitan's February**: Samkoff, 'How To Attract Men,' pp. 163–73.

129   **At Mademoiselle**: Personal interview with *Mademoiselle* editors, 1988; Cathryn Jakobson, 'The Return of Hard-to-Get,' March 1987, p. 220.

129   **And a New Woman**: Dr Joyce Brothers, 'Why You Shouldn't Move in With Your Lover,' *New Woman*, March 1985, p. 54.

129   **'Singlehood seems so'**: Jeffrey Kluger, 'Dangerous Delusions About Divorce,' *Cosmopolitan*, Sept. 1984, p. 291.

129   **She cautioned**: Trudy Culross, 'Whatever You Do Don't Get Divorced,' *She*, June 1991, pp. 118–19.

129   **CBS revived**: Sue Adolphson, 'Marriage Encounter, Tube Style,' *San Francisco Chronicle* Datebook, Jan 22, 1989, p. 47.

129   **'How to Stay Married'**: Barbara Kantrowitz, 'How To Stay Married,' *Newsweek*, Aug. 24, 1987, p. 52.

130   **'How times have'**: *Ibid.*

130   **'Is this surge'**: NBC News Special, *The Baby Business*, April 4, 1987.

130   HAVING IT ALL: 'Having It All: Postponing Parenthood Exacts a Price,' *Boston* magazine, May 1987, p. 116.

130   THE QUIET PAIN: Mary C. Hickey, 'The Quiet Pain of Infertility: For the Success-Oriented, It's a Bitter Pill,' *Washington Post*, April 28, 1987, p. DO5.

130   **As a New York Times**: Fleming, 'The Infertile Sisterhood,' p. B1.

130   **'Have You Left It Too Late'**: Vivienne Parry, *Options*, Oct. 1991, p. 66.

130   **She investigated**: Diana Howard, 'Infertility: Is It Harder To Get Pregnant Now?', *She*, Aug. 1989, p. 30.

131   **Newsweek devoted two**: Matt Clark, 'Infertility,' *Newsweek*, Dec. 6, 1982, p. 102; Barbara Kantrowitz, 'No Baby on Board,' *Newsweek*, Sept. 1, 1986, p. 68.

131   **The magazine warned**: Kantrowitz, 'No Baby,' p. 74.

131   **The expert that Newsweek**: *Ibid.*

131   **Not to be upstaged**: Anna Quindlen, 'Special Report: Baby Craving: Facing Widespread Infertility, A Generation Presses the Limits of Medicine and Morality,' *Life*, June 1987, p. 23.

131   **'It's hard to tell, but'**: Clark, 'Infertility,' p. 102.

131   **'There are few'**: Quindlen, 'Baby Craving,' p. 23.

131   **Mademoiselle, for example**: Laura Flynn McCarthy, 'Caution: You Are Now Entering the Age of Infertility,' *Mademoiselle*, May 1988, p. 230.

131   **And a 1982**: Georgia Dullea, 'Women Reconsider Childbearing Over 30,' *New York Times*, Feb. 25, 1982, p. C1.

132   **'Career women are opting'**: J. D. Reed, 'The New Baby Bloom,' *Time*, Feb. 22, 1982, p. 52.

132   **Time made that**: Claudia Wallis, 'The Medical Risks of Waiting,' *Time*, Feb. 22, 1982, p. 58.

132   **'More and more'**: Reed, 'New Baby Bloom,' p. 52.

132   **McCall's gushed**: 'Hollywood's Late-Blooming Moms,' *McCall's*, Oct. 1988, p. 41.

132   **'Motherhood is consuming'**: Leslie Bennetts, 'Baby Fever,' *Vogue*, Aug. 1985, p. 325.

132   **Actress Patricia Hodge**: 'Love and Patricia Hodge,' *Daily Mail*, Jan. 7, 1992, p. 13.

132   **Interviewed in the Sunday Express**: Douglas Thompson, 'Crying Out For Moore,' *Sunday Express Magazine*, Dec. 8, 1991, p. 12.

133   **'In our personal life'**: 'The Marriage Odds Improve,' *San Francisco Chronicle*, May 1, 1987, p. 38.

133   **'Some college alumnae'**: 'Mothers a la Mode,' *New York Times*, May 8, 1988, p. E28. The *Times* editorial writers appeared to have forgotten their own words. Only two months earlier, they had noted that there was no change in the birthrate: 'New Baby Boom? No, Just a Dim Echo,' *New York Times*, March 30, 1988, p. A26.

133   **'You can't pick up a magazine'**: Kim C. Flodin, 'Motherhood's Better Before 30,' *New York Times*, Nov. 2, 1989, p. A31.

133   **'I wasn't even thinking'**: Bennetts, 'Baby Fever,' p. 326.

134   **In the US, formerly**: Renee Bacher, 'The Ring Cycle,' *The New York Times Magazine*, Aug. 31, 1989, p. 20; Dava Sobel, 'Face to Face With the New Me,' *The New York Times Magazine*, April 9, 1989, p. 26; Carolyn Swartz, 'All That Glitters Is the Tub,' *The New York Times Magazine*, Nov. 5, 1989, p. 36.

134   **And many smaller**: Julie Pechilis, 'What Happened to the Women's Press? No Newspaper of Her Own,' *MediaFile*, Feb.–March 1989, p. 1.

134   **'We give you permission'**: Susin Shapiro, 'The *Ms.* Guide to Minimalist Grooming,' *Ms.*, Oct. 1989, pp. 43–6.

134   **The first magazine**: Peggy Orenstein, '*Ms.* Fights for Its Life,' *Mother Jones*, Nov.–Dec. 1990, p. 32.

135   **What was most curious**: 'Carbine Says Sale of *Ms.* to Australian Will Open New Opportunities for the Magazine,' *Media Report to Women*, Nov.–Dec. 1987, p. 4.

135   **When Summers**: Personal interview with Anne Summers, April 1988.

135   **This point was**: *Ms.* promotional literature to advertisers. See also Susan Milligan, 'Has *Ms.* Undergone a Sex Change?' *Washington Monthly*, Oct. 1986, p. 17.

135   **(It was, weirdly)**: See *Media Watch*, Summer–Fall 1988, p. 2.

135   **Only women in households making**: Personal interview with Anne Summers, April 1988.

135   **'They complained'**: *Ibid.* (Subsequent quotes are from personal interview unless otherwise noted.)

136   **This was, after all**: *Ibid.*

136   **'As for the Women's Movement'**: Shana Alexander, 'A Woman Undone,' *Ms.*, Sept. 1988, p. 40.

137   **Meanwhile, the magazine's publishers**: Orenstein, '*Ms.* Fights,' p. 82.

137   **Finally, with *Sassy's***: *Ibid.*, pp. 82–83.

137   **Relaunched with a full-colour**: Nicci Gerrard, 'Small Noises, Loud Voices,' *Guardian*, March 11, 1986.

137   **Where other, short-lived**: Rosie Boycott, in conversation with Jane Hill, Nov. 1991.

137   **Where in the beginning**: Janice Winship, 'Reading Between the Images: A Look at the Glossies,' *Spare Rib*, July 1987, no. 180, pp. 35–7.

138   **British *Cosmopolitan* 'came out'**: Heather Formaini, '*Spare Rib* Comes of Age!', *Cosmopolitan*, Jan. 1991, p. 60.

138   **Not *Men* or *Men's Life***: Patrick M. Reilly, 'New Magazines Offer "Real" Guy Stuff,' *The Wall Street Journal*, Aug. 29, 1990, p. B4; Deirdre Carmody, 'Magazine Market Targets the Men,' *San Franciso Chronicle*, June 23, 1990, p. C4.

138   **Not *Elle***: Brenda Polan, 'The Age of Confusion,' *Elle*, Nov. 1986, cited in Janet Lee, 'Care to Join Me in an Upwardly Mobile Tango? Postmodernism and the "New Woman",' in *The Female Gaze: Women as Viewers of Popular Culture*, ed. Lorraine Gamman and Margaret Marshment (Seattle: The Real Comet Press, 1989) pp. 166, 171.

138   **'We want to'**: *Media Report to Women*, Nov.–Dec. 1988, p. 3.

Chapter Five. Fatal and Foetal Visions

140   **'I don't get it'**: Personal interview with Sabrina Hughes, Oct. 1987.

141   **As Darlene Chan**: Personal interview with Darlene Chan, Oct. 1987.

142   **'It's amazing what'**: Personal interview with Adrian Lyne, Oct. 1987; Susan Faludi, 'Single Wretchedness,' *West Magazine, San Jose Mercury News*, Nov. 15, 1987, p. 14.

142   **The words of one**: Marjorie Rosen, *Popcorn Venus: Women, Movies and the American Dream* (New York: Coward, McCann & Geoghegan, 1973) p. 151; Molly Haskell, *From Reverence to Rape: The Treatment of Women in the Movies* (Chicago: University of Chicago Press, 1973) pp. 117–18; Julie Burchill, *Girls on Film* (New York: Pantheon Books, 1986) pp. 24–5.

142   **West infuriated the**: Rosen, *Popcorn Venus*, p. 153.

142   **In the 1930s she**: *Ibid.*, p. 153; Kathryn Weibel, *Mirror Mirror: Images of Women Reflected in Popular Culture* (Garden City, NY: Anchor Books, 1977) p. 233.

142   **The biggest Depression**: Haskell, *Reverence to Rape*, p. 123; Danelle Morton, 'Shirley Temple Black,' *West Magazine, San Jose Mercury News*, Jan. 8, 1989, p. 5.

143   **During the Second World War**: Hartmann, *Home Front*, pp. 191–2; Rosen, *Popcorn Venus*, pp. 190–3.

143   **A crop of films soon**: A few examples: *And Now Tomorrow, The Spiral Staircase*, and *Johnny Belinda*. Rosen, *Popcorn Venus*, pp. 219–20; Hartmann, *Home Front*, p. 202.

143   **As film historian**: Rosen, *Popcorn Venus*, p. 219.

143   **In the 1950s as**: Haskell, *Reverence to Rape*, pp. 270–1; Rosen, *Popcorn Venus*, p. 250.

144   **In *The Good Mother***: Sue Miller's *The Good Mother*, the 1986 popular novel on which the movie is based, at least takes note of the injustice behind society's double standard for divorcing husband and wife. But the film version just moralizes, laying out only the dangers that await the woman who challenges convention. If the film's makers aimed to criticize such repressive codes, they kept that intention well hidden.

144   **And soon after**: Marilyn Beck, 'She Did Her Best Work Up Real Close,' *San Jose Mercury News*, Sept. 11, 1987, p. F6.

145   **All of these films were**: Rosen, *Popcorn Venus*, p. 151.

145   **Story after story**: Richard Corliss, 'Killer!' *Time*, Nov. 16, 1987, p. 72; James S. Kunen, 'Real Life Fatal Attractions,' *People*, Oct. 26, 1987, p. 88.

145   **A headline in one**: Cited in Dan Goodgame, 'Getting Close to Stardom,' *Time*, Nov. 16, 1987, p. 81.

145   ***People* promoted**: Kunen, 'Fatal Attractions,' cover line.

146   **British director**: Personal interview with James Dearden, Oct. 1987. For a longer version of the story of the making of *Fatal Attraction*, see Susan Faludi, 'Fatal Distortion,' *Mother Jones*, Feb.–March 1988, p. 27.

146   **In the early 1980s American**: Personal interview with Stanley Jaffe, Oct. 1987.

146   **Lansing had left**: Aljean Harmetz, 'Sherry Lansing Resigns as Fox Production Chief,' *New York Times*, Dec. 21, 1982, p. C11.

147   **'I kept coming back'**: Personal interview with Sherry Lansing, Oct. 1987.

147   **'Michael Eisner turned it down'**: Personal interview with Adriane Lyne, Oct. 1987.

147   **'My short film was'**: Personal interview with James Dearden, Oct. 1987. (Subsequent quotes from Dearden are from personal interview unless otherwise noted.)

147   **'The intent was'**: Personal interview, Oct. 1987.

148   **Kim Basinger, the actress who**: Nina Darnton, 'How 9½ Weeks Pushed an Actress to the Edge,' *New York Times*, March 9, 1986, p. C1; personal interview

with Adrian Lyne, Oct. 1987; personal interviews with film's production staff, Oct. 1987.

148   **But Lyne tried to change:** Personal interviews with production staff, Oct. 1987; Faludi, 'Fatal Distortion,' p. 30; Pat H. Broeske, 'The Cutting Edge,' *Los Angeles Times*, Calendar, Feb. 16, 1986, p. 1.

148   **'Where is the new':** Personal interview with Billy Hopkins, Oct. 1987.

149   **Close was determined:** Faludi, 'Fatal Distortion,' p. 30.

149   **Close was anxious:** Lawrence Van Gelder, 'Why a Fury's Furious,' *New York Times*, Sept. 25, 1987, p. C10.

149   **'I wanted her':** Personal interview with Stanley Jaffe, Oct. 1987.

149   **Casting agent Risa:** Personal interview with Risa Bramon, Oct. 1987.

149   **Concurrently, Lyne:** Personal interview with Adrian Lyne, Oct. 1987.

149   **To inspire this:** *Ibid.* (Rest of Lyne's quotes are from personal interview unless otherwise noted.)

150   **'If you want to know, I'm really':** Joan Smith, *Misogynies: Reflections on Myths and Malice* (New York: Fawcett Columbine, 1989) pp. 31–2.

151   **Close consulted:** Gelder, 'Why a Fury's Furious,' p. C10.

151   **Originally, *Fatal Attraction*:** Faludi, 'Fatal Distortion,' p. 49.

151   **The film's creators:** Aljean Harmetz, 'Fatal Attraction Director Analyzes the Success of His Movie, and Rejoices,' *New York Times*, Oct. 5, 1987, p. C17.

152   **Lansing concedes that:** Personal interview with Sherry Lansing, Oct. 1987. (Rest of Lansing quotes are from personal interview otherwise noted.)

152   **Just as silent-era:** Kay Sloan, 'Sexual Warfare in the Silent Cinema: Comedies and Melodramas of Woman Suffragism,' *American Quarterly*, Fall 1981, pp. 41–36.

153   **At the time, the female audience:** Pauline Kael, *Reeling* (Boston: Little, Brown, 1976) p. 430.

153   **'It was very important':** Personal interview with Nancy Meyers, Feb. 1988.

155   **As Schrader explained:** Glenn Collins, 'Natasha Richardson, on Portraying Patty Hearst,' *New York Times*, Oct. 5, 1988, p. C19.

159   **'Remember the troubles':** Andree Aelion Brooks, 'When Fast Trackers Have Kids: Can a Baby Mix with Business,' *Child*, Sept.–Oct. 1989, p. 88.

159   **'There are certain women':** Jim Jerome, 'Annie Hall Gets It All,' *Savvy*, Oct. 1987, pp. 37–41.

159   **'I don't see women having it all':** Personal interview with Nancy Meyers, Feb. 1988.

160   **'They were very nervous':** Personal interview with Charles Shyer, Feb. 1988.

162   **'She was so torn':** Personal interview with Nancy Meyers, Feb. 1988.

162   **'Well, I know it's Hollywood':** Personal interview with Nadine Bron, 1988. (Rest of Bron's quotes are from personal interview.)

164   **(In the 1912 *A Cure for*:** Sloan, 'Sexual Warfare,' p. 420.

166   **Field was turned away:** Personal interview with Gwen Field, March 1988.

167   **In a 1988 essay:** 'Bewitched, Bothered and Bewildered,' *New York Woman*, Feb. 1988, p.58.

169   **In such films as *Field of*:** For two good discussions of this phenomenon, see Caryn James, 'It's a New Age for Father–Son Relationships,' *New York Times*, Arts and Leisure section, July 9, 1989, p. 11; Stephen Holden, 'Today's Hits Yearn for Old Times,' *New York Times*, Aug. 13, 1989, Arts and Leisure section, p. 1.

169   **Not surprisingly:** Streep, 'When Women Were in Movies,' p. 15.

169   **In 1988, all but:** See *Media Watch*, Spring 1989 issue, 3, no. 1.

170   **'If anyone thinks this movie':** Bob Strauss, 'Hollywood's "Has-It-All" Woman,' *San Francisco Examiner*, Oct. 14, 1988, p. C6.

170   **'Until I saw':** *Ibid.*

Chapter Six. Teen Angels and Unwed Witches

171   **'Under no circumstances'**: Personal interview with Tony Shepherd, 1988; personal observations at the Fox press conference for *Angels '88*, May 5, 1988.

171   **This May morning**: D. Keith Mano, 'So You Want to Be an Angel,' *Life*, May 1988, p. 145; Lisa Wren, 'Hundreds Wing It for a Chance to Be Angels,' *Fort Worth Star Telegram*, March 5, 1988, p. 1; Zay N. Smith, 'Angels Tryout Not So Divine,' *Chicago Sun-Times*, March 5, 1988, p. 3; Bill Givens, 'Fox Hunt for Charlie's Angels of the Eighties,' *Star*, March 22, 1988, p. 2.

173   **Later that same day**: Personal interview with Brad Markowitz, May 5, 1988.

173   **Spelling, who later**: Personal interviews with Aaron Spelling, May 1988, August 1990.

174   **In America in the 1987–88**: Joanmarie Kalter, 'What Working Women Want from TV,' *TV Guide*, Jan. 30, 1988, p. 3.

174   **In a sharp**: Sally Steenland, *Women Out of View: An Analysis of Female Characters on 1987–88 TV Programs*, Washington, DC: report by National Commission on Working Women, Nov. 1987, pp. 2, 4.

174   **In a resurgence of**: Jay Martel, 'On Your Mark, Get Set, Forget It,' *TV Guide*, Feb. 4, 1988, p. 28.

174   **On Australian television**: Alison Carter, 'Behind the Myth of Women's Equality', *Australian Financial Review*, Dec. 20, 1991.

174   **Women's disappearance: Diana M. Meehan**, *Ladies of the Evening*: Women Characters of Prime-Time Television (Metuchen, NJ: The Scarecrow Press, 1983) pp. 42, 109–10.

175   **On *Lady Blue***: Sally Steenland, *Trouble on the Set, An Analysis of Female Characters on 1985 Television Programs*, report by National Commission on Working Women, Washington, DC, 1985, p. 9.

175   **An analysis of**: Donald M. Davis, 'Portrayals of Women in Prime-Time Network Television: Some Demographic Characteristics,' *Sex Roles*, 23, no. 5–6 (1990), 325–30.

175   **The 'return of'**: Peter J. Boyer, 'Television Returns to the Hard Boiled Male,' *New York Times*, Feb. 16, 1986, II, p. 1.

175   **And the networks**: John Carman, 'Networks Playing It Bland,' *San Francisco Chronicle*, TV Week, Sept. 17–23, 1989, p. 3.

175   **In audience surveys**: Michael A. Lipton, 'What You Want to See in the New Decade,' *TV Guide*, Jan. 20, 1990, p. 11.

175   **Nonetheless, Brandon**: Boyer, 'Hard Boiled Male,' p. 1.

175   **Glenn Gordon Caron, producer**: *Ibid.*

176   **Glen Charles, co-producer**: *Ibid.*

176   **As Sue Phipps**: *A Woman's Place? The Portrayal of Women in Advertisements* (London: The Advertising Association, 1991).

177   **The majority of complaints**: Information from Patricia Albans, Independent Television Advertising Control Division, Dec. 1991.

177   **A 1986 study**: Livingstone and Green, cited in Barrie Gunter, *Television and Sex Role Stereotyping* (London: John Libbey, 1986), p. 24.

177   **A 1990 Broadcasting Standards**: Jane Thynne, 'TV Ads Condemned As Sexist,' *Daily Telegraph*, Nov. 21, 1990.

178   **In the UK**: Lynda Myles, in conversation with Jane Hill, Dec. 1991.

178   **Independent women were 'seizing'**: Harry F. Waters, 'Networking Women,' *Newsweek*, March 13, 1989, p. 48.

178   **Behind the scenes**: Michael E. Hill, 'Murphy Brown: F.Y.I., We Like Your Show, Sort of,' *Washington Post*, TV Week, Feb. 26, 1989, p. 8.

178   **The media declared her**: 'People,' *Orange County Register*, March 29, 1990, p. A2; Michael McWilliams, 'Pauley and Barr: Two Notions of Womanhood,' Gannett News Service, Aug. 8, 1990; Dennis Duggan, 'What, Me Judge a Man on Looks Alone? Guilty!' *Newsday, Newsday Magazine*, Feb. 17, 1991, p. 6;

Jeffrey Zaslow, 'Roseanne Ban Would Be as Bad as Barr's Own Antics,' *Chicago Sun-Times*, Nov. 29, 1990, II, p. 65; Michele Stanush, 'Anti-War Sentiments,' *Austin-American Statesman*, Dec. 16, 1990, p. E1.

179   **TV critic Joyce Millman**: Joyce Millman, 'Prime Time: Where the Boys are,' *San Francisco Examiner*, Sept. 9, 1990, p. F1.

179   **Only two of thirty-three**: *Ibid*.

179   **(And most are men)**: Davis, 'Portrayals of Women,' p. 330.

180   ***Tenko*, a top-rating**: Jill Hyem, 'Entering the Arena: Writing for Television,' in *Boxed In: Women and Television*, ed. Helen Baehr and Gillian Dyer (London: Pandora Press, 1987), pp. 151–62.

181   **A 1987 European Commission**: Gabriel Thoveron, 'How Women Are Represented in TV Programmes in the EEC,' Part I: Images of women in news, advertising, and series and serials (EEC), pp. 67–89.

182   **Jane Aldridge**: Results of a survey, 'Views of Men and Women in Real Life and on Television,' conducted by J. S. Aldridge, Research Officer with the Independent Television Commission, 1991.

183   **'It was terrific'**: Personal interview with Esther Shapiro, Nov. 1989. (Subsequent Shapiro quotes are from interview.)

183   **And the network's**: Todd Gitlin, *Inside Prime Time* (New York: Pantheon Books, 1985) p. 251.

183   **When such right-wing**: *Ibid*., p. 251.

184   **'The original script'**: Personal interview with Barbara Corday, 1988.

184   **'These women aren't soft enough'**: Personal interview with Barney Rosenzweig, 1988. (Subsequent Rosenzweig quotes from interview.)

184   **'I said I can't'**: Personal interview with Harvey Shephard, 1991. (Subsequent Shephard quotes from interview.)

184   **'Meg Foster came across'**: Personal interview with Arnold Becker, April 1991. (Subsequent quotes from Becker are from personal interview unles otherwise noted.)

185   **An additional $15,000**: Julie D'Acci, forthcoming dissertation on *Cagney and Lacey*, Chapter 2, pp. 35–6.

185   **On one segment that dealt**: *Ibid*., p. 35.

186   **Becker complained at**: Gitlin, *Prime Time*, p. 9; D'Acci, dissertation, p. 55.

186   **Another CBS executive**: Frank Swertlow, 'CBS Alters Cagney, Calling It "Too Women's Lib",' *TV Guide*, June 12–18, 1982, p. 1.

187   ***Cagney and Lacey* producer April**: D'Acci, dissertation, p. 37.

187   **On a talk show**: Lorraine Gamman, 'Watching the Detectives,' in *The Female Gaze*, p. 25.

187   **When a women's studies**: *Ibid*., p. 25.

187   **'Nesting will be a crucial'**: 'Changes,' *TV Guide*, Oct. 1–7, 1988, p. 83. See also Andy Meisler, 'Baby Boom!' *TV Guide*, Dec. 30–Jan. 5, 1989–90, p. 4.

188   **'Bill Cosby brought masculinity'**: Boyer, 'Hard Boiled Male,' p. 1.

188   **'I do believe in control'**: Dan Goodgame, 'Cosby Inc.,' *Time*, Sept. 28, 1987, p. 56.

189   **'You see, the wives'**: Bill Cosby, *Fatherhood* (New York: A Dolphin Book/Doubleday, 1986), p. 49.

190   **'Single-woman leads'**: Gitlin, *Prime Time*, p. 23.

191   **Early television actually**: Meehan, *Ladies of the Evening*, p. 154.

191   **She had real**: *Ibid*., pp. 174–5.

191   **In *Mary*, she writes**: For excellent critique, see Joyce Millman, 'What Are Big Girls Made Of?' *Boston Phoenix*, Jan. 14, 1986, p. 5.

192   **Under pressure from the network**: Mark Harris, 'Smaller Than Life: TV's Prime-Time Women,' *New York Woman*, Oct. 1988, p. 104.

192   **Maddie's coerced matrimony was**: Joyce Millman, 'Is the Sun Setting on *Moonlighting*?' *San Francisco Examiner*, April 5, 1988, p. E1.

192   **It mirrored a behind-the-scenes**: Louise Farr, 'The *Moonlighting* Mess – Behind the Feuding That Almost Killed the Show,' *TV Guide*, Jan. 14–20, 1989, p. 9.

192   **'I felt ill when I received'**: *Ibid.*, p. 8.
193   **The show *Murder, She Wrote***: Sally Steenland, 'Prime Time Power,' Report by National Commission on Working Women, Aug. 1987, p. 9.
193   **'Ten years ago'**: Personal interview with Mary Alice Dwyer-Dobbin, Feb. 1988.
193   **In daytime TV**: Deborah Rogers, 'AIDS Spreads to the Soaps, Sort Of,' *New York Times*, Aug. 28, 1988, p. 29.
195   **Talk shows even**: Personal interview with Mel Harris, 1988.
195   **Therapists hailed**: Diane Haithman, 'Therapy Takes to TV,' *Los Angeles Times*, April 19, 1988, section VI, p. 1; Patricia Hersch, 'thirtytherapy,' *Psychology Today*, reprinted in *San Jose Mercury News*, Jan. 4, 1989, p. 1F; Aurora Mackey, 'Angst Springs Eternal: Modern-day Therapy Gets Couched in *thirtysomething* Terminology,' *Los Angeles Daily News*, Dec. 6, 1988, p. 4.
195   **As a professor reported**: Bette-Jane Raphael, '*Thirtysomething*: Can This TV Show Help Your Marriage?' *Redbook*, Oct. 1988, p. 18.
195   **Clergymen used the show**: Haithman, 'Therapy.'
195   **Dating services**: Susan Faludi, 'There's *Something* Happening Here . . . ' *West Magazine*, *San Jose Mercury News*, Feb. 26, 1989, p. 4.
195   **Even George Bush**: *Ibid.*
195   **All this excitement**: Howard Rosenberg, 'That Made-Up Feeling of *thirtysomething*,' *Los Angeles Times*, Oct. 27, 1987, section VI, p. 1.
195   **The majority of *thirtysomething* viewers**: Faludi, '*Something* Happening.'
196   **Jif Peanut butter**: *Ibid.*; James Kaplan, 'The *thirtysomething* Sell,' *Manhattan, inc.*, Dec. 1988, p. 78.
196   **'Watching that show'**: Personal interview with Marcia Greene, Feb. 1988.
196   **'Hope is so hard'**: Personal interview with Ann Hamilton, May 1988.
196   **'Hope is married to'**: 'Biographies,' *thirtysomething* production notes, MGM/UA, 1987.
197   **A former actress**: Personal interview with Liberty Godshall, May 1988.
197   **One day in the *thirtysomething***: Personal interview with Godshall and Edward Zwick, May 1988.
199   **'She was just described'**: Personal interview with Melanie Mayron, Jan. 1989.
199   **Draper recalls that**: Personal interview with Polly Draper, Jan. 1989.
200   **'Yeah, Ellyn's a mess'**: Personal interview with Liberty Godshall, May 1988.
200   **'We opted for a much more'**: Personal interview with Edward Zwick, May 1988.
201   **'When you look at the characters'**: Personal interview with Ann Hamilton, May 1988. (That Hamilton was even writing for *thirtysomething* is, in itself, a story of the backlash. Her speciality was actually writing action-adventure scripts – and 'for a while I got assignments because some of these all-male shows were under pressure to hire women'. But, as she notes, 'that's all let up now'. When she took her action screenplay around to the studios in the mid-1980s she was roundly rejected. The script wasn't the problem: When she changed the author's name to 'Buck Finch' and had her husband sell it, the studio executives optioned it at once.)
201   **'I think I'm a'**: Personal interview with Mel Harris, Jan. 1989; Raphael, '*Thirtysomething*,' p. 26.
201   **'From my perspective'**: Personal interview with Patricia Wettig, Jan. 1989; Dan Wakefield, 'Celebrating "the Small Moments of Personal Discovery",' *TV Guide*, June 11, 1988, p. 35.
201   **In the show, when Nancy**: Joy Horowitz, 'Life, Loss, Death and *thirtysomething*,' *New York Times*, Arts and Leisure section, Feb. 10, 1991, p. 29.
201   **ABC market research vice-president**: Personal interview with Henry Schafer, Jan. 1989.
202   **'I think this is a terrible'**: Stephen Fried, 'What *thirtysomething* Is Saying About Us,' *Gentleman's Quarterly*, April 1989, p. 267.

Chapter Seven. Dressing the Dolls

203   **The pushed-up breasts of:** Julie Baumgold, 'Dancing on the Lip of the Volcano,' *New York*, Nov. 30, 1987, p. 36.

203   **These were clothes:** Jennet Conant, 'Oh La La, Lacroix,' *Newsweek*, Nov. 9, 1987, p. 60.

203   **The Lacroix price tags, however:** 'Christian Lacroix,' *Current Biography*, April 1988, p. 39.

204   **Lacroix's bubble skirts:** Bernadine Morris, 'Lacroix Fever Spreads to New York,' *New York Times*, Oct. 30, 1987, p. A16.

204   **The Luxe gowns:** Martha Duffy, 'Fantasy Comes Alive,' *Time*, Feb. 8, 1988. 'High Femininity' was one name fashion trendsetters gave to the look, 'Fantasy Fashion' another.

204   **After Lacroix's July 1986:** Kathleen Beckett, 'The Frill of It All,' *Vogue*, April 1987, p. 178; 'La Gamine: Fun and Flirty,' *Harper's Bazaar*, April 1987, p. 86.

204   **Between 1980 and 1986:** Data from Market Research Corporation of America, Information Services; Trish Hall, 'Changing US Values, Tinged with Caution, Show Up in Spending,' *New York Times*, Oct. 26, 1988, p. B1.

204   **In one poll:** Martha Thomases, 'Why I Don't Shop,' *The Village Voice*, Dec. 27, 1988, p. 37.

205   **Then, in the High Femininity year:** Trish Donnally, 'Gloomy Fashion Forecast,' *San Francisco Chronicle*, March 23, 1988, p. B3.

205   **That year, even with:** Woody Hochswender, 'Where Have All the Shoppers Gone?' *New York Times*, May 31, 1988. The statistic on the 4 per cent drop in dress sales comes from Soft Goods Information Service, Market Research Corp. of America. As MRCA notes, total dollar sales of women's clothing increased in the first seven years of the decade only because the cost of women's clothes was rising so fast; the unit sales of items of clothing ranged from flat to slightly depressed.

205   **Even during the height:** Aimee Stern, 'Miniskirt Movement Comes Up Short,' *Adweek's Marketing Week*, March 28, 1988, p. 2.

205   **And this was a one-gender phenomenon:** *Ibid.*; Jennet Conant, 'The High-Priced Call of the Wild,' *Newsweek*, Feb. 1, 1988, p. 56. Mail-order men's clothing catalogues profited most, boosting revenues by as much as 25 per cent in this period. At Ruff Hewn, a mail-order business hawking gentrified country wear, sales rose 275 per cent a year, and by 1988 this small North Carolina company had expanded production into seventeen factories and was planning a nationwide retail chain. The cast of characters in Ruff Hewn's catalogue were backlash archetypes: 'Barclay Ruffin Hewn', the company catalogue's fictional hero, was depicted as a late-nineteenth century gentleman and highly decorated war veteran who rode with Teddy Roosevelt's Rough Riders. His wife, 'Elizabeth Farnsworth Hampton Hewn', as company president Jefferson Rives named her, was 'a very traditional and feminine lady who stays home to take care of Ruff and the children'. (Ruff Hewn catalogues and brochures; personal interview with Jefferson Rives, 1988.)

205   **In the spring of 1988:** Hochswender, 'All the Shoppers'; Donnally, 'Gloomy Fashion'; Barbara Deters, 'Limited Fashioning a Turnaround,' *USA Today*, May 20, 1988, p. B3; Stern, 'Miniskirt Movement Comes Up Short,' p. 2; Susan Caminiti, 'What Ails Retailing: Merchants Have Lost Touch With Older Customers,' *Fortune*, Jan. 30, 1989, p. 61.

205   **By the second quarter:** By contrast, sales of men's clothing in the same period rose by nearly $1 billion. Data from Department of Commerce, Bureau of Economic Analysis, Personal Consumption Expenditures.

205   **They were pushing:** Blayne Cutler, 'Meet Jane Doe,' *American Demographics*, June 1989, p. 24; Thomases, 'I Don't Shop,' p. 37. By ignoring the 30 to 40 million women wearing size 16 and over, the fashion industry was passing up a

$6 billion industry. See Jolie Solomon, 'Fashion Industry Courting Large Women,' *The Wall Street Journal*, Sept. 27, 1985.

205   **As Goldman Sachs's**: Joseph H. Ellis, 'The Women's Apparel Retailing Debacle: Why?' Goldman Sachs Investment Research, June 8, 1988.

206   **'What's the matter with'**: Personal interview with John Molloy, 1988.

206   **Or, as Lacroix**: Personal interview with Christian Lacroix, May 1991.

206   **As fashion designer Arnold**: Personal interview with Arnold Scaasi, Feb. 1988.

206   **At a Lacroix fashion**: 'Lacroix Triumphant,' *Women's Wear Daily*, July 27, 1987, p. 1.

206   **Designers wanted to be in**: 'Christian Lacroix,' p. 38.

206   **Women who had discovered**: Weibel, *Mirror Mirror*, p. 209.

206   **The fashion industry fell into**: 'Counter-Revolution,' *Time*, Sept. 15, 1947, p. 87.

207   **More than 300,000 women**: Jeanne Perkins, 'Dior,' *Life*, March 1, 1948, p. 84.

207   **In a poll that summer**: Hartmann, *Home Front*, p. 203.

207   **'The women who are loudest'**: 'Counter-Revolution,' p. 92.

207   **And they were obeying**: Weibel, *Mirror, Mirror*, p. xvi.

207   **'If you want a girl'**: Valerie Steele, *Fashion and Eroticism: Ideals of Feminine Beauty from the Victorian Era to the Jazz Age* (New York: Oxford University Press, 1985) p. 182.

207   **In the last half**: Robert E. Riegel, 'Women's Clothes and Women's Rights,' *American Quarterly*, 15, no. 3 (Fall 1963), 390–401; Elizabeth Ewins, *Dress and Undress* (New York: Drama Books Specialists, 1978) p. 89.

207   **The influential *Godey's***: Kinnard, *Antifeminism*, pp. 289, 304.

208   **'A lot of women'**: Personal interview with Bob Mackie, 1988.

208   **While denying that**: Sarah Mower, 'Meet the Feminist Femme Fatale,' *Cosmopolitan*, Sept. 1987, pp. 40–41.

208   **'We were wearing pinstripes'**: Personal interview with Karen Bromley, July 1989.

208   **Wells Rich Greene**: Personal interview with Jane Eastman, executive vice-president of strategic planning at Wells Rich Greene, Feb. 1988.

209   **'You must look as if'**: Bernadine Morris, 'Self-Confident Dressing,' *Harper's Bazaar*, Nov. 1978, p. 151.

209   **'Dress for the job you want'**: Amy Gross and Nancy Axelrad Comer, 'Power Dressing,' *Mademoiselle*, Sept. 1977, p. 188.

209   **Its September 1979**: 'Your Dress-for-Success Guide,' *Mademoiselle*, Sept. 1979, p. 182.

209   **John T. Molloy's**: Published in the UK as *The Woman's Dress for Success Book* (London: Foulsham, 1980).

209   **That earlier book**: John T. Molloy, *Dress for Success* (New York: Warner Books, 1975).

209   **A former prep-school**: Personal interview with John T. Molloy, 1988; John T. Molloy, *The Woman's Dress for Success Book* (New York: Warner Books, 1977) pp. 23–6.

210   **He even dispatched**: Molloy, *Woman's Dress for Success*, pp. 40–8.

210   **'Dressing to succeed'**: *Ibid.*, p. 21.

210   **A child of**: *Ibid.*, pp. 25, 20–3.

210   **'Many women'**: *Ibid.*, p. 22.

210   **When Molloy's book**: Susan Cheever Cowley, 'Dress for the Trip to the Top,' *Newsweek*, Sept. 26, 1977, p. 76.

210   **Retailers began invoking**: Molloy, *Woman's Dress for Success*, p. 30.

210   ***Newsweek* declared**: Cowley, 'Trip to the Top,' p. 76.

210   **And for the next**: 'Your Get Ahead Wardrobe,' *Working Woman*, July 1979, p. 46; 'Power!' *Essence*, March 1980, p. 68; 'What to Wear When You're Doing the Talking,' *Glamour*, Oct. 1978, p. 250.

211   **'The success of suits'**: 'A Well-Suited Season,' *Newsweek*, Nov. 5, 1979, p. 111.

211   **They had good reason**: *Ibid.*

211 **Between 1980 and 1987**: Statistics from Market Research Corporation of America; personal interview with John Tugman, vice-president and general manager, MRCA, Soft Goods Information Services, 1988.

211 **The $600 million gain**: Statistics from MRCA.

211 **Between 1981 and 1986**: 'Women's Coats, Suits, Tailored Career Wear, Rainwear and Furs,' report in *Fairchild Fact File* (New York: Fairchild Publications, 1987), p. 20.

211 **'When this uniform'**: Molloy, *Woman's Dress for Success*, p. 36.

211 **In 1986, US clothing**: 'Women's Coats,' in *Fairchild Fact File*, p. 12; US Bureau of the Census, Current Industrial Reports, 1987, 'Quantity of Production and Value of Shipments of Women's, Misses', and Juniors' Dresses and Suits: 1987 and 1986,' Table 8; personal interview with Judy Dodds, analyst with Current Industrial Reports, US Bureau of the Census, Commerce Department, 1988.

211 **The sudden cutback**: 'Women's Coats,' *Fairchild Fact File*, p. 30.

212 **And this reduction**: US Bureau of the Census, Current Industrial Reports, 1987, 'Quantity of Production and Value of Shipments of Men's and Boys' Suits, Coats, Vests, and Sports Coats: 1987 and 1986,' Table 2.

212 **Soon department stores**: Mark Potts, 'Thirteen Britches for Women Stores to Close,' *Washington Post*, Dec. 9, 1989, p. 10; personal interview with Harold Nelson, vice-president and general manager of Neiman Marcus's Washington, DC store, 1988; Cara Mason, 'Paul Harris Stores Rebounds from 1988 Losses,' *Indianapolis Business Journal*, March 12, 1990, p. A13.

212 **When Molloy**: Personal interview with John T. Molloy, 1988.

212 **'Bye-bye to the'**: Terri Minsky, 'The Death of Dress for Success,' *Mademoiselle*, Sept. 1987, p. 308.

212 **It was one of many**: Patricia McLaughlin, 'The Death of the Dumb Blue Suit,' *Philadelphia Inquirer*, Feb. 7, 1988, p. 35; 'Dumb Blue Suit: A Uniform for Submission Is Finally Put To Rest,' *Chicago Tribune*, May 8, 1988, p. C5.

212 **As a fashion consultant**: Betty Goodwin, 'Fashion 88: Dressing Down for Success,' *Los Angeles Times*, April 15, 1988, V, p. 1.

212 **'Why intelligent women'**: Aisling Foster, *Options*, April 1987, p. 145.

212 **Cosmopolitan agreed**: 'Bold Shoulders!', *Cosmopolitan*, Feb. 1987, p. 22.

212 **John Molloy was the obvious**: The defrocking of John Molloy recapitulates in many respects the attack on Gabrielle 'Coco' Chanel, the original designer of the power suit in 1920. Chanel fashioned her classic boxy jacket and comfortably low-waisted skirt after the male business suit, and, like Molloy, she spoke to the aspiring New Woman on the lower rungs of the class ladder. (She was one of these struggling women herself, having been consigned to an orphanage as a teenager after her father deserted her.) Her era's backlash put her out of business, and when she tried to make a comeback in the early 1950s, her fellow designers unleashed unmitigated scorn – most especially Christian Dior, who reportedly told her that a woman 'could never be a great couturier'. See Weibel, *Mirror, Mirror*, pp. 201, 213–4; Lois W. Banner, *American Beauty* (New York: Alfred A. Knopf, 1983) pp. 275–6.

213 **A major daily**: Personal interview with John T. Molloy, 1988.

213 **His book did not champion**: Molloy, *Woman's Dress for Success*, pp. 43, 52.

213 **And a whole section**: *Ibid.*, pp. 27–9.

213 **'My book recommended'**: Personal interview with John T. Molloy, 1988.

213 **With the suits**: Martha Duffy, 'Fantasy Comes Alive,' *Time* (International Edition), Feb. 8, 1988, p. 44.

214 **Instead of serving**: Louis Trager, 'Nordstrom Abuzz,' *San Francisco Examiner*, Oct. 6, 1988, p. C1.

214 **'We made a conscious decision'**: Personal interview with Harold Nelson, May 1988.

214 **For inspiration**: Duffy, 'Fantasy,' pp. 46–7.

214 **In 1982, while chief**: 'Christian Lacroix,' p. 37.

214 **(As Lacroix explains)**: Personal interview with Christian Lacroix, May 1991.

214   **Nonetheless, he clung**: Duffy, 'Fantasy,' p. 47.

214   **He timed the grand opening**: 'Christian Lacroix,' p. 38.

214   **While the fashion press**: 'Patou's Baby Dolls,' *Women's Wear Daily*, July 25, 1986, p. 1.

215   **As *Women's Wear Daily* remarked**: Christa Worthington, 'Fantasy Fashion Rebounds in Paris,' *Women's Wear Daily*, July 29, 1986, p. 1.

215   FASHION GOES MAD: 'Fashion Goes Mad,' *Women's Wear Daily*, July 29, 1986, p. 1.

215   **Lacroix has 'restored'**: Worthington, 'Fantasty Fashion,' p. 1.

215   **He dressed his**: Videos of Lacroix's Paris and New York shows; Bernadine Morris, 'For Lacroix, a Triumph; For Couture, a Future,' *New York Times*, July 27, 1987, p. C14.

215   **Then he sent them down**: Martha Duffy, 'Welcome to the Fresh Follies,' *Time*, Feb. 9, 1987, p. 76.

215   **John Fairchild, the magazine's**: Baumgold, 'Dancing on the Lip,' p. 49.

215   **The following July**: Morris, 'For Lacroix a Triumph,' p. C14.

215   **The president of Martha's**: *Ibid.*; 'Lacroix Triumphant,' *Women's Wear Daily*, July 27, 1987, p. 1.

216   **Hebe Dorsey of**: 'Lacroix Triumphant,' p. 3.

216   **The next day the *New York Times***: Morris, 'For Lacroix, a Triumph,' p. C14.

216   ***Time* and *Newsweek***: Duffy, 'Fantasy'; Conant, 'Oh La La, Lacroix.'

216   ***People* celebrated**: 'Paris' Daring Darling Shakes Up High Fashion with High Jinks,' *People*, May 19, 1986, p. 138.

216   **Lacroix, who stocked**: Baumgold, 'Dancing on the Lip,' p. 38.

216   **'Primitive people'**: Duffy, 'Fantasy,' p. 46.

216   **'He looks like Brando'**: *Ibid.*, p. 46.

217   **His last effort**: Nina Hyde, 'The Real Lacroix,' *Washington Post*, March 17, 1988, p. 1.

217   **In May 1988 big ads**: 'Introducing Christian Lacroix's Prêt-à-porter first at Saks Fifth Avenue,' *Washington Post*, May 19, 1988, p. A4.

217   **'It's ridiculous'**: Personal interview with Mimi Gott, May 24, 1988. (The comments from Saks employees and shoppers are also from personal interviews the same day.)

218   **A month later**: 'Lacroix Avoids Markdown Blues,' *Houston Chronicle*, Jan. 4, 1990, p. 5; Pete Born, 'How the French Do in US Stores,' *Women's Wear Daily*, March 17, 1989, p. 1; 'Stores Lament Designer Sales,' *Women's Wear Daily*, June 12, 1990, p. 1; Bernadette Morra, 'Mix Master Lacroix Designs with Gusto,' *Toronto Star*, Oct. 25, 1990, p. D2.

219   **To this end, Bullock's**: Lisa Lapin, 'Jeepers! Cool is Hot, Ralph Kramden Is a Folk Hero and Business Discovers There's Money To Be Made From Reviving the '50s,' *Los Angeles Times*, Jan. 4, 1987, IV, p. 1.

219   **'There has been a shift'**: Maureen Dowd, 'The New Exec,' *The New York Times Magazine*, Aug. 24, 1986, p. 145.

219   **In 1987, for example**: Statistics from Market Research Corp. of America.

219   **'This thing is not about designers'**: Genevieve Buck, 'Hemline Lib,' *Chicago Tribune*, June 3, 1987, p. 7.

219   **'Older women want'**: Goodwin, 'Fashion 88,' p. 1.

219   **'Gals like to show'**: Buck, 'Hemline Lib,' p. 7.

219   **'Girls want to be girls'**: 'La Gamine,' p. 86.

219   **'Women change not at all'**: Personal interview with John Weitz, Feb. 1988; Morris, 'The Sexy Look.'

220   **As a publicist**: Personal interview with Sarah O'Donnell, Alcott & Andrews publicist, 1988.

220   **Bloomingdale's, which dubbed**: Bloomingdale's advertisement, *New York Times*, Aug. 24, 1988, p. A5.

220   **'Saks understands'**: Saks Fifth Avenue two-page ad, *Vanity Fair*, March 1988.

220   **The fashion press pitched in**: 'New Season, New Looks,' *Cosmopolitan*, Feb.

1988; 'Dressing Cute Enroute,' *Mademoiselle*, Aug. 1985, p. 56; 'The New Success Looks: Young and Easy,' *Harper's Bazaar*, Oct. 1987, p. 76.

220 **Women could actually**: Goodwin, 'Fashion 88,' p. 1.

220 **'A man shortage?'**: 'Little Dating Looks,' *Mademoiselle*, Nov. 1987, p. 226.

220 **A 1988 New York Times**: Men, however, were far more enthusiastic; 71 per cent said they preferred skirts that didn't drop below the knee. Trish Hall, 'No Surprise Here: Men Prefer the Mini,' *New York Times*, March 31, 1988, p. C1. An earlier 1982 survey by Audits and Surveys for the Merit Report found that 81 per cent of women and men either didn't want miniskirts to come back into style or just didn't care. See 'Opinion Roundup – Light Fare: Of Legs, Locks, Love and Lancelots,' *Public Opinion*, April–May 1982, p. 37.

221 **'I will wear'**: Kathleen Fury, 'Why I'm Not Wearing Miniskirts, I Think,' *Working Woman*, Nov. 1987, p. 184.

221 **Nina Totenberg, legal affairs**: For printed version, see Nina Totenberg, 'Miniskirt, Maxi Blunder,' *New York Times*, March 21, 1988, p. A19.

221 **The miniskirt has thrown**: Sanford L. Jacobs, 'Claiborne Says Miniskirts May Mean Mini-Increase in Earnings for 1988,' *The Wall Street Journal*, Feb. 26, 1988.

221 **'I think it's really a trend'**: Personal interview with Yvette Crosby and observations at California Mart's Market Week, April 9, 1988, p. 20.

221 **'Last year, the miniskirt was'**: Personal interview with Bob Mallard. (Following scenes from personal interviews and observations at Mallard's showroom, April 9, 1988.)

223 **Jean-Paul Gaultier**: Holly Brubach, 'The Rites of Spring,' *New Yorker*, June 6, 1988, p. 80.

223 **Pierre Cardin produced**: Bernadine Morris, 'In Paris Couture, Opulence Lights A Serious Mood,' *New York Times*, July 26, 1988.

223 **Romeo Gigli**: Brubach, 'Rites of Spring,' p. 81.

223 **The Lacroix brand**: Gladys Perint Palmer, 'Top to Toe at Paris Show,' *San Francisco Examiner*, Oct. 29, 1989, p. E3.

223 **By 1990 Valentino**: Marylou Luther, 'Young and Restless: Haute Couture Sports a New Attitude for the '90s,' *Chicago Sun-Times*, Aug. 1, 1990, II, p. 25.

223 **The woman who steps down**: Brubach, 'Rites of Spring.'

224 **'I see it changing'**: Personal interview with Bob Mackie, 1988.

224 **Frustrated by slackening sales**: Personal interviews with staff and board members of the Intimate Apparel Council. See also Susan Faludi, 'Artifice and Old Lace,' *West Magazine, San Jose Mercury News*, Sept. 10, 1989, p. 14.

224 **The committee immediately issued**: Press kit, 'Intimate Apparel: How History Has Shaped Fashion,' Intimate Apparel Council, Summer 1989, p. 5.

224 **'It's not that we aren't'**: Personal interview with Karen Bromley, July 1989.

224 **In anticipation of the**: 'Underwear and Nightwear,' Current Industrial Reports, 1987, US Department of Commerce.

225 **Du Pont, the largest**: Personal interview with Du Pont spokeswoman Ellen Walsh, July 1989. See also 'Dupont Says, "What A Body!"' *Body Fashions/Intimate Apparel*, Oct. 1987, p. 2.

225 **'Women have come a long way'**: 'The Intimate Market: A Profile,' E. I. du Pont de Nemours & Co., Intimate Apparel Marketing, 1987.

225 **'Bra sales are booming'**: Jane Ellis, 'Bra at 100: Big Biz,' *New York Daily News*, June 15, 1989.

225 **Enlisting one fake**: Woody Hochswender, 'Lounge Wear for Cocooning,' *New York Times*, Jan. 3, 1989, p. B4.

225 *Life* **dedicated**: Claudia Dowling, 'Hurrah for the Bra,' *Life*, June 1989, p. 88.

225 **In an interview later**: Personal interview with Claudia Dowling, July 1989.

225 **'The "Sexy" Revolution'**: 'The "Sexy" Revolution Ignites Intimate Apparel,' *BFIA*, Oct. 1987, p. 1

226 **'That Madonna look'**: Personal interview with Bob Mackie, 1988.

226 **Late Victorian**: Steele, *Fashion and Eroticism*, p. 192.

226   **'Whenever the romantic'**: Personal interview with Peter Velardi, July 1989.

226   **'I don't want to sound arrogant'**: Personal interview with Howard Gross, July 1989. (Subsequent Gross quotes are from interview.)

227   **'You can put'**: Personal interview with George Townson, June 1989.

227   **A Stanford MBA**: Personal interview with Roy Raymond, June 1989. (Subsequent Raymond quotes are from interview.)

228   **'Oh God, the panty table'**: Personal interview with Becky Johnson, July 1989. (Following scene and quotes are from personal interviews and observations, July 1989. See Faludi, 'Artifice and Old Lace,' p. 18.)

229   **That year, women's annual**: Data from MRCA, Soft Goods Information Services.

229   **In the UK, *Company***: Madeleine Kingsley, 'Ooh, la la!,' *Company*, March 1987, p. 73.

229   **In 1982 Jockey's**: Personal interviews with Jockey president Howard Cooley, and Don Ruland, vice-president of merchandising, July 1989. (Subsequent quotes from Cooley are from personal interview.)

230   **Jockey's researchers invited**: Personal interview with Gayle Huff, Jockey's national advertising director, and Bill Herrmann, senior vice-president of advertising, July 1989.

230   **The brand became**: Faludi, 'Artifice and Old Lace,' p. 21.

230   **'The women complained'**: Personal interview with Jay Taub, 1988.

231   **In the windows**: Stephanie Salter, 'Short Skirts, Long Battles,' *San Francisco Examiner*, Oct. 20, 1989, p. A25; Jean Kilbourne, *Still Killing Us Softly: Advertising's Image of Women*, 1987, Cambridge Documentary Films.

231   **In *Vogue***: 'Hidden Delights,' *Vogue*, March 1987, p. 462.

231   **Other mainstream fashion magazines**: These images come from *Vogue*, *Glamour* and *Cosmopolitan*. I am indebted to Ann Simonton, director of *Media Watch*, for sharing her collection of these images of women in advertising in the 1980s.

231   **By the late 1980s**: Linda Frye Burnham, 'Rear Window,' *LA Weekly*, Nov. 5, 1987.

231   *Company* **magazine surveyed**: *Company*, April 1987, p. 75.

232   **According to company lore**: 'The Guess? Success,' Guess press kit, 1988.

232   **But soon Guess would make**: From Guess? promotion video.

233   **'You should hear'**: Personal interview with Lisa Hickey, April 1988.

233   **'When I came here'**: Personal interview with Paul Marciano, April 1988. (Subsequent Marciano quotes are from interview.)

233   **In the American West**: *The Panhandle* (Los Angeles: Guess? Inc., undated).

235   **For the role of 'the other woman'**: Following scene and quotes are from personal interviews and observation at the Guess fashion shoot, May 1988.

235   **'The only way'**: Personal interview, May 1988.

Chapter Eight. Beauty and the Backlash

237   **'There are no imperfections'**: Personal interview with Robert Filoso and personal observations, April 1988. (Subsequent Filoso quotes are from personal interview.)

237   **This year he is making**: At the same time, sculptors of male mannequins were producing more macho models. Pucci Manikins, for example, was elevating its male dummies' height from 6′ to 6′2″ and inflating 40-inch chests to 42-inch pectorals. See Sam Allis, 'What Do Men Really Want?' *Time*, special issue, Fall 1990, p. 80.

237   **'It seems like'**: Personal interview with Laurie Rothey, April 1988.

239   **'Is your face paying'**: Ad for Nivea Visage, 1988.

239   **'The impact of work stress'**: Jeanne M. Toal, 'Stress and the Single Girl,' *Mademoiselle*, Sept. 1987, p. 293.

239   **This message was barely**: Kinnard, *Antifeminism*, p. 307, 20.

240   **In 1981 Revlon's**: 'Charlie's Back,' *Barron's*, May 13, 1985, p. 34.

240   **Beauty became medicalized**: A medically oriented and physically punishing beauty standard is another backlash hallmark. Late Victorian doctors conducted the first 'face skinning' operations and breast enlargements – called 'breast piercing' because they inserted a metal ring to irritate and swell the flesh. In the 1930s, face-lifts were popularized; in the 'feminine mystique' era, silicone injections were introduced and intensively promoted. See Rosen, *Popcorn Venus*, p. 181; Maggie Angeloglou, *A History of Makeup* (London: Macmillan, 1970), p. 103.

240   **(One doctor even)**: Ann Louise Bardach, 'The Dark Side of Cosmetic Surgery,' *The Good Health Magazine, New York Times*, April 17, 1988, p. 24.

240   **Hospitals facing**: By 1988, hospital weight-loss programmes were generating $5.5 billion a year and diet clinics $10 billion – not bad for an industry with a 95 per cent failure rate. See Molly O'Neill, 'Dieters, Craving Balance, Are Battling Fears of Food,' *New York Times*, April 1, 1990, p. 1.

240   **Historically, the backlash**: See, for example, Bram Dijkstra, *Idols of Perversity: Fantasies of Feminine Evil in Fin de Siècle Culture* (New York: Oxford University Press, 1986) pp. 25–9.

241   **During the late Victorian**: *Ibid.*, p. 29; Banner, *American Beauty*, p. 41.

241   **The wasting-away look**: Banner, *American Beauty*, p.47; Joan Jacobs Brumberg, *Fasting Girls: The Emergence of Anorexia Nervosa as a Modern Disease* (Cambridge, Mass.: Harvard University Press, 1988) pp. 101–40.

241   **In times of backlash**: This was an equation John Ruskin made explicit in his 1864 lecture on female beauty, 'Of Queens' Gardens': 'What the woman is to be within her gates, as the centre of order, the balm of distress, and the mirror of beauty; that she is also to be without her gates, where order is more difficult, distress more imminent, loveliness more rare.' See Banner, *American Beauty*, p. 12; Steele, *Fashion and Eroticism*, pp. 104–5.

241   **In the late 1910s and**: Banner, *American Beauty*, p. 277; Angeloglou, *History of Makeup*, pp. 109, 116–17, 119.

241   *Again, during the Second World War*: See, for example, 'The Changing Face of the American Beauty,' *McCall's*, April 1976, p. 174.

241   *Harper's Bazaar* **described**: Tina Sutton and Louise Tutelian, 'Play It Again, Roz,' *Savvy*, April 1985, p. 60.

241   **With the war over, however**: Angeloglou, *History of Makeup*, p. 131; Weibel, *Mirror Mirror*, p. 161.

242   **Under the 1980s backlash, the pattern**: See, for example, 'Action Beauty,' *Mademoiselle*, April 1979. The beauty magazines of the 1970s are filled with editorial and advertising tributes to athletic, tanned and all-natural looks.

242   **In the winter of 1973**: Personal interview with Revlon executive vice-president Lawrence Wechsler, 1989.

242   **(It actually wasn't)**: Angeloglou, *History of Makeup*, p. 126.

242   **The Revlon team code-named**: Personal interview with Lawrence Wechsler, 1989.

242   **'Charlie symbolized'**: *Ibid.* (Subsequent Wechsler quotes are from interview.)

243   **Suddenly in 1982**: Philip H. Dougherty, 'Defining "A Charlie" for Revlon,' *New York Times*, Nov. 28, 1986, p. D7.

243   **The new campaign, however**: *Ibid.*

243   **'In the past few years'**: 'Light Scents with Strong Appeal,' *Glamour*, Sept. 1987, p. 386.

243   **A host of eighties perfume makers**: Ronald Alsop, 'Firms Push "Aroma Therapy" to Treat Flat Fragrance Sales,' *The Wall Street Journal*, March 20, 1986, p. 31.

244   **In a new round**: At the same time, men's colognes went macho, as fragrance makers issued such new offerings as 'Boss' and 'Hero', the latter endorsed by baseball hero Hank Aaron. See Woody Hochswender, 'Men's Fragrance: The

Scent of Money Has Attracted a Striking Number of New Products,' *New York Times*, Oct. 4, 1988.

244 **In the first half:** Lisa Belkin, 'Cosmetics Go on Gold Standard,' *New York Times*, Oct. 11, 1986, p. 52; 'Selling Scents Gets Tougher,' Retailing: A Special Report, *The Wall Street Journal*, May 7, 1987, p. 1.

244 **To promote Passion:** Kathleen A. Hughes, 'Perfume Firms Go All Out in Effort to Lure Buyers,' *The Wall Street Journal*, Dec. 10, 1987, p. 29.

245 **'You're a wholesome':** Jean Kilbourne, *Still Killing Us Softly*, 1987, Cambridge Documentary Films.

245 **The flood of:** Mark Honigsbaum, 'Dollars and Scents,' This World, *San Francisco Chronicle*, Oct. 16, 1988, p. 9.

245 **At Avon:** Walecia Konrad, 'The Problems at Avon Are More Than Skin Deep,' *Business Week*, June 20, 1988, p. 49; Denise M. Topolnicki, 'Avon's Corporate Makeover,' *Working Woman*, Feb. 1988, p. 57.

245 **By appealing to:** Topolnicki, 'Corporate Makeover,' p. 59.

245 **As a feature headline:** Cynthia Robins, 'The Makeup Message for the Summer: Be Seen But Not Heard,' *San Francisco Examiner*, July 31, 1986, p. E5.

245 *Mademoiselle's* **cosmetics:** 'Now You're Chic . . . Now You're Cheap – Do Not Cross That Fine (Beauty) Line,' *Mademoiselle*, April 1988, p. 230.

245 *Vogue* **placed:** 'The Impact of a New Year . . . And a Difference in Makeup,' *Vogue*, Jan. 1987, p. 140.

246 **The heaviest users:** Laura Sachar, 'Forecast: Industry Analysis – Cosmetics,' *Financial World*, Jan. 5, 1988, p. 21; Joseph Weber, 'Why Noxell Is Touching Up Its Latest Creation,' *Business Week*, July 11, 1988, p. 92.

246 **The make-up companies':** 'Cosmetics Shows Its Age,' *Financial World*, May 29–June 11, 1986, p. 87.

247 **The labels of dozens:** Biotherm's anti-wrinkle cream claimed to use 'human placental protein'. Barbara Kallen, 'Facing Facts,' *Forbes*, May 19, 1986, p. 178.

247 **The ad agency that created Oil of:** Personal interview with Jane Eastman of Wells Rich Greene, 1988; Kathleen Deveny and Alecia Swasy, 'In Cosmetics, Marketing Cultures Clash,' *The Wall Street Journal*, Oct. 30, 1989, p. B1.

247 **Chanel adverts even:** Ronald Alsop, 'Chanel Plans to Run Ads in Magazines with Less Cachet,' *The Wall Street Journal*, Jan. 27, 1988, p. 30.

248 **By 1985 a cosmetics trade:** Cynthia Robins, 'The Quest for Flawless Skin,' *San Francisco Examiner*, July 27, 1986, p. A19.

248 **By 1986 skin-cream:** *Ibid.*

248 **The claims made on:** Melinda Beck, 'Peddling Youth Over the Counter,' *Newsweek*, March 5, 1990, p. 50.

248 **Skin-care companies cashed in:** Cynthia Robins, 'Blocking the Sun's Rays,' *San Francisco Examiner*, July 30, 1986, p. E4.

248 **A century earlier:** 'The Pale Pursuit,' *Ms.*, Sept. 1987, p. 52.

249 **Retin-A, however:** Kathy Holub, 'Does Retin-A Really Work?' *West Magazine*, *San Jose Mercury News*, May 15, 1988, p. 14; Marilyn Chase, 'Looking for Miracles, Young and Old Flock to Purchase Retin-A,' *The Wall Street Journal*, Feb. 12, 1988, p. 1; Beck, 'Peddling Youth,' pp. 50–1.

249 **In the one study testing:** Jonathan S. Weiss, Charles N. Ellis, John T. Headington, Theresa Tincoff, Ted A. Hamilton and John J. Voorhees, 'Topical Tretinoin Improves Photoaged Skin,' *Journal of American Medical Association*, 259, no. 4 (Jan. 22–9, 1988), 527–52.

249 **Despite the apparent:** Holub, 'Retin-A.'

249 **In one year Retin-A sales:** Susan Duffy Benway, 'Youth for Sale: Anti-Aging Is the Hottest Thing in Cosmetics,' *Barron's*, Dec. 22, 1986, p. 24.

249 **Starting in 1983:** Lisa M. Krieger, 'New Face of Plastic Surgery,' *San Francisco Examiner*, Jan. 1, 1989, p. A1; press kit from American Society of Plastic and Reconstructive Surgeons Inc. and its Plastic Surgery Education Foundation.

250 **'There is a body':** Krieger, 'New Face of Plastic Surgery,' p. A1.

250 **A single issue of:** Bardach, 'The Dark Side of Cosmetic Surgery', p. 24.

250   **Cosmetic surgery can even**: Ad entitled 'Cosmetic Surgery Can Enhance Your Life,' *The New York Times Magazine*, April 17, 1988, p. 57.

250   **With liposuction, 'you can feel'**: Ad in *Los Angeles* magazine, Feb. 1989.

250   **From *Vogue* to**: Teri Agins, 'Boom in Busts,' *The Wall Street Journal*, reprinted in *San Francisco Examiner*, Dec. 15, 1988, p. D1.

250   **'Go curvy'**: 'Go Curvy!: The Right Inches/The Right Places,' *Mademoiselle*, Jan. 1988, p. 108.

250   **'Attention, front and center'**: 'Breasts . . . the Bare Truth: A Beauty Report,' *Mademoiselle*, April 1988, p. 221.

250   ***Options* asked**: Alix Kirsta, 'If Those Are Laughter Lines . . . Why Are You Crying,' *Options*, Sept. 1984, p. 104.

251   **American TV talk shows**: *Good Morning Bay Areas*'s Jan. 13, 1989, segment offered a cosmetic-surgery contest judged by local cosmetic surgeons; the finalists were women who showed the 'most potential for positive change'. In Dec. 1988, *Donahue* named a plastic-surgery patient 'The Perfect Woman'. See Ryan Murphy, 'It's Not Easy Being Perfect,' *San Jose Mercury News*, Feb. 14, 1989, p. D1. For radio stations, see Barbara Lippert, 'Vanna Doesn't Speak,' *Adweek*, July 6, 1987, p. 10.

251   **Even *Ms.* deemed**: Wendy Kaminer, 'Of Face Lifts and Feminism,' *New York Times*, Sept. 6, 1988, p. A23.

251   **In Britain surgeons**: Alix Kirsta, *Options*, Sept. 1984, p. 104.

251   **By 1988 the cosmetic**: Steven Findlay, 'Buying the Perfect Body,' *US News and World Report*, May 1, 1989, p. 68; Susan Jacoby, 'Appearance Anxiety,' *The New York Times Magazine*, Aug. 28, 1988, p. 26.

251   **More than 2 million**: Krieger, 'New Face of Plastic Surgery' p. A22.

251   **A 1987 survey**: 'Facial Plastic and Reconstructive Surgery Study,' cited in Susan L. Wampler, 'Mirror: The Changing Face of Beauty,' *Indianapolis Business Journal*, Feb. 19, 1990, III, p. 28.

251   **In 1988 a congressional**: A six-month investigation by the US House of Representatives' Small Business Subcommittee; its findings were released in spring 1989.

252   **Other studies found**: Rita Freedman, *Beauty Bound* (Lexington, Mass.: Lexington Books, 1986) p. 213.

252   **Follow-up operations to correct**: Elizabeth Bennett, 'Choice of Doctors May Determine Success in Quest for Youth and Beauty,' *Houston Post*, May 29, 1987, p. G1.

252   **For breast implants**: Sandra Blakeslee, 'Breast Implant Surgery: More Facts Are Sought in the Battle Over Safety,' *New York Times*, Dec. 28, 1989, p. B6.

252   **A 1987 study in**: John B. McCraw, Charles E. Horton, John A. I. Grossman, Ivor Kaplan and Ann McMellin, 'An Early Appraisal of the Methods of Tissue Expansion and the Transverse Rectus Abdominis Musculocutaneious Flap in Reconstruction of the Breast Following Mastectomy,' *Annals of Plastic Surgery*, 18, no. 2 (Feb. 1987), 93–113.

252   **In 1988 investigators**: Bardach, 'Dark Side of Cosmetic Surgery', p. 54. In fact, no comprehensive epidemiological studies of breast implants had been conducted since the devices were first introduced in 1964.

252   **Contracture of scar tissue**: *Ibid.*; Blakeslee, 'Breast Implant Surgery'; 'Breast Implants Delay Diagnosis of Cancer,' *San Francisco Chronicle*, July 8, 1988; 'Breast Implants Hinder X-Ray Mammography,' *The Wall Street Journal*, June 14, 1989, p. B1.

252   **In 1989 a Florida**: 'Dying for Beauty,' *Media Watch*, 3 (Summer 1989), 2.

252   **In 1982 the FDA**: Sybil Niden Goldrich, 'Restoration Drama,' *Ms.*, June 1988, p. 20.

252   **'The risk to humans'**: Warren E. Leary, 'Silicone Implants Tied to Cancer in Test Rats,' *New York Times*, Nov. 10, 1988, p. A8.

253   **Not until April 1991**: Jean Seligmann, 'The Hazards of Silicone,' *Newsweek*, April 29, 1991, p. 56.

253   **Former *Howard's Way* star**: Edward Verity, 'Stars in Breast Scare Who Must Wait And Worry,' *Daily Mail*, Jan. 7, 1992, p. 3.

253   **The American Society**: 'Plastic Surgeons' Society Issues Statement on Breast Implants,' news release from the American Society of Plastic and Reconstructive Surgeons, Jan. 1988.

253   **Between 1984 and 1986**: Data from American Society of Plastic and Reconstructive Surgeons, 1988: 'Five-Year Updated Evaluation of Suction-Assisted Lipectomy,' paper prepared by the ASPRS Ad Hoc Committee on New Procedures, Sept. 30, 1987.

253   **The procedure could also**: 'Five-Year Updated Evaluation of Suction-Assisted Lipectomy.'

253   **Furthermore, the plastic surgery**: *Ibid.*

254   **On March 30, 1987**: Carrie Dolan, 'Fat-cutting Gains Wide Popularity But Can Be Dangerous,' *The Wall Street Journal*, June 26, 1987, p. A1; Bennett, 'Choice of Doctors'; Fred Bonavita, 'Pasadena Doctor's License Revoked,' *Houston Post*, July 25, 1987, p. 1A.

254   **'This literature she got'**: Hope E. Paasch, 'Widower Suing Doctor,' *Houston Post*, April 8, 1987, p.3A.

254   **Ramirez operated**: *Ibid.*, Bonavita, 'Pasadena Doctor.'

254   **By 1987, only five years**: 'Five-Year Updated Evaluation of Suction-Assisted Lipectomy,' pp. 8–11.

254   **A 1988 congressional subcommittee**: Laura Fraser, 'Scar Wars,' This World, *San Francisco Chronicle*, May 20, 1990, p. 7.

254   **A woman in San Francisco**: Personal interview with a close friend of the woman who asked not to be identified, 1989.

254   **The society's 1987 report**: 'Five-Year Updated Evaluations of Suction-Assisted Lipectomy,' p. 2.

255   **As even the report**: *Ibid.*, p. 12.

255   ***Vogue* described**: Janice Kaplan, 'Fix vs. Lift?' *Vogue*, Jan. 1985, p. 205.

255   **One Los Angeles plastic**: Bardach, 'Dark Side of Cosmetic Surgery,' p. 51.

255   **In fact the number of**: Statistics from American Society of Plastic and Reconstructive Surgeons. Between 1984 and 1986 the number of breast reconstructive procedures performed fell from 98,800 to 57,200, and the number of burn reconstruction operations slipped from 23,200 to 20,400. Overall, the number of all reconstructive (as opposed to aesthetic) procedures declined from 1,388,700 to 1,259,500.

255   **'To me,' said plastic surgeon**: Rodney Tyler, 'Doctor Vanity,' *Special Report*, Nov. 1989–Jan. 1990, p. 20. Wagner also performed cosmetic surgery on his mother, mother-in-law and wife's sister. This wasn't just one doctor's peculiarity. In a 1987 survey of plastic surgeons, nearly half of them said they remodelled their wives, mothers and daughters.

Chapter Nine. The Politics of Resentment

259   **'The politics of despair'**: Seymour Martin Lipset and Earl Raab, *The Politics of Unreason: Right-Wing Extremism in America, 1790–1970* (New York: Harper & Row, 1970) p. 3.

259   **'I have hope'**: Personal interview with Paul Weyrich, 1988. (Subsequent Weyrich quotes are from interview unless otherwise noted.)

260   **As a New Right minister**: Personal interview with Edmund Haislmaier, Heritage Foundation fellow, who was present at this meeting, 1988.

261   **On the airwaves**: Arbitron's 1981 study, *Prime Time Preachers*, found that their weekly audience fell from 21 to 20 million between 1977 and 1980; A. C. Nielsen's 1980 *Report on Syndicated Programs* found that only two of the top ten independent TV preachers reached as many as 2 per cent of the households in broadcast range. See John L. Kater, Jr, *Christians on the Right* (New York:

The Seabury Press) p. 18; William Martin, 'The Birth of a Media Myth,' *Atlantic*, June 1981, p. 9. As the decade progressed, support for TV ministers eroded still further: A 1987 Louis Harris poll found that 70 per cent of Americans believed the electronic preachers were a more destructive than beneficial influence.

261   **Even at the peak:** Falwell overstated his viewership by 23.4 million people. See Flo Conway and Jim Siegelman, *Holy Terror: The Fundamentalist War on America's Freedoms in Religion, Politics and Our Private Lives* (New York: A Delta Book, 1984) p. 83.

261   **A Harris poll found:** Louis Harris Poll, May 1987.

261   **'Backlash politics,' political:** Lipset and Raab, *The Politics of Unreason*, pp. 29–30.

261   **'America has largely':** Richard Hofstadter, *The Paranoid Style in American Politics* (New York: Alfred A. Knopf, 1965) pp. 23, 43.

261   **As Weyrich himself:** Thomas J. McIntyre with John C. Obert, *The Fear Brokers* (Philadelphia: Pilgrim Press, 1979), p. 156.

261   **The New Right movement has:** Hofstadter, *The Paranoid Style*, pp. 67, 73–4; Lipset and Raab, *Politics of Unreason*, p. 30.

262   **As Conservative Caucus:** McIntyre, *The Fear Brokers*, p. 156.

262   **In 1980 Weyrich:** *Conservative Digest*, 6, no. 6 (June 1980), 12, cited in Rosalind Pollack Petchesky, 'Antiabortion, Antifeminism, and the Rise of the New Right,' *Feminist Studies*, 7, no. 2 (Summer 1981), 232.

262   **That same year:** Jerry Falwell, *Listen, America!* (Garden City, NY: Doubleday-Galilee, 1980) p. 151.

263   **One New Right group:** Charlene Spretnak, 'The Christian Right's "Holy War" Against Feminism,' in *The Politics of Women's Spirituality* (New York: Anchor/Doubleday, 1982) pp. 470–96; Walda Katz Fishman and Georgia E. Fuller, 'Unraveling the Right-Wing Opposition to Women's Equality'; *Interchange*, Report by Interchange Resource Center, Washington, D.C., 1981, p. 1; Marcia Fram, 'ERA Foes Exploit "Women vs. Women" Myth,' *National Catholic Reporter*, July 30, 1982.

263   **'The women's liberation':** Petchesky, 'Antiabortion,' p. 211.

263   **In a 1989 survey:** 'Women Shun Clergy's Advice,' *San Francisco Chronicle*, April 14, 1989, p. B4.

264   **When a researcher:** 'A Poll for Women: A Survey of Protestant Evangelical Opinion About Self-Image and Social Problems,' Feb.–May 1982. See Carol Virginia Pohli, 'Church Closets and Back Doors: A Feminist View of Moral Majority Women,' *Feminist Studies*, 9, no. 3 (Fall 1983), 542.

264   **In their sermons:** Dan Morgan, 'Evangelicals: A Force Divided, Political Involvement, Sophistication Growing,' *Washington Post*, March 8, 1988, p. A1; Janet E. Burks, 'Changing Roles of Women: Two Views, the Religious Right Moves Backward into History,' *Sequoia*, July–Aug. 1986, p. 9.

264   **'Wife beating is on':** Barbara Ehrenreich, Elizabeth Hess and Gloria Jacobs, *Remaking Love: The Feminization of Sex* (Garden City, NY: Anchor Books, 1987) pp. 155–6.

264   **In a smear campaign:** Conway and Siegelman, *Holy Terror*, pp. 275–6.

264   **'They really came':** *Ibid.*, p. 276.

264   **Howard Phillips charged:** Leslie Wolfe, 'The Unfinished Agenda: Women and Girls in Education,' Women's Way Conference, Nov. 9, 1987, Philadelphia, PA., p. 11.

264   **Jerry Falwell seemed to:** Falwell, *Listen, America!* pp. 142–3, 157–64.

265   *Mandate for Leadership*: *Mandate for Leadership: Policy Management in a Conservative Administration*, ed. Charles Heatherly (Washington, DC: Heritage Foundation, 1981) p. 180.

265   *Mandate for Leadership II*: Stuart M. Butler, Michael Sanera and W. Bruce Weinrod, *Mandate for Leadership II: Continuing the Conservative Revolution* (Washington, DC: Heritage Foundation, 1984), p. 157.

265   **And Cultural Conservatism:** *Cultural Conservatism, Toward a New National Agenda* (Lanham, Maryland: Free Congress Foundation, 1987), p. 2.

265   **'One need not wander':** *Ibid.,* p. 7.

265   **The publications list:** *Family in America* publications list, Rockford Institute, 1989.

266   **'Feminism kind of':** Personal interview with Edmund Haislmaier, 1988.

266   **The Act's proposals:** Onalee McGraw, 'The Family Protection Report: Symbol and Substance,' Moral Majority Report, Nov. 23, 1981, p. 4; Petchesky, 'Antiabortion, Antifeminism', pp. 224–5; Frances Fitzgerald, 'The New Righteousness – Changing Our Laws, Your Life,' *Vogue,* Nov. 1981, p. 236.

267   **Under this provision:** Marilyn Power, 'Women, the State and the Family,' p. 155.

267   **The Republican convention's:** For an insightful discussion of this phenomenon, see Zilliah Eisenstein, 'Antifeminism in the Politics and Election of 1980,' *Feminist Studies,* 7, no. 2 (Summer 1981), 187.

267   **And their candidate:** Fishman and Fuller, 'Unraveling the New-Right Opposition,' p. 1.

268   **Richard G. Hutcheson:** Richard G. Hutcheson, Jr, *God in the White House* (New York: Macmillan, 1988). Similarly scant attention is paid to the role of feminism in many other chronicles. See Samuel S. Hill and Dennis E. Owen, *The New Religious Political Right in America* (Nashville, Tenn.: Abindon, 1982); McIntyre, *The Fear Brokers.*

268   **'[T]he "hearth and home" ':** Alan Crawford, *Thunder on the Right: The 'New Right' and the Politics of Resentment* (New York: Pantheon, 1980), p. 149, Petchesky, 'Antiabortion,' footnote 2, p. 239.

268   **'We are different':** McIntyre, *Fear Brokers,* p. 156.

268   **Reverend James Robison:** Conway and Siegelman, *Holy Terror,* pp. 60, 161.

268   **'Jesus was not':** Kater, *Christians,* p. 38.

268   **Yet the fundamentalist:** 'Beause we have weak men,' he complained, 'we have weak homes, and children from these homes will probably grow up to become weak parents leading even weaker homes.' Falwell, *Listen, America!* p. 129.

269   **'Paradoxically, conservatism':** Sidney Blumenthal, *The Rise of the Counter-Establishment: From Conservative Ideology to Political Power* (New York: Harper & Row, 1988), p. 6.

269   **'For twenty years':** Butler *et al., Mandate for Leadership II,* p. 155.

269   **Earlier, the anti-ERA:** Fram, 'ERA Foes Exploit "Women vs. Women" Myth.'

270   **Now, Weyrich could:** For an example of Weyrich's use of this rhetorical tactic, see Conway and Siegelman, *Holy Terror,* p. 116. The New Right even renamed battered-women's shelters 'anti-family' institutions. See Barbara Bergmann, *The Economic Emergence of Women* (New York: Basic Books, 1986), p. 206.

270   **In the 1920s the Ku Klux:** Lipset and Raab, *Politics of Unreason,* p. 117.

270   **These 'pro-life' advocates:** For atom bomb quote, see Conway and Siegelman, *Holy Terror,* p. 417.

270   **Under the banner:** Falwell, *Listen, America!* p. 129.

270   **'Women's liberationists':** Phyllis Schlafly, *The Power of the Positive Woman* (New York: Jove/Harcourt Brace Jovanovich, 1977) p. 72.

270   **'Feminism is more than':** Beverly LaHaye, *The Restless Woman* (Grand Rapids, Mich.: Zondervan, 1984) p. 54.

271   **The woman who opposed:** See Carol Felsenthal, *The Sweetheart of the Silent Majority: The Biography of Phyllis Schlafly* (New York: Doubleday, 1981).

271   **In her anti-feminist treatise:** Schlafly, *Positive Woman,* pp. 40–1.

271   **All the women:** *Ibid.,* pp. 12–13, 33–4, 49, 53–4.

271   **To her mind:** *Ibid.,* p. 53.

271   **'The Positive Woman in America':** *Ibid.,* p. 33.

271   **It was the 1977:** Rebecca E. Klatch, *Women of the New Right* (Philadelphia: Temple University Press, 1987) p. 123; Ann Hulbert, 'The Baltimore Bust,' *The New Republic,* June 28, 1980, p. 20. See also Beverly LaHaye, *Who But a*

Woman? (New York: Thomas Nelson, 1984) pp. 25, 29, 43, 49. As LaHaye, founder of the New Right group Concerned Women for America, herself wrote, 'I know this is going to sound unusual, but I am truly indebted to Bella Abzug, Gloria Steinem, Betty Friedan, and other radical feminists for the existence of Concerned Women for America.' The 1977 convention, she noted, 'opened my eyes and the eyes of other Christian women across the nation who were involved in it'.

272   **'IWY was our "boot camp" '**: Klatch, *New Right*, pp. 123–4.

272   **'I had never'**: *Ibid.*, pp. 143–4.

272   **'A woman's nature'**: Connaught C. Marshner, *The New Traditional Woman* (Washington, DC: Free Congress Research and Education Foundation, 1982) p. 12.

272   **'If anywhere'**: Personal interview with Connaught Marshner, May 1988.

273   **'Oh yeah'**: *Ibid.* (Following quotations are from personal interview with Marshner unless otherwise noted.)

274   **Both cerebral and**: Connaught C. Marshner, *Why the Family Matters: From a Business Perspective* (Washington, DC: The Free Congress Foundation, 1985) p. 8.

274   **Abortion, for example**: *Ibid.*, p. 14.

276   **Just quit whining**: Schlafly, *Positive Woman*, pp. 70–1.

276   **'Women need to know'**: Klatch, *New Right*, p. 45.

277   **'She is new'**: Marshner, *New Traditional Woman*, p. 1.

277   **It had unleashed 'a new image'**: *Ibid.*, p. 3.

278   **'Macho feminism has'**: *Ibid.*, pp. 3–4.

278   **'Marshner's out of it now'**: Personal interview with Paul Weyrich, 1988.

278   **As he speaks**: Personal interviews with staff members, 1988.

279   **'The woman who is truly'**: Beverly LaHaye, *The Spirit-Controlled Woman* (Eugene, Oregon: Harvest House Publishers, 1976) p. 71.

279   **'God didn't make me'**: Personal interview with Beverly LaHaye, May 1988.

280   **'Betty Friedan doesn't'**: *Ibid.* (Following LaHaye quotations are from interview unless otherwise noted.)

280   **At the time, LaHaye was a 'fearful'**: LaHaye, *Spirit-Controlled Woman*, p. 13.

280   **'I refused most invitations'**: *Ibid.*

280   **'One very well-meaning'**: *Ibid.*, pp. 13–14.

281   **'In my case'**: *Ibid.*, p. 89.

281   **When her youngest child**: Personal interview with Beverly LaHaye, May 1988.

281   **The speaker, the popular**: *Ibid.*

281   **'This is what I needed!'**: LaHaye, *Spirit-Controlled Woman*, pp. 13, 14, 30, 34.

282   **By tapping 'spiritual power'**: *Ibid.*, pp. 14, 34.

282   **A spirit-controlled woman must**: *Ibid.*, p. 34.

282   **LaHaye's journey toward**: Personal interview with Beverly LaHaye, May 1988.

283   **'Modern research'**: Tim and Beverly LaHaye, *The Act of Marriage: The Beauty of Sexual Love* (London: Bantam Press, 1978), p. 109.

283   **'Regrettably some husbands are carryovers'**: *Ibid.*, p. 121.

283   **'Many women are'**: *Ibid.*, p. 126.

283   **The LaHayes even declared**: *Ibid.*, pp. 73, 258.

283   **As if all this weren't**: *Ibid.*, pp. 240–1.

284   **She declared herself**: LaHaye, *Who But a Woman?*, p. 53.

284   **'I discovered an organization'**: Mary Schmich, 'A Spokeslady of the Right,' *Chicago Tribune*, March 23, 1986, p. 1.

284   **She organized what she claimed**: Barrie Lyons, Beverly LaHaye's sister and CWA's vice-president, told an interviewer that the organization arrived at a figure of half a million constituents by counting as a member anyone who expressed 'interest' in the group by requesting a newsletter or signing a petition. About 150,000 women, on the other hand, were actually official members who paid the minimum $15 dues each year. Most of the media, however, accepted CWA's inflated membership claims: a *Time* cover story, for example, described

CWA as having more members 'than the combined following of the National Organization for Women, the National Women's Political Caucus and the League of Women Voters' ('Jerry Falwell's Crusade,' *Time*, Sept. 2, 1985.) NOW, in fact, had more dues-paying members than CWA.

284 **'Father, we pray'**: Randi Henderson, 'In the Tradition,' *Baltimore Sun*, March 26, 1986, p. C1.

285 **Tim LaHaye offered**: The CWA's National Advisory Council, for example, included Jerry Falwell's wife Macel, Senator Jesse Helms's wife Dorothy, and Jimmy Swaggart's wife Frances, to name just a few.

285 **'She has the kind of'**: Geoffrey Aronson, 'The Conversion of Beverly LaHaye,' *Regardie's*, March 1987, p. 105.

285 **She refused**: *Ibid.*, p. 120; Morgan, 'Evangelicals as a Force Divided,' p. A1; Maralee Schwartz, Lloyd Grove and Dan Morgan, 'Kemp Loses Endorsement,' *Washington Post*, March 3, 1988, p. A15.

286 **One year she went to**: Mary Battiata, 'Beverly LaHaye and the Hymn of the Right,' *Washington Post*, Sept. 26, 1987, p. C1.

286 **While on the road**: Cathy Trost, 'Conservatives Enter into the Fray on Child Care, Arguing for Tax Breaks, Against Regulation,' *The Wall Street Journal*, May 6, 1988, p. 44.

286 **And she made it clear**: Nadine Brozan, 'Politics and Prayer: Women on a Crusade,' *New York Times*, June 15, 1987, p. C1.

286 **'I think the women's movement'**: Personal interview with Beverly LaHaye, May 1988.

286 **'Mrs LaHaye had that'**: Personal interview with Rebecca Hagelin, 1988.

287 **(Her latest anti-feminist book)**: Beverly LaHaye, *The Restless Woman* (Grand Rapids, Mich.: Zondervan Publishing, 1984) pp. 88, 108, 109.

287 **'I just love it'**: Personal interview with Elizabeth Kepler, 1988.

288 **'I change the car'**: Personal interview with Susan Larson, 1988.

288 **'Now, let's see'**: Personal observation and interview with Rebecca Hagelin, 1988.

Chapter Ten. Ms Smith Leaves Washington

290 **On the bench**: Jane Mayer, 'Unfair Shake? Women Charge They Don't Get Their Share of White House Jobs,' *The Wall Street Journal*, Sept. 10, 1985, p. 1.

290 **On the White House staff**: Barbara Gamarekian, 'Women Are Liberating a Citadel of Male Power,' *New York Times*, May 18, 1988, p. 24.

290 **In fact, even 62**: Information from Federally Employed Women.

290 **But as Joan Smith**: *Misogynies* (London: Faber & Faber, 1990 pbk edn), p. 114.

290 **As Prime Minister**: Quoted by Hilary Burden, 'Are Women MPs On Our Side?', *Cosmopolitan*, Oct. 1990, p. 8.

291 **At the start of**: Mayer, 'Unfair Shake?' p. 1.

291 **At the Justice Department**: There were, as well, no women in the Justice Department's twenty-one presidentially appointed jobs. Meese's record was no better among minorities, in his first two years he named no black senior policymakers either. In Reagan's first six years he appointed only two women out of the 93 US attorneys and 27 women out of 292 federal judges. See Howard Kurtz, 'Affirmative Action: A Vacuum at Justice? Meese Puts No Blacks or Women in Top Jobs,' *Washington Post*, Nov. 26, 1986, p. A19.

291 **The Federal Women's Program**: Personal interviews with staff of the Federal Women's Program, 1989, 1991.

291 **'Each year, our budget'**: Personal interview with Betty Fleming, May 1991.

291 **In Australia, some**: Information supplied by Eva Cox of Distaff Consultancy, Camperdown, NSW, Australia.

292 **UN ambassador**: Mayer, 'Unfair Shake?' p. 1.

292 **The Reagan administration, she**: Lindsy Van Gelder, 'Countdown to Motherhood,' *Ms.*, Dec. 1986, p. 37.

292   **'I know the president'**: Whittlesey, 'Radical Feminism in Retreat,' Dec. 8, 1984.

292   **As she headed for**: Mayer, 'Unfair Shake?' p. 1.

292   **First, anti-abortion activist**: Steve Chapple and David Talbot, *Burning Desires: Sex in America* (New York: Doubleday, 1989) pp. 77–88. The squeal rule was eventually blocked by the courts.

293   **Jo Ann Gasper, *Conservative Digest***: *Ibid.*, pp. 78–82; Conway and Siegelman, *Holy Terror*, p. 372.

293   ***Mandate for Leadership* demanded**: *Mandate for Leadership*, pp. 179–80.

293   **'I was a "known feminist" '**: Personal interview with Leslie Wolfe, Feb. 1988.

293   **In a flurry of internal memos**: See, for example, 'A Brief Look at the Women's Educational Equity Act', a Heritage Foundation 'training' paper (which complained that the programme 'operated as a taxpayer-subsidized effort to insert the "feminist outlook" into the US school curriculum'); 'Feminist Network Fed by Federal Grants: Insider Exposes Education Department Scandal,' *Conservative Digest*, special issue, 8, no. 4 (April 1982), 26.

294   **It had been hailed**: Judy Mann, 'Two Faced,' *Washington Post*, Sept. 14, 1983, p. C1.

294   **The projects WEEA funded**: Judith Paterson, 'Equity in Exile,' *Ms.*, Nov. 1984, p. 18.

294   **Nonetheless, to the men**: Testimony from Charles Heatherly, Heritage fellow and former deputy under-secretary for management in the US Education Department, at hearings before the House Education and Labor Committee, Aug. 2, 1983.

294   **Charles Heatherly, Heritage**: Personal interview with Charles Heatherly, Nov. 1989.

294   **Heatherly recruited**: Congressional hearings on WEEA transcript, Sept. 27, 1983.

294   **They found a**: Paterson, 'Equity in Exile,' p. 20.

295   ***Human Events: National***: 'Education Department Uncovers Grants to Feminist', *Human Events: National Conservative Weekly*, Jan. 30, 1982.

295   ***Conservative Digest*, the publication**: 'Feminist Network Fed,' pp. 26–7.

295   **Again, on a talk show**: Congressional WEEA hearings, Sept. 27, 1983.

295   **Just a week after**: Personal interview with Leslie Wolfe, 1988; 'Statement of Dr Leslie R. Wolfe,' Sept. 27, 1983, testimony before the Congressional WEEA hearings, pp. 17–19.

295   **When Wolfe reported**: Personal interview with Leslie Wolfe, 1988; 'Statement of Dr Leslie R. Wolfe,' p. 20.

296   **Every year, the programme**: Deborah R. Eisenberg, 'Evaluating in the Department of Education's Field Readers,' *GAO Review*, Fall 1984, pp. 32–5.

296   **'There was a general'**: Personal interview with Charles Heatherly, Nov. 1989.

296   **As one of them**: 'Statement of Dr Leslie R. Wolfe,' p. 38.

296   **One reader, whose job**: *Ibid.*, pp. 32, 35–6.

296   **Finally, the General Accounting**: 'Procedures for Making Grant Awards Under Three Department of Education Discretionary Grant Programs,' General Accounting Office, July 26, 1983.

297   **A year later**: Personal interview with Leslie Wolfe, 1988.

297   **All five other**: 'More on the Women's Issues,' *New York Times*, Aug. 18, 1983, p. B12.

297   **'The values taught on'**: 'Can Uncle Sam Cure What Ails the Family?' *US News and World Report*, Sept. 1, 1986.

297   **What Bauer found most**: Personal interview with Gary Bauer, 1988.

297   **But he was ignored**: Julie Johnson, 'Fanning the Flames for Conservatives,' *New York Times*, Oct. 12, 1988, p. A15; John B. Judis, 'The Mouse That Roars,' *The New Republic*, Aug. 3, 1987, p. 23.

298   **When the administration**: Judis, 'Mouse That Roars,' p. 23.

298   **'If the mother does not do'**: 'The Family: Preserving America's Future,' A

Report to the President from the White House Working Group on the Family, Dec. 1986.

298 **'I'm sorry, Sam'**: *Ibid.*, p. 13.

298 **Even female poverty**: *Ibid.*, p. 16. Actually, female-headed households are estimated to have contributed to only 1.2 per cent of the increase in poverty among the nation's children between 1979 and 1986. See Joan Smith, 'Impact of the Reagan Years: Gender & Restructuring,' Paper for 1st Annual Women's Policy Research Conference, Institute for Women's Policy Research, May 19, 1989, pp. 2–3, 26.

298 **Of the offspring**: *Ibid.*, pp. 13–14. The Rockford Institute's *The Family in America*, for example, a New Right publication that features 'research' on the family, focused primarily on divorce's ill effects on sons. With only Mum in charge, the newsletter warned, boys can become emotionally stunted, develop insomnia, and turn into 'sissies'. If girls lose sleep over their parents' divorce, it's apparently not worth noting. See, for example: 'Needing Dad' and 'Just Like His Dad,' *The Family in America*, July 1989, pp. 2, 3.

298 **Bauer's 'recommendations' to**: 'The Family' p. 38. See also follow-up report, *Report to the President on the Family*, Office of Policy Development, July 25, 1988, p. 7.

298 **On the other hand**: 'The Family,' p. 45.

299 **'We're running at'**: Personal interview with Gary Bauer, 1988. (Subsequent Bauer quotes are from interview unless otherwise noted.)

300 **(It's unclear how this is)**: *Child Care: The Time Is Now*, Children's Defense Fund, 1987, p. 9.

300 **'Actually, I went back'**: Personal interview with Carol Bauer, 1988. (Subsequent quotes are from interview.)

302 **The $5,000**: 'Report Urges President to Strengthen Families,' *Washington Post*, Nov. 14, 1986, p. A1.

302 **The measure did not go**: Geraldine Ferraro with Linda Bird Francke, *Ferraro: My Story* (New York: Bantam Books, 1985) pp. 194–5.

302 **The number of women running**: Data from Center for the American Woman and Politics, Eagleton Institute of Politics, Rutgers University.

302 **Ferraro's nomination also**: Sara Diamond, 'Women on the Radical Right: Meeting Our Needs?' *Plexus*, Nov. 1984, p. 4.

303 **'There were rumors'**: Personal interview with Geraldine Ferraro, 1988.

303 **They even followed her**: Ferraro with Francke, *Ferraro*, pp. 223–4, 227–8.

303 **Ferraro herself**: 'Ferraroblip,' *The Nation*, Sept. 1, 1984, p. 131.

303 **Rumours about Zaccaro's**: James Ring Adams, 'The Lost Honor of Geraldine Ferraro,' *Commentary*, Feb. 1986, p. 34.

303 **The *Philadelphia Inquirer* assigned**: *Ibid.*, p. 35.

303 **'The stoning of'**: Ferraro with Francke, *Ferraro*, p. 234.

303 **In the end, as myriad**: See, for example, the 1984 *Newsweek* Poll; 'Bad News for Mondale,' *Newsweek*, Sept. 24, 1988.

304 **In fact, a national**: National Women's Political Caucus poll, 1984.

304 **Moreover, exit polls**: Exit polls by the *Los Angeles Times*, ABC, and Democratic pollster Dotty Lynch. See Peggy Simpson, 'Myths and Realities: Did Ferraro Attract Voters?' *Working Woman*, Feb. 1985, p. 54.

304 **'Polling indicated'**: 'The Ferraro Problem,' *National Review*, Nov. 1, 1985, p. 20.

304 **Democratic party leaders**: Peggy Simpson, 'What Happened in '84: Did Women Make a Difference?' *Working Woman*, Feb. 1985, p. 52; Robin Toner, 'Democrats and Women: Party Shifts Approach,' *New York Times*, July 11, 1987, p. 10.

304 **Writer Nicholas Davidson**: Nicholas Davidson, *The Failure of Feminism* (Buffalo, NY: Prometheus Books, 1988) p. 149.

304 **Washington Post columnist**: Richard Cohen, '. . . And Wobbling,' *Washington Post*, July 3, 1984, p. A15.

304 **In subsequent press:** 'The Hurt Was Even More Than What's In the Book,' *Newsweek*, Oct. 7, 1985, p. 81.

304 **'[T]he defeat of one woman':** Ferraro with Francke, *Ferraro*, p. 312.

304 **In 1984, 53 per cent:** Mark Clements Research, Annual Study of Women's Attitudes, 1984, 1987.

305 **By 1988, recruiters:** Personal interview with Jane Danowitz, executive director of the Women's Campaign Fund, 1988; personal interview with Ruth Mandel, 1988; Ellen Hume, 'Women Grow Reluctant to Run for High Office As Ferraro Euphoria Fades and Scandals Mount,' *The Wall Street Journal*, Oct. 16, 1987, p. 62.

305 **The popular California:** Hume, 'Women Grow Reluctant,' p. 62.

305 **On election day, only two women:** Statistics from Center for the American Woman and Politics. These figures include nominees of the two major parties only.

305 **When the election results:** *Ibid.*

306 **Not one of:** 'GOP Candidates Snub Women's Conference,' *Dallas Times Herald*, Jan. 21, 1988; personal interviews with conference organizers, 1988.

306 **As the organization's executive director:** 'GOP Candidates Snub Women's Conference.'

306 **The 'gender gap' appeared:** Information from Gallup poll, 1982, p. 35; analyses by Center for American Women and Politics; Thomas G. Exter, 'What Men and Women Think,' *American Demographics*, Aug. 1987, p. 34. Among college graduates, the gap was 15 per cent in this election. See Susanna Downie, 'Decade of Achievement: 1977–1987,' p. 34.

306 **On the top of the ticket:** The *New York Times*/CBS News exit poll, 1988. See 'Portrait of the Electorate, *New York Times*, Nov. 10, 1988, p. A16. According to the exit polls, 8 per cent, or about 3 million, fewer women than men voted for Reagan. See Eleanor Smeal, *Why and How Women Will Elect the Next President* (New York: Harper & Row, 1984) p. 3; Simpson, 'What Happened in '84,' p. 43.

306 **Women's rights, in fact:** Klein, *Gender Politics*, p. 159.

306 **The first substantial feminist:** *Ibid.*, p. 161.

306 **It was 'the first election':** *Ibid.*, pp. 159–60.

307 **By 1988, in fact:** Fund for the Feminist Majority poll, 1988.

307 **As the decade progressed:** 'Gender Gap Found in All Areas, Social Levels,' *The Gallup Report*, March 1983; 'Reagan Popularity: Men vs. Women,' *The Gallup Report*, March 1983; Smeal, *Why and How Women Will Elect the Next President*, p. 3.

307 **By 1986 the gender:** 'The Gender Gap,' *WEJC Update*, Women's Economic Justice Center, 2, no. 1 (Spring 1989), 3; 'Women and the Vote – 1988; Women's Impact at the Polls,' National Commission on Working Women, 1988.

307 **The tendency for more women:** Maggie Drummond, 'Women and Politics,' *Options*, June 1991, p. 48.

307 **A 1989 MORI poll:** *Ibid.*

307 **By 1988 the voting preferences:** ABC News/*Washington Post*, Nov. 8, 1988; NBC News/*Wall Street Journal*, Nov. 8, 1988; *Los Angeles Times*, Nov. 8, 1988. See 'The Exit Poll Results,' *Public Opinion*, Jan.–Feb. 1989, p. 26; the *Washington Post*/ABC News Survey, June 15–19, 1988; R. W. Apple, Jr, 'Bush's Growing Appeal Fails to Include Women,' *New York Times*, Oct. 27, 1988, p. B15.

307 **It was single women:** 'In Review,' *The American Woman 1990–91*, p. 49; 'Quayle's Votes on Gender Gap Issues,' *Eleanor Smeal Report*, 5, no. 24 (Aug. 19, 1988), 3.

308 **'We are particularly':** David Hoffman, 'Reagan Coalition's Not Yet Bush's: Women, Blue Collars May Be Drifting from GOP, Polls Show,' *The Washington Post*, May 11, 1988, p. 1A.

308 **This shouldn't have:** Women represent more than 90 per cent of the federal

AFDC (Aid to Families with Dependent Children) recipients, 66 per cent of those depending on federally subsidized housing, 66 per cent of those needing legal services, 60 per cent of Medicaid beneficiaries, and 60 per cent drawing food stamps. Power, 'Women, the State and the Family,' p. 55.

308   **Instead, Republican leaders:** Amy Brooke Baker, 'Low Marks for GOP on Women's Issues,' *The Christian Science Monitor*, Jan. 21, 1988, p. 3; Kenneth H. Bacon, 'Bush Backs Away From Birth-Control Program As Congress Braces for a Tough Fight on Issue,' *The Wall Street Journal*, Feb. 2, 1990, p. A12.

308   **At the 1988 Republican:** Sara Rimer, 'For Women, Taking on One Role at a Time,' *New York Times*, Sept. 23, 1988, p. B1.

308   **Bush hoped especially:** *Newsweek* turned the 'wimp' issue into a cover story: 'Fighting the Wimp Factor,' *Newsweek*, Oct. 19, 1987, p. 28.

309   **'I get furious':** 'Flash! Bush Is Angry (Or Maybe He Isn't),' 'Campaign Notes,' *New York Times*, Nov. 7, 1988, p. B17.

309   **'Maybe I'll turn':** George Will, 'The Pastel President,' *Newsweek*, April 24, 1989, p 86.

309   **'We're not running:** E. J. Dionne, Jr, 'Why Bush Faces a Problem Winning Women's Support, ' *New York Times*, June 19, 1988, p. A1.

309   **When Bush summoned:** Peggy Simpson, 'Games Republicans Play,' *Ms.*, July 1988, p. 42.

309   **His youthful blond:** Ellen Goodman, 'Envelope, Please, for Equal Rights Winners,' *Boston Globe*, Aug. 23, 1988, p. A19.

309   **(Indeed, the 1988 Los):** *The People, the Press, and Politics*, Los Angeles Times Mirror Survey, 1988.

309   **Paul Kirk, chairman:** 'Women's Groups Meet with Kirk,' *Eleanor Smeal Report*, 5, no. 10 (Dec. 23, 1987), 1; Elizabeth Drew, 'Letter from Washington,' *New Yorker*, Aug. 15, 1988, p. 65.

310   **Meanwhile, the Democratic Leadership:** Toner, 'Democrats and Women,' p. 10.

310   **'The major accomplishment':** 'Gender Gap,' p. 1.

310   **But the exit polls:** 'Election '88: What the Voters Said,' *Public Opinion*, Jan.–Feb. 1989, p. 26.

310   **Donna Brazile, the one:** George E. Curry, 'A Season in Hell,' *Ms.*, Oct. 1989, p. 59.

311   **When a few women:** Mary Jo Neuberger, 'Nice Girls Don't: Women's Caucus Shuns Conflict in Atlanta,' *The Village Voice*, Aug. 2, 1988, p. 24.

311   **When feminist writer:** Barbara Ehrenreich, 'The Heart of the Matter,' *Ms.*, May 1988, p. 20.

311   **In a final press mailing:** *America's Families Need Our Votes*, Women's Vote Project and National Women's Political Caucus, Oct. 28, 1988.

311   **('I do hope we'):** Peggy Simpson, 'Child Care: All Talk, No Action,' *Ms.*, Dec. 1988, p. 81.

312   **Not only was this:** And when the US Senate finally passed a watered-down version of the Family and Medical Leave Act in 1990, a bill that only covered 5 per cent of all US employers, President Bush promptly vetoed it.

312   **The day after:** The *Washington Post*'s special section ran on Nov. 9, 1988, pp. 22–43.

312   **In the week after:** Personal review of the *New York Times*, Nov. 9–16, 1988.

313   **In January 1989, days after:** Nadine Brozan, 'Women Meet, Ideology in Back Row,' *New York Times*, Jan. 9, 1989, p. A10.

Chapter Eleven. The Backlash Brains Trust

314   **These middlemen and women did not ally:** What ideology these experts *did* subscribe to was often difficult to determine. Political scientist Jean Bethke Elshtain is one such bewildering example – a seemingly staunch conservative

scholar who called herself a feminist and wrote for such liberal and leftist journals as *The Progressive* and *Dissent*. She produced a steady stream of anti-feminist articles, essays and books, in which she accused the women's movement of destroying the family. See Judith Stacey, 'The New Conservative Feminism,' *Feminist Studies*, 9, no. 3 (Fall 1983), 559. For a discussion of attacks on the women's movement from the left, see Arlie Hochschild, 'Is the Left Sick of Feminism?' *Mother Jones*, June 1983, p. 56.

314 **By the early 1990s Reaganite:** Lasch proposed such a ban both in a forum sponsored by *Harper's* and in a speech before a marriage and family therapists' convention in 1991. See 'Who Owes What to Whom: Drafting a Constitutional Bill of Duties,' *Harper's*, Feb. 1991, p. 48.

317 **When the United States:** George Gilder, *Naked Nomads: Unmarried Men in America* (New York: Quadrangle/The New York Times Book Co., 1974) pp. 106–7.

317 **'In their view':** *Ibid.*, p. 107.

317 **'Not only was I':** *Ibid.*

317 **'A good run':** *Ibid.*

317 **As Gilder was puffing:** *Ibid.*, p. 108.

317 **It hadn't actually:** *Ibid.*, p. 110.

317 **'As I stood':** *Ibid.*

317 **The following year:** Personal interview with George Gilder, 1989. (Subsequent Gilder quotes are from interview unless otherwise noted.)

318 **As he recalls later:** Personal interview with George Gilder, 1989; Gilder, *Naked Nomads*, p. vii.

318 **After he wrote:** Personal interview with George Gilder, 1989.

319 **In each of them:** George Gilder, *Men and Marriage* (Gretna, Louisiana: Pelican, 1986) pp. 108, 139.

319 **Feminists are turning:** *Ibid.*, pp. 149, 108.

319 **'Let us dream':** George Gilder, 'The Princess's Problem (All the Good Ones Are Married, Sort Of),' *National Review*, Feb. 28, 1986, p. 28. (The essay is also in *Men and Marriage*.)

319 **'What does Liberty ask':** *Ibid.*, p. 28.

320 **Simon won't leave:** *Ibid.*, p. 30.

320 **Women 'have to bet':** *Ibid.*, p. 29.

320 **He was past thirty:** Personal interview with George Gilder, 1989; Gilder, *Naked Nomads*, pp. 5, 22.

320 **'The single man is':** *Ibid.*, p. 141.

320 **Unlike some other backlash:** *Ibid.*, pp. 14–21, 27–8, 65–6, 74, 152.

321 **'As in the case of':** *Ibid.*, p. 65.

321 **'Although they may make':** *Ibid.*, pp. 6–7, 10.

321 **'[V]irile masculinity,' he writes:** *Ibid.*, pp. 129, 158.

321 **Gilder's version of:** *Ibid.*, p. 75.

321 **'[T]he older a man':** *Ibid.*, p. 27.

321 **'[T]he peripheral men':** *Ibid.*, p. 75.

321 **They will 'rape and':** Gilder, *Men and Marriage*, p. 39.

322 **The sales figures declined:** Personal interview with George Gilder, 1989.

322 **Throwing away his liberal Republican:** Blumenthal, *The Rise of the Counter-Establishment*, pp. 203–4.

322 **Reagan's men acted:** *Ibid.*, pp. 204, 208, 210.

323 **'The man has the gradually':** George Gilder, *Wealth and Poverty* (New York: Basic Books, 1981), p. 115.

323 **Nini was, as he:** Gilder, *Men and Marriage*, pp. xiii, xi.

323 **When they met:** Personal interview with George Gilder, 1989.

323 **'The latest enemy':** Allan Bloom, *The Closing of the American Mind* (New York: Simon & Schuster, 1987), pp. 65–6, 74–6, 79, 80, 100–1.

324 **'The feminist project':** *Ibid.*, pp. 100–1, 104–5, 124.

324   In *The True and Only Heaven*: Christopher Lasch, *The True and Only Heaven* (New York: W. W. Norton, 1991) pp. 33–4.

324   In *Tenured Radicals*: Roger Kimball, *Tenured Radicals: How Politics Has Corrupted Our Higher Education* (New York: Harper & Row, 1990) pp. xi, xvii, 15.

325   By 1991 in California: Stephen Schwartz, 'Challenge to Campus Policies,' *San Francisco Chronicle*, Jan. 5, 1991, p. A4.

325   A few years after: Personal interview with Allan Bloom, 1989. (Subsequent Bloom quotes are from interview unless otherwise noted.)

326   Women, feminist or otherwise: Deborah L. Rhode, 'Perspectives on Professional Women,' *Stanford Law Review*, 40, no. 5 (May 1988), 1175, 1179–80. A 1982–83 survey by the American Association of University Professionals of 2,500 higher-education institutions found that despite a decade of affirmative action, 'women have achieved very little'. The association's report found the least progress at the most elite colleges: at Harvard University, women represented only 4.2 per cent of full professors; at Yale, 3.9 per cent; at Princeton, 3.2 per cent; at Stanford, 2.6 per cent. This wasn't because of a shortage of women: about one-third of job-seeking PhD holders were women.

326   Nor are feminist professorships: Mariam Chamberlain, 'The Emergence and Growth of Women's Studies Programs,' *The American Woman: 1990–91*, p. 318.

326   As for dominance: Ellen Carol DuBois, Gail Paradise Kelly, Elizabeth Lapovsky Kennedy, Carolyn W. Korsmeyer and Lillian S. Robinson, *Feminist Scholarship: Kindling in the Groves of Academe* (Chicago: University of Illinois Press, 1987) pp. 165, 168–9.

326   If scholars like: Anne Matthews, 'Deciphering Victorian Underwear and Other Seminars,' *The New York Times Magazine*, Feb. 10, 1991, p. 42.

326   'The guns at Cornell': Bloom, *American Mind*, p. 347.

327   'I was lost': James Atlas, 'Chicago's Grumpy Guru,' *New York Times*, Jan. 3, 1988, p. 25.

327   Two years into his: *Ibid.*

327   He writes wistfully of: Bloom, *American Mind*, p. 126.

327   He is upset about: *Ibid.*, pp. 120, 16.

328   'Women, it is said': Allan Bloom, 'Liberty, Equality, Sexuality,' *Commentary*, April 1987, p. 24.

328   Feminists are against pornography: Bloom, *American Mind*, p. 103.

328   A bachelor himself: *Ibid.*, p. 127.

328   He writes that women are: *Ibid.*, p. 124.

328   It is the standard paradoxical backlash: *Ibid.*, pp. 107, 131.

328   'And here is where': *Ibid.*, pp. 12, 129.

328   When he surveys: *Ibid.*, p. 137, 114.

329   Modern men are: *Ibid.*, p. 124.

329   '[A] man without': *Ibid.*, p. 84.

329   The closest he comes: *Ibid.*, p. 125.

329   In his 1988 book: Michael Levin, *Feminism and Freedom* (New Brunswick, NJ: Transaction Books, 1987) pp. 3, ix.

330   'The Hier-Crowley': *Ibid.*, p. 83.

330   '!Kung juvenile': *Ibid.*, p. 90.

330   'If you want to interview': Personal interview with Margarita Levin, 1988. (Subsequent quotes are from this interview unless otherwise specified.)

330   Despite his position in: Levin, *Feminism and Freedom*, p. 270.

331   'My wife does': Personal interview with Michael Levin, 1988. (Subsequent quotes are from this interview unless otherwise specified.)

332   In a 1988 article: Margarita Levin, 'Caring New World: Feminism and Science,' *The American Scholar*, Winter 1988, p. 100.

333   She found a welcoming: Margarita Levin, 'Babes in Libland,' *Newsweek*, Dec. 28, 1981, p. 8.

334   'Men are hurting more': Personal interview with Warren Farrell, 1988. (Sub-

sequent quotes and observations are from this interview unless otherwise specified.)

334   **Feminism may have:** Warren Farrell, *Why Men Are the Way They Are* (New York: McGraw-Hill, 1986), p. xv.

335   **'I had seen her':** *Ibid.*, p. xxi.

335   **'Soon after my':** *Ibid.*

336   **'I was surprised':** *Ibid.*, pp. xv–xvi.

336   **He organized:** 'Getting Men to Hold Handsd – On the Road to Liberation,' *People*, Jan. 20, 1975, p. 48.

336   **'A boy who is not':** Warren T. Farrell, 'The Human Lib Movement I,' *New York Times*, June 17, 1971, p. 41.

336   **'The truth is that':** Michael Korda, *Male Chauvinism* (New York: Random House, 1973), p. 160; Marc Feigen Fasteau, *The Male Machine* (New York: McGraw-Hill, 1974), pp. 5, 11.

337   **A flattering four-page:** Farrell, 'Getting Men to Hold Hands,' p. 48.

337   **As Farrell himself:** Farrell, 'Human Lib Movement.'

337   **Independent women were:** Farrell, *Why Men Are*, p. 355.

339   **It is a massive:** Robert Bly, 'Fifty Males Sitting Together,' in *Loving a Woman in Two Worlds* (New York: Harper & Row, 1985), p. 3.

339   **'All of you men':** Personal observation at Black Oak Books, 1988.

340   **'Since we are':** Jill Wolfson, Make Poetry,' *San Jose Mercury News*, April 16, 1983, p. F1.

340   **'I began to feel':** Robert Bly, *The Pillow & the Key* (St Paul, Minn.: Ally Press, 1987) p. 19.

340   **It wasn't his loss:** *Ibid.*

341   **'If someone says':** 'Robert Bly,' *Whole Earth*, Winter 1988, p. 68.

341   **Mainstream newspapers hailed:** Jerry Carroll, 'Father Figure to the New, New Man,' *San Francisco Chronicle*, March 19, 1986, p. 36.

341   **By 1990 his self-published:** Robert Bly, *Iron John: A Book About Men* (London: Element Books, 1991).

341   **Bly's success inspired:** See *Men's Resource Hotline Calendar*, 5, nos 1–3, The National Men's Resource Center, 1989; Trip Gabriel, 'Call of the Wildmen,' *The New York Times Magazine*, Oct. 14, 1990, p. 36; Phil McCombs, 'Men's Movement Stalks the Wild Side: Lessons in Primitivism,' *The Washington Post*, Feb. 3, 1991, p. F1.

342   **In New York City and Oakland:** Personal observation and interviews with staff at the Sterling Institute and participants in the weekend seminars, 1988.

342   **Bly's weekend retreats:** 'The Gender Rap,' *The New Republic*, April 16, 1990, p. 14.

342   **On Bly's retreat roster:** Chapple and Talbot, *Burning Desires*, p. 200.

342   **'I remember':** Robert Bly, *Pillow & the Key*, p. 2.

343   **'I see the phenomenon':** Robert Bly and Keith Thompson, 'What Men Really Want: A New Age Interview with Robert Bly,' *New Age*, May 1982, p. 30.

343   **'Men's societies are':** Bly, *Pillow & the Key*, pp. 13–14.

343   **Too many women:** *Ibid.*, p. 14.

343   **The single mother's son:** *Ibid.*, p. 2.

343   **To restore the nice:** *Ibid.*, p. 5.

343   **The young man:** *Ibid.*, p. 9.

343   **At Bly's all-male:** Jon Tevlin, 'Of Hawks and Men: A Weekend in the Male Wilderness,' *Utne Reader*, Nov.–Dec. 1989, p. 50.

344   **As he [Bliss] spoke:** *Ibid.*, pp. 53–4.

344   **'In two full days':** Trip Gabriel, 'Call of the Wildmen,' p. 37.

344   **'Men young and old':** Chapple and Talbot, *Burning Desires*, p. 189.

344   **When one of:** *Ibid.*

345   **Indeed, the Bly retreat:** *Ibid.*, pp. 187, 195–6.

345   **'What's the matter?':** Personal observation at Jung Center seminar, 1988. (Sub-

sequent quotes are from personal interview with Robert Bly and observations of the same event.)

346 **'I grew to understand'**: Personal interview with Sylvia Ann Hewlett, 1988.

346 **'In a profound way'**: Sylvia Ann Hewlett, *A Lesser Life: The Myth of Women's Liberation in America* (New York: Warner Books, 1986), pp. 208, 216.

346 **In one case**: *Ibid.*, pp. 202–3.

347 **'Women's liberation wants'**: Hewlett, *A Lesser Life*, p. 329; George Gilder, *Sexual Suicide* (New York: New York Times Book Co., 1973), p. 6.

347 **'I don't have'**: Personal interview with Sylvia Ann Hewlett, 1991.

347 **'The American [women's] movement'**: Hewlett, *Lesser Life*, p. 217.

347 **But most American women**; *Ibid.*, p. 216.

347 **By concentrating**: *Ibid.*, p. 179.

347 **Feminism 'threw the baby'**: *Ibid.*, p. 188.

347 **Hewlett's book proposal**: Personal interview with Sylvia Ann Hewlett, 1988.

348 **As a *Washington Post***: Beryl Lieff Benderly, 'Motherhood and the Fast Track,' *The Washington Post Book World*, April 6, 1986, p. 6.

348 **As Hewlett observes**: Hewlett, *A Lesser Life*, pp. 406, 413.

348 **'GALS ARE BEING HURT'**: Arline and Harold Brecher, 'Gals Are Being HURT – Not Helped – by Women's Lib,' *National Enquirer*, July 22, 1986, p. 32.

348 **Hewlett indicts**: *A Lesser Life* also claims that the infertility rate is climbing sharply, citing the 1982 French study published in *The New England Journal of Medicine*, which, as we have already seen, had been widely rejected by demographers by the time she was at work on her book. See *Lesser Life*, pp. 194, 443.

348 **'It is sobering'**: *Lesser Life*, p. 211.

348 **The majority of women**: *Ibid.*, pp. 208, 201.

348 **The only other**: *Ibid.*, p. 203.

349 **If she had checked**: By May 1987, the Harris Poll found that this figure had risen to 75 per cent. The Louis Harris Poll, April 1982, found 63 per cent support.

349 **According to a 1982**: The Gallup Poll, June 1982, pp. 139–41.

349 **But the ERA would have had**: Deborah L. Rhode, 'Equal Rights in Retrospect,' *Law & Inequality: A Journal of Theory and Practice*, 1, no. 1 (June 1983), 19–21; Wendy Kaminer, *A Fearful Freedom: Women's Flight from Equality* (Reading, Mass.: Addison-Wesley, 1990), p. 80; Catherine East, 'Critical Comments on *A Lesser Life*,' National Women's Political Caucus, unpublished paper, p. 27; Barbara R. Bergmann, *The Economic Emergence of Women* (New York: Basic Books, 1986), p. 153.

349 **These were men**: Rhode, 'Equal Rights in Retrospect,' p. 51.

349 **Hewlett's second charge**: Hewlett, *Lesser Life*, pp. 61, 66–7.

349 **The women's movement, she charges**: *Ibid.*, pp. 184, 190.

349 **The 'anti-children'**: *Ibid.*, p. 185.

350 **This negligence she contrasts**: *Ibid.*, pp. 143–4, 167–74.

350 **But in fact the European**: East, 'Critical Comments,' pp. 7–8.

350 **In the early 1970s**: Klein, *Gender Politics*, p. 24.

350 **Three of the eight**: *Sisterhood is Powerful: An Anthology of Writings from the Women's Liberation Movement*, ed. Robin Morgan, (New York: Vintage Books, 1970) pp. 576–7.

350 **When the Yankelovich**: Yankelovich Clancy Shulman poll, Oct. 23–25, 1989, for *Time*/CNN.

350 **(The Chamber triumphed)**: Alice H. Cook, 'Public Policies to Help Dual-Earner Families Meet the Demands of the Work World,' *Industrial and Labor Relations Review*, Jan. 1989, pp. 201–15.

351 **Hoping to bring**: Personal interview with Sylvia Ann Hewlett, 1988; Hewlett, *Lesser Life*, pp. 367–82.

351   **'It became this'**: Personal interview with Sylvia Ann Hewlett, 1988. (Subsequent quotes are also from the interview unless otherwise noted.)

351   **Like some of the**: Personal interview with Sylvia Ann Hewlett, 1988.

351   **She would later**: Hewlett, *Lesser Life*, p. 405.

352   **'I specifically invited'**: Personal interview with Sylvia Ann Hewlett, 1988.

352   **'Our failure was'**: Betty Friedan, *The Second Stage* (New York: Summit Books, 1981), p. 203.

352   **Not only that**: *Ibid.*, pp. 202–3; 244–5, 248, 254, 333–5, 337. Strangely, and as is often the case in this work, Friedan flatly contradicts herself on this very point on other pages. 'The women's movement,' she writes on page 247, 'was perhaps the first large-scale political application of the Beta style.'

352   **'Feminism, which once'**: Dinesh D'Souza, 'The New Feminist Revolt: This Time It's Against Feminism,' *Policy Review*, no. 35 (Winter 1986), 46.

352   **After *The New York Times Magazine***: Phyllis Schlafly, 'Betty Friedan and the Feminist Mystique,' *Phyllis Schlafly Report*, 19, no. 8 (March 1988), 3. (This issue of Schlafly's report also pounced on Lenore Weitzman's divorce figures and gleefully noted the new fluffiness of *Ms.* magazine.)

352   **Literary scholar Camille Paglia**: Camille Paglia, *Sexual Personae: Art and Decadence from Nefertiti to Emily Dickinson* (New Haven: Yale University Press, 1990); Francesca Stanfill, 'Woman Warrior,' *New York*, Mar. 4, 1991, p. 22; Camille Paglia and Neil Postman, 'She Wants Her TV! He Wants His Book,' *Harper's*, Mar. 1991, p. 44; 'A Scholar and a Not-so-Gentle Woman,' *Image, San Francisco Examiner*, July 7, 1991, p. 7.

353   **Formerly the media's favourite**: Germaine Greer, *The Female Eunuch* (London: MacGibbon & Kee, 1970), frontispiece.

353   **Greer herself billed**: Germaine Greer, *Sex and Destiny: The Politics of Human Fertility* (London: Secker & Warburg, 1984), pp. 94, 104–5, 243, 257.

353   **Clitoral orgasms are**: *Ibid.*, p. 253.

353   **By 1986, anti-feminist**: D'Souza, 'Feminist Pioneers,' p. 21.

354   ***Femininity* pondered such**: Susan Brownmiller, *Femininity* (London: Hamish Hamilton, 1984), p. 129.

354   **In her 1989 memoir**: Germaine Greer, *Daddy, We Hardly Knew You* (London: Hamish Hamilton, 1989), p. 12.

354   **Meanwhile, Brownmiller**: Susan Brownmiller, 'Hedda Nussbaum, Hardly a Heroine,' *New York Times*, Feb. 2, 1989, p. A25; Susan Brownmiller, *Waverly Place* (New York: Grove Press, 1989); Stefan Kanfer, 'Out to Make Killings: Crime Pays, At Least for Many Authors Who Write About It,' *Time*, Feb. 20, 1989, p. 98.

354   **Women of 'my generation'**: Erica Jong, 'Ziplash: A Sexual Libertine Recants,' *Ms.*, May 1989, p. 49.

355   **Yet here she was**: Friedan, *Second Stage*, pp. 31–2.

355   **'I don't use'**: Personal interview with Betty Friedan, 1989.

355   **Feminists, she says**: Friedan, *Second Stage*, p. 362.

355   **They shouldn't have devoted**: *Ibid.*, p. 257.

355   **(Her words recall)**: Gilder, *Men and Marriage*, pp, ix–x.

355   **They lost the ERA**: *Ibid.*, p. 207.

355   **'I do not think'**: *Ibid.*, p. 365.

355   **'Aging, in the right-wing'**: Judith Stacey, 'Are Feminists Afraid to Leave Home? The Challenge of Conservative Pro-family Feminism,' in *What Is Feminism? A Re-Examination*, ed. Juliet Mitchell and Ann Oakley (New York: Pantheon Books, 1986) p. 229.

356   **Friedan may say she 'easily'**: Friedan, *Second Stage*, p. 245.

356   **Much of the book is**: See, for example, *ibid.*, pp. 101–3. For a particularly 'I'-strewn passage, in a book that frowns on such 'masculine' ego-directed behaviour, see p. 28.

356   **In 1970 she retired as**: Marcia Cohen, *The Sisterhood* (New York: Simon & Schuster, 1988) pp. 273, 317, 336–7, 351.

357   **In this new stage she envisages:** Friedan, *Second Stage*, p. 230.
357   **'The power of':** *Ibid.*, p. 297.
357   **If men haven't:** *Ibid.*, p. 363.
357   **In the 'second stage':** *Ibid.*, pp. 333, 335, 343.
357   **To liberate themselves:** *Ibid.*, pp. 333–4.
357   **Friedan is convinced that:** *Ibid.*, p. 333.
357   **In one of the book's:** *Ibid.*, p. 334.
358   **Betty Friedan's: 'female machismo':** *Ibid.*, p. 56.
358   **Friedan sketches a grim:** *Ibid.*, pp. 113–14.
358   **She is reacting:** *Ibid.*, pp. 31, 45, 53.
358   **At times in the book:** *Ibid.*, p. 41.
358   **In the 1980s popular works:** Sally Helgesen, *The Female Advantage: Women's Ways of Leadership* (New York: Currency/Doubleday, 1990); Sara Ruddick, *Maternal Thinking: Toward a Politics of Peace* (Boston: Beacon Press, 1989).

359   **Suzanne Gordon, in her 1990:** Suzanne Gordon, *Prisoners of Men's Dreams: Striking Out for a New Feminine Future* (Boston: Little, Brown, 1991) pp. 12, 14. Gordon was not rejecting feminism. She made a distinction in her book between 'equal-opportunity' and 'transformative' feminism, the latter being the purer, non-commercial version, and defined herself as a supporter of the unadulterated variety. But this distinction was lost on the backlash press.

359   **In the late 1970s:** 'Relational' feminist scholarship has gone by other names, among them, 'neofeminism', 'social feminism' and 'difference feminism'. For convenience sake, I will refer to it here as the 'relational' school, an umbrella term meant to cover varying shades of feminist thought that have arisen out of this new emphasis on women's 'different' or 'special' status. For discussions of the rise of 'relational' scholarship and its diversity, see Joan C. Williams, 'Deconstructing Gender,' *Michigan Law Review*, 87 (February 1989), 797; Hester Eisenstein, *Contemporary Feminist Thought* (Boston: G.K. Hall, 1983), pp. xii, xviii–xix, 134–5; Ellen DuBois, 'Politics and Culture in Women's History,' *Feminist Studies*, 6, no. 1 (Spring 1980), 28; Wini Breines, Margaret Cerullo and Judith Stacey, 'Social Biology, Family Studies and Antifeminist Backlash,' *Feminist Studies*, 4 (Feb. 1978), 43. This preoccupation with sex differences also, of course, spilled over into the media, generating one cover story after another that played up the biological, rather than the cultural, barriers between the sexes. See, for example, Merrill McLoughlin, 'The New Debate Over Sex Differences: Men Vs. Women,' *US News and World Report*, Aug. 8, 1988, p. 50; Ethel S. Person, 'Some Differences Between Men and Women,' *The Atlantic Monthly*, Mar. 1988, p. 71; Laura Shapiro, 'Guns and Dolls: Scientists Explore the Differences Between Girls and Boys,' *Newsweek*, May 28, 1900, p. 56.

359   **By 1987 the American:** Barbara Reskin, 'Bringing the Men Back In,' *Gender & Society*, 2, no. 1 (March 1988), 76.
359   **'The task,' as she:** Miller, *Toward a New Psychology*, p. x.
360   **As feminist scholar Ellen DuBois:** DuBois, 'Politics and Culture,' p. 31.
360   **The eminent feminist scholar Alice:** Breines *et al.*, 'Social Biology,' p. 48.
360   **Women are willing to forgo:** DuBois, *et al.*, *Feminist Scholarship*, pp. 128–9; Elizabeth Wolgast, *Equality and the Rights of Women* (Ithaca: Cornell University Press, 1980).
361   **As one commentator noted:** Williams, 'Deconstructing Gender,' p. 803.
361   **Beyond academia:** 'Men's and Women's Reality – Making the Differences Count,' Candle Publishing press release, Sept. 30, 1988, p. 1.
361   **Even *Vogue*:** Kathleen Madden, 'Femininity: Do You Buy It?' *Vogue*, Mar. 1987, p. 445.
361   **In the media, *Ms.* named:** Lindsy Van Gelder, 'Carol Gilligan: Leader for a Different Kind of Future,' *Ms.*, Jan. 1984, p. 37; Francine Prose, 'Confident at 11, Confused at 16,' *The New York Times Magazine*, Jan. 7, 1990, p. 23.
361   **And when Radcliffe convened:** Heather R. McLeod, 'The Radcliffe Conferences: Women in the 21st Century, *Radcliffe Quarterly*, Sept. 1989, p. 11.

361 **Gilligan's work grew out**: Personal interview with Carol Gilligan, May 1991. (Subsequent Gilligan quotes are from personal interview unless otherwise noted.)

362 **Psychologist Lawrence Kohlberg**: Carol Gilligan, *In a Different Voice: Psychological Theory and Women's Development* (Cambridge, Mass.: Harvard University Press, 1982) p. 18).

362 **'The different voice'**: *Ibid.*, p. 2.

362 **'Clearly, these differences'**: *Ibid.*

363 **Jake says to steal**: *Ibid.*, p. 26.

363 **Amy waffles**: *Ibid.*, p. 28.

363 **Jake, Gilligan writes**: *Ibid.*, p. 26.

363 **Amy's reasoning, on the**: *Ibid.*, p. 29.

363 **Gilligan goes on**: *Ibid.*, p. 35.

363 **Gilligan's 'studies'**: *Ibid.*, pp. 2–3.

364 **'No effort was made'**: *Ibid.*, p. 3.

364 **In a written defence**: Carol Gilligan, 'Reply by Carol Gilligan,' from 'On *In A Different Voice*: An Interdisciplinary Forum,' *Signs*, 11, no. 21 (Winter 1986), 326, 328.

364 **While the young women**: Catherine G. Greeno and Eleanor E. Maccoby, 'How Different Is the "Different Voice"?' *Signs*, 11, no. 21 (Winter 1986), 313–14. These studies involve helping a stranger; research on which sex is more caring to friends and relatives has yet to be done. Other researchers who study sex differences have concluded that being cooperative or sympathetic – 'niceness', as it's been dubbed – is virtually the only human trait that is *not* significantly affected by genetics. See Deborah Franklin, 'The Making of a Personality: New Light on the Debate Over Nature vs. Nurture,' *San Francisco Examiner-Chronicle*, 'This World,' Sept. 17, 1989, p. 15.

364 **'If there is one statement'** Zella Luria, 'A Methodological Critique,' *Signs*, 11, no. 21 (Winter 1986), p. 318.

365 **The *New York Times Magazine*'s**: 'Confident at 11,' p. 25.

365 **'It seems almost philistine'**: Greeno and Maccoby, 'How Different,' p. 314.

365 **Newsweek used**: Salholz, 'Feminism's Identity Crisis,' p. 59.

365 **Anti-feminist scholars such as**: Levin, *Feminism and Freedom*, p. 38. Neoconservative writer George Gilder invokes Gilligan, too. See Gilder, *Men and Marriage*, pp. 169, 218.

365 **'Was it really?'** Davidson, *Failure of Feminism*, p. 230.

365 **'I am well aware'**: Gilligan, 'Reply by Carol Gilligan,' p. 333.

Chapter Twelve. It's All in Your Mind

369 **Inside the Center**: Personal observation and interviews with Melvyn Kinder and Connell Cowan, 1987. (Subsequent Kinder and Cowan quotes are from interview unless otherwise noted.)

370 **[Margaret Kent's book]**: Margaret Kent, *How to Marry the Man of Your Choice* (New York: Warner Books, 1988).

372 **Get 'power' by**: Dr Toni Grant, *Being a Woman: Fulfilling Your Femininity and Finding Love* (New York: Random House, 1988) pp. 157, 146, 16.

372 **Don't talk back**: *Ibid,*. p. 74.

373 **'Take charge'**: Dr Stephen and Susan Price, *No More Lonely Nights* (New York: G. P. Putnam's Sons, 1988), pp. 221, 68.

373 **The pseudo-feminist**: Judith Kurianksy, *Women Who Marry Down and End Up Having It All*, forthcoming from Doubleday from Fall 1989 Upcoming Publications List, p. 14.

373 **This is a view that**: Lynn Z. Bloom, Karen Coburn and Joan Pearlman, *The New Assertive Woman* (New York: Delacorte Press, 1975) pp. 23–42.

373 **The diagnosis was, underneath it all**: Chafe, *American Woman*, pp. 203–5.

373   **In the popular 1988**: Susan Page, *If I'm So Wonderful, Why Am I Still Single?* (London: Grafton Books, 1989) p. 8.

373   **'I want to accept'**: *Ibid.*

374   **'[L]ately it seems'**: Dr Connell Cowen and Dr Melvyn Kinder, *Smart Women/Foolish Choices* (London: Bantam Books, 1986), p. 6.

374   **It's not the men**: *Ibid.*, p. 37.

374   **Women are just**: *Ibid.*, p. 9.

374   **All would be well**: Dr Connell Cowen and Dr Melvyn Kinder, *Women Men Love/Women Men Leave* (London: Bantam Books, 1988), p. 182.

374   **Women would be happy**: Cowen and Kinder, *Smart Women*, pp. 250, 245.

374   **'Women could have'**: Personal interview with Dr Melvyn Kinder, 1987.

374   **But it is exactly**: Cowen and Kinder, *Smart Women*, p. 264.

375   **'You have been deeply influenced'**: Price and Price, *Lonely Nights*, p. 71.

375   **'These obsessive'**: Personal interview with Dr Stephen Price, 1988. (Subsequent quotes are from interview unless otherwise noted.)

375   **'We're both feminists'**: Personal interview with Susan Price. (Subsequent quotes are from interview unless otherwise noted.)

376   **They advise women to 'deal with your'**: Price and Price, *Lonely Nights*, pp. 23, 611.

376   **'It's Up to You to'**: *Ibid.*, p. 207.

379   **More than a year**: Susan Faludi, 'Addicted to Love,' *West Magazine*, *San Jose Mercury News*, Nov. 29, 1987, p. 6.

379   **In 1987, when**: *Ibid.*

379   **Then excerpts from**: Robin Norwood, *Letters From Women Who Love Too Much* (London: Arrow Books, 1989): see Bernice Andrews, 'A Kind of Loving,' *Guardian*, May 23, 1989.

380   **'Many, many of us'**: Robin Norwood, *Women Who Love Too Much: When You Keep Wishing and Hoping He'll Change* (London: Arrow Books, 1986), p. 2.

380   **Instead of encouraging**: *Ibid.*, pp. 239, 43, 211.

380   **'Spiritual practice calms you'**: *Ibid.*, pp. 210–11; taped lecture by Norwood in San Francisco, 1987.

381   **'I feel it was'**: Personal interview with Robin Norwood, 1987; Faludi, 'Addicted to Love,' p. 35.

381   **'Oh, it isn't me'**: James, *The Bostonians*, pp. 69–70.

381   **It helped to double**: It rose from an estimated 5 to 8 million in 1976 to 12 to 15 million in 1988. See Patricia Leigh Brown, 'Troubled Millions Heed Call of Self-Help Groups,' *New York Times*, July 16, 1988, p. 1.

381   *The professional medical*: Kathleen Bell Unger, 'Chemical Dependency in Women,' *The Western Journal of Medicine*, Dec. 1988, p. 747.

381   **(The individual)**: Wendy Kaminer, 'Chances Are You're Co-Dependent Too,' *The New York Times Book Review*, Feb. 11, 1990, p. 1.

382   **'The codependency movement may'**: Audrey Gartner and Frank Riessman, Letters column, *The New York Times Book Review*, March 18, 1990, p. 34.

382   **Norwood herself compared**: Personal interview with Robin Norwood, 1987.

382   **As feminist writer Charlotte Perkins**: Ann J. Lane, *To Herland and Beyond: The Life and Work of Charlotte Perkins Gilman* (New York: Pantheon Books, 1990), p. 121.

382   **As *Ms.*'s 1972 guide**: 'A Guide to Consciousness-Raising,' *Ms.*, July 1972, reprinted in *Women's Liberation in the Twentieth Century*, ed. Mary Lynn (New York: John Wiley, 1975), pp. 111–18.

383   **'Most of the women'**: Anna Gilchrist, quoted in 'Are You *Addicted* To Love?' by Liz Hodgkinson, *She*, Feb. 1990.

383   **Research by research psychologist**: 'A Kind of Loving.'

384   **'I'm like a mother'**: Personal interview and observations, 1987.

385   **For more than a year**: Personal interview with publicist in Pocket Books' publicity department, 1987.

385 **As Judith Staples:** Personal interview with Judith Staples, 1987.
386 **Norwood's congregants:** *Ibid.*
386 **'It was an inside job':** Taped lecture by Norwood in San Francisco, 1987.
387 **Just like 'Pam':** Norwood, *Love Too Much*, pp. 149–56, 1–5, 262–71.
387 **'I never claimed':** Personal interview with Robin Norwood, 1987; Faludi, 'Addicted to Love,' p. 36.
387 **In the spring of:** *Ibid.*
388 **Her daily life there, she reports:** *Ibid.*
388 **'The heart of [consciousness]':** Hester Eisenstein, *Contemporary Feminist Thought* (Boston: G. K. Hall, 1983), p. 37.
388 **As psychoanalyst:** Susan Quinn, *A Mind of Her Own: The Life of Karen Horney* (New York: Addison-Wesley, 1988), p. 14.
389 **That year, Dr Teresa Bernardez:** Personal interview with Dr Teresa Bernardez, 1988.
389 **'Premenstrual dysphoric':** Constance Holden, 'Proposed New Psychiatric Diagnoses Raise Charges of Gender Bias,' *Science*, Jan. 24, 1986, p. 327.
389 **This was obvious:** Herb Kutchins and Stuart A. Kirk, 'The Future of DSM: Scientific and Professional Issues,' *The Harvard Mental Health Letter*, Sept. 1988, pp. 4–6.
389 **They included anyone who:** Dr Frederick Kass, 'Self-Defeating Personality Disorder: An Empirical Study,' *Journal of Personality Disorders*, 1, no. 2 (Summer 1987), 168–73.
390 **The APA panel included these traits:** *Ibid.*, p. 170; Thomas A. Widiger, 'The Self-Defeating Personality Disorder,' *Journal of Personality Disorders*, 1, no. 2 (Summer 1987), 157–9.
390 **The panel illustrated:** Widiger, 'Self-Defeating,' p. 159.
391 **The panel was dominated by:** Bruce Bower, 'The Diagnostic Dilemma,' *Science News*, 135 (Feb. 25, 1989), 120.
391 **The masochism disorder's backers:** Nearly half of psychologists are women, compared with less than 10 per cent of psychiatrists. In surveys within the profession, psychiatrists were expressing increasing displeasure and anxiety as competition from more affordable therapists and counsellors caused their earnings to drop. See 'Unhappy People,' *San Francisco Chronicle*, May 23, 1990, p. A22.
391 **As APA vice-president:** Deborah Franklin, 'The Politics of Masochism,' *Psychology Today*, Jan. 1987, p. 53.
391 **'The anger we':** Personal interview with Dr Teresa Bernardez, 1988.
391 **It wasn't until:** Paula J. Caplan, *The Myth of Women's Masochism* (New York: Signet, 1985), p. 257.
391 **And the mostly male:** Personal interviews with Lynne Rosewater, director of the Feminist Therapy Institute, who attended the meeting, 1988; personal interview with Dr Robert Spitzer, 1989.
391 **Then he revealed:** F. Kass, R. A. MacKinnon and R. L. Spitzer, 'Masochistic Personality: An Empirical Study, *American Journal of Psychiatry*, 143, no. 2 (1986), 216–18.
392 **One of the feminist:** Personal interview with Lynne Rosewater, 1988.
392 **The APA panel's 'data':** Dr Richard C. Simons, 'Self-Defeating and Sadistic Personality Disorders: Needed Additions to the Diagnostic Nomenclature,' *Journal of Personality Disorders*, 1, no. 2 (1987), 161–7; Franklin, 'Politics of Masochism,' p. 57.
392 **The poll, however:** Paula J. Caplan, 'The Psychiatric Association's Failure to Meet Its Own Standards,' *Journal of Personality Disorders*, 1, no. 2 (Summer 1987), 178.
392 **Next, psychological researcher:** Lenore E. A. Walker, 'Inadequacies of the Masochistic Personality Disorder Diagnosis for Women,' *Journal of Personality Disorders*, 1, no. 2 (Summer 1987), 183.
393 **'It's irrelevant':** Personal interview with Dr Robert Spitzer, 1989.

393   'I didn't think': Personal interview with Dr Paul Fink, 1989.
393   The female therapists again: Caplan, *Women's Masochism*, pp. 259-61.
394   As a senior APA: *Ibid.*, p. 270.
394   'I began to speak': Personal interview with Dr Teresa Bernardez, 1988.
394   When Bernardez's term on the: Personal interviews with Dr Paul Fink, 1989, Dr Teresa Bernardez, 1988. Asked about the purge of the feminists from the committee on women, APA president Dr Paul Fink says: 'I think that human nature says if you're having a lot of trouble with some groups then you might think twice, more carefully, about who[m] you appoint.' Asked about Bernardez specifically, he says: 'There's one of them I can think of [whose tenure he did not want to see continued]. I won't say her name. I think her time was up.' Then he adds: 'Nothing you've heard has any validity in terms of our going out of our way to disenfranchise people. People whose time was up just couldn't be reappointed.'
394   In this case, however: Caplan, *Women's Masochism*, pp. 270-1; Robert Spitzer and Janet Williams, *A Guide to DSM-III-R* (Washington, DC: American Psychiatric Association, 1987), p. 15.

Chapter Thirteen. The Wages of the Backlash

397   Newspaper editorials applauded: See, for example, '70 Percent of a Man,' editorial, *San Jose Mercury News*, Feb. 7, 1988, p. P8.
397   Women working full time: US Bureau of Census, Current Population Reports, Consumer Income, Series P-60, no. 157, 1987.
397   The press got the 70-cent figure: 'Male–Female Differences in Work Experience, Occupations, and Earnings: 1984,' US Bureau of Census, Current Population Reports, Series P-70, no. 10, Aug. 1987; personal interviews with statisticians at the Census Bureau and the Bureau of Labor Statistics, 1988. See also 'Briefing Paper on the Wage Gap,' National Committee on Pay Equity, Sept. 18, 1987. That same year, the US Office of Personnel Management was also promoting its own 'good news' on the wage gap for federal employees – through similar data fudging. This agency 'adjusted' the figures to reflect a spurious claim that full-time working women work many fewer hours than men, and they claimed the rest of the gap could be explained away by such factors as geography and 'personal choices'. Through these sleights of hand, federally employed women were now suddenly said to be earning 75 cents to a man's dollar. The actual figure was 69 cents, a paltry 3 cent improvement on 1976. See 'Comparable Worth for Federal Jobs: A Wrong Turn Off the Road Toward Pay Equity and Women's Career Advancement,' US Office of Personnel Management, Washington, DC, Sept. 1987.
397   By that year: US Bureau of Census, Current Population Reports, Consumer Income, Series P-60, no. 157, 1987.
397   And as much as . . . : Mishel and Frankel, *The State of Working America*, pp. 83-5, 105; 'Briefing Paper no. 1: The Wage Gap,' National Committee on Pay Equity.
397   By 1988 women with a college: 'Average Earnings of Year-Round Full-Time Workers by Sex and Educational Attainment, 1987,' US Bureau of Census, Table 35, Feb. 1989; US Bureau of the Census, Current Population Reports, Consumer Income, Series P-60, no. 166, 1988. For data on older women, see James P. Smith and Michael Ward, 'Women in the Labor Market and in the Family,' *Journal of Economic Perspectives*, 3, no. 1 (Winter 1989), 10.
397   In Britain, according to: 'The Pay Gap Between Men and Women in 1991,' Low Pay Unit, 1991.
397   Full-time women still earn: Tony Blair MP and Jo Richardson MP, 'A Woman's Lot: Poverty and Inequality in Women's Pay,' Labour Party, 1991, p. 5.
397   Three-quarters of the workers: *Ibid.*, p. 15.

397 **Equal pay legislation**: *Beyond the Barriers: the State, the Economy and Women's Employment 1984–1990*, National Advisory Council on the Employment of Women (Wellington, 1990), p. 84.

397 **In Australia**: Information from Eva Cox, Distaff consultancy, Camperdown, NSW, Australia.

398 **While the level of**: Cynthia Taeuber and Victor Valdisera, 'Women in the American Economy,' US Bureau of the Census, Current Population Reports, Special Studies, Series P-23, no. 146, pp. 21–3; *American Woman 1990–91*, p. 358; O'Neill, *Everyone Was Brave*, p. 148; *Women's Work, Men's Work: Sex Segregation on the Job*, ed. Barbara F. Reskin and Heidi I. Hartmann (Washington, DC: National Academy Press, 1986) pp. 32–3. Between 1900 and 1960 occupational segregation remained the same. A 1986 study of 61,000 workers found that only 10 per cent had job assignments that were held by both men and women. See William T. Bielby and James N. Baron, 'Sex Segregation Within Occupations,' *American Economic Review*, May 1986, pp. 43–7.

398 **A resegregating work force**: Bennett Harrison and Barry Bluestone, *The Great U-Turn* (New York: Basic Books, 1988), Table A.2, p. 199. Bizarrely, their findings were reported in one press article under this inappropriate headline: 'Women Are Beginning to Make Big Gains In the Workplace.' See Carol Kleiman, *San Francisco Examiner*, Jan. 15, 1989, p. 27.

398 **The already huge proportion**: Nancy Barrett, 'Women and the Economy,' *American Woman 1987–88*, p. 119. The 40 per cent figure is from 1982. The following year the Labor Department changed this job classification, so it's not possible to compare this group of workers after 1983.

398 **By the late 1980s**: *American Woman 1990–91*, p. 385.

398 **A long list of**: The secretarial pool, for example, went from 98.9 per cent female in 1979 to 99.2 in 1986. See 'Male-Female Differences,' p. 5.

398 **In Britain, according to**: 'Putting Equality into Practice,' a Shadow Ministry of Women consultation document, Labour Party, 1991.

398 **The worst-paying occupations**: 'A Woman's Lot, Poverty and Inequality in Women's Pay,' p. 14.

398 **Australia has a highly**: Alison Carter, 'Behind the Myth of Women's Equality', *Australian Financial Review*, Dec. 20, 1991.

398 **In New Zealand**: *Women in New Zealand*, Department of Statistics and Ministry of Women's Affairs (Wellington, 1990), p. 62.

399 **In the US, black women**: Personal interview with Natalie J. Sokoloff, sociology professor at John Jay College of Criminal Justice, City University of New York, 1991; Natalie J. Sokoloff, 'Are Professions Becoming Disintegrated? An Analysis of Detailed Professional Occupations by Race and Gender,' unpublished paper, Aug. 1989; Natalie J. Sokoloff, 'The Gender/Race Interaction: Toward a More Complex View of Black Women in the Professions,' unpublished paper, Aug. 1990; Natalie J. Sokoloff's study is forthcoming in *Black and White Women in the Professions, 1960–1980: An Analysis of Changes in Job Segregation by Race and Gender* (Winchester, Mass.: Unwin Hyman).

399 **Between 1976 and 1986**: 'Comparable Worth for Federal Jobs'; unpublished data from US Office of Personnel Management; Susanna Downie, 'Decade of Achievement: 1977–1987,' The National Women's Conference Center, May 1988, p. 37. The lowest rungs are grades 1–8.

399 **In 1988 in the UK**: Jo Richardson MP, 'A New Ministry for Women', Labour Party, 1991, p. 14.

399 **And even though, in the law profession**: Lesley Abdela, 'It Is Like Waiting for Fish to Grow Feet,' *Independent*, Sept. 25, 1991.

399 **In the end, the *Guardian***: Edi Smockum, 'Putting Women in Their Place,' *Guardian*, Dec. 3, 1991, p. 33.

399 **A 1991 survey**: 'What the Statistics Say,' *Guardian* Women, Oct. 22, 1991.

400 **In 1991, Australia's**: Alison Carter, 'Behind the Myth of Women's Equality', *Australian Financial Review*, Dec. 20, 1991.

400   **And in New Zealand**: *Women in New Zealand*, p. 119.

400   **As a job-integration study**: Barbara Reskin, 'Occupational Resegregation,' in *American Woman 1988–89*, pp. 258, 263; personal interview with Barbara Reskin, sociology professor at University of Illinois, 1988. I am grateful to Barbara Reskin for sharing her research and several chapters of *Job Queues, Gender Queues: Explaining Women's Movement into Male Dominated Occupations*, by Barbara Reskin and Patricia Roos, forthcoming, Temple University Press.

400   **Other studies**: Chloe E. Bird, 'High Finance, Small Change: Women in Back Management', unpublished paper, Jan. 1989; Myra H. Strober and Carolyn L. Arnold, 'The Dynamics of Occupational Segregation Among Bank Tellers,' in *Gender in the Workplace*, ed. Clair Brown and Joseph A. Pechman (Washington, DC: The Brookings Institution, 1987) pp. 107–57.

400   **And still another**: Smith, 'Impact of the Reagan Years,' pp. 4, 12–13.

400   **Professional athletes**: 'Employment and Earnings: 1983 Annual Averages,' US Department of Labor, Bureau of Labor Statistics, Jan. 1984; 'Employment and Earnings: 1988 Annual Averages,' US Department of Labor, Bureau of Labor Statistics, Jan. 1989; William T. Bielby and Denise D. Bielby, 'The 1987 Hollywood Writer's Report: Unequal Access, Unequal Pay,' The Writers Guild of America West, Hollywood, Calif., 1989; 'The Female in Focus: In Whose Image?: A Statistical Survey of the Status of Women in Film, Television and Commercials,' Screen Actors Guild, Inc., Hollywood, Calif., Aug. 1, 1990; EEO-1 Employment Analysis Report Program, 'Producers, Orchestras and Entertainment,' Nationwide Summaries, 1987, 1984, 1981. (It should be pointed out that the EEO-1 reports probably understate women's declining status. These figures are based on the corporations' own equal opportunity reports to the federal government, and, as subsequent audits have found, these corporate self-reports have frequently exaggerated the numbers of women and minorities hired. During the Reagan years this tendency toward embellishment got far worse – as the administration scaled down monitoring and enforcement of affirmative action and turned a blind eye to companies that inflated hiring data.)

400   **Under Reagan, women's progress**: Marc Leepson, 'Women in the Military,' The Women's Movement: Agenda for the '80s, Editorial Research Reports (Washington, DC: Congressional Quarterly, 1981) pp. 83–100; Robert Landers, 'Should Women Be Allowed in Combat?' Editorial Research Reports, Congressional Quarterly, 2, no. 14 (Oct. 13, 1989), 570–82.

401   **After 1983**: 'Employment of Women in Nontraditional Jobs, 1983–88,' US Department of Labor, Bureau of Labor Statistics, Report 756, second quarter 1988.

401   **By 1988, the tiny proportions**: 'Employment and Earnings: 1983'; 'Employment and Earnings: 1988'; 'Male–Female Differences,' Table G, p. 5; *American Woman, 1990–91*, Table 19, p. 358.

401   **'Virtually all large'**: Peggy Simpson, 'Why the Backlash is a Big Bust,' *Working Woman*, Nov. 1986, p. 164.

401   **Discrimination was dropping**: Gretchen Morgenson 'Watch That Leer, Stifle That Joke,' *Forbes*, May 15, 1989, p. 69.

401   **Women's sex discrimination**: Statistics from the Equal Opportunity Commission. A 1988 survey by the Merit Systems Protection Board found 42 per cent of federally employed women said they had been sexually harassed. A 1988 US Navy survey the same year found more than half of women in the Navy were victims of sexual harassment.

402   **Australia's Sex Discrimination**: 'Human Rights and Equal Opportunity Commission Annual Report,' 1989–90, pp. 75, 82.

402   **Case studies, Bryce says**: Quentin Bryce, AO, 'Challenges for the 1990s – Employment Discrimination,' Occasional Papers from the Sex Discrimination Commissioner, no. 3.

402   **In Britain, as journalist**: Angela Phillips, 'The Salary Scandal: Are You a Victim?', *Options*, Dec. 1991, p. 104.

403   **But even with all the discouragements**: 'Industrial Tribunal Statistics,' *Employment Gazette*, April 1990, p. 214; 'Industrial Tribunals – An Update,' *Employment Gazette*, May 1991, p. 304.

403   **At the same time that**: 'Equal Employment Opportunity: EEOC and State Agencies Did Not Fully Investigate Discrimination Charges,' US General Accounting Office, Oct. 1988; Report on the EEOC by the House Education and Labor Committee, 1986; Reskin and Hartmann, *Women's Work/Men's Work*, p. 86.

404   **In the early 1970s**: In 1969 the Federal Communications Commission first added sex to its anti-discrimination rules. In 1970, NOW petitioned the FCC for affirmative action reports and challenged broadcast licences under the Fairness Doctrine. The legal challenge failed, but in 1971, for the first time ever, the FCC began requiring broadcasters seeking licences to file affirmative action reports on female employees. Women in journalism organized and filed sex-discrimination suits, FCC and EEOC complaints, and negotiated favourable settlements involving almost every major national news outlet in the country, including all three networks, the *New York Times*, the *Washington Post*, *Newsweek*, *Newsday*, The Associated Press, *Time* and *Reader's Digest*.

404   **Under his tenure, the FCC**: Downie, 'Decade of Achievement,' p. 52; 'Numbers Not There for Employment of Women, Wilson Says,' *Media Report to Women*, 16, no. 2 (March–April 1988), 11.

404   **'Eighty per cent of'**: Janice Castro, 'Women in Television: An Uphill Battle,' *Channels*, Jan. 1988, p. 42.

404   **The networks took**: A 1988 study of network anchors by the Gannett Center for Media Studies, which tracked anchors over three years, found that the men had become greyer and older, the women blonder and younger. See Edwin Diamond, 'New-Girl Network,' *New York*, June 10, 1991, p. 20.

404   **In 1989, at the ripe**: Harry F. Waters, 'If It Ain't Broke, Break It,' *Newsweek*, March 26, 1990, p. 58.

405   **'Paula's married'**: Jennet Conant, 'Broadcast Networking,' *Working Woman*, Aug. 1989, p. 58.

405   **By 1983, the number**: Vernon A. Stone, 'Newswomen's Numbers Level Off,' *RTNDA Communicator*, July 1984, p. 22; *Media Report to Women*, May–June 1988, p. 5; Terri Schultz-Brooks, 'Getting There: Women in the Newsroom,' *Columbia Journalism Review*, March–April 1984, p. 25.

405   **By 1989 only eight**: Judy Southworth, 'Women Media Workers: No Room at the Top,' *Extra!*, March–April 1991, p. 6.

405   **In the UK, female newsreaders**: Gillian Dyer, 'Women and Television: an Overview,' in *Boxed In: Women and Television*, ed. Helen Baehr and Gillian Dyer (London: Pandora Press, 1987), p. 8.

405   *Skill Search*: *Skill Search: Television, Film and Video Industry Employment Patterns and Training Needs, Part 1: The Key Facts*, by Carol Varlaam, Richard Pearson, Patricia Leighton and Scott Blum (University of Sussex: Institute of Manpower Studies, 1989), pp. 9, 28.

405   **Although women make up**: Lisa Buckingham, 'The Distorted Picture of Women in Television', *Guardian*, July 24, 1990, p. 10.

405   **Despite initiatives like**: Information from Maggie Sanson, Director, Joint Board for Film Industry Training.

405   **Margaret Gallagher**: Quoted by Rowena Evans, 'Women At the Top of a Man's World,' *Television Business International*, March 1990, p. 44.

406   **The *Today* newspaper**: *Today*, Oct. 12, 1990.

406   ***Broadcast* magazine reported**: Peter Goodwin, 'Some Are More Equal Than Others,' *Broadcast*, Nov. 1, 1991.

406   **Progress in improving**: 'The Changing Face of the Newsroom,' *American Society of Newspaper Editors (ASNE) Bulletin*, May 1989, p. 28.

407   **At the *Washington Post*:** Statistics from the Washington-Baltimore Newspaper Guild; 'Complaint of Unlawful Discriminatory Employment Practices,' *The Washington-Baltimore Newspaper Guild v. The Washington Post*, No. 88-540-P, July 12, 1988.

407   **While the *New York Times*'s:** Statistics from the *New York Times* Women's Caucus and the Newspaper Guild. By the end of the decade, the *New York Times*'s top executives apparently decided it was wiser to keep women in the dark on salary differences. When the *Times*'s Women's Caucus pressed for the numbers, the paper's management told them it wasn't releasing the figures any more because it was 'too expensive' to collect them. See Emily Weiner, 'Status of Women in the Professions: Media & the Arts,' Committee on Women Hearing, Council of the City of New York, March 16, 1989, p. 2.

407   **After having reached:** Dorothy Jurney, 'Tenth Annual Survey Reports Women Editors at 12.4 Percent,' *American Society of Newspaper Editors (ASNE) Bulletin*, Nov. 1986, p. 5.

407   **Despite this pathetic:** 'ASNE Panelists Poles Apart on Status of Women Journalists,' *Media Report to Women*, 16, no. 3 (May–June 1988), 1.

407   **The numbers of:** Data from studies by Jean Gaddy Wilson, journalism professor and research fellow of University of Missouri Journalism School; Jean Gaddy Wilson, 'Taking Stock: Women in the Media,' speech, Dec. 1988; *The Changing Face of the Newsroom*, ed. Lee Stinnett, American Society of Newspaper Editors, special report, May 1989, pp. 19, 27–8.

408   **At NBC, two female:** Personal interview with Janice Goodman, attorney who handled the NBC suit, 1988.

408   **At the *New York Times*:** Personal interview with Betsy Wade, 1988.

408   **'There's apparently':** Betsy Wade, 'From Lawsuits to Caucuses: Promoting Women in the Newsroom,' Women in American Journalism lectures, Graduate School of Journalism, University of California at Berkeley, Dec. 1988, p. 16.

408   **'The group's response':** K. Kaufmann, 'Since When Is Feminism So Unfashionable?' *Mediafile*, Dec.–Jan. 1987–88, p. 3.

409   **Soon afterwards, in September:** Judy Flander, 'Women in Network News,' *Washington Journalism Review*, March 1985, p. 39.

409   **After a while:** *Ibid.*, p. 40.

409   **It had the worst record:** Diane Landis, 'Women from ABC Air Grievances,' *Washington Woman*, March 1986, p. 13; Bob Brewin, 'ABC's Trouble with Women,' *The Village Voice*, Feb. 11, 1986, p. 46.

409   **In 1983 Rita Flynn:** Personal interview with Rita Flynn, 1989. (Subsequent Flynn quotes are from interview unless otherwise noted.)

410   **ABC management made only:** Brewin, 'ABC's Trouble,' p. 46.

410   **Cecily Coleman:** Flander, 'Network News,' p. 39; Marlene Sanders and Marcia Rock, *Waiting for Prime Time* (Urbana: University of Illinois Press, 1989) pp. 150–1. (ABC officials declined to discuss this case or the other grievances raised by the women's committee.)

410   **'It was like':** Flander, 'Network News,' p. 39.

410   **Soon the committee's spokeswoman:** Berwin, 'ABC's Trouble,' p. 46.

411   **While 146,000 American women were:** 'Employment and Earnings, 1990,' US Department of Labor, Bureau of Labor Statistics, Jan. 1991, Table 22, Current Population Survey. (Retail trade expanded by about 5 million jobs in the 1980s).

411   **American saleswomen suffer:** Bergmann, *Economic Emergence*, p. 72.

411   **The average female sales assistant:** *Ibid.*

411   **The result: women selling clothing:** Barrett, 'Women and the Economy,' p. 122.

411   **The Commission had received:** Personal interview with James P. Scanlan, litigation attorney on the Sears case, US Equal Employment Opportunity Commission, 1988.

412   **The average salesman:** Ruth Milkman, 'Women's History and the Sears Case,' *Feminist Studies*, 12, no. 2 (Summer 1986) 374–400.

412   **The agency calculated that:** Plaintiff's Pretrial Brief – Commission Sales Issues,

revised Nov. 19, 1984, *EEOC v. Sears*, p. 4; Closing arguments, *EEOC v. Sears*, June 28, 1985, p. 18958.

412   **By the end of the 1970s:** Reskin and Hartman, *Women's Work*, pp. 91–3.

413   **As soon as Sears:** Closing arguments, *EEOC v. Sears*, June 28, 1985, p. 18958; Alice Kessler-Harris, 'Academic Freedom and Expert Witnessing,' *Texas Law Review*, 67:429 (1988), 429–40.

413   **A Sears personnel manager:** Written testimony of Rex Rambo, *EEOC v. Sears*, pp. 8433, 8439, 8437, 6.

413   **'It does require':** Testimony of Ed Michaels, *EEOC v. Sears*, pp. 12071, 12085–6.

413   **And Ray Graham:** Testimony of Ray Graham, *EEOC v. Sears*, Feb. 19, 1985, p. 8537.

413   **The company's hiring:** Testimony of Ray Graham, *EEOC v. Sears*, Feb. 19, 1985, p. 8432.

413   **All applicants for:** 'Psychological Tests – For Use in Sears Retail Stores,' Plaintiff's Exhibit 113, *EEOC v. Sears*, p. 4.

414   **Though Sears told:** Closing arguments, *EEOC v. Sears*, June 28, 1985, p. 18970. Sears did make some cosmetic alterations in its revised test manual in 1973, such as changing the title for the section on commission sales from 'Big Ticket Salesmen' to 'Big Ticket Salespeople'.

414   **But in Rosenberg's testimony:** Barbara Winkler, 'Scholars' Conflict in Sears Sex-Bias Case Sets Off War in Women's History,' *Chronicle of Higher Education*, Feb. 5, 1986, p. 8.

414   **'Many women choose jobs':** 'Offer of Proof Concerning the Testimony of Rosalind Rosenberg,' March 11, 1985, reprinted in *Signs*, Summer 1986, pp. 761, 762.

415   **But at Sears:** Closing arguments, p. 18992.

415   **Rosenberg was initially drawn:** Personal interview with Rosalind Rosenberg, 1989.

415   **'My gut personal':** *Ibid.* (Subsequent quotations are from interview unless otherwise specified.)

416   **'This is not an argument':** Personal interview with Alice Kessler-Harris, 1989.

416   **For example, Rosenberg:** Testimony of Rosalind Rosenberg, *EEOC v. Sears*, June 22, 1985, pp. 18284–5. Nonetheless, in the press, efforts by such feminist scholars as Kessler-Harris to defend their own work from misrepresentation were presented as an attack on *Rosenberg*'s academic freedom. In the *Washington Post*, for example, columnist Jonathan Yardley complained that Rosenberg was being 'maliciously vilified' by 'feminist thought-control wardens'. 'They may call it feminism but it sounds for all the world like totalitarianism,' he wrote. 'One can only wonder how well these people sleep at night.' See Jonathan Yardley, 'When Scholarship and the Cause Collide,' *Washington Post*, June 16, 1986, Style section, p. 2.

416   **With words that:** Memorandum of Points and Authorities in Support of Defendant's Motion to Dismiss, *EEOC v. Sears*, p. 15; Memorandum in Support of Defendant's Motion to Reconsider Order Denying Defendant's Motion to Dismiss Or, in the Alternative, to Reopen Discovery on Conflicts of Interest Issue, *EEOC v. Sears*, pp. 2, 4; Closing arguments, p. 19059; Defendant's Interrogatories, *EEOC v. Sears*, pp. 17–21; Plaintiff's Opposition to Defendant's Motion to Reconsider Order Denying Defendant's Motion to Dismiss, *EEOC v. Sears*, pp. 60, 52–4, 57–8.

417   **When Sears's lawyers:** Plaintiff's Opposition to Defendant's Motion to Reconsider Order Denying Defendant's Motion to Dismiss, *EEOC v. Sears*, pp. 28–30.

417   **The whole fishing:** *Ibid.*, pp. 26–35.

417   **Sears even submitted:** Reply Brief of Cross-Appellant, Sears, Roebuck and Co., *EEOC v. Sears*, p. 17.

417   **The trial judge:** Decision of US Court of Appeals Judge Harlington Wood, Jr, nos 86-1519 and 86-1621, pp. 104–10; personal interview with Charles Morgan,

Jr, 1989. In this interview and elsewhere, Morgan has said he supports the goals of the women's movement. But his courtroom and press pronouncements suggest a less friendly view of feminism's influence: 'My heavens, what did the pill do?' he erupted at one point in closing arguments. 'Said to women, you can determine when you want to have a child. . . . You don't have to have children at all. You can devote and dedicate yourself to a career.' In the media he expressed displeasure with efforts to apply landmark civil rights laws to women. 'The government has to get its priorities straight,' he complained to the *New York Times*. 'There's just no equation between minorities and women. . . . Look I know who the 13th, 14th and 15th amendments were intended for.' See Closing arguments, *EEOC v. Sears*, p. 19093; Milkman, 'Women's History,' p. 379.

418   **Far from desiring:** Personal interview with James P. Scanlan, 1988.

418   **A high-ranking:** Juan Williams, 'Despite Class-Action Doubts, EEOC Presses Sears Bias Case,' *Washington Post*, July 9, 1985, p. A1.

418   **'I've been trying to get out':** *Ibid.*

418   **Thomas maintained that:** Juan Williams, 'A Question of Fairness,' *The Atlantic Monthly*, Feb. 1987, p. 70.

418   **Thomas was, in fact:** Williams, 'Despite Class-Action Doubts.'

418   **'It was very bizarre':** Personal interview with Karen Baker, 1988.

418   **If women weren't working in:** Decision of Judge John Nordberg, Jan. 31, 1986, *EEOC v. Sears*, 628 F. Supp. 1264 (N.D. Ill. 1986), p. 1306.

419   **'I was after commission':** Personal interview with Lura Lee Nader, 1988. (Subsequent quotations are from interview unless otherwise noted.)

419   **'I needed to get out':** Trial transcript, p. 16466.

419   **Alice Howland, the other woman:** Personal interview with Alice Howland, 1988. (Subsequent quotations are from interview unless otherwise noted.)

421   **In an admittedly:** Personal interviews conducted in Sears store, San Francisco, 1988. (All of these women have since lost their jobs. By the end of the decade, with profits plunging, the retailer cut back its work force and shut down a handful of stores, including the San Francisco outlet.)

422   **In the backlash decade, as:** 'Employment and Earnings,' US Department of Labor, Bureau of Labor Statistics, Annual averages, 1983–1988. And in a cruelly ironic development, many of the major retailers, from Sears to Nordstrom, began requiring their mostly female clerks to work on commission in the *small-ticket* 'ladies' ' departments – where commission pay yielded *less* than straight wages because of the low price tags on the merchandise handled in these departments. See Susan Faludi, 'Sales Job: At Nordstrom Stores, Service Comes First – But at a Big Price,' *The Wall Street Journal*, Feb. 20, 1990, p. A1.

423   **'Women are far more':** Personal interview with Mary Ellen Boyd, executive director of Non-Traditional Employment for Women, 1987.

423   **Diane Joyce arrived:** Personal interview with Diane Joyce, 1987. (Subsequent Joyce quotations from interview unless otherwise noted.) See also Susan Faludi, 'What Women Are Up Against in the Fight for Equal Pay,' *West Magazine, San Jose Mercury News*, Sept. 27, 1987, p. 18.

425   **One day, the stockroom storekeeper:** Personal interview with Tony Laramie, 1987; personal interview with Diane Joyce, 1987.

425   **At a construction site:** Mary Ellen Boyd and Elizabeth Edman, 'Women in Non-Traditional Employment,' unpublished 1987 paper, p. 20; personal interview with Mary Ellen Boyd, 1987.

425   **'It's pervasive':** Personal interview with John Longabaugh, 1987.

425   **A maintenance worker:** Faludi, 'What Women Are Up Against,' pp. 20–1.

426   **Another new woman:** *Ibid.*

426   **They got similarly:** The county's 'Rule of Seven' hiring policy mandates that the applicants with the top seven scores be treated as equally qualified for the job, because the differences in the top scores are usually minimal. Later in the press, Johnson would nonetheless make much of the two-point difference between his and Joyce's scores – citing it as proof that he was 'better-qualified'.

What Johnson failed to mention when he made this claim, however, was that when Joyce had applied for a county foreman's job in 1985, *she* ranked first on the orals test – yet lost out to the man who scored fifth. See Faludi, 'What Women Are Up Against'.

426   **The three interviewers, one of whom**: Trial transcript, *Johnson v. Transportation Agency*, Santa Clara County, pp. 153, 161–2.

426   **'What's wrong with'**: Personal interview with James Graebner, 1987.

426   **'I just said'**: Personal interview with Ron Shields, 1987.

426   **'I felt like tearing'**: Personal interview with Paul Johnson, 1987.

427   **'Something like this'**: Personal interview with Gerald Pourroy, 1987.

427   **Several months after**: Personal observation, 1987.

427   **'She thinks she is'**: Personal interviews, 1987.

428   **Women's numbers in the**: Faludi, 'What Women Are Up Against,' p. 26; personal interviews with Santa Clara County Equal Employment officers and union officials, 1987, 1991.

428   **The court ruled**: *Lorance v. AT&T Technologies*, June 12, 19889.

428   **The court made this ruling**: Personal interview with Bridget Arimond, plaintiff's attorney in the *Lorance v. AT&T Technologies* case, 1989.

429   **And ironically enough**: *Martin v. Wilks*, June 12, 1989.

429   **As long as anyone**: Personal interviews with employees at the plant, 1989.

429   **She had been working since**: Personal interview with Pat Lorance, 1989. (Subsequent Lorance quotations from interview unless otherwise noted.)

430   **As several women**: Personal interviews with Pat Lorance, Jan King and three women who were called in to the personnel office, 1989. The three women, who still work there, asked that their names not be used.

430   **'We have found no'**: Personal interview with Charles Jackson, April 1991.

430   **Some of the men began**: Personal interviews with workers in the testing division, 1989.

431   **'I looked around'**: Personal interview with Jan King, 1989. (Subsequent King quotations from interview.)

433   **'The ladies hadn't'**: Personal interview with Charles Jackson, April 1991.

433   **'The irony of it all'**: Personal interview with Bridge Arimond, 1989.

Chapter Fourteen: Reproductive Rights Under the Backlash

436   **'Don't kill me'**: Personal observations at National Day of Rescue II, April 29, 1989, in Sacramento, Calif.

437   **'We're not allowed to speak'**: Personal interview, April 29, 1989. (Subsequent quotes from this event are also from personal interviews.)

437   **Like the 'anti-vice' crusade**: 'Anthony Comstock,' *Dictionary of National Biography*, Vol. II (New York: Charles Scribner's Sons, 1958), p. 330; Colin Francome, *Abortion Freedom: A Worldside Movement* (London: Allen & Unwin, 1984), p. 47.

438   **Virtually all of**: See Susan Faludi, 'Abortion Obsession,' *Mother Jones*, Nov. 1989, p. 22. This demographic information is pieced together from police arrest records of Operation Rescue events, reports of law-enforcement officers and civil liberties organizations that monitor the activities of anti-abortion groups, and the Operation Rescue staff's own estimates. Many other key players in the 1980s anti-abortion movement fit this demographic: Samuel Lee and Andrew Puzder, who drafted the restrictive Missouri abortion law that was upheld by the US Supreme Court's landmark Webster decision, were thirty-one and thirty-three years old. Lee did not have a place to live and slept on friends' couches. See Cynthia Gorney, 'Taking Aim at *Roe v. Wade*,' *The Washington Post Magazine*, April 9, 1989, p. 18. An earlier study of participants in the anti-abortion and pro-choice movements found that anti-abortion activists disproportionately belong to the lowest income brackets: one-third make less than

$20,000, compared with one-fifth of pro-choice advocates. See Kristin Luker, *Abortion and the Politics of Motherhood* (Berkeley: University of California Press, 1984) p. 221.

438 **Twenty-two American Rescuers**: Eileen Fairweather, 'Theatres of War,' *Guardian*, Nov. 2, 1989.

438 **One Sydney clinic**: Abortion Rights Coalition (ARC), NSW, Fact Sheet, January 1988.

438 **New Zealand saw clashes**: Madeleine Simms, 'Abortion and Democratic Politics,' *The New Humanist*, 1977.

439 **Pro-choice women, he charged**: Petchesky, *Antiabortion, Antifeminism*, p. 221.

439 **'God didn't create'**: Personal observation, 1989.

439 **In his 1986 *Men and Marriage***: Gilder, *Men and Marriage*, p. 107.

440 **In the case of**: The judge sympathized: he granted a temporary restraining order without even giving the wife a chance to speak in court on her own behalf. Later, he forced her to testify in an *open* court, then barred the abortion. Even after his ruling was overturned on appeal – a month later – the state Supreme Court granted the husband's request to extend the injunction against his wife's abortion for another week. See Reproductive Freedom Project Legal Docket, 1988, ed. Diana Traub, American Civil Liberties Union Foundation, p. 77.

440 **'I just didn't like'**: Pat Milton, 'Husband Sues Wife and Doctors for Abortion Without Knowledge,' AP, April 21, 1988; personal interview with David Ostreicher, May 1988.

440 **In upstate New York**: Susan Church, 'Woman Has Abortion Hours Before Appeal Heard,' *Press and Sun-Bulletin*, Sept. 21, 1988, p. 5.

440 **In fact, women have been**: Luker, *Politics of Motherhood*, p. 19; Carl Haub and Mary Kent, 'US Abortions Up? Down?' *Population Today*, Nov. 1987, pp. 6–7; Tamar Lewin, 'US Abortion Rate Shows 6% Decline,' *New York Times*, April 26, 1991, p. A14. Conversely, banning abortion doesn't necessarily stem the number of abortions either: in Brazil, where abortion is illegal, the abortion rate is three times higher than in the United States. Banning abortion, however, does make the operation more lethal: before the legalization of abortion, about 10,000 women a year died from illegal abortions that went wrong, and illegal abortions were the leading cause of maternal death and mutilation.

440 **While the number of abortions**: 'Abortion: Statistical Trends,' Family Planning Information Service Fact Sheet, Jan. 1989, pp. 1–2.

440 **The number of legal**: 'Abortion Review,' Autumn 1991, no. 41, The Birth Control Trust.

440 **According to Margaret McDonald**: Letter to Jane Hill, Nov. 28, 1991.

441 **Despite an annual increase**: *Women in New Zealand*, Department of Statistics and Ministry of Women's Affairs (Wellington, 1990), pp. 102, 103.

441 **As a result, in the half**: O'Neill, *Everyone Was Brave*, pp. 297–8; Steven D. McLaughlin, Barbara D. Melber, John O. G. Billy, Denise M. Zimmerle, Linda D. Winges and Terry R. Johnson, *The Changing Lives of American Women* (Chapel Hill: University of North Carolina Press, 1988) pp. 84–6.

441 **By 1980 a landmark sex survey**: 1980 *Cosmopolitan* Sex Survey. See Linda Wolfe, 'The Sexual Profile of That *Cosmopolitan* Girl,' *Cosmopolitan*, Sept. 1980, p. 254.

441 **In these decisions**: The 1990 Virginia Slims Opinion Poll, pp. 53, 41; Mark Clements Research Women's Views Survey, 1987.

441 **The Abortion Act**: Madeleine Simms, 'Abortion and Democratic Politics,' *The New Humanist*, 1977.

441 **A National Opinion Poll**: *Ibid*.

442 **A Marplan poll**: 'Legal Abortion in Britain,' Co-ordinating Committee in Defence of the 1967 Abortion Act, May 1991.

442 **Despite attempts in Parliament**: *Ibid*.

442 **'Males have almost'**: Gilder, *Men and Marriage*, p. 107.

442 **'The harridans'**: Tom Bethell, 'Operation Rescue,' *The American Spectator*,

Dec. 1988, p. 11. The connection between supernatural women and cultural rites of abortion or infanticide is longstanding. During the witchcraft burnings of the sixteenth and seventeenth centuries, a popular image that theologians advanced was of sorceresses who rubbed themselves down with the fat of murdered infants so they could slip through keyholes. See Page Smith, *Daughters of the Promised Land: Women in American History* (Boston: Little, Brown, 1970) p. 31.

442 **In his 1988 anti-abortion**: George Grant, *Grand Illusions: The Legacy of Planned Parenthood* (Brentwood, Tenn.: Wolgemuth & Hyatt, 1988) pp. 17, 21, 24, 176.

443 **Anti-abortion leader Father**: Stanley Interrante, 'The Rescue Movement Comes to Southern California,' *The Wanderer*, Feb. 16, 1989.

443 **In Joseph Scheidler's**: Joseph M. Scheidler, *Closed: 99 Ways to Stop Abortion* (San Francisco: Ignatius Press, 1985) p. 68. The anti-abortion leader also tried to convince modern women that they would be more *liberated* if they opposed abortion. 'A true feminist,' Scheidler argued, 'would believe in herself enough not to have an abortion.' Personal interview with Joseph Scheidler, 1989.

443 **'Let's be positive'**: Dr and Mrs. J. C. Willke, *Abortion: Questions and Answers* (Cincinnati, Ohio: Hayes, 1985) p. 240.

443 **The Willke handbook**: *Ibid.*, p. 241.

443 **'The baby has to have a choice!'**: 'Abortion Showdown: Hearing Begins in Supreme Court,' *San Jose Mercury News*, April 26, 1989, p. A1.

443 **Women didn't**: Women Exploited by Abortion, or WEBA, a satellite group of Operation Rescue, 'treated' women said to be suffering from 'Post-Abortion Syndrome'. WEBA offered two-month courses in which counsellors instructed their female patients to write letters of apology to their aborted 'children' and sign them, 'Love, Mommy'. Personal interviews with counsellors at WEBA in New York and San Jose, 1989. See also Stephanie Salter, 'She Spied on Operation Rescue,' *San Francisco Examiner*, Aug. 6, 1989, p. A19.

443 **One Australian leaflet**: C. D. O'Loughlin, 'Is This What They Mean by Family Planning?', Life Lobby, Leichhardt, Australia.

444 **Women who were unhappy**: Post-Abortion Syndrome was an ailment that even Surgeon-General C. Everett Koop, who opposed abortion, could find no scientific evidence to support. See Warren E. Leary, 'Koop Says Abortion Report Couldn't Survive Challenge,' *New York Times*, March 17, 1989, p. A10.

444 **National Right to**: Willke and Willke, *Abortion*, p. 273.

444 **Pro-Life Action**: Personal interview with Joseph Scheidler, 1989; Mary Suh and Lydia Denworth, 'The Gathering Storm: Operation Rescue,' *Ms.*, April 1989, p. 92.

444 **'I was conceived out of'**: Personal interview with Randall Terry, 1989. For a longer version of the Terry story, see Faludi, 'Abortion Obsession.' (Subsequent Terry quotations and biographical information are from personal interviews unless otherwise noted.)

445 **'Randy Terry's backlash'**: Personal interview with Dawn Marvin, 1989.

445 **Terry's three aunts**: Personal interviews with Dawn Marvin, Diane Hope, Dale Ingram and Doreen Terry (the DiPasquale sisters), 1989.

446 **He offers an example**: Sanger's sexual behaviour became a subject of almost obsessive interest in 1980s anti-abortion circles. Her 'sordid and promiscuous affairs' were attacked with particular intensity in one of the more popular anti-abortion treatises of the decade, George Grant's *Grand Illusions*. See Grant, *Grand Illusions*, p. 58.

447 **His father, Michael Terry**: Personal interview with Michael Terry, 1989.

448 **She tells how she**: Personal interview with Cindy Terry, 1989.

449 **Alex Aitken, a clinic**: Personal interview with Alex Aitken, 1989.

449 **In her place, Terry**: Personal interviews with Margaret Johnston, administrator of the Southern Tier Women's Services, and other clinic counsellors at Southern Tier, and Binghamton, NY, police investigators, 1989. This sort of behaviour wasn't peculiar to Terry. Joseph Scheidler hired a private detective to hunt down

a pregnant teenager whom he heard was seeking an abortion. See Garry Wills, 'Evangels of Abortion,' *The New York Review of Books*, June 15, 1989, p. 15.

449   **By 1985 Terry had:** Personal interviews with clinic counsellors at Southern Tier, 1989; personal interviews with police investigators in Binghamton, 1989.

449   **During still another:** Personal interview with woman who was assaulted, 1989; personal interview with police investigators, 1989.

449   **By 1989, Operation Rescue:** Personal interview with staff members at Operation Rescue headquarters, 1989.

450   **The day I visited:** Personal observation and interview with office manager of the Crisis Pregnancy Center in Binghamton, NY, 1989.

450   **As for the homes:** Personal interview with staff members at Operation Rescue headquarters, 1989.

450   **At their instigation:** 'Incidents of Violence and Disruption Against Abortion Providers,' National Abortion Federation, Washington, DC, May 15, 1989; 'The Threat to Health Care Workers and Patients: Antiabortion Violence and Harassment,' National Abortion Federation, Washington, DC, May 1988; 'Violence Against Clinics Remains Serious Problem,' *Reproductive Rights Update*, II, no. 23: 4–5; 'Repro Woman,' *Ms.*, Oct. 1989, p. 50.

450   **In 1800, abortion was legal:** Luker, *Politics of Motherhood*, pp. 14–15; Linda Gordon, *Woman's Body/Woman's Right: A Social History of Birth Control in America* (New York: Penguin Books, 1977 edn) pp. 52–3.

451   **Suddenly, the *New York Times*:** Luker, *Politics of Motherhood*, p. 267; Gordon, *Woman's Body*, p. 52. Luker observes that the *New York Times* printed no stories at all on abortion from 1851 (the start of the *New York Times* index) until the mid-1860s. In the 1870s, however, the newspaper became preoccupied with the threat of the procedure; at the peak of its obsession, 1871, the *New York Times* ran sixty-nine stories on the subject.

451   **Suddenly, the American:** Luker, *Politics of Motherhood*, pp. 27–32, 20.

451   **Suddenly, 'purity' crusades:** Francome, *Abortion Freedom*, p. 47; Gordon, *Woman's Body*, p. 65; David M. Kennedy, *Birth Control in America: The Career of Margaret Sanger* (New Haven: Yale University Press, 1970) p. 45.

451   **By the end of the:** Francome, *Abortion Freedom*, p. 76; Luker, *Politics of Motherhood*, p. 15.

451   **'Whether we are':** Cott, *Modern Feminism*, p. 48.

451   **In the hundreds of:** The Helms Amendment did not even permit abortion to save a woman's life. See Harriet F. Pilpel, 'The Fetus as Person: Possible Legal Consequences of the Hogan-Helms Amendment,' *Family Planning Perspectives*, 6, no.1 (Winter 1974), 6; 'Special Report: Anti- and Pro-Choice Ballot Initiatives Scheduled,' *Reproductive Rights Update*, 2, no. 8 (April 13, 1990); 'Josephine County Voters Defeat Birth Control Consent Initiative,' *Reproductive Rights Update*, 2, no. 11 (May 25, 1990); *Who Decides? A State by State Review of Abortion Rights in America*, The NARAL Foundation, 1989, pp. iv–v; Guy Coates, 'Louisiana OKs New Anti-Abortion Bill,' *San Francisco Examiner*, July 9, 1990, p. A8; Margaret Carlson, 'Abortion's Hardest Cases,' *Time*, July 9, 1990, p. 22; 'Anti-Abortion Law Is Passed by Idaho House by 47 to 36,' *New York Times*, March 10, 1990; Maralee Schwartz, 'Utah Enacts Abortion Limits, Prepares for Bitter Court Test,' *Washington Post*, Jan. 26, 1991, p. A2; Dan Balz, 'Guam Surprises Abortion Activists, New Restrictive Law Puts Pacific Island in Middle of Controversy,' *Washington Post*, March 24, 1990, p. A11.

452   **There have been several attacks:** See 'Abortion, Legal and Ethical Issues,' Family Planning Association Fact Sheet, Jan. 1989, pp. 2–3; Joan Smith, 'Abortion: It's Time to Defend Your Rights', *Cosmopolitan*, April 1990, p. 8.

453   **The *Guardian* reported:** David Brindle, 'District Cuts NHS-Funded Abortions,' *Guardian*, Nov. 15, 1991, p. 24.

453   **Members of 'Doctors for a Woman's Choice':** 'Backward Step on Abortion Rights,' Letters to the Editor, *Guardian*, Nov. 18, 1991.

453   **Australia has seen:** Women's Electoral Lobby (Perth), 'Inequality of Access to

Abortion Services in Australia: a Report to the Committee on the Elimination of Discrimination Against Women (CEDAW),' 1988, pp. 13–15, 45, 50.

454   **In the last two years:** Tiffany Devitt, 'Abortion Coverage Leaves Women Out of the Picture,' *Extra!*, March–April 1991, p. 5.

454   **The American Bar Association:** 'ABA Rescinds Pro-Choice Position,' *Reproductive Rights Update*, 2, no. 16 (Sept. 14, 1990), 7.

454   **Even moderate religious denominations:** The American Baptist Church retracted its longstanding support for a woman's right to legalized abortion, replaced it with a 'neutral' posture, and withdrew from the Religious Coalition for Abortion Rights. The Presbyterian Church, USA, empanelled a task force to review the pro-*Roe* stance it had held since 1970. And the United Methodist Church modified its endorsement of *Roe*, too. Information from the Religious Coalition for Abortion Rights, 1990.

454   **The Catholic bishops:** Ari L. Goldman, 'Bishops Hire Pros to Sway Public Against Abortion,' *Sacramento Bee*, April 6, 1990, p. A1; Nadine Brozan, 'Cardinal Proposes Order of Nuns to Fight Abortion,' *New York Times*, Nov. 4, 1989; 'New Jersey Governor Quits Knights of Columbus,' *Reproductive Rights Update*, 2, no. 12 (June 8, 1990), 7; Robin Toner, 'Catholic Politicians See Line on Duty,' *New York Times*, June 25, 1990, p. A1; 'Bishop Excommunicates Abortion Clinic Administrator,' *Reproductive Rights Update*, 2, no. 14 (July 6, 1990), 5; Eric Pace, 'No Unanimity on Abortion Excommunication,' *New York Times*, June 16, 1990, p. 10.

455   **By 1987, 85 per cent:** Barbara Ehrenreich, 'Mothers Unite,' *The New Republic*, July 10, 1989, p. 30; 'Guttmacher Study: Rural Abortion Providers Drop by Half,' *Reproductive Rights Update*, 2, no. 14 (July 6, 1900), 7; Tamar Lewin, 'Abortions Harder to Get in Rural Areas of Nation,' *New York Times*, June 28, 1990, p. A18.

455   **In Missouri:** Stephen Wermiel and Michel McQueen, 'Turning Point? Historic Court Ruling Will Widen Disparity in Access to Abortion,' *The Wall Street Journal*, July 5, 1989, p. A1.

455   **Federal funding was no longer:** Data from National Abortion Rights Action League.

455   **(Moreover, eight states):** *Economics of Abortion*, National Abortion Federation, Fact Sheet, Nov. 1985, p. 1.

455   **In Michigan, a state ban:** The ranks of welfare babies also rose 31 per cent in this same period. At the same time, the numbers of low-income women seeking sterilization increased drmatically and the proportion of poor babies being put up for adoption rose by about 50 per cent, according to a survey of adoption agencies in the Detroit area. See Patricia Chargot, 'Abortion and the Poor,' *Detroit Free Press*, Aug. 5, 1990, p. F1.

455   **The handful of private:** Barbara Brotman, 'Private Agencies Filling Abortion Funding Gap,' *Chicago Tribune*, Jan. 22, 1990, p. C1.

455   **Rosie Jimenez:** Gina Seay, 'Abortion-Rights Group to Launch Campaign to Recruit Young Teens,' *Houston Chronicle*, Aug. 25.

456   **When Spring Adams:** 'Slain Girl Was to Have Abortion,' *Argus Observer*, Aug. 31, 1989; Margie Boulie, 'Now He Admits It, Now He Doesn't,' *Portland Oregonian*, Mar. 13, 1990, Editorial Section, p. 1.

456   **Federally funded sex-education:** Linda Greenhouse, 'Anti-Abortion Aid Stirs Church-State Questions,' *New York Times*, March 17, 1988, p. 12; Karen Gustafson, 'The New Politics of Abortion,' *Utne Reader*, March–April 1989, p. 19.

456   **Whether as a:** 'College Paper to Ban Abortion Clinic Ads,' *New York Times*, Aug. 18, 1989; Lisa Stansky, 'Group Seeks Ads in School Papers,' *The Recorder*, Oct. 19, 1990, p. 1; 'Florida TV Stations Refuse to Air Pro-Choice Ads,' *Media Report to Women*, Nov.–Dec. 1990, p. 4; 'Abortion Bulletin,' *Eleanor Smeal Report*, 6, no. 11 (March 25, 1989), 2.

456   **A NOW ad that simply:** 'Briefs,' *Media Report to Women*, May–June 1989, p. 10. In 1989, at the *Press Journal* in Vero Beach, Florida, a reporter was fired

after she wrote some letters in support of legal abortion to state legislators. That same year, after the student newspaper at Marquette University published an ad for the Washington march for abortion rights – which read 'Stand Up. Be Counted. While You Still Have the Choice' – the university administration ordered the firing of the school paper's business manager and suspended both the editor and advertising director.

456   **The *Los Angeles Times* and:** Personal interview with Tamar Raphael, The Fund for the Feminist Majority, 1989.

456   **(And women who wrote):** Letter from Don Clark, executive vice-president of marketing of the *Los Angeles Tiems*, Aug. 8, 1989. Mr Clark also said that the newspaper hadn't turned down the ad outright, only refused to print it unless it was 'toned down' and made 'less graphic'.

457   **On the other hand:** 'Should an Innocent Child Pay for a Brutal Father's Mistake . . . With Her Life?' Advertisement, American Life League, Inc., *USA Today*, Jan. 22, 1991, p. A11.

457   **An ABC radio:** Joanne Lipman, 'Barbara Walters Radio Special on Abortion Shunned by Sponsors,' *The Wall Street Journal*, June 16, 1989, p. B1.

457   **In 1988 United Way:** Stephanie Salter, 'Long Line, Small Social Conscience,' *San Francisco Examiner*, April 5, 1990, p. A25; 'AT&T Shareholders Vote Down Anti-Choice Resolution,' *Reproductive Rights Update*, 2, no. 9 (April 27, 1990), 7.

457   **By 1990, the National:** Statistics from the National Center for Health Statistics, 1990. A rise in unmarried teenage births first registered in 1987, jumping 10 per cent among fifteen- to seventeen-year-olds between 1986 and 1988.

457   **England, too, saw a substantial rise:** Birth Statistics, OPCS, 1989.

457   **Even Establishment groups:** Rose Shapiro, 'Britain's Sexual Counter-Revolutionaries', *Marxism Today*, 29, no. 2 (Feb. 1985), pp. 7–10.

458   **Most direct provision:** Rose Shapiro, *Contraception: A Practical and Political Guide* (London: Virago Press, 1987).

458   **This was later confirmed:** Chris Mihill, 'GPs "Fail" Young for Birth Control,' *Guardian*, Nov. 28, 1991.

458   **By the end of the decade:** Philip J. Hilts, 'US Approves 5-year Implants to Curb Fertility,' *New York Times*, Dec. 11, 1990, p. A1.

458   **Insurance companies retreated:** Dorothy Wickenden, 'Drug of Choice,' *The New Republic*, Nov. 26, 1990, p. 24.

458   **A 1990 Institute of Medicine:** Kenneth H. Bacon, 'Health: US Birth Control R & D Lags,' *The Wall Street Journal*, Feb. 15, 1990, p. B1.

458   **Sterling Drug:** Dr Scott Zeller, 'The Abortion Pill,' *San Francisco Weekly*, Sept. 13, 1989, p. 1; Emily T. Smith, 'Abortion: A Vocal Minority Has Drugmakers Running Scared,' *Business Week*, Nov. 14, 1988, p. 59.

458   **In 1989, the Food and Drug Administration:** Wickenden, 'Drug of Choice,' p. 27.

458   **In 1990 the makers:** Laura Fraser, 'Bringing the Abortion Pill to California,' *California*, July 1990, p. 58.

458   **And these researchers:** *Ibid.*, p. 61.

459   **Meanwhile, when a:** 'Shareholder Proposal on RU-486 Nixed by Management,' *Reproductive Rights Update*, 2, no. 7 (March 30, 1990) 5.

459   **Only one American company:** Smith, 'Vocal Minority,' p. 59.

459   **One right-to-life:** 'Diary of an Unborn Child,' Knights of Columbus flyer, 1989.

459   **The Willkes' manual:** Willke and Willke, *Abortion*, pp. 240–1.

459   **Dr Bernard Nathanson:** Janet Gallagher, 'Prenatal Invasions and Interventions: What's Wrong with Fetal Rights,' *Harvard Women's Law Journal*, 10 (1987), 57–8.

459   **'Her body is a haunted house':** Scheidler, *Closed*, p. 138.

460   **In 1982 a group of:** Gina Kolata, 'Operating on the Unborn,' *The New York Times Magazine*, May 14, 1989, p. 34.

460 **In the waiting rooms**: Personal observation at the Pacific Fertility Center, San Francisco, 1989.

460 **Some infertility specialists**: Personal interviews, 1989; Robyn Rowland, 'Decoding Reprospeak,' *Ms.*, May/June 1991, p. 38.

460 **At the Jones Institute**: Jean Seligmann, 'Tempest in a Test Tube,' *Newsweek*, Aug. 21, 1989, p. 67.

460 **In Australia there have been**: Letter from Margaret McDonald, Chief Executive Officer, The Family Planning Association of NSW Ltd, to Jane Hill, Nov. 28, 1991.

460 **In the UK, the Whittington**: Tim Lawrence, 'Funeral Rite or wrong?' *New Statesman & Society*, April 19, 1991, p. 22.

461 **The *Observer* commented**: Frankie Rickford, 'Virgin Prose and Cons,' *Observer*, March 17, 1991.

461 **'Whose body is it'**: Roger Scruton, 'Whose Body Is It Anyway?', *Sunday Telegraph*, March 17, 1991, p. 24.

461 **The *Daily Mail***: 'Storm Over Virgin Births,' *Daily Mail*, March 11, 1991; 'Nightmare Vision of Baby Production Line,' *Daily Mail*, March 12, 1991.

461 **Virginia Bottomley**: Quoted by Celia Hall, ' "Virgin Births" Ban Seen as Unlikely,' *Independent*, March 12, 1991, p. 2.

461 **A New Hampshire court even**: 'Court Rules Fetus a Resident,' *Reproductive Rights Update*, 2, no. 21 (Nov. 21, 1990), 5.

461 **By the mid-1980s**: Dawn E. Johnsen, 'The Creation of Fetal Rights: Conflicts with Women's Constitutional Rights to Liberty, Privacy and Equal Protection,' *The Yale Law Journal*, 95, no. 3 (Jan. 1986), 599–625; Joseph M. Harvey, 'Fetus a "Person," in Car-Death Law,' *Boston Globe*, Aug. 17, 1984; David Sellers, 'Fetus is "Person," DC Appeals Court Rules for First Time,' *Washington Times*, Oct. 10, 1984, p. A1; Nan D. Hunter, 'Feticide – Cases and Legislation,' Reproductive Freedom Project, unpublished paper, May 5, 1986.

461 **In a 1989 divorce**: Seligmann, 'Tempest in a Test Tube,' p. 67.

462 **By the late 1980s**: Ted Gest, 'The Pregnancy Police, On Patrol,' *US News and World Report*, Feb. 6, 1989, p. 50.

462 **'Surely the most'**: 'The Most Sordid and Terrifying Story,' *California Advocates for Pregnant Women Newsletter*, Sept.–Dec. 1990, no. 12, p. 3.

462 **Meanwhile in the states**: Johnsen, 'Creation of Fetal Rights,' Dawn E. Johnsen, 'A New Threat to Pregnant Women's Autonomy,' Hastings Center Report, Aug. 1987, p. 33; 'Legislative Alert,' *California Advocates for Pregnant Women Newsletter*, May–June 1990, p. 2, and July–Aug. 1990, p. 3; Marianne Takas, 'Eat Right, Stay Off Your Feet – Or Go to Jail,' *Vogue*, May 1987, p. 148; personal interviews with Dawn Johnsen, Lyn Paltrow and Janet Gallagher, 1989. I am grateful to the staff of the ACLU Reproductive Freedom Project for generously sharing its voluminous research.

462 **Other legislative initiatives**: 'Statutes That Unfairly Punish Pregnant Women for Behavior,' *Reproductive Rights Update*, 2, no. 1 (Jan. 5, 1990), 4.

462 **By 1988, half of the people**: Ronni Sandroff, 'Invasion of the Body Snatchers,' *Vogue*, Oct. 1988, p. 330.

462 **Medical and legal**: Marjorie Shaw, 'Conditional Prospective Rights of the Fetus,' *Journal of Legal Medicine*, 63 (1984), 67–9; Johnsen, 'Creation of Fetal Rights,' pp. 607–8; Gallagher, 'Prenatal Invasions and Interventions,' p. 11.

462 **In Seattle in 1991**: Barbara Kantrowitz, 'The Pregnancy Police,' *Newsweek*, April 29, 1991, p. 52.

463 **Poor pregnant women were hauled**: Molly McNulty, 'Pregnancy Police, the Health Policy and Legal Implications of Punishing Pregnant Women for Harm to Their Fetuses,' *Review of Law and Social Change*, 16, no. 2 (1987–88), 285; Reproductive Freedom Project Legal Docket, ACLU, 1988; *Reproductive Rights Update*, 2, no. 3 (Feb. 2, 1990), 6; Lynn M. Paltrow, 'When Becoming Pregnant Is a Crime,' *Criminal Justice Ethics*, 9, no. 1 (Winter–Spring 1990), 2–3, 14; Janet Gallagher, 'The Fetus and the Law – Whose Life Is It Anyway?' *Ms.*, Sept.

1984, p. 62; Gallagher, 'Prenatal Invasions and Interventions'; Ellen Willis, 'The Wrongs of Fetal Rights,' *The Village Voice*, April 11, 1989, p. 41; Susan Lacroix, 'Jailing Mothers for Drug Abuse,' *The Nation*, May 1, 1989, p. 587.

463   **In Michigan:** *In the Matter of J. Jeffrey*, no. 99851, Michigan Court of Appeals, April 9, 1987; Paltrow, 'When Becoming Pregnant Is a Crime,' pp. 8–9.

463   **In California:** *People of the State of California v. Pamela Rae Stewart*, 1987. See Angela Bonavoglia, 'The Ordeal of Pamela Rae Stewart,' *Ms.*, July–Aug. 1987, p. 92; Memorandum of Points and Authorities in Support of Demurrer to Complain Without Leave to Amend, *Calif. v. Pamela Rae Stewart*, p. 3; Jo Moreland, 'Neighbors Cite Mother's Troubled Past,' *Daily Californian*, Sept. 30, 1986, p. A1.

463   **In Iowa:** Associated Press, 'Baby Placed in Foster Home; Doctor Claims Prenatal Abuse,' *Des Moines Register*, April 3, 1980, p. A11.

463   **In Wyoming:** *State of Wyoming v. Pfannenstiel*, no. 1–90–8CR, Laramie County Court, Jan. 5, 1990; Paltrow, 'When Becoming Pregnant Is a Crime,' p. 9; 'Pregnant Drinker Faces Trial for Child Abuse,' *San Francisco Examiner*, Jan. 1, 1990, p. A13.

463   **In Illinois:** *Stallman v. Youngquist*, 125 Ill. 2nd 267, 531 NE 2nd 355, 129 Ill. App. 3rd 859 and 152 Ill App. 3rd 683; *Reproductive Rights Update*, 2, no. 4 (Feb. 16, 1990), 7.

464   **In Michigan:** *Grodin v. Grodin*, 102 Michigan Court of Appeals 396, 301 NW 2nd 869 (1980); Johnsen, 'Creation of Fetal Rights,' p. 604.

464   **In Maryland:** 'Hospital Transfers Pregnant Woman Against Her Will,' *Reproductive Rights Update*, 2, no. 4 (Feb. 16, 1990), 7.

464   **In South Carolina:** 'Pregnant and Newly Delivered Women Jailed on Drug Charges,' *Reproductive Rights Update*, 2, no. 3 (Feb. 2, 1990), 6.

464   **In Wisconsin:** 'Girl Detained to Protect Fetus,' *Wisconsin State Journal*, Aug. 16, 1985, p. 2.

464   **Police loaded:** 'Pregnant and Newly Delivered Women,' p. 6; Debra Lucero Austin, 'Prosecution Plan Draws Fire. "A Cop in the Delivery Room?" ' *Chico Enterprise Record*, Nov. 3, 1988, p. A1.

464   **Judges threw:** Ellen Barry, 'Quality of Prenatal Care for Incarcerated Women Challenged,' *Youth Law News*, National Center for Youth Law, 6, no. 6 (Nov.–Dec. 1985), 2–4; Tamar Lewin, 'When Courts Take Charge of the Unborn,' *New York Times*, Jan. 9, 1989, p. A9. A California study in 1983 found that less than half of prison pregnancies ended in live births and 30 per cent of them resulted in miscarriages. In Alameda County's Santa Rita Jail, 73 per cent of the pregnant women were miscarrying, fifty times the state average.

465   **'In my mind':** Personal interview with Ray Narramore, 1989.

465   **In the District:** Courtland Milloy, 'Who Will Save DC's Babies?' *Washington Post*, July 23, 1989, p. 3.

465   **By the end of the decade:** Sonia L. Nazario, 'Midwifery Is Staging Revival as Demand for Prenatal Care, Low-Tech Births Rises,' *The Wall Street Journal*, Sept. 25, 1990, p. B1.

465   **In New York State, a health department:** *Ibid.*

465   **In California:** 'Medi-cal Maternity Care and AB 3021: Crisis and Opportunity.' National Health Law Program, May 1986, cited in 'Memorandum of Points and Authorities in Support of Motion to Dismiss,' *People of the State of California v. Pamela Rae Stewart*, Feb. 23, 1987, p. 15.

466   **In a 1986 survey:** Veronika E. B. Kolder, Janet Gallagher and Michael T. Parsons, 'Court-Ordered Obstetrical Interventions,' *The New England Journal of Medicine*, 316, no. 19 (May 7, 1987), 1192–6. More than a quarter also believed that women in their third trimester who weren't already being treated inside the hospital system should be under state surveillance.

466   **Their recommendations:** Johnsen, 'Creation of Fetal Rights,' p. 607.

466   **A Washington, DC, Superior Court:** 'In the Matter of Madyun Fetus,' *The Daily Washington Law Reporter*, 114, no. 209 (Oct. 29, 1986), 2240.

466   **A review of**: Kolder *et al.*, 'Court-Ordered Obstetrical Interventions,' p. 1192.

467   **Judges granted**: *Ibid.*, pp. 1193–4.

467   **The women's wishes were**: *Ibid.*, p. 1194.

467   **And most of these**: *Ibid.*, p. 1193.

467   **In a 1981 court**: *Ibid.*, p. 1192; *Jefferson v. Griffin Spalding County Hosp.*, Auth., 247 GA. 86, 274, SE 2nd, 457, 1981.

467   **At a time when**: Gallagher, 'The Fetus and the Law.'

467   **In Chicago, a woman**: Gallagher, 'Prenatal Invasions and Interventions,' p. 9.

467   **In at least two**: *Ibid.*, p. 46.

467   **In a 1982 Michigan case**: *Ibid.*, p. 47.

467   **In two key cases**: Johnsen, 'Creation of Fetal Rights,' pp. 615–17.

468   **'To compel'**: *McFall v. Shimp*, 10 Pa. D.&C. 3rd 90, 91, Allegheny County, 1978.

468   **On a June day**: Carol O'Brien, 'Patient's Lawyer Calls A.C. Case Human Sacrifice,' *American Medical News*, March 11, 1988, p. 46.

468   **Doctors had told her twice**: *Ibid.*; personal interview with Carder's mother, Nettie Stoner, 1989.

468   **She was in fact**: Affidavit of Dr Jeffrey A. Moscow, *In Re: Angela Carder*, 1986, p. 3.

468   **Her cancer had been**: Personal interview with Nettie Stoner, 1989.

468   **Her long-time oncologist**: Affidavit of Dr Jeffrey A. Moscow, p. 2.

468   **'She told the doctor'**: Personal interview with Nettie Stoner, 1989.

469   **But the doctors**: *In Re: Angela Carder*, Superior Court of the District of Columbia, Transcript, June 16, 1987.

469   **'She said, "No",'**: Personal interview with Nettie Stoner, 1989.

469   **Even the hospital's**: David Remnick, 'Whose Life Is It, Anyway?' *The Washington Post Magazine*, Feb. 21, 1988, p. 14.

470   **'No one told me'**: Personal interview with Nettie Stoner, 1989.

470   **Each of the physicians**: *In Re: Angela Carder*.

470   **'Well, I suppose'**: *Ibid.*

470   **The judge's questions**: *Ibid.*

470   **When Carder's attorney observed**: *Ibid.*

470   **'If I wanted to'**: Personal inerview with Barbara Mishkin, 1989.

471   **'There's been some'**: *In Re: Angela Carder*.

471   **He asked**: *Ibid.*

471   **This time, she told**: *Ibid.*

471   **'The court is still not'**: *Ibid.*

471   **The judges, told that**: *In Re: Angela Carder*, District of Columbia Court of Appeals, Transcript, June 16, 1987, p. 4.

471   **Was her 'mental frame'**: *Ibid.*, p. 7.

471   **'Does this woman'**: *Ibid.*, pp. 6–7.

471   **The foetus's attorney**: *Ibid.*, p. 9.

471   **It was 'not'**: *Ibid.*

472   **The law 'is'**: *Ibid.*, p. 16.

472   **'With the time'**: *Ibid.*

472   **A short while later**: Remnick, 'Whose Life,' p. 21.

472   **It was 'like trying to'**: *Ibid.*

472   **'They wanted a live'**: Personal interview with Nettie Stoner, 1989.

472   **Her mother held**: *Ibid.*

472   **An autopsy report**: 'First Amended Complaint for Damages,' *Nettie and Daniel Stoner v. George Washington University, et al.*, p. 9.

472   **Five months later**: 'In the Matter of A.C.,' No. 87–609, 53 A.2d, p. 611 (DC App. 1987).

472   **Three years later**: Linda Greenhouse, 'Forced Surgery to Save Fetus Is Rejected by Court in Capital,' *New York Times*, April 27, 1990, p. 1.

473   **'They took'**: Personal interview with Nettie Stoner, 1989.

473 **Starting in the:** 'Reproductive Health Hazards in the Workplace,' US Congress, Office of Technology Assessment, 1985.

473 **By mid-decade:** Joan E. Bertin, 'Reproductive Hazards in the Workplace,' in *Reproductive Laws for the 1990s*, ed. Sherrill Cohen and Nadine Taub (Clifton, NJ: Humana Press, 1989) pp. 277–305.

473 **And a survey:** Ronald Bayer, 'Women, Work and Reproductive Hazards,' The Hastings Center Report, Oct. 1982, p. 14.

473 **Passed off as:** Freeman, *Politics of Women's Liberation*, p. 76; Kessler-Harris, *Out to Work*, p. 211.

474 The proponents of these: Kessler-Harris, *Out to Work*, pp. 180–214.

474 **'We cannot drive':** *Ibid.*, p. 202.

474 **Working women were exposed:** 'Women, Work and Health Hazards,' National Commission on Working Women, Washington, DC, 1984.

474 **These companies:** Michael Rose, 'Reproductive Health Hazards for High-Tech Workers,' in *American Woman 1988–89*, pp. 281–3; Lynne Lohmeier, 'Making Work Safe for Childbearing Couples,' *East West*, Aug. 1987, p. 52.

474 **The Reagan administration:** Rose, 'Reproductive Health Hazards,' pp. 283–5.

474 **When the National:** A 1986 congressional review of the Office of Management and Budget's handling of this study found that OMB *intentionally* selected reviewers who had little concern for occupational health and OMB itself 'unreasonably delayed, impeded and thwarted governmental research efforts ... on serious public health questions'. See *ibid.*, pp. 284–5.

474 **AT&T, for example:** *Ibid.*, p. 279.

475 **Officials at Allied Chemical:** Gail Bronson 'Issue of Fetal Damage Stirs Women Workers at Chemical Plants,' *The Wall Street Journal*, Feb. 9, 1979, p. 1.

475 **Johnson Controls, the nation's:** Richard Carelli, 'Court Calls Job Hazard Policies Sex Bias,' *San Francisco Examiner*, March 20, 1991, p. A1.

475 **In a federal survey:** Bayer, 'Reproductive Hazards,' p. 17.

475 **One industry group:** Rosalind Petchesky, *Abortion and the Woman's Choice: The State, Sexuality and Reproductive Freedom* (Boston: Northeastern University Press, 1990), p. 351.

475 **To the Synthetic:** Bayer, 'Reproductive Hazards,' p. 17.

475 **These same companies:** Lohmeier, 'Childbearing Couples,' p. 52; Mary Sue Henifin, 'Making Healthy Babies Not Just Women's Work,' *Womanews*, April 1983, p. 4.

475 **A study by the OSHA:** Carolyn Marshall, 'An Excuse for Workplace Hazard,' *The Nation*, April 25, 1987, p. 532.

476 **Johnson Controls barred:** *Ibid.*, p. 534.

476 **A 1989 survey of 198:** Anne J. Stone, 'In Review: January 1, 1988–July 3, 1989,' in *American Woman 1990–91*, p. 50.

476 **Du Pont based:** Bertin, 'Reproductive Health Hazards in the Workplace,' unpublished paper, 1988.

476 **Of the tens of thousands:** Marshall, 'Workplace Hazard,' p. 533.

476 **In fact, the Reagan:** Under Carter, OSHA drafted new rules that encouraged employers to protect both sexes from reproductive hazards. The Reagan administration scuttled them, slashed OSHA's budget by 25 per cent, and cut industrial inspections, citations and court actions. See Betty Holcomb, 'Occupational Health: The Fetus Factor,' *Ms.*, May 1983, p. 40.

477 **They even hired:** Personal interview with Faith Popcorn, 1989.

478 **'After we interviewed':** Deposition of Glenn E. Mercer, *Christman v. American Cyanamid Co.* (Civil Action No. 80–0024, N.D. West Va.), Oct. 19–20, 1982, p. 100.

478 **At the time, Betty Riggs:** Personal interview with Betty Riggs, 1988; Deposition of Betty June Riggs, *Christman v. American Cyanamid Co.*, Dec. 8, 1980, p. 8.

478 **When Riggs pressed:** Personal interview with Betty Riggs, 1988.

478 **As a number:** Personal interviews, 1988.

479 **When she went:** Deposition of Donna Lee Martin, *Christman v. American Cyanamid Co.*, Dec. 9, 1980, p. 22.
479 **Six weeks later:** *Ibid.*, pp. 22, 28.
479 **Barbara Cantwell:** Deposition of Barbara Cantwell Christman, *Christman v. American Cyanamid Co.*, Dec. 9–10, 1980, pp. 16, 27.
479 **In her job interviews:** *Ibid.*, pp. 16–17.
480 **'Women shouldn't':** Deposition of Christman, p. 39.
480 **He complained that:** *Ibid.*, p. 28; Deposition of Riggs, p. 101.
480 **'SHOOT A WOMAN:** Deposition of Martin, p. 158.
480 **Another day:** Personal interview with Betty Riggs, 1988.
482 **American Cyanamid's corporate medical:** 'Reproductive Health Hazards in the Workplace,' Office of Technology Assessment, 1985, p. 253.
482 **The protection plan:** Deposition of Dr Robert M. Clyne, *Christman v. American Cyanamid Co.*, May 16, 1983, p. 141.
482 **The company's medical department:** 'Reproductive Health Hazards in the Workplace,' pp. 253–5.
482 **As Clyne explained:** *Ibid.*, p. 253.
482 **'We just did not':** Deposition of Clyne, p. 476.
482 **'Other steps':** *Ibid.*, p. 1052.
482 **The company later:** Personal interview with American Cyanamid representatives, 1988, 1991; American Cyanamid press release.
482 **A government inspection:** Decision of Judge Cecil L. Cutler, *American Cyanamid Co.*, OSHRC Docket No. 79–2438, Oct. 14, 1980.
483 **'We recognize':** Deposition of Clyne, pp. 240–1.
483 **In a series:** 'Reproductive Health Hazards in the Workplace,' p. 257.
483 **As Mercer put it:** Deposition of Martin, p. 184.
483 **'He told us':** Personal interview with Betty Riggs, 1988.
483 **The women began:** *Ibid.*; Deposition of Martin, pp. 42–5; Deposition of Christman, pp. 62–5.
483 **Mercer said he didn't:** Deposition of Christman, p. 65.
483 **Then a company nurse:** 'Reproductive Health Hazards in the Workplace,' p. 257.
483 **With that:** Personal interview with Betty Riggs, 1988.
483 **Donna Martin listened:** Deposition of Martin, pp. 47, 173.
484 **'Mentally, I couldn't':** *Ibid.*, p. 173.
484 **She had some painkillers:** *Ibid.*, pp. 166–7, 169.
484 **Within a week:** *Ibid.*, p. 168.
484 **She went to:** *Ibid.*, p. 77.
484 **Afterwards, frightened:** *Ibid.*, p. 80.
484 **Finally, that September:** 'Reproductive Health Hazards in the Workplace,' p. 257.
484 **Like Martin:** Deposition of Christman, p. 90.
484 **When Christman surfaced:** *Ibid.*, p. 95.
484 **The doctor, Rymer:** Deposition of Lola Rymer, *Christman v. American Cyanamid Co.*, December, 10–11, 1980, pp. 46–7.
485 **'I did what I did':** Personal interview with Betty Riggs, 1988.
485 **In the end:** 'Reproductive Health Hazards in the Workplace,' p. 257.
485 **Q: Did she tell:** Deposition of Clyne, p. 780.
485 **'I wondered':** Personal interview with Betty Riggs, 1988.
485 **He warned her:** Deposition of Riggs, p. 108.
485 **When she took:** Deposition of Christman, p. 103.
485 **Soon after Donna Martin:** Deposition of Martin, p. 147.
486 **The men in the department:** Deposition of Christman, p. 150; personal interview with Betty Riggs, 1988; Deposition of Riggs, pp. 143–4.
486 **In early 1979:** Opinion of Circuit Judge Robert Bork, *Oil, Chemical and Atomic Workers International Union v. American Cyanamid Co.*, 741 F.2d Series, 444 (1984), pp. 444–50.

486   **'You women are'**: Personal interview with Betty Riggs, 1988; Deposition of Christman, p. 113.

486   **That October**: Opinion of Bork, pp. 446–7.

486   **American Cyanamid responded**: 'Reproductive Health Hazards in the Workplace,' p. 257.

486   **In 1980 American**: Opinion of Bork, p. 447.

486   **Meanwhile, the women**: Personal interview with Joan Bertin, 1988.

487   **The foetal protection**: Opinion of Bork, pp. 445, 449.

487   **In 1983 they accepted**: Personal interview with Joan Bertin, 1988.

487   **The women who participated**: Personal interviews, 1988.

487   **One day in 1987**: Personal interview with Betty Riggs, 1988.

487   **'I suppose'**: Nat Hentoff, 'Is Anyone There Underneath the Black Robes?' *The Village Voice*, Oct. 27, 1987, p. 32.

487   **And at the hearings**: Amy Wallace, 'Bork Version of Sterilization Case Disputed,' *Atlanta Journal-Constitution*, Sept. 20, 1987, p. A1.

488   **'Everybody had a'**: Personal interview with Steve Tice, 1988.

488   **'I feel these women'**: Personal interview with Dr George Gevas, 1988.

488   **'I don't care to'**: Personal interview with Glenn Mercer, 1988.

488   **In the years since**: Personal interviews, 1988.

489   **'I became cold and'**: Personal interview with Betty Riggs, 1988.

Epilogue

494   **Between 1914 and 1918**: Sheila Rowbotham, *Hidden from History* (London: Pluto Press, 1973), pp. 86, 110, 120.

495   **As political scientist**: Klein, *Gender Politics* p. 22.

495   **The 1970 Women's**: Freeman, *Politics of Women's Liberation*, p. 84.

495   **Afterwards, seventy-one women's**: Klein, *Gender Politics*, pp. 22, 124.

496   **Among female students, too**: Alexander M. Astin Student Survey, 1990. The survey polled 200,000 undergraduates.

496   **Their vast numbers**: Dan Balz and Ruth Marcus, 'In Year Since Webster, Abortion Debate Defies Predictions,' *Washington Post*, July 3, 1990, p. A1.

496   **'Let the governor'**: David Shribman, 'Gov. Andrus Worries about Threat to Boycott Idaho Potatoes in Fight Over Abortion Rights Bill,' *The Wall Street Journal*, March 29, 1990, p. A16.

496   **'Anytime someone'**: *Ibid.*

497   **'Women are not'**: Kate Rand Lloyd, speech, 'Women, Men and Media,' University of Southern California, 1988.

497   **(A record gender gap)**: The Gallup Poll, 1991.

497   **'The reason men'**: Personal interview with Eleanor Smeal, 1989.

498   **'I get press calls'**: Sara Frankel, 'Women Go to the Pols,' *San Francisco Examiner*, May 6, 1990, p. C4.

Index

and divorce 39, 43–5, 46
feminist 336–7, 338
and marriage 34–6, 319–23, 374, 375
mental health of 35–6, 60–1
single 34–5, 88–9, 127–8, 320–2
threat of women's equality to 9, 22, 25,
80–1, 86–9, 323, 328–9, 331, 334, 337,
342–3
women's attitudes to 7, 9, 24, 495
and women's rights 60, 81, 82–3, 87–8, 444,
495
see also 'man shortage'; masculinism, New
Age; masculinity
men's liberation 337, 338
men's movement 85–6, 314, 337, 339, 341–2,
343–6
mental health see women's mental health
Mercer, Glenn 478, 483, 485, 488
Meyers, Nancy 153, 159–60, 162
Milken, Michael 92
Miller, Jean Baker 14; Toward a New
Psychology of Women 359–60
Mills, Barbara, QC 399
miniskirts 219, 220–1, 222
miscarriage 48
Mishkin, Barbara 470, 471–2
Miss America pageant 70–1, 99, 136
Molloy, John T. 206, 212–13, 223
Woman's Dress for Success Book 209–11,
213
'mommy tracking' trend 101, 106, 114–16,
194
Mondale, Walter 304
Moonlighting 175–6, 192
Moore, Demi 132
Moore, Mary Tyler 191–2
Moorman, Jeanne 29–32
Moral Majority 261, 262, 279, 285, 289
Morgan, Charles, Jr 415, 416, 417
motherhood 162, 348, 349–51, 441, 489
media promotion of 105, 106, 116, 118,
130–1, 132–3, 188
mothers:
foetal rights and 459–73
single 10–11, 42–3, 72, 144, 298, 308, 343
working 107–8, 161, 167, 190, 191, 201, 351
see also motherhood
movies see films
Ms. 79, 116, 134–7, 138, 251, 260, 281, 338,
354, 361, 382–3
'mummy tracking' see 'mommy tracking'
trend
Murder, She Wrote 193
murders, sex-related 11, 89, 456
Murphy Brown 178, 193
My Brilliant Career 155
mystique, feminine 59, 74

Nader, Lura Lee 419
Nation 123

National Abortion Rights Action League
(NARAL) 446, 496
National Center for Health Statistics, US
47–8, 56
National Enquirer 348
National Health Service, British 51
National Opinion Research (US) 82
National Organization for Women (NOW)
266, 294, 295, 346, 350, 356, 358, 417,
446, 456
National Review 2, 304
National Right to Life 439, 444
National Survey, US 33
National Woman's Party 70, 71
NBC 104, 129, 408, 409, 473
Nebecker, Judge Frank 471, 472
Neiman Marcus 207, 212, 214
'neotraditionalism' see New Traditionalism
'nesting' see 'cocooning'
Neustatter, Angela 114
New England Journal of Medicine 46, 48
New Right 12, 15, 45, 62, 69, 102, 259,
314–15, 327, 442, 443
abortion, the ERA, and 262–4, 267, 268
'pro-family' agenda of 266–7, 269–70,
297–8, 358
women's leadership in 270–89
women's movement attacked by 260,
262–8, 280, 286, 287, 293, 350
Newsday 100, 106, 353
Newsweek 2, 3, 22, 62, 86, 91, 115, 210–11,
216
backlash supported in 102, 103, 107, 119,
120, 123–5, 129–30, 131, 333, 365
marriage 'study' by 123–5, 141
New Traditionalism 36, 77, 105, 107, 117–19,
133, 243, 277, 286, 492
New York 121, 128, 353
New York Daily News 91, 225, 379
New York Times 63, 127–8, 175, 176, 250,
287, 309, 312, 336, 337, 348, 354, 370,
379, 407, 408, 451
fashion covered by 204, 209, 216, 219, 223,
225
on 'infertility epidemic' 48, 130, 131, 133
on 'man shortage' 1, 25, 31, 32, 122, 124,
195
New Traditionalism and 36, 107, 116, 117,
133, 134
on 'spinster boom' 120–1, 122, 124, 195
women's equality and 3, 8, 12, 72, 82–3,
101
New York Times Magazine 45, 91, 101, 341,
361, 365
New York Woman 55
New Zealand:
abortion campaigns and legislation 438, 441
cohabitation rate 34
discrimination in employment 398, 400
Equal Pay Act (1972) 6

588

Family Proceedings Act (1980) 38
feminist press 138
Nile, Rev. Fred 453
9½ Weeks (film) 144, 148
Nordberg, John A. 418, 434
North, Colonel Oliver 92, 449
Norwood, Robin 377–8, 379–81, 385–8;
  Women Who Love Too Much . . . 377–8,
  379, 385, 387
NOW see National Organization for Women

Observer 114, 461
obstetric intervention 466–73
Occupational Safety and Health Act (OSHA)
  475, 483, 486
O'Connor, John, Cardinal 454
one-parent families 10–11, 72, 144, 298, 308,
  343
  and child maintenance 42–3
One Plus One 38
Operation Rescue 436, 437–8, 443, 444, 445,
  447–8, 449–50, 493
opinion polls 88, 115, 118, 123, 204, 221,
  304–5, 441–2, 462, 495
  on marriage 33, 44–5, 57, 61
  on men's attitudes 44–5, 81, 83, 87–8, 495
Opportunity 2000 399
Oprah Winfrey Show, The 106, 369
Options 24, 113, 121, 128, 130, 212, 250
Oranges Are Not the Only Fruit 178
Overboard 144, 163

PAA see Population Association of America
Page, Susan: If I'm so Wonderful, Why Am I
  Still Single? 373–4
Paglia, Camille: Sexual Personae . . . 352–3
Paramount 145, 146, 147, 151, 164
Parenthood 163, 164, 176
Parsons, Elsie Clews 67
Patti Rocks (film) 165–6
Pauley, Jane 404–5
pay, equality of 5, 6–7, 8, 10, 14, 44, 70, 71,
  72, 81, 284, 310, 312, 350, 395–7, 401–3,
  407, 411–12
People 145, 216, 348
perfume industry 242–5
personal ads 34
Petchesky, Rosalind Pollack 263
Petersen, Lisa Marie 27
Phillips, Angela 402
Phillips, Howard 262, 264, 294, 295
Phipps, Sue: A Woman's Place? 176
Planned Parenthood 285, 443, 445, 446, 450,
  457
plastic surgery 249–50, 251–2, 253–5
Pleck, Joseph 83
PMS see premenstrual stress
Polan, Brenda 15, 119
politics:
  gender gap and 306–12

women in 6, 302–5, 312–13
  see also Democratic Party; Republican
  Party
Popcorn, Faith 107–9, 477
popular culture 3, 9, 93, 289
popular psychology 2, 4–5, 55, 122, 281, 365
  see also backlash psychology
Population Asociation of America (PAA)
  Conference 30–2
pornography 16, 166, 328
positive discrimination 26, 82, 325, 404,
  426–7, 428, 429
post-feminism 14, 15, 70, 95, 101, 236, 287
poverty 5, 11, 17, 43–4
  and pregnancy 462, 464–6
Powell, Enoch 452
preachers, New Right 15, 260–5, 268, 269,
  451
pregnancy 46–55, 131–3
  compulsory caesareans in 466–73
  drug users and 462, 463–4
  'foetal neglect' and 462–5
  low-income women and 462, 464–6
  and mother v. foetus 459–63, 466–73
  teenagers and 457–8, 464
premenstrual stress (PMS) 389, 394
Pretty Woman 167
Price, Susan and Stephen 375–7; No More
  Lonely Nights . . . 375
Prima 119
Private Benjamin (film) 153, 154, 159
professional women 1, 4, 21, 48, 55, 112, 158,
  212, 247; see also career women
Pro-Life Action League 443, 444
psychoanalysis 388–94
Public Health Service, US 26–7
Punch 85
Purves, Libby 114

Quayle, Dan 309, 310

Radclyffe, Sarah 178
Raising Miranda 190
Rambo, Rex 413, 414, 418
Ramirez, Hugo 254
rape 4, 8, 11, 16, 77, 89, 104, 170, 321–2, 328,
  353–4, 355, 372, 433, 456
Raymond, Roy 227
Reagan, Ronald 4, 12, 13, 62, 82, 89–90, 93,
  267, 276, 286, 291, 294, 306, 307, 322,
  400, 403, 404, 423
Reagan administration 7, 26, 30, 49, 265, 285,
  290–301, 302, 322, 395, 400, 401, 418,
  474, 486
Reeves, Richard 303
Refractory Girl 138
Republican Party 13, 259, 267, 305, 496
  and gender gap 306, 307–11, 312
Reskin, Barbara 400
Retin-A 249

retroprogramming, television 188
Revlon 242–3, 245
Reynolds, Burt 177–8
Rich, Adrienne 66
Richardson, Natasha 155
Riches, Valerie 38, 457
Riggs, Betty, 478–9, 480–1, 484–5, 487, 489, 492
rights, women's 71–3, 103
   backlash against 12, 13, 16–17, 60, 66, 70–95, 182–6, 239, 492–8
   campaigns for 3, 9, 69–72, 82, 121, 263, 265, 276, 444, 450–1, 494–5
   men's attitudes to 60, 81, 82–3, 87–8, 444, 495
   New Right opposition to 267–70, 277–8, 280, 284–6, 289, 293
   spiral of progress in 68, 75–6
Robertson of Oakridge, Lord 452
Roe v. Wade 440, 452, 455
Roosevelt, Theodore 69, 84, 298, 309
Roper Organization surveys 9, 11
Roseanne 178–9, 195
Rosenberg, Rosalind 414–16, 421
   Beyond Separate Spheres 414
Rosenzweig, Barney 184–6
Rossi, Alice 360
Rowe, Marsha 137
RU-486 (abortion pill) 458–9
Rymer, Lola 484–5

Saks Fifth Avenue 217–18, 220
Salaam, Yusef 89
salaries *see* pay, equality of
San Francisco Chronicle 128, 133
San Francisco Examiner 106
Sanger, Margaret 70, 446, 451
Sarich, Vincent 325
Sarler, Carol 137
Sassy 137
Savvy 25, 82
Scaasi, Arnold 206
Schafer, Henry 201–2
Scheidler, Joseph 444; *Closed: 99 Ways to Stop Abortion* 443
Schlafly, Phyllis 38, 270, 271, 276, 296, 346, 348, 350, 352
Schrader, Paul 155–6
Schwartz, Daniel 46–7
Schwartz, Felice 114–16
Scruton, Roger 461
Sears, sex discrimination by 411–22
self-help 281–2, 361, 369–72, 380–2, 388
sex discrimination 5–7, 76, 111–12, 115–16, 156, 161, 186–7, 294, 296, 492
   complaints about, to EEOC 401–3, 411–13, 415, 429
   lawsuits filed over 9–10, 350, 361, 406–7, 408, 409–10, 428–9, 433–4
   Sears lawsuit over 411–22

women's resistance to 408–11, 430–5
sex roles, 'natural' 330, 331, 334–5, 359–60
sexual freedoms 347, 353, 375, 376, 438–9, 441
sexual harassment 10, 77, 134, 187, 284, 328, 372, 401–2, 409, 410, 430–1, 480–1
sexuality, women's *see* women's sexuality
sexual revolution 4, 263–4, 321, 324
sexual violence 379–80; *see also* domestic violence; rape
Shapiro, Esther 183
Sharif, Omar 231
Sharon and Elsie 181
She magazine 58, 128–9, 130
Sheila Levine Is Dead and Living in New York 153
Shephard, Harvey 184, 185
Shepherd, Cybill 192
Shepherd, Tony 171, 172
She's Having a Baby 168
Shyer, Charles 153, 160, 162
Siegler, Ava 121
Signs 365–6
Silent Scream, The 457, 459
silicone injections 255
Simons, Dr Richard 392
Single in America (TV documentary) 126–7
single men *see under* men
single women 1, 3–4, 17, 32–3, 76, 101, 119–30, 265
   marriage and 33–6, 68, 105, 123–30, 154, 319–20, 369–77
   mental health of 35–7
   movie images of 141, 144, 147, 151, 152, 153, 157–8, 163–6
   television images of 176, 180–1, 182, 184–5, 190–4, 196, 198–201
   see also mothers, single
situation comedies, TV 174, 187, 188, 191
skin creams 240, 247–9
Slutsky, Laura 126
Smeal, Eleanor 266, 497
Smith, April 187
smokers, female 59
Spare Rib 137, 138
Spelling, Aaron 171, 172–3, 235
spinsters *see* single women
   'boom' in 105, 119, 123
Spitzer, Robert 390–2, 393, 394
Stanton, Elizabeth Cady 69
Staples, Judith 385
Stapleton, Ruth Carter 264
Startz, Dr Jack 255
Steinberg, Joel 92
Steinem, Gloria 135, 185, 337, 339, 350, 356–7
sterilization 475, 477, 482–6, 487, 488–90
Stevens, Doris 71, 80
Stewart, Pamela Rae 465
Stoner, Nellie 468, 470, 472
stress 2, 58–9, 248, 474